Phyllis Blauer

¹/₀

WALLABY

Sun Sign: Capricorn (cusp)
Rising Sign: Sagittarius

CAPRICORN

December 22–January 20

ASTROSCOPE PROFILE

A WALLABY BOOK
Published by Simon & Schuster
New York

Copyright © 1981 by Datura Verlagsanstalt
All rights reserved
including the right of reproduction
in whole or in part in any form
Published by Wallaby Books
A Simon & Schuster Division of
Gulf & Western Corporation
Simon & Schuster Building
1230 Avenue of the Americas
New York, New York 10020

WALLABY and colophon are registered trademarks
of Simon & Schuster

First Wallaby Books Printing November 1981

10 9 8 7 6 5 4 3 2 1

Manufactured in the United States of America

Library of Congress Catalog Card Number: 81-51340

ISBN 0-671-43511-6
Book design: H. Roberts Design

Contents

Introduction to the
Astroscope Profile System

Astroscope Profile—
Your Personal Horoscope

How will this book help you, a distinct individual, know yourself better? Whether you are a Gemini or a Virgo or any other "sign," your experience tells you that you are different from other Virgos or Geminis. This *Astroscope Profile* series of books confirms your experience. *Astroscope Profile* presents the elements of a personal horoscope—an astroscope, as we call it—that are often missing in traditional descriptions of the basic types Aries through Pisces.

To be a Gemini or a Virgo or any other sign simply means that the Sun was in a particular part of the Zodiac on the day of birth. If the position of the Sun was all that mattered, there would be only those twelve types of people. Although the descriptions of the twelve Sun types are astonishingly accurate, they are nevertheless limited.

Our individuality arises from the fact that there are *ten other factors* to consider: the Ascendant (Rising), the Moon, and the planets Mercury, Venus, Mars, Jupiter, Saturn, Uranus, Neptune, and Pluto! All these have distinct and inescapable influences on individual character and personality. Their combined effect on us as individuals is equal to that of the mighty Sun's!

Every genuine astrologer knows that the traditional Sun sign descriptions, as valuable as they are, tell only half the story about the individual. The other half of the story, contributed by the Rising, the Moon, and the planets, seldom ever gets told short of a visit to a professional astrologer.

The problem has always been in devising a system for publication whereby the positions and interpretations of all the planets are worked out in advance for everyone. This problem has been solved in the *Astroscope Profile* series. Each book in the series provides, in addition to a full description of your Sun sign, complete positions and interpretations of the Rising, the Moon, and the other planets for all signs! Now you have the opportunity to read both sides of your own astrological story.

HOW TO USE THIS BOOK

With the book for your Sun sign, you can construct your own astroscope. Tables of planetary placements are conveniently located on colored/banded pages at the end of the book, so you won't have to skip around to list the various placements for your astroscope. Interpretations of each placement are presented in separate chapters, so you can easily find the ones that apply to you. You won't have to make any guesses, calculations, or interpretations. All the tables and interpretations have been done for you, based on the data of professional astrologers.

You might be interested to know how these astrological data are obtained in the first place. What an astrologer does when erecting a personal horoscope is to plot on paper a minimap of the heavens at your moment of birth. But the minimap cannot be made until the astrologer pinpoints the positions of all the planets at the time of birth. To do this, prepared tables of planetary positions, called ephemerides (from the Greek *ephemeris,* meaning "calendar"), are used. Years ago the positions of the planets had to be laboriously worked out each time a horoscope was cast, which introduced a wide margin for error. Today ephemerides are prepared years ahead, mainly by computer, ensuring accuracy within seconds of a degree.

If you glance at your birthday tables—the Planetary Tables that end on page 477—you will see that they are given up to the year 1990. Because the planets move in mathematically predictable orbits, astrologers can predict their positions for the future.

Here is what you need to chart your astroscope, and how this book organizes your search.

Your Sun sign. You know your birthday, but it may be on the cusp, or edge, of a sign for that particular year. Check the Cusp Tables for all Signs, pages 379–83, to find out for sure which Sun sign is yours.

Your Rising sign—the Ascendant. If you know the time of your birth, consult the Ascendant Tables, pages 387–92, to discover your Rising sign. If you don't know the time, a suggestion is given to help you identify your Rising sign.

Your planetary positions: Moon, Mercury, Venus, Mars, Jupiter, Saturn, Uranus, Neptune, and Pluto. Use the Planetary Tables, pages 397–477, to discover what signs each planet is in.

Once you've listed the various placements for your astroscope, you will want to interpret them. This book provides the following material for that purpose.

Sun sign description. Separate chapters on character analysis, work and business, love and romance, and parents and children for your Sun sign.

Cusp sign description. A chapter describing each cusp combination from Aries and Taurus through Pisces and Aries.

Rising sign description. Separate chapters for each of the twelve signs Aries through Pisces.

Moon and planets in the signs. Separate chapters for each planet covering the twelve signs Aries through Pisces.

Look through the Contents for the chapters that apply to you specifically. Then you may want to read up on your friends. Or peruse other chapters of interest as you go along.

You can also construct your astroscope on a wheel, just as professional astrologers do. The next chapter, "Planets of the Solar System and the Signs of the Zodiac," shows you how. Read through the chapter first, so you have a visual picture of the heavens that corresponds to your wheel.

ADVANTAGES OF THE *ASTROSCOPE PROFILE* SERIES

The first advantage of the *Astroscope Profile* series is simplicity. Simply by turning to the birthday tables—the Planetary Tables—for any day in the eighty-one years covered, it is possible to see at a glance the astrological makeup of the person concerned. Reading across the page from the birth date, you can see instantly that each planet is in a certain sign.

The second advantage is the in-depth profile. You match the placement with its interpretation. Take a random example. Moon in Taurus, which makes a person artistically practical. Then Mercury in Leo, giving a dominant turn of mind. Venus in Cancer, making someone deeply protective of loved ones. Mars in Aries, which gives great energy and determination. Jupiter in Aquarius, endowing a detached, scientific capability. Saturn in Scorpio, an intense urge to discover the truths of life and sex. Uranus in Pisces, love of the unusual and a psychic sensitivity. Neptune in Virgo, fondness for detail, artistic precision, and wit. Pluto in Leo, the desire to operate creatively on a grand scale.

Fun and enlightenment are two other advantages. Astroscope can be a game for friends and at parties. Or it can be a means of developing a hobby, more serious study, finally even a career. Astrology's growing popularity creates the demand for new astrologers.

A fourth and very important advantage is understanding other people. The *Astroscope Profile* series helps you estimate the types of people you deal with: relatives, friends, mates, lovers; teammates and bosses; prospective employees and employers; rivals in love or work; professional contacts; children and their companions.

A final advantage concerns children. The birthday tables are supplied up to the year 1990. Parents and expectant parents can assess their children's qualities and needs. People who are planning families can look up the influences that will be present when they become parents. Teachers and other guardians can understand more about their youthful charges.

Most of us have had some experience of youngsters being forced to take up interests, studies, or jobs incompatible with their natural inclinations and abilities. Even a bit of astrological knowledge can help parents and teachers prevent this. The *Astroscope Profile* series provides insights that enable the caretakers of the young to build nurturing, encouraging environments for each child's development.

We create much of our own fate, as well as influence the fate of those we are responsible for. The *Astroscope Profile* series helps us to see what can be done, what probably cannot be done, and what may be possible. Applying these understandings is a safe and sure way of taking destiny out of the hands of chance and putting it firmly in our own.

Planets of the Solar System and the Signs of the Zodiac

Planet Earth is part of the Solar System. This huge solar family has nine planets that revolve around the Sun, our star, and any moons that belong to a planet. Earth has one moon. Jupiter has twelve moons! Figure 1, on page 14, shows the Solar System in space.

Planet Earth is also part of the larger environment defined by the space around the Solar System. That environment stretches billions of miles and contains billions of stars. One fascinating series of stars, which could be seen to early cultures observing the nighttime sky, is the Zodiac.

The Zodiac—a far, far distant series of stars—seems to extend around the Solar System. The Zodiac seems to occupy, at least to the Earth observer, a band of space around the Solar System. The Zodiac contains twelve characteristic star groups, or constellations, that have been variously studied by astronomers and astrologers both ancient and modern. The twelve constellations are known as the twelve star signs or, simply, as the twelve signs of the Zodiac.

A model of the Solar System and the signs of the Zodiac is pictured in Figure 1. This model, though fancifully artistic, is similar to the model astronomers and space scientists use. When they depict the constellations of the Zodiac, they use dot patterns instead of animal or human forms. It doesn't take much imagination to see that their dot patterns resemble the sign symbols used in astrology.

Astrologers have always believed that the Solar System and the Zodiac interact to produce cosmic influences. Astronomers and space scientists confirm that the Solar System and the Zodiac constitute an interacting field of matter and energy. Astrologers talk about the qualities and forces of matter and energy. Astrophysicists and astronomers talk about gravitational forces, electromagnetic fields, and the transformations of matter and energy.

Although the terms are different, the concept is the same. The planets and signs constantly interact, affecting all life on Earth. Their interaction, measured on a day-to-day basis, is the fact on which the system discussed

Figure 1   Model of the Solar System and Constellations of the Zodiac

in the *Astroscope Profile* series was built. That is why Ascendant Tables and Planetary Tables are provided for you to find your own placements. And the chapters on the meanings of each planet in each sign help you zero in on your personal characteristics.

THE RELATIONSHIP OF PLANETS TO SIGNS

In Figure 1, look at the outer band depicting the signs of the Zodiac. Notice that the band is drawn so that the sign of Aries is on the left center. Then all the other signs follow Aries counterclockwise until the band is completed with Pisces.

Why start with Aries? Why not start with Gemini or Capricorn or any other sign, for that matter? In fact, Aries doesn't even correspond with our January 1, the beginning of a calendar year. Starting the Zodiac with Aries is a correct convention, respecting the wisdom of our first astronomers. These early peoples were the first to classify the planets and the signs as well as to develop other fundamentals of astronomy that exist today in every textbook.

Aries is the sign that begins on March 21. That date is called the spring (vernal) equinox. It is the date when the length of day and night is *the same everywhere on earth.* (The Sun's rays at the time shine vertically on the equator.) So it is an appropriate time. It is springtime in the Northern Hemisphere, where our early astronomers observed the nighttime sky. It is the beginning of a new growing season, the herald of summer, the expectation of harvest.

Aries is the Rising sign of the natural Zodiac.

Look back again at Figure 1, noting the rest of the signs in the Zodiac. The Zodiac is so far distant from the Solar System that it is considered to be a relatively stationary system in space. It is not moving *relative* to the motions of the Earth and the other planets around the sun.

The Earth, for example, moves around the Sun completely in one year. Other planets take shorter or longer times to revolve around the Sun, as you can tell from the lines that represent their orbits. But relative to the Earth's motion and the motions of the other planets, the Zodiac seems to stay put. So we always draw the natural Zodiac starting with Aries on the left and going around as shown in Figure 1.

As the Earth or any other planet revolves around the Sun, it passes through the space defined by each of the twelve signs of the Zodiac.

THE SUN SIGN

As the Earth revolves around the Sun, the Sun and Earth together appear to be in line with one sign of the Zodiac approximately once a month. The Sun is said to be "seen" in that sign; then it is "seen" in the next sign, and so on. By the time the Earth has made one complete revolution—a year—the Sun has been in every sign of the Zodiac.

You can check this for yourself by referring again to Figure 1. Put your finger or a pencil point on the planet Earth. Trace an imaginary straight line connecting the Sun, the Earth, and the closest zodiacal sign. Be sure to start from the Sun, then draw the line through the Earth, and go out to the Zodiac band. Try it. What sign do you hit? Your line should hit Gemini. So for the day shown by Figure 1, the Sun is in Gemini. Or, more accurately stated, the Sun is in direct line with the Earth, which is in line with Gemini.

This is how the Sun sign is determined throughout the year. From astrological calculations, generalized dates for the Sun signs are used. Sometimes the dates vary slightly from year to year. The *Astroscope Profile* series takes this fact into account by providing for you the cusp dates (see Cusp Tables for All Signs, pages 379–83) if you need them. The generalized Sun sign dates are given below.

Sun Sign	Date
Aries	March 21–April 20
Taurus	April 21–May 20
Gemini	May 21–June 20
Cancer	June 21–July 20
Leo	July 21–August 21
Virgo	August 22–September 21
Libra	September 22–October 22
Scorpio	October 23–November 22
Sagittarius	November 23–December 20
Capricorn	December 21–January 19
Aquarius	January 20–February 18
Pisces	February 19–March 20

Cusp

For your particular birth year, you may need to check the Cusp Tables, pages 379–83, to be sure which is your Sun sign. If you are born near the cusp—say, within six days from the end of one sign to the beginning of another—you may want to read the cusp description that applies to you in the chapter "The Cusps of All Signs," pages 139–47.

THE MOON AND PLANETS IN THE SIGNS

Sun and Earth were considered together for the Sun sign. What about the signs for the Moon and for the eight other planets in the Solar System? The planets, too, fall into different zodiacal signs as they revolve around the sun.

Astrologers use the same method as was used for the Sun sign to figure out the signs for the Moon and planets. These are the data in the Planetary Tables, which the *Astroscope Profile* series has provided for you on pages 397–477. For your Sun sign, the Planetary Tables give the signs for the Moon and each planet on each day of the eighty-one years from 1910 to 1990 inclusive.

You could play with Figure 1, taking a planet, imagining it revolving around the Sun, stopping every now and then at a point on its orbit, then drawing a line from Sun to planet, and seeing in what sign the planet is at that moment of its year. But can you imagine doing that challenge for *every planet* on *every day* of the *eighty-one years!* This is the compiled work given to you by the Planetary Tables of the *Astroscope Profile* series.

CHARACTERISTICS OF THE PLANETS AND SIGNS

Our Solar System forms one huge interacting force (gravitational) and energy (electromagnetic) field, as you can imagine even from the simple model shown in Figure 1. Each of the planets is a cosmic force. And each has a special brand of energy. That the planets continuously radiate energy is documented by evidence from space probes. We moderns have been lucky enough to see infrared photographs taken at night from space showing the Earth's otherwise invisible energy glow.

Every planet receives the Earth's energy. (If Martians are constructing their astroscopes, they will certainly note what sign the Earth was in when they were "born.") And the Earth receives the planets' energies. The Sun's energy is so powerful it is easy to see why so much emphasis is placed on the Sun sign. But the Moon and the other eight planets, each with their characteristic energies, significantly modify the Sun sign character. (You may know or have noted in reading that the Sun is a star and that the Moon is a satellite of Earth. From the astrological framework of force and energy, the Sun and Moon are considered planets.)

The Solar system also interacts with the Zodiac, as we saw in the last section and in Figure 1. Now that we have introduced the idea of the Solar System as an energy field, the fanciful depiction of the Zodiac as a band of stars takes on a new meaning. There is nothing abstract about the Zodiac. Though pictured as an animal or human form, each sign is in reality one or more groups of stars. Like our Sun, these stars generate tremendous energy. Our Sun is only one star. Each sign consists of many stars, and so generates energy fields many times more powerful than the Sun's. These fields stretch across space, intersecting and interacting with the energy fields of the Sun and planets.

Even though the signs are very far away, their energy fields affect us here on Earth. Their energy fields also affect the Sun and planets. Each sign, consisting as it does of different kinds of stars—white, blue, red, yellow—has its own brand of energy. So each sign is associated with specific modes of energy expression and specific elements of matter.

Energy Keys

Energy principles or modes of expression for the planets and signs are as follows:

Planet	Energy Principle
Sun	Being, Life
Earth*	Embodiment, Physicality
Moon	Response, Instinct
Mercury	Mind, Intellect
Venus	Attraction, Union
Mars	Action, Force
Jupiter	Expansion, Wisdom
Saturn	Restriction, Responsibility
Uranus	Change, Independence
Neptune	Dissolution, Spirituality
Pluto	Upheaval, Renewal

*This may be the first time you have ever seen the Earth included as a planet in an astrology book. Because the *Astroscope Profile* series is based not only on your Sun, Moon, and planets, but also on your Rising sign, the Earth is included. Our Rising sign is most important because it transmits the Earth's own energies to the individual as an indestructible part of self from the moment of birth on. The Earth's energy principle, in positive form, is the human body; its negative form is pure materialism.

Sign	Energy Expression
Aries	Assertive
Taurus	Possessive
Gemini	Communicative
Cancer	Protective
Leo	Creative
Virgo	Critical
Libra	Related
Scorpio	Intense
Sagittarius	Enthusiastic
Capricorn	Conservative
Aquarius	Detached
Pisces	Impressionable

Element

Fire, earth, air, and water and the four natural divisions of matter associated with the twelve signs of the Zodiac. Each element is associated with three signs, as you can see in Figure 2. Fire represents an energetic and assertive person. Earth denotes a practical and cautious person. Air represents an intellectual and communicative person. Water signifies an emotionally sensitive person.

Quality

Cardinal, fixed, and mutable are three other designations associated with the twelve signs. Each quality represents four signs. Cardinal signs tend to produce outgoing people, oriented to action, movement, and change. Fixed signs tend to produce stubborn people, resistant to change but determined to build and create. Mutable signs tend to produce adaptable people, intuitive, creative, and responsive to change.

Polarity

Signs have been represented by dualities of nature or convention. Positive and negative, aggressive and passive, expressive and repressive, introverted and extroverted, male and female have been used. The duality shown in Figure 2, active and receptive, is suggestive but no sign is completely one or the other. Some of the signs themselves show opposites or doubles. Pisces, the Fishes swimming in opposite direction; Gemini, the Twins; Sagittarius, the Archer, half man, half beast. Note that these signs are also mutable ones.

THE ASCENDANT: YOUR RISING SIGN

The Rising Sign, or Ascendant, is the second most important placement in your astroscope, almost equal in importance to the Sun sign. The Sun sign was determined by considering the Earth's revolution, its yearly trip around the Sun. The Rising sign is determined by considering the Earth's rotation. The Earth turns, rotates, completely around once every twenty-four hours on the circuit of night and day.

The Rising sign is your Earth placement. At the moment of your birth, it is the sign "rising" with the Sun somewhere on Earth at that moment of time. That's why astrologers say it is the sign rising on the eastern horizon at the moment of birth. The eastern horizon marks sunrise, where daylight is breaking. Even though you may have been born at night on a certain day in a certain place, somewhere on Earth at that very moment sunrise is also occurring. And that place designates the eastern horizon for that moment of time.

SIGNS OF THE ZODIAC

Signs and Symbols			Element
Aries	Ram	♈	Fire
Taurus	Bull	♉	Earth
Gemini	Twins	♊	Air
Cancer	Crab	♋	Water
Leo	Lion	♌	Fire
Virgo	Virgin	♍	Earth
Libra	Scales	♎	Air
Scorpio	Scorpion	♏	Water
Sagittarius	Archer	♐	Fire
Capricorn	Goat	♑	Earth
Aquarius	Water Bearer	♒	Air
Pisces	Fishes	♓	Water

Quality	Polarity	Planetary Ruler	
Cardinal	Active	Mars	♂
Fixed	Receptive	Venus	♀
Mutable	Active	Mercury	☿
Cardinal	Receptive	Moon	☽
Fixed	Active	Sun	☉
Mutable	Receptive	Mercury	☿
Cardinal	Active	Venus	♀
Fixed	Receptive	Mars,	♂
		Pluto	♇
Mutable	Active	Jupiter	♃
Cardinal	Receptive	Saturn	♄
Fixed	Active	Uranus,	♅
		Saturn	♄
Mutable	Receptive	Neptune,	♆
		Jupiter	♃

Figure 2 Signs of the Zodiac. Each sign is ruled by one or more planets. Where there are co-rulers, each planet is considered equally important.

The Earth is constantly turning. Every place on it is turning also, as you know when you experience the full range of day and night in and out of sunlight. As the Earth turns, the eastern horizon is in line with a specific sign of the Zodiac at any given moment. And, as the Earth turns, about every two hours another zodiacal sign comes into line with the eastern horizon. This means that within the twenty-four-hour period of rotation, all the twelve zodiacal signs appear to rise. (No observer on Earth can actually see the sign that is rising. The light of the Sun blocks a view of the signs at sunrise. We see signs only at night.)

If you know the time of your birth, you can use the Ascendant Tables on pages 387–92 to find your Rising sign quickly. These Ascendant Tables give the Rising sign for each hour of the day for every day in your Sun sign. If you do not know the time of your birth, consult the chapters for each Rising sign. Read a few paragraphs of each, or skim through. See which Rising sign description best fits you.

RISING SIGN AND THE HOUSES OF THE ZODIAC

The Rising sign is a major indicator in your personal astroscope. The Rising sign influences how other people see you. It influences your body type, appearance, temperament. It helps to fashion your "face" to the world. It is a very real part of your identity.

The Rising sign always "starts" the astroscope. Look at Figure 3. It shows a flat model of the Zodiac without sign names or symbols. The Earth is in the center of the model. Lines like spokes of a wheel radiate from the Zodiac band to the center, and mark twelve equal divisions. Each division is called a house.

The Rising sign is always placed *on* the first house—that is, on the line dividing the twelfth house and the first house. The bubbles in the drawing are merely artistic devices so that a sign can be placed *on* the house and not *in* it.

Your Rising sign determines the sequence of signs around the wheel from the second house through the twelfth house. Figure 4 shows a sample wheel for someone whose Rising sign is Leo. See how each sign follows in natural zodiacal sequence once Leo is placed on the first house. In Figure 4 there are no planets listed, so the astroscope wheel is not complete.

Let's take another example based on obtaining from the appropriate Planetary Tables all the positions for this person with Leo Rising. See Figure 5. First we list the planetary positions. Then we transfer the planets to the wheel and put them *in* the houses where their signs fall. The signs are *on* the lines. The planets are *in* the houses. The astroscope wheel is complete. There remains only the job of interpretation.

You see from Figure 5 that planets are in certain houses. The term "house" is an apt one, and the Zodiac wheel is aptly termed "the wheel of life." The twelve houses are regarded as spheres of life experience. Together these twelve houses represent most of what makes up everyday living. Brief meanings of the twelve houses of the Zodiac are sketched on the wheel of life in Figure 6.

Figure 3   The division of the Zodiac into 12 houses. The Rising, or Ascendant, sign is always placed on the 1st house (left center of the wheel). The houses go around counterclockwise from 1 to 12 as shown in the inner circle surrounding Earth.

The twelve chapters "Your Rising Sign" for each specific sign detail the meanings of these houses for the individual. When you read the chapter that applies to you, you will see how you react and relate to these life experiences defined by the houses of the Zodiac. As the *Astroscope Profile* system has emphasized all along, your Rising sign modifies the characteristics of your Sun sign.

For example, a Capricorn Sun sign tends to make an individual conservative, especially with money. But a Capricorn Rising sign tends to make an individual unpredictable about money. These distinctions and modifying influences are thoroughly covered in each of the twelve chapters describing a different Rising sign (pages 151–245).

RISING ASCENDANT

USING SIGN NAMES

USING SIGN SYMBOLS

Figure 4 Astroscope wheels showing how to sequence the signs on the houses for someone with Leo Rising. The Rising sign is placed always on the 1st house. On each successive house, the natural sequence of the Zodiac follows.

Positions

Rising in Leo
Sun in Gemini
Moon in Sagittarius
Mercury in Cancer
Venus in Leo
Mars in Libra
Jupiter in Virgo
Saturn in Pisces
Uranus in Taurus
Neptune in Virgo
Pluto in Cancer

Figure 5 Completed astroscope wheel. The names of the planets, followed by their symbols, are written in the appropriate houses.

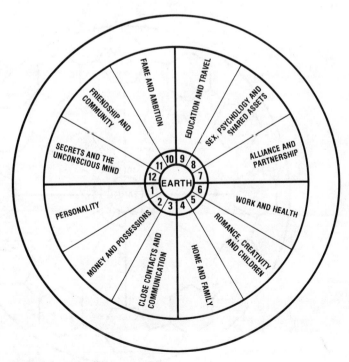

Figure 6 The 12 Houses of the Wheel of Life.
Each house defines specific life experiences.

CONSTRUCTING YOUR ASTROSCOPE WHEEL

This page is reserved for you. Fill-in blanks are provided to list your planetary positions. The astroscope wheel is reproduced. Go ahead! Write in this book. It's yours, and you will have a permanent record for study and fun.

YOUR ASTROSCOPE WHEEL

Planet	Sign	Birth Date
Rising	_____	Time _____
Sun	_____	Day _____
Moon	_____	Year _____
Mercury	_____	
Venus	_____	
Mars	_____	
Jupiter	_____	
Saturn	_____	
Uranus	_____	
Neptune	_____	
Pluto	_____	

Astrology:
Tradition and Frontier

SCIENCE AND THE STARS

Tuesday, July 20, 1976, was a triumphant day for science—and astrology. America's *Viking* spacecraft had just bumped gently down to a perfect landing on Mars.

For twenty-five hundred years, astrology had associated the red planet Mars with the metal iron. To science, such an assumption was laughable. It was impossible for an ancient tradition to know such detail about a cosmic object thirty-six million miles from the Earth.

Yet one of the first signals received from the spacecraft confirmed that the planet's red surface was formed of oxidized iron. The Martian rocks were covered with rust. In fact, the probe indicated that the planet's pink sky and its reddish appearance from the earth were probably caused by the iron dust particles in the atmosphere scattering the Sun's rays.

The Mars probe indicating its iron composition confirmed something astrologers have always known. As a planetary influence, Mars in the individual astroscope adds its ironlike qualities of courage and strength to the character. Mars is associated with many aspects of life on Earth, as was emphasized in the preceding chapter.

Each of the planets has its own particular qualities, as were described in that chapter. No doubt existing and future space probes traveling even farther than Mars will reveal similar astrological parallels.

The recent probe of Saturn in 1980 is evidence of this thinking. Saturn was shown to be shrouded in ice crystals and frozen gas particles. Its chilly atmosphere surrounding the planet is only slightly colder than the freezing temperatures on its surface—equivalent to about −270° Fahrenheit. Again, modern science has confirmed certain astrological qualities assigned to the planet Saturn.

Where did the ancient astrologers get their information? How did they know?

No one can answer this question. Astrology is so old that it predates history. We cannot even say *why* astrology works. But we can satisfy ourselves that it *does* work by observing the amazing accuracy of its insights into our characters, together with the discoveries of science that are constantly confirming its principles and beliefs.

THE WORLD'S OLDEST TRADITION

Astrology is one of the oldest ideas in the world. It also was the world's first science. It goes back so far into antiquity that it is the basis for much myth and legend. Mercury, Venus, Mars, Jupiter, Saturn—all the planets were said originally to have been gods. How this could be possible defies any rational speculation, much the same as applies to ancient religious traditions. But it does help to make the point that in that imponderable beginning of history, astrology was there.

Astrology is the science of circles or cycles. It is founded on the principle that people and the world evolve to the rhythm of circular motion, wheels within wheels, symbolized by the planets orbiting the Sun, and the Solar System as a whole appearing to move against the background of the Zodiac, an even larger "circle" in space. (See Figure 1 in the preceding chapter.)

The end of every zodiacal round or cycle heralds a fresh new start in which a person, or on a larger scale a society or the world, is wiser and more capable of handling life's challenges. Out of this idea emerges the strong astrological suggestion that reincarnation or recurrence is a fact. According to that tradition, every individual gets another crack at life, having been all the better equipped for it by their previous experience.

FROM THE AGE OF LEO
TO THE AGE OF AQUARIUS

Astrological cycles have a curious connection with one of the most pressing problems facing the world today—the search for an alternative power source to our fast-diminishing oil supplies. It looks as though history might be about to repeat itself with the recurrence of a very ancient cycle.

The connection goes way back to around 12,000 B.C., into fables and astrological traditions. That was the time when the world was passing through the Age of Leo. According to traditions, it was a very different world indeed from that of today.

Most people have heard about the Age of Aquarius, which the world is said to have entered recently. Each astrological age lasts approximately twenty-one hundred years. The age just ended was the Age of Pisces, which started a bit before the birth of Christ. The ages succeed each other around the zodiacal circle in a direction *opposite* to the Aries to Pisces sequence we are familiar with. In other words, after the Age of Aries comes Pisces, and now Aquarius.

Way back in the Age of Leo, we are told, there was a civilization called Atlantis, an island just west of the Strait of Gibraltar. Atlantis was developed socially, economically, and politically beyond our wildest dreams. The Atlanteans had mastered the problem of obtaining power from the Sun. They powered their space vehicles with solar energy and had even succeeded in using it to regenerate human bodies. The whole Atlantean world was run on Sun power!

Atlantis, according to the tradition, was literally ripped apart as a result of Leonine power struggles among its rulers. It finally vanished beneath the Atlantic ocean. Does history repeat itself?

Astrologically, there is no justification for suggesting that our civilization over the next two thousand years is going to reach Atlantean heights of harnessing solar power. But the law of astrological cycles does indicate that this Aquarius Age could at least be a beginning toward that end.

Aquarius is the sign of scientific discovery, originality, progress, radical change, and invention. It is exactly opposite Leo across the Zodiac. So we are now halfway around the circle from the days of Atlantis. The "dark" ages that followed the loss of Atlantean technology are at last behind us.

The cycle is on the way up and heading toward Leo again. This point will be reached in 12,600 years. It is to be hoped people will have evolved and matured enough not to repeat the same disastrous mistakes.

HOW ASTROLOGY BEGAN

There are two main schools of thought about how astrology began. The first is that it was the product of divine inspiration handed down by the sages of Atlantis. These sages included the spiritually evolved guides of the human race, the legendary figures who during this epoch gradually withdrew from the world and became known as Hermes, Minerva, Apollo, Isis, Osiris, Dionysus, Diana, and Vesta—in other words, the gods and goddesses.

The other and more popular idea is that the science of astrology must have evolved purely out of man's observations of celestial phenomena. These supporters picture early peoples observing phases of the moon, eclipses, meteors, and comets, then correlating them to such earthly events as floods, famines, wars, disease, earthquakes, and, later on, the characters of people.

But when the principles, functions, and formulas of astrology are studied as a whole, it becomes clear that the idea of astrology having been invented and put together piecemeal, like assembling a model of some new animal, is even more preposterous than giving it a "divine" or inspirational origin.

The answer probably lies somewhere in between.

There can be no doubt that astrology existed in prehistoric times. Out of early man's fears and dreads in coping with a hostile and cruel environment emerged a natural yearning for order. For this, his closest example was nature itself. Even its extremes of floods, droughts, and gales offered a predictable cyclic pattern. And there was the regularity of the seasons and the rhythm of the tides and the repetition of the climates year in and year out.

Early peoples linked these periodic phenomena with the apparent path of the Sun and the motions of the Moon which followed periodic and predictable routes. It must not have taken early peoples long to rationalize that almost every aspect of human existence was dependent on these two mysterious heavenly bodies.

Alexander Marshack, writing in the journal *Science,* has suggested that nicks found cut into mammoth ivory and reindeer bones dating back to the Upper Paleolithic period (up to around 20,000 B.C. were "records" of such observations of the lunar cycles.

Early man's inability to explain celestial phenomena probably led him to identify them with the work of superhuman intelligences and spirits. He even invested the Sun and Moon with "characters" of their own, giving rise to religion, rites, and unlimited superstitions. But magic was the beginning of science!

THE EGYPTIANS

For written evidence we leave early peoples' possible inferences and move forward to around 4200 B.C., to the Egyptians. It is a giant leap in time from the first human beings to these sophisticated people of the Nile who by this date had been able to erect finely accurate charts of the fixed stars. Some of these charts survive today; they evidently are copies of even earlier charts.

There is no concrete evidence from this time that the Egyptians practiced astrology. They were, though, extremely skilled astronomers. Their calendar was so accurate that only in relatively recent times was it possible to improve on it.

But it is inferred by many modern scholars that astrology was practiced by the Egyptians before any other Mediterranean race. The Egyptians practiced it in the strictest secrecy, something like an exclusive cult. This hypothesis is supported by folk traditions that maintain that the original astrological knowledge, presumably issuing from Atlantis, first passed to the Egyptians, who later disseminated it to the Babylonians. The main wave of the knowledge, it is said, was from Egypt to India to China, and then across the Bering Strait between Russia and Alaska down to the vanished civilizations of South America, where innumerable astrological relics have been discovered.

The supporters of the Egyptian theory point to the findings of a French scholar, R. A. Schwaller de Lubiscz. During the last thirty years, de Lubiscz produced extraordinary evidence to show that astrological principles were built into Egyptian art and architecture in such as way as to be obvious only to those who were in sympathy with the idea of a harmonious, unified universe—the actual basis from which astrology begins.

It is said that the whole Egyptian astrological tradition was handed down orally from master to pupil and only allowed to be expressed publicly in art and architecture. Some examples exist among the acknowledged masterpieces surviving today.

THE BABYLONIANS AND THE EGYPTIANS

On purely historical evidence, the Babylonians, or Chaldeans, were the first people to develop astrology systematically. These were the ancestors of the people of old Mesopotamia and today's Iraq. Their civilization grew up between and around those two most famous rivers of the ancient world—the Tigris and Euphrates, which empty into the Persian Gulf.

On the evidence, it was the Babylonians also who were the first to put 2 and 2 together and so to invent mathematics. It was a fairly simple system, but it did allow them to translate their observations of the heavens into meaningful records and especially calendars.

The Babylonians were originally desert people. For thousands of years their acenstors had been shepherds. They had every opportunity to observe the ceaseless comings and goings of the heavenly bodies in the clear and cloudless desert sky and to make mental notes. In fact, skywatching probably was their equivalent of TV!

By 3,000 B.C. the Babylonians had developed a relatively advanced system of organized observation and interpretation of celestial phenomena. They were a people who had always depended on divination, including the examination of animals' entrails for "signs." It was a natural step for them to see a correlation between the movements of the stars and certain earthly events.

The Babylonians erected a series of watchtower observatories, which for those times were impressive structures. These watchtowers, set around the kingdom and manned full time by the priests, were up to two hundred feet high and hundreds of feet long. Some consisted of seven terraces, one on top of the other, representing the seven known planets. They were lined with glazed brick, and the topmost chambers were sometimes finished elaborately in gold and precious stones.

The Tower of Babel mentioned in the Bible is a likely reference to one of these towers, which were said to "reach unto heaven."

The Babylonians had no telescopes. Yet they were able to discover and name at least two constellations—Orion and the Pleiades. The Babylonian priests were deeply steeped in the occult. To them, there was no doubt that the brightly shining planets were gods, and they had no difficulty identifying them with mysterious forces and powers that affected terrestrial affairs.

For two thousand years they charted and studied the heavens, discovering the ecliptic—the apparent annual path of the Sun around the Earth. They eventually divided this path into twelve divisions, the signs of the Zodiac, although they did not identify them as such.

Astrology in those early days was practiced differently, though the principles were the same. No individual horoscopes were cast, at least not for ordinary people. It was the custom of the early priest-astrologers to link the fortunes of the nation with the fate of the King. If the King prospered, so did everyone. If ill luck befell him, it was bad times for all. So only the King's horoscope was erected and interpreted. This one horoscope was the basis for a continuous reading that helped to guide the running of the country from day to day.

Across more than four thousand years of history have come down to us some of the written maxims of these ancient astrological pioneers. In fact, more than thirty thousand of their cuneiform clay tablets have been recovered near the site of ancient Babylon.

The most famous Babylonian predictions in existence are those of Sargon the Old (2470–2430 B.C.). These are mainly concerned with the Sun and the Moon.

He wrote: "If the moon can be seen the first night of the month, the country will be peaceful; the heart of the country will rejoice. If the moon is surrounded with a halo, the king will reign supreme.

"If the setting sun seems twice as large as usual, and three of its rays are bluish, the king of the land is lost.

"If the moon is visible on the 30th, good tiding for the land of Akkad, bad for Syria."

It is not reported whether the astrologers were able to predict the end for Babylon, which came around 1000 B.C. Then the country was overrun by the Assyrians from the north.

Meanwhile, however, to the south, Egyptian astrology was becoming more mundane and Babylonian in flavor. It was losing any purely esoteric connections with art and architecture. It had begun the long journey toward the marketplace.

The argument that the Egyptians learned astrology from Babylonian sources receives support from the evidence of the Old Testament. It could well be that the old esoteric system became "lost" through excessive secrecy and that the later system developed along conventional lines.

The Bible shows that the Israelites were well versed in the subject. Abraham, the prophet, actually lived in Ur, part of the Babylonian Empire. According to another old work, Abraham "wore an astrological clay tablet on his chest." The enslavement of the Hebrews by the Egyptians around 1300 B.C. also would have resulted in a wide exchange of ideas, no doubt including astrological ones.

On the other hand, the oldest horoscope relic in the world is one that was cast in 2767 B.C. by Imhotep, the architect responsible for the first of the Great Pyramids of Zoser. The earliest Egyptian horoscope known to have been drawn up was for Nectanebo II in 358 B.C., more than two thousand years later. But this, of course, proves nothing. as earlier relics may yet be found.

Using their tremendously advanced astronomical knowledge, the Egyptians were able to align the pyramids to the cardinal points of the compass within a few seconds of a degree of error. The Great Pyramid of Gizeh, finished around 2800 B.C., was originally 481 feet high and covered 13 acres. It incorporated measurements said to correspond to astrological relationships and cycles.

Also at Giseh, in front of the Great Pyramid, was built the Sphinx, claimed to be another example of astrological symbolism.

Pliny, the Roman scholar writing about A.D. 50 observed: "In front of the pyramid is the Sphinx, a still more wondrous object of art, but upon which rests a spell of silence, as it is looked upon as a great deity." The Sphinx even then was more than twenty-five hundred years old. Wrote Plutarch, the Greek biographer about the same time: "The Sphinx symbolizes the secret of all occult wisdom."

Nevertheless, with Ptolemy's works astrology no longer needed to defend itself. Ptolemy's works were the bible of astrology for more than twelve hundred years—until Copernicus.

But trouble was coming. Although the early Christian fathers seemed to have no trouble living with astrology, the later leaders of the Church came out hard against it as a pagan practice. By A.D. 323 the first Christian Emperor, Constantine, sat on the throne of Rome. And under the fierce attacks of St. Augustine, who had once been an adherent, the science virtually disappeared from Europe.

Meanwhile, however, astrology was thriving in the Middle East, where it had begun. The Mohammedan conquests of the seventh century interfered for a time, while millions of people turned to embracing the new faith. Then Islam became the center of astronomical and astrological effort.

In Baghdad, the successors of Mohammed surrounded themselves with the greatest mathematicians and scholars from the Arab world. They were employed in making observations of the heavenly bodies, measuring distances along the meridian, redetermining the size of the Earth, and inventing a new calendar for civil affairs based on the Moon.

At the same time, a "House of Wisdom" was established where translations were made of Ptolemy's *Almagest* and *Tetrabiblos* as well as many Greek texts. Over the next six hundred years the Arab contribution to the world's knowledge of astronomy, mathematics, medical chemistry, biology, and geology was enormous. From the point of view of astrology, it was these gifted people who kept the science alive while Europe lay prostrate under priestly rule and the ignorance of the Dark Ages.

THE COPERNICAN MODEL OF THE UNIVERSE

With the Renaissance, the period of renewed cultural and intellectual endeavor around the start of the fifteenth century, astrology once again attracted the leading minds of the day. One was Roger Bacon, the English philosopher and scientist whose writings contain prophecies of the telescope, microscope, steam engine, and airplane.

Bacon believed that the nature or character of an individual was determined by the sky at conception and birth. Bacon also thought that health and disease of the body were under the influence of the stars, so "the wise physician should be aware of the fact that hour by hour the bodily states vary with changing positions of the planets."

Thomas Aquinas (1225–74), one of the guiding lights of the Church, also averred that "no wise man doubted that all natural motions of the inferior bodies are caused by movements of the celestial bodies." Dante, the devotional poet of the same period, believed that the power, wisdom, and love of the Almighty were transmitted to man through the stars and planets.

Shakespeare wrote: "The fault . . . is not in our stars but in ourselves that we are underlings."

Then came Nicolaus Copernicus (1473–1543). He spent several years studying in Italy, where he became familiar with the Ptolemaic model of the

Aristarchus made the incredible deduction from mathematical calculations that the Sun and Moon must be of very different sizes, even though they appear in the sky to be approximately the same. He also concluded from the shadow of the Earth cast over the Moon at an eclipse that the Earth was twice as large as the Moon. (It is actually about four times larger.) Eratosthenes was the first to estimate accurately the circumference of the Earth. And under Empedocles and especially Hippocrates, often called the father of modern medicine, a system of medical astrology was started.

It was Empedocles also who formulated the doctrine of the four elements in astrology: earth, air, fire, and water. These elements were said to distinguish the temperaments of people.

THE PTOLEMAIC MODEL OF THE UNIVERSE

From the Greeks, astrology passed to the Romans. Greek slaves are reported to have first brought this art and science to Rome. But it was coldly received by the traditional Roman diviners, who, feeling their power and livelihood would be threatened, had the star readers banned from the city.

However, the appeal of the old science lingered. With the support of the Stoics and other schools of philosophers and intellectuals, it gradually gained ground. By the first century A.D. it was firmly entrenched. Every leading citizen, including Emperors Caesar and Octavius, had their horoscopes cast in great detail.

Nevertheless, astrology did have its ups and downs, usually due to the fluctuating temperature of the Roman political scene. Emperor Augustus, although a firm believer, outlawed the astrologers in 33 B.C. because he feared Marc Antony, his archrival, would cause unfavorable predictions to be made about him by his enemies. As soon as Antony had been removed, Augustus restored astrology to its former respectable place in Roman society. And, as though to reaffirm his own allegiance, he had a special coin struck showing Capricorn, his Moon sign, dominating the world!

In A.D. 137 astrology received probably the greatest boost in its history by Ptolemy's publication of his two books the *Almagest* and *Tetrabiblos*. Ptolemy (Claudius Ptolemaeus of Alexandria) was the greatest astrologer and astronomer of that time. His two books brought together all the known astrological and astronomical knowledge to that date.

Ptolemy's model of the solar system had the Sun and all the planets moving around the Earth. The planets moved in tiny circles, called epicycles, as they revolved in larger circles around the Earth. It seems quite natural to think that the Earth is at the center of the universe. It is also natural to assume that the Sun and stars move around the Earth, since every day and night we see these objects appear to rise, move across the sky, and set.

But predictions of the positions of the planets did not always work out based on the Ptolemaic model. It kept being revised, and it was still clumsy. Not until Nicolaus Copernicus revolutionized the model in the sixteenth century could celestial motions be accurately explained.

And understandably so. The riddle of the Sphinx and its hidden astrological significance are intriguing.

THE GREEKS

According to Greek mythology, the Sphinx originally was a living monster, part man and part beast. It used to ask passersby to answer a riddle, and when they failed ate them alive.

The riddle was: What creature walks in the morning upon four feet, at noon upon two, at evening upon three?

Oedipus, the future King of Thebes, guessed the riddle. In amazement the Sphinx turned to stone.

The answer was: man. The allusion is to his walking on hands and knees as a baby, on two feet later, and with a staff in old age.

Astrologically, the Sphinx is said to represent the fixed signs in a cross: the Bull (Taurus); the Lion (Leo); the Eagle, which was the ancient symbol used for the Scorpion (Scorpio); and Man. It also is said to embody the four elements: Bull, earth; Lion, fire; Eagle, water; Man, air.

After the Babylonians, the Greeks became the main custodians of astrological lore in the Western world. Babylonian astrologers, fleeing from the Assyrian conquest of their country, filtered through the Hellenic islands and gradually passed on their knowledge.

Under the keen minds of the Greeks, astrology developed even more swiftly. But for a while, around 600 B.C., it was somewhat neglected. The Greeks had other things on their mind. This was the unique period of Greek enlightenment during which philosophy and the arts received an impetus that was to influence succeeding civilizations for thousands of years.

The period also marked the foundation of the scientific method as it is understood today. The result was that when the Greeks once again turned their attention to astrology, they were better equipped than ever to pursue it.

The Greeks welcomed astrology as the natural partner to the divine science of mathematics. Their philosopher scientists pursued the subjects with extraodinary insights. Over the next three hundred years they added tremendously to the concepts of astrology. This plus their astronomical achievements resulted in a completely new intellectual view of the world and the universe. It was the era of such memorable names as Thales, Anaximenes, Pythagoras, Empedocles, Anaxagoras, Aristotle, Plato, and Hippocrates.

Although Copernicus of the fifteenth century A.D. is credited with being the first to propose that the Earth orbited the Sun, this fact had already been discovered and recorded by Aristarchus of Samos in 300 B.C. Democritus correctly surmised that the Milky Way consisted of myriads of stars. Leucippus declared that the Moon's markings were caused by hills and valleys casting shadows on its surface. Empedocles taught that the solar eclipses were due to the Moon passing between the Earth and the Sun.

These are all well-known facts today. But it has to be remembered that the invention of the telescope was still a long way off. With no instruments, all the Greeks had to assist them were their extraordinary minds.

Solar System. Copernicus returned to his native Poland and took about thirty years to develop a new model of the Solar System.

The Copernican model, with slight improvements, is the model of the Solar System used today. In it, the Sun is at the center. The planets and their satellites, including our Earth and Moon, revolve around the Sun. Now the planets' positions could be accurately predicted.

The Copernican model also explained the apparent daily motion of the Sun, Moon, and stars. He suggested that the Earth is rotating on its axis from west to east, and that the celestial objects appear to us Earth observers as passing scenery. But it is we, not they, who are moving. Because we are not aware of our rotation, the objects we see appear to be moving.

The Copernican model has been one of the most useful tools of discovery in science. It, together with Newton's theory of gravitation, made it possible, for example, to predict the position of the unknown planet Neptune in 1843 and the even more distant planet Pluto in 1930.

After Copernicus came the scientific discoveries of Galileo (inventor of the telescope), Tycho Brahe, Johannes Kepler, and Isaac Newton. All of these scientists took an interest in astrology.

Brahe, by his meticulous observations of planetary orbits, paved the way for the genius of Newton to define the laws of gravitation in 1693. A practicing astrologer, Brahe predicted the years of birth and death of Gustavus Adolphus of Sweden, a hero of the Thirty Years' War.

Johannes Kepler, a student of Brahe, used Brahe's observations of planetary orbits to refine the Copernican model. Kepler discovered that the orbits of the planets were ellipses, not circles as Copernicus and the others had assumed. Kepler, also an astrologer who published astrological calendars, put the finishing touches on the model of the Solar System that is used today by astronomers, space scientists, and astrologers.

THE SPACE ERA

The Copernican model of the universe, Kepler's laws of motion, and Newton's laws of gravitation, inertia, mass, and acceleration were the scientific "launching pads" for the space era. Now astrology was put to the real test. Could the world's oldest tradition and first science possibly survive in such a climate of supertechnology?

Astrology has certainly survived, and it is booming. Never in the history of the world have so many people taken such an intelligent interest in astrology. Each week, hundreds of thousands of copies of specialist books, magazines, and other publications on astrology are bought and studied.

Astrology today has demonstrated the validity of its principles in modern scientific terms.

Despite official obstinacy, more and more individual scientists, especially those of the last couple of generations in this new Age of Aquarius, are acknowledging the validity of astrology as a tool for helping them unravel the mysteries of the universe. It makes absorbing reading to bring together some of the major scientific discoveries of recent years, which help to confirm astrological practice and theory. It is, in fact, quite an astounding record.

THE MOON AND BEHAVIOR

The Moon's effect on aspects of life around us is so much a part of normal experience that it often passes without being noticed. However, its vital influence on terrestrial existence has been a key factor in astrology since time immemorial.

As everyone knows, the Moon controls the tides. Scientists also have established its connection with the menstrual cycle, births, and blood flow. Medical astrologers of old were respectfully aware of the latter connection. They would refuse to perform operations during certain phases of the Moon because of the danger of patients bleeding to death.

In modern times, it was the observation of an alert nurse in Florida that prompted research into this old belief. The nurse reported to Dr. Edson Andrews of Tallahassee that his patients seemed to be hemorrhaging more frequently at certain times than at others.

Ignoring his first impulse to dismiss the idea, Dr. Andrews made a quick check, which convinced him that here indeed was something that needed closer investigation. In subsequent tests covering a thousand cases of tonsillectomy, he found that 82 percent of the bleeding crises occurred between the Moon's first and third quarters. "These data have been so conclusive and convincing," he is reported to have said, "that I threaten to become a witch doctor and operate on dark nights only!"

Japanese and American researchers, in studying the frequency of more than 530,000 births over a period of years, found a significant peaking one or two days before the Moon's first and last quarters. Similarly, studies of thousands of menstruation cases over a period of fourteen years showed a maximum at Full and New Moons.

Leonard J. Ravitz of Duke University, by comparing the electrical potential of normal and disturbed people, found that patients were markedly more affected at times coinciding with Moon phases and seasonal changes. Astrology has always linked the Moon with mental disorders, a tradition perpetuated by the word "lunatic."

One of the first medical men to publicize the apparent connection between lunar cycles and physical illness was William Peterson of Chicago. He reported that deaths from tuberculosis were most frequent seven days before the Full Moon. In 1961, a significant correlation among lunar phases, pneumonia cases, and uric acid in the blood was discovered by a German scientist, Hans Heckert.

Perhaps the most interesting and revealing experiment is what has been called "The Strange Case of the Evanston Oysters." Frank A. Brown, professor of biology at Northwestern University, had done a tremendous amount of research work into "biological clocks." It was known that every living organism, from man to the tiniest living cell, operates according to predetermined rhythms. But the disputed question was: What controls those rhythms?

From rhythm tests with beans, flies, and rats and from color changes in fiddler crabs, Brown and his colleagues found that solar factors, probably the Sun and Moon, must be responsible, not climatic changes, as had been generally supposed. His next experiment with oysters gave the breakthrough and forced a major, though somewhat reluctant, change in scientific thinking.

It had been long assumed that the trigger for the oysters' biological clock, telling them when to open their shells to feed, was the movement of the tides. No one ever bothered to check this assumption. Brown did. He took a batch of oysters fresh out of the sea from New Haven, Connecticut, to Evanston, Illinois, a thousand miles from the nearest tidal waters. There he placed them in specially prepared pans of salt water in a dark room.

For two weeks, the oysters opened and closed to the tidal rhythms back in New Haven. But then they began to alter their timing, soon settling into a routine of opening their shells when it would have been high tide in Evanston—had there been tides there!

Brown's experiment proved conclusively that gravitational forces coming from the Moon, and not immediate external conditions, were responsible.

THE SUN AND BEHAVIOR

From the Moon we now switch to the Sun. The Sun is the most powerful of all the cosmic influences in astrology, for the simple reason that it is the source of life for us and the brightest object in the sky.

In the 1920s, a Russian historian, Tchijevsky, was struck by the cyclical pattern in which wars, epidemics, and major social changes occurred. Science by then had discovered sun spot activity. Huge electromagnetic storms on the Sun every 11.1 years spew into space huge flares of solar gases. Tchijevsky figured that there might be a connection between sunspot activity and world-shaking events. Over the next fifteen years, he assembled historical data from seventy-two countries dating back twenty-five hundred years. His findings revealed that peaks in sunspot activity coincided with the world's major epidemics and plagues, including the Black Death.

Since then, a great new world of scientific research into cyclical rhythms has opened up, especially in America and Russia. These cyclical patterns have been found to exist in a range of phenomena—flu epidemics, heart disease, world rainfall, icebergs, and even droughts in India. Russian scientists were able to link the solar activity, especially a particularly violent eruption in 1959, with a blood deficiency due to destruction of lymphocytes, a form of white blood cell.

But it was a persistent and brilliant Japanese professor, Maki Takata, who put his finger on the Sun's power to affect the human bloodstream. Takata found that the composition of human blood changes in relation to the sunspot cycle, solar flares, and eclipses. He also found that just before sunrise the blood becomes enormously active. For some astrologers this immediately suggested a correlation with the Sun sign and the Ascendant, or Rising, sign (the sign that was rising on the eastern horizon at the time of an individual's birth).

Solar activity has been found to affect the incidence of road accidents. Russian scientists and engineers reported that research carried out over a number of years at the Tomsk Medical College had found a relation between roads accidents and solar activity. Their statistics show that the day after the eruption of a solar flare, road accidents increased, sometimes as much as four times above the average. Similar findings had also been obtained by investigators in Hamburg and Munich.

THE IGY EXPLORATION AND
PLANETARY INFLUENCES

The existence of an electromagnetic link between the Sun and the planets, which would help to prove the functional validity of astrology, was actually established as a result of discoveries made during the International Geophysical Year (IGY), 1957–58.

During the IGY exploration, rocket probes and brilliant deskwork led scientists to the discovery that the Earth was "cocooned" in vast "local" radiation layers. These were named the Van Allen Belts, after American scientist James A. Van Allen, who first explained the phenomenon.

The Earth's own magnetic field interacted with the Van Allen Belts. In the vast space around Earth was created a tremendous electromagnetic field. This field is called the magnetosphere.

For a further fifteen years, the space scientists labored. Finally, through the U.S. *Pioneer* space probes, they established that the other planets also had magnetospheres of their own. This meant that one secret of the Solar System was at last solved. It consisted of a single gigantic electromagnetic field of force and "information," in which the orbiting planets act as magnets and "cut" and change the field continuously.

Electromagnetic radiation is "sensed" by all organisms in different ways. What "information" is conveyed has become a rich area for speculation and organized research. For example, scientists investigating earthquake areas found that shortly before an earthquake occurred, the local magnetic field collapsed. This was immediately sensed by the wildlife in the area, which promptly fled. The magnetic field had acted as a warning system.

Medical science for years has been utilizing the electromagnetic fields in the human body to evolve more effective and precise diagnostic techniques. Much research still remains to be done. But it has been established that during magnetic storms in cosmic space, the incidence of heart attacks and mental and nervous disorders increases.

To astrologers, all this is yet another demonstration of their much-maligned craft being made scientifically respectable.

The work of a famous German geophysicist, Rudolph Tomascheck, has helped to give scientific credence to one of the most ridiculed aspects of traditional astrology. This concerns the astrological tradition of assigning to each planet a symbolic character, which is either intensified or diminished by the planet's position relative to other planets. Even that most benign planet Jupiter, which is supposed to symbolize luck and good fortune, can create very disturbing conditions when in an adverse aspect.

Tomascheck, an ex-chairman of the International Geophysical Society, is one of those rare Western scientists who also takes an active interest in astrology. In making a statistical analysis of 134 major earthquakes and comparing them with the positions of the planets at those times, he found that Jupiter, Uranus, and Pluto were in bad or stressful aspect "to a statistically significant degree."

This becomes even more interesting when it is remembered that modern astrology attributes qualities of revolution and drastic change to Uranus, and upheaval and chaos to Pluto. Pluto also was "god" of the underworld. According to the Greeks, the benevolent god Jupiter was not beyond turning nasty and throwing thunderbolts when his cronies and mere mortals upset him.

Another physicist who believes in applying traditional astrological principles to modern scientific research is Konstantin Kobysev of Moscow University. His researches have produced such positive results he is confident that one day it may be possible to predict natural disasters such as earthquakes, floods, and epidemics from the study of relationships between and among celestial bodies. He thinks the laws behind these phenomena could eventually be clearly defined, thus ushering in a new era of hope for thousands who die annually in natural disasters.

Two Western scientists who were not afraid to suggest that astrology might deserve more respect from official scientific circles are John R. Gribbin, a British astrophysicist, and Stephen H. Plagemann, an American astronomer who worked with eminent astronomer Fred Hoyle, as well as for NASA. "To the surprise of many scientists," they said, "there has come evidence . . . that the astrologers were not so wrong after all: it seems that the alignments of the planets can, for sound reasons, affect the behavior of the earth. The trail [of evidence they had assembled] links astrology—for that is really what the study of planetary alignments is even though we can explain their effects in sound scientific terms—astronomy, meteorology, geology, geophysics and other sciences."

SUN SIGNS AND PERSONALITY STUDIES

Hans Eysenck, professor of psychology at London University, has come up with some extraordinary results. His research has shown that astrology can and does make accurate assessments of personalities. Eysenck says that the position of the planets when a person is born is an accurate guide to how introverted or extroverted the person will become and also to how emotional the person will be.

His research was based on the traditional astrological premise that extroverts are born when the Sun is in Aries, Gemini, Leo, Libra, Sagittarius, and Aquarius, and that introverts are born when the sun is in Taurus, Cancer, Virgo, Scorpio, Capricorn, and Pisces. According to astrologers, people born under the three water signs—Cancer, Scorpio, and Pisces—are the most emotional types.

Professor Eysenck asked more than two thousand people to complete a personality questionnaire, which included their dates of birth. The answers were computer-analyzed and gave "an overwhelming verdict supporting the predictions of astrology."

Publishing his findings, the professor said: "I must admit this was a great surprise to me. My instinctive skepticism had led me to expect failure from an investigation of astrology."

Sybil Eysenck, also a psychologist and the professor's wife, has found that the position of the planets Mars, Jupiter, and Saturn at the moment of birth is significant in the forming of an individual's personality. In France, she studied the research of another famous husband-and-wife team, Dr. Françoise Gauquelin and Dr. Michel Gauquelin.

PLANETARY PLACEMENTS AND CAREER STUDIES

Michel Gauquelin, who originally set out to disprove astrology, has done more perhaps than any other scientist in modern times to prove the validity of its assumptions.

With his wife, he traveled through Europe collecting data from birth registers to combine with similar statistics obtained from his native France. His object was to discover any correlation between the positions of the planets at the time of birth and the professions people follow.

The two researchers compiled data for large groups of eminent professors of medicine, soldiers, politicians, artists, sportsmen, clerics, writers, and musicians. In all cases, their comparisons showed an inexplicable correlation between the planets and the chosen professions.

In the horoscopes of scientists and academicians, as astrology would maintain, Mars and Saturn figured prominently. Sportsmen were strongly influenced by Jupiter and Mars, as tradition would predict. In the charts of musicians and painters, the influence of the not-so-artistic planets Mars and Saturn was noticeably diminished.

At the odds of half a million to one against, Mars occupied dominant positions in the charts of scientists. At astronomically greater odds against chance, the hard-driving, energetic planet Mars was prominent among the 1,485 athletes surveyed. And among 3,142 military leaders whose charts were examined, Mars, the planet that symbolizes war and self-assertion, was strong in 634 cases—at odds of a million to one against.

An interesting point about the leading Nazis of the Third Reich came out of Michel Gauquelin's research. It concerns the position in their horoscopes of the planet Jupiter. Jupiter symbolizes expansion and power. Strongly positioned in a chart, it also induces a fondness for exaggerated ceremony and theatrical display. In the horoscopes of Hitler and his henchmen Himmler, Heydrich, Goebbels, and Bormann, all of whom hungered for power and possessed a love of the dramatic, Jupiter was the dominant factor in the power-sensitive angles.

SUN SIGNS AND CAREER STUDIES

Other scientists have also done studies to ascertain whether the twelve zodiacal Sun sign types are inclined to be drawn to particular jobs, careers and professions. In both America and England, two independent research teams have culled through hundreds of thousands of birth dates and come up with much the same answer. Astrological notions are correct to a statistically significant degree.

The English team comprised Alan Smithers of Manchester University, and his colleague, Bradford sociologist Joe Cooper. In the United States, Edmund Van Deusen, a scientific consultant, and his team of researchers checked through the birth dates of 163,953 individuals to ascertain which of the Sun signs had been successful in 37 specific professions.

In an interview with Ann Leslie in the *London Daily Mail,* April 25, 1977, Van Deusen explained: "Let's suppose, for example that it takes a certain type of personality to become a good doctor. By the law of averages the birth pattern of doctors should match the birth pattern of general population. If (in the final analysis of such a research project) to a statistically significant degree the doctors' birth pattern is very different—then something extraordinary is happening."

And so it was.

Van Deusen and the British team, although working independently on the evidence of more than 750,000 birth dates between them, found that the birth dates of 6,413 British and American doctors clustered well beyond chance in the summer and autumn months, with the British Army medical officers peaking in Scorpio. Scorpio, according to astrologers, is the sign of natural-born soldiers and surgeons.

Samples of 6,677 British and American lawyers revealed that they tend to be born in early summer and midautumn, with the American birth dates peaking particularly in Gemini. The sign of the Twins, astrologers say, is noted for the ability to argue any issue or case from either side.

Geminis also came out on top as the people most likely to become diplomats and advertising executives. Traditionally, Gemini is the sign of communication, salesmanship, quick thinking, and a facility for learning languages.

Of the 2,696 bankers studied by Van Deusen, a statistically disproportionate number were Virgos. "Astrologically speaking," Van Deusen is quoted as saying, "this would be predictable. Virgos are supposedly accountants by nature—life is a ledger in which every event must be neatly entered."

American and Birtish composers, the researchers found, tend to be born between late autumn and late winter—that is, in Sagittarius, Capricorn, Aquarius, and Pisces.

Of the 5,111 American and Canadian librarians surveyed by Van Deusen, the dominant sign was Libra. And Librans "according to astrologers need to work in a quiet, congenial, harmonious environment."

British politicians, according to the researchers, tend to be born under Aries, the sign of go-getting, self-asserting, and often crusading people.

Both surveys bore out the astrological tradition that Scorpios (and Leos because of their leadership qualities) are drawn to the army. The birth dates of 16,000 British Army officers and 12,000 American Army officers showed that 34 percent more than would be expected were born in late summer and early autumn, with the peaks occurring in Leo and Scorpio.

Of 5,056 schoolteachers, the dominant signs were Leos and Virgos. Said Van Deusen: "A schoolroom can quickly degenerate into chaos unless the teacher exercises a degree of authority. This, an astrologer would maintain, makes it the right setting for Leos, who can command a situation by their very presence. And it is also appropriate for the everyone-in-his-place Virgos.''

Virgo also was the sign under which a disproportionate number of the 3,927 leading British and American authors were born. Virgos are methodically analytical, as the distinguished classical Virgo writers Tolstoy, Goethe, and H. G. Wells showed.

Top signs in the laughter stakes are Aquarius, Pisces, Aries, Taurus, and Gemini. The British survey found that the most comedians were born between January 21 and June 20.

ASTROSCOPE PROFILES

Astrology, as it is practiced today, is far easier to follow and understand than at any other time in its long history. Still, you can recapture that old-time magic and mystery even as you read here the commonsense, factual connections between the planets and the signs that make you a unique individual. Astrology is a personal art and science. The *Astroscope Profile* series, which enables you to construct your own profile, opens up that exciting new world of discovery. The subsequent chapters of this book take you on a journey through your Sun sign, your Rising sign, and the signs in which the Moon and other planets appear for you. *Bon voyage!*

Sun Sign Capricorn

Capricorn:
Character Analysis

T he Sun in Capricorn at birth produces a thoughtful, strong, enterprising, practical, and intriguing character of extraordinary endurance and courage. Capricorns persevere in the face of difficulty and hardship. They are cautious and methodical individuals. If they seem to take a chance, it is usually because they have worked out all the angles in advance and know the odds are more than with them.

The Capricorn boy and girl, in spite of a youthful freshness and exuberance, have a distinctly serious side. These youngsters seem older than their years, far wiser at times than adolescence normally suggests. They are a bit of a puzzle, not easy to fathom or work out.

Capricorn men and women, no matter how humble or ordinary their beginnings, usually make something special of their lives, at least to their own satisfaction. Quite frequently they end up in positions of power and authority. They are the stuff tycoons are made of. But it does take time.

FROM THE SEA TO THE SUMMIT

The modern astrological symbol for Capricorn is frequently a Goat heading to the summit of a mountain. The most ancient astrologers depicted it as a goat with a curling fish's tail—half goat, half fish. They associated this figure with the culture gods who came out of the sea (the unconscious) each day to teach man the ways of civilization, before returning at night.

Like the myth and the old symbol suggest, men and women born under Capricorn have an exceptional ability for organizing and taking command of worldly affairs. They are constructive realists. They face up to the world as it is. Facts are their building stones. Unlike many other zodiacal types, Capricorns aren't daunted by the size or complexity of a project.

Their schemes are of the kind that can encompass and serve an entire community. The civilizing or organizing urge expressed through order and correct procedure is dominant. In fact, the bigger, harder, and more challenging an undertaking, the more they revel in the exertions of mastering it.

The secret of these people's strength and success lies in their patience and fortitude, in the remarkable way they can fix a long-term goal and drive relentlessly toward it. Opposition and obstacles are expected, responsibilities and obligations never shirked.

Capricorns are not belligerent individuals who go looking for a fight. They prefer to conserve their energies as much as possible for climbing— to the top. If forced, they can give a good account of themselves in any kind of scrap. At their best, they do indeed exemplify the qualities of the hardy Goat who can attain to head-spinning heights of achievement.

And what of the sea, the other world, the unconscious that the half goat, half fish comes from? How does this part of the character reveal itself?

Capricorn men and women are deep and unknowable. Their profoundest thoughts and feelings are never expressed. They would truly love to be able to release these to show the world that they are as feeling and as sensitive as others, and possibly more so. But it never happens. It's as though an invisible wall existed between their inner emotions and the outer world.

Capricorn people are not idle dreamers or talkers. Certainly they are idealists with a desire to set the world to rights according to their view of it. They bring their dreams to earth and materialize them. While others may look hopefully to a bit of good luck for help, the Capricorn way is to make the best of what is available and get on with it. These men and women are invincibly self-reliant. The typical Capricorn person takes very little for granted. The motto of the sign is: "I use."

A LONG AND LONELY SEARCH

The ruling planet of Capricorn is Saturn. Saturn is the planet of limitation, restriction, and discipline. Astrologically, Saturn is said to represent the pinnacle of achievement—after hard, long, and self-sacrificing exertions.

This explains why Capricorns often come into their own in later life. The second half of their existence is usually the most rewarding and personally fulfilling, as then their conscientious and persevering labors begin to pay off. They reach their goals and begin to sit back a little. Although never inactive, they then find more time to work for the benefit of others.

The Saturn influence tends to make the childhood of many Capricorn people less happy and smooth than what might be normally expected. Separations from loved ones can have traumatic effects and leave deep psychological scars. They may lose a parent, or through other circumstances have to be raised by a stepparent or a foster family. Frequently, a stern and authoritative parental figure is involved in their early years.

Capricorn men and women suffer frequently from loneliness. But they are able to bear it better than most. Due to their self-imposed reserve and aloofness, they accept it with patient resignation. Loneliness, to a Capricorn, is just one of the many afflictions man has to bear. There is something of the fatalist in their nature, although to them it is realism.

Capricorns seldom make enemies. As long as a person shows them respect and does not try to put them down, they are easy to please and are tolerant. They don't have any great expectations of the human race. Their nature is basically pessimistic, so they tend to look on the dark side.

Being realists, they can understand the necessity in the world for lying, deceiving, and trying to take advantage. These frailties of human nature they can forgive. But any action by another that embarrasses and humiliates them personally is a devastating blow.

The less-evolved Capricorn type is vindictive. Insults and slights are brooded on until the desire for revenge becomes another goal. But, as always with Capricorns, nothing is rushed. Unlike Scorpios, they don't plan how they will even a score. The Goat, in his or her long trek from the sea to the summit, knows the value of time, that in the end somehow the opportunity or time to get even will come.

This great respect for time insinuates itself through every level of the Capricorn nature. It is part of their astrological inheritance. Saturn, the powerful ruler of the sign, is identified with time, with the old god Cronus bearing a flint scythe. Astrologically, Saturn represents the guardian of higher consciousness or knowledge. Until man surrenders his selfish will by humbly accepting the restrictions of time and the need for self-discipline, he can't earn the right to pass to immortality.

Capricorn people, Saturn creatures all, are distinguished by their preparedness to plod on conscientiously and persistently regardless of difficulties and hardships. These men and women work better with encouragement. But even without it, they'll accept their lot while patiently, methodically, and responsibly striving on. They expect nothing, except that time will run its natural course. There is no need for hurry.

THE VIEW FROM THE TOP

Capricorn is the tenth sign of the Zodiac. It stands for worldly acclaim, prestige, and honor through accomplishment. The primal desire of this group is attainment. They are success-oriented. They do not have a great deal of time for the lighter side of life once they've found the job they want to do. Other interests gradually become secondary, even nonexistent, as they concentrate on the goal fixed. Usually, this is to reach the top, whether in business, employment, or a profession.

Capricorn is the sign in which Mars, the most energetic and physical planet of all, is exalted. That is, Mars reaches the height of its power in Capricorn. Mars is the planet of aggression and masculine strength. It is this influence that gives Capricorn men and women their indomitable drive. Of course, it makes the sign very tough and hardy, which is somewhat difficult for the females, who appear to be very much able to look after themselves. However, Capricorn is a female sign. So Mars, burning under its frozen beauty, provides the very attractive suggestion of smoldering fire.

Capricorns are not ones to dramatize their qualifications or abilities, or to draw attention to themselves for fear of creating a scene. So their progress is often slower than they deserve. They tend to wait for promotions to be handed out rather than to ask. They are head down, hard at work most of the time. So intent are they on doing a good job, they have little time for frivolity or aimless talk.

Rewards and honor, not so much fame, are what Capricorn people desire most. They are prepared to work hard for the honors they covet, to give all they've got in punctilious concentration and application. But too often, they disregard the value of personal relationships. Seeing achievement as the only virtue of work, they give little of themselves to others. People as people are frequently excluded from their calculations.

Capricorns tend to cut themselves off, to back into a corner surrounded by their files, systems, phones, and buzzers, and to lose touch with the rest of working humanity. The farther they advance in an organization, the more isolated they become. Although respected for their abilities, in positions of authority they can be feared rather than liked or loved. This becomes irksome. They can yearn for company, for the human touch, yet with their stern, uncompromisingly aloof manner keep any hand from reaching out toward them. In these circumstances, they often end up with all the power and security they craved—but desolate and unhappy.

WORKING TO STAY ON TOP

To compensate for desolation and unhappiness, Capricorn people release their pent-up feelings through more work. What they feel they can't attain in love, they determine to win through achievement and success. They are seldom idle. Most of their waking moments are spent attending to some organized activity. Even as homemakers, they work untiringly, dividing the day into specific chores so that their time is used efficiently and well.

Nothing, not even their families, is allowed to interfere with work. Although family life means a good deal to Capricorn men and women, those who go out to work insist that the problems of their mates and children be kept completely separate. Work is considered the nucleus of their existence, and around that everything else spins in its allotted place. There are not many empty spaces in a Capricorn's life.

These men and women are so work-involved that frequently they put off taking vacations until the last moment. When they do get a break, it is often their style to spend it working on the house or some other project or hobby.

They are so absorbed in work that even unpleasant and uncomfortable conditions do not intrude. A Capricorn person is likely to carry on just as efficiently at work through sickness, depression, and major family upheavals. Their sense of purpose and responsibility is undeviating.

Being one of the most success-oriented of the twelve zodiacal types, and willing to work night and day for it in the face of hardship and frustration, they often prove to be the superachievers.

Capricorn men and women are especially suited for working in big companies and organizations. The larger the concern, the farther they are likely to go. Often they manage to climb to the very top executive positions.

They have an amazing ability for controlling diverse operations of the kind found in multinational conglomerates of the type involving oil, banking, land, investment, and finance. Federal, state, and local government often attract them. They become trusted senior administrators and advisers to governors, ministers, and heads of state.

Their dependability is one of their great strengths. They can sustain a great output of work over long periods. The more they feel needed and appreciated, the harder they work. Money is often considered to be secondary to the power and authority that can be won through high positions.

Capricorn people can make successful journalists, accountants, secretaries, educators, engineers, mathematicians, farmers, ranchers, builders, construction bosses, and office managers. These people can become great scientists and leaders of industry. With their indomitable spirit and rare talent for taking command and controlling labor, there is hardly any field or responsibility in which they can't become top man or top woman.

What Capricorn men and women have to remember all the way is to rise above their fears and to share themselves more with the people around them.

PUBLIC VS. PRIVATE IMAGE

It is in their emotional affairs that these December–January-born men and women are most vulnerable. Otherwise, they are very self-centered, rocklike in their convictions. Although not in the least vain, they refer the remarks of everyone around them to their exterior self-image, their sense of self-importance, which is exalted. They are very opinionated people, often snobs. The slightest slur or criticism is secretly regarded as an offense to dignity. Though too diffident or reserved as a rule to protest, they remember. Every little disrespectful act, real or imagined, is noted.

Capricorn men and women usually put ambition before all other considerations. Once they have fixed their sights on a goal, personal relationships may be given second place or swept aside. Those not helpful or involved in the worldly aim tend to be expendable. This is not as callous as it may sound.

The Capricorn person considers his or her home and family as the foundations for worldly success, a solid base from which to operate. These Saturn-ruled individuals are willing to work very hard at making a good job of both. The Capricorn instinct, as the urge to construct and control, is to use everything at their disposal to further their objectives.

Left to their own devices, these sons and daughters of Saturn are not optimistic people. They get the jitters about the future, start worrying, and get down in the dumps. Being with friends invariably bucks them up, gives them a more positive outlook. But they are too cautious and suspicious to believe anything until it happens.

The Capricorn ambition, unlike Leo's, is not obvious. Capricorn's highly developed sense of dignity demands a minimum of spectacle and no show of emotional involvement. Their approach at all times is serious, mature, and businesslike. They put more store by ideas and actions than words and promises.

They don't blow their own trumpets. When praised, they are inclined to be self-effacing, to play down their expertise and skills. Compliments give enormous enjoyment, but self-consciousness quickly sets in. When exposed to the limelight, Capricorns become easily embarrassed, uneasy, even furtive in their anxiety. But praise or recognition is seldom forgotten, and the person responsible will be well received the next time they meet.

A very poor opinion of their own worth typifies Capricorn men and women. Here again is the contradiction between the outgoing goat and the ingoing fish. On one hand, they have enormous faith in their efficiency and ability to perform and command. They have no difficulty imagining that the world would be far more productive if they were in charge.

But inwardly they are tyrannized by self-doubt. It is difficult for Capricorns to believe that anyone could think well of them, let alone love them for themselves. They feel like abysmal failures even when there is nothing in their worldly record to merit it. They are people at war with their own personality because the Goat is too frightened to jump into the sea of unconscious self.

TO SHARE OR NOT TO SHARE

The result is that Capricorn people give an impression of stiff and cool reserve. They can seem unfriendly, offhand, and brusque. Their words are few but meaningful, very often so much to the point that they stab and cut. Yet underneath is a truly tender and emotionally intense person who is looking for the warmth of true friendship and companionship—and especially love.

Capricorn people seldom manage on their own to erect a bridge between their inner and outer selves. The people who love and respect them have to do this. Capricorns are one of the loyalest and probably the most dependable types in the Zodiac. They have an enormous amount to give, not only to the world, but also to those who can manage to penetrate their deep reserve and establish inner contact.

Although never doubting their convictions, Capricorn men and women seldom understand themselves, mainly because their true selves are repressed and never see the light of day. They are so taken up with the material civilizing urge that they present an austere, aloof, no-nonsense exterior for people to take them seriously. They are weighed down like armor-suited Crusaders by a heavy sense of duty. So identified are they with maintaining a thoroughly respectful outer image, they can't bear the thought of failure and the loss of face it might bring. Better to show no feeling under any circumstances than to risk making a fool of oneself in public.

And so Capricorn men and women constrict their natural selves and suffer deeply for it. They long to share their complex and bewildering emotions, yet can't bring themselves to reach out to do it. There is, in fact, something of a saint, a Joan of Arc, trying to get out of these people. If this impulse surfaces, they can be extraordinarily kind and humanitarian, dedicating themselves to the improvement of society and the lot of human beings.

In spite of their cool-headed deliberateness, they are highly strung. In the face of obstructions, tensions build up. But these are kept well under control deep within. Self-containment is one of the hard lessons of Saturn. The trouble is that such stoic self-discipline in the end can make an individual too severe and exacting.

Capricorn men and women have to guard against becoming narrow-minded and unfeeling. It is terribly important that they don't make self-denial a way of life. This way they tend to cut themselves off from the rest of the world, most of which does not possess their Spartan will nor see the necessity for it. They can become derisive of fun and pleasure. The margin of experience they allow themselves can become so narrow that there is little left but ingrained habit.

At their worst, Capricorn men and women are suspicious and resentful. They are easily depressed and often go around for days in blue moods. Usually, these are induced by feelings that they are failing or that they are not appreciated sufficiently.

Self-forgetfulness is the one way people born under this sign can overcome discontent. It is significant that the birth of Christ is celebrated just after the Sun enters Capricorn. The self-sacrificing qualities of the sign are very often demonstrated by Capricorns. Once they discover the pleasure and fulfillment they get from serving and giving to others, instead of rigidly pursuing their own hardheaded schemes, they begin to realize the hidden potential of this sign. In India, the goat is still the sacrificial animal.

FRIENDSHIP: HONOR THROUGH DISTANCE

Capricorns normally do not take other people into their confidence. Friendship seldom means sharing intimate secrets. Good friends are few. But acquaintances are many, and Capricorns are usually well known in their communities.

At first meeting, a Saturn-ruled man or woman may seem unapproachable, somewhat forbidding. But this self-protective attitude starts to melt as confidence is gained. Then Capricorns emanate a gentle warmth.

These people are often active members of societies and clubs. By identifying with group aims, they can enhance their prestige. Although in many ways loners, Capricorns love and need company. They are more at ease in an objective atmosphere, though. With their organizational abilities and resourceful, enterprising minds, they usually gravitate to some form of group leadership. They are likely to take on the job of honorary secretary, treasurer, or some other key functional post.

Although undoubtedly the most serious types in the Zodiac, Capricorns have a delightful sense of humor. They are witty. Once relaxed in company, they are charming and can keep others cheerful and amused. Their humor is subtle, notable for its aptness and economy of words.

The typical Capricorn man or woman is a faithful, kind, and loyal friend. Although cautious and discriminating in accepting close friendship, these Saturn children often make wrong choices. This usually is in cases where they choose with their heads instead of with their hearts. They can seek friends with power and position believing they may be helpful in the future. In the usual Capricorn way they give a great deal to a friendship initially, but when the people involved turn out to be unworthy or when things go wrong, they suffer very badly.

To their true friends, Capricorn men and women are rocks to stand on in times of trouble. Their self-sacrificing quality comes to the fore. Although not ones to show much sentiment, their sympathetic efforts to be of as much practical help as possible are a great comfort.

What Capricorns promise, they do, They can't stand being betrayed themselves, and they won't do it to others. Having a sense of duty and honor, they never talk behind a friend's back or allow others to do so in their presence. In such cases the subject is quickly changed. They have their own way of estimating people and find that quite sufficient until a person proves to be otherwise.

It is in times of crisis that the glacial calm of Capricorn people wins them respect and admiration. Harassed and pressured by circumstances or events, they seldom lose their composure or ability to think clearly. In emergencies they are a tower of strength, constructive and realistic. Others have no fear about entrusting their interests or personal safety to the Capricorn judgment.

TRUSTING TRADITION AND THE TRIED AND TRUE

Tradition means a good deal to Capricorns. Although not sentimental types, they have a respect for the old and the past. They are attracted by the idea of their ancestors. Underneath their formality, they are patriotic and proud of any contribution they are able to make to the progress of society. All true Capricorns would like to see a statue of themselves erected by a grateful public in recognition of some worthy community achievement. The perennial problem at the bottom of the male and female's frustration is to find a way to channel their enormous self-oriented capabilities into worthy service.

Self-criticism is a pernicious habit of Capricorns. Among strangers, they feel people are staring at them and will perceive the humiliating truths about themselves that they have seen. In maturity, the urge to run away and hide is controlled. But often young Capricorns can't stand the imagined scrutiny of others, and abruptly leave the room without explanation or apology.

Capricorn men and women are secretive. A great deal of their time is spent in their complex feelings behind the veil that keeps these emotions hidden from the world. Here is the wellspring of their intuition, which can give them tremendous insights into truth and reality.

But they are very cautious about communicating any unorthodox views or mystical experiences. These they keep very much to themselves, in the deep subconscious from where they arose, and only briefly became known. They are too afraid of ridicule to be pioneers in the realm of the spirit.

Also, they tend to doubt their own insights. What was real one moment is soon engulfed by the practical, rationalizing considerations that dictate their worldly responses. Capricorns tend to trust only tangibles. In the absence of continuous revelation, they put their faith in concrete facts. And if these are not available, they tend to embrace the doctrines of established religions.

Capricorn is the sign of law and order. These people normally are skeptical of abstract ideas and philosophies. They prefer systems of thought that have developed over the ages and that they can equate with their experience. They are strong-willed, strong-minded people who believe implicitly in the correctness of their opinions. They have to guard against allowing their views and beliefs to degenerate into dogmatism. These people usually are pillars of propriety, staunch supports of the rules and regulations of their communities.

CONSERVING MONEY, TIME, ENERGY, AND EMOTION

Both the Capricorn man and woman do not like waste. Although they like their creature comforts, they seldom can be accused of extravagant living. They are careful with money, but not miserly unless the placements of the other planets are unfavorable.

Typical Capricorns are wizards at making money and controlling it. They are not necessarily fast earners. But as the years go by and as they persevere toward their long-held goals, the money usually keeps coming in. Their conscientious, responsible, resourceful, patient, and industrious efforts invariably earn them good wages as employees and satisfactory profits as business owners.

They are not the kind of people to speculate or gamble. Their money mounts slowly, steadily, and surely. Once they start to get some cash together, it invariably grows. They have a flair for financial transactions and a natural urge to save and economize. When obliged to, they can make money go a very long way.

In hard times, they have the self-discipline to deny themselves any luxury required as well as what others might consider necessities. Yet they will never allow their families to go without while they can possibly help it.

Often these people worry about their financial security when there is not the slightest need to. They are not the types to starve. They are too hardworking, shrewd, versatile, and self-concerned for that. Capricorn men and women never doubt their ability to succeed in the world. Whatever they choose to do for a living they invariably do well.

In most areas of their life, Capricorn people are shrewd and prudent. They are just as economical with words as with money and emotion. Nothing is wasted, not even their never-ending supply of energy. Although continuously active, they seldom start anything and not finish it. However, they are capable of handling several projects at the same time and keeping them under their personal control. Usually, their diversified activities have a common long-range objective where all will come together in one bigger-than-life finale.

HEALTH AND THE OUTDOOR LIFE

People born under Capricorn usually get healthier as the years roll by. By the time they reach a mellow age, they're tougher than leather and a great deal lighter and cheerier of heart than in the earlier days. They grow into well-rounded, relaxed, and far less self-conscious personalities.

Older Capricorn men and women are often doyens of the professions, the business world, and industry. Happily surrounded by respectful and numerous family members, they frequently wonder in maturity what all their earlier fears and hangups were about. As a rule, these male and female Goats live long lives, having active and capable minds right to the end.

Healthwise, it is in the earliest years that their exacting and demanding planetary ruler, Saturn, seems to afflict them most. As youngsters, they are often weak, thin, and slow-growing. They are types to get frequent colds, coughs, and flu. They seem susceptible to every known child's disease. Although not serious, these ailments force them to stay away from school and interfere with their studies.

In adulthood, the main health problems are likely to be caused by worry and gloom. Illnesses can be brought on by anxiety. Just to think about some disorder can produce symptoms of it and create more worry. It is a vicious circle that often can be broken only by Capricorns mixing with people and getting more fun out of life.

Discontent and depression can gradually attack the digestive system, causing painful stomach ailments. Once psychosomatic disorders get a hold, they tend to become chronic. Capricorn people often suffer from totally unnecessary discomfort brought on by nervous tension.

Relaxation and vacations are especially important. Of all the types, the Goat needs to get away from the arid workaday mountain. Green pastures, laughter, travel, and new faces are all part of the essential therapy for these workaholics. Both the male Goat and the female Goat are good dancers.

Emotional low tides and the need to compensate for a massive inferiority complex often drive these Saturn-ruled individuals to drink. Although they need to relax in convivial company, they often tend to go overboard and make a habit of excessive alcoholic intake.

Capricorn people either have very good teeth or very bad. Much depends on the placement of their ruler, Saturn, which governs the bone structure as well as the skin. They should be careful not to get sunburned. Infections of the skin may be difficult to get rid of even with medical treatment.

The mind of these people is so much linked with their deepest emotions that they should try to avoid brooding and suspiciously working out the intentions of others who may have offended them. Behind the façade, deep inside the unconscious, is an unfathomable whirlpool of negative emotions, a disaster area for any Capricorn to try to explore.

These men and women love open-air life. They are often good at sports, especially skating and skiing. They have tremendous resistance to cold weather. One Capricorn man walks through the woods to the train for work every morning, even in midwinter snow, wearing just a suit, his glowing face and confident, lively gait showing his absolute delight. These people seldom get fatigued after long periods of physical exertion.

They enjoy gardening because it allows them to get out of the house and to root around in the soil. They will plant anything, proudly displaying the fruits and flowers of their efforts. They also reclaim from the soil any materials that can be recycled and put back into good use. Capricorns are creative conservationists. What is rubbish to some folk is coin for a new realm in Capricorn's book.

HOMELIFE AND FAMILY LIFE

Their typical Capricorn home is a very practical place. It is as clean and tidy as human hands and a good assortment of equipment can make it. Often, the Capricorn woman will go through the place twice a day: once in the morning and again in the evening. These women can't stand the thought of disorder in their domain; no dirty dishes will pile up in this house while the house is their niche.

Both the Capricorn man and woman love color and comfort. Their home is usually bright and airy, perhaps sometimes a bit on the chilly side in winter—but not because they're too stingy to pay the heating bills. With their love of fresh air and natural resistance to cold, they like to have at least one window open most of the time.

Flowers abound. Or if that is unfeasible, there will be outdoor scenes represented. There's usually at least one brightly colored wall or a large vivid painting, perhaps executed by the woman of the house, that provides a lighter feeling when Capricorn gets down in the dumps and needs cheering up.

Typical Capricorns usually have more than one child. Sometimes they have several. Although they love their kids and provide them with every material need, they don't make them their entire life. To the Capricorn parent, children are more of an ideal to be served than an individual attachment.

Children represent the fulcrum of home and family, life that is essential to the Capricorn idea of security. Here Capricorn lays down his or her roots. Here are the foundations from which these ambitious people start to build. Their worldly pursuits may often seem to absorb far more of their time. But it is the family, the home that they rationalize as being the reason for it all.

Above all, these are rational people who must have a good reason for everything they do. Spontaneity is not one of their foremost qualities. It is important that the home of a Capricorn man or woman is a source of delight. Otherwise, Capricorns are likely to spend more and more time away from home, working late and pursuing their goals. Their mates will be happier if they remember this.

Entertaining is usually a correctly elegant affair. Dinner parties are organized with all the efficiency and flair of a majordomo. And if friends drop in unexpectedly, Capricorn is equal to the occasion. Something appropriate is always stored away in the pantry or the freezer. Seldom are Capricorn people ever caught napping. ''Be Prepared'' is another of their mottos.

The typical Capricorn, especially the female, is very attached to his or her parents, probably more to one than the other. People who marry Capricorns are usually taken home very early in the affair to get Mom or Dad's approval, tacit or otherwise. After marriage, the Goat invariably maintains close or regular parental contact. Frequent visits are likely to be the accepted routine.

RELATIONSHIPS

How Capricorn people get along with and react in love and marriage with the other signs of the Zodiac are given in detail in the next chapter, titled "Capricorn: Love and Romance." Here we will deal generally with the Capricorn love nature, and take a brief glimpse at what makes the Capricorn female and then the Capricorn male tick.

In their approach to love, Capricorn men and women often are late starters. Their reserved and rather standoffish manner does little to encourage close relationships. Other amorously precocious types are inclined to experiment as soon as possible. However, the seemingly hard-to-get appeal of the younger Capricorn attracts the attention of deeply sexual signs such as Scorpio or Taurus. So an initiation into the mysteries of romantic excitement and sex takes place very early for some Capricorn individuals.

Underneath the pretentious Capricorn frigidity is a volcano of love and sex waiting to be released. It takes a real man or woman to bridge the gap, someone who truly knows how to love. Capricorn men and women can be reached only by love. The awakening fire has to come to them from outside. They may yearn and long for love, but seldom can they bring themselves to make the move toward it. They are shy. They are timid. They are vulnerable.

In the game of love, Capricorn men and women lose all the confidence that makes them such formidable business or professional people. Although they try to discriminate and choose their partners with great care, their judgment in the early days is often woefully wrong. Their introduction to romance is frequently heartbreaking.

They tend to believe what they've read about starry-eyed love, to be misled by superficial qualities. They don't make the same mistake twice. But not being emotionally resilient people, once is enough. The hurt lasts for a long time. And the damage done often makes them more suspicious and distant than is their nature.

Capricorn men and women need love like bodies need air. Only through love, and particularly physical love, can they adequately express and release the repressed creative fire that burns within. Capricorn is not a sign renowned for its artistically creative talent. This is because few of these people ever really find the love they need to awaken or manifest this side of their nature. Love is their inspiration. Love is the fountain that can lift them up out of their earthbound rational world to the heights of artistic attainment.

This does not mean that Capricorn people who have found true love are necessarily going to be great artists, painters, sculptors, and suchlike. Where Capricorn usually expresses its most self-fulfilling creative talent is in service to other human beings, especially to humanity as a whole. Enlightened by the discovery of true love, the often brilliant Capricorn mind can win distinction and the grateful thanks of the community in science, medicine, politics, and other civilizing fields.

Love and art can't be separated in the Capricorn person. Without love, his or her life can be materially constructive but aesthetically sterile.

Capricorn is probably the best sexual performer of all the zodiacal types. The sexual appetite of these men and women is often voracious and insatiable. Few people would ever guess that under that quiet, reserved exterior boils such a cauldron of physical passion and need.

The Capricorn woman is looking for total love. She makes mistakes only when she settles for less. She tends to rationalize her feelings, so that love often becomes a search for someone who can satisfy her desire for material security. She wants to go places socially and financially. Her dream is to accomplish something worthwhile in life and to find a man with whom she can make her dreams come true.

She is not interested in big talkers with grandiose plans but little energy. This is an action female. As a teenager she probably was more interested in sports and studies than in boys. She liked the company of young men who were friends but nothing more. She was the type who likes to study with a boy. But when it comes to him walking her home and trying to steal a kiss, forget it. This girl even then was serious. She wasn't going to fool with any Tom, Dick, or Harry, fall in love, and sell herself short.

The Capricorn woman always sets high standards for men as well as for all other areas of her life. She is a high climber, a summit female. The boyfriends of her classmates she never considered good enough. Sometimes she treated them with undisguised disdain. They probably were too immature, undisciplined, and intent on pleasure for her liking.

Capricorn is not a woman a man can hope to win by reading poetry, singing under moonlit skies, or displaying a gardenful of posies. If there are any love fairies in these childish games, she would have to see them to believe in them. She is not the imaginative, romantic type. Boxes of chocolates, perfume, soft lights, and secluded restaurants are all nice and appreciated—but not sincere.

The Capricorn woman, by nature and through experience, has learned not to judge a book by its cover. Tokens of affection are all very well and good. But it is the man behind them she wants to see. And she knows that only time reveals all. She will make no quick decisions. She is terrified of making mistakes where her emotions are concerned.

Because Capricorn has always been emotionally unsure of herself, she has made a point of developing a technique for attracting men. Being a rational and methodical person, she has noted since her first serious affair what turns them on and what turns them off. The self she puts across to a man is not really her at all. It is usually her serious, cautious, sensible self. In love, though, she can be magnificently abandoned.

The problem is that deep down inside, the female Goat has such a poor opinion of herself that she can't believe any man would be interested in her apart from her body or her brain. She wants to be loved for herself. Yet even she can't find herself, although she feels that her self is in need of love, incessant and true.

She can be a problem for the men who do not care enough to reach her. She can be moody, suspicious, untrusting—the kind who would follow and spy on a man she thought might be two-timing her. She's got little vanity but a lot of pride. Any double-crosser will never do it twice to her.

A Capricorn woman is very demanding to live with. She needs to be reassured constantly that she is appreciated and loved. She is such an ex-pert, responsive physical lover that what she can't say in words to com-municate her love and affection she does with her body.

This female can be an ego downer for any man who does not care enough to tear aside her cool and logical veil. Men who are looking for emotional reassurance from a woman had better pass her by. She does not try to amuse the man she takes seriously. She won't flirt with him or com-pliment him needlessly. She needs the reassurance, but she is not giving any away to get it back.

If she really likes a man and wants to go to bed with him, she is quite capable of making this very clear very quickly. When she wants to make love, she does not beat around the bush. But usually, the man she ap-proaches she has had under observation for some time. So she knows how to seduce him without complications.

One exceedingly attractive Capricorn woman in her early thirties was living with a family for some months after terminating a long love affair. The son of the family, in his early twenties, had always admired her but never imagined he would have a chance. She seemed too beautiful, aloof, self-contained, and serious for him. And, obviously, she could have any man she wanted. One astonishing day they were alone in the house. She looked at him with that straight, deep, serious gaze. And he knew she wanted him to make love to her. She had observed him for a long time to make sure he was right for her, that he would not rebuff her nor be unkind.

Typical Capricorn women are not promiscuous. They are choosy. They select their lovers with the same care that a connoisseur chooses a wine. Indiscriminate bed hopping is beneath their dignity. Besides, it contains too many risks of their being ridiculed or dishonored.

Capricorn women who put off taking lovers do not often recognize their own sensuality. In the moment of conquest, they are often surprised at their responses to the actions and words of lovemaking. They frequently discover for the first time what it is like really to be alive. The pleasure of the senses is something they can revel in without inhibitions.

After marriage, a Capricorn woman who does not keep up her career is likely to center all her ambition on her husband. It will be a happier relationship if he is a hard worker, determined to make a name for himself in the world. This woman will be a tower of strength to him. If he loves her, she will never be unfaithful. She wants to excel in every way as a wife and homemaker.

The typical Capricorn man wants a woman who will stand beside him all the way to the top. He is not interested in the flirtatious, flighty kind, although he won't mind an affair with a few of them while he searches for the woman of his dreams. These dream images are pretty fancy for such a quiet, reserved fellow like honorable Capricorn.

Capricorn's dream woman is extremely feminine, yet tough and vital enough to keep up with him speeding down the ski slopes, hiking through the mountains, or roughing it on a camping vacation. He wants her to be intelligent, but does not mind if she frequently seeks his advice and help. Although he wants her to stand on her own two feet, he enjoys the idea of being lord and master. His fantasy is a contradiction. What he really wants is an androgynous female who is sexy.

This man has low-key charm and authority. He knows what he wants. He doesn't waste words. Some of them are blunt and off-putting until a woman gets to know him. But he conveys a genuine air of seriousness and sincerity. When he shows interest in a woman, he means it. This man takes his promises and obligations very seriously.

He can be flirtatious in a mild way. He is very amusing with his sharp, quick wit. But with a woman he wants to make his mate or wife, he rarely plays around. He is not the dramatic type, however. A woman might be uncertain for some time whether he is really trying to make it with her. His approach is cautious, tentative. He wants to be sure she's absolutely right for him before revealing his intentions. Although he would not admit that he likes a woman to take the lead and try to woo him, he often has to be encouraged gently and coaxed in the right direction.

When Capricorn does make up his mind that a certain woman is for him, he doesn't fool around. He pops the question, and announces all his plans for the two of them for the future. He wants a marriage that will last and that goes places. Often he tries to put off marrying too early, but somehow he gets maneuvered into it. When the time comes for starting a family, he would prefer just one or two kids. But frequently he has several, and does well by all of them.

He is impressed by a woman's refined background, especially her academic qualifications. He is very happy if she comes from an influential family. And if there happens to be money on her side, he is even more delighted. The Goat is prepared to work for all he gets. But the idea of a little something that might benefit him in later years tends to stop him from worrying about material security in the middle years.

The Capricorn man has to be boosted continuously. Otherwise, he tends to feel like a failure and will fall into deep depressions. His woman has to remember that his lovemaking is the most voluble way he has of saying he loves her. Either he does not see any need to utter those words, or he just can't manage to get them out. The verbalizing of love or affection makes him feel foolish.

His woman should never kiss him or throw her arms around him in public. He hates having attention drawn to him, unless it is out of respect or esteem, the more formal the better. Emotional displays make him freeze. His need for warmth is hidden. What is revealed is his cool exterior, a rocklike self-image. This man's image of himself is a person of worth, responsibility, and good standing, and he wants to be considered as such. No emotion, please!

In familiar situations he quickly settles into a rut. It will be up to his woman to make sure he gets out, sees people, has fun, and exercises his joints and muscles. He likes good company, but can retreat into a world of work and little play if left to his own devices.

Even the sports that in his youth were so important are likely to be dropped gradually. A woman who can play a round of golf with him or get him out walking regularly in the fresh air or get him rooting around in a flower or rock garden will be one of the best things that ever happened to him.

ALTERNATIVELY ... *Unevolved ♑*

Every sign of the Zodiac has a negative side. No one is perfect. Most people have their fair share of mean, destructive, and antisocial traits. But there are individuals in this world who are absolutely rotten, villains to the core.

One of the values of astrology is to provide the opportunity for people to see themselves as they really are, and then to make any personality corrections they themselves decide are necessary. The following is a description of the negative side of the Capricorn character.

Perverse Capricorn people are selfish and egotistical. They are determined to present their exalted self-image to the rest of the world, regardless of who suffers in the process. One thing is sure: They won't!

They use everyone in their lives. Very little is sacred in their desperation to get to the top. It is very easy for an unevolved Capricorn man or woman to cross the borderline of ambition into crime. Unable to wait for the rewards that usually come to Capricorns through patience and persistence, these exploiters take Easy Street and become mobsters.

But they do not risk their own necks. Being extraordinarily good schemers, they make sure that others are the scapegoats for their own failures. These people have a thirst for power. They are the organizers, the syndicate bosses who try to get others in their clutches and then exploit them. They are the greedy ones who milk the poor and underprivileged.

Seldom are these unprincipled Capricorns happy for long. They suffer from fierce depressions and paranoia. They like to work out their negative emotions by being cruel and autocratic to their subordinates and dependents. They hurt the communities they live in and represent.

They are pessimists, killjoys, and wet blankets. To live and be associated with them is an exercise in gloom and despair. Sometimes their black moods can become so desperate that they seem suicidal.

These people usually work so hard at whatever they do that they become overstrained. Chronic fatigue makes them even more pessimistic. They seldom have a good word to say for anything or anyone. They want to be honored by the world, but seldom are in the least honorable. They are sneaky, mean, and two-faced. Often these uncultured Capricorn men and women are misers. They expect others to spend money on them, but they won't buy anything in return.

Because they have so many weaknesses and faults themselves, they have a very low opinion of the rest of society. In business, they trade on lower instincts and encourage others to surrender their principles. These highly opinionated and self-centered characters expect to be catered to. Anyone who does not show them the respect they believe is deserved is invariably punished in some way sooner or later. These are vindictive and revengeful people.

Older Capricorn men often marry women younger than themselves whose strength will restore their own youth. They may not care if their young wives lie or deceive them, as long as these females pay them all due respect and constantly admire them, especially in public.

The female Capricorn gone wrong does not like other women. She encourages acquaintances, whom she uses at every opportunity. Her friends tolerate her because she will always organize things for them. But generally she takes much more out of a friendship than she puts back.

Perceptive people stay clear of a self-serving Capricorn man or woman because they sense the Goat's desire to get control of them and root them under the ground. Perverse Capricorns try to prove their superiority at other people's expense. They scoff at the accomplishments of others, making out that such success is due to unfair tactics or worse. They will destroy a person's reputation to make themselves appear more important and influential.

To superiors, they are grovelers and yes-men. Yet they are among the greatest snobs on earth. They are arrogant and condescending. They love to talk about themselves and to tell others what to do.

In positions of power or authority, Capricorns can make the lives of those around them a misery. They are demanding, critical, and narrow-minded. They have no consideration for the feelings of others. The higher they progress, the more unfeeling and out of touch they get.

These Saturn-ruled people are inclined to regard themselves as martyrs rather than leaders or helpers if they are unevolved types. If they have to perform helping tasks for others or to contend with the illness of others, they complain, scheme, worry, or bolt. They won't serve, stand, and wait for judgment the way the noble Capricorn man or woman chooses to serve humanity.

Capricorn: Love and Romance

How successful will you be in sex and romance, love and marriage? And doesn't that depend on with whom? In the preceding chapter you read a description of how you react in relationships in general. Here the following sections describe your attitudes and behavior and the likely attitudes and behavior of individuals born under each of the twelve different Sun signs.

First there are the sections for the Capricorn woman in combination with each of the twelve zodiacal signs Aries through Pisces. Then there are the sections for the Capricorn man in combination with each of the twelve signs Aries through Pisces.

You can build on this in-depth view of yourself if you read the appropriate sections of chapters that apply to your Moon, Venus, and Mars placements. The Planetary Tables at the end of the book give you your placements. The chapters "The Moon in the Signs," "Venus in the Signs," and "Mars in the Signs" describe each placement in your profile.

The Moon, Venus, and Mars figure prominently in love, sex, affection, passion, response, instinct, unconscious motivation—the whole ball of wax. Venus essentially influences affections. The Moon influences emotions. And Mars influences sexuality. But how these broad capacities are expressed specifically varies with the individual, as described in the chapters mentioned.

You can also learn more about an individual born under a certain Sun sign this way. You may want to buy the relevant book in the *Astroscope Profile* series to read his or her Moon, Venus, and Mars placements. For this individual, you might also want to read his or her Rising sign, for as has been emphasized, the Rising sign indicates how a person appears to others on the basis of what he or she is showing the world. Perhaps a person's come-on is so much a part of the nature that it can't be changed. And you, Capricorn, don't want to be fooled!

WHEN CAPRICORN WOMAN
MEETS ARIES MAN

The Aries man is likely to tune in to the Capricorn woman's basic sexual allure. Underneath that smooth, butter-wouldn't-melt-in-the-mouth poise, this female is sexy to the core. The Ram and the Goat share Mars, the planet of sexual energy, in common. Mars rules Aries, and Mars reaches its highest vibration in Capricorn. These two are kissin' cousins under the skin. Sex will bring them together, and through it they can learn that they have other things going for them.

Capricorn is likely to be immediately attracted to the Ram. Although a rather introverted woman, she often is drawn to guys who rush in head first and ask questions later. He is a creative person and a born leader. It is quite possible they will meet under working conditions of some sort.

Many a Capricorn female has been secretary or personal assistant to an Aries guy and ended up marrying the boss! This is the kind of relationship that is likely to start off on a platonic level and grow into something deeper. Many of the best marriages follow this pattern. It can be an advantage to know someone really well before getting deeply involved romantically with him or her.

The Aries man is a pioneer. He always is looking for the big score. With the Goat behind him to give him a push if his confidence happens to wane on occasions, he really cannot go wrong. The Ram is an aggressive man. He is willing to fight for what he believes is right and his. He is the no-nonsense type. His directness certainly will appeal to a Capricorn woman, who sometimes can get confused about the direction she wishes to take.

Aries is an old-fashioned type as far as close personal relationships go. She may find it difficult to accept some of his attitudes. He may not want her to pursue a career after marriage if it takes her away from home and family life. He is a born flirt, but Capricorn should not read too much into this. He is unlikely to get involved with another woman once he has pledged his everlasting love to her.

Aries men are not very good with money. It would be advisable in this liaison for the Ram to pay attention to what his Capricorn woman has to say about putting cash to one side. If she can get him to take her advice, it will save him from making a lot of stupid mistakes.

A Capricorn woman will have no difficulty keeping a swinging sexual relationship going with the Ram. She will love his aggressive approach to lovemaking. Being a Capricorn, she will soon realize how important it is never to put a damper on this guy's enthusiasm.

Both are good with children, and they could end up having a larger-than-average family. She will have to exercise the discipline with the children, however, as Aries can be a pushover with kids. It is important that he does not allow her to sink into a rut when she becomes contented with children, for instance. He could get bored with this. And ultimately so will she.

WHEN CAPRICORN WOMAN MEETS TAURUS MAN

Both being earth signs, these two partners should find they have a lot in common. Taurus is the no-nonsense type. For a woman who often gets mixed up and confused, he will have many of the qualities she is looking for in a mate. She can look up to the strong-willed, determined Taurus man.

Family means a lot to a Capricorn female. It is extremely important to her to please her folks by the decisions she is making regarding her personal life. The folks should be delighted if she chooses the Bull for a marriage partner. He undoubtedly will have many of the qualities they will be looking for in a son-in-law.

He is kind, considerate of others' feelings, a home lover, and a man who believes in living up to his responsibilities and providing for his loved ones. Capricorn could be the woman of his dreams. He does not give his love easily, but when he does it is total. He could never live with a woman he did not trust absolutely.

Taurus will feel that in the Goat he has found the female he has been looking for all his life. However, he will expect her to be more of a romantic than perhaps she sometimes appears. With the trust and confidence that she is likely to feel for this man, she should be able to let herself go and show her true feelings.

The Taurus man is also sentimental, sometimes more so than sexual and sensual. He will expect his Capricorn woman to express the appropriate feelings for family life and the in-laws. The female Goat, though, is frankly and thoroughly sexual. She will constantly challenge the Bull to prove himself in bed. If he lives up to her expectations, she will meet his demands for loyalty to family and the past.

These two are definitely traditionalists. He does not like change for the sake of it, and holds fast to the old values. He prefers to employ methods that have proved themselves over the years. It would be wise for Capricorn to remember that he cannot stand to be put down in front of other people. She should never let on in front of friends that she knows more than he does about subjects on which he considers himself expert.

He will love the way she runs a home. He is a guy to whom the domestic environment is very important. He will enjoy bringing people home. This pair will have luxurious dinner parties. Entertaining within the confines of his home is likely to appeal more to the Bull than wasting money in expensive restaurants. She will concur with this point of view.

As regards money, both are security-conscious and do not believe in throwing cash around. He will offer this woman the sort of protection she needs. Capricorn will feel secure when her Taurus man holds her tightly in his arms.

WHEN CAPRICORN WOMAN MEETS GEMINI MAN

The Gemini man thinks in terms of brief affairs, conquests for the season. If he's hitched, he'll flirt, but will be honest about where he's at. If he's single, he'll just seek the conquest. He can come on as the lost boy on the mountainside. This will definitely catch the heart of the Capricorn woman, who knows the terrain and will take a special delight in guiding this son of Mercury to a safe ledge, a secure hiding place where they can abandon themselves to a few moments of pleasure.

What is likely to attract a woman to the Twins is his sense of humor, that "naughty boy" streak in his nature, and the fact that he can be such fun. It is quite possible that if a Capricorn female does get hooked on this guy, she will meet him at a crisis point in her life.

He is not the sort of man that a down-to-earth woman like Capricorn usually gets involved with. The Goat would have to be in a very special frame of mind to fall for Gemini. The sudden changes the Twins are capable of would be most unsettling to Capricorn. She likes both feet planted firmly on the ground.

Maybe she is getting over a miserable love affair, or perhaps she is just fed up with men in general. So for a good time the Twins will be fine. But if she is looking for a permanent relationship, it would be wise for the Saturn-born woman to think again.

Gemini is charming and has a ready wit. He is great fun to be with at a party or gathering. He is the type she will feel she can confide in. This relationship might start out on a platonic level. It may be some time before Capricorn realizes just how much this guy has come to mean to her.

He certainly knows the right places to take a woman. He probably will be a member of the latest fun clubs in town. The trouble is that when she needs him, elusive Gemini simply will not be there. He cannot stand to think that anyone is too dependent on him. He is not very good at permanent relationships. Although he craves security, the Twins are terrified of losing their freedom.

The trouble with this man is that he often gets confused about what he really wants out of life. He always can see all sides of any situation and so may end up sitting on the fence. He is a great talker and loves discussing his dreams. But when it comes to transforming those dreams into realities, he can be found woefully lacking.

A Capricorn woman would be extremely good for Gemini if only he will realize it. Maybe, if he meets her when he has taken a few knocks in life, he will know just how lucky he is. He really needs looking after. She will provide him the with the soothing atmosphere in which he can unwind. He is great with kids, but makes a more responsible parent if he starts a family late in life.

WHEN CAPRICORN WOMAN
MEETS CANCER MAN

The Cancer man, on first meeting and in the most formal of circumstances, is sweet, shy, and serious. This could be just the right combination in a mate for urbane, glamorous Capricorn. If she's looking for a mate, she's very sure of herself. Cancer could be the one, if his exterior holds up. She needs a mature guy. Cancer has to be skilled both socially and sexually, in public and in private, to win this woman. But he can pretend when he is wooing. When they get to know each other, though, his true persona emerges.

The Crab finds it very difficult to come to terms with life. When he is faced with a big problem, his main desire is to run away from it or to pass the buck to someone else. He has a way of being able to blame others for the difficulties he so often finds himself in.

Often he is a very talented, artistic man. But very often, because he lacks honesty with himself, he does not achieve his true potential. He will be lucky, indeed, if Capricorn is smitten by the love bug and falls for him. This is a woman who could give this guy just the push he needs and the confidence in himself to get to the top.

She will not stand for any of his nonsense. She has enough ambition for two, and will do her best to see that the Cancer man does not waste his undoubted talents. He is a complex character, as Capricorn soon will discover if she gets on intimate terms with him. To meet him at a party, one may think he does not have a care in the world. He is very good at hiding his true feelings when it suits him.

It also is true that when he has the blues, he is capable of depressing a room full of people with his cries of woe. If only he could face up to the fact that he is responsible for the upsetting situations he so often gets into. He can be a hard worker, but sometimes lacks the drive to aim for the top. He would like to be chairman of the board, but may not welcome the challenge and the struggle that are involved getting there.

What are the chances of these two making a go of life together? That will depend very much on the Capricorn woman. Surprisingly, they have quite a lot in common. Both are home lovers; family life is terribly important to them. He will not mind her pursuing her career after marriage. That will be a blessing to a woman who has so much more to offer the world than a place at the kitchen sink.

Cancer is sentimental and romantic. He is very good at remembering those special days like birthdays and anniversaries. He is entertaining and amusing. He loves to take a trip down memory lane, reviving happy memories of the good old days.

He may take his time about proposing marriage. The Crab rarely is one to rush the big decisions. He is the faithful type. A Cancer man will not stray when he has decided on his partner for life.

WHEN CAPRICORN WOMAN MEETS LEO MAN

Leo's head is always turned by an urbane, put-together woman. Add sex appeal, and Leo is gone. The Capricorn woman, besides having a subtle glamor, is usually successful. Leo's blood runs hot at the prospect of getting to know intimately such a perfect woman, one who is subdued but who exudes sexual excitement. Leo's come-on is winning: strong, flattering, protective, flamboyant, serious. He's already decided to marry this woman before the first date.

Leo could be the man of her dreams. Certainly, he will have many of the qualities that a Capricorn woman has been searching for in a partner. He is a born leader, good at making decisions. Once he has decided what the best course of action is likely to be, he usually sticks to his guns. Capricorn women do have difficulty in making up their minds. They need a man who is prepared to play the dominant role in their relationship but who also is gentle and caring.

The Lion will help this woman find herself. He is the loyal type. He will make her feel loved with all the attention he lavishes on her. Although he is careful with money, he will never be stinting as far as his mate is concerned. He has pride. So he will want his lady love to look her best at all times, not only for her sake, but also because he will feel it reflects on him.

Surprisingly, on first meeting, the Goat is not likely to be all that impressed by the Lion. He may come on too full of himself for her liking. If he perseveres, however, she may find that behind that great big ego is a gentle and caring man. Leo will be good for her in many ways. He will help her overcome her social and intellectual inhibitions.

She needs appreciation and constant reassurance. This guy will help her to grow and to come to terms with herself. He will not mind his Capricorn woman pursuing her own career, as long as it does not interfere in any way with their life together, or the way she carries out her family responsibilities. In fact, he will be eager for his woman to be happy in life. He knows that if she does not fulfill her real potential, she always will feel lost and unsure of herself.

He makes a giving partner in bed. It will be important to him that his lovemaking satisfies her. He has loads of confidence in bed and out. It is rare for a Leo man to be found in a subservient position as far as his job is concerned. He likes a feminine woman, although he does believe in equality of the sexes. So he will help out with domestic routine. He is a great one with kids as long as Junior does not try to usurp his position as head of the household!

Although this couple will have their disagreements, they won't be serious ones. A certain amount of conflict will keep the relationship alive and growing.

WHEN CAPRICORN WOMAN MEETS VIRGO MAN

This couple will have plenty of good things in common. One thing is certain: Capricorn will have a great deal of respect for Virgo. His respectful, slightly old-fashioned manners will please her. He will treat her as he feels a woman should be treated—with dignity and sensitivity.

He is a gentle, caring man. They are likely to be in agreement in many areas, especially on politics, religion, and codes and standards of living. It can be said that a certain amount of conflict is important in any relationship to keep it sparkling. This viewpoint could be relevant as far as a Virgo and Capricorn link is concerned. They may find themselves in such complete unity over so many points that life together over a long period becomes a little dull. Capricorn, although a home-loving female, does require plenty of stimulation to keep her interest going.

The Virgo man can be intimate, if carefully taught. Once she gets him into the swing of lovemaking, he can be a sexy guy. He will know just what to do to turn her on and keep her happy when they make love. He's also friendly during sex, a rare trait, and able to talk as well as use his body in a sensitive way. The Virgo man is there for keeps with his Capricorn dream woman. Her glamor, depth, and sensuality keep him on his mettle.

Virgo is a man who keeps his word. Once he has decided she is the woman of his dreams and he has plucked up the courage to tell her so, Capricorn can be sure he means what he says. He has a fine mind and usually is a great lover of art, particularly music. He is quite the conservative type and is tidy to the point of fussiness.

But then, Virgo does have his faults. Perhaps he is not quite passionate enough for a Capricorn female who is so highly motivated on the sexual plane. He is a great romantic, but may lack the abandon she requires in a partner when it comes to making love. However, this female is not lacking in imagination. She should soon be able to help her Virgo man overcome his inhibitions and reticence and let himself go.

Marriage is a big step for any person, but particularly for the Virgo guy. This type tends to marry late in life and is unlikely to walk up the aisle after a whirlwind courtship. He does not mind sharing the household chores. He will be quite content if his woman wishes to pursue her career after they are hitched.

He cannot stand criticism and is likely to be quite blind to his own faults. This couple should have children, but it may be a while before he is convinced he can really afford to bring up a family. However, once he becomes a father, he will have no regrets and usually is terrific in the paternal role.

These two will find it the most natural thing in the world to sink into a rut together. It would be a good idea for them both to realize this and to do what they can to prevent it. Both of them should try to keep up as many outside interests as possible.

WHEN CAPRICORN WOMAN
MEETS LIBRA MAN

The Libra man is seldom without a close personal relationship. He can function in a casual affair better than most other zodiacal types. This is a man who needs other people. He is not very good at living alone. Communication is terribly important to him. Most of all, he needs a woman to share his aspirations.

The point to be remembered about Libra is that he is one of nature's givers. If he is not deeply involved in a close personal relationship, he finds it very difficult to operate. He is not all that good at self-motivation. Capricorn could be just the woman to fire his imagination.

Libra is a charming, attractive, and fun-loving character. Most women find themselves magnetically drawn to him, and the Goat probably will be no exception. He usually is very good at playing the game of love. He knows how to flirt and how to treat a woman.

During the early days of courtship he is likely to suggest a variety of outings. It is important to him to give pleasure. As soon as he discovers what his partner likes and wants most out of life, he will do all in his power to make sure she gets it. He will make a Capricorn female feel like a million dollars. He has that gift for looking for the best in people and not trying constantly to find fault.

He also will expect his mate to be similarly tolerant. He is likely to be quite honest about his shortcomings and, having accepted them himself, will expect others to do the same. However, in spite of having mutual respect, these two lovers will have to face quite a few problems before seriously contemplating a permanent relationship.

Libra basically is a social animal. The love that Capricorn has for her home, and the many evenings that she wishes to spend in it, may not appeal to his gregarious nature. He loves parties and mixing with people from different walks of life. Seven nights a week away from home would not be too much for him if he is enjoying himself.

This woman takes a great pride in the home. Capricorn will do all she can to make it as comfortable and attractive as possible. It will be rather disheartening for her to discover that Libra has hardly noticed her efforts.

Occasionally, he requires a shove to get him going. If Capricorn is prepared to be the power behind the throne, she could really help him make his mark in the world. Libra is marriage shy. It may take a few hints from Capricorn to get him to pop the all-important question.

WHEN CAPRICORN WOMAN
MEETS SCORPIO MAN

Scorpio is a guy people may love or may hate, but they cannot pretend he is not there. His presence is intense. There could be a clash of personalities between Scorpio and Capricorn on first meeting. In fact, she may not be able to stand the sight of him. However, a Capricorn female might find herself thinking a lot about Scorpio, and wondering what it is that seems to attract her in spite of her better judgment. It may be that she senses a great challenge if she takes on this man.

He is not the one for beating around the bush. He lays it right on the line. If he wants to go to bed with a woman, she will be under no illusions about his intentions. That openness may be what draws a Capricorn female toward the Scorpion. His honesty and forthrightness have to be admired. In fact, if she does decide to let the guy get farther than first base, she will discover he has many admirable qualities.

A Capricorn woman will feel the vibes when he walks into a room. His approach is not the most romantic in the world, either. He is quite capable of acting in a rough and sexually dominant way when suggesting it would be a suitable time to move off in the direction of the bedroom. However, it is not likely that this caveman approach would appeal to a sensitive woman like Capricorn.

To the Scorpio man, sex in its highest form should be communication and communion, an attempt to develop intimacy and commitment. Sex should not be merely for selfish pleasure, an act that makes Scorpio feel guilty, even when he's initiated it that way. And he often punishes the woman in retaliation for this mortal act. The Capricorn female will have none of this bigger-than-life stuff. If Scorpio can't enjoy and honor sex, pure and simple, she won't capitulate by helping him turn it into a private vision of spirituality.

When he loves, however, it is a total affair. If he decides he has met the woman of his dreams, he will not readily take no for an answer. He is a jealous man and a possessive one. Woe betide the guy who makes a pass at his woman. He strives for power and will do all he can to provide a good home for his dependents.

He will love the feminine qualities of a Capricorn woman. Although he can be stingy with cash, he will make sure his partner never really wants for anything. His dress sense usually is appalling. Oddly enough, he is still capable of looking like a slouch even if his woman does talk him into wearing an expensive suit.

It will be very important to Scorpio to have children. He will want his name to carry on after him. He is a hard worker and never shirks his duties. He is terribly ambitious, too. If his kid rushes home from school full of excitement, shouting, "Hey, Dad, guess what! I came in second in the class!" the reply typical of a Scorpio father would be, "Why didn't you come in first, son?"

WHEN CAPRICORN WOMAN MEETS SAGITTARIUS MAN

The Sagittarius man and the Capricorn woman might meet in a group, on a camping expedition or political conference, single each other out from the crowd, and decide to do their own camping and conferring on a one-to-one basis—for a couple of nights. By the time their weekend is up, they have to decide what to do with their mutual enjoyment of the outdoors life, their shared sexual spontaneity, and their lusty though different dreams.

Sagittarius and Capricorn might decide to continue their tryst on a trial basis, the condition for doing so being separate but equal lifestyles and distinct individualities. The chances are that these two could make a swell pair on a short-term basis. This couple is likely to have a swinging affair, then decide quite amicably to go their separate ways.

The Archer is a difficult guy to keep tabs on. He is an outgoing man. He is never happier than when he is out gallivanting or holding forth in the friendly neighborhood bar. Although he is a sexy type, he prefers the company of his own sex. He has a great love for sports and gambling.

Capricorn, with her love for the home and preference for the quiet life, may find his driving personality too much to accept at times. Freedom is more important to him than almost anything else. He finds it difficult to cope with a one-to-one relationship very long. Marriage is a union he will fight to avoid.

Sagittarius can be counted as one of the luckiest signs of the Zodiac. He manages to come unscathed through scrapes that others simply would not survive. He takes his chances, all right, but it would be wrong to write him off as a fool.

It is possible that this duo would get on extremely well on a platonic level. He is a loyal pal, and his friends mean a great deal to him. Although he may seem to be a fly-by-night type, he would never let down a pal who turned to him for assistance. If Capricorn can come to terms with his roving ways and has enough of her own interests to occupy herself when he is not around, they may have a chance of making a go of life together.

In fact, as he gets older and matures, he quite likely will calm down and cease his wandering ways. He will decide to marry. It is unlikely that he will get involved in serious romantic relationships then; his marriage would be far too important for him to endanger it.

Sagittarius individuals do not always make the best of fathers. They have particular problems dealing with sons. It may be that these parents try to mete out discipline when they are in a sober mood, but fail to give a consistent example by the way they conduct their own lives.

However, if a Capricorn woman does fall under the spell of Sagittarius, she could find herself forgiving him for almost anything, sometimes in spite of herself. Perhaps he could best be summed up as an irresistible rogue.

WHEN CAPRICORN WOMAN
MEETS CAPRICORN MAN

Female Capricorns are not quite so set in their ways as the male of the species. A Capricorn man tends to be more of an introverted character than his female counterpart. His inward-looking nature poses something of a problem in a beginning sexual relationship.

The Capricorn man may be the first to make the pass, but she will have to be flanker back, tackle, and linebacker all the way in this rugged sport of sexuality. He can fumble a lot until she gets him skilled in knowing and calling the plays. Basically a sexual creature, the Capricorn male does not emerge until he has a super coach. And the Capricorn woman fills that bill.

He is not an easy man to get to know. It will be up to her to help him get more fun out of life. A Capricorn female will show him how to let his hair down and really enjoy himself. If anyone can get through to him, it is likely to be a woman born under the same sign. In fact, it is amazing how many Capricorns end up sharing an extremely happy and contented life together.

He needs a woman behind him who believes he has what it takes to get to the top and who will give him a push. Success is very important to this woman. It is possible that she will be content to be the power behind the throne, as this in itself can be a full-time job. She will be prepared to make all sorts of sacrifices as long as she feels her man is getting to the top.

Although a shy and retiring man, the Goat does have a big ego. It would be unwise for any woman to attempt to usurp his position as head of the household. These two will have many interests in common; that is why this pairing makes so many successful marriages. They will be very much on the same wavelength.

Their tastes in friends and art and their general likes and dislikes are going to tally in many areas. He may not be the most romantic guy in the world. His shyness sometimes makes it difficult for him to express himself in poetic terms. He is the cautious type and is likely to want a long courtship before he entertains the idea of matrimony. He likes to be organized, but then so does she. He will be proud of her tidy ways and her ability to entertain his business associates so charmingly and competently.

He is an old-fashioned type in many ways. He believes in holding onto values that are tried and trusted and that have proved themselves down the years. He will be faithful. He may desire another woman from time to time, but his flirting probably will be harmless. Although quite a jealous female, his Capricorn mate should not take it seriously.

They will make good parents. But they must be sure they give Junior freedom to express himself or herself. They must try not to impose their wills too strongly on the child. They will see that their children are law-abiding and have respect for their elders.

WHEN CAPRICORN WOMAN
MEETS AQUARIUS MAN

An Aquarius man might get to the mature Capricorn woman where it counts—on a matter of principle. Both of them share the weighty planet of responsibility, Saturn. Saturn rules Capricorn and corules Aquarius. If the Capricorn woman is beyond the pleasures of the moment—sexual gratification, for one—she and Aquarius meet at a crossroads. The Aquarius male never stood at the corner for a good time, and continues to shun sex as he grows older.

So if the male Water Bearer and the female Goat meet at a certain time and stage of their lives, they are definitely simpático. Against all the odds and the advice of their respective friends, this is likely to be an extremely successful pairing. In many ways they appear to be opposites. But this may work as a stimulant in the relationship. They could be good for each other. Of course, certain sacrifices would have to be made. But there has to be a give-and-take in all successful partnerships.

The Goat may find herself alone quite a lot of the time. Aquarius people simply refuse to allow themselves to be ruled by the clock. Still, she is a fairly practical female. A certain amount of solitude and living in her own world are likely to appeal to her.

He is a great talker and reformer. When he starts to voice his opinions on the way the world's problems should be dealt with, she will think he is a man who really knows where he is going. The trouble with the Water Bearer is that he is a dreamer, always thinking about utopia. But when it comes to setting it up, his ideas are not always workable.

An earthy woman like Capricorn will be good for getting him to face the reality of this world. He is not a stylish dresser. He often walks around looking like an absent-minded professor. She will be able to keep him looking neat in reasonably up-to-date clothes. He will love the way she fusses over him and looks after his needs.

It is possible that Capricorn has never met a man like Aquarius. She will be constantly surprised by him. His unpredictability will confuse and shake her traditional values. But this woman likes a challenge, and there is no bigger challenge than the Water Bearer.

This guy is not a great home lover, although he will appreciate the way she runs the domestic scene so smoothly. He will make her stop worrying about herself. He will help her stave off those Saturn-induced depressions that occasionally overtake her.

It would be advisable for the Capricorn partner to have control over the finances. Aquarius is not too good at handling money. If he is convinced that a person needs help or that a cause is worthy of support, he can be generous to a ridiculous degree. Once he realizes how much his Capricorn woman loves and needs him, he may channel all that caring and compassion in her direction. When that happens, they will indeed live happily ever after.

WHEN CAPRICORN WOMAN MEETS PISCES MAN

When a Capricorn woman first comes across the Pisces man, she may feel he is a weak-willed, dreamy character. That faraway look in his eyes may make her think that here is a guy who lives in a world far removed from reality.

This would be a false assumption. The two Fishes, the symbol of Pisces, may be swimming in opposite directions, but when it comes to making important decisions, they can be absolutely ruthless about getting what they want. His manner and general demeanor serve him very well in business; this come-on puts his competitors off guard.

Pisces and Capricorn can be a very powerful team. Joined together, they could conquer the world, if they make the best use of the positive aspects of their personalities. She is a very practical person and could be an excellent stabilizing influence when he gets carried away with one of his many new and ambitious projects. His trouble is that when he gets an idea in his head, he is unable to see the possibilities of failure.

The Capricorn female, being cautious yet totally focused, will get Pisces to slow down a little. But still waters run deep with this water sign. He will be something of a mystery to an earthy woman like the Goat. There will be certain problems that should be faced squarely in order to be overcome.

He loves to be on the move, meeting people from all walks of life, and constantly trying to satisfy his great curiosity. She is more of the home lover. However, it is imporant for him to have an anchor, and he will learn to love those evenings when they can be alone together.

Unless Pisces has the right person by his side, he tends to drift along with no real purpose in life. He needs someone to work for, someone to share his possessions and his dreams. One thing that a Capricorn woman may have trouble adapting to is his vagueness. Sometimes, when he is trying to solve a problem connected with his work, he may appear to ignore her completely. She must learn not to trouble him when he is wrestling with important matters that only he and he alone can figure out.

He requires a certain amount of excitement in his life. He will help his Capricorn woman conquer her dark moments. His ready wit can turn the most difficult situation into an occasion that can be laughed off. He is likely to make a faithful husband. He is not the kind of guy to put in jeopardy a relationship he values.

Perhaps the greatest value a Pisces man holds is his sexual relationship with his Capricorn woman. He better hold on tight. She is thoroughly un-inhibited. He, an incurable romantic, has always wanted a woman who could live up to his fantasy expectations. She can do that and more. She can bring dreamy Pisces back to the flesh-and-blood reality of a woman for him to love, honor, and, in her case, obey.

WHEN CAPRICORN MAN
MEETS ARIES WOMAN

A personality clash could loom here. The Capricorn man can be a difficult character to get along with at times. He is somewhat introverted. He needs to be in the company of optimistic people who bring out the positive side of his nature. Aries is a fiery and impulsive woman. She is born under the percussive first sign of the Zodiac. She is very wrapped up in herself and her own interests. The Goat may find her moods and sudden flashes of temper too much to take.

He tends to go for a woman who is perhaps a little more charming of manner and gentle of nature. This female tends to put her foot in it at times. She believes in speaking her mind no matter who she's with and regardless if what she says gives offense. For diplomatic Capricorn, the Ram's jump-in-feet-first attitude to life could be embarrassing in the extreme.

This woman is dominant in every area of her life. She is not content to take a back seat in a relationship. If the Goat is not careful, his Aries mate may end up wearing the pants in his house. She also is a career woman. This is another factor that is not likely to go down too well with the Capricorn male. He is looking for a woman to provide him with a smoothly and efficiently run home.

Success is very important to the Ram. She will not be happy playing the tame role of housewife and mother. This woman also may be in too much of a rush for a quiet and methodical person like Capricorn. She may be too nervy and too demanding as far as he is concerned.

However, the prospects are not all negative. There are numerous interests they can have in common. A sense of humor, for one thing, will help to overcome many of the difficulties. In their love relationship, he is likely to find her passionate and demonstrative. He will display that happy mixture of aggression and gentleness she needs to satisfy her lusty sexual appetite. She is very highly strung, and the Capricorn man will have to learn to be understanding of her depressions.

The Ram is a very resilient creature, however. Capricorn cannot fail to admire her ability to bounce back and come out fighting. A long courtship would be advisable. If they do decide on marriage, it also would be wise to wait a while before starting a family. The Aries female will want to enjoy herself before accepting any part of domesticity.

The Aries woman will not put up with a mate who flirts or strays. But her demands may not end with that traditional demeanor between husband and wife. She will also want to share her man's inner life. If the Goat is focused inward and too shy to reveal his innermost feelings, the ardent Aries woman will rebel. She expects more than silence and reserve from him in those quiet hours when they are alone together.

WHEN CAPRICORN MAN MEETS TAURUS WOMAN

Taurus and Capricorn predictably make a very successful pairing. Both are earth signs, so both have their feet firmly planted on the ground. Neither likes to get too deeply involved with people who are always changing their minds. Reliability is a very important attribute in both their books.

Taurus and Capricorn individuals are not quick to take people into their confidence. But when they do, it is a total commitment. They feel terribly hurt if they are ever let down or proved wrong. Both like to have their quiet moments. Some people may call it moodiness, but a truer characterization is reserve. It is important to these two individuals to have areas where they can be on their own.

Taurus people sometimes get a reputation for being bossy. This, however, is really a reaction to people who try to regulate their affairs without being asked. The Bull just does not like to feel pushed around. Left to herself, this woman will make the important decisions in her life when she feels it is right and not when dictated to by outsiders.

Being stubborn is very different from being bossy. And when the lady Bull digs her heels in, there's no budging her. This woman takes love relationships very seriously indeed. She is ruled by Venus, the love planet. She will appreciate the gentleness with which the Capricorn man treats her. She responds with warmth and affection to charm and respectful manners. A Taurus woman may seem cold on occasion, but she just feels things deeply and knows that for her own good she must control her emotions.

She loves pretty things, so she will be pleased at the way this guy remembers special days like anniversaries and birthdays. Both are hard workers, and will do all they can to make their union a successful one. A successful and secure home life is probably the greatest thing in her life.

Taurus is not extravagant, except perhaps where fashion is concerned. She loves dressing up and taking hours over her makeup and hair. A Taurus female is a bundle of passion in the bedroom. She has much more sexual drive than one might imagine on meeting her socially. Both these types are home lovers, and do not believe in spending fortunes on expensive entertainment. Curled up together in front of a fire on a winter's evening will be bliss for them both.

The Taurus woman can certainly reach deep into the heart, mind, soul, and, of course, body of a Capricorn man. Sex is the coinage of their realm together. She will have to use their physical and sexual communication to get him out of that stony reserve he adopts when things are going wrong in his outer life. She will not want to abandon her role as hostess and homemaker, but she will know that after the guests have gone she needs to reassure her Capricorn mate in the privacy of the bedroom.

WHEN CAPRICORN MAN
MEETS GEMINI WOMAN

Gemini is capable of blowing hot and cold, which could be an infuriating thing for a Capricorn guy. It is essential for him to know where he stands, especially in something as important as a romantic involvement. This woman could drive him to distraction with her dizziness.

A Gemini woman will challenge the Goat to a series of unexpected leaps and bounds over the rocky terrain of love. The Goat is so surefooted that he boasts to his friends that this lightweight daughter of Mercury is no burden for a brief fling on the side of the mountain. But the Gemini woman can make the path treacherous. She will discover obstacles and want to stop, then she will sight peaks and want to start up again—right away. She could run the Capricorn male ragged.

It is not that Gemini means to upset or mislead people. The plain fact is she does not know what she wants out of life for much of the time. There are quite a number of difficulties that would have to be overcome if this couple has any chance of making a relationship permanent.

Gemini is a split sign symbolized by the Twins. These individuals always seem to have two answers for every problem life throws at them. And very often they end up doing precisely nothing when the time comes for action. Taking the line of least resistance often adds to their problems.

The Gemini woman also can have an irritating habit of involving other people in her troubles. What is terribly frustrating for her friends is that when they have gone to a great deal of trouble advising her, their wise counsel is totally ignored.

This woman finds it very difficult to settle down with one man. Alas, hers is one of the most promiscuous signs of the Zodiac. This is fine for a swinging affair. But it would put a big dent in Capricorn's ego if he were looking for something more lasting than a one-night stand. Gemini females find it very hard not to burn the candle at both ends.

One wonders if a conservative, stay-at-home guy like Capricorn could take this lifestyle very long. However, the Goat is patient, if nothing else. If he could help his little girl lost grow up and mature, he would have something most worthwhile. If he loves her enough, perhaps he could give her the sort of stability she really is yearning for.

The important thing for any man to remember about a Gemini woman is that she must never be made to feel hemmed in or trapped. Having children would be an important step in her life, although she may need lots of reassurance that she is capable of being a responsible mother. If they do set up home together, the Goat may find himself doing more than his fair share of the household chores. He likes a tidy home. Quite a lot of his time may be taken up trying to keep it that way with the Twins around.

WHEN CAPRICORN MAN
MEETS CANCER WOMAN

On first meeting a Cancer woman, Capricorn may think he has come across a vivacious female without a care in the world. She has a distinctive and contagious laugh that will get any party or social occasion off the ground. However, when he gets to know her a little better, he will find her to be a woman of many moods and emotions.

It is impossible to know which way a Cancer female will turn. Just when she seems to be won, she can change her mind about a relationship in the wink of an eye. Her passions are heavy and deeply felt. She is intuitive, ruled by her heart and not her head. She is, in fact, ruled by the Moon. Her instincts are most important to her.

Capricorn may find this approach to life rather wearying. Although a very giving person, Cancer also is extremely self-centered. She loves to be the center of attraction and cannot stand to be in the same room with someone who is stealing what she considers to be her limelight. She is egocentric to the core.

A Cancer female in a good mood is great fun to be with. But it is best to stay out of the way when she has the blues. She has a way of imposing her moods on others. When Cancer is in a state, it is impossible to cheer her up. But her moods never last too long.

There are pluses, of course. Both Cancer and Capricorn are incurable home lovers. Many a pleasant evening is likely to be spent within the confines of their house or apartment. The lady Crab will be pleased to discover that she has a man who keeps his word. She cannot abide being two-timed. She would not allow a relationship to continue if she felt she was being cheated.

This woman takes quite a while to make up her mind about marriage. It is unlikely she will get hitched to her girlhood sweetheart. When she loves, she loves deeply but may hold back until she is sure she has met the real thing. Cancer is a wonderful homemaker and usually a great cook. She knows how to look after her man. She will make him want to rush home to be with her after a tough day at the office.

This woman needs to be controlled. Basically, she needs a man who can dominate her. Capricorn will have to brush up on the masterful side of his nature. But the Crab cannot stand to be criticized. It will be up to him to give her the right sort of guidance and control. She will want a family. Motherhood is very important to people born under her sign. Also, she is a romantic. The Goat must keep alive the romance in their marriage.

The Cancer woman seeks always to enhance the home and traditional ties. The love and respect she and Capricorn share may take on a new dimension for them in the middle years of their union. They may turn their attention to a mutual interest outside the home, either community work or a business partnership. Both of them have a fine head for making money. With her artistic sense and his organizational skill, they can start building in tandem again—a second honeymoon.

WHEN CAPRICORN MAN
MEETS LEO WOMAN

The Leo woman is all glamor and sparkling lights. She represents to the Capricorn man all he's ever yearned for in success and social status. Besides, her warm and open and flamboyant personality awakens in him those repressed sexual urges. Spontaneously drawn to her, he makes his interest felt. But the Lioness may not be playing his game. She is all that he thinks, but she's not giving herself away. She is no one's sexual object, dream woman, or female on a pedestal. She's real, and she'll tear the Goat's ear proving it.

The Capricorn male, although rather shy, is an arrogant sort of guy. If he is honest with himself, that much he will admit. It should be very interesting if he gets deeply involved with a Leo female. He will soon find that he has met his match in the ego stakes! This is a woman who not only thinks she's right but also usually proves it.

The Lioness is a very together woman. She can take care of herself. The Goat is careful with money; he's not exactly stingy, but he knows the value of a buck. If he has ideas about wooing this sophisticated cat, he will have to blow the cobwebs out of his wallet. The Lioness will expect to be taken to all the right places on a date.

A Leo woman is not really extravagant; it's just that her tastes are stylish, so they are expensive. Her dress sense is up to the latest fashion, if not ahead of it. Although conservative in many ways, she is an experimentalist as far as her clothes go. Some may say she dresses outrageously, others say flamboyantly.

She would prefer to go out a couple of nights a week and really enjoy herself blowing the wad. She can't see stinting on entertainment, spreading money thin to make it last. The Leo female has a commanding air about her. She expects to be treated like a lady. If the Goat is the diplomatic type, she will go for his natural charm and good manners in a big way. If he's not, he's done for!

It is quite likely that most of her friends will be men. She may have one or two close female friends. But she is happier in the company of the opposite sex, and many of these relationships are purely platonic. Leo likes to keep herself occupied. She cannot stand to idle away her waking hours. All through her life she probably will be taking lessons in one thing or another.

Leo is a very passionate woman. When she loves, there are no holds barred—it is total. In many ways she will be extremely good for the Capricorn man. She is a great asset as a hostess. She is terrific for a man to have by his side. Leo will wish to retain her individuality though. She can stand on her own two feet and will expect the man in her life to do the same.

It may well be that they wait a while before starting a family. Then she will want to go back to work as soon as Junior is old enough to say "Daddy." Leos are great with children, but do not want to devote twenty-four hours a day to them. Papa Capricorn will have to be prepared to look after the baby part of every day.

WHEN CAPRICORN MAN
MEETS VIRGO WOMAN

Many men find hitting it off with a Virgo woman rather difficult. They may feel she is standoffish and hard to get to know. Capricorn is unlikely to be faced with any such problem. In fact, of all the signs of the Zodiac, he is one she will find most compatible. Virgo is a discriminating female. She immediately assesses the fine points about a Capricorn man.

This has all the makings of an excellent match. The Virgo woman will have many qualities that appeal to the Goat. For a start, she is dependable and sincere. When she gives her word, she will keep it. It is really terribly important to her not to let people down. A sensitive man like Capricorn will be particularly conscious of how valuable and rare is her integrity.

Home life is a big thing to her and to him. Virgo is houseproud, and as a result can be fussy when it comes to tidiness and hygiene. These two individuals are both realistic and know what they want out of life. A Virgo woman is not the flirtatious type. In fact, true love may come only once in her life. If the Capricorn guy wins her, he will soon realize how lucky he is.

The Goat will have to be more pushy than usual. He may need to persevere before she agrees to go on a date alone with him. She is shy, and he will have to make most of the romantic overtures early in the relationship. There is a strong sense of female responsibility with her. When she takes on a challenge, she will do all she can to see it through to a successful conclusion.

Sexually, the Virgo woman is something of an experimenter when she gets going. The Goat, whose sexual appetite is unbridled, will learn a thing or two from this modern, intellectual female. Who says that lovemaking must be a natural art and not a learned skill? When Virgo loses her inhibitions with the loyal and trustworthy Capricorn man, they will be able to write a new lovers' manual. The challenge of sexuality is one the Virgo woman will pursue with a loving vengeance.

As a wife, she will do all she can to live up to her marriage vows. She can be anxious and a worrier, though. It will be up to her Capricorn man to get her to see the funny side of situations she might otherwise get in a tizzy about. She needs lots of understanding. She sometimes has difficulty letting go and showing her true feelings.

Virgo-born people are very good judges of character. Her astuteness sizing up people will be invaluable to Capricorn in work and business. If he is not sure about someone he's negotiating a deal with, he should take the person home to meet his Virgo mate. She will give the Goat an instant analysis. She will realize early in their life together how important it is for the Capricorn man to succeed. She will do all in her power to help him.

WHEN CAPRICORN MAN MEETS LIBRA WOMAN

The Libra female is a bright light who likes to spark optimism in people and things. She has a fabulous sense of humor, which helps her ride out many a storm. She can be diplomatic, too. She is not the sort of woman to put her foot in it and say the wrong thing, thereby creating an embarrassing situation. Her tactfulness will be very much appreciated by Capricorn. If there is one thing he cannot stand it is an unnecessary scene or tantrum.

A Libra woman wants a man who is always attuned to her moods and attitudes, and who will help her negotiate them. She never announces the changes going on inside her; she merely acts them out abruptly. Capricorn, so focused on his own inner life, may not be aware of Libra's churning emotions. When he learns, too late, he may try to squelch that lively temperament by preaching discipline. Libra reads it as repression, and may walk out if she feels put down or misunderstood.

Libra has an outgoing personality. She cannot stand to be alone for long spells. She excels at gatherings, especially at parties where people get together for a good time, pleasure pure and simple. Underneath the bright exterior is a sensitive person who worries about the fate of humanity.

It is not brightness and cheer all the way for her. In many ways she is a mass of contradictions. Libra is subject to sudden mood changes, which can catch off guard people who know her intimately. The Goat may feel he knows her well after a few months of an affair. But she's full of surprises. It would be wise never to take her for granted.

A Libra woman is not easy to live with. With her constant desire to be on the move, life could become unsettled for the Goat, who is so fond of his creature comforts. This is a very determined female. It is no good if he tries to change her into something else. The relationship will not last long unless Capricorn learns to love her for what she is.

Libra-born women are extremely good at coping with people from different walks of life. These females excel in jobs that give them plenty of variety. For a Capricorn man, it may be hard to comprehend the ease with which she fits into almost any group. This woman is no snob. She will accept people for what they are, not for what they've got. Very often women born under the sign of the Scales are career-conscious. Would a Capricorn man be able to accept a woman who is determined to retain her individuality after marriage?

With Venus her ruler, Libra obviously is a loving and sexy woman. As a rule, Libra females are very attractive and ultrafeminine. The Capricorn male will be forever drawn to her. And she will forever admire the fact that he is such a conscientious worker. Libra is a winner at home entertaining. She can arrange a spread fit for a king if Capricorn has to bring the boss or an associate home, even on short notice.

WHEN CAPRICORN MAN
MEETS SCORPIO WOMAN

The Scorpio woman knows how to seduce a man. She is one of the most seductive and sexual females in the Zodiac. Her quiet, magnetic appeal will attract at a distance, working wonders across a crowded room. If a shy Goat is over there, and if she is looking for a steady mate, she will draw him out and over. She fixes Capricorn with her frank, magnetic gaze. She will permanently magnetize him so he is always in her force field—if she is looking for a steady mate.

The Scorpio woman will be very attractive to a Capricorn man on an intensely physical level. It could be one of those slam-bang affairs that starts up almost before either party really knows what is happening or what they have let themselves in for. He may feel he is being drawn into a mysterious whirlpool. She is extremely voluptuous and totally frank where sex is concerned. Many men find her too hot to handle, but cool Capricorn is not afraid to tread.

A Scorpio female has a very powerful personality, and not just on first meeting. When she gets involved with a guy, there are no half measures. Women born under this sign do not play silly games. She plays to get something she wants, not points in a popularity poll. If she digs a guy, she will let her feelings be known in no uncertain terms. This female does not put on airs and graces about fundamental needs—sex and love for her.

There are many things she will admire about a Capricorn man. His ability to keep a secret is one of them. She can be secretive herself. If she confides in someone, she likes to feel she can trust him forever. Scorpio is the jealous type. If he lets her down once, she will never forget it. She has a revengeful streak in her nature. If she feels she has been taken for a ride, she will get back in some way, even if it takes her years.

From a long-term point of view, Scorpio and Capricorn do not seem to be a promising match. The Goat is really seeking a peaceful life. Living with a woman who is always looking for heightened sensations may be too much for him to cope with. She is not a woman to sit at home while her man goes out with the boys. She likes to be in on the action. The kitchen sink is not an area of her house she treasures or is contented to manage for long.

The Scorpio female is honest to the point of cruelty. It never pays to ask her opinion if one is looking for flattery. She will do all she can to help her man get to the top, but she won't lie to save hurting his feelings. She believes it is better for him to hear the truth from her than to get a battering in the outside world.

She is honest about sex and her sensual desires. She needs a physical guy. This woman is a great survivor. With her curiosity about life, she can get herself into some tight corners. But as a rule she manages to come through reasonably unscathed. It is important to her to have children, even though she has some difficulty casting herself in the role of mother. As parents, Scorpio and Capricorn may differ on how to bring up the baby.

WHEN CAPRICORN MAN
MEETS SAGITTARIUS WOMAN

Sagittarius and Capricorn may seem mismatched, but actually such a liaison could work out extremely well. The Goat undoubtedly will admire the honesty of the female Archer. Her blunt approach to life can be too much for many people to take, but she means well and is not a vindictive female. The Goat tunes in to her sincerity.

Capricorn, being a sensitive soul, is likely to admire many of the fine attributes this woman possesses. She is one of life's experimenters. She never gives up without a fight. She may take more than her fair share of knocks, but she has the grit to get up off the ground, shake the dust off her clothes, and start all over again.

She has great charm without being sugary. The lady Archer is a winner in the popularity department. The more people know her, the more they come to love and admire her. She gets on with the job at hand without a big fuss. This woman is prepared to suffer in silence while she aims toward a goal. Many people are unaware of her dedication, but a Capricorn man sees it and is full of appreciation.

A Sagittarius woman is ambitious, not only for herself but also for her man. If she sees it is in her man's best interests that she takes a back seat from a career viewpoint, she would do so—for a while. It will be important to her that her Capricorn man makes the best of himself, and the sooner the better. Her hope has little to do with the financial rewards. It has a lot to do with their relationship. Will it be successful if he is doing well in his job? Or should she get out of the back seat and go back to work?

She can be very outspoken. She will say her piece without thinking who may be offended or embarrassed. Her jumping-in-feet-first attitude could make the Goat cringe a little. He is one of the most fearful and, as a result, diplomatic types in the Zodiac. "Anything for a Quiet Life" is likely to be his motto—a vain hope with the female Archer around.

It will be good for him, however, to have to cope with her outgoing and cheery personality. The Goat can get too introspective. This daughter of Jupiter is sensitive, but she is not sentimental. She does not believe in showing hurt feelings. It may be a fault that she never lets go when she feels bad. An occasional emotional outburst would do her good, as it would the Goat.

The female Archer will never lie to her guy. She may withhold information if she feels it is in their best long-term interest. But if confronted, she will come clean. She must not be pressured, however. It is important that she be given her privacy. Although an extrovert, she does need to be left on her own and alone when she needs to conserve energy and emotion.

The Sagittarius female will excel in the lovemaking department, and she will delight in the praise given her by a Capricorn guy. She is a lustful and loving woman. Sex is natural to her. It's fun and it makes the world go round. If the Goat gets the blues, he can be sure that his Sagittarius woman will fix him up with a hot pack, a warm drink, and a lot of fiery affection. She will burn out his gloom by creating the fires of love and sexual desire. If he decides to come out, they will go from strength to strength in their sexual joy.

WHEN CAPRICORN MAN
MEETS CAPRICORN WOMAN

Surprisingly, many partnerships between two people born under the same sign of the Zodiac simply do not work out as well as might be expected. It may be that the couples involved too quickly recognize their own faults in their opposite numbers. In the case of Capricorn, however, it is interesting to note how many couples born under the sign of the Goat do end up living happily ever after. Perhaps it is because of all the signs, Capricorn is the least guilty of making value judgments about other people.

A Capricorn male will have a lot of understanding for the problems of his Saturn-ruled lady. Both are romantics at heart, as well as sentimentalists and traditionalists. Basically she is a very correct person. Like him, she also is reliable and trustworthy. This is not a woman to play games with. If a Capricorn guy is looking for a passing affair, he would be wise to look elsewhere and not waste this woman's time. She is not interested in ships that pass in the night.

Being born under Capricorn should guarantee a certain stability in his nature. He, too, is probably looking for a lasting relationship. What he may find he has most in common with her is the search for true love. Success is very important to this pair—success in career as well as in their private lives. Although she has a desire to get to the top herself, she is quite capable of channeling these feelings into her hopes for her guy. This is a wonderful woman for a man aiming high.

As he must know, the Goat, male or female, is extremely sensitive. He will have to watch his quick-to-be-irritated temper, and those sudden hurtful statements. This is a woman who could get involved in many affairs before she finds Mr. Right. But when she really falls in love, it is total. She is capable of being the most faithful and dependable woman in the world. And she'll stand behind her guy, pushing him all the way to the top.

The Capricorn woman's fidelity has delightful fringe benefits. The greatest is her loyal and lusty sexuality. Central to her happiness is a satisfactory sex life, and she aims to be satisfied by the guy in her life, whether he is a natural lover or whether she has to teach him the art of lovemaking. The Capricorn woman is no shy female in bed. She knows all the plays and ploys to get her man excited, and all the ways she can be gratified while making her lover feel masterful.

Her family is likely to mean a great deal to her. It is to be hoped that her Capricorn man will show the same respect for her parents as she will show to her in-laws. She is a superb homemaker. She will keep the home organized and modern without appearing to make any special effort. These two will make terrific parents, but they must refrain from being too strict with their children.

WHEN CAPRICORN MAN
MEETS AQUARIUS WOMAN

Capricorn will have to hold on tight here. He is in for a bumpy passage if he gives his heart to an Aquarius woman. She is a mystery, even to herself. It is very difficult to keep tabs on this female. Just when he thinks he really has her number and understands her, she will act in a way that seems entirely out of character.

The Aquarius woman also might be unpredictable when it comes to lovemaking. If there is anything that the male Goat cannot tolerate, it is an up-and-down sex life. Though loyal and loving, the Aquarius female may not be lusty enough for this highly sexed guy. He doesn't want to create a theater piece every time they go to bed. Sex should be natural, not high drama.

The Water Bearer is a difficult female to pin down. She belongs to everyone and to no one. To a man who is possessive, it might be hard for him to accept the way she makes new friends so readily. The Goat also likes privacy in his own home. Yet an Aquarius woman will bring home all sorts of people, many of whom he will not get along with at all.

It may be that an affair with an Aquarius woman would be a better idea than a long-term relationship. As long as these two do not expect too much from each other, all will be well. Being a down-to-earth and stable character, the Capricorn man may find her crazy notions too unsettling for his cool blood.

The female Water Bearer does have a way of getting what she wants out of life, although usually by employing extraordinary methods. Or perhaps remarkable circumstances and events just magically follow her around. She may find the Goat too restrained, too stable, and too traditional for her liking. It would be unwise for a man to run away with the idea that Aquarius will settle down as the years roll by. She is unlikely to change, and it would be foolish for Capricorn to enter a long-term relationship expecting it.

This woman deep down is looking for utopia. She is out to change the world. The trouble with her philosophy is that she is not very practical in the way she goes about putting her theories into practice. The Water Bearer has too many outside interests to concentrate on one to fulfillment. And she certainly is no stay-at-home. But she is a trusting female. So she won't ask suspicious questions if her Capricorn man is home late from the job.

Marriage is a subject that should be approached very carefully. It is important that these two get to know each other really well before they contemplate walking up the aisle together. It may surprise Capricorn to discover that his woman knows all about money. In spite of her zany ways, she knows the value of a buck. Possessions, however, mean very little to her, but they do mean a great deal to him. Perhaps they could make a go of life together. Having a family would do a great deal to stabilize the relationship.

WHEN CAPRICORN MAN
MEETS PISCES WOMAN

When the angels sing, when lovers pledge a ring, their joy is forged in the heavens. Such is the union between Jupiter and Capricorn. So when the Pisces woman and the Capricorn man, born of Jupiter and Saturn, respectively, get together, the heavens open. Life on Earth, too, has some interesting possibilities.

Together, Pisces and Capricorn are an intriguing pair in whatever they do publicly. Privately, though, they may have a few skirmishes. Sometimes it is difficult for a Capricorn man to play a totally dominant role in close relationships. But he must play master to the hilt with a Pisces woman. She wants her man to be top dog.

A Pisces woman will be very good for a Capricorn in many ways. She will boost his confidence and get him to believe much more in himself and in his ability to get to the top in his chosen career. She is an intuitive female.

The Goat may think some of her ideas are way off the mark, but she has a way of getting to the root of problems and solving them in unconventional ways.

She possesses qualities that make her the dream woman of many men. For all her apparent vagueness, she has great patience and understanding. If she really loves a man, she will do almost anything to make him happy and contented. This woman is very adaptable. Although fond of the good things in life, she is prepared to take the knocks if she feels it will be worth it in the long run.

The Goat is a home-loving guy. And so is his Pisces woman. She is feminine in the extreme. She is very artistic, too, and will design the home to be a comfortable and desirable place. He will have to learn to laugh at himself and enjoy company. The two little Fishes, the symbol of Pisces, may find his approach to life too serious, too dogmatic, and too isolating.

The Capricorn man will be helpful to her when she becomes confused and frightened about facing the harsh realities of life. Underneath her sophisticated pose is a shy person who can be easily hurt. She will love this man's sensitivity and the way he puts a protective arm around her when she needs it.

The influence of Jupiter, the planet of optimism, is very strong in a Pisces woman. She will inspire a Capricorn man to believe in himself and to be a little more adventurous. Romance is very important to her. She is inquisitive about life and people, as well. Life never will be dull and routine with a Pisces woman satisfying her curiosity.

In lovemaking, she needs to be treated with gentleness and respect at all times. She is great with kids. As a couple, these two will give kids a great start in life. She is not too good at discipline, though, and that task is likely to fall to Papa Capricorn.

Capricorn:
Work and Business

No matter how important ambitions and desires may be, happiness is usually decided by human relations—the ability to get along with others. The preceding chapter, "Capricorn: Love and Romance," gave you insights into the deeply personal relationships of love, sex, and marriage.

How do you relate to other people as a friend? An employer? A partner? What is the best career field for you? And if you strike out on your own and seek a partner, what can you expect from him or her in a work and business relationship?

The chapter describes your personality as a friend, as an employer, and as a partner. It highlights your career motivations and capacities. It details your work and business relationships with individuals born under each of the twelve Sun signs.

You can extend the in-depth view of yourself as a friend, employer, and partner if you read the sections that apply to you from the chapters "Your Rising Sign," "Mercury in the Signs," "Jupiter in the Signs," and "Saturn in the Signs." The pertinent descriptions there will add to your understanding of yourself as developed in this chapter and in the chapter on character analysis.

The Rising sign, as the *Astroscope Profile* series has emphasized, indicates how others see us and how they may relate to us on the basis of what we are showing the world. Mercury, Jupiter, and Saturn are significant in work and business partnerships, too. Mercury influences the individual's capacity for mental work and communication. Jupiter indicates how an individual might develop and expand a venture, and the capacity for taking chances and risks. Saturn indicates how an individual might deal with money, obstacles, and the plain hard work involved in a venture.

You can also add to the descriptions of specific business partners given in this chapter. If you are interested in finding out more about a particular individual, you may want to read the relevant book of the *Astroscope Profile* series for that person. The tables in that book will give you the Rising, Mercury, Jupiter, and Saturn placements for him or her. These descriptions should be read together with the person's Sun sign description.

CAPRICORN AS A FRIEND

Capricorns have a wonderful way of accepting the bad with the good. People admire them for their sense of realism, and find a sturdy strength in their ability and willingness to accept responsibility. Many a friend has a Capricorn person to thank for getting him or her through a crisis in life.

Capricorn men and women believe more in action than in words. Once given, their promises can be relied on. They have a great deal of energy, which is waiting to be directed into worthwhile humanitarian efforts. But their reserve and their desire not to intrude often mean that the compassionate side of their nature never gets adequate expression.

Friends are something that Capricorn people can and do serve. But they are cautious. They make friends only with people they are sure will understand them. It is not easy to understand a person who holds back feelings. As a result, Capricorns often look at life from the sidelines. Their longing for companionship, which would bring responsive friends, remains repressed. It is never revealed in their attitude or demeanor.

When Capricorn does make a friend, it is usually for a long time. Capricorns are loyal, with a steadfast sense of duty. They will not make friends with unsuitable people. So true friendships will endure and flourish.

But Capricorn men and women, in spite of their rocklike qualities, are extremely sensitive. It is very easy for these people to feel they are unloved and unliked. The slightest remark can send them into deep gloom and self-recrimination.

Capricorns need to be told they are appreciated. Although they may seem indifferent or matter-of-fact about praise or gratitude, they are deeply offended if they have made an effort, and a reward is not forthcoming.

Friends can help Capricorn people through their periodic moods by being sympathetic and understanding. But it is very important not to try to use sentimentality in dealing with these down-to-earth men and women. Any excessive emotion irritates them, and is likely to draw an apt and penetrating remark that can be severely cutting.

CAPRICORN AS AN EMPLOYER

Capricorn employers are inclined to put work before any other consideration in an enterprise. They are success-oriented and are determined to achieve their goals no matter how long it takes and whatever effort is required. Invariably, working for them is not going to be any hayride.

But with a Capricorn boss, a worker certainly gets the impression that here is someone who at least knows what he or she is doing. And there is no chance of the employee being left alone working overtime in the office or shop at night while the boss stretches out at home, feet up, watching TV.

Capricorn employers are so hardworking that they usually see more of their staff than they do of their own families. They are first to arrive and last to leave. They are always trying to do a little more. They enjoy work like others enjoy Sundays. Often they are slave drivers. Capricorn people use work as compensation for their own feeling of inadequacy. They have to achieve to maintain faith in themselves.

Although they keep a vigilant eye on the pennies, they can be unpredictable with finances, especially expense and development money. But with wages, they will pay the going rate, and no more. What you give is what you get. A bonus is for superior work. The Capricorn boss likes methodical and self-disciplined workers. People who are not afraid of responsibility get big pay raises and promotions.

It is not a good idea for an employee to try to get too friendly with these cool and resourceful operators. They like to keep their personal life and feelings completely separate from their working situation. But it is not all hard grind with the Capricorn employer. These people have their tender but rarely sentimental moments, and will respond generously with time off and even a loan if they feel a worker's problem is genuine.

CAPRICORN IN A CAREER

Capricorn people are highly organized. They shine in any position demanding constructive systems of production and administration. The more complex and widespread the operation, the better. They make first-rate government administrators and business directors. On the way up, they should finally choose a career that has no limits to the power that can be achieved—because that is their subconscious motivation.

As long as the Goat doesn't run out of something—ideas, materials, or heart—he or she has it made. And it takes a little bit of each of these ingredients to get Capricorns started. If and when they do, they can go from strength to strength, starting out as a menial worker and ending up with a fine business or directorship. They make top-notch engineers, scientists, journalists, and administrators in the private and public sectors.

In spite of a leaden tendency to sink into a rut, Capricorn men and women will change careers if they think it is advantageous. Although careful to plan and think through every detail of every move in advance, once a decision has been reached they act quickly. Once resolved, they have push and confidence. This sign produces many great men and women in politics and big business.

CAPRICORN AND ARIES
IN BUSINESS TOGETHER

These two people are very ambitious, but for different reasons. Aries wants to be the leader—out front where everyone can see that he or she is setting the pace and giving the orders. Capricorn wants to control—to be the power, if necessary, behind the scenes. It is obvious that with a little give-and-take both these characters can be satisfied in tandem. They certainly have all the other ingredients between them to make a first-rate business combination.

Aries is the pioneer of the Zodiac. The Capricorn person will admire the way this partner is able to see the start and the end of an enterprise in a flash. It takes Aries no time at all to sum up a situation calling for action, and an even shorter time for this dynamic character to get going.

This raises a small problem. The Capricorn person is going to find it hard to get used to the Aries impulsiveness. Capricorns are cautious and deliberative types. They do not like to embark on any exercise, especially a business project, without having made thorough preparations. They believe in planning, and especially in having all the facts on hand.

Aries cannot wait. Aries charges in head down. The Capricorn Goat, with his or her need for a firm foothold before leaping, is not going to be very happy at all to see Cousin Ram failing to take the necessary precautions.

Finances also could be a problem. Capricorn people like to keep some reserves aside for emergencies. They do not believe in spending any more than is necessary. Aries individuals regard money as the means to reach their many objectives. Their objectives are seldom just to make money, as Capricorn's can be. The Ram lives for action. To reach the inaccessible, whatever that might be, the cost can be high.

The Aries partner will be good for the Capricorn side of the outfit because he or she will never allow the Goat to get caught in a rut. Aries is a go-getter. The ambitious Capricorn person will find that there is no one better at coping with difficult situations or people.

Capricorn people do not like arguments and emotional scenes. Aries thrives on conflict and fails to acknowledge the emotional hangups of others. Capricorn will have to be a little less thin-skinned, as the Ram is often blunt to the point of rudeness.

CAPRICORN AND TAURUS IN BUSINESS TOGETHER

Both Capricorn and Taurus work very well together in partnership. In business, they could really get something going. But it will be extremely important for both to have around them some bright and interesting types off whom they can bounce their ideas. Two earth signs together can get into a self-satisfied rut and fail to exploit their full potential.

Together, Capricorn and Taurus are ideally suited for any business or profession that follows traditional, conventional lines. The Goat and the Bull are the types behind the most successful partnership firms of lawyers, accountants, real-estate agents, and engineering consultants. The bigger and more institutional the concern becomes, the better. These two earthy characters can make a great deal of money, although it may take a great deal of time.

The Taurus touch also will open up a whole new range of business possibilities. Taurus people are ruled by Venus, the planet of beauty and comfort. They have a gift for making money out of beauty aids, hairdressing, fashion, interior decorating, furnishings, antiques, paintings, and art objects. The Capricorn person will have much to learn from this partner, who is a good teacher. A Capricorn, with characteristic patience and perseverance, may easily finish up knowing more than the teacher!

But Capricorn will have the good sense never to show that he or she knows more about the Taurus person's special subject. The Bull, the symbol of Taurus, is fairly fixed and possessive. He or she can jealously guard knowledge and skills. It is no good trying to reform Taurus in any way. He or she has very fixed ideas, and, when confronted, can be as stubborn as a mule.

The Taurus side of the outfit will work hard, but not for long stretches. The need to take a break after a few days is sure to appear in some guise or other. This may only take the form of a day spent visiting various business contacts. There is sure to be a lavish lunch involved. Taurus people love their creature comforts, especially food.

This combination may eventually get into the restaurant, motel, or catering business. The Capricorn partner is much more austere by nature, and there could be some disagreements over the way Taurus spends money. What other people may consider luxuries, Taurus regards as essentials.

CAPRICORN AND GEMINI
IN BUSINESS TOGETHER

A love or marriage partnership between Capricorn and the Twins is not an idyllic union. Usually, when these two people meet, they do not take a second glance at each other. Gemini is far too frivolous for the Goat to relate to. The Goat gives off those serious and stern vibes that make the Twins run a mile. These two will come together only in a business partnership, when a combination of their particular talents is needed. In this case, they can make money and enjoy doing it.

Both these partners can be calculating. They always have a fair idea what they are up to when it comes to business or money. Capricorn, despite his or her modest qualities, has a surprisingly ruthless streak underneath the diplomatic pose. This often shows itself in business when the Goat feels the urge for power, or when power is within grasping distance.

Gemini is often regarded as something of an opportunist. The Twins have a reputation for jumping on bandwagons. Their agile and intelligent minds are like quicksilver, another name for mercury, the metal associated with the sign and its ruling planet, Mercury. The metal mercury in liquid form expands with heat and contracts when cooled, as its rise and fall in a thermometer show. Geminis, too, blow hot and cold according to the wind or fortune of the day.

Both these signs are rather cool characters, especially Capricorn, who are at their best handling a crisis. But whereas Gemini is basically unemotional, the Goat just cannot manage to express emotion. Capricorns hate displaying their feelings. With extraordinary willpower, they exercise a great deal of self-discipline.

The Gemini Twins will soon start getting some black looks from the Goat if they start getting too talkative or nervously excitable. It would be a good idea for the Capricorn person contemplating a business link to check the astroscope profile of the Gemini person. The Twins are naturally lightweight by Capricorn standards. With a planet in Capricorn or one of the other earth signs, Gemini's compatibility will be much stronger.

Gemini would make an excellent partner in charge of the sales or marketing half under the wise guidance of the Goat. The Twins are smart enough to accept direction, which they often realize is lacking in themselves. Capricorn, being an extremely sensitive person, is not likely to start putting on any heavy pressure, which would be intolerable to the Twins.

CAPRICORN AND CANCER
IN BUSINESS TOGETHER

In their more personal relationships, both Cancer and Capricorn may be timid and uncertain of themselves. But in business, although uniquely different, each of these characters can be a very tough customer in his or her own way.

Both the Crab and the Goat are very easily hurt. They yearn to be respected and appreciated. Business gives them the opportunity to express the more positive side of their nature. Together, and as long as they do not waste time trying to determine what makes the other tick, they can build up a very successful operation.

The Goat is a realist and relies on reason. Every move is patiently thought out. Basically he or she wants power, not by revolution but by making the best possible use of traditional methods and all the facts that can be gathered. The Crab, on the other hand, is an idealist, an incurable romantic who aims toward some utopia he or she cannot even define. The Cancer person would far rather sit down and discuss what could be done than do what can be done. Yet Cancer people, almost against their will, are drawn into the thick of things, into the center of the commercial world.

The Cancer approach even in business is more a live-and-let-live one. Cancer also has a hunger for power, but not at any price. Cancer likes people to be emotionally dependent on them. It will not be long before the Capricorn partner is pouring out his or her pent-up feelings to this very obliging listener, and then possibly hating themselves for it.

Cancer in business drives a hard bargain. People are often lulled into a false sense of security by the Crab's easygoing manner. But when the Crab is negotiating a deal, the sentimentalist inside takes a vacation. The hard shell and the claws remain. Many a business rival has regretted underestimating this sensitive and intuitive man or woman.

It will be necessary for both partners to show their respect for each other. Capricorn will appreciate the old-fashioned charm of the Crab, and will be the first to agree that in many ways modern life has deteriorated since the good old days.

They must be careful that the business does not get into a rut. Capricorn may have to give the Crab a reminder sometimes that he or she is not making the most of their undoubted talents. And the Goat's imagination may need a transfusion of Cancer imagination to prevent him or her from holding too fixed opinions or getting behind the times.

CAPRICORN AND LEO
IN BUSINESS TOGETHER

A Capricorn man or woman has lots of ambition and a hearty appetite for authority, but often fails to make the most of opportunities available. Capricorns lack that extra drive and initiative needed to get to the top of the tree. They are inclined to stop to admire the view and then become part of the scenery. A Leo partner could be just the person to get the Goat really motivated.

Once Capricorn people start climbing in the right direction, they seldom fail to achieve their objectives. They can work under great pressure and hardship without showing the strain. It could be that Leo, the born leader, eventually finds himself or herself happily hanging onto the shirttails of the Goat as the partnership aims for the summit.

Leos do not like emotional hangups introduced into their business world. They let others know where they stand and expect the same treatment. The trouble with the Goat is that he or she gets uncomfortable trying not to show feelings. Capricorn people seldom feel relaxed and comfortable in the company of others. It will be up to the cheery and enthusiastic Leo partner to help bring the Capricorn businessmate out from gloomy self-doubt.

The Leo side of the outfit will be quick to see that the male or female Goat is often their own worst enemy. Capricorns are so afraid of being laughed at or made a fool of that they often end up venturing nothing and standing still. Their decisions are often made in terms of security, both material and emotional. A Leo partner will be a great help in showing them there is not so much to fear in the big wide world of people.

The Goat has a great deal of potential locked up inside. If Leo can manage to get close to this person, not only as a business partner but also as a friend, he or she will discover there is a very capable and deeply human person underneath.

The Leo partner will certainly be impressed by the way his or her opposite number can shift the work. Leo also is a hard worker, but is not so fastidious with details. Leo is an organizer and a leader. With these two characters, in spite of their love of power, it is unlikely they will clash over leadership. Each is after something different in authority. And each will respect the other's ability to wield it in their own particular area of the partnership.

CAPRICORN AND VIRGO
IN BUSINESS TOGETHER

Virgo and Capricorn are motivated by a desire, almost a compulsion, to find security. In business together, there is no doubt they would see things from much the same angle. Their practical and shrewd outlook on life would be very reassuring to each other. It could be that a commercial operation would not only be successful but would also lead to a lifelong friendship. Also, the possibility could not be ruled out that if they were man and woman, they could end up husband and wife.

These two earth signs produce thoughtful and methodical characters. Not for them the risky speculation or daring venture, which could land them on Easy Street overnight. Capricorn and Virgo believe in working for what they get. Anything extra is bonus, but it must not be counted on. They believe in looking before leaping, in making thorough plans, and in striving patiently toward one goal.

In combination, these two very conservative and cautious people are likely to miss some golden opportunities. Both are uncomfortable exploring new ground, especially when meeting new people. Virgos like to sit back in the crowd, analyzing the character of everyone in the room before attempting to make their own presence felt. And even then they are likely to wait patiently until someone addresses them.

Capricorn, because of agonizing hidden feelings of inferiority or self-doubt, may put on an aloof or brusque front that frightens everyone off. These two partners will have to do something about their hangups. The danger is that each will understand the other's feelings, sympathize, and do nothing positive to rectify the public-relations side of the business.

Although Capricorn can be pessimistic and critical, it will be difficult for this partner to take the constant criticism likely to come from the Virgo partner. Virgo people are always trying to improve the world by making it more efficient. They often think they are helping people by pointing out their faults. Capricorn will react to this very severely.

Virgos also can be fussbudgets around the office or shop, putting things back after Capricorn has deliberately taken them out to use. Both are careful with money, but could not be described as tight. Either could take charge of the finances. It would be a good idea if when the business prospers, they take on staff members who stimulate their thoughts and feelings and provide contrasting points of view.

CAPRICORN AND LIBRA IN BUSINESS TOGETHER

A love or marriage relationship between the Goat and the Scales might be a difficult combination. But a business tie-up contains very promising possibilities. The reason is that the realistic and responsible planet Saturn, ruler of Capricorn, reaches its strongest vibrations in Libra. This means that in a moneymaking business partnership these two people will see things in much the same light.

Even so, the Libra nature does have some lighthearted aspects that may at times get on the nerves of the Capricorn partner. Libras are extremely charming and easygoing. They love meeting people, especially at the social level. Libras seem to put more emphasis on being diplomatic and cooperative than on getting down to the nitty-gritty.

Libras also can be difficult people to pin down. Reaching decisions is not one of their strong points. These people see so many sides of a question that the answers often cancel each other out. Or they are inclined to sit on the fence waiting for the best suggestion and then going along with that, as though it were their own idea.

But it must not be thought that a Libra business partner would not have a great deal to contribute. It is likely that for a Libra to be interested, the partnership would have to have some connection with color, food, design, beauty aids, or social work. Because of their great interest in justice and the rights of the underdog, Libras also are attracted to the legal profession. Libras have excellent judgment. When faced with nonpersonal decisions they can weigh the pros and cons with remarkable clarity.

When it comes to meeting and entertaining clients, the Libra partner would be a great asset. Libra people have a knack for putting others immediately at ease. Even cautious and reserved characters like the Goat soon feel comfortable and more relaxed in their company. Libras also are great peacemakers. They have a way of bringing people with opposing ideas or attitudes closer together.

With their splendid capacity for work, Capricorn people will find that a Libra partner helps to keep them in circulation and current with all that is going on in the outside world. The Goat can become too engrossed in the practicalities of the business. Libras can be big spenders, and the Goat will have to monitor this tendency.

CAPRICORN AND SCORPIO IN BUSINESS TOGETHER

Scorpio people usually are prepared to take on the world to get what they want. They have a yearning for power and are single-minded about earning money. Capricorn people are the controllers of the Zodiac. They love the responsibility that comes from authority. There is no reason why Scorpio and Capricorn should not make a mint out of a business enterprise together.

Both are realists. Each will appreciate the other one's skills and talents. Their assets are different, but they will mesh into operation like matched gears. But the partnership has to be finely organized, with checks and balances. Neither of these powerful characters is going to allow the other one to dominate.

The Capricorn person is deeply emotional. Although not a water sign like Scorpio, Capricorn's mental processes are very much integrated with feelings and emotions. When a Capricorn person is not happy with a job, he or she will shrivel and brood, worrying whether or not to quit. On the other hand, once the Goat finds a comfortable niche, he or she will stick there forever. The world may pass such Capricorns by. But what do they care? They are happily involved.

Fortunately, the Scorpio person is a different kettle of fish. Scorpio also can get in a rut. But it is the sort of rut that definitely will be going places. A Capricorn partner in business with the fiercely ambitious Scorpion will somehow be made to make the most of his or her undoubted talents.

Both these characters are set in their opinions. They need to get out and exchange ideas with other people to make sure they keep up with the times and that they are heading in the right direction. It is easy for both of these individuals to fix their aims, then to put their heads down without ever looking up. Both are extremely hard workers and can bear all sorts of hardship until the goal is reached. But in partnership together both must be sure to check that the goal is still there.

There can be some difficult days ahead if these two get down in the dumps together. Both are subject to black depressions. They may at times get on each other's nerves. The Scorpio person is rather blunt and can easily offend the Capricorn partner's finer feelings. The Capricorn person has to know he or she is appreciated to prevent moody self-doubt. Scorpio may not be interested in this game.

CAPRICORN AND SAGITTARIUS IN BUSINESS TOGETHER

There is much in the Sagittarius personality that the Capricorn person is trying to flee from. In fact, the Goat is just about a total reaction against everything the Archer stands for. This sort of thing is not helpful to a close personal relationship. But in business together, these two are hardheaded enough to forget their personal differences and to accentuate the positive side. There is much to recommend this commercial link.

The Capricorn partner will have to get used to the fact that the Archer does business in strange ways. At least it will look strange from the cool and lofty peaks where the Goat stands. Sagittarius people always like to be on the move. Unlike Capricorn, who is rooted, they cannot bear to stay in one place for more than a few hours.

Also, unlike these earthy sons and daughters of Saturn, Sagittarius folk enjoy meeting as many people as possible and exchanging laughs and ideas. Sagittarius people have numerous friends. They seldom walk down the street without hailing or being hailed by someone. The Archers invariably have a great number of contacts in business, many of whom are bound to be prominent and influential. All this can be very good for a partnership.

The Sagittarius person also has a quick business brain, with an amazing facility for summing up the good and the bad points of a proposition and giving quick answers. One often suspects that the Archer fits the description of an "expert"—someone who makes quick decisions and is sometimes right; only in the Archer's case, these people usually *are* right.

People born under the sign of Sagittarius are ruled by the lucky planet Jupiter, which may bring good fortune to a business enterprise. They are not serious types like the Goat who prefers a cautious and methodical approach to the commercial scene. The Archer will take the most hair-raising risks. He or she often seems unable to turn down any venture that contains some novelty or speculative twist. Such irresponsibility will horrify the Capricorn partner until he or she gets used to the Archer's way of operating.

The Sagittarius partner will be quite happy to leave the details of running the business to Capricorn. The Archer is a born salesman, not an organizer. Capricorn, too, will be the one to oversee the finances.

CAPRICORN AND CAPRICORN
IN BUSINESS TOGETHER

These two Capricorn people believe in the importance of work. Neither could be associated for long with anyone who was lazy or wanted the easy way out when faced with a difficult task. In fact, they are two very hard workers who thrive on responsibility and self-discipline. When two people of this caliber get together in a commercial partnership, they can go right to the top.

There are, of course, a few difficulties. These fortunately will not be at the personality level, as two Goats together will get along famously. Each will appreciate the other's sensitive feelings and need to be respected. There will be no game-playing with each other's emotions. Each will know exactly how much the other hurts even when he or she is putting on a cool, brave face after an argument with someone in the office or on the phone.

But this partnership could start coming apart if it fails to move with the times. Usually, Capricorn people choose a line of business that does not depend on taking any chances. They work with the long term in view. They are resourceful but very careful people who prefer to stick to traditional methods and procedures rather than experiment.

It will be easy for the business to sink into a rut. Capricorn tends to stay in one place. The Goat, once settled in a secure niche, is very reluctant to make any changes. He or she is a person who does not make many friends. Capricorns are afraid of their own emotions, and especially of being rebuffed or criticized. They tend to hide their true and rather lovable selves behind a façade of authority and undoubted competence.

Capricorn people are at their best in business requiring their responsible and economizing qualities. Together, they can build a fine partnership firm of lawyers, accountants, real-estate agents, farmers, or engineers. They can make money in the construction or sale of scientific instruments. They have a great ability for constructing systems of production and administration.

It is important that the two partners do not spend all their life working. They should aim to get time off for recreation or exercise every day. If the partners play any sport before they team up, they probably will drop it under the pressure of business, which would be unfortunate. They must endeavor not to become solely career people.

CAPRICORN AND AQUARIUS
IN BUSINESS TOGETHER

A Capricorn person would have to be the power behind the scenes in a business partnership with the Water Bearer. It will need Capricorn's down-to-earth and focused method to hold the whole thing together. Aquarius people are very good at whatever job they take on. But the routine of business life tends to bore them. To succeed, the business will have to be in a field that serves humanity in some way and is not just a moneymaking concern.

Aquarius individuals are offbeat and prefer offbeat careers. They think differently from other people, but not all the time. Mostly, they are conventional and moderate. Then they do something extraordinarily extreme, seeming quite out of character.

However, the Water Bearer has much to contribute to any undertaking that maximizes his or her talents. Aquarius people are extremely intelligent. They are among the most progressive thinkers in the Zodiac. Often they are inventors. They are terribly interested in making the world a better place to live in. They aim to help, reorganize, and improve everyone or anyone. If this business partnership is connected with scientific research, social welfare, writing, broadcasting, publishing, and even space technology, the mental skills of this partner will soon be apparent.

The Capricorn person is an understanding human being. He or she will want to direct the Water Bearer. This could be a problem. Aquarius people are very independent. They may appear terribly friendly and cooperative, but they will not be told what to do. They have to be maneuvered very carefully or they will walk out in a huff.

Aquarius individuals outgrow the people around them and get bored with a steady scene. They are interested in everyone and everything from an intellectual point of view. But once they have discovered what the person or situation is all about, they lose interest and drift away. Before entering this partnership the Capricorn person should think very seriously about whether the line of business will offer sufficient scope to sustain the Water Bearer's interest.

The Aquarius partner is unpredictable. This could make the more settled and methodical Capricorn person feel uncomfortable. Aquarius folk change direction in midair. But they are friendly and civilized people who bring a distinct touch of meaning to whatever they start.

CAPRICORN AND PISCES
IN BUSINESS TOGETHER

Capricorn people believe in hard work and responsibility. They realize at a very early age that this is a tough and demanding world. Even in their teens and early twenties, when they can appear to be living it up and not to have a care in the world, they are aware of the realities and the seriousness within themselves that will soon start to show.

Pisces is completely the opposite. Pisces is unrealistic and dreamy, does not like hard work, and is tremendously optimistic. Could such a pairing of partners succeed in a business link? Most certainly it could because it combines two different sets of expertise.

Capricorn will make an excellent balance for the Pisces side of the outfit. No one in the Zodiac has greater talent than the Fishes for being able to come up with moneymaking ideas. Pisces people may seem as though they are wandering around in another world, but really their minds are ticking away at high speed. In business, they may seem to be lax, daydreaming or relaxing, while in fact they are scheming how to pull off a big deal for the partnership. Although many of the Pisces' propositions are hopelessly impractical, it is rare indeed that the odd one does not turn out to be a real moneymaker. It will be up to the Capricorn partner, with his or her practical good sense, to see that Pisces does not get carried away with enthusiasm for the less likely schemes. The Fishes, when they do come up with ideas for making money, often are unable to see any possibility of failure.

Before contemplating a business partnership, however, the Capricorn person will have to make sure that the Pisces person is an evolved type. The underdeveloped type is a weak fish. Unless he or she has managed to face their own weaknesses instead of constantly running from them, such an individual will drift along with no real purpose in life. Pisces needs someone to keep him or her headed in the right direction. No one would be better for this task than a Capricorn partner.

A Pisces partner will be very good for the Goat in business. The Fishes will teach the logically minded Goat that there is another way of approaching life other than through the rational mind. The Fishes are one of the most intuitive types in the Zodiac; they rely almost totally on their emotions to inform them of what's going on. It would be wise for Capricorn to keep the books and money accounts.

Capricorn:
Parents and Children

How will a child born under a different Sun sign respond to a Capricorn parent? And how will the youngster be as a toddler, an adolescent, a teenage boy or girl? Will there be changes? What kind?

These questions and suggested answers make up one of the most overlooked aspects of astrological psychology. The *Astroscope Profile* series provides in-depth discussions of these questions and answers in this chapter.

Parents who take the trouble to read and understand the Sun sign descriptions of their children may certainly save the kids from future psychological problems, and at the same time make life easier for themselves. The child's natural urges can be anticipated, and opportunities provided for the youngsters to express these in positive ways. The negative side of the nature also can be watched for and handled with intelligent understanding as soon as it appears.

But parenthood is a kind of partnership. Success usually means turning out a balanced and integrated young personality capable of coping with adult pressures and creating a reasonably fulfilling life. This depends a great deal on the temperament and character of *both* child and parent. How will each take to the other despite the natural bond of parental and filial love?

This chapter describes the likely interaction and compatibility between Capricorn parents and children born under each of the twelve Sun signs. Each section first describes family togetherness and likely modes of behavior and response. Then there follow points about the child's developing character as an infant, a youngster, and a teenager.

CAPRICORN PARENTS
AND ARIES CHILDREN

The Capricorn parent will provide a very desirable balance for the fiery nature of an Aries youngster. The Aries child is impulsive, so eager for action and instant results that very often there is no pause for caution or thought. But the earthy Capricorn mom or dad will slow Aries down. Capricorns like to be sure of their ground so that the margin for error is as wide as possible.

The young Ram will not be short of discipline in a Capricorn family. The natural adventurous urge, which often can become foolhardiness in these young people, will be curbed. Whereas the Aries nature often is impractical, the Capricorn parent is extremely down-to-earth and will teach the worthwhile lesson of looking before leaping.

However, it is important that a Capricorn parent does not allow his or her own cautious approach to life to inhibit the Aries offspring's innate spontaneity. In many ways, Capricorn and Aries temperaments are as different as night and day. Restraint, patience, and practicality are certainly qualities that will enhance the Aries boy or girl's chances in the world as long as these traits are not carried to extremes.

The Capricorn parent will induce in the restless Aries youngster an appreciation of family life. This boy or girl will grow up with the certainty that he or she needs a solid family base from which to operate in the vigorous pursuit of worldly ambitions. Aries kids will be better suited to settling down in married life when the time comes for them to be on their own.

The Capricorn mother runs an efficient and well-organized home. If she has an Aries daughter, it would be advisable for her to entrust the girl with certain functions important to the operation of the family unit. Aries love to take up a challenge. But they must be allowed to cope with it in their own way. Interference by a parent would ruin the value of the exercise and probably result in a very rebellious and frustrated young person around the house. It is not always easy for the Capricorn nature to hand over responsibility.

In this household, all birthdays and family celebrations will be duly honored. It will be a very disappointed mom or dad if teenage Aries has other arrangements made for the day when a family get-together or reunion is planned. Capricorn types are clannish.

The Aries youngster will have some dedicated help from Mom or Dad when it comes to school studies and homework. Home study times are likely to be fixed rigidly, and this could create some anxiety for the Aries boy or girl. These children do have to have a sense of freedom and room for maneuvering to do their best work. It would pay the parent to devise a system of trust wherever possible in training the Aries child rather than to depend on a fixed routine or the power of parental authority.

The Capricorn parent has a deep need to be respected by his or her children. This can best be achieved with Aries youngsters by giving them the opportunity to display their initiative and enterprise, and being sure to acknowledge their efforts. Like Capricorns, Aries individuals love to be praised and appreciated when they have done a good job. Sometimes a Capricorn parent may withhold praise out of a desire not to spoil the child. In the case of an Aries youngster, this would be counterproductive.

The Capricorn parent has to resist any urge to put up unnecessary restrictions, or to impose discipline for its own sake. Capricorns should try to take life a little less seriously by seeing the funny side. This is not to say that Capricorns do not have a sense of humor; they do, and it is deliciously subtle. Subtlety is something unfamiliar to young Aries. The power of a Capricorn parent to be relaxed and charming also will be a good influence on the restless and blunt young Ram.

Infant Aries

The Aries infant will soon demonstrate to doting Mom and Dad that he or she was born under the restless first sign of the Zodiac. "Me first" will be the message right from the start. Words will not be necessary: just a boisterous, full-blooded cry for instant attention. Aries types, young and old, never can wait. If a thing is in reach, they grab it. If it catches the eye outside the crib, they are up and over—and possibly down, with a fall.

Aries is the sign of pioneers and adventurers. Falls, bumps, bruises, cuts, and scratches, especially from the cat, are all in a day's experience to these young daredevils. It is especially important not to leave boiling saucepans on the stove or other dangerous things within tumbling distance of an Aries infant. Somehow they can usually manage the impossible when it comes to action.

These are very active and energetic little people. They are early talkers and walkers. They are as bright as buttons and full of life. They are angry in a flash and forget it the next moment. They can be destructive, especially of toys that they cannot work. If they can't master a game, they are likely to throw it down and break it just to have the last word.

Young Aries

At school, Aries youngsters will not learn too well if they are forced to delve into detail. They excel in work and activities that allow them to show off their lively imagination. Once their interest is aroused, they learn very quickly. But the danger is that they will race ahead, depending on their quick mind and good memory for answers, instead of understanding what they are doing. They are very impatient young people. They become easily bored by repetition.

Aries boys and girls are extremely curious. They always ask questions. They are eager to experience life to the full and to learn all about it in three seconds flat. Parents have to make sure these children understand the basics of what they are supposed to be learning. Often they skip over fundamentals. When exam time comes round, they flunk—to everyone's surprise, especially their own.

These youngsters are likely to roam. Parents of Aries children have to be prepared for them getting lost. They can't resist the urge to explore the unknown, even if it is only hopping on a passing bus or streetcar. Usually they are good at sports. But unless they can take a leading or impressive role, they are inclined to lose interest.

Teenage Aries

Aries teenagers are very independent young people. They are inclined to think they know more than everyone else. At least they are very sure of what is best for them.

They are often brash and inconsiderate, a law unto themselves. Unless they have received a good deal of understanding and love in the early years, they can start to take it out on the rest of the world.

Aries teenagers exude an air of self-sufficiency that can make adults believe they are not in need of much affection and love. They are inwardly sensitive; they need more loving guidance and attention than their independent airs indicate.

These young people are naturally honest and trusting. It is only through others that they learn to be otherwise. They should be put into positions of trust. They should be given the opportunity to meet challenges that will win them admiration and praise, instead of pursuing dares that get them in trouble.

Sex is one of the dares that Aries teenagers will meet when challenged by their peers. Sex is an area in which the young Aries has not had much independence and precious little experience. So early experimentation serves a dual purpose: showing off to friends and proving something to themselves.

Here is where the parents must come in. Their teenage Aries youngsters are too likely to plunge into sexual freedom without knowledge or protection. Pregnancy is one danger, worse for their daughter than their son. But the wise parent is not likely to preach the double standard. Escapades in fast cars are another danger, often attracting the unfavorable attention of the law.

Suitable parental guidance, and it can't be too subtle, can forewarn their teenage Rams. They can discuss the dangers of freedom without responsibility, as well as the intricacies of social acceptance and pressure with all the price tags. The parents' message to their teenage youngsters should help to modify any behavior the kids show with companions outside of the home.

CAPRICORN PARENTS
AND TAURUS CHILDREN

A Capricorn parent will have a deep understanding of the needs of a Taurus youngster. These two characters will often know exactly how the other is feeling without a word being exchanged. Both are united in nature by being earth signs. This makes them hardheaded and practical when it comes to material security.

At first, the Taurus child may seem to be a crybaby. These kids are inclined to want everything their own way. They may scream or stubbornly sulk to the bitter end to get it. Fortunately, the Goat, who has a good idea of how children should behave, is stubborn, too. The Capricorn parent can be counted on to crack down on any tantrums by the obstinate young Bull. This is a good thing because Taurus is one of the most potentially self-indulgent signs in the Zodiac.

As a rule, the Capricorn parent is good with money. Capricorns could never be described as stingy when it comes to providing for their loved ones or building a comfortable home. But they don't throw their money around, nor do they lose any sleep about having more comforts and luxuries than they need. The Taurus nature, on the other hand, is to exist and work for just these things.

Mom or Dad will admire the way Junior at an early age starts to put the pennies away. But the Goat may feel a little dismayed at the way this boy or girl always seems to choose the most expensive item on the shelf. Taurus is ruled by the pleasure-loving planet of beautiful things, Venus. This influence, coupled with their practicality, makes Taurus people aware of comfort and luxury. It will be obvious to the Capricorn parent that the indulgent side of the Taurus nature will have to be watched. Any excessive move in teenage toward enjoying aspects of the good life, or overdependence on the delights of the senses, can mean future trouble.

On the positive side, Taurus youngsters have great promise. Their love of beautiful things can be channeled into a productive hobby and later a lucrative occupation. Often they are very good at making things with their hands, such as pottery, paintings, handicrafts, and tapestries. The Capricorn parent should encourage any aptitude for combining colors or designs or materials.

Once Taurus kids are past the early years, when they are most likely to be spoiled, they are easy to encourage to take up activities and training courses that may serve to prepare them for a future career. These youngsters have a sound sense of material values, and they are prepared to work diligently to obtain what they want.

Taurus is one of the most affectionate signs of the Zodiac. This young person will be able to communicate love, not always an easy thing to do with a Capricorn. Taurus kids also love their home. They will give Mom or Dad a great amount of pleasure with the interest they display in whatever is done to make the home a more attractive and efficient place.

It will be a good idea for the parent to make sure that Junior does not eat too much candy or cake. Taurus people are inclined to have waistline problems if they can't resist the temptations of the table.

Taurus teenagers are sensible kids as a rule. Unless they get into bad company, they are not the experimental types. They are more likely to follow the group and become innocently involved if trouble does come their way. The Capricorn parent believes in law and order, and Junior will find that this attidtude accords with his or her own cautious and conservative nature.

Neither Capricorn nor Taurus enjoys change. It might be up to the other parent to make sure that these two individuals do not get into a comfortable living style that becomes a rut. Both the Goat and the Bull need to be encouraged to take up regular exercise or recreation.

Infant Taurus

This child is very easy to spoil. The young boy or girl Bull is usually very soft, round, and cuddly. They are not demanding types. That comes later. They are not silly, either. But when Mom or Dad can't resist picking them up often enough, they soon get the idea and start squealing for attention.

It has to be remembered that Taurus is a luxury-loving sign. So anything that comes near to making life more comfortable and congenial will quickly be seized on even by infant Taurus. If handled intelligently, this little boy or girl will probably be a model of quiet and contented babyhood.

As long as they feel comfortable, Taurus infants are easy to keep amused. They receive most of their assurances through their highly developed senses. They love to be cuddled and made a fuss of, to feel warm and loved. Even having soft and fine materials next to their skin can mean more to these children than to other infants. Furry toy animals and squeezable objects are good company in the crib.

Very early it will become apparent that Taurus infants have a mind of their own. If challenged, they can become very difficult. It is easier for a parent to go along with them or change the subject or distract their attention than to persist in trying to make them do what they do not want to do.

Young Taurus

Taurus children learn slowly. They are more physical than mental. They have to absorb the feel and situation of things by handling and touching. Parents and schoolteachers have to remember that it is no good rattling off facts and numbers and expecting these young people to remember them. They won't! And if this is the attitude of a teacher, these youngsters will be unfairly labeled dull or backward.

Above all, Taurus children need educational toys. Handling them and moving them around and playing with them help the youngsters learn their arithmetic and spelling. Given the time to take things in their own way, they learn mathematics and language arts thoroughly.

It is seldom that the young Bull cannot be stimulated to take an interest in music. Music is something that people born under this sign seem to have a natural aptitude for and appreciation of. Any musical talent should be encouraged as soon as it is revealed. Taurus youngsters often make good singers as well as instrumentalists.

It is easy to teach a Taurus youngster to be methodical. They fall quickly into habits. They should be given little chores to do around the house; they will take pride in doing these chores if given a good example. Touching, moving, or putting anything into place reinforces a careful and systematic approach to problem-solving.

Teenage Taurus

Taurus youngsters are usually attractive physically at an early age. They grow into fine-looking teenage boys and girls, who are very much in demand among their friends and acquaintances. Their ear for music and ability to dance make them popular in the disco scene.

Taurus teenagers always make a point of understanding in depth what interests them. They can build a reputation among their friends for being a whiz or an expert in one hobby or another. They are fairly serious, but cars turn them on. It's possible that the Taurus teenager likes cars more for the comfort and status they confer than for any love of mechanics or driving.

However, they have a great love of entertainment and being entertained. These teenage Taurus boys and girls can quickly become bored, especially if they have been spoiled by their parents, and can get into selfish habits. Indulgence can be a problem in sharing situations.

Taurus teenagers are much more cautious than their confident manner may suggest. They are not inclined to take physical risks. They would much rather stay safely in the group than take the lead. Sports that require strength catch their interest more than show-off sports of skill, speed, and daring.

Sex on the experimental level may not become a pursuit of the Taurus teenager. Slightly shy and lacking the natural curiosity that may characterize other youngsters, they express sexual urges and sexual interests more through clothes, the company they keep, and the extracurricular activities they pursue. The alert parent can easily tune into these strategies and help their teenager learn the social graces so important to dating.

Some Taurus teenagers secretly wish to go steady, but may be too emotionally immature to handle such a situation. So they make a big splash with one set of costumes, companions, and cliques. Then they abandon these for new fashions, fads, and friends. Such behavior is uncharacteristic of the adult Taurus or of one who has matured beyond the family scene. Again, the alert parent can point out how extravagant behavior creates problems and dangers, especially in relating sincerely to people.

CAPRICORN PARENTS
AND GEMINI CHILDREN

For a Gemini boy or girl, a Capricorn parent will be a tower of strength and good sense. It will not be easy to figure out just what makes this young person tick. Mom or Dad will often shake his or her head in bewilderment trying to stabilize and pin down, with few results, this restless and impulsive mercurial character.

There is no doubt that the Gemini youngster is as bright as they come. But the question that will always be in the back of a Capricorn mom or dad's mind will be whether Gemini will ever learn to apply himself or herself long enough to anything to fulfill all that potential.

The Capricorn parent is patient, cautious, and methodical. The Goat is a down-to-earth person who believes that the rewards in life come from persistence and hard work. The Gemini nature is almost completely different. These kids are outgoing and communicative personalities. They cannot stand the thought of being tied down. They will sacrifice just about anything for their freedom. And this could mean not turning up at school, or changing their minds and doing something else in the middle of an important project.

The Capricorn parent will not stand for this inconsistency. And this is a good thing, for Geminis are very easy people to influence and condition if they are trained early enough in their lives. It is the worst thing in the world for these youngsters to be given all the liberty they incessantly demand. The Capricorn parent will inculcate in this adaptable and versatile young character a greater sense of responsibility.

It is important for Gemini youngsters to have a good parental example to follow. The Gemini nature is not immoral by any means to begin with, but it does tend to take the shape or the outlook of the people closest. Geminis can go either way, picking up admirable or undesirable traits that will be with them to the end of their days.

Geminis like to please. They are loving and affectionate young people. They will genuinely do all they can to be a good son or daughter. If they respect their parents, they will turn out like them in many ways.

It must be remembered that Gemini is the sign of the Twins. The Capricorn mind is deliberate and practical, able to follow a line of inquiry without being distracted. But the dual nature of Gemini youngsters makes them changeable and unreliable. It is often as though one Twin going one way is taken over by the other Twin going the other way. The result is inconsistency and frequently confusion in the Gemini mind.

With intelligent and patient handling, the Gemini youngster's clever and versatile mind can be directed along positive lines. The Gemini character is well suited for any vocation that exploits brain power or intellect to the fullest. The job should provide opportunity to do, learn, and see new things, as well as to make fresh personal contacts. Geminis shine as reporters, secretaries, linguists, lecturers, teachers, writers, agents, and sales representatives.

It is extremely important for Mom or Dad Capricorn not to nag this sensitive young boy or girl. Although the Goat will be exasperated at times by the Twins' incessant restlessness, the Capricorn parent must resist any urge to keep pointing out their faults.

With a Gemini teenager around, a Capricorn parent may find that life is a lot more interesting and lighthearted than it used to be before Junior arrived on the scene. Geminis can often perform two or even three things at one time. They can be more productive in their disjointed and versatile way than more serious and plodding types.

Infant Gemini

A Gemini infant is very quick to learn and to mimic. It will not be long before this child is amazing its parents with the things it can do and say. It is especially quick at picking up words and actions.

The parent of a Gemini toddler will soon learn that this little boy or girl cannot be left alone for more than a few seconds without getting into some sort of mischief. They are extremely quick at moving, whether on their knees or feet. They can be out the door in no time, or into the cupboard where the best china is stored.

Gemini children at a very early age show an intelligent interest in what is happening around them. They should be given crayons and pencils and paper as soon as their deft little hands can hold them. Then they can express themselves and work off their abundance of mental energy.

The curiosity of these children makes it very difficult for them to concentrate on any one thing for very long. They need great variety in their toys and games. It is not unusual for parents of these kiddies to become wearied, either chasing after them or answering their incessant questions, which they frequently cannot wait to be answered before asking the next.

Young Gemini

The immediate environment is of vital interest to young Geminis. They will draw what they see and think. Soon they are stringing letters into words, and words into phrases on paper. It is important to get the Gemini child down to silent reading and written expression as soon as possible. Otherwise they will interrupt classmates and teachers and parents with endless though spirited recitations.

At school, young Gemini is likely to have some problems. He or she will be among the brightest in the class, probably first up with the hands when questions are being asked about current events or controversial topics. But when it comes to anything old or routine, the Gemini youngster is likely to be disinterested or just plain bored.

Young Gemini may disturb his or her parents by the number of activities that are started but never finished. Parents may despair at their child's inability to concentrate. But this is typical of the Gemini nature. Parents should encourage them in each new project, helping them to see the broad overview, even though they won't see the project through to a conclusion.

The Gemini urge is to learn by experimentation. Anything novel is immediately absorbed. Their minds are always active. It is not a good idea to allow them to become too excited before going to bed. Chances are, they will not sleep. Sometimes Gemini children develop a stutter because their minds work faster than their tongues. Nevertheless, this impediment doesn't stop them from verbalizing.

Teenage Gemini

As a rule, the Gemini teenager does not spend as much time at home as most other types do. Geminis are often among the first teenagers to leave home. It is not that they can't stand the family or their homes. They just need constant variety and change. These youths are not runaways or truants, just absentees for short periods of time.

Gemini teenagers probably will roam often but not far, especially if they are handled with understanding. Although their curiosity often leads them into dubious company and dangerous situations, they have a knack for avoiding trouble. They are survivors once they have learned something of the ways of the world. And it does not take them long to absorb a little knowledge and put it to use.

But it seems to take a long time for Gemini teenagers to grow up. Not only do they look younger than their years (which is often annoying to them), but also they refuse to satisfy their parents' expectations by settling down eventually. Geminis can be in their thirties before they start to show a desire to quit their restless, chattering, gallivanting ways.

It is essential for parents to see that their teenage Geminis get sufficient sleep and rest, or their health may suffer. But the youngsters themselves usually have a hand on whatever regime is plotted for them. They will show up at mealtime, maybe; they will endure piano lessons, sometimes; they will abide by curfew, seldom.

Romance and sex usually interfere with Gemini teenagers' regime of exercise, rest, and nutrition. Studies and sports certainly do not get these youngsters off stride. But the excitement of the unknown can upset all their daily routine.

Sex and romance, their final youthful plunge into knowledge, can take them far afield, making them abandon piano lessons or basketball practice or early snacks at the hangout. They even can stay away from the house for a few days, or sneak out when they have been punished. But this little knowledge does not lead them into danger.

Somehow Gemini teenagers manage to avoid violence, pregnancy, venereal disease, and the long hand of the law or their companions' family when they break into this new frontier of experience and feeling and insight. Their own parents usually are amazed at the scrapes they get into and out of.

But then, of course, Geminis, teenagers notwithstanding, have lots of knowledge they picked up somewhere or other, here and there. They are always using this knowledge to protect themselves and their companions.

A mature head for responsibility on youthful shoulders seems to be a contradiction. But Geminis, contradictory to the core, perform splendidly in emergency situations. Romantic and sexual adventures to the teenage Gemini are appreciated as emergency situations. The novelty and knowledge gained may be the only feature of the situation that Gemini will brag about later.

CAPRICORN PARENTS
AND CANCER CHILDREN

A good relationship can be established between a Capricorn parent and a Cancer boy or girl. Astrologically, they are opposites, facing each other across the Zodiac. But both have a great amount of love in them. The problem could be that Mom or Dad will not demonstrate that love in the emotional ways that mean so much to this very sensitive son or daughter.

Capricorn people are very practical and down-to-earth. These parents will know they love and cherish their youngster. They prove it in the innumerable overt ways in which they provide a comfortable and secure home and family life. However, Cancer types need lots of displays of love and affection. The Capricorn parent can be a bit neglectful in the sensitivity and sentimentality areas.

Mom or Dad must make a point of cuddling and making a fuss of this youngster even though this may go against the grain. Capricorns should remember that although they have difficulty expressing their feelings in a showy or sentimental way, not to try to do so will leave a gap in their relationship with a Cancer child.

Cancer boys and girls often seem to be a lot tougher and more self-assured than is the case. They create for themselves an armor plate like the hard shell of the Crab, their symbol, because they are so soft inside and would often be walked over by others. They are sympathetic youngsters, always looking for something or someone to love and protect.

What has to be understood by the Capricorn parent is that Cancer is a water sign. That means a Cancer child is deeply emotional and not nearly as practical or rooted as Mom or Dad. Young Cancer kids are passive and receptive. They need constant reassurance to build up their ego so that they can cope with the world.

The Capricorn parent usually is temperamentally steady. The Goats have their emotional ups and downs, of course, but compared to the fluctuating moods of Cancer people they are as steady as rocks. It has to be remembered that the Moon, the ruler of Cancer, also rules the tides. The emotions of these Moon children follow similar rhythms.

For part of the month, Cancer individuals are likely to be seized with an instinctive outgoing urge, which can lead to considerable achievements. They have an enterprising quality that will surprise and delight Mom or Dad. But during the remainder of the month, these Moon children may retreat within themselves and be unable to face the pressures of the world. The Capricorn parent has to recognize that these periods of apparent moody isolation are necessary for such emotionally motivated types.

However, it is a good idea with Cancer children not to allow them to sit around too much chatting with their pals about all the things they are going to do, and then doing nothing. Cancer people, when they are not withdrawn, are very social creatures. They are not particularly physically active, though. Their bodies can be clumsy and slow-moving. They would rather exercise their imagination than muscle and nerve.

The Cancer youngster will be a great help around the house. Both the male and female Crab love the warmth and togetherness of family life. Young Crabs often have extraordinarily accurate hunches. They can be extremely shrewd when it comes to business transactions, something that will be admired by Mom or Dad, who are no slouches themselves when it comes to putting over a deal. Cancer and Capricorn are two types who sometimes manage to do well in business together.

The artistic inclinations of the young Crab should be encouraged, as such assets may lead to a worthwhile career. Success often comes to Cancer people through their style of moving sideways like the Crab. Other people who forge ahead in the ordinary way are often surprised to find that the faltering Cancer person in the end is up with them in achievement and recognition.

Infant Cancer

These children need love more than anything else. Whereas Taurus infants need the reassurance of cuddling and touch, Cancer infants need even more. These little ones born under the sign of the Crab are deeply emotional beings. They need, above all, to feel they are wanted. Loving words and sound help.

The Cancer child needs to be brought up in harmonious surroundings. Parental and family arguments create emotional strains in the child, even in the tenderest years or months. Any excessive crying and fretfulness that cannot be explained are often attributable to anxiety about a hostile environment.

During the infant stage, Cancer children are not very demanding as long as they feel affection around them. They will sit for hours playing quietly by themselves. They are usually very good with younger brothers or sisters, being quick to accept them as members of the family, for whom they want to feel responsible in some small way or other.

Often the Cancer infant is a slow developer. These little ones learn more through their feelings about things than through any concentrate mental or muscular activity.

To encourage the growing Cancer infant, music and art should be introduced into the environment as early as possible. Musical toys and objects representing people, animals, and buildings should be available for the little one to play with and relate to.

Young Cancer

Growing up is often a painful process for the Cancer youngster. In spite of all the love and care lavished on these little people by their parents, their sensitivity causes them to feel hurt more often than most other types of children.

School days sometimes are an agony for them. They do not mix easily in the beginning. They tend to wait on their own for someone to approach them, rather than making any attempts at contact themselves. Often they are teased, sometimes because they are inclined to be a bit fat or dumpy. Every hurtful gibe and comment, even though it may not really be meant, goes straight to the soul of the young Cancer person.

Parents should try to remember that appearances with a Cancer child do not always tell the full story. They may suffer in silence. Sympathy and understanding will help to bring them out of themselves, and perhaps help the parent to remedy a situation.

Cancer boys and girls, once they feel accepted by a group, are very active and vivacious. The more familiar they become with their surroundings and companions, the more likely Cancer children are to start showing their considerable initiative.

Teenage Cancer

By the time Junior Cancer reaches teenage, he or she is likely to be showing a good deal of swagger and self-assurance, at least on the outside. There can be something of the rebel in the late teenager. They are not nearly as quick to obey as they were in the earlier years.

Also, in teenage, Cancer youngsters are likely to start showing the moody side of their nature. For a while they can be sunny and bright and outgoing. Then without warning they retreat deep inside themselves. They transmit inexplicable waves of gloom that are likely to affect everyone else in the household.

The slightest criticism is likely to send the Cancer teenager into a black mood. Even imagined hurts and slights will have the same result. There is something of the martyr in the Cancer nature, which makes these young people inclined to keep their problems to themselves. An intelligent parent has to endeavor to get them to open up, or the mood may go on for days. Love and sympathy displays can be the solutions.

The Cancer teenager has to be encouraged as much as possible to see his or her own emotional weaknesses. Otherwise, they can become intolerably demanding in later life.

Dating and sex could be the areas where Cancer teenagers first discover how painful their emotions are. They want a steady boyfriend or girlfriend, but they may have a reputation for being difficult. It is not that the Cancer teenager is picky. Just moody!

Also, peer pressures around cars and clothes and spending money and sexual experimentation might be hard for the Cancer teenager to handle. This youngster may not be daring enough either to rebel against parental restrictions or to tell his or her friends off. And he or she is not likely to confide these worries to the parent.

Parents should try to draw their Cancer teenager out on such subjects as dating, sex, and peer pressures. Appearance and good looks, so important to these youngsters, must be considered. Also, it is never too early to explain the consequences of sexual freedom. The Cancer teenager, deeply attached to home and family, may be thinking of starting his or her own family prematurely!

CAPRICORN PARENTS
AND LEO CHILDREN

Having an outgoing and exuberant young Leo around the house is going to give a lot of pleasure to a Capricorn mom or dad. But there will be times when the racket of self-assertion and vitality from this bundle of energy will get on the parent's nerves. There is a fundamental difference between Capricorn and Leo. The former is a restrained earth sign, the latter an assertive fire sign.

Very early in the game, Mom or Dad Capricorn will frown on and tone down this boy or girl's tendency to show off in company. Capricorns are quiet, self-disciplined people. It may come as a shock to this parent to find a youngster so noisily determined to make a mark, to occupy center stage when anyone is around. When the young Lion is not being applauded or admired, he or she will find some way to draw attention to himself or herself, including sulking and temper tantrums.

The Capricorn parent's serious and responsible attitude to life may save this boy or girl from growing into an arrogant and overbearing type of person. But the Goat must not be too strict or stern. The Leo son or daughter must be guided to know the limits of other people's tolerance, while at the same time maintaining the juvenile optimism appropriate to the Lion. The Goat is an expert at fancy footwork, and that skill should be transmitted to the developing Leo youngster.

Leo kids are filled with spontaneous good feelings and good qualities. Excessive restriction or restraint can inhibit their natural talents. Self-repressive types like Capricorns sometimes fail to understand the vitality and passion that fire outgoing signs like Leo. Leos, as Mom or Dad will soon discover, are born leaders. Through their enthusiasm and love of life, they are able to inspire others to live lives more fully and actively.

The youngster's talent for leadership and organization and love will give Mom or Dad a great deal of satisfaction. Capricorns, underneath their relaxed exterior, are very ambitious people who believe in getting to the top. They may be prepared to wait longer and work more methodically than the young Lion, but both share the same craving for success. But love, a unique Leo expression, will have the Goat beaming.

One thing the Capricorn parent may never get used to is the Leo youngster's powerful self-assurance. Sometimes Capricorns will feel themselves curl up inside at the confidence this youngster has. Capricorns are unsure of themselves in unfamiliar situations. It will amaze this parent how the young Lion is able to stride into strange company without the slightest trace of self-consciousness.

For the Leo youngster, it will be good to see how cool and collected Mom or Dad remains in a crisis. Leos, being passionate types, tend to overreact and to start shouting or crying when the pressure is on. They can handle it ultimately, but are often noisy, teary, and demanding; they waste a lot of their energy in unnecessary action.

However, the Capricorn parent cannot help but be struck by the powerful presence that Leo youngsters exhibit as they mature. It should be remembered that Leo is a sign associated with the kings and queens of old, so a regal and dignified bearing comes naturally. However, there is a great sense of pride in Leos. If it gets out of hand, it can become intolerable conceit.

The Leo son or daughter is a born romantic. These kids love to imagine themselves in heroic situations. There is no deceit in their nature; they say what they think. They will do anyone a good turn whom they regard as worthy. But if not given the recognition they think is due, they can cut a person down with imperious disdain.

When the Capricorn parent gets into his or her occasional down moments, the cheery, sunny, and warmhearted presence of the Leo youngster will help to snap the Goat back to reality. Although this young Leo person may seem dauntingly self-sufficient, he or she needs plenty of love.

Infant Leo

It will soon become evident to the parent of a Leo infant that this little person has to be the center of attention. The Leo child, even at the tender age of a couple of years, starts showing off. This behavior will not be quite the same as when other children go through a state of juvenile exhibitionism. Other children grow out of it. The Leo child grows into and perfects it.

Any parent who shows a Leo infant true love will seldom have to worry about being lonely and neglected in old age. The Lion, like the elephant, never forgets. A loving mother or father always will have a secure place in the Leo heart.

This child knows unconsciously whether a parent really needs him or her. Leo is the sign of children, and so is intuitive on this level. Although a natural show-off, right from the start the Leo child is extremely sympathetic. He or she should never be loaded even in jest with any sort of responsibility that is not intended. There is a tremendous seriousness in these toddlers under all the lightheartedness that compels them to do what is expected of them.

Although they will be as naughty and as mischievous as the rest, Leo children will fret about letting their parents, or those who love them, down. Their anxiety may express itself in unexpected bursts of tears or tantrums, especially when they are not able to converse more than with baby talk.

Young Leo

Young Leo's mind is quick. But his or her instinct to grab the limelight is quicker. At school, Leo children will work in the direction that gives them the most recognition. They are likely to be good scholars or tops at sports or the best fighters or the leader of the gang.

Seldom are Leo adolescents successful both academically and physically. These young people put their heart and soul into whatever they attempt. They do not divide their energies.

Leo youngsters may take up numerous activities and then abandon them while they endeavor to find one that suits them. When they do, they work imaginatively and conscientiously and seldom fail to reach their objectives.

Leo is a born leader. But it takes some time for these youngsters to understand themselves. Until they do, they cannot assume the powers of rulership that lie dormant within them. They can be little devils and bullies, boasting more than they can deliver. They need intelligent direction—and plenty of loving understanding.

Teenage Leo

Parents should try to set their Leo youngsters on a positive course early in their teens. These boys and girls want to make a success of their lives. And if a certain direction seems to offer this, they will be inclined to cooperate and work toward it.

Teenage Leos can be extremely proud and arrogant. They are not easy young people to control, especially if there is any attempt to boss them around. In their eyes they know all the answers, and any they don't know they will not admit to. Leo teenagers are not the type ever to admit they are wrong. Even when standing in the ruins of their own disastrous decisions, they are likely to justify their actions.

But these Lion-hearted boys and girls will be inclined to follow the advice of their parents, as long as Leos respect their parents and their opinions. Once they are disillusioned, however, as often happens in teenage, they are not likely to take advice from that place again.

Underneath the bravado of Leo is a loving and warmhearted individual who is trying only to find a mission in life. Youthful sexual and romantic experiences can temporarily sidetrack the Leo teenager from discovering his or her true mission in life. Leo adolescents get hung up in love, possibly more so than other people of the same age.

Leo in love radiates immense happiness and enthusiasm, but often the enthusiasm is focused strictly on the girlfriend or boyfriend. Homework and sports practice can go by the boards. Unrequited love will send the Leo teenager into a spell of gloom and inactivity. Moping around the house and refusing invitations from friends, this lovesick cat will abandon all the things that gave him or her such pleasure before.

It is not unusual for Leo teenagers to put off college or job training to hang around with the object of their affection. They may take a "leave" from school or a year off before pursuing future goals just to travel with their romantic partner.

Such situations may result in an early marriage and a premature family. Leo is the sign of children. So when Leo teenagers outgrow their childhood, they think it's perfectly natural to start the next generation.

Parents are wise to help their Leo teenagers see the options open to them, as well as the consequences. Love, romance, and children, pursued too early, might interfere with these youngsters' mission in life. On the other hand, these pursuits might very well be Leo's true mission.

CAPRICORN PARENTS AND VIRGO CHILDREN

No youngster is more in tune with the earthy Capricorn nature than a Virgo boy or girl. This household will be graced by the presence of this easy-to-manage child, who also will be very easy to love if Mom or Dad Capricorn can show loving and tender care.

Capricorn parents should understand that this youngster, like themselves, has a good deal of difficulty expressing love and affection. Virgo kids should not be allowed to get into the habit of living purely in their minds. Both parent and child must endeavor to get closer together emotionally. Mom or Dad from the first day must get this child used to being affectionately cuddled and physically embraced.

The Capricorn parent probably will feel compelled to correct the Virgo tendency to find fault in others. Capricorns are sensitive and easily hurt. This parent will realize that a critical faculty in Junior could add up to unpopularity in the future unless restraining action is taken early.

An understanding of the Virgo nature will help. Being born under the sign of Virgo endows a child with a great deal of discrimination. All their life Virgo individuals will be looking unconsciously for some kind of perfection. Their way of finding it is to analyze and try to sift the good from the bad, whether it is in a person or a situation. They are specialists at heart. They are looking for that tiny essence among a host of details that will pull the whole picture together. Their motivation is to solve the world's problems by pointing out what is wrong with the world.

Virgos are renowned for being able to put their finger on faults with great accuracy, even though it often hurts another. So the Virgo boy or girl is a smart cookie in the mental department. These kids will spend long hours with their head in a book, reading, drawing, working out puzzles, trying to understand everything as clearly as possible.

Virgo children will be a great help around the house as they grow up. These young people are among the easiest in the Zodiac to train. They spend their lives trying to devise methods for doing things better. Any sensible suggestion such as would come from this Mom or Dad with their practical Capricorn natures will be acted on.

However, as easily as Virgo children can be taught good habits, they can pick up bad habits. Virgos are known for being neat and tidy. Yet some of them are so sloppy and dirty around the house that people start to doubt the astrological description. In many cases, this careless and slovenly attitude is a bad habit picked up from the parents or from early conditioning.

A future career will present no problems when the time comes for choosing. Virgos, like Mom or Dad, take life fairly seriously. They appreciate the need for material security, as well as knowledge and study as means of achieving it. A Capricorn parent will be a sensible adviser. Virgo is the zodiacal sign of work. Virgos will not shirk what has to be done, even though it means a good deal of monotonous routine.

It is important for this parent to see that Junior has plenty of young friends. Virgos can put too much time into their own specialized mental activities. They need to feel the common touch, and to release their feelings and emotions in normal play and group games. As a teenager, there is a tendency in Virgos to feel inferior and unliked. Often these youngsters are unusually attractive, but cannot believe that anyone really wants to be with them for themselves.

Infant Virgo

This child is quite an early developer. Mercury, the planet that rules mental ability, governs the sign of Virgo. In a very short time, the parent of a Virgo toddler will be struck by the little one's quick comprehension. Even before he or she begins to talk, the child will be noticed to listen intently to what is being said.

These children are good mimics. It is important always to set a good example for them, or their antics in company may cause some embarrassment. Not that they are pushy or show-off types. Far from it! Virgo children are more inclined to sit in the background observing everything that is going on. As they develop and learn to converse, which is astonishingly early, they make very adult and wise comments or answers to questions.

Good common sense will start to be evident in this child at a very early age. A tendency to be shy may have to be corrected. Virgo toddlers learn very quickly and can be taught to put away toys and to keep their rooms tidy. To these little ones, helping around the house comes naturally and is often played as a game.

Young Virgo

At school, Virgo youngsters are likely to be regarded as ideal students. Their minds are very orderly, and they do things methodically. They have a love of sorting out detail, which many other children despise, and are quick to learn mathematics. Soon they become proficient at writing and speaking.

Young Virgos are very sensitive. It takes these youngsters a longer time than usual to mix freely in company. They are inclined to sit apart, reading books or concentrating on writing or drawing. They would dearly love to join in, but find it extremely difficult to make the first move.

Parents have to be careful not to try to push this child into company. The entrance should be slow and natural, possibly through the device of a party where children can informally get to know each other. It is important for Virgo children to have at least one little friend early in life who can help them across the relationship barrier.

Once sure of their ground, Virgo children are active and happy in play as well as in formal company. They are popular among their playmates for their ability to think up interesting games for wet afternoons. Their minds naturally go to activities requiring pencils, paper, counting, and problem-solving. Usually they are good at puzzles and games.

Without materials for writing or drawing and without puzzles or games to work out, the Virgo child nevertheless is a master at entertainment. Virgo youngsters can spin tales of mystery and adventure that keep their companions delighted for hours.

Teenage Virgo

The Virgo teenager is not usually rebellious. For this there will need to be some unsettling influences from other planetary placements. The Virgo teenager is likely to be fairly serious, aware of what is going on in the world and what needs to be done to make it a better place to live in.

Virgo teenagers are inclined to be studious, often avid readers. They enjoy discussions and debates. They have an excellent memory for details. They can be interested in religion and any other formalized system of morality or philosophy.

But by this time, the Virgo youngster's main fault is likely to be evident. Virgos cannot help being critical. The Virgo teenager is likely to turn his or her critical eye on parents, friends, relatives—anyone at all—and make the most bone-chilling and disturbingly accurate observations.

Virgo people do this because they strive to make the world a perfect place, an obvious impossibility. They try to correct any fault or disorder that they spot. And with their discerning attention, they can find a lot to criticize. Virgo teenagers can be precocious in their knowledge of worldly affairs.

Precociousness, however, is not apparent in the Virgo teenager's attitude and approach to sex. These young people already may have an obsession with neatness and cleanliness. Fears about personal well-being may be aroused at the thought of actual sexual experiences.

Virgo kids are fairly knowledgeable about sex, even if they are completely innocent, because they read and listen so much. They probably know more about abortion, birth control, and pregnancy than some adults do. But young Virgos, whose concerns around health and hygiene may become phobic, are afraid to experiment.

The parents of a Virgo teenager probably sigh with relief, thinking they don't have to worry about the youngster getting in trouble. But if not intelligently guided, the Virgo teenager can get into another kind of trouble— unpopularity.

The teenager may avoid all physical demonstrations of affection and even mild sexual fun. Parents must help him or her develop prudence, rather than prudishness, and so go forward to enjoy dating and romantic attachments.

CAPRICORN PARENTS
AND LIBRA CHILDREN

Capricorn parents are down-to-earth people. As the mother or father of a Libra boy or girl, they will have much to teach their youngster. The Libra nature can be a bit flighty if left to its own development. Under the sensible, practical guidance of a mother or father born under the sign of the Goat, the necessary self-discipline will be inculcated in the Libra child.

This parent has to avoid a tendency to put too much emphasis on responsibility and practicality. Libra is an air sign, so Libra people are naturally chatty and communicative. They have to socialize a lot and have a variety of company to keep them mentally stimulated. They would become very unhappy and their mental faculties would decline if they had to stick to a monotonous regimen.

Libras can't abide routine. They are not known for their staying power unless they are doing what interests them. They are easily distracted by others. As a result, they do not get around to making the most of their natural skills and abilities.

The Capricorn parent will be very good for young Libra in this respect. This parent will teach the youngster the value of receiving a good education. Under this guidance, Junior probably will gravitate toward an interest or hobby connected with art. Libra has a natural ability to evaluate harmony, color, beauty, and form. The parent must observe if this youngster shows an early aptitude for painting, designing, and other creative work.

With a cautiously ambitious Capricorn mom or dad at their side, Libra boys and girls will be encouraged to become doers and not just dreamers. Sometimes they are too idealistic. Libras, in spite of their early promise, are inclined to slip back into inaction if they are not pushed.

This youngster has all the charm in the world. It will delight the Capricorn parent to have friends in and to see the mature way in which Junior responds to introductions and helps the conversation along. This will be especially helpful when formal guests or work associates come to dinner. Capricorns sometimes find it difficult to be natural with unfamiliar people in social situations.

But to young Libra, especially the teenager, such occasions are a piece of cake. Libras are among the best hosts and hostesses in the Zodiac. So while the Capricorn parent is preparing a superb dinner and making final touches, young Libra keeps the guests entertained.

There is much in the Capricorn nature that Libras will react against as they grow older. For one thing, Mom or Dad can get into a rut. The Goat can be a stay-at-home and an old fogy. The Libra youngster is not going to settle down into a comfy family existence of watching TV and going to bed early. These young people need and have lots of friends.

Libras have bright minds. They believe in living for human contact, not just for work. If the Capricorn parent can guide them toward a vocation that satisfies their need for social interaction, it will save arguments later on. Libra, with a highly developed sense of cooperation and harmony, is suited for work as an artist, diplomat, beauty specialist, hairdresser, social worker, restaurateur, or interior designer.

But the Capricorn mom or dad must be warned that there is no purpose in putting this young person into a work environment lacking congenial or harmonious conditions. It would be very rare indeed to find a Libra of any age working in a noisy construction job or in a physically punishing professional sport.

Infant Libra

A Libra infant usually has something attractive about him or her that goes beyond good looks or a sturdy body. Parents who feel that their newborn Libra baby is the most beautiful in the world may not be all that far-out.

Libra is ruled by Venus, the planet of beauty and love. And this universally attractive though subtle quality of Venus tends to pervade all her little children born at this time of the year. The placements of the other planets, and especially the child's Venus, will have an important moderating effect. But generally, Libras tend to be beautiful people.

As a toddler, the Libra child will be popular with aunts, uncles, and all the family friends. "Cute" and "adorable" will be words frequently heard. There will be a constant succession of young friends coming in to play. And young Libra will hardly miss a birthday party in the whole neighborhood.

But there will be a fair number of squabbles in the neighborhood as this youngster grows a bit older. Then he or she learns to play off one playmate against another. Surprisingly, Libra doesn't get too much dust on hands or clothing. They prefer wheedling or crying to a parent or nearby authority figure. They have a real fear of pushing, shoving, tumbling, or fistfighting.

Young Libra

At school, the Libra child will be regarded as bright, intelligent, and cooperative. These boys and girls often become teachers' pets and are able to think like adults at an early age. Libra children assume social and neighborly responsibilities that threaten other youngsters their age.

Young Libras are more likely to be interested in mental and creative activities than in sports. Although they may join school teams to keep up identification with their group, they will prefer to remain on the sidelines organizing the off-field and after-game activities.

This youngster has a natural love of harmony, which may be expressed in color, music, or human relations. Parents should be alert for any particular artistic aptitude their Libra child may show. Libra adolescents are often drawn to painting and sculpturing.

The Libra child should not be exposed to harsh or uncongenial surroundings. These young people have a temperament that is particularly sensitive to any kind of discord or conflict. They never will be able to do their best under such conditions.

The Libra youngster thrives in an atmosphere of refinement and good taste. The kids themselves have learned the difference between charm and force. They always prefer a charming technique to get what they want, though they will resort to street violence when they are pushed beyond endurance.

The alert parent, anxious about his or her Libra youngster's development, may be undecided whether to send the youngster to private school or to public school. Private school has all the benefits of selectivity and tact that encourage the Libra child in learning. But public school teaches him or her how to get along with other kids, sometimes the hard way, and to mistrust the easy and extravagant ways of charm and refinement.

Teenage Libra

Libra teenagers, especially the girls, usually are very conscious of appearance. They are likely to spend a great amount of time in front of the mirror. They can tie up the bathroom for hours, luxuriating in hot baths or attending to their well-cared-for hair.

Sometimes Libra teenagers are a bit lazy. They can drive their parents mad by not being able to make up their minds about what they want to do. They may go in one direction one moment and in another direction the next. But when they eventually find what they want to do most, they can be very determined and independent.

Since Venus is the ruler of Libra, an interest in the opposite sex usually occurs very early in the teens. Libras are aware of their innate ability to attract others and make the most of it, often leaving behind them a trail of wounded young hearts.

Libra teenagers are not rebels. Usually they depend on their charm and tact to get their own way. They are cheerful, easygoing, seemingly cooperative. They know the value of compromise, which is often the key to their success.

Sex is of vital interest to the Libra teenager, but not so much for adventure or learning purposes. Libras do not get kicks out of cheap thrills or foolish experimentation. And they are not burning to discover the great mysteries of life.

Libra teenagers' curiosity about sex has to do with their popularity. And the niceties of partnership, even the most innocent attachment. How far can Libras go? How far should they go? What is the appropriate line to draw before they turn off their date, on the one hand, or get a fast reputation, on the other?

Libra teenagers discover a middle ground very quickly. They show an almost adult ability to be coy, play the field, and promise but never dare. They always keep their date or steady dangling but interested, while they toy with the next eligible partner hankering for a chance. Libra boys and girls are terrible flirts, and charming heartbreakers.

CAPRICORN PARENTS AND SCORPIO CHILDREN

A Capricorn parent and a Scorpio son or daughter will get along fairly well together. However, there will be some stresses and strains as Junior gets older. Basically, Capricorn wants a quiet and harmonious life. But young Scorpio loves drama, and just can't help involving everyone around him or her in emotional scenes.

What the Capricorn parent has to understand and accept is that this youngster is born under the most mystifying, yet fascinating, sign of the Zodiac. It will be a good thing for young Scorpio to have that solid, down-to-earth guidance of a parent born under the steady and reliable sign of the Goat.

If Junior is one of the evolved Scorpio boys or girls, there are not going to be many problems, and Mom or Dad will end up extremely proud of the way young Scorpio turns out. If the youngster, though, is an undeveloped Scorpion, he or she can cause endless problems, presenting a hard and ungratifying discipline job for the parent.

What will be good for this young person is the early influence of such a conventional and decent character as the Goat. Capricorns are patient and dependable. They do not put on airs and graces. They do their best to be themselves.

The Scorpio youngster has an unerring ability to see through people and to spot their pretensions and weaknesses. It is a good thing that this parent is content to be real. Otherwise, Junior may get the idea too early in life that duplicity is the nature of all people. And a Scorpio young person cannot afford to have these impressions.

The parent should be warned to watch for any signs of vindictiveness or cruelty. Capricorn must not, however, be unduly concerned if this boy or girl shows a pronounced secretive side. This trait is natural to all the water signs, which are emotional signs, although it is more essential and intense in the Scorpio character.

The Capricorn parent is fairly discerning, a good judge of character. But Mom or Dad does not have the same talent for delving into the depths of the unconscious the way Scorpio does. The intuition of Scorpio, even at a young age, is amazing.

As much as a Capricorn person enjoys working out what makes others tick, Mom or Dad should not try it on Junior. Junior's love of secrecy starts with himself or herself. This young person will become furious if anyone tries to probe. This boy or girl wants to know all about others, but will never reveal his or her own true feelings. Scorpio can be blunt to the point of rudeness.

The Scorpio youngster becomes more and more intense as he or she matures. These kids may not have a lot to say at times, but when they do speak it is usually worth listening to. These young people are severely self-repressive. They are continuously sitting on their highly volatile emotional natures to keep them from being expressed. A tremendous buildup of energy potential is the result. A constructive outlet has to be found or there will be trouble.

Scorpio youngsters, like the Capricorn parent, deal in realities, not trivialities. The Goat will see that Junior receives a thorough grounding in the ways of the world. But Scorpios do have a reputation for being compartment thinkers—that is, they have fixed ideas about things and rigidly refuse to change these ideas even in the light of experience.

The teenage Scorpio boy or girl has a deeply passionate nature. These kids tend to seek heightened sensations. Sometimes they even look for danger, enjoying the sensation of keeping one jump ahead. There can be a tendency to experiment with drugs and alcohol. Scorpio also is the sign of sex. The parent must help young Scorpio experience things in moderation armed with a knowledge of the consequences.

Infant Scorpio

Scorpio infants need plenty of love and attention. Even though these little people may seem strong and tough and able to look after themselves, the parent who demonstrates how much they are loved will be doing much to prevent problems for the child when he or she grows up.

Inside every Scorpio-born human being is an affectionate and jealous person. If they are not shown the love they need in childhood, they can become disillusioned and bitter people who are likely to take it out on the rest of the world.

Parents of Scorpio toddlers should remember that the Scorpio nature is fixed. Once these kids get an idea in their head, it is very difficult to change it. They need to be shown the value of flexibility in dealing with their friends and playmates. They should be discouraged from taking rigid attitudes and putting people into compartments of their own making.

Young Scorpio children are sensitive and sweet to animals and babies younger than themselves. Here they can show an incredible kindness, almost an instinctive understanding of the other creature. Scorpio infants are not likely to get scratched by the cat or bitten by the dog.

But as Scorpio children grow older, they may get into rough-and-tumble fights with playmates and friends. Here they may develop cruel and insensitive speech and actions, a capacity to hurt and hurt hard.

The alert parent, always proud when their youngsters defend themselves, may not fully appreciate how defense for the Scorpio child can take on antisocial attributes. This is an area where the parent can help the child learn to fight fair, get over failures, and not hold grudges.

Young Scorpio

Scorpio youngsters have good intellects. They are not the frivolous kind. They like to delve into things with their minds, to get to the bottom of what they think are mysteries and challenges.

It is a good thing if at an early age they are encouraged to take up some hobby or study that will utilize their analytical capacities. Chemistry sets, a telescope, or a microscope are the kind of educational toys that may have an important bearing on the child's future development.

Scorpio children can be loners. They are not the type to engage in silly and superficial games for long. It is also a good idea for parents to try to encourage them to join groups such as the Scouts, where they can get used to working with others.

A Scorpio child needs constant though unobtrusive supervision. Both boys and girls can get into bad company. They have deep emotional needs, and often they think they can get their kicks through taking unnecessary risks.

There is a strong secretive streak in these youngsters. Wise parents will acknowledge it by respecting their privacy. A good strategy is to allow the youngsters to have a "secret" drawer of their own with a key where they can keep writings and relics free from probing eyes.

Teenage Scorpio

The good sense and understanding parents have shown to the Scorpio child in earlier years will start to pay off in the teenage years. If the child has been neglected or unloved, there is likely to be trouble.

Scorpio teenagers are direct, often blunt. They say exactly what they mean, even though they often resort to sarcasm. Any scars of disillusionment with parents are likely to show in independent and aggressive behavior.

The Scorpio person is a great survivor. If these teenagers leave home early, they are very capable of looking after themselves. However, their tendency to look for heightened sensations can lead them to experiment with drugs and alcohol.

Sex is an area that Scorpio teenagers are almost sure to investigate. These youths have plenty of knowledge under their belts by the time they are ready to leave home. And they're not the shy or inhibited type. These youthful experimenters may already have won, or lost, a reputation with their friends.

There is little in the way of practical knowledge that the parent can offer a Scorpio teenager when he or she is set on discovering their own sexuality. But the parent can advise the teenager on the tricky ins and outs of each tender relationship, and help him or her decide the emotional and ethical conduct appropriate to each relationship.

By impressing on the Scorpio youngster from an early age the qualities of honesty and consideration for others, the parents will help to ensure that this teenager realizes his or her considerable potential. Consistency is especially important in raising a Scorpio successfully. Scorpios are practical,

CAPRICORN: PARENTS AND CHILDREN

down-to-earth people who are not impressed by anyone who does not practice what he or she preaches.

CAPRICORN PARENTS
AND SAGITTARIUS CHILDREN

A Capricorn parent will be very good for a Sagittarius son or daughter. Capricorn will keep a restraining hand on the shoulder of this impatient and impulsive youngster. But the Goat will never understand how anyone could ever want to be constantly on the move the way young Sagittarius does.

The spirit of adventure throbs in the heart and mind of all Sagittarius individuals. They cannot stand the humdrum of routine living for long. It is very important in the early years that Mom or Dad gets the young Archer into the habit of concentrating on school studies and completing homework. The Sagittarius boy or girl has a good mind, but it is not easy persuading these kids to give up their games and love of company to attend to their studies.

This young person will turn the home into a place of laughter and joy. His or her coming along may be one of the best things that ever happened in this parent's life, especially if the other parent is also an earth sign like Capricorn. Earth signs can get into a rut, finding it too much bother to venture outside the home for entertainment or to pursue anything but work and material things as a way of life.

Sagittarius is a fire sign, exactly the opposite in temperament. This boy or girl has a self-assertive, outgoing nature. Young Archers are very active and entertaining little people. The Capricorn parent, patient and persevering in all things, will set a good example. The Goat's steadiness will produce a balanced and down-to-earth young person.

Where Junior and Mother or Father will have a lot in common is in their love of the great outdoors. Sagittarius kids are more sports-minded, but the two should be able to get together regularly in the swimming pool or on the tennis court. There is always a danger of people with such different natures growing apart, even though the love always remains.

One of the problems that may create a generation gap in adolescence is the Sagittarius youngster's almost pathological love of freedom. Although these kids have a lot of good sense and will listen to the cautioning words of Capricorn, the young Archer just does not have this parent's self-disciplined nature. This boy or girl lives for new experience, the riskier the better. They have little fear of anything.

The Capricorn parent will have to get used to the fact that young Sagittarius does not have a great sense of time. If the action is still on, these kids will not bother to come home. They believe so much in freedom that it would not occur to them that Mom or Dad may be worried about them.

Yet these two will have a good deal in common. The Capricorn parent will not try to stifle a Sagittarius youngster with demanding love and affection. Neither is particularly good at demonstrating their feelings, although both are able to love as much as anyone.

The problem with Sagittarius is that he or she is an other-people lover.

Sagittarius people will do anything they can to help someone who is in trouble or out of luck, even to the extent of handing over their own last dollar. Or they will travel long distances to help people, forgetting or ignoring their own other responsibilities. Those closest to them often have to suffer for the Archer's generosity and compassion.

It is not a good idea for a Sagittarius youngster, especially the male, to get into the gambling habit. The Archer is often lucky with money, and would rather take a chance on winning it than earning it the hard way.

Mom or Dad Capricorn is just the person to teach the young Archer to save for a rainy day.

Infant Sagittarius

The Sagittarius toddler needs plenty of fresh air and space outdoors to play in. Frequent visits to the park to see the bigger kids playing football and steering toy vehicles will help to keep this active and curious little person entertained.

Sagittarius children usually are fairly healthy and robust types. They are likely to crawl early in their attempts to find out just what is happening around the corner or up the stairs. They may also disappear smartly out the front door, if it is left open.

Due to their clumsiness, these infants seem to get more bruises and bumps than other children. It takes Sagittarius infants some time to get their bodies properly coordinated in spite of their incessant physical activity. Sports help them get mind, eye, and body synchronized.

They do not like to be hemmed in. They are inclined to put up a raucous fight when stopped from doing what they want. It is easier to coax and humor a Sagittarius toddler into submission than to use force.

Young Sagittarius

Sagittarius youngsters are bright and intelligent. But they are more likely to distinguish themselves on the sports field than in the classroom. Sagittarius kids have the brains to make good students, even scholars, but seldom have the time to devote to their homework.

These young people should be handled with a fairly firm hand so that homework and chores around the house get done. Sagittarius children long to be outdoors. They relish any kind of games and sports requiring physical movement and prowess. They are inclined to treat the whole of life as a bit of a game.

These youngsters usually love pets. A cat, a dog, and especially a horse can mean more to these young people than imaginable. Sagittarius children often find it easier to express love by caring for animals than by trying to communicate it to human beings. Sagittarius youngsters are spontaneous little people with a strong desire to share without a great need to possess emotionally, as many people are inclined to do.

Teenage Sagittarius

Sagittarius teenagers usually are extremely popular among their young friends and do not spend a great deal of time at home in one sitting. If they do, it usually is spent in the company of friends who come and go, day in and day out, at a bewildering rate.

These teenagers seldom go through the moody-blues period that so often afflicts the adolescent. They manage to remain cheery and optimistic most of the time. Their sense of humor is well developed and matches their love of fun.

There is often a strong religious interest in Sagittarius individuals that develops in their teens. They respect the need for the golden rule and tend to remember it all their lives, though they may abandon regular church attendance. In spite of their rash and rascally ways, they have a due regard for moral and social responsibilities.

These teenagers have to be trusted, and usually they are worthy of it. Otherwise, with any kind of narrow supervision, the parent will have an adolescent rebellion on his or her hands.

Sex is a lot of fun and games to typical Sagittarius teenagers. These youths are not too fond of passionate attachments. They think that the mysteries of love and sex are a bit too heady for them. "Nothing Heavy" is their motto. Easy come, easy go characterizes their dating patterns.

The girls are just as independent as the boys and can chase and hunt with the best of the Archers. Sagittarius teenagers may get a love-'em-and-leave-'em reputation. As far as actual sex is concerned, Sagittarius teenagers often retain their innocence while they are promoting their reputation.

Crushes, even the most romantic attachment, will not lure these kids too far from their sports and hobbies. Of course, they will use their boyfriend or girlfriend as an excuse to get out of homework. And they may make a big thing about each new steady. Their enthusiasms burn brightly for a while, then disappear as they discover a new horizon.

CAPRICORN PARENTS
AND CAPRICORN CHILDREN

Capricorn parents often come to a full stop when Junior arrives. With this blessing, they gradually give up their outside interests, apart from their work, and concentrate on the family and the home. They can get deeper and deeper into the bind that leads from the office to the nursery. This would be a pity with a Capricorn child in the house.

A Capricorn child, more than most other youngsters, needs to be exposed to a constantly shifting environment. Mom or Dad must try to raise this child with lots of activity and attention involving other people as often as possible. The Capricorn boy or girl, like Mom or Dad, will soon enough tend toward a one-track life if left without adequate stimulation.

Capricorns enjoy an open-air life, the great outdoors. They like to garden, to go for long walks, to participate in sports, especially winter sports.

And they are very good dancers. Junior Capricorn should be encouraged to try all these and any other activities blending coordination and movement, with Mom or Dad joining in as often as possible.

Capricorn youngsters will respond very well to parental efforts to give them a good education. However, it should be remembered that these boys and girls are not quick learners in the early years. They need to take their time in developing their mental faculties. They are slow, but they are thorough. When they are interested, they are superb students.

In the teenage years, the Capricorn youngster can be a rebel and a discipline problem. But Capricorns are by nature serious young people. Even though they have some living to do, there is an unmistakable quality of maturity about them that no amount of gallivanting or trouble can obscure.

Capricorn is ruled by Saturn, the weighty planet that takes its responsibilities very seriously. Sooner or later Capricorn youngsters will settle down and aim toward making a name for themselves in this world. Chances are, because of the tremendous capacity they have for perseverance and hard work, they will succeed in becoming influential in their field.

The Capricorn parent will not have to be reminded that Junior Capricorn is a cautious and restrained youngster. Inside, there is a lot less self-assurance than the commanding and aloof attitude may suggest. Capricorns are born worriers. They are always suffering from the frustration of never quite succeeding enough in their own eyes. They crave respect and recognition. But people are often rebuffed by their coolness. Usually, the Goat has all the respect and admiration of those around him or her, but does not get to hear about it.

The Capricorn boy or girl should be praised and encouraged. These kids are inclined to take responsibilities very seriously and to do the very best job they can. Because they are silent and efficient workers, it should never be assumed they are machines.

However, there is a selfish streak in the Capricorn nature. But this trait can be largely eliminated by proper parental treatment. Because of their basic feelings of insecurity, young Goats are inclined to take what they can without giving back. Through love and affection and plenty of recognition for their efforts, young Goats can learn to share, and their sense of isolation can be remedied.

The Capricorn mother or father will be wise to see that Junior is receiving enough demonstrated love. One of the parents has to show love and affection constantly. Expressions of caring are difficult for a Capricorn, whether parent or child. Capricorns hate any kind of emotional scene, especially in public. The danger is that with two Goats in one family, they may not get around often enough to demonstrating their feelings, and Junior could grow up emotionally frustrated.

It is easy for a Capricorn person to become peeved and gloomy. These Saturn-ruled creatures take offense more easily than they show. Their nature is inclined to be pessimistic and suspicious. To counteract this tendency, there should be as much laughter, humor, and optimism as possible around the house. A Gemini or Sagittarius baby-sitter is just the thing for the young Goat growing up.

Infant Capricorn

The Capricorn infant may seem to be developing a bit more slowly than other toddlers of his or her age. But the proud parents—and proud they will be—should not be disturbed by this. The Capricorn influence tends to be slow to express itself at all stages of early development.

Although these children take their time, they are absorbing their surroundings. They should not be hurried. They are much more sensitive than they may appear. They need plenty of love and affection, especially the physical kind.

Capricorn children need to feel that they are really needed. They need to be cooed over and told how good they are. This is more important than one would think, for as they grow up, these little ones can very easily obtain a poor opinion of themselves and become too self-conscious.

Brother, sister, or other children of other signs may show more promise than little Capricorn. But parents should know that in this lovable bundle is a character who will develop into a conscientious, patient, and courageous individual. In maturity, this person is likely to have a prominent and responsible place in society.

Young Capricorn

At school, these children are likely to be good students. Study comes naturally to them. They are not easily distracted by the regular pastimes of children and are likely to be avid readers and eager listeners to adult conversations.

It is important for the parent of a Capricorn boy or girl to see that he or she gets out and plays with the other children. If these youngsters born under the sign of the Goat get interested in collecting stamps or coins or a similar isolated hobby, they are likely to pursue it to the exclusion of other interests.

It is a good thing if they can be persuaded to take up a sport. They should be given some coaching lessons, so they can prove their ability in front of their schoolmates early. If left to their own devices, Capricorn youngsters may become more conscious of their failings than their successes. A mediocre performance pushes them more than ever to retreat where they feel secure.

Young Capricorns usually are not the type to have many close friends, but are very selective and take their time to make sure the other child does not criticize or ridicule them. They find it hard to take a joke against themselves. They are extremely sensitive about what others may be thinking about them.

This young person should not be allowed to mope around the house. They will respond to any parental request for help in running the house. They should be given small chores to their liking, which they can regard as their own personal contribution to the efficient operation of the household.

Teenage Capricorn

Capricorn adolescents usually have a fair idea of what they want to do in life. Although this may be in the distant future, they are inclined to work assiduously toward that objective. Their interests and pastimes probably will be connected with it in some way. These are serious young people who like to prepare themselves.

Capricorn teenagers in normal circumstances are not likely to be rebels. They enjoy the warmth and closeness of family life. They respect their parents and are not a problem in learning the merits of law and order. They are not particularly adventurous and would rather keep things as they are.

However, they do have a keen regard for social injustice, especially if they have seen their parents or families deprived by the system.

Contact with the opposite sex is not easy for Capricorn adolescents. They are shy and painfully determined to avoid rebuffs. Yet more often than not, Capricorns go steady in their teenage years. They seem to attract outgoing types who want someone to nurture.

Such a warm and private attachment is perfect for the Capricorn teenager. Their steady won't be fooled by Capricorn's reserve or seeming detachment. Capricorn thaws with a loyal steady who can show him or her the ropes. And Capricorn thrives if the girlfriend or boyfriend is popular in the gang and insists on dragging Capricorn along.

Through this attachment and vicarious popularity, the Capricorn teenager is introduced to social and cultural events that this introverted type might be too frightened to attend alone. Parents of Capricorn teenagers are wise to encourage such love affairs, especially when they include plenty of socials, sports, and fun activities that their son or daughter might otherwise skip.

CAPRICORN PARENTS
AND AQUARIUS CHILDREN

Capricorn and Aquarius have only one thing in common: the planet Saturn. Saturn rules Capricorn and corules Aquarius. So in a parent-and-child combination, the influence of Saturn will make itself felt in the areas of discipline and responsibility. These two Saturn creatures will see eye to eye on a matter of principle.

But the Capricorn parent will need to adjust very early to the fact that Aquarius is a mental creature, an air sign, and also ruled by the unpredictable planet Uranus. Unlike Capricorn, Aquarius is not particularly interested in a regulated, orderly life. Aquarius people do not care that much about material possessions. They certainly do not want to work all their life just to make a name for themselves.

It will be a good idea if Mom or Dad Capricorn reads up on world affairs and encourages this youngster from an early age to take an interest in what is happening to people outside the immediate family and community circle. That interest will develop anyway. But young Aquarius kids will marvel at how Mom or Dad in infinite wisdom got them interested in the problems of mankind.

Inside the young Aquarius person is the great humanitarian of the Zodiac. Sooner or later, these kids will start displaying their need to help others. They are not interested in the physical problems of people, but they do want to change ideas that bind people to narrow, selfish ways. The typical Aquarius individual wants to see everyone free from any kind of authority that is not thoroughly accountable every minute for its actions. As Junior grows into teenage, there might be some fierce disagreements about parental authority as well.

Aquarius individuals are basically erratic and unpredictable. But they are so filled with good sense and reason that it is difficult to imagine at times that within them lurks a very unorthodox person. They can go on for ages seeming to be regular. Then suddenly, they shoot off at a tangent, leaving everyone gasping and upset.

Aquarius kids, as bright and intelligent as they are, do not take easily to routine book learning. They become bored with facts and figures; their minds start to wander. These youngsters need to know that what they are learning has a purpose. They will believe this only if it is demonstrated to them by making the subject relate to people and life in general. These youngsters have very definite ideas about what is worthwhile and not worthwhile.

As they grow older, Aquarius kids form strong political and social opinions; they can't be swayed. But in their youth, Aquarius kids show great promise. They can be encouraged to follow any career that will make the world a better and happier place to live in. They have strong reformist urges, which fit them for a life in politics or government. They are suited for training in all branches of science. Their minds are quick and inventive. They are often endowed with musical ability.

These youngsters in adolescence and teenage are found at the head of banner-waving demonstrations and haranguing crowds on the street or campus. Aquarius individuals are original thinkers and often go to extremes in their political beliefs. They can become fanatics and revolutionaries if not sensibily restrained.

The Capricorn parent will have to work hard to make sure that he or she and Junior do not grow apart as the years roll by. It is quite possible that a conservative and law-abiding person like Capricorn would fail to understand just what an Aquarius is driving at when seeming to undermine authority without putting something better in its place.

Aquarius kids have the kind of mind that believes that when the undesirable is destroyed, the more desirable arises. These youngsters have strong artistic leanings. It is important that any creative talents be tapped and encouraged in adolescence. These youngsters also refuse to conform to behavioral patterns accepted by the rest of society. If this does not go down too well with Mom or Dad Capricorn, the Goat had better fashion another image of the world.

Infant Aquarius

When this little one starts toddling around and taking an interest in things, it will not be mere childish curiosity. Aquarius endows a child with an unusual type of intelligence that can best be described as the ability to synthesize, to put ideas together, and to draw the essential meaning out of that combination. It will not be long before the parents of this kiddie will start remarking, with justifiable pride, that he or she is a bit unusual and bright.

These boys and girls of Uranus, the unconventional planet that rules Aquarius, are not concerned about being kissed and cuddled. They do, of course, need to be surrounded by love and affection. But the demonstration of these in emotional ways is not so important to them.

Intellectual rapport—even for baby Aquarius—is the vital thing. Somehow parents communicate their interest in the unformalized ideas of baby Aquarius just by listening intently to their coos and squeals and watching carefully the thrusts and grasps of hands and legs.

Aquarius is a high-octave mental sign. Parents should gradually establish common ground in interests and mental pursuits. These children will enjoy playing. But they want to know how and why things are done in a particular way. They are likely to be very good at inventing games and things to do.

Young Aquarius

At school, the young Aquarius boy or girl will have a lot of friends, but perhaps not many close ones. He or she will be regarded as intelligent and full of strange ideas and imaginings. These children are too alert and observant to be called daydreamers. But they do make fanciful and inventive use of their imagination.

The Aquarius youngster's chief interest is experimentation. This can range from dressing up in bizarre combinations of clothes to becoming absorbed in the wonders of the glassware and chemicals in the school laboratory or the intricacies of system and design in architectural and electronic models.

Aquarius kids often begin an early fascination with adult topics, such as questions of law and ethics, justice and politics. Philosophical issues turn them on. They can spend more time reading and researching the whys and wherefores than in recreational pursuits.

They don't take to sports and games, especially the strenuous variety. But all study and no play cannot become too much the rule, or these youngsters get an unbalanced picture of life—the very thing they're trying to understand. Parents can guide them here.

Aquarius youngsters are truthful. They look to their parents and teachers to guide them with honesty. They should not be fobbed off with superficial answers to questions, and should certainly not be misled by "white lies."

Aquarius children will quickly lose respect for anyone who lies to them. This could largely account for the fact that in adult life, all Aquarius people tend to question, and deride as necessary, established authority in the person of mere mortals.

Teenage Aquarius

Parents of Aquarius teenagers will have learned by now that these young people can be very fixed in their opinions. It's true they have some amazingly advanced ideas at times for their age. And they show a great capacity to move even ahead of the times.

But these teenagers can be as stubborn as mules when it comes to such familiar things as household chores, attendance at family gatherings, curfews, clothes, and appearance. Once these kids get an idea into their head—their own idea of these things, of course—they will not abandon it until experience has proved it to be misguided, or until their defiance has been met by restriction of their personal liberties.

Normally, Aquarius teenagers are not a rebellious type. They are extremely independent, but not unreasonable. They will listen to the good advice of their parents and genuinely do not want to make trouble for those they love. Their motivation is to be helpful. Although inclined to go to extremes when their feelings are strong about certain issues, they tend to lead a fairly moderate kind of existence.

They have many casual friends, some of whom may have ideas as strange as their own. When it comes to romance, the Aquarius teenager is more likely to act like a friend most of the time than a youthful lover. There usually must be a mental compatibility and a sharing of intellectual interests before any more serious attachment starts.

Sexual experimentation, though, is likely to start for the Aquarius teenager with a good friend or even a casual pal. These youngsters do not have to wait for the love of their life, or even a serious crush, before getting down to what makes the world go round.

Pursuing kicks, they manage to experience sex but not necessarily the emotions of the attachment. Somehow, in their love for kicks, they do not even give the impression that they are capricious.

Their seriousness, though, should be a comfort to their parents. Methodical and cautious, typical Aquarius teenagers are not likely to be caught in embarrassing situations, risk pregnancy, or set the law on their trail. The latter they reserve for their more purposeful forays into political agitation.

CAPRICORN PARENTS
AND PISCES CHILDREN

A Capricorn parent and the affectionate, sweet-tempered Pisces son or daughter will get along fine together, with one possible reservation. Mom or Dad is not renowned for being able to demonstrate love and affection. Affection could be a one-way street in this relationship, with young Pisces pouring out love and not receiving enough in return.

This is not to say that Capricorns' love is less profound or caring than any other type. It just means that the male Goat and the female Goat are practical people who believe that love is expressed in action. This parent must realize that this youngster is a totally different individual. The Fishes need to be kissed, cuddled, fondled, and frequently reassured that love is the warm, comforting feeling they crave it to be. No one becomes starved for affection more quickly or pathetically than a young Pisces boy or girl.

However, there will be much that is good for the youngster in having a Capricorn parent. The Goat will do a splended job in keeping Junior's feet on the ground. Pisces children are daydreamers. If they are not sympathetically restrained in the early years, the dreams rather than the reality can take over their lives. They need to be allowed to use their imagination, and the usual fairy tales will help to provide this. But they must be discouraged from living these tales in their minds; otherwise, the fantasy world gets mixed up with the real world.

A Capricorn parent is a doer. The Goat is methodical, thorough, and conscientious. The Pisces youngster growing into the teenage years will be well served by this example. Pisces are very easygoing people who shy away from any kind of pressure or harsh reality if they can. They are not usually the type to face their problems; they would prefer to ignore them and hope that they go away. If they are not disciplined to find solutions, adolescence is the time they slip into dreamland.

However, the Capricorn parent must remember that these youngsters born under the sign of the slippery Fishes are highly emotional types. Capricorn is a serious and self-contained sign. It would be an error for the Goat to attempt to regulate Pisces' days and ways rigidly. Like water, the element that rules their sign, Pisces youngsters need to be able to take the shape of the surroundings and circumstances of the moment, and respond spontaneously. They are very adaptable and changeable by nature.

Pisces are not as reliable as Capricorn types when it comes to work and action. Pisces boys and girls need a good grounding in taking responsibility or they can become directionless. However, such guidance should be given as sympathetically and encouragingly as possible every bit of the way. Harsh methods can do psychological damage. When Pisces find something that they want to do, they are very capable and productive. This may not add up to a nine-to-five routine, though.

These youngsters are compassionate, kindly, and quickly moved to tears. They cannot bear to witness suffering, either real or in their imaginations. They either collapse emotionally under the feeling of suffering in themselves, or offer the utmost help.

The Pisces boy or girl has strong artistic inclinations. These aptitudes should be cultivated at every level. The Capricorn mom or dad should not dismiss any poetry their son or daughter writes as just a foolish stage that many juveniles experience. It could be a thread leading to an iceberg of artistic talent.

Pisces people often make fine writers, dancers, actors, and musicians. Often they are drawn to the nursing profession, where they can fulfill their instinct for self-sacrifice.

Infant Pisces

There is something about the Pisces child that most people take to. Although all infants are lovable and cuddly, this tiny baby seems more vulnerable than others. Its skin is so soft and translucent, its miniature fists and feet curl so close to its body. Parents, even brothers and sisters, are moved to hold the little creature just a little more tightly in order that nothing may befall it.

There is nothing delicate about baby Pisces, soft and sweet and silent though it may be. Baby Pisces, boy or girl, is just expressing the basic Pisces nature. It is made for love and loving. A little older, and this infant will be showing salty tears, rough tantrums, and tough rebellions that its babyhood never betrayed.

The Pisces kiddie is extremely affectionate. Both boy and girl relish the demonstrations of love. They feel comfortable in loving arms. They respond immediately to any show of warmth aimed in their direction. They love to be loved and liked.

This toddler is usually spoiled. Parents, relatives, and friends seldom resist indulging the child's desires. The child's delight in receiving attention of any kind is most charmingly expressed.

Parents should be warned, however, that these children of the deceptive planet Neptune, which rules Pisces, can be very demanding emotionally. They may cry at being left alone or in unfamiliar surroundings. They can have inexplicably odd likes and dislikes.

Young Pisces

Pisces children are extremely sensitive and cannot stand harsh treatment or surroundings. Although quite able to take care of themselves when left to their own devices, they are inclined always to be on the lookout for others who will help them. This can lead to dependence and lack of initiative.

Pisces youngsters start out full of life and enthusiasm. They love plenty of change and excitement. They are often at their happiest when they are looking forward to something. Because of their heightened expectations, they frequently are disappointed and disillusioned.

Pisces children are more emotional beings than mental ones. At school they may be regarded as slow learners. They need to be taught with patience and understanding. They have to be emotionally involved in what they are learning to absorb and retain it. Otherwise it is like water off a duck's back.

These children, born under the water sign of the Fishes, are daydreamers. They tend to go off into a world of their own at the first sign of pressure or hostility. They do not like to be criticized. They are very easily hurt and put out.

Sometimes these young people worry their parents by not eating much, or they can be finicky and inclined to pick. They do not need a great deal of food as children.

Teenage Pisces

The secretive side of the Pisces nature usually surfaces in the teenage years. This side must be respected by their parents if these young people are ever to develop their full potential.

Pisces teenagers need privacy. They must be allowed enough spare time from homework, household chores, sports, games, and lessons to cultivate their own hobbies. In fact, these adolescents need more extensive periods alone than most other teenagers do.

It may be difficult for parents to understand this, especially if they are outgoing types themselves. Pisces is essentially a self-repressive and passive sign.

These teenagers can be the life of the party one moment, down in the dumps or in tears the next. Their emotions change with bewildering swiftness. Often they appear to be two people who never seem to meet each other.

As teenagers they are inclined to overeat, believing they are indulging sophisticated tastes.

Pisces teenagers need discipline, not the harsh but the understanding kind. Without being taught restraint, they can become self-indulgent and demanding. They may grow into very discontented and uncertain people. The Pisces charm, their favorite device, should not be allowed to win them their own way all the time.

Sex, drugs, alcohol, and daredevil sports may become lures and possible dangers for Pisces teenagers. Their tendency to go to excess, on the one hand, and their idealistic belief in romantic purity, on the other, make them careless of chances and risks.

Here is where the parents must take a firm hand. They should demonstrate by subtle and not so subtle means the need for knowledge, protection, and responsibility. The real world can be more hurtful and sordid than even the Pisces teenager ever imagined it would be.

Cusp Signs: Aries Through Pisces

The Cusps of All Signs

Being born on the cusp means that you were born between the nineteenth and twenty-fourth of any month. This is the period when the signs change. The actual day a sign changes is different from month to month and from year to year because the time used to measure planetary motion differs from calendar time. The actual day the signs changed from 1910 through 1990 is given in the Cusp Tables for All Signs, pp. 379–383.

Being born on the cusp means that you exhibit characteristics of two signs. If you were born on any of the days nineteenth through twenty-fourth of a month, you will want to read the cusp description that applies to you in the following sections. Through it, you will learn another set of influences that make you uniquely you.

Cusp Days for the Signs

Aries and Taurus Cusp	April 19 through April 24
Taurus and Gemini Cusp	May 19 through May 24
Gemini and Cancer Cusp	June 19 through June 24
Cancer and Leo Cusp	July 19 through July 24
Leo and Virgo Cusp	August 19 through August 24
Virgo and Libra Cusp	September 19 through September 24
Libra and Scorpio Cusp	October 19 through October 24
Scorpio and Sagittarius Cusp	November 19 through November 24
Sagittarius and Capricorn Cusp	December 19 through December 24
Capricorn and Aquarius Cusp	January 19 through January 24
Aquarius and Pisces Cusp	February 19 through February 24
Pisces and Aries Cusp	March 19 through March 21

CUSP OF ARIES AND TAURUS

People born between April 19 and April 24 are on the cusp of Aries and Taurus. These people have some of the drive of Aries and some of the slowness of Taurus. They have wonderful ideas and great energy to implement them as well as tremendous enthusiasm, all of which they get from the Aries side of their personality. The Taurus side gives them a practical, thorough approach and an ability to finish what they have started. Together, these energies can be a formidable combination.

Individuals born on this cusp will take risks, but not unnecessary ones. They will try new things but with a practical approach. They have the ability to initiate *and* to follow through. They will start new businesses on a thoroughly practical foundation. The chances of success with this combination are very high.

On the negative side, people born on the Aries and Taurus cusp can be at war with themselves. They want to take risks, but may be too afraid. They may feel that their innovative ideas are not practical enough. The Taurus resistance to change is at odds with the Aries need to create something new. Taurus wants to be slow and sure, and Aries is too impatient to wait. Taurus wants to be secure and will not take risks, while Aries wants new challenges and hates the too familiar. People born on this cusp may feel that they are going through life with one foot on the accelerator and one foot on the brake.

CUSP OF TAURUS AND GEMINI

People born between May 19 and May 24 are born on the Taurus and Gemini cusp. They combine strong practicality and a lightning-quick mind. The Taurus brawn and the Gemini brains make them particularly well suited for athletics. The Taurus placidity can make the person not want to move at all, so the Gemini restlessness is a perfect balance.

These people are much more open-minded than a Taurus is likely to be, and much more practical and patient than a Gemini. They can give practical application to their ideas. They will see a project through, and not take the rest of their lives to do it. They are excellent students and probably have more than one degree. They are often found improving their homes. They have a whole library of do-it-yourself books. They like all kinds of handywork. Some of them write books. These people are generally successful in life because they have good mental discipline.

On the negative side, people born on the Taurus and Gemini cusp can be so intent on getting all the information they need that they never get started. Some of them are professional students, being attracted to learning but afraid of the real world. They spend a lot of time talking about what they are going to do and very little time actually doing it.

The Taurus resistance to change can be well supported by the Gemini inability to make a decision. These are people who are mentally agile but never move beyond square one. They spend a lot of time doing crossword puzzles and other brain teasers. They like nothing more than a wonderful dinner and stimulating conversation. They give away many good ideas because they do not have the drive to use the ideas themselves. They also find it easy to think up excuses for not changing. Some of these individuals can be accident-prone; their mind moves faster than their body, and so they have a tendency to trip over their feet.

CUSP OF GEMINI AND CANCER

People born between June 19 and June 24 are on the Gemini and Cancer cusp. This combination of energies provides the intellect of Gemini and the intuition of Cancer. These people have tremendous communication skills. Not only do they instinctively know the right words to say, but they also put feeling into those words, so they can move any audience. They are well suited to political speechwriting, public relations, and advertising. They know what the public wants to hear. They can also write best-selling novels. Their understanding of people's feelings plus their facility with words make them particularly well equipped to create characters and situations.

Cancer and Gemini cusp individuals are social animals, providing excellent food and scintillating conversation. Some love to entertain and do it so well they make a career of it. Other Cancer and Gemini people are psychologists and teachers, and still others do very well writing cookbooks.

On the negative side, people born on the Cancer and Gemini cusp spend too much time talking about their feelings. They want sympathy so much they think that if they tell you how bad they feel, you will provide the appropriate amount of sympathy. When they don't get the emotional support they think they deserve, they assume it is because they haven't explained their needs well enough. They will explain and explain, feeling that they have not found the right words, rather than the right person. They go back and forth between their intuitive side and their thinking side rather than integrating these two sides. As a result, they will mistrust their intuition if their logic does not agree, or try to reason out matters when their intuition already knows the answer. Their reasoning tends to be circular because the clarity of their intellect is clouded by their feelings.

CUSP OF CANCER AND LEO

People born between July 19 and July 24 are on the Cancer and Leo cusp. These people have excellent dramatic skills. The flamboyance of Leo together with the sensitivity of Cancer make them award-winning actors and actresses. Even those not involved in the entertainment field create drama in their everyday lives. Their lives *are* soap operas.

These people also have a great sensitivity to the feelings of others. They are very generous with time and affection. These are natural nurturers. They will make such a dramatic event out of your being sick that you almost hate to get well.

They are particularly sensitive to the needs of children, having the mothering quality of Cancer and the childlike quality of Leo. Cancer and Leo cusp people give memorable parties; they are particularly fond of costume parties. These people provide entertainment for everyone around them.

On the negative side, Cancer and Leo cusp people are extremely demanding emotionally. They must be the center of attention at all times. They throw temper tantrums if someone else has the limelight for even one minute. The Cancer insecurity together with the Leo need for ego gratification can make them very difficult to live with. When they do not receive all of the other person's attention, they feel unloved and they sulk. They can be very possessive and manipulating, and no matter what is done for them, it is never enough.

They blame everyone else for whatever goes wrong in their lives. They feel indignant and outraged at what they consider the lacks in their lives, and refuse to take any responsibility for them. They see themselves as tragic figures on the stage of life, and no amount of evidence to the contrary will change their mind. They prefer dramatic suffering to undramatic happiness.

CUSP OF LEO AND VIRGO

People born between August 19 and August 24 are on the Leo and Virgo cusp. These people combine the drama of Leo and the service of Virgo, and so are often teachers of dramatic arts. They produce children's plays, teach in acting schools, and use dramatic expression as a tool in psychotherapy.

The precision of organizational ability of Virgo, together with the executive ability of Leo, makes these people particularly well suited to run any business. The Leo and Virgo person appears at home in any situation because the poise and competence of Virgo, together with the Leo confidence and flair, command attention and respect. Because of Virgo's communication skills and Leo's dramatic skills, these people are naturally suited to writing plays, television scripts, and best-selling novels. They are generally wealthy in later life.

On the negative side, the Leo and Virgo cusp person never feels adequately rewarded for his work. The Virgo side of him feels no one could ever do it as well, and the Leo side demands to be in charge. As a result, he has to do everything and feels that no one appreciates his contribution. He is intensely sensitive to criticism, as he cannot admit his mistakes. In an effort to get a job done, he bosses others around, points out their imperfections, and then wonders why others do not like him; he is therefore often quite lonely. He cannot understand their attitude, because he feels he was only trying to be helpful.

Leo and Virgo individuals tend to overdo everything. They are flamboyant with details and showy about the amount of work they do. They sometimes have trouble distinguishing between the essential and the trivial. They tend to make an opera out of blowing their nose, yet will handle a car with perfect ease.

CUSP OF VIRGO AND LIBRA

People born between September 19 and September 24 are on the Virgo and Libra cusp. The precision of Virgo together with the artistic quality of Libra make them particularly well suited for fine arts. They have an eye for line and color, and like to design their own pictures or needlework. Their creations are often meticulous and lovely. They make very charming hosts and hostesses because of the Virgo need to serve and the Libra need to bring peace to the environment.

These people are very popular because they listen well and provide adequate solutions to people's problems without becoming emotionally involved. They are found most often helping other people dealing with their lives. They are fair and unbiased in their dealings with others. They work hard at their relationships. They try to help other people work as hard. They are usually very attractive, and take great care with their appearance and their surroundings.

On the negative side, they can be too cold and calculating in their relationships. They can find it difficult to be emotionally involved and are often considered very distant. This is hard to deal with because they always want to keep everything pleasant. Others find it hard to believe that such an attractive person would have so little feeling. The Virgo inability to accept criticism together with the Libra refusal to confront situations make it very difficult for these people to deal with the emotional problems of their own lives. It can also be frustrating for those people who have to deal with them.

Virgo and Libra cusp individuals can be very indecisive because of the Virgo insecurity and need for perfection and the Libra need to consider both sides of a question before taking action. Their inability to make decisions leads many of them into escapist activities such as living in a fantasy world of perfection and harmony.

CUSP OF LIBRA AND SCORPIO

People born between October 19 and October 24 are on the Libra and Scorpio cusp. The charm of Libra and the intuitive qualities of Scorpio make these people extremely attractive. The Libra side knows how to please and the Scorpio side knows what others want. They can often achieve prominence in the field of their choice. The Scorpio stamina and persistence together with the Libra ability to create harmonious working conditions enable them to rise at a meteoric rate. There is no one more skilled at drawing people out and finding out what makes the other person tick, often without that other person's realizing what is happening.

Such individuals have an ability to manipulate others so gracefully that people seldom feel used and actually give them what they want joyously. They can move mountains because they can charm other people into helping them.

On the negative side, the Libra and Scorpio cusp person can be cold and calculating to the point of being insensitive to the feelings of others. He can manipulate those around him to serve his needs with little regard for what they need. Such a person charms others into service, and it isn't until after he is gone that they realize they have been had. A master at illusion, he will create whatever environment is necessary to achieve his ends.

He is secretive in the extreme, hardly letting his right hand know what his left hand is doing. He is conceited, as he truly believes he is more attractive and brighter than almost everyone. He is possessive of his family and expects them to adhere to his rules. He can be extremely vindictive when his feelings are hurt. He can ruin a career without the victim's ever realizing what has happened. This is one to be wary of. He would never forgive you if you disappointed him.

CUSP OF SCORPIO AND SAGITTARIUS

People born between November 19 and November 24 are on the Scorpio and Sagittarius cusp. These people have the Sagittarius optimism and the Scorpio realism. Such a combination enables them to fulfill their dreams. They are spontaneous and enthusiastic as well as passionate and deep. They accomplish what they set out to do and have unbelievable energy and drive.

The Sagittarius curiosity and the Scorpio need to get to the bottom of things lead them to learn everything possible about the subject of their choice. Their powers of concentration are formidable, as is their physical stamina. They are able to accomplish goals that others aspire to but rarely achieve. The Sagittarius side gives them high ideals, and the Scorpio side gives them the fixity of purpose to achieve those ideals. The Sagittarius desire for travel and the Scorpio need for constancy lead them often into careers in which travel is an integral part.

On the negative side, the Sagittarius and Scorpio cusp person has trouble trusting others. The Sagittarius need to believe the world is wonderful, and the Scorpio realization that it is not, make it difficult for them to be open and honest about their feelings. These people can be very immediate in their relationships, and they are the ones who invented the phrase "out of sight, out of mind."

Although they are most charming, they can disappear without a trace, leaving people wondering what happened. Their humor can be sarcastic or black, and they are not above destroying somebody for the sake of being funny, a combination of the Sagittarius humor and the Scorpio sting. Their rapier wit is their greatest tool, and they thrust it where it will do the most damage. These people are extremely secretive and sometimes have two separate lives, complete with aliases. They are not trustworthy.

CUSP OF SAGITTARIUS AND CAPRICORN

People born between December 19 and December 24 are on the Sagittarius and Capricorn cusp. The Sagittarius optimism that everything will work out well is combined with the Capricorn willingness to make things work. The Sagittarius immediacy is tempered by the Capricorn foresight and planning. The natural curiosity of Sagittarius to cover as many bases as possible, together with the innate ambitiousness of Capricorn to get to the top, enable these people to achieve professional success early in life.

The Capricorn side enjoys working hard, being responsible, and keeping his finger on the pulse of things. The Sagittarius side is able to deal with multiple factors simultaneously with efficiency and good humor. These people are successful because they can set more far-reaching goals and see possibilities that others would miss, and then design and implement the methods by which the goals can be attained. There is often therefore a fruitful combination of idealism and practicality.

On the negative side, the Sagittarius and Capricorn cusp person has trouble integrating his idealism with his innate practicality. The natural conservatism of the Capricorn side is at odds with the flamboyance of the Sagittarius side. Here is a person with idealism, but his Capricorn pessimism makes him think he can never realize it. He wants the best of all possible worlds, but doesn't think he will ever achieve it.

These people resent all authority, whether parental or organizational, because the Sagittarius need for freedom is in conflict with the Capricorn need to be in control. They are difficult to work with because they are either too bossy or too cavalier, and sometimes alternate between the two. The Sagittarius belief that he knows the truth and wants to share it, together with the Capricorn need to be an authority figure, can make these people tyrannical in their dealings with others. They can be extremely self-righteous, even when they are wrong.

CUSP OF CAPRICORN AND AQUARIUS

People born between January 19 and January 24 are on the Capricorn and Aquarius cusp. The Aquarius ability for abstract thinking, together with the Capricorn practicality, make this combination formidable for problem solving of all kinds. Since Aquarius individuals are usually the most scientifically minded people of the Zodiac, and Capricorns are the people who deal with the practical details of daily living, people born on this cusp are often very good troubleshooters.

They often have mechanical ability and are amateur as well as professional inventors. The Aquarius desire to improve the quality of life plus the Capricorn ability to see practical solutions to problems leads these people into social reform and political organizations. They are clear-thinking and unbiased by the emotional environment in which they are operating. They tend to see life's problems as solvable like a mathematical equation. These people will establish social structures that will guarantee the freedom of each individual.

On the negative side, the Capricorn and Aquarius cusp person can be too detached from the people around him. He can be so busy organizing the community that he neglects his family. He has trouble establishing close emotional relationships. He's more comfortable being a friend to all. His natural intellectual gifts may make him arrogant and condescending to those around him. He can run into difficulty because he keeps his eye on the goal and forgets the needs of the people doing the work.

Such a person can have a pessimistic view of life and deal with every situation with too much seriousness. Although he can get things done, it is not necessarily enjoyable to work with him. He can push the people around him unmercifully because he has no tolerance for emotional weakness. His lack of success in relationships often leads him into dealing with abstract ideas and mechanical devices.

CUSP OF AQUARIUS AND PISCES

People born between February 19 and February 24 are on the Aquarius and Pisces cusp. These people combine the Aquarius ability for logical reasoning and the Pisces ability to fantasize and imagine. Many of these people are talented in the arts, particularly in areas in which they can create an illusion out of time, such as science fiction, fairy tales, or allegories. They have an abiding awe of the universe and a great desire to understand how it works. Many are led into the study of higher physics. They can often envision future events. They are sensitive to the harshness of life and will often turn to music for solace.

Basically the Pisces side has faith that things will work, and the Aquarius wants to know how. The Pisces creativity is given expression by the logic and fixity of Aquarius. Many Aquarius and Pisces cusp individuals are exceptionally fine painters and musicians. Many others are excellent psychiatrists because of the Pisces sympathy and the Aquarius analytical ability.

On the negative side, the Aquarius and Pisces cusp person is caught on the horns of the dilemma of wanting to know, which is an Aquarius quality, and having faith, which is a Pisces quality. Such a person may have trouble integrating the creative and logical sides of his nature. He is likely to have very structured thinking and deny his creative impulses. As a result, he stalls in his progress and accomplishes very little. He can be facile in his talk but lazy in his accomplishments. Such a person will escape into fantasy and abstract thinking. He will construct crossword puzzles and Double-Crostics. He would tend to be a dabbler, rather than pursue anything thoroughly.

Because of the Aquarius need for freedom and the Pisces confusion about this world, such a person can have a great deal of trouble surviving in the real world. The problem is that he can be too easily distracted, so that he has difficulty finishing things and therefore has no sense of accomplishment.

CUSP OF PISCES AND ARIES

People born between March 19 and March 21 are on the Pisces and Aries cusp. It should be noted that because the Sun moves into Aries on

March 21 of each year, this cusp is very small. These people combine the creativity of Pisces with the drive of Aries, so they often achieve renown in some artistic field. The Aries need to be first, coupled with the Pisces ability to generate fresh ideas from the imagination, often puts these people in the forefront of their field.

The enthusiasm and energy to initiate is tempered by a sensitivity to the needs of others, so that such a person often has an enthusiastic team working with him. He can encourage others to take risks, and is sympathetic to their fears. He appreciates creativity in all forms. He encourages his associates to express their own creative urges. He has great compassion, and will think of new ways to take care of people's needs. His optimism inspires others to have faith in themselves.

On the negative side, the Pisces laziness together with the Aries impatience can cause this person to give up any creative endeavor before he has completed it. He tries everything once, perfecting nothing. This person wants to be a leader and be respected for his executive abilities, but will get very hurt and upset if this does not happen. He can get arrogant about his own ideas.

Such individuals have an ability to create a fantasy world for themselves, and they do not let the facts interfere with that fantasy. They are past masters at not dealing with issues whenever they so choose. They put the Aries energy into the Pisces fantasy. They are willing to take risks, but are terribly upset when those risks fail. In an effort to overcome the insecurity of Pisces, the Aries side can make such individuals domineering. They can become angry if others do not share their fantasy. They find it difficult to live with themselves, so naturally it is difficult for others to live with them.

Rising Signs:
Aries Through Pisces

Consult the Ascendant Tables at the end of the book, pages 387–92, to find your Rising sign for the hour and day of your birth. When you have determined your Rising sign, read the chapter relevant to you.

Your Rising Sign: Aries on the Ascendant

A ries Rising people are self-starters. Like the Ram, the symbol of Aries, these people are headstrong. And like Mars, the planet that rules Aries, these people give the impression of fiery energy, courage, speed, and skill. With the iron and steel of Mars in their sinews, they are tough and commanding. But whatever they do, Aries Rising individuals relate everything back to the self, which gives their personality a sharp focus and colors how they experience the twelve life houses as described below.

FIRST HOUSE: PERSONALITY

People born with Aries Rising make their presence felt. Even their gait and manner suggest an attitude of "Here I come!" Their bodies and minds are finely attuned to their immediate environment. This gives them a sense of urgency and the confidence that they can handle whatever happens.

These people are prepared to take on anything or anyone around them. They are so lacking in fear that often they will take great physical or professional risks to carry out the most ordinary tasks. Their friends may ask, "Is it worth it?" Aries people will reply, "It is, if I do it." They are fiercely self-reliant.

Never are these people prepared to sit back and let life come to them. They are the self-starters of the Zodiac, men and women who create their own destiny and are often followed by the multitude. They have great faith in their stamina, their survival power. They love nothing more than action, especially if it involves challenges and dares.

People with Aries Rising are often more idealistic than practical. They can quickly be talked into supporting hopeless causes, particularly if they see themselves as the rallying point. Their imaginations are extremely active. New ideas and schemes crowd their minds, often forcing them to abandon pending projects for new ones. Once a project catches their imagination, though, their enthusiasm is unlimited. But a desire for instant results makes them ignore proper planning and detail. Impatience is a major flaw.

Aries Ascendant people tend to have quick tempers. Feelings of frustration or indignation can trigger immediate action, sometimes anger or even violence. But such rages are usually short-lived. When temper subsides, Aries Rising people are not too skilled at coping with subtler situations. Masters of action and direct thought, they are bewildered by the less direct and more emotional sides of life.

Their hearts and feelings are vulnerable. Sensitive to the self but insensitive to others is more the rule than the exception. Thoughtless actions and blunt words often hurt the people they care for most. Such behavior can occasion loss or regret. Yet Aries can take the bitterest of blows and start all over again.

SECOND HOUSE: MONEY AND POSSESSIONS

Money and possessions are more important to Aries Rising people than one would think by casually knowing them. A lifestyle geared to being constantly on the go and involved in endless activities may suggest slight interest in things material. But Aries Rising people are keenly aware of the advantage of a stable base. And then they like to build on it.

They also like to acquire their own property—bought independently, owned independently, and managed independently. They have more faith in land and buildings than in cash or credit. Money in the bank is idling, and it should be active. So they pick one of two general alternatives: spending cash impulsively or tying it up safely in property investments.

Aries Ascendant people can be surprisingly conservative as far as their assets are concerned. Sometime they can be almost rigid. In spite of their spontaneous and open ways in other areas of daily life, they can miss valuable opportunities by sitting on investments and not moving with the trends or varying their assets to get a broad mix. Many people with Aries Rising have complained that inflation has left them behind the eight ball; their holdings have dwindled or the interest on their holdings is lower than for other available investments.

Such people can be obstinate about taking good financial advice, believing they already have all the answers. Mistrust of experts and professionals is a trait developed in order to survive independently. But once it backfires, Aries will reluctantly admit that good advice is also an asset to acquire. Although slow to make changes, Aries Rising people show a sound practicality in financial matters, sometimes even flashes of brilliance. Once they start building and acquire a feel for wealth, they can amass fortunes.

The most important asset of all to Aries Ascendant people is the physical body. Although they will not hesitate to risk it to achieve their objectives, they like to keep it in fine shape. A fit and agile body is their best security.

THIRD HOUSE: CLOSE CONTACTS AND COMMUNICATION

Close contacts and communication keep Aries Rising people continuously active. They are forever on the move, visiting people, writing letters, making phone calls, and generally spreading their ideas and themselves about. Getting in touch rather than being in touch is the hallmark, and it is for the sake of moving pet projects along rather than an interest in other people.

Aries Ascendant folks have brilliant notions about most of the problems facing their friends and society. There is no subject that stumps such people. But too often their brainstorms lack the maturity of experience. Solutions are plucked out of thin air with admirable dexterity, but not out of the solid ground of consideration and analysis.

These individuals make first-rate speakers. Indeed, Aries Rising people are known to be fast and voluble talkers. Sometimes, though, they may develop a verbal block because too many swift ideas crowd the mind and cancel each other. Words come so easily that they can be careless about the way they put things; often they are guilty of putting their foot in their mouth, creating long silences of embarrassment or resentment.

Aries Rising finds it fairly easy to keep emotion out of debate. Being able to see and adapt to many points of view, such people can take a stand fully aware of the legitimate arguments of the other side. This sometimes make them appear to be opportunists, a reputation that can destroy their credibility and persuasive power. They may come on as individuals who do not believe in what they say. But come what may, Aries does not stop expounding.

FOURTH HOUSE: HOME AND FAMILY

Home and family attachments can be unexpectedly strong for Aries Ascendant people. Their action-packed, on-the-go existence can create a false impression, as though outside activities are far more important. But the basic Aries impulsiveness leads to idealistic attitudes about close ties, so that home and family are never ignored or abandoned for other alliances.

Home and family affairs are areas where the emotions of Aries Rising people can be surely touched—and touched in ways that may render the Aries brand of relating inadequate. Even single Aries like to keep in touch with home base. But verbal contact of a simple and direct variety is easier than sentiment. Although they may spend a lot of time away from house and kin, the home is a place they long to return to, even if it is only to leave quickly.

Aries Ascendant people are often softies at home. These individuals believe in the old-fashioned family traditions. They are inclined to feel that the modern approach to family life is not as desirable as the good old days when "families were families," staying together and playing together.

Aries people with their own family are likely to move many times in their adult life. Rather than leave their families behind, they like to take them along—at whatever expense. The isolated Aries for whom such an endeavor is not possible makes frequent return trips over long distances or sends regular caring communications so that the feeling of separation is not allowed to become excessive.

FIFTH HOUSE: ROMANCE, CREATIVITY, AND CHILDREN

Love and romance, creations of the mind or body are resources of immense pride for Aries Rising people. In romance, they are romantics. They love to give fine and expensive gifts, to dine and wine in the best places, to put on a show. A casual date or an intimate dinner party at home can have all the excitement of Aries on a dare. He or she love to dramatize their part as host or hostess, doing all the right things, and especially creating spectacular little surprises to add to the occasion's entertainment.

Aries Rising people can be arrogant about their talents, but they have every right to be because they guard them so jealously. They often will take all sorts of risks, financial or otherwise, for the opportunity to display their particular abilities. Sometimes they appear to be gambling all. But this is unlikely to be the case; they are very clever at creating the effects of suspense.

The Aries Ascendant person has a great need to show off. When he or she becomes a parent, children become the focus of their zeal. Aries parents strive to give children every advantage in order to be proud of them, as well as to develop young ones in the Aries model who can do and think and say everything. Aries parents try hard to spend a lot of time with children, but inevitably other activities interfere. The justification for absences is that the child will learn to be a loner, just like their parent.

Aries craves applause for personal efforts. The appeal of being accepted by glamorous people or being in glamorous situations is often a compulsive drive for Aries Rising individuals.

SIXTH HOUSE: WORK AND HEALTH

In work and health matters Aries Ascendant people are not afraid to be analytical, as long as emotion is kept out of the problem-solving. At work they are likely to display an impressive talent for getting to the heart of the matter instantly and for offering sharp ways to proceed.

They are not great ones for getting immersed in detail, but they quickly size up a problem. If given control, they will do their energetic best to remove the difficulty in record time. These are no clock-watchers or slouches once they accept an assignment—and stick to it.

They are inclined, though, to get distracted from their labors unless they are physically involved or in a position where they can set the pace. Aries Rising folks can be perfectionists, always on the lookout for ways of introducing greater efficiency. This aggressive manner can appear self-serving and get on the nerves of associates. When Aries perceives resentment, criticism of coworkers' effort is quick to be expressed, though never in a vicious way. Given the chance to do better, they take swimmingly to a leadership role, but are not always as effective as they imagined they would be.

People with an Aries Ascendant take an intense interest in diet, analyzing for themselves and by themselves its possible effects on their total health. They are then inclined to adopt delicately contrived measures—which others may call fads—to improve their resistance to illness. The Aries person really believes in purity of mind and body, but never quite manages to achieve this high ideal.

SEVENTH HOUSE: ALLIANCE AND PARTNERSHIP

Partnerships are not so easy for people born with Aries on the Ascendant. They resent a yoke. But if there is a basic compatibility and understanding, they can work loosely in tandem with a mate.

The trouble is that Aries cannot help trying to be boss. They are often accused of trying to control people and to dominate situations. On the one hand, if they link up with a similar forceful and independent type, there is little chance of a harmonious relationship, let alone a permanent one. On the other, more reserved and placid folk become ruffled and uncomfortable under the aggressive, get-up-and-go Aries influence.

But Aries Rising people do need others, even if only to be admired and encouraged. Sharing can become fairly one-sided. To be completely happy in partnership, Aries must feel they are in charge of the people and the events around them.

In business and social alliances and often in marriages, Aries can be very choosy, carefully selecting a suitable type who will put up with their need to give orders, their frankness, and their lack of diplomacy. However, if they impulsively fall in love, they often manage to choose exactly the wrong partner, with disastrous results.

In partnership, it is extremely important for Aries to be associated with someone who does them credit or whom they can look up to. It is then easier for them occasionally to surrender those independent and self-assertive ways.

EIGHTH HOUSE: SEX, PSYCHOLOGY, AND SHARED ASSETS

The Aries approach to sex is straightforward. There is very little sentiment involved. When a suitable mate has been found and the romantic preamble, if any, is over, they are concerned with getting to the point as quickly as possible, expressing themselves through the action rather than unnecessary words or game-playing.

The Aries psychology is expressed in a similar rugged realism. These people do not like pretense or pose. They can be rude to a fault in the company of others or on social occasions where great delicacy and tact are required. Their no-nonsense directness often arouses hostility and hurt feelings.

Aries Rising people seldom confide their inner secrets to others. They may be aware of a compelling urge to achieve a higher freedom, a sense of being beyond the limits of the physical body. Sex often is felt to be a way of achieving this freedom, as well as the means of self-renewal.

A person with an Aries Ascendant often can make money through alliances and marriages. The presence of a partner, perhaps even a silent one, helps them to maintain a sense of financial responsibility. A lover or mate, a teammate or colleagues help them to conserve and improve shared money and resources.

Aries people like to impress. Increasing joint funds often is a painless way to win admiration and respect.

NINTH HOUSE: EDUCATION AND TRAVEL

In their more relaxed moments people with Aries Rising believe in looking beyond the limited horizon of immediate circumstances in which they are so often deeply involved. They feel that only by looking to the future can they receive the insights that help them cope with today.

Aries Ascendant people's strong faith in themselves helps them to be philosophical about the ups and downs of life. They are highly intuitive, sometimes prophetic. They often are inspired in their ability to cope with fast-moving situations. They are optimistic. They like to believe in something. In religious matters they are broad-minded but cannot help adhering to convention.

These people love to travel—the farther the better—and to observe the cultures of other nations. They learn more easily from people and experience than from books and lectures. Time-consuming and complex studies can be a bore for most Aries Rising folks. Trying their hand at a situation is far more appealing.

Aries people often visit strange and exotic places in an effort to find something new to believe in. But usually they return to the accepted religious and philosophical views. It is difficult for them to change their opinions once they have been formed. It may take an emotional upheaval in their personal lives for them to develop a workable philosophy of their own.

TENTH HOUSE: FAME AND AMBITION

Success and image figure prominently in the thinking of Aries Rising people. Because they must always be out in front, they have strong urges to get way ahead of the pack. Fame for its own sake doesn't interest them so much as the public recognition of being a leader.

Their basic motivation is to get to the top where they will be respected and free from the demands that interfere with their need to be in charge and give orders. It is not so much the prospect of material reward that impels these people, as the prize of power. Such power will allow them to implement their schemes and enterprises without having to refer them to higher-ups.

Aries people are particularly fitted to control large organizations. Their tremendous capacity for physical work often enables them to outflank rivals who may have more smarts and persistence. The Aries stamina, gift of initiative, and pioneering spirit are tremendous assets for reaching a chief executive position.

Aries have little taste for monotonous desk jobs, no matter how important the job may be regarded. Their ambition is to rise to such a position of authority or prestige that they can select the adventurous assignments and leave the mundane operations to others.

ELEVENTH HOUSE: FRIENDSHIP AND COMMUNITY

Aries Rising people cannot stand dull companions. They are very selective about the company they keep. As a result, they have many acquaintances but few close friends.

An emphasis on physical fitness makes Aries sports-minded and exercise-oriented. So they continually join recreational or health clubs, searching for the perfect formula. Here they pick up pals and casual acquaintances. Aries also knows a lot of people at work or from business on a first-name basis, and enjoys the endless socializing such contacts provide. Some of these people may regard themselves as friends, but few ever reach this degree of intimacy with Aries.

Basically Aries people are attracted to others for their ideas. Aries Ascendant types like to be associated with free thinkers whose beliefs are so advanced that they have not yet been accepted by society. Only in their religious and philosophic views do they tend to be conventional, and their friends often help them gradually to change such beliefs. Aries people surround themselves with odd types whose eccentric ways are tolerated as long as their minds are sharp and stimulating.

Aries people often have radical ideas, which can attract an extreme type of person. Although fairly socially conformist when it comes to action, they can be drawn unsuspectingly into political intrigues in which their fearlessness may be exploited. They are not very good at playing people off against each other; their frankness gets in the way.

TWELFTH HOUSE: SECRETS AND THE UNCONSCIOUS MIND

Aries Ascendant people seldom come to terms with their own emotions. They are so used to being brave and self-assertive, they fail to notice that the tender side of their nature is constantly repressed. This tenderness pops up unexpectedly, most embarrassing for steely Aries, and is immediately pushed down again.

Emotions and sentiment are things Aries Rising people associate with their homes and families. Here their feelings are nicely compartmentalized, so there are no unforeseen problems.

The area in which Aries individuals are least equipped to handle their emotions is in their love lives. This is a secret they frequently manage to keep even from themselves. They confuse boldness with openness.

Emotions are involved in every facet of life, even for clear-thinking Aries. If they are constantly repressed, they have to surface somewhere. For Aries, they break out as compulsive urges and sudden impulses—so often the cause of problems, loss, and regret.

A bit of self-analysis and introspection, especially by Aries men, would help them to understand their emotional complexes. But pioneering Aries folk, forging ahead in the world of action, seldom have the time and patience.

Your Rising Sign: Taurus on the Ascendant

People born with Taurus Rising tend to be security-conscious in everything they undertake. An inhospitable environment makes them anxious. But money, things, and love (a possession to them) make them feel comfortable. Taurus Rising folk sometimes amass possessions more for the sake of security than for the pleasure or prestige they offer. This need affects how Taurus Rising people experience each of the twelve life houses as described below.

FIRST HOUSE: PERSONALITY

Taurus Ascendant people are slow to start, but long and strong on the finish. They are particularly tenacious. Once they decide to take on a project, they can be counted on to complete it. The quality of follow-through makes them desirable workers and partners.

You always know where you stand with Taurus Ascendant people. They are renowned for their straightforward and honest approach. But it isn't always easy to get them to change their mind once it is made up. Taurus can be very stubborn. Strongly opinionated, too, they do not sheepishly follow what other people say.

The symbol of Taurus is the Bull. Like the Bull, Taurus Rising people usually have powerful constitutions, which enable them to work long stretches at a time without tiring. And, like the Bull, they resent being pushed or pressured. Methodical and deliberate, they plod along at their own pace. In one day Taurus can often achieve more than flashy and dynamic types.

Loyalty is an outstanding characteristic of Taurus Rising people. Once they give their word, their heart, or their hand, they would rather suffer than let a person down. And suffer sometimes they do. Their loyalty can

159

land them in tricky situations. But even when betrayed, they refuse to acknowledge it until the fact is driven home in a painful way.

Taurus Ascendant people are uncomfortable with doubts and insecur-
ities, so much so that they prefer to shut their eyes to difficult realities.
They are reluctant to doubt the sincerity of loved ones and friends until
they themselves have examined all the possibilities. When Taurus people
finally accept the fact of betrayal, their hearts turn to stone as far as the
betrayer is involved. He or she is written off without another thought.

Taurus Rising people sometimes find it hard to make decisions. They
try to avoid radical changes. They try to leave nothing to chance. They
prefer to fix a goal well into the future and then work slowly but construc-
tively toward it. Change puts them off balance. Their thought processes are
geared to follow accepted and reliable patterns.

Taurus is not the gambling type. Security in all its forms means more
than virtually anything else. Such people like to surround themselves with
solid possessions. Their ruling planet is Venus, planet of attraction, harmony, and beauty. But being an earth sign, they express their fondness for
beautiful things in practical ways. They are good with their hands, and they
have an eye for design and texture. Taurus craftspeople enjoy fashioning
jewelry, clothes, furniture, and objects of art out of the sturdy materials of
the earth.

Taurus people love their homes. They take great pride in their families.
Their sense of possessiveness dominates the people in their life. Taurus can
treat loved ones like "things." And because Taurus folk like the things
around them to be desirable to others, they unwittingly foster situations
where flirtation and competition go on right under their noses. When the
Bull finally gets a whiff, the jealous rage is something to behold!

SECOND HOUSE: MONEY AND POSSESSIONS

Money and possessions mean security to Taurus Ascendant people.
Their peace of mind depends on it. They have no illusions about the world
and its worship of material things. Taurus people are not grabbers, but they
know the value of money. For them, there may never be enough tokens of
ownership to give them an adequate sense of security. When they do have
the funds, they put them into tangible assets—especially those they can
touch and gaze upon.

Jewelry and precious metals, paintings and ceramics, stamp and coin
collections give Taurus the feel of wealth. If they cannot afford these things,
they dream about having them. When Taurus people invest in land or buildings, you can be sure they are not absentee owners. They enjoy the experience of seeing and feeling part of the earth they own.

Taurus Rising folk often reach their goal of stability and comfort because they do not divide their time. They tend to fix on one aim early in
life—to acquire enough material wealth to feel good—and never get distracted from it. Even though they marry, raise families, and enjoy the good

life, all these activities are geared to the driving ambition to be as well off as possible.

Taurus people are naturally conservative. If they buy something, it must be the best quality. Their possessions are durable and eye-appealing; some of them last long enough to become valuable antiques. The home is the place where Taurus Rising people like to show off their artistic sense. They strive to make everything attractive and comfortable.

Extravagance is the middle name for some of those with Taurus on the Ascendant. They like rich food, heady drink, flashy clothes, and fast cars. These flamboyant desires are in direct contrast to the steadfast and sober nature of most Taurus Ascendant folk. And even though they watch their pennies grow into nickels, dimes, and quarters, they cannot help spending on luxuries for themselves and loved ones.

Taurus Rising people seldom have all their eggs in one basket. They manage to spread their savings in various ways so that a disaster in one sphere will not wipe them out. When Taurus people complain they have no money, they don't mean cash in hand; they mean a large and comfortable margin in savings or investments. They try to allow nothing to threaten their very precious feelings of security.

THIRD HOUSE: CLOSE CONTACTS AND COMMUNICATION

Taurus Ascendant people are neither garrulous nor gregarious. Casual contacts can frighten them. But close ties are very important. Taurus people make a point of keeping in touch with their nearest relatives and all associates with whom they feel a close bond of affection.

Quick visits and brief phone calls can rattle the Taurus Rising person. He or she needs time to react to a new situation, then settle into it. So letter writing and overnight or weekend trips are the preferred means of keeping in touch. Taurus people like to talk and think about things gone by, and to return to places to which they were attached in the past.

Taurus people operate at a far deeper emotional level than would seem to be the case for these practical, down-to-earth types. They are not quick thinkers. They deliberate; they weigh all the pros and cons before reaching a decision. Some of these people seem to be slow learners because teachers fail to give the subject matter an emotional content to which Taurus Rising can relate.

People with their Ascendant in the sign of the Bull are sensitive to their immediate environment. They are more dependent on what they feel than on what they think. If they rely on their minds too much, they often make mistakes. Having learned this lesson once, they tend to mistrust snap judgments in themselves as well as in other people.

Taurus Rising folk feel most comfortable in an environment that appeals to all the senses. They rely on touch and sight and sound more than many other people do. Taurus people love nature in all its splendid variations. It is important that these people settle in a neighborhood where beauty, balance, and harmony can be achieved and maintained.

FOURTH HOUSE: HOME AND FAMILY

Home life is a matter of personal security for Taurus Ascendant people. It also reflects their own value and status in the world. So do their loved ones, whom they often regard as objects to be admired and shown off. Family members for whom they are responsible must be clothed and presented in the best possible light. They are adamant about schooling youngsters in good manners and socially acceptable ways.

Their pride in their home and family borders on fierce possessiveness. It is not unusual for Taurus people to treat loved ones as if they were precious china dolls. Nor is it unusual for loved ones to feel objectified and stifled.

Taurus Rising folk are happiest entertaining at home. Here they can bestow the kind of hospitality they enjoy receiving, but seldom get, when they go out. Their surroundings must be plush. But no matter how modest their incomes and circumstances, they always try to be lavish in one way or another. What they cannot do because of lack of money, they will say in other ways—eye-catching flower arrangements or pleasing combinations of color and fabric.

Taurus Ascendant people often deprive themselves of certain pleasures to make their home more luxurious and comfortable. Food and drink must be of the best quality, and quantity is no object. If Taurus folk have a lot of money, they can become gourmets or gluttons. At the very least they are self-indulgent to an extreme.

Everything to do with the home and hearth is performed with a flourish. Here is the unconscious urge to impress. People whose Rising Sign is under the Bull would love to own a mansion and stock it with every lovely object imaginable. But their practical nature balances this expansive urge. That ever-present need for security prevents them from stretching fantasy to the reality of bankruptcy.

FIFTH HOUSE: ROMANCE, CREATIVITY, AND CHILDREN

People with Taurus on the Ascendant are not gambling types. They would never dream of approaching love life or artistic ventures with a speculative eye. Such matters are earnest ones for Taurus, who typically see them in terms of security. Will security be threatened or can it be relaxed? With that as the abiding question, Taurus folk go forward with a good deal of common sense and discrimination.

In romance, Taurus Rising people have a bent toward the sensuous and sensual. But this tendency is offset by a cautious, even prim, approach. They do not make bold advances, and they abhor this trait in people whom they are dating. A flamboyant come-on from a prospective partner can turn Taurus right off. They like their romantic companions to be modest and conventional, at least in public.

Taurus people experience strong emotions, but have a hard time expressing them verbally. Statements of ardor and passion embarrass them. They frown on displays of affection and emotion, which they believe are unnecessary and tend only to make them look frivolous to the onlooker. Reserved and shy out of bed, in bed the story is different. With a responsive lover, Taurus people abandon inhibitions for the full gratification of their senses.

Taurus Rising people can be extremely critical in romantic matters. Their usualy live-and-let-live attitude fails them in this area. They set high standards of morality, and then find it hard to live up to them. They try to choose lovers and mates who share the same moral code. Fidelity is paramount. Taurus people are severely threatened when promises are broken and commitments betrayed.

A common-sense attitude characterizes the Taurus approach to creativity and artistic endeavor. They don't daydream about talents they don't have or those that cannot be made practical and lucrative. Such people usually know their limitations. They try to make the most of their abilities. Applied arts and handicrafts are areas where Taurus Rising folk excel. Rather than being original and pioneering, their imagination is more suited to rearranging ideas that have already been absorbed by experience.

Children are a source of pride for Taurus Ascendant folk. It is not unusual for Taurus to plan well in advance when to have a family. The job of overseeing the family never quite ends. Taurus people want their youngsters to be a splendid advertisement of their fine parenting tradition. So they can be strict with the kids, not putting up with any nonsense. Taurus Rising people spend a great deal of time with children, seeing they get a good education and that they practice all the social graces.

SIXTH HOUSE: WORK AND HEALTH

Taurus Ascendant people are often drawn into trades or professions connected with music and art. The application of beauty is their special skill. But it is terribly important to them that the work surroundings be harmonious. They become uptight and irritable if conditions grate on their senses. Thrust among noisy and unruly people, Taurus will quit the job before adjusting to it.

It is the noise that really bothers Taurus Rising folk. They like sweet and melodious sounds, a gift from the planet Venus. Otherwise they probably would get along swell with teammates, no matter how distracting job relationships and job politics become.

Taurus folk work well with others. They bring tact and diplomacy to disputes. They are reasonable and cooperative workmates. They have a knack for bringing together people with clashing opinions. They are good peacemakers. And they have a strong sense of justice. They will not stand around indifferently while their coworkers are exploited or badly treated.

But Taurus Rising people do have a stubborn streak. It can infuriate bosses and colleagues. On the other hand, this trait enables them to follow through with painstaking detail all the requirements of a task and to complete it to near perfection. Only their bosses and colleagues would complain that the Taurus method is too exacting, too trivial, and too time-consuming. But for Taurus it is the only method!

The health of people influenced by the sign of the Bull depends on their working and living conditions. Their feeling of well-being is attuned to peace and quiet. Sensitive to jarring impressions, they can easily be upset. If conditions are harmonious, fine. If not, all manner of imagined ailments plague them.

They are inclined to worry unduly about minor health problems, despite the fact that they have a naturally robust constitution. Strong as an ox, nevertheless they often feel weak as a kitten. But when the question of professional diagnosis and treatment comes up, Taurus Rising people characteristically ask, "How much will it cost me?"

SEVENTH HOUSE: ALLIANCE AND PARTNERSHIP

Personal relationships for people with Taurus Rising cover the vast terrain where angels fear to tread. Close relationships, especially of love and marriage, make these people uptight and skittish. Taurus Ascendant people are not afraid of commitment. They are afraid of betrayal. They guard their security by adopting whatever pose seems to work with a partner or mate who could threaten them.

The truth is that their emotions are intensely concentrated, not casual, and always ready to blow the calm, cool, and collected pose. Taurus Rising people try to handle partnerships with a matter-of-fact grace, but a great deal of ferment is going on under the surface.

Taurus Rising is possessive and jealous. These people suffer agonies when a lover or mate keeps them pawing at the air, seeking solid ground. Uncertainty is the brink of a pit of terror. They cannot endure to be dangled on a string or kept at bay. Their emotional tranquillity and happiness demand their knowing exactly where they stand.

Marriage is a matter of great moment. Taurus Ascendant people do not enter it lightly. Serious planning must go on before the commitment is made. As long as Taurus feels that his or her love and affection are returned, faithfulness will override all. Except frustration! Once intimacy is established, Taurus folk demand a fulfilling physical relationship.

In business and social alliances, Taurus Rising people expect open and aboveboard behavior. They want full disclosure; no detail, no secret, no nuance of feeling is too trivial for their partners to omit. But Taurus people themselves may not be as emotionally honest or straightforward as they expect others to be.

Nevertheless, Taurus people work well in business partnerships, and business partnerships usually work out well for them. Their dislike of financial risks combined with their capacity for dogged effort usually ensures that the partnership reaches a solid financial footing.

EIGHTH HOUSE: SEX, PSYCHOLOGY, AND SHARED ASSETS

Modern attitudes about sex are not likely to meet with the full approval of people who have Taurus on the Ascendant. They believe in maintaining a strict code of behavior. Their tendency toward prudishness makes them regard sexual freedom as a threat to the traditions of family, loyalty, and security.

Taurus people might be surprised to hear themselves criticizing the effects of "loose morals" on society as a whole. Until the subject comes up, they probably never realized they worried about the subject. If questioned closely, and if they give in to their basic honesty, Taurus folk will admit that there really is nothing wrong with sexual freedom except the uncertainty it generates—and that is a Taurus bugaboo.

A live-and-let-live attitude is the Taurus psychology. They are prepared to take people and conditions as they find them. If the conditions are too grating, Taurus will leave. And if people are too upsetting, Taurus will flee. But they won't seek to change the environment. The exception is when people and conditions interfere with their money and possessions. Then they react in a narrowly focused way. It is not unusual for them to stand pat and fight to the finish.

People with Taurus Rising often inherit money or a position of prestige. Through a desirable marriage some of them achieve wealth and fame that would not be theirs otherwise. Although they do not take marriage lightly, they have an eye for improving their financial position. If marriage involves more than material security and prestige, all the better. It can be said that the number of Taurus folk who marry poorly is fewer than those who marry into money.

Taurus Ascendant people bring fine personal assets to business partnerships, and help to increase shared assets. Their tireless energy and patience carry an endeavor far beyond the initial stages. They work hard to develop a project and bring it to completion. Preferring to work in the background and avoid upfront risks, nevertheless they are able to teach other people how to achieve a good image and material success.

NINTH HOUSE: EDUCATION AND TRAVEL

People born with Taurus as the Ascendant are not the types to fall for highfalutin doctrines or creeds. If any aspect of learning is not true in their experience, it is suspect. Although many of them adhere to traditional philosophic or religious codes, it is not with zeal; it is the expected thing to do to get ahead.

These people are the pragmatists of the zodiac. They feel their way as they go. They test every idea and suggestion by their own practical leanings. They would never mislead anyone. The only trouble is that they can often miss the spirit of an idea.

Taurus Rising folk are sticklers for the letter of the law, whether it is religious, philosophical, or legal. They must guard against being too cautious and conservative. On the one hand, they accept only what can be proved by concrete evidence. On the other, they easily experience the subtleties of art and beauty through pure sensation.

These people are inclined to support established authority whenever they are in doubt. In spiritual matters they are often orthodox, until their

own experience teaches them otherwise. Then they can rise to great heights
of enlightenment.

Knowledge for its own sake is seldom a priority for people with Taurus
Rising. Many of them, as youngsters, were chided for being slow learners.
Of course, that was probably because the subject matter was so abstract.
Taurus people need to feel that whatever they study has a definite and
tangible purpose, a purpose that immediately or ultimately improves their
basic security.

Taurus Ascendant people are not the type to travel long distances without a good reason. Long journeys to other nations purely for pleasure do
not motivate them. And the expense of the tickets can turn them off! But
if they can combine travel with commercial goals, they are happy to slip the
anchor that holds them so securely to home ground.

TENTH HOUSE: FAME AND AMBITION

The Taurus desire for fame and attainment is not so self-centered as it
is in many other zodiacal signs. The Taurus Ascendant person genuinely
wants his or her job and career to benefit as many people as possible. The
fact that his or her prestige is enhanced is swell, but it is not vital to involvement or performance.

Taurus Rising needs to feel needed. Such people want to be of service
in their vocation. Although not highly original in other areas, in business
and public affairs these men and women display ingenuity and invention.
They have a way of turning unexpected changes to advantage, as long as
they themselves are not too unsettled by the changes.

Determined to build something out of their lives, they do their very
best even without approval. If they feel secure, they will work with a persistence unmatched by other zodiacal signs. Although they like to measure
their personal success in wealth and status, they are capable of working day
in and day out on pursuits aimed solely at benefiting society as a whole.

It is not unusual for Taurus people to become involved in scientific
projects. Their inventive minds, pragmatic goals, and tolerance for detailed
technical work enable them to sustain long periods of frustrating work. In
music or art, technology or trade, they endeavor to contribute something
tangible to the sum total of human knowledge in that area.

ELEVENTH HOUSE: FRIENDSHIP AND COMMUNITY

No one is more loyal to their friends than a person with Taurus on the
Ascendant, except perhaps someone whose Sun sign is Taurus. When Taurus makes a friend, it is not a casual occurrence. And it is not an event that
takes place at an intellectual level.

Taurus Rising people are particular about whom they call friend. They
are not fussy, but there has to be the right chemistry. The link is emotional,
and the bond can be deep. That bond won't be broken as far as the Bull is

concerned. When a friend lets Taurus down, there can be a definite cooling-off period. But if the friend sincerely apologizes, Taurus is prepared to forgive and forget.

They are no fools, of course. They are too practical to be used by so-called friends. You can't force a Taurus person against his or her wishes. Opportunists don't get far with these folk. And high-pressure types might just as well not try to develop that special bond called friendship.

The way to lead a Taurus is not by the ring through the Bull's nose, but by love. Taurus people give love and affection freely, and they expect their close friends to reciprocate in kind and quantity. These sons and daughters of Venus feel hurt at the slightest evidence of neglect.

Taurus Ascendant people are not types to join clubs and groups that highlight intellect over sentiment, or that feature large-scale impersonal goals over the nitty-gritty everyday ones. A group must have a useful purpose for them.

Yet Taurus people easily become involved in humanitarian efforts if they feel secure with the group members. They often are dedicated for purely altruistic motives. They can immerse themselves in projects that seem to have no extrinsic or material rewards for them. Taurus Rising people do not resent volunteer work or the helping and caring services.

Taurus people need to exchange ideas with others, but superficial contacts are difficult for them. Acquaintances are few. Taurus folk are a bit too insecure to approach strangers or newcomers merely on the basis of group interest. Friendship, preferably of an intimate and long-standing nature, is preferable to casual companionship.

Taurus are wonderful listeners. They are staunch and understanding; theirs is the shoulder to cry on. Their practical turn of mind offers solutions to problems that baffle their friends. They have a deep, seemingly endless, well of sympathy. They often sacrifice for their friends, providing a sense of total support and caring.

When a person is in need, a Taurus friend is a friend indeed.

TWELFTH HOUSE: SECRETS AND THE UNCONSCIOUS MIND

People born with Taurus on the Ascendant have strong and sympathetic imaginations. Their fears and compulsions have a terrifying reality. They worry, especially as youngsters, that their imaginations will take them over.

The slightest fear can be exaggerated into enormous proportions. Once their vigorous fantasizing gets going, it often gives rise to compulsive behavior that they cannot understand. Such uncontrollable impulses shock the cautious and reserved side of their nature.

This is their big secret. They would not care to admit that there was a time in their life when they were unable to control a longing for pleasure, pure and simple. A large part of their adult psychology centers around pleasure and its forbidden aspects. They try to control their constant need for sensual gratification. Or they learn to live with the consequences of overindulgence in food, drink, and erotic experience.

Strong-willed and patient, these people try to control their actions by repressing their emotions. They also try to put down feelings of rage or sadness even when such feelings are justified. They do succeed in avoiding a lot of trouble this way. But repression is repression. Taurus Rising folk repress their passions to such an extent that they can explode at the slightest thing.

Your Rising Sign: Gemini on the Ascendant

People with Gemini on the Ascendant inherit the mercurial characteristics of the Sun's closest neighbor. These daughters and sons of Mercury are indeed "neighborly." They need to be constantly in touch with all facets of their environment, especially the people in it. They are forever rushing around, checking on this one and that one, asking questions, noting replies, and trying to complete what they started. Communication for Gemini Rising people is a two-way street, coloring how they approach the twelve life houses described below.

FIRST HOUSE: PERSONALITY

Gemini Rising people are adaptable and communicative. They are restless individuals in mind and body. They are, or try to be, continuously active and on the go. Their favorite pastime is getting out and about, meeting as many new people as they can, touching base with the regular crowd.

Being the first air sign, Gemini bestows a keen and active intellect in these people. They love to exchange ideas. Geminis are often accused of chattering rather than speaking. Their ideas come so fast that they hurry their speech to keep up with their minds. Talking, performing, and traveling come naturally to them.

Gemini is a dual sign. Its symbol is the Twins, for Castor and Pollux, the two bright stars in Gemini. Gemini Rising people are very changeable, often contradictory. They set out to do something with great zeal, get distracted after a short time, and end up doing several other things without returning to their original intention.

Change and variety are their spices in life. Unexpected events and interruptions often disturb other zodiacal signs. But Gemini Rising people thrive on such developments. They can adapt with lightning quickness to virtually any situation that arises.

Excitement and stimulation are basic requirements if Gemini people are to pursue an activity to its end. They become bored and irritable if they are forced to stick to a routine. It is not easy for them to perform in a routine occupation if it does not offer changing surroundings and contacts.

Gemini Rising people are quick-witted, always eager to learn new things. The speed with which they absorb facts makes them appear merely to skim the surface. They seem to be incapable of deep and profound study. This is probably not the case. Gemini people have a serious bent. You would be surprised at the deliberation going on in their heads while they appear to skip from one concern to another.

People with a Gemini Ascendant appear to suffer from a lack of concentration. What is really going on is a powerful mind beaming on all angles of a question. Just one more bit of data is needed to weigh all that has been absorbed. But Gemini people then have a hard time resolving the issue. It is their own fault. They have gathered so much information, it may be impossible to cut through the nonessentials to the heart of the matter.

Gemini Rising folk have a fine knack of doing several things at once. They are usually deft with their hands. They are fine inventors, able to fix any gadget or tool. Some of them can write with both hands; many play musical instruments. Artistic and witty, they have a keen aptitude for languages, writing, lecturing, and teaching.

Geminis are great to have around in emergency situations. Logical and quick, their bright ideas more often than not provide an instant solution. They will help to carry it out, too, because they do not worry about danger or consequences. Their ability to adapt makes them accept the unexpected as a challenge to their considerable mental abilities.

Gemini people are nearly obsessive about their personal freedom. They will not be tied down long. They can walk out without explanation if they find themselves trapped in a relationship. They cannot stand pressure. Hard manual work is something they seek to avoid. They are mental creatures whose silvery qualities tarnish under prolonged physical effort.

SECOND HOUSE: MONEY AND POSSESSIONS

Gemini Rising people are romantic about money. It should be used for having a good time, according to them. They seem to throw it around as they go on their merry way from one person or event to another. They give the impression that money is not very important to them.

But they know exactly what they are doing with their cash. Their agile minds are as efficient as computers, noting everything they and other people are doing. They are always aware of whose turn it is to pick up the tab, and who has missed out. Their nonchalance masks a real concern about every penny, nickel, and dime. Perhaps Gemini folk are too embarrassed to expose this petty concern to view. So they are not above posing as a spendthrift or wastrel.

They can be extravagant. But seldom do Gemini Ascendant people waste all their money. They like to have a solid core of funds invested for a rainy day. They tend to put funds into their home or into a family enterprise. What is not invested can be spent lavishly at times.

They like to have variety in things, especially for the home and their families. They think nothing of abandoning old things and buying new ones to fit the trends. The intrinsic value of things is of little importance to them. Possessions for them must be exciting and appeal to the senses. But their senses get easily wearied. Gemini can have a million gadgets around the house, all performing the same task.

Although not emotional themselves, Gemini Rising people are sensitive to others in their environment. They often depend on their ability to excite people's emotions as a means of earning money. This talent enables them to range successfully from actor to con artist. They can be financially successful in the role of agent, broker, merchant, or banker.

A Gemini Ascendant person uses his or her ability to communicate with the public as a means of increasing income. They may take part-time jobs as actors, writers, agents, and teachers. They are modern people who keep up with the times. Their ideas have a fashionable appeal. And they know how to excite the minds of their audience.

THIRD HOUSE: CLOSE CONTACTS AND COMMUNICATION

Close contacts, and plenty of them, are lifelines for Gemini Rising. People are most important assets in the lives of these mercurial types. They sincerely want to know what makes you tick. If anything is askew, there is Gemini trying to figure it out for you.

They take great pride in their ability to persuade and influence people. They realized, probably early in life, that they have the gift of gab. And they make the most of it in their social and occupational affairs.

Gemini Ascendant folk are clever talkers and apt writers. They are chatty and witty. They easily entertain a crowd of people with fascinating stories. They can spellbind the individual with amusing conversation. They never tire of injecting everyday life scenes with the unusual. They have a childlike interest in everything, and it helps them to see with a fresh perspective.

Geminis appear to be intense talkers. They think so fast that words tumble out in a great urgency. Sometimes their tongues cannot keep up with their thoughts. In youth some of these people develop a stutter or other speech impediment.

Gemini Rising folk are habitual telephone users. They like to keep in touch with relatives and pals, although they try to avoid a deep involvement with relatives. They love hearing other people's troubles and discussing them. The logical Gemini mind can always find something of interest in the most trivial detail.

Gemini Ascendant people make many short trips and visits. They prefer traveling by public transportation. It gives them an opportunity to chat briefly with people from all walks of life. Besides, if they drive alone, they probably wind up talking to themselves.

They love listening to news from other people and about other people. Sometimes they get a reputation for being gossips. Gossip, though, is an important tool for Gemini Rising. It enables them to learn about the world and communities and people with whom they are not directly involved.

FOURTH HOUSE: HOME AND FAMILY

A Gemini Ascendant person is fussy about where she or he lives. Although such people like to be on the move, they need to have a place to unwind and retool. A quiet and small niche is all they really need in order to relax and renew their spent energies.

But Gemini Rising people get bored fast. They are unlikely to spend a lot of time at home, especially if they live alone. They are not prone to loneliness. But visiting other people's homes has an instant appeal. Nevertheless they do need the psychological assurance that something solid is waiting for them at the end of their restless day.

If their own private niche has outlived its usefulness, Geminis are quick to make a family of their own. Geminis like the emotional freedom of being single, but they like the physical security of having a family or at least a mate to come home to. Another dilemma for the dual Gemini!

Geminis can be chaotic in the house, either maddeningly sloppy or maddeningly neat. They may throw their belongings around with abandon, leaving them strewn about without any regard. But sooner or later they confront the mess as if they just discovered it. Then they vehemently attack the job of tidying up and putting everything back in its place. Until the next whirlwind change descends!

They can be quick-tempered with their families. Little things that others do or do not do in the house annoy them. Although their lives are usually lived as a constant revolt against routine, they like their home to be run on methodical lines.

They find it easier to organize their home and the people in it than adjusting to the demands of an outside workplace. It is not unusual for people influenced by the sign of Gemini to work at home. Here they can do the writing or make the handicrafts and artistic objects that suit their temperaments at their own sequence and pace.

Gemini Rising people sometimes feel that they want to live in the country, away from the hectic pace. Especially away from the telephone! But isolation rarely works. Living in a rural commune or near a big city is a choice that fulfills the dual needs for privacy and stimulation.

FIFTH HOUSE: ROMANCE, CREATIVITY, AND CHILDREN

Romantically, Gemini Ascendant people are not too reliable. When they are in love, they are charming, attentive, and eager to please. They mean what they say at the moment. But unfortunately it is often difficult for them to maintain a close personal relationship for a long time. After the initial passion has receded, they tend to lose interest and to go their own way.

Gemini Rising folk are often flirts. They can have too or three affairs going at the same time. They are mentally curious rather than physically passionate or emotional. But their love of variety enables them to be skilled and inventive lovers. They can be cold and aloof when it suits them or when the party is over.

Gemini Ascendant people have strong artistic and mechanical abilities. Sometimes they do not spare the time to develop them. Writing and speaking come naturally. They also like to fool around with any and all conceivable machines, tools, and appliances. Their hands and minds are nimble and quick. Gemini is a bit of a culinary whiz, too. They make first-rate actors, entertainers, and caterers.

Children are second nature for Gemini Rising people. Being something of an eternal Peter Pan themselves, they get along splendidly with youngsters of most ages. They do prefer children who have passed the nursing and baby stage, for such tiny creatures baffle Geminis and also tie them down. They truly believe in a live-and-let-live attitude, so they are not too concerned with discipline. Their own forever-young approach to life helps them to understand and to teach youngsters at most stages of development.

SIXTH HOUSE: WORK AND HEALTH

Gemini Ascendant people take their work more seriously than they are given credit for. An observer only sees them flitting from task to task without seeming to finish any of them. But Gemini people do not rigidly adhere to an expected sequence of beginning, middle, and end. In fact, they abhor routine. So they usually vary the way in which they will perform—and ultimately complete—a job.

The Twins have a heaven-sent gift for doing several things simultaneously, without sacrificing efficiency or neglecting any detail. They have an extraordinary memory. Many an employer thankfully remembers the day a Gemini worker joined the staff—and probably regrets the day Gemini, as is his or her tendency to do, left it.

Geminis are exceptional at getting to the bottom of things and finding facts. They make topnotch reporters, researchers, and investigators. Often they are born psychologists and sociologists, with a shrewd and discerning logic. Even if they do not pursue such professions, they nevertheless develop a keen insight into people because they have a tireless interest in what makes people tick.

Gemini Rising folk must find a job that utilizes most of their skills and interests. Otherwise boredom sets in fast. Repetitive tasks unvaried as to time and space chafe at them. If they don't quit, they will rebel by giving far less to the job than it deserves. They will spread themselves thin by becoming involved in outside activities that assume more importance than the job. To be truly happy, they need work that thoroughly challenges the application of their talents and the absorption of their mental energies.

The Twins never seem to run out of energy. In fact, they revitalize by pushing themselves to the limit. They work frantically, sometimes till the wee hours. They seem to get a second, third, and even fourth wind through this incessant activity. With just a tiny bit of peace and quiet, even a refreshment break, they quickly recover.

The health of Gemini Ascendant people is fairly stable, despite their nervousness and intensity. They work off a lot of repressed energy by having their mouths and their hands constantly engaged. So they are not too likely to succumb to psychosomatic ailments. With a great fondness for food and a love of variety, it is predictable that many Gemini Rising folk are diet faddists and exercise bugs.

SEVENTH HOUSE: ALLIANCE AND PARTNERSHIP

Partnerships òf an intimate variety are something of a one-way street where Gemini Ascendant people are concerned. Impersonal or group alliances, on the other hand, are eminently suitable for these dual folk. In business partnerships and other mutual endeavors, the Twins often find the variety of experience necessary for them to work as a team.

Marriage is regarded as a meeting of the minds. But Gemini changes his or her mind so often, it is hard for them to find a partner whose personality is exciting enough to sustain their interest. Gemini people also have the capacity to think about their partners while not being with them. After the honeymoon Geminis think nothing of roaming here and there by themselves.

Gemini Rising people cannot stand to be fenced in. The responsibilities and obligations that go with married life may be experienced as intolerable bonds. It is important for people born under the influence of the restless Twins to find a partner who is capable and who knows his or her mind. Then Geminis won't have to do all the work in the marriage.

Gemini people are inclined to need looking after. They want to be looked after, babied even. Although they present a fiercely independent front, they secretly yearn to be taken care of and given direction. They feel guilty about their aimless ways, and imagine that a strong and helping hand can lead them from childishness to sober adulthood.

With a partner who takes charge, but still allows Gemini plenty of latitude, the marriage can be a happy one. But these people need a long leash, and they will revert to those aimless and childish ways if their sense of freedom is threatened. Geminis do not like to be bothered with the details of domestic life that have nothing to do with other people. They prefer to organize the social side.

EIGHTH HOUSE: SEX, PSYCHOLOGY, AND SHARED ASSETS

Gemini Rising people are unsentimental about sex. Although they have a sweet line of patter and a charming approach, they are down to earth, almost businesslike, when it comes to lovemaking. Nevertheless, they are inventive lovers. They like experimentation. They approach sex naturally, and they usually have few, if any, inhibitions or hangups.

But a love of variety and experimentation does not lead them into promiscuous ways. Geminis are fussy about whom they want to play games with. Either they are interested or they are not. It's hard to seduce them. They, of course, can be the seducers. But their flirtatious ways are often a game that never comes to anything. In fact, flirtation may be their strategy for fending off real sexual contact. It is their way of saying "Nothing doing!"

Gemini-influenced people do not dwell on abstract issues, nor do they worry about the abstract sides of such everyday issues as death and survival. They will not probe too deeply into the problems of life unless those problems happen to be affecting them at the moment. It is enough for them to keep moving with the moment, and not to presume that the moment is ever going to end.

But when Gemini people do put their minds to deep investigation, they can become seriously involved. Invariably they discover a truth that is meaningful to them. And they assume that the truth will be meaningful to others. Their need to communicate with other people leads them to share their insights generously.

Sharing resources as well as insights can be a bond of interest that keeps a partnership going long after Gemini Rising people become bored with other aspects of the partnership. When money and possessions are involved, Geminis can display an admirable degree of responsibility.

It is often best if Geminis are allowed to manage shared assets. The responsibility brings out the best in them. Flighty Geminis often settle more comfortably into double harness when they have the obligation to oversee joint funds. If a partner insists on taking control of the financial side, Geminis as a rule will forget about economizing. Sooner or later they will spend whatever they can get, even if it means dipping into the cookie jar.

NINTH HOUSE: EDUCATION AND TRAVEL

Gemini Ascendant people learn quickly and easily. They are interested in everything. They appreciate knowledge for its own sake and also in order to communicate tidbits of information to their cronies. If they get deeply involved in studies, they will not keep the project to themselves. It is important for these people to share their knowledge with others.

But Gemini is a rebel. He or she will not accept orthodox doctrines merely on faith or as a fashion. Some of these people do belong to established religions, but probably because belonging offers social contacts or because the rigorous logic of the belief challenges the Gemini intellect.

Gemini Rising folk can be fanatical about their love of freedom. Their dislike of established authority often makes it difficult for them to pursue college or university studies to the end. They become distracted or rebellious. They spend a lot of time supporting worthy causes on campus. They like to spread their own ideas on philosophy, religion, and the law. Nonconformists to the end, they enjoy exhorting others to rebel.

Gemini-influenced people like to roam among people of all persuasions and beliefs. They travel at any and every opportunity. Trips to new and different lands intrigue them. Culture contrasts fascinate them; they enjoy discovering how people of other cultures think. It is not unusual for Gemini visitors to shun the tourist role and live with the people. Going "native" is easy because Geminis quickly pick up a new language.

TENTH HOUSE: FAME AND AMBITION

Gemini Rising people have lofty dreams about what they would like to be. But when it comes down to the reality of making decisions, they often are uncertain. Too many careers have appeal for them to decide, once and for all, that this is it. And they have too many talents to focus on one and cordon off the others.

Their ambitious urges tend to take the form of enthusiastic spurts. They get a romantic notion of a field of endeavor, then pursue it only to discover that it really isn't as glamorous as they thought. When the drab reality starts to show through, they lose interest.

It isn't easy for typical Gemini-influenced people to know exactly what they want out of life. Undefined dreams of fame and glory make it almost impossible for them to put up with routine. They want to fly before they can walk. But their mercurial wings are not made to soar like those of eagles, and sometimes they do not get off the ground.

Gemini people are extremely versatile. They can do and adapt to just about anything that requires swiftness of mind and movement. They often achieve maximum fulfillment when they are handling several jobs at once. One job must be mightily challenging to hold their interest for long. The danger is that their versatility may lead them to go from one job to another.

Public image is not a priority concern for Gemini Rising people. Of course, they want to be recognized for their alert minds and their easygoing ways. But they are too nonconformist to assume the conservative pose that befits high standing in the community. In fact, they rather enjoy the reputation for being mischief makers and scandal lovers.

ELEVENTH HOUSE: FRIENDSHIP AND COMMUNITY

No one in the Zodiac makes more contact with people than does the typical Gemini Ascendant person, except possibly someone whose Sun sign is Gemini. The act of communicating is fun. It is also a reason for existence. Geminis do not care whether the ideas exchanged are inconsequential tidbits of information or serious insights about life problems. The important thing is the communicating.

Geminis are vigorously enterprising at establishing relationships. Among their many acquaintances are usually just the right people to help them at any particular time and for any particular situation. If they are isolated from people for even a few days, they start to show strain. They become irritable and stale and frustrated. Their health can be affected.

Typical Gemini Rising people have many friends, associates, and acquaintances. They love to debate. Arguing the issues of the day keeps them vital and young. Their agile minds are usually more than a match for their companions, but they do not always try to win. They will start a verbal dispute for the pure pleasure of exercising their intellectual muscles.

Gemini Rising folk are often in the forefront of radical movements. They are good at starting clubs, associations, and collectives. They like to get involved in community work or burning social issues. They get along well in groups. They have an extraordinary ability to inspire others to support causes they believe are important. But once the initial enthusiasm fades, they move on.

TWELFTH HOUSE: SECRETS AND THE UNCONSCIOUS MIND

Gemini Ascendant people are determined that no one will ever get close enough to them to discover their motives. What makes them tick is a private affair, although they certainly can be nosy about the lives of other people.

Geminis sometimes feel that their true emotions are buried so deep that they can never express them. They often are aware of their own coldness and lack of sympathy. They worry that their interests and intensity might be shallow.

Gemini Rising folk assume many poses and play many games: mischief maker, storyteller, gossip, scandalmonger, petty tyrant, jack or jill of all trades. They appear to be flighty and superficial. But underneath, and not as deep as Gemini fears, is another facet of the Gemini nature.

They possess a solid core of seriousness. This can surface easily in their approach to material matters. Their possessions are more important to them than their breezy manner suggests. They also yearn for security. But it is hard for them to admit that fact and to stay put long enough to attain it.

The underlying need for security is reflected in the way Gemini people refuse to put all their financial eggs in one basket. They depend on their versatility to see to it that the baskets are tended, and that there is more than one source of income.

Gemini-influenced people are often secretly anxious about what others think about them. They want to be accepted. As a result, they are generous and hospitable. They give expensive gifts to mark special occasions. Their memory always serves them in this regard, much to the amazement of their friends. They have a sixth sense about what will give others pleasure, so generally they are able to select just the right gift.

Your Rising Sign: Cancer on the Ascendant

Cancer Rising signifies instinct and response. People with Cancer on the Ascendant are deep ones, but changeable. Like the Moon, ruler of Cancer, their enthusiasms wax and wane. Like the waters of the Earth, their element, their spirits rise and fall, trickle and stream, then take a sudden turning. Cancer Rising people seek to stabilize themselves through links with tradition and the past. Ties to home and family become a central theme, affecting their experiences in the twelve life houses as described below.

FIRST HOUSE: PERSONALITY

People born with Cancer on the Ascendant are extremely sensitive. They live in and on their emotions. They display a brave front to the world, which manages most admirably to hide the uncertainty within. Like the Crab, their symbol, they scuttle away when they sense danger.

Cancer Rising people know what it is like to be hurt. They feel miserably offended at the slightest criticism. They are often thin-skinned, imagining slights and insults where none are intended. They yearn to be respected and appreciated. No one can ever seem to love them enough.

Deep, black moods are one of the prices Cancer Rising people have to pay for their hypersensitivity. They can get so far down in the dumps that it is sometimes impossible to coax them out until the emotional buildup has been worked out. In these moods they can be demanding of the people around them.

But their sensitivity has a positive aspect. Cancer Ascendant people are very understanding. They will listen for hours to other people's problems. Their sympathy is unbounded. A person in trouble pouring out his or her heart to a Cancer feels truly understood. And the Crab's ability to relate emotionally to others is so great that these people can at times actually feel what the other person is going through.

Cancer Rising people are spasmodically active. When the pressure is on, they can wade into the work and get a lot done. But they are not the staying type. Dogged, unremitting effort leaves them exhausted and lethargic. They need frequent breaks from any prolonged physical or mental effort.

Excessive pressure, which many other signs regard as the normal strains of living, is something Cancer people cannot stand. They put on the toughest and bravest front possible. But at the first opportunity they scurry off to a quiet place where the pace is easy and undemanding, and the surroundings comfortingly familiar.

Cancer Rising people love their homes. They try to make them as attractive and comfortable as possible, in keeping with their strong artistic leanings. They make excellent cooks and considerate hosts. Cancer people are very protective of their loved ones, so much so that they often make their nearest and dearest feel stifled.

SECOND HOUSE: MONEY AND POSSESSIONS

Cancer Rising people like to use their money to put on a show. One of their fondest possessions is their home. They love to entertain. They spoil their guests with the best of everything. They enjoy having a reputation for being attentive and generous hosts. They are prepared to work hard at maintaining that image.

Cancer people are generally conservative with their cash. They like to save up for a home and for all the nice things that go into it. They make it a most desirable place, because they like to spend much of their time there. They frequently collect old books, antiques, and relics of the past. They have a flair for displaying their nostalgic treasures in most attractive ways.

The typical person with a Cancer Ascendant has a great need for security. If they cannot feel materially secure because of lack of money, they will attempt to surround themselves with people or family who love them or are dependent on them.

They try to put something away for a rainy day. They are quite happy to spend as much as necessary to give their children a good education and start in life. They often regard their youngsters as possessions and may be reluctant to let them grow up and go their way.

THIRD HOUSE: CLOSE CONTACTS AND COMMUNICATION

Cancer Ascendant people like to keep in touch with their kin, no matter how distant they are from relatives and family friends. They also like to have more than a nodding acquaintance with their neighbors. Close relationships, near or far, are the stuff of life for Cancer-influenced folk.

Although they are particular about choosing close friends, they have many informal contacts. Cancer people love to invite people to their home. Chatting and exchanging ideas are fine in familiar or domestic situations.

Cancer people worry a good deal about the future. Details and little things seem to stick in their minds. Mistakes get blown up beyond all proportion by their vivid imaginations. They also tend to brood about the past, remembering this and that minor thing that most others have long ago forgotten.

Cancer Rising people usually express themselves very precisely when they want to. They can be quite sharp-tongued and critical. They are seldom entirely happy with any current state of affairs. They tend to feel that life was far more desirable in the good old days.

As a rule, people strongly influenced by Cancer are great storytellers, with an eye for quaint and romantic detail.

FOURTH HOUSE: HOME AND FAMILY

Home and family affairs are usually the most important part of a Cancer Ascendant person's life. At the hearth of the home and the heart of the family—here is where they imagine themselves to be.

They want their home to be as attractive as possible and to fill it with the nicest of people. They are often disappointed with the way their families turn out, possibly because their expectations are so high. But their love of their nearest and dearest, as well as their dependence on them as a guarantee of future security, allow these rather critical people to live with human frailty.

Cancer Rising people will forgive anything if they feel appreciated and loved. But if neglected by their families, they are likely to be gloomy and disgruntled. They complain how little they have received in return for all the sacrifices they have made.

Cancer people are charming and diplomatic in their close relationships with friends and neighbors. But they can be picky and mean with lovers or mates. They allow the spiteful side of their nature to surface in the bosom of family.

People born under the influence of Cancer do not like to live alone. If they cannot find a lover or mate who meets romantic or idealistic standards, they are likely to spend much time in intimate clubs or community activities.

FIFTH HOUSE: ROMANCE, CREATIVITY, AND CHILDREN

Cancer Rising people can suffer terribly from jealousy. They desire a love that is complete and perfect. They see anything less, even a harmless word or action, as betrayal of their faith. When badly hurt, these people scuttle back to a safe place. It is almost impossible to reach them then.

They can be passionate lovers but rely on their vivid imaginations to maintain their erotic interest. They are in love with the idea of romantic love. The want to get to the bottom of the mystery of love, and they use their emotions, true or false, to do so. They often put their loved ones on pedestals, failing or refusing to see the faults or shortcomings.

Secret love affairs have a fascination for Cancer Ascendant people. The element of risk provides an extra stimulation that excites their emotions.

The natural talents of people influenced by the sign of the Crab lean toward the artistic. They have an inborn appreciation of beauty and an extremely reliable intuition. They make splendid painters and designers; fine arts and applied arts utilize their moody talents. Their sensitivity and sympathy make them ideally suited for the caring and helping services.

Cancer parents can be rather strict one moment with their children, lovingly indulgent the next. They find it difficult to maintain a middle-of-the-road emotional course.

SIXTH HOUSE: WORK AND HEALTH

Cancer Rising people are excellent workers as long as they believe in the importance of what they are doing. It also is essential for thcm to feel they are among congenial people and surroundings. They are good organizers who can bring together masses of details.

They are always looking beyond the immediate task to the future. If they are not happy with their present position, they are inclined to dream and speculate without taking much action. Or they leave and drift with their moods, longing for a perfect and safe niche.

The work of Cancer Ascendant people often requires them to travel. Or they are in frequent contact with other countries. They may be obliged to take on extra study and to develop their minds.

Cancer-influenced people shine in any job that makes use of their quality for protecting and caring for others. They are often attracted to the medical and nursing professions, as well as social and child-welfare occupations.

They cannot work efficiently or happily if they have to submit to a rigid or harassing authority. They are easily hurt and start worrying and brooding. Their moods affect everyone around them.

The health of people born with the influence of the Crab demands that they have plenty of change, either in people or surroundings. They are drawn to people who share their fondness for occasional isolation, especially for communing with nature. If they become ill, they recover much more quickly with tender loving care. Their loved ones must not allow these sensitive folk to worry.

SEVENTH HOUSE: ALLIANCE AND PARTNERSHIP

Partnerships are never entered into lightly by typical Cancer Rising people. They like to weigh every angle, especially in love and marriage unions, before taking the plunge. But often they load themselves with partners who have difficulty coping with the pressures of life.

Cancer Ascendant people have an inborn desire to protect and look after others. Often the prospect of having to shoulder a partner's particular problems or responsibilities provides them with a sense of purpose and fulfillment. They may complain from time to time if they feel they are not being appreciated, but otherwise are quite prepared to play a nurturing role.

The Cancer woman can be the makings of her man as he is trying to get to the top. She will be prepared to accept more than her share of any sacrifice that may be necessary. Cancer men and women are ambitious for their partners; they want them to make the very best use of their skills and talents.

Nevertheless, people born with the Crab as their Rising sign often feel restricted by the partnership role. They can become especially demanding and even nagging if they feel their partner is not making the full effort.

With an aggressive and fairly competent business partner, Cancer Rising people happily submit to the alliance. They are dependable and encouraging; they would never think of abandoning ship for the kinds of picky reasons that so often mar their love relationships.

EIGHTH HOUSE: SEX, PSYCHOLOGY, AND SHARED ASSETS

Cancer Rising people are fairly strict about marriage vows. They do their very best to stick to the straight and narrow. But if they are not committed in marriage or partnership, they are inclined to believe in sexual freedom. They are more outspoken about these matters than their reticent natures would normally suggest.

They are often in the forefront among advocates of a more liberal approach to abortion, homosexuality, and birth control. They may not personally support any particular issue, but they do champion the right of the individual to make his or her own decisions.

People born with a Cancer Ascendant have a natural interest in occult subjects, unless they have been frightened off by their own experiences. These individuals are strongly intuitive and very impressionable to psychic influences. They frequently are mediumistic.

People with Cancer on the Ascendant have a strong desire to share what they have with those who are closest to them. Where shared resources and finances are concerned, such folk are very dependable. They would never as a rule do anything to endanger joint security. They are the sort of people who are very good at managing community funds.

NINTH HOUSE: EDUCATION AND TRAVEL

Cancer Ascendant people fall into two types. There are the wishful thinkers who only dream about what they would like to do or be. And there are those who relentlessly pursue their objectives.

The more evolved Cancer type is not a follower where education and learning are concerned. These people as a rule do not conform to orthodox religious beliefs unless they have some sort of personal reality for them. They are not prepared to accept other people's explanations of what life is about, or why they are here.

Cancer folk have a strong urge to serve others, or at least to protect and help them. Therefore a Cancer person's personal ethics embody the highest religious principles of service and surrender.

At the wordly level, people born under the influence of the Crab frequently have a strong desire to improve their minds. They delve into history and traditions. From these studies they extract the most desirable aspects and try to apply them to improving present conditions.

They love to travel physically, as well as mentally and emotionally. Journeys of the mind are enlightening. Through their vivid imaginations they discover new worlds of creative thought, which inspire them to artistic expression. They also may journey through their emotions into psychic experiences.

TENTH HOUSE: FAME AND AMBITION

The urge of ambition is often extremely strong in Cancer Rising people. This is something of a contradiction in their nature, for much of the time these people are retiring types. They like to be in a comfortable position where demands upon them are not too great.

But the desire to get ahead in the world and possibly make a name for themselves periodically overtakes them. And they become filled with new enthusiasm and a strong determination that often catches their competitors napping.

Cancer Rising folk have a way of putting on an air of self-assurance. Such a pose may not be matched by any feelings of certainty within. They can carry off the big bluff. They have a way of appearing detached, which often forces others to act along the lines they wanted. Cancer can be a manipulator.

People born under the influence of the Crab are often difficult to get close to in business and career affairs; they are more suited for occupations where they can operate on their own.

Cancer people are often more interested in honor and prestige than in the material gains from their ambitious efforts. They have a strong desire for power. They enjoy being in a position of authority, which leaves them free to pursue their lives without reference to superiors.

ELEVENTH HOUSE: FRIENDSHIP AND COMMUNITY

Cancer Ascendant people enjoy doing things for their friends. They like to be of some practical value. A Cancer person is the type who will help a friend to decorate or build a house, giving up a great amount of his or her spare time and thinking nothing at all of it.

Although Cancer Rising people can be difficult and demanding in close relationships, they are far more easygoing and tolerant with their friends. Their affectionate and caring ways usually guarantee them a staunch circle of good friends. They will never let a friend down if it is up to them. And they will forgive their friends any human frailties except disloyalty.

Cancer folk regard their friends as essential to their enjoyment of life. Although loners in many ways, they cannot stand to be prevented from circulating regularly among their many acquaintances.

Ties within the community are most important for Cancer Rising people. They like to number among their friends or acquaintances a few important people. The Cancer generosity is geared for public events, which they enjoy hosting. They enjoy sharing the customs and traditions that keep the community together.

It is the desire of Cancer Rising people to leave something lasting where they have been. They make very good members of clubs and societies. They endeavor to make a solid contribution that will be remembered by posterity.

TWELFTH HOUSE: SECRETS AND THE UNCONSCIOUS MIND

Cancer Ascendant people are frequently not very sure of themselves. They have far more faith in their feelings than in their intellectual ability. They are highly intuitive and not a little mistrustful of so-called facts.

In childhood there may have been the possibility that parents or teachers put a mistaken emphasis on learning, putting too much store in memorization or other mental tricks. This could make the Cancer Rising youngster seem a bit slow on the uptake. Both youngsters and adults are more suited to learn through feeling and experience. They also are best at expressing themselves in these ways.

Cancer Rising people are often moody. Whereas other types spend much of their time in their thoughts, Cancer people spend much of their time in their emotions. They are introspective and need time alone to try to work out some of the ideas that enter their heads.

Cancer folk have such vivid imaginations that they can create, at times, an inner world that competes with the real world for their attention.

Like all water signs, Cancer people are inclined to be secretive. This is because they are emotional creatures. They regard their feelings as something very private. They prefer to chat about their problems rather than analyze the causes of them. They often feel that deep down inside there are other parts of their personality they are never quite in touch with.

Some of the pressures from the unconscious mind of Sagittarius people relate to sex. As long as they do not dwell on the subject they have no difficulties, being fairly direct and straightforward in their lovemaking. Any tendency to brood about sex or become preoccupied with sex can trigger conflicts leading to excess or unnatural attempts at repression.

Your Rising Sign:
Leo on the Ascendant

L eo Rising beams the radiance and creativity of the Sun, as well as its power, centrality, and domination. Leo Rising people want love and pleasure, but they also need to rule. They want a mate and family, but they also must be alone with their hobbies. Will the Lion play or will the Lion stalk? What is the Lion's domain? Self-expression can be a dilemma for Leo Rising people, coloring how they experience the twelve life houses as described in the following sections.

FIRST HOUSE: PERSONALITY

People born with Leo on the Ascendant have a strong taste for leadership. There are powerful and intense personalities, with all the qualities that fit them for positions of authority.

The sign of Leo has always been associated with monarchs and rulers. In this liberated Aquarius Age, it is possible for Leo to overdo the power act and to alienate the admirers he or she is so intent on attracting.

Leos are theatrical. Showpeople at heart, they have a keen sense of the dramatic. They cannot help but imagine themselves always at the center of attention. In any kind of gathering, they endeavor to dominate the conversation, often becoming quite dogmatic and overbearing in the way they put their opinions across. Leo Ascendant people find it very difficult to concede that others may know as much as they do about one of their pet subjects.

People influenced by the sign of the Lion are extremely good organizers. They have a talent for directing others and for getting the very best out of them. They are often able to inspire their associates with their creative imaginations and their boundless enthusiasm. Leos are great optimists.

But they do have faults. If they are not receiving sufficient attention and admiration, they are inclined to demand it. They become noisy, sulky, or boisterous. Too much applause and acknowledgment often make them conceited and patronizing. The less evolved type of Lion is often snobbish, boastful, and pompous. They love to throw their weight around and to lord it over others.

Typical Leo Rising people have a strong sense of justice and great pride. They find it difficult to do anything underhanded. They are truly sincere people, but mainly they don't want their actions to reflect on their image. They like to think they are above the need to be shady or petty.

At their best, Leo-influenced individuals are generous, warm, and outgoing. They have a great capacity for attracting friendship, loyalty, and respect. Although they expect others continuously to praise their good points, they are always the first to admire and encourage the talents of others.

Leo Ascendant people are ambitious and usually seek a career in a field in which there is a chance for them to become a leader or public figure. They like to do things with a flourish.

SECOND HOUSE: MONEY AND POSSESSIONS

Money and possessions are things that Leo Ascendant people like to keep careful track of. In spite of their rather fancy and often extravagant lifestyle, they usually know where every penny is and exactly how liberal or generous they can be.

The typical Leo Rising person can often be a bit of a contradiction where money is concerned. They can argue and perform endlessly with dependents over the spending of a few pennies. Then they go and buy them a gift that costs the earth! Even then, Leos tend to spend their money only on those who have proved themselves to be loyal and appreciative of what they do.

However, money can be wasted or misspent on the hangers-on. Anyone who satisfies the strong Leo need for compliments and flattery has a good chance of cashing in.

Leo-influenced people are shrewd and discerning when it comes to buying property, or large resources. Although they are not great ones for attending to detail where their possessions are involved, they are seldom neglectful. They take good care of their investments. They see that insurance premiums are paid up and that property is kept in good repair.

Financial problems can affect the health of Leos. They are a fixed sign. As long as there is a chance of holding onto what they own, they will fight to the end without respite. They worry about money more than their confident natures will allow them to admit.

THIRD HOUSE: CLOSE CONTACTS AND COMMUNICATION

Leo Ascendant people are very persuasive. They exude a magnetism that at the physical level is difficult to ignore. When a Leo person walks into a room, everyone seems to know about it. Their vibes are intense and often provocative.

Leos are always trying to get others to agree with their ideas. They are the "professors" of the Zodiac, always trying to teach someone something. They often have deep insights. It pains them not to share this knowledge with their companions. To their companions, they can seem to be "know-it-alls." Leos have to learn that not everyone wants to know what is good for them.

The typical Leo Rising person can often become argumentative if his or her ideas are challenged. Although they will endeavor to be tactful and diplomatic, these devices are often cast aside at the first sign of opposition.

Leos usually have little difficulty in winning the sympathy of an audience, even if there is not unanimous agreement with the points that are being made. They seldom try to speak on any subject they do not believe in wholeheartedly. So their sincerity comes across.

Leos love to bring sunshine into other people's lives. They often are instruments for matchmaking. Love is so important to Leo people, they figure it must be equally important to others.

FOURTH HOUSE: HOME AND FAMILY

Home is the "King of the Jungle's" castle. Leo-influenced people are inclined to rule both home and family with a fairly strong hand. Although they are kind and considerate, they do not stand for any rebellious talk or action on the home front.

But the very dominating manner of Leo brews trouble on the home front, rather than quelling it. Leo people often have to contend with domestic difficulties. Their partners and dependents are seldom as submissive and obedient as the Leo nature expects.

People born under the influence of Leo are often not aware of their own faults. They think in a compartmentalized way, failing to recognize the contradictions in their own actions. Leos will insist on certain procedures in the home or in family affairs, and then fail to follow the guidelines. They offer a transparent excuse that they really believe to be true but that fools no one else.

Leos do not like family laundry washed in public. Their pride requires that skeletons be kept in the closet. They can be very secretive and hedgy about such matters.

Leo Rising people also tend to be quite proud of their roots and traditions. The family tree is immensely valuable if it contains important ancestors, scoundrels notwithstanding.

FIFTH HOUSE: ROMANCE, CREATIVITY, AND CHILDREN

Romance is Leo's sphere. Leo Ascendant people can be romantic about anything, given half a chance. They approach many of life's activities with the unspoiled pleasure of a child on a romp. Recreation, sports, theater, art, and of course love—these are the pleasure-filled niches for these romantic people.

Leos are inclined to gamble. If they don't gamble with their cash, they certainly gamble with their hearts. Leo Rising folk seldom do anything by halves. When they love, they go all the way.

When they fall in love, they fall hard. They put their sweethearts on pedestals, usually far above the limits to which human frailty can aspire. As a result, they are frequently disappointed and sometimes brokenhearted.

Leos have considerable creative talent. They are often good with words and can be writers and lecturers. Their enthusiasm for high ideals often inspires others to make creative efforts and to discover unsuspected or undeveloped talents in themselves. Being dramatic types, Leo men and women often make fine actors.

With children, Leo-influenced people endeavor to bring them up with a good knowledge of the ways of the world. Leos make very conscientious teachers. They can be fairly strict, but this is usually to instill some particular lesson in the child. They often can spoil their children, being far too generous when the times for giving come around.

SIXTH HOUSE: WORK AND HEALTH

Leo Rising people are very conscientious employees as long as they are doing the type of work that makes full use of their capacities. They have a strong sense of duty once they have taken on a task. Their natural pride will not allow them to do any less than their very best. To them, failure to deliver the goods is a self-inflicted insult.

They can often push themselves to the point where their health is affected. Although they usually have strong constitutions, they make heavy demands on themselves. However, Leos are quite health-conscious. They like to look after themselves and to keep fit.

Leo Ascendant people have a natural ability for leadership. They seldom stay on the same rung of the ladder for long. Although they are prepared to follow orders in which they believe, they are always moving toward the top. Higher-ups soon learn to trust them and to admire their way of organizing people and work.

Leos prefer to stay in one job or profession in which they can make a name for themselves. But they will make changes in direction if they find their way blocked. Their driving urge is to be able to express their sense of power and authority.

Their enterprising qualities and reliability seldom go unrecognized by people in charge.

SEVENTH HOUSE: ALLIANCE AND PARTNERSHIP

Leo Rising people do not find partnerships particularly easy, especially those of the love and marriage kind. Although they love to be with their partners, they cannot stand any interference with their independence. Partnership being a two-way affair, there are often domestic fireworks in the Lion's household.

One of the problems for Leo-influenced people in their close relationships is that they frequently choose partners who are as independent-minded as themselves. Even if they picked a more docile type, the Leo nature is to try to awaken the sense of independence in others. The more they succeed in doing this with their partner, the more they add to their own troubles.

Leos want their associates to be free but cannot stand rebellion against their edicts. This is a basic contradiction in the Leo nature. It affects their close relationships more adversely than business and social ones.

In business partnerships, Leo-Ascendant people are more down-to-earth. They are prepared to give and take more for the sake of the business. They can maintain a more detached attitude when their personal emotions are not involved.

Social and intellectual alliances can be a boon for Leos working on a project. An atmosphere of teamwork triggers original and progressive ideas for making money. They also prefer a mutual endeavor to have some sort of benefit for the community. In harness, they like the idea of serving a cause.

EIGHTH HOUSE: SEX, PSYCHOLOGY, AND SHARED ASSETS

Leo Rising people are inclined to be sensual. But their sexual relationships usually have a sense of the romantic about them. This romantic idealism can prevent Leo from surrendering to passionate lust.

They are prepared to make sacrifices as a rule for people with whom they have an intimate association. Their sense of responsibility and justice does not allow them to exploit others for long. There are, of course, the romantic scoundrels. But even they find their Don Juan ways unsatisfying after a while.

Leo-influenced individuals are inclined to use their many attributes to indulge their personal desires. They often live a very active social life. But to mature and reach the highest state of development the sign is capable of, they have to learn eventually to serve others in some selfless way.

Where partnership funds are concerned, Leo Ascendant people are inclined to run into difficulty. Other people may be to blame, through woolly-headed thinking or actions. Some confusion for Leos is never very far away when they have to combine their money or resources with others.

Legacies and inheritances may not come up to expectations. Or there may be misunderstandings due to the imprecise instructions of the person who made the bequest.

NINTH HOUSE: EDUCATION AND TRAVEL

The starting point of the Leo pattern of destiny is the desire for knowledge. Leo Rising people at every level of development are continuously endeavoring to broaden their minds. The less evolved Leo type cannot help showing off his or her knowledge and can be quite a bore. They are often boastful and conceited.

The more mature Lion or Lioness is a born teacher. They pursue the highest knowledge they are capable of absorbing. They spend their lives trying to impart it to others. People influenced by the Sun's own sign often feel they have a mission in life. This, of course, can lead to delusions of grandeur.

Leos are often natural philosophers. They are more interested in the inspiration behind the world's religions than in particular dogmas. They like to make up their own minds—and then to spread their own dogmas!

They have great faith in the future. They like to envision a worthwhile goal and then to stick to it. They know the importance of ideas as the fount of effective action.

The more serious-minded Leos regard travel as the best learning tool. Of course, the pursuit of pleasure is never entirely absent from the numerous trips and visits Leo people undertake. But long journeys to faraway places satisfy their craving for knowledge. And they prefer such travels to formal studies.

TENTH HOUSE: FAME AND AMBITION

Fame and ambition are very important to a person with a Leo Ascendant. It probably would be safe to say that in most cases such people would rather be famous than rich. They love the idea of being surrounded by applauding and admiring crowds.

Leo Rising people are prepared to work very hard to get to the top. Although they enjoy their leisure, they are ready to postpone recreation, even vacations, to satisfy their driving ambition. They will not give up once an objective is firmly fixed in their mind.

Leos take to power like ducks take to water. When recognition and fame do come to them, they are never in doubt that they deserved it. They have a natural ability for handling the public. They use their keen sense of the dramatic to obtain as much publicity as possible.

They enjoy the trappings and ceremonials of power and status. They are secretly offended if anyone fails to observe the formalities they think are due. They entertain in a regal manner. Queenly or kingly to all in their realm, their generosity is truly a magnificent thing.

The trouble with Leos is that they often continue to perform and to demand applause, even after the act is over. In retirement, forced or otherwise, they can be very disillusioned people. They find it very difficult to cope with the fickleness of the public when the tide has turned.

ELEVENTH HOUSE: FRIENDSHIP AND COMMUNITY

Leo Rising people are seldom short of friends. They have an easy way with people, which guarantees that wherever they go they make numerous new acquaintances. The Leo person likes engaging in conversation and trying to win others over to his or her ideas.

Leos are good listeners—as long as the talker is being informative. Otherwise they would prefer to do most of the talking. They believe that what they have to say is more important or entertaining. They cannot stomach bores and know-it-alls, often other Leos.

Leo Ascendant people often associate with the younger, intelligent crowd. They frequently make links with youth clubs. They like to have around them people who represent the thinking of the day. They are stimulated by discussions and debates, which give them the opportunity to display their knowledge and understanding of difficult subjects.

These people born under the influence of the Lion usually hold down prominent positions in clubs and groups. Here they are capable of a relatively impersonal attitude toward problems, projects, and progress. Their personal pride does not get in the way of promoting endeavors that have benefit for the community or society at large.

Leos are inclined to select their closest friends from among the people who support their humanitarian ideals. When and if they change these ideals, they usually change their friends.

TWELFTH HOUSE: SECRETS AND THE UNCONSCIOUS MIND

The greatest fear that a Leo Ascendant person can imagine is not to be loved or appreciated. It is the compelling desire for love and appreciation that makes Leos capable of giving up just about everything else. Their loved ones and admirers hardly expect this sacrifice.

Until he or she realizes some worthwhile purpose to their existence, the Leo person will tend to substitute daydreams. Their vivid imaginations can place them in positions of authority where, in exchange for loyalty and obedience, they take on the problems of the world.

Leo Rising people are more easily slighted than their self-assurance would suggest. Although they are forward-looking characters, they can be inclined to brood about incidents in which people have not shown them sufficient appreciation or respect.

Leos often give out vibrations that make them unapproachable. Their expectations of special treatment often come across to others as pomposity and pretentiousness.

Leo Ascendant people can become sulky and disagreeable if they feel they are being neglected—which is fairly often. Their demands for equal time and treatment in the spheres of love and appreciation are impossible for most people to fulfill.

Your Rising Sign:
Virgo on the Ascendant

Virgo Rising signifies "worldliness." The symbol of Virgo is the Virgin, or Maiden. This ancient designation is not synonymous with chastity. The Virgin is the woman, fertile and productive, the only zodiacal sign that is a human female. Virgo is an earth sign; Mercury, her ruling planet, is the planet of mind and communication. Worldliness means instruction in such vital matters as inheritance and progress. The process is personal. Virgo Rising people, rooted in their own minds and bodies, are the guardians and teachers of other people. The identification of Virgo Rising people with productivity and well-being—work and health—affect their experiences in the twelve life houses as described below.

FIRST HOUSE: PERSONALITY

Virgo Rising people are active, practical, and sharp. Work is their context, service their aim. They appear to be unemotional, impersonal, and detached, as though their efforts were obligatory. But these people are totally absorbed in their projects. Their sense of self comes from the involvement, the more complex and the more intellectual the better.

Nevertheless, Virgo Ascendant people appear to be unassuming. They are not ones to put on airs and graces, or to go on ego trips. They just like to do the job to the very best of their considerable ability, and without drawing much attention to themselves. For them, work is natural and work is cyclical. It goes on without rules being imposed or rewards offered.

But it must go on, especially when there is stress. So Virgo Rising people are the great teachers, mediating what is natural and what is imposed. And they are critical teachers, sparing neither feeling nor defense. They often upset their associates by pointing out their faults and failings. The fact that their criticisms are usually right on the mark does not help, either.

192

Virgo Rising people have a fine analytical talent. In fact, they enjoy analyzing things. Confronted with a great mass of complicated detail, they coolly and methodically translate it into a straightforward and intelligible pattern.

They also enjoy analyzing people. Their sharp logic enables them to define other people's weaknesses. And their sharp tongues express such weaknesses succinctly.

Virgo people have strong intellects. They are fond of art, literature, science, and mathematics. They have very good memories but are not particularly original, despite their strong reasoning powers. They are better at getting things in order, especially the messes left behind by muddled and confused minds.

These people influenced by the sign of the Virgin can be prudish. They tend to follow the letter of the law rather than the spirit of it. They have a good respect for authority. They would rather trust to precedent than break new ground reaching decisions.

Virgo-influenced people are often health faddists. They are particularly careful about following a healthful and balanced diet. Of course, their quirks in this regard can make them go to unbalanced extremes. The results often surface in unusual ailments.

Virgos are the hypochondriacs of the Zodiac. They are also worrywarts and fussbudgets. They focus intensely on their health and personal well-being. No ailment, real or imagined, is too slight to arouse their anxiety and care.

Down-to-earth Virgo types like to maintain a low profile. They often immerse themselves in their work, not worrying unduly about promotion or pay raises. They often hide their light under a bushel. They can become too subservient. They would rather persevere in a dead-end job on many occasions than face the disturbance of moving on.

Virgo Ascendant people do not like changes. They tend to be old-fashioned. They have a passion for orderliness and neatness. These qualities help to make them careful and conservative administrators.

SECOND HOUSE: MONEY AND POSSESSIONS

Virgo Ascendant people seldom live beyond their means. They like to budget their monthly income and stick to it. They are good savers, mainly because they follow the method of putting a fixed sum away out of each paycheck.

But Virgo-influenced people do have their extravagant and expansive moments. They like to spend their money on finely made objects. They are often collectors of works of art, musical instruments, manuscripts, and old books. They do not like cheap and shoddy articles.

Virgos are not spendthrifts as a rule. They are shrewd shoppers, cautious consumers. They believe in getting their money's worth as well as getting an attractive item. They also have an idea about resale if that should ever be necessary. They are no fools.

People born with a Virgo Ascendant are security-conscious. They like to be prepared for the proverbial rainy day. Fussy and conservative, they manage their money well.

They are extremely good at handling other people's money or possessions. They make fine brokers, accountants, managers, and auctioneers. With their methodical and meticulous minds, they know where every penny is.

But Virgo Rising people often have their well-laid financial plans upset and even ruined by their partners or associates. Virgo Rising people are often the victims of extravagance by others.

THIRD HOUSE: CLOSE CONTACTS AND COMMUNICATION

Because of their mercurial nature, Virgo Ascendant people enjoy a variety of contacts. They like the changing scene—as long as it is not personally unsettling. They are the type of individuals who like to stand unobtrusively on the sidewalk and observe the rest of the world go by.

Virgo Rising people tend to be shy in groups and with new acquaintances. They do not like to intrude until they are very sure of their ground. Then they come out with shrewd but extremely critical remarks about what they have seen in situations and in people.

Virgos maintain fixed opinions. They believe in order. They are looking for perfection in the world around them. Anything they see out of place irritates them. They can be blunt in their attempts to weed out the faults in other people. But they often fail to see their own imperfections.

People with a Virgo Ascendant have a natural flair for writing, especially the analytical variety. However, they are not especially communicative when it comes to their personal affairs. They would rather deal with others than have the spotlight put on thmselves.

Virgos are among the most logical characters in the Zodiac. They can be relied on to stick to the facts and to adhere to traditional systems. They are easy people to educate.

FOURTH HOUSE: HOME AND FAMILY

The home is one place where the Virgo Ascendant person feels confident to insist on establishing rules and order. With family members, the usually modest and unassuming Virgo can become something of an authoritarian. The object is not to impose a rule of power on the household, but one in which neatness or tidiness dictates the state of things.

Their homes are frequently larger or more spacious than their needs require. They do not like to feel hemmed in, especially if there are more than two people in the household. Virgo, the hypochondriac, tends to be claustrophobic.

There are some Virgo Rising types who can be surprisingly untidy, even sloppy, around the house. Much will depend on the positions of the planets other than the Sun. In these cases, domestic disorder is ignored.

The emphasis is placed on mental order. There can be a wearying insistence on logic and rational method.

Virgos have a strong belief in the power of the home and family to keep society morally intact. They are inclined to be very critical of any doctrine, or person, who opposes this belief.

These people like the idea of traveling to broaden their minds. Short trips and visits have a magical appeal. But Virgos often feel restless and at loose ends when far away from home.

FIFTH HOUSE: ROMANCE, CREATIVITY, AND CHILDREN

Virgo Ascendant people are rarely able to let themselves go in pleasurable or romantic situations. They often have the reputation for being a bit staid and straight-laced. They are people who enjoy themselves most by being part of the scene, rather than at the immediate center of it. They are self-conscious.

The Virgo-influenced woman finds it difficult to be unrestrained in romance, especially lovemaking. She needs a very understanding and patient lover to make her gradually abandon her preconceptions about sex. Once this is done, she can be free. The Virgo male is more sex-oriented because he is driven to prove his masculinity.

Virgo Rising people have a great talent for devising methods. They are often able to introduce new methods into areas of art that artists themselves are incapable of. Virgo Rising people have computerlike minds. They often have a talent for music. And their sharp minds and sharp tongue make them splendid critical writers or satirists.

Virgos as a rule prefer not to have large families. They are cautious types who do not like to take on more than they can afford. They are factual and straight with children. But they do have to be careful not to neglect children's emotional needs. It is hard for Virgos to give love and affection. They are not usually the types who go in much for physical displays.

SIXTH HOUSE: WORK AND HEALTH

Virgo Ascendant people are happiest when working as part of a team. They are extremely cooperative and very considerate toward the people they work with. They like to be appreciated. But they are rarely guilty of putting on temperamental scenes. They like to do a good job and to keep personality problems out of it.

These people influenced by the sign of the Virgin are conscientious and dependable employees. They would prefer to work under someone and with instructions. Being a boss frightens them. But they do make capable administrators; they have an extraordinary ability to cope with details and to create systems. They are not the types to lose their heads in an emergency.

Virgo-influenced people are often employed in scientific and industrial laboratories. Their ideas about food and hygiene can be innovative. They are especially good at setting up production lines and devising methods for dealing with delays and logjams.

Virgo is the sign of health. People with Virgo Rising are health-conscious to an extreme. They may not be the best at getting regular exercise, but they do try to keep fit and trim through a sensible diet. They have to avoid excessive worry, which can upset their nervous system as well as lead them into spurious health fads.

SEVENTH HOUSE: ALLIANCE AND PARTNERSHIP

Virgo Ascendant people often turn out to be the long-suffering partner in love and marriage relationships. Once they commit themselves to a partnership, they will do all in their power to make it work. They are the types who will constantly forgive and forget in their efforts to discover a perfect harmony.

These people seldom walk out until all else has been tried and has failed. Their kind and considerate natures can be exploited if they are unlucky in picking a partner. They need a sympathetic mate who can appreciate their finer points.

Virgo-influenced people are easily upset by conflict in love. They do not like wrangling and arguing. They would rather give in to the partner than try to live in a depressing or unharmonious atmosphere. They will make considerable sacrifices to keep a marriage together.

It is not difficult for Virgo people to remain single. Unsatisfactory experiences early in life can put them off forever. Or they will wait for the right person to come along, without making any aggressive effort to find that person. Sometimes they appear to be unpopular or left on the shelf. But Virgo people are not short of admirers. Any decision not to marry is a considered one.

In social and business alliances, people with Virgo Rising take conflict situations more in their stride. Their caustic wit and acid tongue often provoke clashes with their partners. Virgos enjoy the ensuing debate or argument, for in the long run it improves the relationship.

EIGHTH HOUSE: SEX, PSYCHOLOGY, AND SHARED ASSETS

The Virgo reputation for chastity is farfetched. Virgo Ascendant people enjoy sex as much as any other sign. But because of their self-consciousness, they are slow to get started. And their desire for inner purity often clashes with their ideas of sex. However, Virgo-influenced people think a great deal more about sex than would seem. Often their sexual complexes are expressed in indirect ways.

The Virgo nature personifies the desire to be rid of everything less than perfect. As this is impossible, these are usually highly strung, nervous people. They tend to know what they don't like very definitely and to be outspoken about it.

But what they want out of life, they are not so sure of.

Virgo Rising people are considerate and conservative when it comes to assets or resources shared with a partner. They can be depended on to treat as carefully as their own anything left in their care. They are impelled by an urge to achieve maximum efficiency. They will never allow their own personal interests to interfere with a shared asset.

Virgo-influenced people like to take control of joint finances and possessions. They endeavor to turn them into something better. They have a way of getting rid of unnecessary expenditures and poor investments. They make very good accountants and financial advisers.

NINTH HOUSE: EDUCATION AND TRAVEL

In their search for knowledge, Virgo Ascendant people prefer to stick to tried and trusted ways. They do not have much faith in speculation and experimentation. As a rule, they are more likely to support an established religion or philosophic method. Virgo-influenced people are often the staunchest members of the local church.

The Virgo nature does not like any idea that does not have a practical value. These people will translate lofty teachings into down-to-earth ethics. They truly believe that brotherhood and sisterhood will bring peace and harmony into the world. They probably could not accept a philosophic code that has no concrete application.

Virgo Rising people can be dedicated teachers. They know the value of a higher education. They have a great deal of patience and understanding with slower-thinking people. They like people to have an appreciation of the artistic side of life. They often spend their time writing and simplifying for popular consumption lesser-known aspects of music, painting, poetry, and classical literary works.

Virgo-influenced people usually travel for a purpose rather than for pure sightseeing or pleasure. Curious about other customs and systems of belief, Virgos will take long journeys to observe, compare, and classify people of other cultures.

TENTH HOUSE: FAME AND AMBITION

Virgo Ascendant people often appear to have very little ambition. They may seem content to accept what comes. They appear to make the best of their lot without going out of their way to push their interests.

Virgo Rising people often become famous, just as often as people of other signs. Their modest and unassuming ways have a great appeal, especially to the dynamic folk who try to run this world. But Virgos seldom allow fame and position to go to their head.

Virgo Rising people are intelligent and shrewd. They do not complain about hard work. They are practical and love solving problems. They are great with detail, which usually drives others up the wall. To employ a Virgo is often the answer to the harassed boss's prayer.

Virgo-influenced people have no difficulty doing two jobs or handling several things at once. In fact, they enjoy a variety of small challenges in whatever work they do. They become completely absorbed. If they are happy, money becomes a secondary consideration.

Virgos do not have many enemies. They are likable people who never give the impression that they are after another person's job. Sometimes when rivals are angling for senior positions, the unassuming Virgo is promoted over them as the reasonable compromise choice.

ELEVENTH HOUSE: FRIENDSHIP AND COMMUNITY

Friends are very important to Virgo Ascendant people. They like to gather around them a select circle of companions who appreciate them for themselves and who do not resent their tendency to be critical. Virgo-influenced people and their friends both know that no offense is meant.

Virgo people's friends usually are the quiet and sensitive types. But Virgo does enjoy occasional outings with boisterous acquaintances, observing their antics from the sidelines. Virgos are always interested in how other people behave.

Virgo-influenced people like to entertain their friends at home. They enjoy the intimacy of a small dinner party, and will go to a great deal of trouble cooking and presenting the meal in an artistic way. They love to talk about the past with their closest friends. In familiar company they are often good storytellers.

Virgo Rising people take close friends to their bosom. They enjoy fussing around any pal who is in trouble, endeavoring to make things as easy as they can. They try to provide a nurturing environment for anyone hurt or ailing.

They also are inclined to join or support groups whose aim is improving the lot of less fortunate people. Virgos can be active animal lovers and frequently possess pets of their own.

TWELFTH HOUSE: SECRETS AND THE UNCONSCIOUS MIND

Virgo Rising people love secrets. They keep their own secrets well hidden. But they like to unearth other people's motives and compulsions. They make a mystery out of it. Prodding and prying, detecting and solving give Virgos an enormous sense of glee.

Virgo Ascendant people have a tendency for self-sacrifice. It may appear quite normal to them. It lies behind their ability to perform work that other people might consider boring or beneath them.

Virgo-influenced people have a most admirable modesty. It often expresses itself in doing the dirty work of society, such as cleaning up after others. They make first-class nurses and institution workers. They care for the sick and weak uncomplainingly.

These people influenced by the sign of the Virgin draw their strength from within. They are not dependent, like many others are, on outside recognition of their accomplishments. They do what they do because to them it is worth doing. Sometimes Virgos feel more inwardly fulfilled and satisfied if they exert themselves on behalf of others.

These are people who often rule behind the scenes. They possess a quiet sense of dignity. It soon communicates itself to anyone who tries to impose on them or take them too much for granted.

Your Rising Sign:
Libra on the Ascendant

Individuals born with Libra Rising are people-oriented. Sharing activities with date or mate, lover or spouse, partner or ally makes life more interesting. Venus, the planet that rules Libra, is the planet of love. Libra, being an air sign, does not foster possessive love. Libra's affections are breezy, and Libra Ascendant individuals like to circulate. But they always seek some kind of personal relationship. Their need for relatedness colors how they experience the twelve life houses, as described below.

FIRST HOUSE: PERSONALITY

People born with Libra on the Ascendant are constantly striving for harmony and balance. Like the Scales, their symbol, they seek equilibrium, poise. These people try to avoid any kind of conflict or disagreement. But when they are pushed to an extreme, they will take a stand.

If their basic beliefs are at stake, they can hit out as hard and effectively as anyone. Usually, however, they do all they can to bring about compromise. If they cannot mediate an argument, they tend to disappear from the scene. They flee to peaceful surroundings.

Libras are basically mental creatures. They have to be surrounded by people who interest them. Once a person has been understood by a Libra, there may be little mystery or originality remaining. If they are not constantly amused, Libras tend to lose interest. They usually have many friends, but not of the intimate type. They are inclined to go from one friend to another, sometimes neglecting old friends for a newly discovered one.

It is not that Libra Rising people are disloyal or would abandon any of their friends who are in trouble. On the contrary, they are very sympathetic and understanding people. But it has to be remembered that Libra is the sign of partnership. Relating to others is their basic impulse. They need to spread themselves around as much as possible.

Libra Ascendant people usually are physically attractive. If they are not beautiful or handsome, their skin, hair, and bodies usually have an indefinable attractive quality. They tend to be vain about their appearance. Their friendliness, charm, and dislike of conflict make them popular.

In social situations the Libra personality reaches its glittering best. These people are natural hosts and hostesses. They do not consider expense when they are entertaining, either at home or in restaurants. They select the best places and food, often being prepared to run themselves into temporary debt to make an occasion just right.

Libra-influenced people sometimes are unable to face up to their difficulties. Their love of harmony makes them put off disagreeable tasks. Their dislike of conflict tends to make them postpone decisions. They would prefer to wait for something to happen to provide an alternative.

Libras have the reputation for being lazy. It is more that they refuse to do what their hearts are not in. Because they are people who are attracted mainly to beautiful things and pleasant activities, there is much in this world that they tend to shy away from and to neglect.

SECOND HOUSE: MONEY AND POSSESSIONS

Libra Ascendant people tend to have a basic contradiction in their personality where money is concerned. Their strongest impulse is to spend their money on beautiful things. They tend to select the most expensive of objects, being shrewdly aware that as a rule you get the quality you pay for. But deep down, they tend to worry about financial insecurity. Though aware of their extravagances, these trouble-hating people seem unable to compromise their taste for luxury.

Libra-influenced people seldom manage to avoid financial problems for long. They are extremely generous with gifts, often going beyond the bounds of good sense. In addition to the lavishness of the gifts, they often hand them out to people who are mere acquaintances and who have no particular connection to justify such generosity.

The Libra influence also makes a person enjoy the good life. They like fine food, flashy cars, rich clothing, and posh accommodations. They often cannot earn enough to support their taste for exotic things. Characteristically, they depend on a partner or lover to help pay their way.

Libra Rising people are successful with property investments. Their shrewd business minds are capable of seeing the resale value in land and other products of the earth, especially finely crafted pieces of furniture, jewelry, fabric, and metal. Libras tend to buy art objects and other valuable things for trade purposes rather than for lifelong possessions.

THIRD HOUSE: CLOSE CONTACTS AND COMMUNICATION

Close contacts and communications keep the Libra Ascendant person very active mentally. They love to be in touch with one segment of their considerable circle of friends and acquaintances, then to move on to a new segment. In this way they obtain the variety and change that are so necessary to their feeling of well-being.

Libra Rising people also like to communicate with their relatives and to visit them from time to time. They usually leave a longish interval between calls to particular relatives, so that the contact is stimulating and informative. They do not stay long in any one place. Daily routine easily bores Libra.

Libra-influenced people love to travel long distances, especially to other countries. They often write books or keep diaries about their travels. They are not the type to journey without due attention to maps, food and hotel guides, and information on local beauty spots and interesting things to see.

Libras are talkative but also good listeners. They make many casual contacts wherever they go, some of whom become firm friends. They often have numerous pen pals. Libras prefer letter writing to phone calls as a means of communication, because it is more formal and doesn't put them on the spot to make quick decisions.

These people have good judgment. Sometimes, though, they weigh things in the balance so long that they become indecisive. Easily distracted by petty details, they have to work hard at keeping their mind focused on the task at hand.

FOURTH HOUSE: HOME AND FAMILY

Home and family affairs are extremely important to Libra Ascendant people. Although they appear to be easygoing and even a bit flighty in other matters, they have a no-nonsense attitude about family life. Here they are very much down-to-earth. Their sense of luxury is tempered by an uncharacteristic thriftiness.

Libras organize their households to operate efficiently. They take responsibility to see that the home is well equipped with the latest gadgets and labor-saving appliances. Although they probably work harder in their homes than anywhere else, they always have an eye for anything that will save them time and effort.

Libra-influenced people are neat and tidy. They regard their homes as a reflection of themselves. They would hate to be criticized for the way they run or furnish their homes. In keeping with the Libra fondness for being surrounded by beautiful things, they do all they can to make their homes attractive and comfortable.

Libras like to be proud of their families and will work conscientiously to win their respect. Their keen sense of fair play enables Libra folk to see all sides of a family dispute. Playing the role of referee or peacemaker, they manage to keep family squabbles to a minimum.

Libra Rising people regard the home and family as the cornerstone of a successful society. They believe that justice and fairness on the home front help family members see the wisdom in the law and order of the larger society, as well as help them to enjoy a better life.

FIFTH HOUSE: ROMANCE, CREATIVITY, AND CHILDREN

In romantic affairs, Libra Ascendant people do not easily fall in love. They love the game of love but do their best to keep their emotional distance. Even so, they frequently underestimate the degree of involvement that others are capable of. So they tend to get embroiled in complicated situations. They are quite capable of walking away from a situation once it becomes too demanding.

Libra-influenced people often fall in love with an idea, and then attach that idealism to a person. However, they usually choose attractive or socially desirable people as their romantic companions.

Libra Rising people have a talent for combining mind with beauty. They are especially gifted for bringing social improvements into community life. Libras have been responsible for making many towns and cities more harmonious and attractive through their efforts in local government.

Libras are very good with children. They have a natural way of winning their confidence and respect. They are neither too strict nor too easygoing. Children regard them more like friends and learn quickly under their instruction. Libras have a happy knack of being able to treat all children the same; their own do not receive special treatment. They make very good elementary school teachers.

SIXTH HOUSE: WORK AND HEALTH

Libra Ascendant people are not enthusiastic about hard physical work. They lack the necessary stamina and will. They need an occupation that stimulates their mind and interest. They do not like to remain in one place for too long. They get bored in mind and body very easily.

Libras have a way of getting others to do the more strenuous and monotonous work for them. They are quite prepared to do nothing or make no move in a situation that cries for volunteers. They rely on tactful and cooperative noises as a smoke screen. They do not like making commitments that might tie them down for long.

Libra Rising people are very good at maneuvering behind the scenes. They are first-rate diplomats, able to convey disagreeable information in the nicest of forms. Often they are accused of being connivers. But it is just the situation Libras want to manipulate, not the people; for in a harmonious environment, Libras believe that all sides can come to a compromise.

They work best in occupations that allow them to express their strong sense of social duty. Any job that taps their arbitrating and peacemaking skills suits them very well. They also gravitate toward artistic fields that enable them to blend color, line, and texture in harmonious patterns.

Libras worry a great deal about failure. That fear affects their performance. They are not the type of people to take chances; they tend to swing back and forth in a debate. They stay alert for the first sign of a winner, to whom they can give their support.

Libras often suffer from health problems that are difficult to diagnose. They can worry about their health and yet do nothing about it. The twin fears of conflict and of failure make them prone to psychosomatic ailments affecting the nervous system. Their obsession with appearance lures them into diet, exercise, and beauty fads.

SEVENTH HOUSE: ALLIANCE AND PARTNERSHIP

Partnerships are the most important thing in the life of the typical Libra Ascendant person. These people are happiest and most efficient when living and working in a close relationship. They have a gift for getting along with others, more so than probably any other sign in the Zodiac.

Libras are prepared to accept other people as they find them. This takes a lot of the tension out of a partnership. Although they may recognize the slightest failing in their partner, they are not the kind to argue about it. They look for peace and quiet in their close relationships. Anyone looking for heightened emotional responses or kicks would have to look elsewhere than at Libra.

However, Libras also have a way of provoking aggressiveness in others. When they do, they are not the type to sit back and take it. They have an unexpected fiery streak. They will allow no one to impose on their rights without their permission. Nor will they allow others to undermine the rights of people with whom they feel identified.

Libra-influenced people receive pleasure out of bringing together potential romantic partners. They often arrange to have unattached men and women at their social functions in order to couple them off.

Social, intellectual, and professional alliances are lifelines for the typical Libra Rising person. He or she works splendidly in tandem on a job. Projects are always more interesting if they are mutual endeavors. The chitchat and back-and-forth relieve the boredom of routine that Libra people so abhor.

EIGHTH HOUSE: SEX, PSYCHOLOGY, AND SHARED ASSETS

Libra Ascendant people are romantics at heart. But where sex is involved, they can be detached enough to be mercenary. Sex, for many of these people, is a function of their security. And security is always measured in material terms. Libras can flirt, often meaninglessly. But they won't commit themselves unless the affair heightens their social or professional prestige.

Libras are not shy once past the flirting or courting stages. Even though they are matter-of-fact in bed, there is always the Libra vanity to contend with. Suitors get much father with a Libra Rising person if they remember to flatter him or her, and bring plenty of expensive presents to arouse Libra's desire for lovemaking.

Libras are often lucky. They tend to attract good things and good people consistently. What they gain through their relationships is often more than they earn through solitary efforts and endeavors.

Although their lives are seldom without financial strains and crises, they have a way—especially when the chips are down—of turning troubles to profit. They frequently manage this through partnership. They sometimes marry into money. And their financial problems are more than occasionally solved through legacies, insurance policies, the stock market, and business transactions.

Libras are usually financially successful in partnership. They have good business heads when they apply themselves. They have a knack for spotting lucrative investments. They often make successful husband and wife teams in business.

Libra Ascendant people have to feel they are responsible for joint funds or resources. If not, they can easily become extravagant and cause their partner considerable worry and anxiety. They are usually quite prepared to take the easy way out if the other person is foolish enough not to involve them.

NINTH HOUSE: EDUCATION AND TRAVEL

Libra Ascendant people are constantly endeavoring to broaden their minds. They love to meet people from all walks of life, to listen to their problems, and to exchange ideas. It is essential that they try to find a consistent philosophy for life. Until they do, they are always in danger of flitting from one belief to another.

They can easily become dabblers in religious and philosophic subjects. They have an ability for expressing the most abstract ideas in down-to-earth terms. But much of their outlook is based on pure reason and logic; the emotional and experiential sides may be neglected.

Libra Rising people enjoy any kind of travel, from short trips to world journeys. They often regard the world as their university, and the people in it as their teachers. Even when tied to the home by a family, they always manage to get out and about and to meet interesting people.

People influenced by the sign of the Scales are usually avid readers, especially if they cannot travel. Being mental types, they easily enter the world of adventure through the written word. And not being particularly energetic individuals, unless an exciting journey lures them, they often are happy to settle down with a good book and travel in their minds.

TENTH HOUSE: FAME AND AMBITION

Any success in the world that Libra Rising people have is reflected in their home. The home is a status symbol to them. They aim with all their heart and soul to make it as attractive, comfortable, and luxurious as possible.

Libras feel deeply about their careers. They are ambitious but choosy about the kind of work they are prepared to do. They like to feel respected and appreciated; they would rather do nothing than a job that others might regard as inferior.

Many people born with the sign of the Scales as their Ascendant make a name for themselves by catering to the public taste. They often own or manage good restaurants, beauty establishments, interior decorating concerns, and motels or hotels. They have a superb way of making people feel at home and at ease.

Their professional lives frequently have ups and downs. Depending on their moods, they make hasty changes, which may not always be well advised. Sometimes Libras will quit a career for solitary pursuits. This may be a mistake, because these people need to work with others in a harmonious environment.

Libra Ascendant people often work from home. If not, they rearrange their work space to suit their own concepts of harmony and design. They are not trendy, relying more on traditional schemes of color and line balance. A Libra's cubicle, shop, or office is a pleasant and inviting niche.

ELEVENTH HOUSE: FRIENDSHIP AND COMMUNITY

Libra Rising people love to mix with famous and socially prominent people. They are at ease in any company and have no trouble taking their place among celebrities. They are flattered to number such people among their friends.

Venus-ruled Libra has a weakness for beautiful people and beautiful things. But Libras do not always look deep enough below the surface when selecting their companions. They often go by appearances—and are then let down. But they have a natural ability to attract others, which means that they seldom are lonely.

People born under the influence of Libra know how to give their friends the royal treatment. They are generous and charming hosts and hostesses. They know just the right thing to say. They have a gift for avoiding controversial subjects if people of opposing beliefs are present.

Although they are not disloyal to their friends, they do tend to blow hot and cold. All over their friends one day and seemingly disinterested the next, Libras expose this unbalanced and contradictory side of their nature. It is maddening to their friends.

Libras like to be members of clubs and societies where their particular enthusiasms can be expressed. They are interested as a rule in humanitarian and cultural projects that propose justice for all. Libras can be equally active in establishing the rules of fair play and in organizing the social functions of such groups.

TWELFTH HOUSE: SECRETS AND THE UNCONSCIOUS MIND

A secret about themselves that few Libra Ascendant people are aware of is that they are constantly trying to suppress an unconscious urge to criticize others. For a sign that is said to epitomize the desire for peace and harmony, this is a very disturbing state of affairs. This urge drains some of

Libra's vital forces. It also explains why Libras sometimes feel inexplicably lethargic, and why to others they may even appear to be lazy.

Libras spend a lot more time in front of the mirror than many other signs do. Although they seldom are guilty of displaying vanity in egotistical ways, they are inclined to work hard at keeping up an elegant appearance. Their sense of style in costuming is highly developed.

Although Libra people usually are among the most naturally attractive types in the Zodiac, they find it difficult not to find fault with their own looks. They often resort to cosmetics and artificial devices to cover up what is more likely to be a form of neurosis than a noticeable defect.

In spite of their easygoing appearance, Libra-influenced people are worriers underneath. They feel obliged to make every effort to keep the peace, even when there is no need. Carried to extremes, this compulsion can make them appear gushing and insincere.

Your Rising Sign:
Scorpio on the Ascendant

Scorpio Rising is a powerhouse placement. The planetary rulers of Scorpio, Mars for force and action, Pluto for control and spirituality, pack plenty of punch. Scorpio Rising individuals can go to extremes. The stinging venom of the Scorpion, symbol of Scorpio, can be destructive as well as protective. Scorpio Rising individuals are deeply involved with the great psychosexual mysteries of life. They are always seeking to understand their own sexual natures and their own psyches, and to transform their everyday reality through such understanding. This search affects how individuals with Scorpio on the Ascendant experience the twelve life houses as described below.

FIRST HOUSE: PERSONALITY

People born with Scorpio on the Ascendant are proud and temperamental. They do not like others to know what they are doing. They are secretive. They feel quite capable of handling their own affairs without help from others. They certainly expect their associates to respect their privacy. They can be cutting and hurtful to anyone they suspect of being personally curious or too friendly.

Scorpio Rising people are often a riddle, not only to others but also to themselves. They are constantly endeavoring to discover the secrets of their own nature. But no one else should pry. They maintain privacy by repressing any emotional displays that would betray them to others.

There is always a danger of Scorpio Ascendant people exploding into an emotional rage. Their self-repression can get too much for them. They need to be handled tactfully and carefully. They are the types to remember insults and slights for a long time—as long as it takes to get revenge.

These people possess great powers of leadership if they are sure of themselves. They are extremely good in situations posing danger. They have steady nerves and steel-trap minds. They can keep their cool and operate efficiently while others around them are in a panic. They are great people to have around in an emergency.

Scorpio-influenced people are often aloof. They do not make close friends easily. And they keep gregarious types at bay. People have to prove their worth in one way or another before Scorpio will allow them into their private world.

These people can be blunt to the point of cruelty. They are especially intolerant of anyone who starts fishing for compliments. Scorpios like to tell the truth. They are not always so talented at seeing their own faults, but they certainly have a way of summing others' up. They are especially good at spotting other people's weaknesses. And if they are in any way competing with them, they play on these weaknesses.

Scorpios have tremendous endurance. Once they fix their mind on an objective, they will work toward it until it is achieved. Time means nothing to them. They also are able to withstand any physical discomfort inherent in the pursuit of their aims. They are intensely ambitious, determined to make a name for themselves in whatever they do.

SECOND HOUSE: MONEY AND POSSESSIONS

Money and possessions are vital to Scorpio Ascendant people. They have been called greedy. But the intrinsic value of things is not as important as the feeling of abundance. Scorpios need to have a sense of plenty around them. And they are prepared to work extremely hard for it.

Scorpio-influenced people are enterprising and shrewd. Their judgment in business and money matters is first-rate. Although their natural astuteness usually ensures that they have an adequate cash flow, they tend to work toward long-term profits. They have an ability to look ahead and imagine conditions in the distant future, then make their day-to-day moves accordingly.

Scorpio Rising people, however, can sometimes be so engrossed in looking to the future that they fail to note current changes and trends. Once they get an idea fixed in their head, it is difficult for them to see any other point of view.

If Scorpios ever do become wealthy, they like to surround themselves with items of value. They can buy enormously expensive works of art, even though their aesthetic appreciation may not be strong.

Scorpio Rising people have a compulsive desire for power. Often they command obedience from others through intimidation. They are not above trying to instill fear in people, especially if they possess the financial muscle to back up their threats.

THIRD HOUSE: CLOSE CONTACTS AND COMMUNICATION

Scorpio Ascendant people play their cards close to the chest. They are not among the most spontaneous or communicative of people. They are at their best, down-to-earth. They express ideas in a purposeful, practical, and economical way. They are most reticent, though, when they have serious business matters on their mind.

However, there is another side to them that their closest companions will recognize. At times, Scorpio-influenced people are extremely talkative. It is often necessary for them to talk out their emotional hangups. Doing so prevents a buildup that would otherwise end in an outburst of rage.

Scorpios honor close contacts within the traditional family unit. They tend to be more respectful of relatives, especially older ones, than of their acquaintances or daily associates. In fact, Scorpios frequently complain to their nearest and dearest about the attitudes and shortcomings of the people who stand in the way of their ambitions.

Scorpio Rising people think nothing of taking weekends off to visit relatives and family friends out of town. They also like solitary trips for the purpose of communing with nature, or possibly communing with a lover whose whereabouts, even existence, is kept secret. Scorpios love to make a mystery out of their contacts, viewing them as much as conquests as routine interactions between people who know each other.

FOURTH HOUSE: HOME AND FAMILY

Scorpio Ascendant people often have odd ideas about how to run their homes and bring up their families. In this area they often display an originality that may not be appreciated by those around them. They can even be ahead of their times. Their innovations, which initially cause raised eyebrows or even domestic rebellions, may one day be adopted by society as the latest thing.

Scorpio Rising people can often appear to run their households with a severe hand. But mature Scorpios know the meaning and importance of discipline in helping to forge character. They try to teach family members a sense of freedom by insisting that each one accept responsibilities for his or her own lives and actions.

People born under the influence of the Scorpion often have to contend with radical changes in their home and family affairs. Unforeseen events can change their place or mode of living overnight. Often these changes are associated with their deeper emotional needs.

Although Scorpios maintain stubbornly fixed ideas as a rule, they do have an extraordinary way of suddenly throwing off their old beliefs for a new truth. Change and renewal are basic to the Scorpio nature. So these people find no contradiction in adopting a new doctrine, especially because they embrace it with characteristic zeal and fanaticism.

FIFTH HOUSE: ROMANCE, CREATIVITY, AND CHILDREN

Romance is something that a Scorpio Ascendant person can enjoy as much as anyone. Romance, though, is usually secondary to the need for intimacy. These people are seriously concerned with what is at the bottom of the attraction between male and female, not the surface effects.

Scorpios need to experience intimacy in its deepest emotional contexts. And as often as they can! Their search for intimacy leads them from experimentation to commitment. The search has also given Scorpio a reputation for sexual excesses.

These people often get involved in secret love affairs. They have a love of danger that is almost suicidal as far as their emotions are concerned. They tend to push events beyond limits, seeming to court disaster in an effort to experience heightened sensations. They are fearless people. They will court disaster to plumb emotion.

Scorpio Rising people are talented in the arts. They bring artistic expression down to earth. They are frequently connected with the entertainment industry because of their love of dramatic effects, as well as their ability to create such effects.

They are often surprisingly compassionate, and may spontaneously give away large sums of money or make other sacrifices when faced with the suffering of others. Scorpios' creative drive is linked with their compassion. They make powerful painters and skilled surgeons when they are dedicated.

Scorpios can be quite sentimental about their children, although they may succeed in hiding the fact. Children represent to them the mysterious life forces of change and renewal. So Scorpio people are either intimidated by their youngsters, or are deeply concerned with understanding their motives and following their development.

SIXTH HOUSE: WORK AND HEALTH

Work is often the Scorpio Ascendant person's reason for being. They throw themselves into work with conviction and purpose that usually leave their competitors straggling behind. The only problem is that they first must find something they want to do. If they do not, they may waste their talents and become discontent and bitter.

They are self-sufficient people. They have no trouble making their home wherever they happen to be. Scorpios make extremely good explorers. They are able to put up with all kinds of discomfort in order to reach their goal.

Scorpio-influenced people have immense physical stamina and enduring powers of leadership. Their aggressive instincts are well developed. They make good soldiers, especially commanders. They also are suited for the stage and public arena, where their qualities of intensity have a magnetic effect.

Scorpio Rising people are usually successful as doctors, engineers, politicians, lawyers, detectives, psychologists, and energy and conservation specialists. They are often in the forefront of attempts to deal with industrial pollution, waste, and recycling of matter and energy.

Scorpio people's main health problems are those that arise from an emotional source, especially through indulging their senses. The pursuit of erotic pleasure can lead them to burn the candle at both ends, neglecting their rest and nutrition. Or they can become obsessed with a part of their body and imagine ailments they do not have.

SEVENTH HOUSE: ALLIANCE AND PARTNERSHIP

Typical Scorpio Ascendant people never enter into a partnership without a great deal of soul searching. Being realists, they weigh all the pros and cons. They are not adverse to marrying into money as a substitute for more idealistic expectations of a partner.

Scorpios are prepared to have their casual affairs before settling down. Often such relationships do not last once brief physical or emotional expression is over. But their more serious love and marriage associations mean a great deal to them.

Scorpio Rising people know exactly the sort of person they want for a permanent partner. It takes time for them to be sure that the person they have selected measures up. They do not intend to make any mistakes. But they often do. Their ideas are too fixed. They frequently fail to see possible areas of incompatibility, especially when they put a lover on a pedestal.

Scorpios are loyal. But they are very possessive. Jealousy often is the cause of much domestic disharmony. However, they do their best to persevere even with an unhappy marriage. They have fairly conservative ideas about marriage. They find it difficult to forgive a partner who cheats. However, their own emotional needs often require them to look elsewhere for physical gratification.

Business and social alliances pose a dilemma for Scorpio Rising people. On the one hand, mutual endeavors challenge their creative and leadership drives. On the other, they can abuse trust and misuse power. If they feel threatened in any way, they can subvert the partnership to serve their own ego needs. The mature Scorpio nurtures alliances by sharing knowledge and offering compassion in need.

EIGHTH HOUSE: SEX, PSYCHOLOGY, AND SHARED ASSETS

The Scorpio reputation for being preoccupied with sex is exaggerated. Scorpio Ascendant people are early experimenters, for they have little shame about their bodies and the sensations of pleasure. They enjoy variety, either in partners or experiences, in their love life. They need a sense of mystery and novelty to maintain their sexual interest.

Scorpio Rising people have a deep intellectual need to get to the bottom of mysteries. They are also keenly curious about death and the afterlife. They often are students of the occult.

Scorpios will write and lecture about their findings in sexuality and spirituality. They enjoy sharing their discoveries with other people. But they prefer to keep private thoughts and emotions a secret. Verbally sharing intimacies on a one-to-one basis is hard for them to do.

Sharing material assets is also something of a problem for them. Scorpio-influenced people are usually shrewd with money, and believe they are better managers of it than their mates or partners. It is sometimes their capable management of joint funds and resources that helps the partnerships to endure. Many a husband or wife who has been prepared to let their Scorpio mate look after the finances has lived comfortably and watched their money grow.

Scorpio people seldom put their investments in one basket. They believe in spreading the risk. Their business interests often cover a variety of fields. In their financial dealings, they are more adaptable and flexible than in most other areas of their life.

NINTH HOUSE: EDUCATION AND TRAVEL

Scorpio Rising people are natural philosophers and psychologists. It is not enough for them to learn what other people have reported; they have to experience the truth of it for themselves. In religious matters, they hold wide-ranging views. They are inclined to look beyond the limited scope of orthodox dogmas.

They are inclined to take up studies later in life that may have been neglected in earlier years. As they get older, they discover the value of education as a means of realizing their ambitions. They have great powers of concentration once they put their minds to a subject.

In their search for the truth, Scorpio Ascendant people depend a lot on their own emotional states. They can sometimes become completely self-absorbed, so much so that they may go into temporary isolation or refuse to converse with anyone. They often become depressed and moody. They can feel deeply identified with the futility of existence.

Scorpio Rising people enjoy the sea and voyages across water. They do not usually travel for sightseeing reasons. When they visit other countries, it is usually in quest of personal enlightenment. Or they undertake journeys on behalf of other people. A long and distant search challenges the Scorpio love for danger and imperiled survival.

TENTH HOUSE: FAME AND AMBITION

Scorpio Ascendant people are intensely ambitious. They are determined to make good in whatever field they choose. They are not as interested in the egotistical side of fame as in the power that it conveys.

Their aim is to be the person in charge of whatever they do. If they enter politics, they would have their eye continuously on the most powerful position in the land. When they do make it to the top, they expect others to show them respect and obedience.

However, Scorpio Rising people have a deep sense of justice. It often prevents them from going to extremes with power in public life. They are more inclined to become protectors of the people than their oppressors. But if they lead minority groups, they can clash with established law and order and be ruthlessly efficient in their tactics.

Scorpio Ascendant people will work day and night to achieve positions of prestige and authority. They are prepared to work under others but usually only while they feel they are on the way up. They do not work well as a member of a team unless they are leading it.

ELEVENTH HOUSE: FRIENDSHIP AND COMMUNITY

People influenced by the sign of the Scorpion are very choosy when it comes to making friends. Although they are affable enough in formal situations, and at first meetings, they are inclined to give an impression of aloofness. They cannot help summing up immediately everyone they meet. And their judgments are usually uncannily accurate.

These self-sufficient people do not make many friends. Few of the people they meet come up to their exacting standards. They can at times be critical of their associates and acquaintances. But to their real friends they are loyal and true. They will work quite selflessly to help a friend.

They do not like much close contact. Too many people in close proximity make them feel uncomfortable. They feel there are not many people they can trust. They sometimes settle for pets instead of friends.

Scorpio Ascendant people will work hard for any clubs or societies of which they are members. These groups usually promote cultural or artistic aims in which Scorpios have a personal interest. Community welfare projects also interest them, especially if the project taps their sense of social and political justice. These people can be tireless fighters against oppression of any kind. Brilliant strategists, they understand that it takes power to challenge authority.

TWELFTH HOUSE: SECRETS AND THE UNCONSCIOUS MIND

Scorpio Ascendant people are suspicious types. They are subconsciously on their guard. They are not at all susceptible to flattery. Displays of charm and tact team to make them suspect another person's motives.

Typical Scorpio Rising people learn fairly early in life that any form of partnership contains deception for them. They are invariably misled at one time or another. Disillusioned by close relationships, they seek privacy and solitude.

Often they are the victims of gossip. They are not usually lucky with lawsuits. They easily become mistrusting and secretive as a result.

There is always a battle between war and peace going on inside a typical Scorpio person. They are often contradictions to themselves. In times of peace, they will be inclined to provoke situations that soon land them in a sea of trouble. In the midst of their emotional storms and self-inflicted problems, they will yearn for peace.

Scorpios live on an emotional edge that is very demanding of the people who share their lives. Their marriages and other close relationships often turn out to be tests of fortitude for both Scorpio people and their mates.

Your Rising Sign: Sagittarius on the Ascendant

Sagittarius Rising signifies a love of freedom that is seldom ever satisfied. Such people won't allow themselves to get stuck for long in dead-end situations. Jupiter, the ruling planet of Sagittarius, propels these people on a search for excitement, wisdom, and truth. Bitten by the wanderlust, they are always seeking. A need to know and to learn colors how people with Sagittarius Rising approach the twelve life houses, as described in the following sections.

FIRST HOUSE: PERSONALITY

Sagittarius Rising people are enthusiastic. Being influenced by a fire sign, they exude seemingly boundless energy, and appear always to have something cooking. Sagittarius Rising people are also restless, both physically and mentally. They are always on the move; new people, new places, new things beckon. They are on the lookout for interesting new ventures, some of which take them far from their starting places.

Sagittarius on the Ascendant inspires a great fondness for travel. Such people will seize any opportunity to visit other countries. Frequently they combine travel with their jobs. They are often professional sportsmen and sportswomen who compete in other countries. They are active and friendly hostesses and stewards who even after exhausting trips, bounce right back to see the sights and sample the local entertainment until the wee hours.

People influenced by the sign of the Archer have a great love of pleasure. They are often born entertainers. They are cheerful, optimistic, and friendly. People feel good in their company and seldom resist laughing with them. They are often the life of the party.

In spite of their easygoing and often lighthearted manner, Sagittarius-influenced people are serious. They enjoy discussing profound subjects, and their views are usually well worth listening to. They have a way of seeing the basic truth in a maze of detail. They make very good teachers and managers.

Sagittarius Rising folk are renowned for their love of the great outdoors. They are animal lovers, having a special attachment to horses and dogs. Sometimes this interest leads them to the racetrack; here they can lose— and sometimes win—a lot of money. Sagittarius people are gamblers at heart. Even if they do not gamble with money, they love to stake themselves against the challenge of life.

These people can easily become involved in the most hair-raising business schemes. And they are great promoters. An untried challenge turns them on. They seldom worry about failing; they have too much faith in the chances of succeeding. They tend to depend a lot on luck. Strangely enough, they often are lucky.

Sagittarius Ascendant people have to guard against making promises they cannot keep. They are so used to expecting the best they can become dangerously optimistic.

SECOND HOUSE: MONEY AND POSSESSIONS

Sagittarius Ascendant people have a deeper regard for money than their open-handed ways suggest. They may be tempted to take more chances than most. They will invest in dubious moneymaking schemes. Or they will gamble a large piece of their financial future on a fast horse or a throw of the dice. But underneath, they like to know that there is something in the kitty. They often fail to look at their actual financial situation because they cannot bear the thought of having no security to fall back on.

With money, Sagittarius people are often contradictions. When they spend, they spend big. They often run into debt, then refuse to consider where the next penny is coming from. They would rather count on something turning up than face facts. More often than not, their philosophy works for them. Their faith in the future can pay off at the very last moment.

Sagittarius people have a great talent for planning for the future. In this way they can amass wealth. Influenced by Jupiter, the sign of abundance and good fortune, Sagittarius Ascendant people see golden opportunities knocking at every door. But they have to be careful not to become impatient and through speculation try to win tomorrow's gains today.

Sagittarius Rising folk like to have valuable possessions around them; it helps to satisfy an unconscious craving for security. But these people are never so attached to their belongings that they would not pick up and go, leaving everything behind. The need to roam, to gather experience, is deeper than any need to acquire and keep material things.

THIRD HOUSE: CLOSE CONTACTS AND COMMUNICATION

Sagittarius Ascendant people never tire of making contacts—here, there, and elsewhere. Like their Gemini cousins, they probably have more acquaintances than most other zodiacal types. And, like Geminis, they often get a reputation for being gadflies of the Zodiac. They do not as a rule form very close relationships; they are terrified of any involvement that might tie them down.

These are very progressive-minded people. Their intellects are sharp and inventive. They are often original. Their writings and commentaries display keen wit and irony without sarcasm. Their understanding of humanity, especially its comic side, is great. They are usually good storytellers with a wonderful sense of humor.

Sagittarius folk believe in free education for all people. They feel that everyone should receive the best education available, not just to earn a living but also to share insights with each other. Communication, they believe, is vital to human progress.

People influenced by the Archer are independent and have a hearty belief in freedom of speech. In spite of their originality, they often become fixed in their ideas and inclined to support orthodox traditions. When they do speak out, it is often from the podium or recording room of an established group. They make good preachers, whether in person, in print, or on radio and TV.

FOURTH HOUSE: HOME AND FAMILY

Sagittarius Ascendant people are roamers. They spend a lot of time away from home base. But they are intensely sentimental about their families. No matter how far they wander, they keep in touch—not on a regular basis, but when an intense longing for loved ones overtakes them. And by phone, which is quicker and more personal than writing.

Sagittarius people are kind to their families. They will listen to their troubles, and do all in their power to fulfill their desires. They go out of their way to make things easier in times of worry. They are a soft touch. They are generous with gifts and seldom fail to remember birthdays and anniversaries.

At the core of the Sagittarius personality is timidity. These individuals are not as sure of themselves as their extroverted ways suggest. They look to their families to provide a sense of belonging. Once assured of this, they can happily pursue their carefree rushes into the world.

Sagittarius Rising folk usually furnish and decorate their homes in quiet harmony, with only a few mementos and trophies proclaiming their worldly enthusiasms. They like to regard where they live as a sanctuary, a place to which they can escape when the world becomes too much.

FIFTH HOUSE: ROMANCE, CREATIVITY, AND CHILDREN

Sagittarius Rising people are fun lovers. They seldom tire of pleasure and entertainment. And they seldom tire of the chase. Hunters of the heart, they pursue variety and challenge. Any conquest is fair game, which often gets them into trouble.

Though ardent lovers, Sagittarius-influenced people do not allow romance to dictate their lives. They seem to put heart and soul into a love affair, but they are really enthusiastic about the lovemaking. They infuse sex with idealism. Then they get on with the next exciting activity.

Their loved ones can at times feel neglected. It is impossible to tie Sagittarius down. Any interference with their freedom makes them unhappy and rebellious. They are inclined to walk out on anyone who consistently tries to put an emotional rope round their neck.

Sagittarius Rising people have a talent for all occupations or hobbies involving plenty of human contact and movement. They are very good at sports. They have a way with animals, especially horses and dogs, and like careers breeding, training, racing, and showing animals. On the intellectual side, they make first-rate teachers and scholars. Politics, promotion, coaching, and exploring also attract them.

Sagittarius Ascendant folks are good with children as long as they do not have to stay indoors with the kids too long. The men, being somewhat boys themselves, never seem to be able to take on the role of father comfortably. They are either too heavy or too indulgent. The Sagittarius woman makes a better all-round parent, blending freedom with discipline in judicious amounts.

SIXTH HOUSE: WORK AND HEALTH

In spite of their fondness for amusements and the good life, Sagittarius Ascendant people are hard workers. They are prepared to put in a full day's work without shirking, as long as this will provide them with the financial means and freedom to do as they please in their spare time.

This often means that Sagittarius folk burn the candle at both ends, working and playing with equal zest and vigor. However, most Sagittarius-influenced people like to keep fit. They are interested in sports and games, which help them to keep the weight down and to stay in balance.

These pleasure-loving people are susceptible to rich food and drink. When they eat or drink too much, an expanding waistline often is a problem. However, people influenced by the fleet-footed Archer are usually diet-conscious. In between their excesses they try to keep to good natural foods.

In both work and health, they aim to establish a good foundation to support their many activities. They usually choose work that will allow them to fulfill their visions of future security. They tend to live for the future, having great faith that they will find the pot of gold at the end of the rainbow.

Their work usually has an element of speculation in it; they often choose to work on commission, or on a time or production basis, so that there is always the possibility of exceeding fixed expectations of one salary.

Sagittarius Rising people, though, do have a strong conservative streak. It often projects them into professions such as teaching, which offer plenty of time for them to follow their other interests.

SEVENTH HOUSE: ALLIANCE AND PARTNERSHIP

Partnerships of the love and marriage kind are not an easy thing, especially for the male Archer. He is terribly conscious of his independence and freedom, and is most reluctant to do anything that may endanger these precious assets. He is one of the most marriage-shy types in the Zodiac. In this age of liberation, female Archers are settling the score. They, too, demand an independent life, free of the usual constraints.

Both male and female Sagittarius require a special kind of partner. They need a mate who is a friend and who will not make undue emotional demands. They look for a partner who is able to share their many interests. It is imperative for a happy marriage that the husband or wife be intelligent, versatile, and easygoing.

Sagittarius people love to share their lives with their friends and acquaintances. They are often away from the home. Or they will invite all manner of companions back to the house for dinner and drinks. Their instant sociability can be tough on mate and the kids at home, giving Sagittarius people a reputation for being somewhat irresponsible. But their social and business allies flock around them.

Sagittarius Rising people make good business partners, provided the field offers scope for them to move around and experience plenty of human contact. Some never wed, preferring to settle down with their intellectual pursuits and studies. As they get older, their preoccupation with physical activity, tripping around, and meeting people matures into a philosophy of life that younger generations can find both illuminating and practical.

EIGHTH HOUSE: SEX, PSYCHOLOGY, AND SHARED ASSETS

Sex means a lot to Sagittarius Rising people. They are passionate and ardent but suffer sudden changes of mind. This can be difficult for their lovers and those seeking a fulfilling union. The Sagittarius male and female are ill equipped for devotion to one partner and long-term or permanent relationships.

There are two distinct types of Sagittarius: one is the playboy type, and one is deeply reflective. The easygoing Sagittarius nature belies a deep emotional connection with such questions as death and survival. These people have the ability to look deep within themselves, but rarely are they able to come to terms with what they sense is there. They are inclined to skate over such subjects or to express their feelings in traditional ways.

Sagittarius-influenced people can be protective of joint funds and resources. In spite of their generous, spendthrift, ways, they manage to respect shared finances and property. Sagittarius folk like a stable foundation. They are wise enough to know that a partnership arrangement can offer this. So they try to brake their irresponsible impulses before they reach such momentum that both the money and the partnership are endangered. With the Sagittarius luck, they squeak through just in time.

NINTH HOUSE: EDUCATION AND TRAVEL

Sagittarius Rising people are justifiably proud of their ideas. They present them with the confidence that comes from knowing they are an expression of themselves. Whatever they learn, from formal sources or from the school of hard knocks, they adapt to suit current needs and purposes.

These people are natural teachers. They are capable of becoming professors and philosophers. Their minds can delve deep into complex subjects and understand them. But they do have to control their urge to move around too much. A diversity of interests can distract their concentration.

When Sagittarius embraces a religious or philosophic point of view, he or she is never in doubt that it is the correct one. They have supreme faith in their ability to see the truth. The only thing that prevents them from being truly original is a tendency to conformity. They often express their truths through established positions. In this they can be stubbornly conventional.

Sagittarius people are the travelers of the Zodiac. Fresh horizons broaden their mind. They regard long journeys and extended stays in other countries as a learning experience. They see them also as a teaching experience. They love to present their own ideas to people of different cultures, even to the extent of trying to convert them. Sagittarius Rising makes an ideal missionary.

TENTH HOUSE: FAME AND AMBITION

Typical Sagittarius people are vigorously ambitious. They aim for the highest in whatever they do, even though their final goal is probably not definitely clear to them at any time. They work toward an indescribably broad future where freedom, space, and opportunity are unlimited. It is not that they are dreamers. They are optimists, with tremendous faith in the unknown.

When famous, Sagittarius Ascendant people have an element of modesty about them. They often enjoy participating in the ceremonies and trappings of their office, but they are able to retain a basic simplicity that comes across. Arrayed in colorful robes or surrounded by worldly splendor, they can still be simple at heart. They also can be swashbuckling and boastful.

Sagittarius people have a gift for critical analysis. They are able to see the merits of a complex proposition. Intuition is keen. They do not like handling details, but they can cope with a variety of claims on their time and talents at one time. They are often writers and lecturers.

In spite of their independent natures, Sagittarius Rising people are good at following orders, as long as they respect the aims of the authority issuing them. They are not too independent to seek conventional careers in the fields of law, politics, and religion.

ELEVENTH HOUSE: FRIENDSHIP AND COMMUNITY

Sagittarius Ascendant people are most expansive among friends. They love nothing more than to be at the center of a group of congenial people exchanging ideas, telling amusing stories, and relating their experiences. They are enthustiastic raconteurs, seldom short of a joke or a parable.

People like their easygoing and jovial manner. They do not have as much interest in making close friends as in collecting acquaintances. Their dearest friends are those who usually share their many interests and accompany them on their ceaseless trips and adventures.

These sons and daughters of Jupiter, which is the ruling planet of Sagittarius, are very good at bringing together people of opposing points of view so that compromises can be reached. They make efficient chairpeople and mediators. Although in their personal lives they are often outspoken to the point of bluntness, in group and community work they can be exceedingly tactful and diplomatic.

Still, they are great believers in justice. They will not shy away from an unpopular decision if they deem it to be necessary. Firebrand Sagittarius speakers can rouse their audience to take action toward some societal or political goal.

TWELFTH HOUSE: SECRETS AND THE UNCONSCIOUS MIND

Deep within the subconscious of the frank and outgoing Sagittarius is a secretive side. This often makes these people feel uncomfortable whenever they are forced to consider the truly mystical elements of their own experience. There is something there they do not want to face. Although they are capable of great insights, they would prefer to stick to the safety of familiar conventional religious and philosophic views.

However, if they can overcome this reluctance, Sagittarius people can delve deeply into the subconscious. They can become perceptive investigators of the occult, and reveal to the world new explanations for psychic phenomena.

Your Rising Sign: Capricorn on the Ascendant

Capricorn Rising people tend to be concerned with their public image. What they do, even what they think, may be measured against conventional standards of acceptability. These people are strongly motivated by a need for success, as it is defined through such wordly ambitions as recognition and prestige. In a broader sense, achievement is what Capricorn Rising people are striving for. It colors their approach to the twelve houses of life experience, as described in the following sections.

FIRST HOUSE: PERSONALITY

People born with Capricorn on their Ascendant are determined and patient. These people have a tremendous capacity for hard work. They are not the types to expect favors. They are down-to-earth realists. Their early life often teaches them that living is no bed of roses. They are prepared to accept conditions as they are and to get on with the job of whatever has to be done.

Capricorn Ascendant people are proud and aloof. They know what they want out of life when they reach maturity. Whereas many other signs are never quite sure what they should, or should not, have done, the developed Capricorn does not look back. He or she is no dreamer. Things are as they are because they had to be that way, as far as they are concerned. With long-suffering patience, these people move inexorably toward their goals.

That doesn't mean such people have never experienced loss or sadness or failure. Capricorn Rising people know there are limits to everything, including their ambitions. But their quality of patience allows them to look at the record, to size up the alternatives, and to work and wait. With restraint and through responsibility, characteristics inherited from Saturn,

222

Capricorn's ruling planet, they work their way steadily upward. Indeed, the Goat, symbol of Capricorn, makes their climb sure-footed and steady.

Capricorn Ascendant people usually succeed in the end because of their sheer persistence. They are not deterred by setbacks or obstacles. They grind away like the "mills of the Gods," wearing down any resistance. What they lack in imagination they make up for in dogged determination to succeed.

People born under this cardinal sign of action are more interested in gaining prestige and respect than in amassing large sums of money. They like to be looked upon as authorities in their particular line. They can become so preoccupied with work that they live for little else. Their loved ones must sometimes see to it that they get enough recreation and leisure.

Capricorn Rising people are more sensitive than their manner often suggests. An inferiority complex often lurks behind their tough, skeptical exterior. They love their homes and families, although they are shy about expressing their feelings. They worry whether their undemonstrative ways will cool off loved ones. Their pride often won't allow them to ask for the affection they need.

These people influenced by the sign of the Goat are also contradictions within themselves, to themselves, and to the world at large. One type of Goat may in youth exhibit a rather irresponsible attitude. Their parents may think such youngsters are never going to settle down. But when their wild oats are sown, they become the most serious and law-abiding of citizens. The other type of Goat can start life being serious and studious, and in maturity become more yielding and young at heart.

There are seldom any half measures about Capricorn. Life demands discipline and restraint, as well as joy and fulfillment. Which sequence comes first and which last seems to vary with the individual. With Capricorn Rising, the sequence tends to be conservative in early life, expansive and enthusiastic later in life.

SECOND HOUSE: MONEY AND POSSESSIONS

Capricorn Ascendant people can be unpredictable where money is concerned. This tendency wars with their basic nature, which is cautious and methodical. They want to take responsibilities seriously, so they try to be conservative. When it comes to saving, they certainly can put the pennies away—but sometimes not long enough to grow.

They will often spend their money on an impulse, frequently without getting much value for it. And they are not the type of people who take unsolicited financial advice easily. They are independent thinkers in this respect. They can even spend their money in unconventional ways, which may seem out of character but is typical for Capricorn Rising.

Capricorn Ascendant people do not allow money to rule their life. They can be quite detached from it, although keenly aware of its practical value. In their business lives, they can amass wealth through bold and original investments. They have a canny way of thoroughly investigating a proposition. And after getting the best of advice from competent authorities, they are able to act swiftly.

Capricorn Rising people usually like to surround themselves with the latest gadgets and scientific equipment. They are the types of people who after acquiring wealth may support worthy causes, especially scientific research into humanitarian problems. They are likely to do this anonymously.

THIRD HOUSE: CLOSE CONTACTS AND COMMUNICATION

The typical Capricorn Ascendant person plays his or her cards close to the chest. They are not ones to confide in all and sundry. They are very careful to whom they tell their inner thoughts and private problems.

Capricorn people, however, do like to listen to others. They enjoy working out the reasons why other people make certain statements. They are especially quick at noting any unguarded statement; they are interested both in the information it may contain and what it reveals about the person making it. Logic and sentiment, according to Capricorn Rising people, should combine to make sense.

People influenced by the sign of the Goat live in a deeply emotional world that seldom gets expressed. They are far more sensitive to what other people say and think about them than they ever let on. They are often deeply hurt and pained, but would consider it weakness on their part to show it. They hide their vulnerability behind a cynical shell, sometimes coming out to express disapproval in verbally cutting ways. Or they bury their vulnerability so deeply, they remain inhibited and silent even with close associates.

These strong and proud individuals have to work harder than most other types to express themselves through language. When they do develop this facility, they can become speakers and writers of rare depth and sensitivity.

Capricorn Rising people often are music lovers who find it easier to enjoy emotions that are communicated without the complication of words.

FOURTH HOUSE: HOME AND FAMILY

Home is where Capricorn Rising people feel most comfortable. Family gives them a basic sense of selfhood and reinforces that image of self that they want to show the world.

No one takes more interest in their domestic affairs than these people. They need a stable base to make them feel psychologically secure while they pursue their ambitious enterprises. Gradually, as they become older and more fulfilled, the Capricorn Ascendant type tends to spend more time in the bosom of his or her home and family.

It is surprising how often Capricorn people are influenced in their formative years by an ambitious mother or father or other parent figure. If adult pressure to succeed has been excessive, there can be a revolt in later years.

If mate or family members have great expectations, Capricorn may perversely fail them or demonstrate a tough, rebellious streak. The Capricorn Goat can be led to water but cannot be made to drink.

These are people who usually know what they want around the home. They can become quite dictatorial. Their know-it-all and bossy ways can provoke arguments with other members of the household.

Capricorn Ascendant people are extremely loyal. They want the very best for their families. They endeavor to provide a comfortable home. In return, they expect to be respected, and their efforts appreciated. They are capable of handling a large family if they blend discipline with tenderness.

FIFTH HOUSE: ROMANCE, CREATIVITY, AND CHILDREN

Capricorn Rising people do not rush into love affairs. But physical affection is terribly important to them. They find lovemaking the easiest way in the world to express their feelings, which often are so difficult for them to put into words.

No one at the beginning of a romance should expect a Capricorn person to bare his or her soul. These people are intensely afraid of being hurt. They will not confide in anyone until they feel they can trust them completely. Where their emotions are concerned, Capricorn types would rather proceed at a snail's pace than risk the possibility of rejection.

Capricorn Ascendant people are resourceful and practical. They are very good at making the most of whatever is available. They have a talent for organization and administration. The women are usually more artistically inclined than the men. Both sexes, however, enjoy their creature comforts. Art and music attract them. Some of these people become the strong, silent artists of their generation, speaking to others through the languages of soul and senses.

Capricorn people are at their creative and enterprising best when they are juggling money problems and investments. They have a way of grasping intricate details of higher finance that would leave others confused and despairing. These are people who can become leaders in handling merger operations and the complications of big business.

With children, Capricorn Rising people are fairly firm. They like to turn out their offspring as socially acceptable individuals having due respect for law and order. They like their children to be a favorable reflection on themselves.

SIXTH HOUSE: WORK AND HEALTH

Capricorn Ascendant people produce their best work when they have plenty of variety. But this does not mean they have to be darting hither and thither. These people have intense powers of concentration. Nothing delights them more than coping with a stream of detail that they can arrange into orderly patterns.

They make very good researchers in scientific fields. They can put their finger on the salient facts among a welter of detail and trivia. They can make boring statistics interesting and more meaningful with their ability to write clearly and concisely. They make competent accountants and engineers.

They also manage to bring versatility into their work. They are good examples to the younger generation of how work can be handled efficiently and without fluster. Capricorn-influenced people are not the types to lose their heads or panic when the pressure is on. They have faith in method and order. They endeavor to bring structure to all their activities, so they do not have to depend solely on imagination.

Capricorn Rising people are usually physically strong. They will stay on a balanced diet trying to keep fit, because they worry so that ill health will interfere with their work. But they tend to ignore leisure activities; they often do not get enough exercise and rest. They sometimes suffer from nerves through keeping their emotions repressed.

SEVENTH HOUSE: ALLIANCE AND PARTNERSHIP

Partnerships represent an emotional area for the usually cool and serious Capricorn-influenced person. They are never sure of their ability to cope with this area of life experience. They don't want to give up control, so they can be suspicious and aloof with a new lover or potential mate.

These people are very protective toward their marriage partners. They try to avoid arguments, even to the point of giving in. Or if their behavior is the cause of complaint, they may refuse to discuss it and walk off. They cannot bear any situation in which their emotions are brought to the surface.

A Capricorn person is not the type to cheat after marriage, unless there is a compelling reason. Once they have given their word, they do their very best to stick to it. The problem is that they have a great need for physical affection. If it is not forthcoming from their mate, they may feel compelled to go elsewhere.

But these people will not break up a close relationship for any trivial reason. They take their responsibilities very much to heart. As long as a marriage is still intact, they will be inclined to let their partner have his or her way.

Capricorn Rising people are usually successful in work and business partnerships. In these relatively nonemotional alliances, they don't worry too much about being tricked or used. They have the patience and endurance to take bad times with good; they would never wittingly let their performance fail the goals of the alliance or their partner's expectations.

EIGHTH HOUSE: SEX, PSYCHOLOGY, AND SHARED ASSETS

Capricorn Rising people usually are good lovers. They enjoy the physical side of romance. This is an area where these naturally cautious and modest people can really let their hair down with the right kind of partner.

Until they find the right partner, though, they tend to feel inadequate about sex and love. They worry about intimacy, how it might expose their sensitive emotions or how it might threaten their need for control. But it is through the intimacy of love and sex that Capricorn Rising people find the true meaning of success and achievement—the joy and fulfillment of sharing with another human being.

These people influenced by the sign of the Goat find hope in their own accomplishments. The more they succeed, the more they tend to relax their stern outlook on life. They become younger at heart. No types in the Zodiac respond more positively to success than Capricorn; to them it can be a reason for living.

A person with a Capricorn Ascendant is often proud of his or her ability to manage money. They enjoy demonstrating this talent to others, especially to their partners. This makes them ideal people to be in charge of shared funds and resources. Besides, Capricorns truly get a sense of pleasure from providing partners and loved ones with a solid base, often exceeding everyone's expectations and building a large nest egg.

NINTH HOUSE: EDUCATION AND TRAVEL

A person with a Capricorn Ascendant is naturally skeptical. They are not the types to accept any radical ideas about religion or philosophy. They find their truths in their own experience or in practical, down-to-earth rules of living.

They are most suspicious of beliefs that engender an emotional response. They feel that whatever is true can be described in rational terms. Their inner feelings may tell them that there are other purposes to life, but these have not been revealed. Until they discover these truths for themselves, they will continue to adhere to their own ethics.

Capricorn Rising people believe in higher education. Often their own education is interrupted in youth. They resume it in later life to help them attain their ambitions.

These people tend to be supporters of law and order. Their general outlook is that in an ordered society, people have the opportunity to reach their own conclusions, political and moral, free from emotional demands.

Capricorn people are seldom interested in extensive travel unless there is a good reason. They will visit other countries for business and educational purposes but seldom for pure pleasure or sightseeing. They believe in having a responsible attitude to life; sometimes they become narrow-minded, with shrunken vistas. The more they learn through formal courses of study, the more they are attracted to travel, mainly to compare book learning with actual, everyday experience.

TENTH HOUSE: FAME AND AMBITION

Many Capricorn Ascendant people become leaders in their field. Their way to the top is usually along a steady gradient. They become so much a regular part of their field that often they are far more renowned than they know. They are the "authorities" to whom others come for advice. Capricorn people usually know their job in and out.

Capricorn Rising people frequently are successful in partnership. They have a flair for being able to control diverse and scattered activities. They make excellent managers, administrators, and public officials. They frequently are attracted to law and accounting. They can handle heavy responsibilities without any sign of stress.

Capricorn rarely appears to get flustered. They often make topnotch arbitrators with a pronounced ability for weighing alternatives.

Capricorns are among the most ambitious people in the Zodiac. But they seldom make any noise about it. They are prepared to work and wait. They do not like to take shortcuts, which they feel may be a sign of shirking.

On many occasions the quiet, hard-working Capricorn person gets to the top ahead of the favorites as well as the whiz kids. People can make the mistake of underestimating the Goat, then end up working for him or her.

ELEVENTH HOUSE: FRIENDSHIP AND COMMUNITY

Capricorn Rising people are steadfast in friendship. But they choose their companions carefully. No one can expect to become a close friend of the Goat just because they have enjoyed a few days or nights out together. Capricorn people regard friendship as a private, intimate relationship in which both parties are likely to know each other's secrets. They want to be sure first that whoever they call a friend is absolutely trustworthy. They do not have many close friends.

Capricorn Ascendant people cannot stand disloyalty. Anyone who lets them down is banished but not forgotten. If the rascals ever ask for favors in the future, their request probably will be turned down. Both the male and female Goat enjoy the kind of friend who does not make excessive demands on their time. They like to spend a good deal of time alone.

Capricorn-influenced people are not indiscriminate joiners. They frown on clubs where company and conversation are the main activities. Their affiliations with groups and societies require more meaningful objectives, work-oriented ones as a rule. Their public image often demands that they join conservative groups whose emphasis is law and order and where radical ideas are suspect.

Capricorn Rising people do have a liking for secret societies. Mystery intrigues them. They often cultivate people who have an interest in the occult, then amuse themselves by being skeptical and demanding demonstrations of proof.

TWELFTH HOUSE: SECRETS AND THE UNCONSCIOUS MIND

A Capricorn person can keep a secret. They have many of their own, which will never be revealed to anyone.

Their deepest religious convictions are seldom discussed. Even if they have mastered the art of communication and can verbalize their feelings, it is unlikely that they will disclose any really private opinion. These people can enjoy an argument or debate, using them as means of discovering the hidden connections that make their opponents tick.

As a result, Capricorn Rising people are very good at making plans in the background. Their minds are alert to what is going on behind the scenes. In their business and work affairs, they usually have figured out all the possible angles well in advance of any decisions that have to be made. They are seldom taken by surprise.

Despite appearances, Capricorn Ascendant people may be secret optimists. They don't believe in chance nor will they rely on other people to solve a problem. But they do put their faith in themselves; they attend to the practical matters of the present, then trust that this preparation will insure a favorable result in the future.

Capricorn Rising people privately nurture their secret hopes and wishes, which are more expansive than their conservative behavior suggests. They also have a hidden rebellious streak. A sudden shift from conformity to radicalism, for example, comes as a shock to friends and loved ones, but it is really the maturing of a long emotional and intellectual process.

Your Rising Sign: Aquarius on the Ascendant

A quarius Rising creates a free spirit, interested more in human considerations than personal ones. Such people look to friendship and community networks for stimulation and satisfaction. Group ties may supplant intimate alliances. But in all involvements, even in day-to-day relationships, people with Aquarius on the Ascendant tend to be detached. An impersonal approach characterizes their experiences in the twelve life houses, as described in the following sections.

FIRST HOUSE: PERSONALITY

Aquarius Rising people are fiercely independent. They are not prepared to follow for long in the footsteps of others. They yearn for change, but not for the sake of variety. Change breaks up old patterns and allows the new to come. Change is progress to these often misunderstood people.

Being born under the influence of Aquarius makes a person impatient to discover new truths. They are sometimes regarded as the truth seekers of the Zodiac. They often are attracted to scientific and humanitarian occupations. Where they can apply their intelligent, intuitive minds to discovering keys to the universe or solutions to society's ills.

Aquarius is an air sign; it bestows intellect and the ability to communicate ideas. Once an idea is planted, it must germinate and grow. The symbol of Aquarius is the Water Bearer, signifying fertility, creativity, and nurturance. The sons and daughters of Aquarius are destined to spread their ideas, then take part in the growth and development. Saturn, one planetary ruler of Aquarius, charges them with this responsibility.

Aquarius Rising people are among the most original thinkers of the Zodiac. Uranus, the other planetary ruler of Aquarius, gives them a quality of genius. Frequently their ideas are so advanced that society turns them down only to adopt them at some later date.

Aquarius Rising people are as a rule friendly and cooperative. They make many acquaintances but few close friends. They resist alliances and friendships that are emotionally demanding. Aquarius like to keep their relationships as impersonal as possible.

These are people who show in some way a love for humanity. Sooner or later, they endeavor to take responsibility for making the world a better place to live in. They are supporters of worthy causes and often at the head of protest groups. The intense believers can become revolutionaries, taking their place in the forefront of movements aimed at radicalizing society and government.

Aquarius Ascendant people are often intent on reforming the people or organizations they associate with. They are quick to notice when others try to become leaders or authorities. Then they do their best to pull them down, often by the very despotic means they have deplored. Their abuse of people in the name of freedom is destructive of their goal of changing society's thinking.

Aquarius can be very stubborn, in spite of a freewheeling personality. Once they get an idea fixed in their heads, they will not amend it until they have proved to themselves that it is unworkable. With their tendency toward intense beliefs, they can go to extremes of fanaticism.

As artists, Aquarius Rising people can make their best statements. Here their attraction to the unusual and their stubborn need for self-expression enable them to produce truly individualistic works.

SECOND HOUSE: MONEY AND POSSESSIONS

Aquarius Rising people are idealistic about money. How they make it and how they spend it are concerns that plague their social conscience. Usually they wind up compromising their idealism with pragmatism.

Money and possessions actually mean more to Aquarius Ascendant people than they are prepared to admit. They need a sense of material security behind them. Then they feel free to pursue their consciously expressed concerns for the betterment of society.

Unless Aquarius folk find some ideal to work toward, they can get too attached to the power of money and the pursuit of money. Attractive possessions and a comfortable life undermine their social values.

Aquarius can be uncharacteristically impractical where money and possessions are concerned. They frequently have a blind spot that can mystify those closest to them. They can be good managers of household budgets, but may easily endanger their assets by investing in fanciful schemes.

They are not stingy with money. They will help people who are down on their luck. They are more inclined to believe a hard-luck story than to reject it. They genuinely want to help people. If they are able to do it with money, as well as progressive ideas, they feel fulfilled.

The basic Aquarius unpredictability is likely to reveal itself at any time in regard to money and possessions. However, home and family responsibilities make these people more stable.

THIRD HOUSE: CLOSE CONTACTS AND COMMUNICATION

Airy and friendly, typical Aquarius Ascendant people stay socially alive and active. They love to circulate among their many friends and acquaintances. They make frequent short trips and use of the telephone. They like to know all that is going on in their immediate environment.

People influenced by the sign of the Water Bearer have alert, logical minds. They are not generally the type to engage in superficial gossip. Their conversations usually have an instructive purpose; they are always endeavoring to communicate the truths they have discovered. Aquarius Ascendant people have a knack of expressing the truth in a few words.

Aquarius Rising people can make quick decisions. They have active imaginations. They can envisage several courses of action at the same time, then draw an acceptable compromise line to follow.

Sometimes these Uranus-influenced characters are a bit eccentric. Their independent attitudes and progressive ideas put them outside conventional opinion. If they believe enough in a cause, these are the types who are not deterred by libel or other man-made laws from declaring their convictions.

It is not unusual for them to get into temporary disfavor with their current circle of friends and associates. Their companions do not like to be lectured on social and political priorities. However, Aquarius Rising people can be so affable and sociable, their idiosyncracies are soon forgiven—but not forgotten.

FOURTH HOUSE: HOME AND FAMILY

When Aquarius Ascendant people fail to make use of their fine minds and natural inventiveness, it usually means they are tied up with their homes and families.

Although these people are fiercely independent and reluctant to fall into a rut, they do settle down quite well. Family life is a minisociety; here they can preach and practice the ideals of brotherhood and sisterhood. Aquarius singles, who before marriage were probably the envy of their friends, may overnight change into responsible and dutiful parents.

Aquarius people have an underlying need for power, which is often satisfied by involvement in family life. In spite of their ideals of brotherhood and sisterhood (these are usually reserved for the kids in the family), they tend to take and hold onto the reins of power at home. They believe wholeheartedly in their own ideas. In a family scene they insist on demonstrating the practical value of their ideas by running a capable household in which they are undisputed boss.

The Aquarius home is usually modern in decor and furnishings, as light and airy and spacious as economy permits. They enjoy entertaining on a large scale where space, or even the lack of it, encourages impersonal contact rather than intimate exchanges. They will, though, invite friends or associates to drop by any time to examine an ingenious household appliance or a bizarre artistic creation.

Aquarius Rising people can settle into a home fast and are not easily threatened when uprooted. Unexpected events may force them to move, a not uncommon occurrence in their lives.

FIFTH HOUSE: ROMANCE, CREATIVITY, AND CHILDREN

Aquarius Ascendant people are not hot-blooded lovers. Their approach to romance is cool and controlled. Their friendly, broad-minded ways make them popular. So they are seldom short of romantic companions or opportunities. They are able to maintain a fairly detached attitude, which often makes them appear more desirable to the pursuer.

The Water Bearer prefers to keep his or her love affairs as free as possible from emotional demands. Articulate and civilized, these people believe that disagreements should be settled by logical discussion. If they do get involved with possessive or jealous mates, they are likely to split. They also seek a lot of experimentation in love and romance before they are willing and ready to settle down.

Aquarius Rising people are innovators, talented in the arts as well as in politics and the sciences. They try to bring progressive and original ideas to whatever work they do. They have vivid imaginations and a natural aptitude for using words. They are fine public speakers and writers.

Aquarius people are good with children. They usually suggest interesting games and things to do, a form of structured play for the child. They are likely to take more interest when a child is older and able to converse. Aquarius parents are not possessive of their children. They try to pass on to them their own love of independence and truth.

SIXTH HOUSE: WORK AND HEALTH

Aquarius Rising makes a person take work very seriously, provided it interests them. They can become so immersed in their work that time means nothing to them. As these people are often attracted to science, logic, mathematics, philosophy, and similar studies, it is not difficult to imagine the absent-minded professor being one of their type.

However, Aquarius Ascendant people are not daydreamers. They are indeed idealist, but they try to give their notions concrete expression. They are usually found in some field or career that is of benefit to society. As owners or bosses, they make a point of providing good working conditions.

Aquarius Rising people make first-rate politicians, social and charity workers, broadcasters, writers, and psychologists. They often are attracted to the study and practice of astrology. Regardless of field or occupation, they like to be involved in both the theory and practice of it.

People with Aquarius on the Ascendant hold strong views about health and nutrition. They can become identified with efforts to feed the world's starving millions. They sometimes become so absorbed in their mental activities that they fail to take sufficient exercise. They are not enthusiastic about sports, especially the strenuous variety. They prefer introspection and meditation as ways of relaxing and putting their thoughts into perspective.

SEVENTH HOUSE: ALLIANCE AND PARTNERSHIP

Aquarius Ascendant people marry for love, but seldom without other considerations. For one, they have to feel proud of their mate. They like to imagine that their friends and acquaintances also share this esteem.

Second, it is vital for a person influenced by the Water Bearer to marry a partner who has similar intellectual interests. Aquarius are mental creatures, foremost, and they need someone equally intelligent with whom to share their creative ideas.

Typical Aquarius people are often attracted to partners who are as stubborn as themselves. Their homelife can be fraught with periodic tension, battles of minds, and struggles for power.

Aquarius Rising people work very well in a team, but usually gravitate toward a leading role. They are often found as prominent members of laboratory teams, orchestras, and other groups concerned with reform and social welfare.

Aquarius are modest people. They would prefer the group with which they are associated to receive the praise rather than themselves. Even when their originality and inventiveness may have been the main reason for success, they generously share the stage with colleagues.

EIGHTH HOUSE: SEX, PSYCHOLOGY, AND SHARED ASSETS

In sex, Aquarius Rising individuals are never lacking in imagination. But they do have a detached approach which can give a wrong impression—that they lack passion. This is not so. People influenced by the Water Bearer must be mentally attracted to their lovers, as well as physically. Often physical love develops out of shared intellectual interests or pursuits.

Aquarius people have fairly strong critical tendencies. But their friendly nature and genuine interest in the welfare of people as a whole check them from expressing these tendencies. They are more inclined to put their analytical faculty to work in practical ways. They become researchers, technicians, scientists, and psychologists.

Aquarius Ascendant people are quite good at managing joint funds and resources, probably better than they can manage their personal financial affairs. They are suited for controlling large investments for business corporations and pension funds, where practical attention to minute detail is required.

However, it must be remembered that Aquarius types need a sense of purpose and plenty of novelty in whatever they do; they will not allow themselves to be bogged down by mere statistics. They make very good investigators of financial frauds; they can keep secrets discovered in the course of their inquiries. It is not easy for a partner to pull the financial wool over their eyes.

NINTH HOUSE: EDUCATION AND TRAVEL

Nothing is higher in the mind of the typical Aquarius Ascendant person than his or her idea of justice. Whereas others have a limited idea of justice, these people believe in justice for all—that all men and women should have equal opportunities. And they are prepared to do something practical about it.

The Aquarius Rising person is not one who just preaches idealism. They are always active in their conversations or writings. They point to what needs to be done. They often assume the role of reformers in politics and social life.

The Water Bearer is diplomatic and tactful as a teacher. He or she will defend individualism, and will encourage students to develop their own philosophies of law and justice. Aquarius teachers like to present their own strong beliefs, then challenge students to debate.

Aquarius Ascendant people are unemotional. They are able to make balanced assessments. They enjoy listening to other people's viewpoints, and do not have preconceived ideas about how others should run their private lives. They are prepared to accept people as they are. Yet at the same time they work toward helping people understand society better.

Aquarius Rising people love to travel as often and as extensively as possible. They are interested in the unusual, and can be snobbish about their exotic journeys. Travel can be a way of life for some of these individuals. They prefer traveling with a like-minded partner. But lone journeys never remain solitary for long; Aquarius people easily join up with strangers at public events and on sightseeing tours.

TENTH HOUSE: FAME AND AMBITION

Once Aquarius Rising people decide on a definite career, they will work vigorously and with great dedication. Although they enjoy fame and renown, these factors are not usually their main motivation. They take on a profession or job because they feel it should be done. Through it, they hope to contribute something to the world's store of knowledge.

But it is not always easy for these people to decide what field to enter. Without a definite commitment, they can waste their talents. They can become absorbed in projects that have no practical use. Sometimes, they get a reputation for being eccentric.

It is in the fields of science, medicine, space research, electronics, engineering, aviation, television, writing, broadcasting, and music that Aquarius individuals usually make their name. They love nothing more than a challenge, the more complex the better. If they can get to the bottom of some problem that is impeding progress or affecting the welfare of society as a whole, they feel they are fulfilling their destiny.

Although they are more mentally inclined than physical, Aquarius Ascendant people have no trouble finding the necessary stamina and vitality to see their enterprises through. No matter how long a project might take, they can be relentless about completing it. Their work and their causes can inspire deep passions not often aroused by other life experiences.

ELEVENTH HOUSE: FRIENDSHIP AND COMMUNITY

People born with Aquarius on the Ascendant have a natural way of getting along with others. They are affable and sociable, enjoy themselves in all company, like to meet new people, and have many acquaintances.

They select as their friends the more liberally minded types like themselves who believe in freedom, justice, and equality. But they are interested in all types and enjoy exchanging views, even with the most conservative people.

On these occasions, Aquarius does his or her best to present the more broad-minded principles in which they so firmly believe. But their friendly and diplomatic natures seldom give the impression that they are imposing their views on others.

Aquarius Rising people are usually active members of associations and societies. They prefer to mix in circles where their original and progressive ideas are likely to have the most effect in bringing about reforms in society. They know that change takes time. But they also know that it is the conditioning of public opinion that provides the ground for improvement.

TWELFTH HOUSE: SECRETS AND THE UNCONSCIOUS MIND

Aquarius Rising people are often unable to express their feelings in personal ways. They rely on expressing their sympathies for other people, usually in practical ways, and hope that other people will not try to probe into their souls. It's hard for Aquarius people to be emotional about themselves, to look at the deep conflicts that surround their self-image.

Sooner or later Aquarius Ascendant people have to face up to some sort of self-discipline. These freewheeling, intelligent people have much to give to the world, especially to their fellow man. But they often want to give too much too soon. As they can be ahead of the times with their inventive and reforming ideas, they can be ahead of themselves, too. They need to keep a firm hand on their enthusiasm for causes—as well as on their preoccupation with their own independence—until they reach a state of maturity.

Aquarius can become frustrated. The slowness of society to accept their brilliant ideas can make them bitter, rebellious, erratic, and perverse. They have to practice patience to reach their full potential.

These people, however, do have a conservative side to their nature, although it usually remains in their unconscious. This allows them to temper their more revolutionary and radical views with good sense. Then they are able to argue their ideas in rational and socially acceptable terms.

Your Rising Sign: Pisces on the Ascendant

Pisces Rising personifies the human dilemma of impression, repression, expression. The two planetary rulers of Pisces present contradictions. Jupiter develops wisdom, but also promotes indulgence. Neptune creates vision, but can offer illusion. Like the Fishes, symbol of Pisces, Pisces Rising individuals caught in turbulent eddies may plunge into the dangers of the deep or swim to the safety of shore. Pisces Rising individuals are always trying to integrate their contradictory natures. They dive into the unconscious, then surface to adapt poses for everyday situations. This approach colors how individuals with Pisces on the Ascendant experience the twelve life houses as described in the following sections.

FIRST HOUSE: PERSONALITY

Pisces Ascendant people are exceptionally intuitive. They know instinctively the right thing to do. They don't have to weigh the pros and cons of a situation with rational thought. When, under pressure, they do try to reach decisions intellectually, they often make mistakes.

Pisces Rising are among the kindest and most compassionate people in the Zodiac. They would never harm anyone if it were up to them. They are conscious of the suffering and sorrows of others, and will do all in their power to alleviate them. They can be generous to a fault. These people are soft touches for the hard-luck story. They are true humanitarians.

Pisces-influenced people are often artistic. They have a fine appreciation of music and poetry, and a love of natural beauty. Their creative talents are multifaceted, leading them into fields where they combine physical and emotional expression, especially theater. They make accomplished dancers, singers, and actors. They have a natural aptitude for psychic communication.

These people influenced by the sign of the Fishes, each swimming in opposite directions, vacillate. They can be vague in their personality and approach to life. They are inclined to live in a dreamland, where everything seems to drift. They have difficulty facing the harsh realities of life. Submerged in their fantasies, it is hard for them to surface and make for shore.

Pisces Rising people as a rule do not stand up well under pressure. Of course, much will depend on the position of the other planets in the astroscope. But these people do tend to shy away from action and decision. Unlike the rosy dreams of their fantasies, the real roses of life have thorns, and they prick.

Their extremely sympathetic natures make them attracted to caring for the sick and underprivileged. Pisces Ascendant people often become nurses and social workers, especially in hospitals and institutions. They love children, who respond to their gentle and understanding ways. Their compassion also extends to animals; they frequently have a peculiar empathy with flowers.

Pisces Rising people have a love of the sea. They are deeply emotional. Sometimes they suffer long depressions. They are inclined to spend a good deal of time alone and in introspection. But they also are happy people in between their emotional lows and highs.

They love the good life. They are frequently extravagant with money and may indulge to excess. Isolation doesn't suit them for long. They are incessant talkers when the sociable side of their nature is foremost. They are not very good at keeping secrets, except their own.

Pisces Rising people are lovable individuals who often have a deep understanding of mystical experience.

SECOND HOUSE: MONEY AND POSSESSIONS

It is typical of the nature of a Pisces Ascendant person to scheme like mad to acquire wealth and security—and then yearn to give them away. Frequently they do, for they are generous and unselfish people. But their innate desire to keep some hold on material reality checks them. They retain a sense of proportion in their charitable and philanthropic urges.

Pisces Rising people are contradictions. They blow hot and cold. When the mood is on them to make money, they are intensely active and capable. They tend to resist outside financial advice. Their intuition serves them extremely well in business, especially in connection with land and other real-estate transactions.

But Pisces are impulsive. They are just as likely to blow their entire savings on one wonderful vacation and refuse to think about tomorrow. When tomorrow comes, they are likely to be depressed at the thought of owning anything. Or they may decide with great enthusiasm to start afresh. Pisces people are usually up or down, wild with joy or confused with self-reproach for having more than the needy person next to them.

Pisces Ascendant people are promoters. They look for a quick profit—

probably so they will not have time to change their mind. They are big spenders when they have it, and quick-to-recover-their-spirits losers.

THIRD HOUSE: CLOSE CONTACTS AND COMMUNICATION

From their first day in elementary school, Pisces Ascendant people tend to find the learning process a bit of a drag. Education taught with an emphasis on detail, facts, and memorization is at the opposite pole from them. Their sensitive, feeling natures intuit. They are capable of absorbing the big ideas, as opposed to the nitty-gritty, and they can make broad generalizations based on seeing things as a whole.

To learn, Pisces Rising people have to be involved emotionally. The best way of doing this is to appeal to their sense of beauty or creativity. Having them observe the natural world around them leads to deep understandings of the interconnections in all of life.

Naturally, in adulthood, Pisces Ascendant people tend to mix in circles where feelings are easily communicated. They are often found in the arty domains of the community, among the poets, writers, dancers, and dramatic performers.

Pisces get most of their kicks out of their feelings. So they look for a constantly changing scene. They love to be in the city one day, yearn for the country the next. They would prefer to have a home in both so that they could pack up and move the instant the mood overtook them.

In spite of their easygoing ways, Pisces Rising people can be extraordinarily obstinate. Once they get an idea in their head, they are extremely reluctant to budge from it. It usually requires a deep emotional experience or shock to dislodge an attitude once it is formed.

FOURTH HOUSE: HOME AND FAMILY

Pisces Ascendant people love their homes. But this does not mean they are prepared to settle down in the vine-covered cottage for the rest of their lives. They like to move fairly regularly, if it is possible. And it seems that they always move toward a more expensive residence. Their thoughts about material security are often more solid than their love of change suggests.

Like the Fishes tied together, Pisces Rising people often are not sure in which direction they want to go. Sometimes they want to get away from it all and live in the country. At other times, they yearn for the bright lights. It is a typical Pisces wish to have both a town and a country residence.

For the less mature Fish, this inclination toward the gypsy life can make them wanderers. It is difficult for them ever to settle down. These are the individuals who cart their young families around in circles while they try to find the impossible ideal they are looking for.

All Pisces people love their families. Being one of the most sympathetic and kindly folk in the Zodiac, they frequently overindulge their loved ones.

Yet at times they can become quite irritated with family members. If they feel they are being unduly tied down or if their ideals are criticized, they may just pick up and go. Certainly, open conflict will be unavoidable.

FIFTH HOUSE: ROMANCE, CREATIVITY, AND CHILDREN

Romantic dreams and ideas are almost more important than reality to Pisces Rising people. They spend a great deal of their time drifting on the currents of their emotions, feeding all sorts of romantic imaginings.

In romantic love, they are idealists and dreamers. Quite frequently, they do not see the man or woman they fall for as a real individual. They see only the romantic vision of a lover. Naturally, Pisces Rising folk can be disillusioned and heartbroken in love.

Pisces Ascendant people have a keen sense of the dramatic. Their emotional sensitivity provides them with a talent for artistic pursuits, including writing, poetry, dancing, entertaining, and acting.

Pisces is the last sign of the Zodiac, and so instills in its children a capacity to see all of life's variety as an interrelated whole. Such a collective view enables Pisces Ascendant people to become the theoreticians of art, science, philosophy, and sociology, always within the framework of the humanities.

Pisces people are very sensitive where their children are concerned. They react strongly to criticism of their youngsters. Yet they do all they can to try to correct any shortcomings in their children. The kids should always appear as attractive in looks and behavior as possible. The Fishes want to be proud of their youngsters, for these creations are reflections of themselves.

Pisces-influenced individuals are not consistent enough to be good disciplinarians. They can be quite strict at times, then forget the rules. They tend to give in fairly easily. They are more likely to spoil their youngsters than to be bothered trying to deny them for long.

SIXTH HOUSE: WORK AND HEALTH

Pisces Ascendant people will seldom do a job they consider beneath their dignity. In their way, they probably have a greater sense of pride about work than any other type in the Zodiac.

Pisces Rising people are a bit of a paradox. They are often prepared to do the most menial and self-sacrificing work for the sick, handicapped, or underprivileged. They make wonderful nurses, caretakers, orderlies, and houseworkers. But on no account will the mature Pisces work as a second-rate citizen in his or her own eyes. These people have a way of "disappearing" or not turning up when the work is likely to fall short of their expectations.

Pisces at heart are show-offs. They love to display their talents in their own way. They prefer work where they feel they are at the center of activity yet not under any pressure to perform in established ways. They like to set their own pace, which usually does not involve much physical exertion.

Mature Pisces Rising individuals do not complain about ill health. They are too proud to let others think they are not up to coping, even though this often is the case emotionally.

The emotional highs and lows that Pisces can experience as a matter of course can affect their constitutions, which are never too robust at any time, making them feel ill when they really are not. Their self-absorption and vivid imagination also lend a tendency to hypochondria.

SEVENTH HOUSE: ALLIANCE AND PARTNERSHIP

Pisces Ascendant people are not particularly efficient in an organizational sense. They are wonderfully kind and understanding human beings. Their artistic and moneymaking ideas are often uniquely brilliant. But generally, they need a mate or partner who can get down to brass tacks and compensate for their rather impractical ways.

Pisces people usually make a point of choosing a solid, down-to-earth partner. Other things being equal, the relationship can work out very successfully. But if Pisces individuals are immature, they may expect everything to be done for them. Or they just refuse to think about their responsibilities to mate or lover. If so, the partnership almost invariably ends up a stormy and emotional affair.

Pisces Rising people can be extremely critical of their mate or lover. They often blame their partner for their own failings and shortcomings. Their emotional sensitivity makes them prey to deep depressions in which they can appear to be cold and unloving.

Pisces individuals are fairly adaptable and easygoing. They can swing with the ups and downs, and so manage to make their partnerships work when they put their minds to it. They are the sort of people, however, who often are happier remaining single.

Pisces Rising people tend to go to extremes in business and work alliances. They throw themselves in and get swallowed up. Then they resent their backstage role and worry about losing their independence. At this point they may either act uncharacteristically bossy or simply walk out on the scene.

EIGHTH HOUSE: SEX, PSYCHOLOGY, AND SHARED ASSETS

Sexually, Pisces Rising people are inclined to be more curious than deeply sensual. They are avidly interested in understanding the emotional subtleties behind the attraction of the sexes. They can blow hot and cold in physical relationships, leaving their partners confused at their sudden changes of mood.

There are Pisces individuals who through their curiosity get so involved at a sensual level that they find it easier to continue their indulgent way of life than to stop. They can be lazily permissive, being able to "forget" their bodies by going into dreamland.

Pisces Rising people are often mystically inclined and psychically sensitive. They often understand people intuitively, without need for verbal explanations. They can so identify with another person that they are in danger of losing their individuality. This tendency may be behind their abrupt changes of partner and the constant search for satisfaction.

Pisces Ascendant people often breeze into money through their partners. But they can just as often make mistakes in their financial partnerships, and end up being let down and losing their cash.

They have to be very careful with whom they decide to share their funds or resources. Agreements that are made today may fall apart tomorrow through no fault of their own. Partnerships can involve them in taxation and insurance worries.

But probably more often than many other signs, Pisces-influenced people do tend to share at some time in their life in inheritances or legacies through mates and partners.

NINTH HOUSE: EDUCATION AND TRAVEL

Pisces Ascendant people are usually keenly interested in subjects connected with the mysteries of existence. They are natural philosophers who tend to disdain formal metaphysical and religious doctrines. They rely on their own deeply introspective natures to reveal to them the truth about life, death, and purpose.

Pisces Rising people are among the most mystically inclined types of the Zodiac. They tend to meditate naturally, even if they have never had a lesson. They love to examine relationships minutely and to work out what makes other people tick.

People influenced by the sign of the Fishes find it easier and more interesting to understand abstract ideas. They follow a true intellectual process. The boring jobs of concentrated study and memorizing are not for them. These are individuals who depend on their sensitive emotions and intuition more than their reasoning abilities when making important decisions.

Pisces Rising people love to travel. They enjoy the variety of emotions that contact with people in other countries rouses in them. They also are compulsive daydreamers, who often are just as happy performing in their own fantasies as in the real world. They often escape into their dream world when the pressures outside become too much for them.

Pisces Ascendant individuals are impressionable. They are wise to avoid excessive use of drugs or alcohol, which can induce in them rougher trips than other people might experience.

TENTH HOUSE: FAME AND AMBITION

Pisces Ascendant people are great optimists where their careers are concerned. Once they have found what they want to do, their enthusiasm is boundless. Their strong sense of fantasy allows them to visualize with great conviction a rosy end to their dreams. And very frequently these highly adaptive and intuitive people manage to make them come true.

Pisces-influenced people will express their full potential only when they are doing what interests them. If they settle for a humdrum job where their vivid imaginations are not utilized in practical ways, they tend to become incorrigible dreamers.

These individuals are anxious to leave their mark on the world. But they are not the egotistical types who strive for power for power's sake. Once they have achieved their ambitions, they are inclined to do all they can to help other people achieve theirs.

It is important for a Pisces Rising person to aim high. They are rather easily discouraged. They need more than one objective, so if one door shuts they do not feel depressed. These people are inclined to judge themselves too harshly. They are often their own strongest critics. They need the support of their loved ones, who should never allow them to lose heart.

Pisces Ascendant individuals usually have many ups and downs in their professional and working lives. But after the knocks, they have a way of getting up again, often due to a lucky break.

ELEVENTH HOUSE: FRIENDSHIP AND COMMUNITY

Pisces Rising people love their friends and need them. Their friends provide them with a feeling of social security, which is so essential. They often suffer from an inferiority complex, hiding guilts and inadequacies that are mostly figments of their imagination. When meeting people for the first time, they may experience agonies of embarrassment that nevertheless are carefully disguised under a cheery exterior.

Their companions love them despite all, and seldom catch on to their poses. Pisces-influenced individuals are capable of playing a part convincingly because they believe in it. They totally immerse themselves in the persona of the moment.

They are not the types to have many close friends. They require a certain sort of person for an intimate companion, one who will be prepared to ignore or put up with their frequent depressions, changes of mood, and desire to be alone. And one who will not rip the mask off their hidden faces.

Pisces Rising people are often helped in their careers by their friends. They tend to cultivate companions who are ambitious, solid, and reliable.

Although not practical and efficient themselves, they generally look for these qualities in their friends.

When their emotions are outgoing, Pisces Ascendant people like to have many casual contacts. They have a fondness for excitement and novelty provided by new faces and new places. They are talkative in familiar company.

But they do not usually become members of groups, clubs, or societies. They are inclined to feel that such affiliations tie them down. They will, however, actively support movements and causes aimed at helping sick and deprived people. They are idealistic, and identify with the suffering and exploitation of other people.

TWELFTH HOUSE: SECRETS AND THE UNCONSCIOUS MIND

Mystery, rather than secrecy, comes naturally to the Pisces Ascendant individual. Neptune, the planet of mystery and illusion, enhances the effects that sleight of hand and sleight of mind can produce. Pisces Ascendant individuals are always playing with these possibilities, perfecting them in the unconscious—or conscious—mind, and practicing them on real-life people. So they get a reputation for being mysterious and secretive.

Nothing could be farther from the truth. Such individuals will tell all, even about themselves once their hidden persona is penetrated. They can be secretive about their private affairs, but only until they have found the right person, or source, in whom to confide.

Then they can be unguarded. They are perfectly willing to divulge other people's confidences, especially if such a disclosure supports a general principle or belief. Idealistic to the core, Pisces Rising individuals think nothing of betraying personal secrets—in order to make an impersonal judgment or point.

Also, Pisces Ascendant individuals need to share their thoughts with other people. So their private affairs can be a vehicle for sharing. So can the private affairs of other people! But when they do tell secrets, it is with the best of intentions.

The hidden personas of Pisces Ascendant people serve definite purposes. Although the conscious mind may not make the connections at the time, the process can be fulfilling as it goes along and when it is completed. The process is one of immersion and analysis and synthesis and creation—all proceeding without noticeable starts and stops.

As a result, Pisces Rising people often appear confused and vague in wordly affairs. Yet they are never short of original and inventive ideas. Their pioneering thoughts often emerge after a period of apparent daydreaming. Pisces-influenced people are the most imaginatively creative types in the Zodiac.

However, they are frequently disillusioned. They yearn to be loved. But often they are linked with people who do not feel the same attachment as they do. The attachment can be personal, as in love and friendship, or it can be impersonal, as in work and study. Yet somehow Pisces Rising individuals have more commitment than their partners do.

The relationship gap and the difficulty in coping with worldly affairs and expectations can lead Pisces Ascendant people into solitary pursuits, such as exploring the frontiers of knowledge.

Through their emotional sensitivity, they often possess an awareness of occult and spiritualistic states that are not normally in the experience of others. Pisces-influenced people are frequently mediumistic and able to receive messages from the psychic world. They have remarkable intuition and sometimes can tell the future.

The Planets in the Signs: The Moon Through Pluto

Consult the Planetary Tables at the end of the book,
pages 397–477, to find the position of the Moon and
the other planets for your individual astroscope profile.
When you have determined your placements, you can read the
descriptions relevant to you in the next chapters.

The Moon in the Signs

The Moon stands for response. Its quality is sensitivity. A positive influence from the Moon enables a person to express sympathy. A negative influence breeds moodiness and suspicion.

The Moon is the planetary representative of the forces of the past, preserved in memory. Instinctive and habitual modes of mind and body are inherited from the Moon.

The Moon is associated with the ebb and flow of the tides, as well as the rise and fall of sensation and emotion. All that is cyclical in nature, and nearly everything is, draws upon the Moon's ever-changing faces, shapes, and movements.

Whereas the Sun vitalizes our senses and makes us conscious of what we have and want to do *now,* the Moon makes us look back. It reflects our tradition and heritage. It makes us cling nostalgically to what used to be, and endeavor to create the past through the present. In so doing, we learn from our mistakes. This is evolution.

The Moon draws us into sleep, into the unconscious. It ensures our safety for a while. Dreams and introspection give us pause. We do not proceed so swiftly into action that we endanger our physical and emotional mechanisms.

But the Moon is constantly changing—moving, turning a new face to Sun and Earth. And sometimes it is hidden, invisible to view. It appears and disappears. Change, changeability, birth, death, and disappearance are phenomena we accept as naturally as we accept the Moon's familiar phases, though not without sentiment.

The Moon also helps us to express such sentiment. Its phases proceed gradually, such as emotions build. First there is awareness of a feeling; then its gradual development; conscious desire, climax, and descent follow in similar rhythms, although they may appear to be stepped up or slowed down.

We think broadly in terms of crests and waves, beginnings and ends.

We forget the gradualness and the connections. The Moon, representing a complete cycle with all the nuances, reminds us, forces memory into impulse.

The Moon is the nature principle, the nurturer, the protector, the mother, the antecedent. The Moon activates our everyday experiences with the expectation of newness and the guarantee of familiarity.

The Moon is associated with the sign of Cancer, which it rules.

THE MOON IN ARIES

This is a good placement if other planetary positions enable a person to handle it. Moon in Aries gives a tendency to stop and start, to swing between action and inaction. One day the person may be fiercely ambitious and ready to mow down any opposition. The next, he or she may feel sorry for their rivals and go out of their way to be helpful, considerate, and understanding.

The marriage of the Moon and Aries can create inner conflict and nervous tension. The Moon tends to make individuals sentimental, while Aries urges them to shake off hindrances or attachments that might hamper freedom of action.

But much can be accomplished in practical ways. Moon in Aries combines intelligence with feeling. These people sense situations because they are attuned to the emotions of others and to their environment. They know instinctively the best thing to do. They are extremely handy to have around in emergencies.

The combination does present problems for emotional relationships. Seldom do attachments of any kind go smoothly. The watery emotions of the Moon often reach boiling point in fiery, impulsive Aries. Arguments and walkouts frequently occur. Despite some moodiness, hard feelings are seldom nursed. These people are quick to forgive. And if they do remember slights or insults, they will not try to get even or be petty.

Moon in Aries people often have a strong desire to work in the public eye. Or their work allows them to influence public opinion. They are confident, enthusiastic, idealistic, and enterprising. Frequently they will be attracted to creative and artistic occupations. In their spare time they may write poetry.

There is likely to be a strong interest in travel, especially to other countries. These people can be surprisingly patriotic. They may be among the first to defend established order and past traditions.

Moon in Aries individuals take an active and somewhat demanding pride in the family. Loved ones are expected to live up to certain standards and to show their affectionate appreciation of what is done for them.

Irritableness can be a problem. Temper has to be controlled. Difficulties can arise in parent-children relationships, especially affecting the mother. Moon in Aries people often can become a bit fussy.

These are people with powerful instincts. Their feelings are easily aroused. Their intuitions often are more reliable than their deliberative decisions. They are especially capable when responding to the challenges of moving situations; a sixth sense seems to guide their reflexes.

The imagination of Moon in Aries individuals is extremely active. They are quick to be drawn into any projects that take their fancy. They can be impetutous and inclined to forget about the consequences of their actions in their eagerness for immediate results.

People with Moon in Aries are independent. They tend to go their own way even when they are working as a team. If they do not occupy a position of authority or leadership in the group, they are inclined to lose interest and look elsewhere.

The danger with Moon in Aries people is that they may start projects and not finish them. They can be restless, forever looking for stimulating changes. They may lack stability. There also is a danger of enthusiasm developing into fanaticism.

Their enthusiasm, though, is often an inspiration to others, especially in the artistic field. Even if they are not particularly creative themselves, they have an eye for art and an urge to encourage self-expression in their associates.

THE MOON IN TAURUS

Here the Moon is especially strong and helpful. Moon in Taurus people are practical, reliable, and earthy. They have a strong feeling for nature and beautiful things. But there is nothing dreamy about their sensitivity. They usually succeed in bringing their ideas into the world, where they can be enjoyed in books, handicrafts, design, and the like.

Success for these individuals often comes through dealing directly with the public. There is a keen sense for business and making money, which often brings material success and enviable reputations.

Moon in Taurus people are among the builders of the Zodiac. Even though they are creative and inventive in artistic ways, they like putting down solid foundations, and especially deep roots. They may travel a bit, or wish to, in order to find just the right place to settle. Surroundings must be harmonious. Ideally, there has to be a link with nature, a lifeline to them, especially if they are crowded in cities. Once they find a suitable place, they settle.

These people are conscientious, imaginative, and keenly productive. They can be relied on to do what they say. They do not undertake things lightly. Nor do they ever give up just because the going gets rough. If they have faith in a person or a project, they will doggedly pursue it to the end.

Moon in Taurus confers an emotional temperament, which enables these individuals to make friends very easily. Such persons are quietly confident, courteous, sympathetic, and unobtrusive. They can be secretive about some of their activities. But they do not try to probe into the private affairs of others, either. They are intensely loyal to their friends.

They are especially fond of the home and their family. Being slow to make changes, they are content to build step by step as the years go by. Their aims are a comfortable home and an affectionate, tight-knit family group.

Moon in Taurus people are not revolutionary in their thinking. They even can be suspicious of new ideas. They like to see first that ideas are workable. They specialize in adapting established ideas—upgrading them with a new or attractive or profitable twist.

Moon in Taurus gives a natural skill in handling money, especially on behalf of others and in connection with public enterprises. These individuals are the perfect guardians of partnership funds and shared assets of a group.

Sex for Moon in Taurus individuals is sensuous. They have a deep need to be loved and cherished and to feel the physical warmth of affection. If they are promiscuous, it is usually because they are looking for the ideal partner. They are great romantics but manage to retain a keen eye for practical advantages and disadvantages of a relationship. They would love to love a partner who could also provide them with the economic security they deeply crave.

Moon in Taurus people have considerable capacity to enjoy life. They love comfort and good things. Although they insist on having their pleasures, they are usually prepared to work hard for them. Once they set their minds on a material objective, they are not inclined to give up.

The Moon signifies instinct; Taurus signifies persistence. So these people can be supremely focused. Their powers of endurance are impressive. But they need an aim outside of merely satisfying their desire for creature comforts. They can become too contented and get into a rut.

Moon in Taurus people often have musical appreciation. Artistic pursuits can help them toward a greater sense of self-fulfillment. On the negative side, they can be fiercely possessive. Their jealousy can make the lives of their loved ones a misery. There is always a danger that early marriages may be based on physical attractions and so fail.

THE MOON IN GEMINI

This person can be a born writer, talker, or speaker, popular to everyone. But Moon in Gemini individuals need to understand themselves if they are to make the most of their talents. They can too easily become superficial and spend their time gossiping, absorbing useless information, and visiting others as a need to share their own restlessness. Not facing up to problems can be a fault. So can the tendency to tell untruths to gain popularity or attention.

But with a little self-understanding, Moon in Gemini people can combine the wonderful feeling world of emotions with the interesting and stimulating world of the mind. They can present to the public all kinds of new ideas and perceptions. Their intellects are extremely sharp. They can reach deep into themselves and express the most complex feelings in clear and entertaining ways.

Moon in Gemini individuals can pick up atmospheres instantly. They are very adaptive but inclined to change their minds or moods without warning. They should try to write down what they think when they are feeling creative. Later, their record of insights and inventions may be put to profitable use.

Moon in Gemini can make a person secretive about home and family affairs. Although they may not want the household to know everything they are doing, they expect to be kept informed of what the others are doing. They enjoy reminiscing about the past. They are very good storytellers if they put their mind to it.

It is sometimes one of their bad habits to insist on getting their own way in close relationships. They can even take pleasure out of rubbing others the wrong way just to trigger a response. Then they try to use their superior mental qualities to win the argument.

Moon in Gemini people find learning very easy. What they can't quite understand with their minds, they pick up with their feelings. This placement of the Moon often gives an aptitude for music, either as a composer or a player. Languages are easily mastered. The imagination is particularly vivid and colorful and can be used to make money and to get ahead in practically any profession or line of work.

Moon in Gemini people are versatile. They can turn their hand and mind to practically anything. In business, they are alert and shrewd, sometimes even described as crafty. They have good ideas for obtaining publicity and influencing public opinion.

These people can make good actors, speakers, and entertainers. They can switch their emotions very swiftly, almost to order. Sometimes they are guilty of using this ability to play on the feelings of their loved ones, especially family members. They can be opportunists who just cannot resist taking advantage of a situation.

The Moon in Gemini often produces individuals who have difficulty finding what they want to do with their lives. Even when they achieve enviable heights of success, they are still likely to be dissatisfied. They always seem to be looking for something else or something more. Because of this, they are often accused of being restless and superficial.

Moon in Gemini individuals need to cultivate a purposeful attitude. They can be too easily distracted from whatever they are doing to have much success in finishing anything worthwhile. They tend to love novelty and change. They seldom stay in the one place for long. They are likely to move house and change their jobs frequently. They can be talkative and may enjoy gossiping.

THE MOON IN CANCER

Cancer is the Moon's own sign. So a person with this combination enjoys the best that the emotional world, represented by the Moon, can give. They are deep-feeling people, who enjoy a rich inner life. But this must not be allowed to take over too much from the external world, or they will become disjointed and lapse into moodiness.

Moon in Cancer individuals are inclined to become mentally lazy; they depend unduly on the sensitivity of their feelings. A Moon in Cancer person needs to mix and talk and give verbal or written expression to feelings and instincts.

These people are nature lovers. Like the Moon and the tides, they easily fall into rhythms and can reach great heights of enjoyment and beauty. They are artistic and very impressionable. They like to think things over rather than make quick decisions. When they get a creative idea or thought, they should try to do something with it. It is easy for them to let their best impressions fade. So they often miss opportunities for having their talents and skill recognized.

With effort, Moon in Cancer people can easily become famous. They have a way with the public. They also possess a remarkably good business sense, which they should apply if they are not already aware of it. They often are much more ambitious than their retiring nature suggests. These people can show uncharacteristic aggression and determination when they are moved to.

Moon in Cancer folk make loving parents and successful marriage partners. The family and the home are extremely important to them. They are great homemakers. They have a knack for creating a haven. They are nurturers, inclined to cluck over their loved ones with the protective care of a mother hen.

Moon in Cancer people are sentimentalists. They look at people through their own deep emotional experiences, and so understand immediately what the other person is feeling. Their sympathy is especially comforting to those in distress, especially those who are experiencing loss of loved ones.

It is easy for Moon in Cancer people to be imposed on. They also must be careful of excessive intake of drugs or alcohol. And they must choose more selectively prospective lovers, partners, and mates—even casual contacts whom they let into their lives.

These are people who love to relive their experiences. They frequently go into daydreams about the past. They love to wander down memory lane, not only in their minds but also by visiting the places in their past, especially of their childhood.

Moon in Cancer individuals are among the most romantic types in the Zodiac. The women are cherishing, loving, emotionally responsive. The men are protective, sensitive, understanding. All of them radiate an Old World style and charm. These are people who love to entertain at home, to prepare succulent and fine dishes. They are the most hospitable folks. They love to make visitors feel at home.

People born with the Moon in Cancer are generally fine raconteurs. Although initially reserved in their talk, they become more and more voluble and communicative as they settle into pleasant company. Their stories usually show an ability to observe the nuances of life and living. They possess a subtle sense of humor.

Moon in Cancer people can be lazy. They may be inclined to discuss their grandiose plans with all and sundry, but never get around to making a start. They can be selfish, demanding, and cranky to live with.

THE MOON IN LEO

Moon in Leo individuals often become very successful in life. They make good entertainers, professional or amateur. They are often among the leaders in creative and artistic fields. Moon in Leo confers an extremely fine ability to gauge the mood of the public.

But Moon in Leo people often get carried away by their importance. They often try too hard to get their own image across, and so fail to give their audiences what they want. Through conceit, and an inordinate desire to be at the center of everything, they can make mistakes that ruin their chances.

Moon in Leo individuals have to be loved. They don't care whether it is family love, romantic love, or hero worship, as long as they feel an emotionally appreciative response from others. They have a flair for dramatizing situations, and are not beyond using these to get the attention they want. They are born actors and actresses, as their loved ones will be the first to attest.

Moon in Leo people take a great pride in their homes. They like them to be comfortable, attractive, and a little out of the ordinary. They are particularly fond of giving dinner parties to which their special friends are invited. To them, the home is the place where they enjoy showing off their social graces, their collections, their good taste in food and wines—and their lovers, mates, or children.

Moon in Leo people are romantic individuals who have no trouble attracting admirers. They fall in love easily and usually very deeply. Their affection can be so intense that the beloved feels smothered. With all the best intentions in the world, the Moon in Leo person can become just too emotionally attached.

But they are loyal and will not go back on any undertakings. They have a high sense of honor that cannot condone pettiness or backbiting. Yet if not appreciated sufficiently, or if they feel left out of situations, they can become moody and sulky.

Moon in Leo individuals have a great deal of initiative. But they can balk getting started. They need to feel a project is going to bring them some form of personal acknowledgment. They would usually rather be famous than rich.

Moon in Leo folk are generous. But their sharing can be a bit heavy-handed. They have a sense of dignity that can make them appear affected and patronizing. They have considerable self-confidence and like to hear themselves talk. They want to be at the center of attention. They can be show-offs and conceited. They are frequently luxury-loving and in danger of self-indulgence.

These people have a capacity for leadership. Their perceptions are geared to other people; they instantly pick up how people receive them and respond to them. They have a persuasive way with groups and a sixth sense for measuring the mood of the public. They make good public-relations consultants.

People born with the Moon in Leo have passionate feelings. They seldom become involved in anything, or with anyone, in a halfhearted manner. They are outgoing and optimistic. They often refuse to recognize personal limitations. They have fertile imaginations and are inclined to get along well with children.

Moon in Leo individuals make loyal friends. They usually have numerous acquaintances from whom they enjoy receiving admiration and

256

THE PLANETS IN THE SIGNS: THE MOON THROUGH PLUTO

praise. Anyone who does not appreciate them to their satisfaction is likely
to be ignored and banished from their inner circle. Although radiating fun
and warmth, these people can be self-opinionated and so run the risk of
alienating friends and realizing their worst fear—isolation.

THE MOON IN VIRGO

People with Moon in Virgo are competent and conscientious. They
have a unique ability to analyze problems and to come up with solutions.
Once involved in a project or task, they become totally absorbed until their
work is completed.

Given even a small share of appreciation, Moon in Virgo individuals
will work as though they really enjoy it—and they do—without fuss about
pay or privileges. Employed in a job, they are usually there as long as it
suits them. Employers find them willing, uncomplaining, trustworthy, and
undemanding.

Moon in Virgo individuals may appear much more self-confident than
is the case. They are likely to have some problem understanding their own
emotions. They may feel in a way that they can't trust their emotions and
therefore get inwardly uptight trying not to show them.

There are chances that childhood misunderstandings, involving a parent
or parent figure, have never been resolved and become the basis for adult
attitudes. The tendency to criticize and find fault is strong. Old prejudices
picked up from elders in childhood may be unconsciously applied.

Moon in Virgo people have very practical minds as long as they do not
allow their emotional uncertainties to get the better of them. They can
become woolly thinkers if they start to worry about what others are thinking
about them, instead of dealing with the facts in hand and getting on with
what has to be done.

Moon in Virgo people are modest and unassuming. They make extremely good teachers who are able to appreciate the feelings of their students without allowing personalities to get in the way. They genuinely wish
to help people. And even their critical tendency has this object behind it.

In business and work, Moon in Virgo people believe in giving service.
They are industrious and unassuming, sometimes inclined to be a bit timid.
They are very good at dealing with detail. Although their personalities can
at times be cold, they have a knack for being able to analyze other people's
feelings. They can remain detached from a problem and are capable of
giving first-rate advice.

They have to be careful that their practical way of looking at things
does not make them calculating. They may need to cultivate a more imaginative outlook. There is a tendency for these people to concentrate on
mental activities to the exclusion of emotionally stimulating ones.

Moon in Virgo individuals can wait for romance to come to them, then
end up let down. They need to make more effort to communicate their
deeper feelings. They can be too sensitive about maintaining appearances.
Displays of affection in public are likely to embarrass them.

These people are inclined to make good doctors, nurses, administrators, and teachers. Even so, they have to work harder at accepting pro-

gressive ideas. They can be too conforming and conventional. They may need to relax and enjoy life more.

With the Moon in Virgo, a person can be particularly interested in health and diet. These people have to avoid becoming unduly imaginative about ailments or feelings; their imaginings can be exaggerated to the point where phobias can develop.

Fault-finding is one of the most annoying traits of Moon in Virgo people. They are usually looking for some kind of perfection. This tendency can make them tidy and efficient around the home. Or they may concentrate all their attention on their family, putting its comfort and welfare before neatness and tidiness.

A love of the past, combined with analytical ability, can lead to hobbies such as souvenir collecting, and tracing family trees.

THE MOON IN LIBRA

This person can make the ideal partner. Libra is the sign of partnership, and the Moon the energy of emotional response. Between them they make the sweetest music.

But the combination of Moon in Libra can confer a changeableness, sometimes a flirtatiousness. It is not conducive to lasting relationships. While everything is going smoothly, an association with this person can be idyllic. They are undemanding, understanding, charming, courteous, agreeable, and diplomatic. They accept their partners as they find them, and are not out to reform or correct them.

Then the mood is likely to change. The attention is likely to shift. If distracted by something out of the past, these people can withdraw deeply and uncommunicatively inside themselves. Or if a new and interesting person or event happens on the scene, they respond.

The need to be accepted by others is extremely strong, so Moon in Libra individuals are never alone for long.

Moon in Libra people have a habit for a while of giving everyone the response he or she wants. They tend to agree with whatever is said without noticing any contradiction in themselves. They feel the need to adapt to the emotions of the other person. It is this that makes them so popular. And after a while so exasperating to the person who takes them seriously!

Moon in Libra people often have a lot of ups and downs in their love life. Not so much because they are sensual, but because they are always out to please. And it's very difficult to please several people at the same time, especially if one of them is the marriage partner or primary lover. Libra, energized by the Moon, responds and relates to every contact, mostly innocently, but this does have its obvious complications.

Moon in Libra individuals seek harmony. Even though they may be the cause of much falling out, they hardly ever see it—they have moved on to a new relationship. And besides, they would not want to be involved in any nasty scene or argument if they could possibly avoid it.

Moon in Libra also produces persons who finds it hard to make up their mind. In their indecisiveness, they often wait for events to pick them up and carry them along. They have a powerful appreciation of beautiful things.

Their tastes in clothes, food, and amusements are expensive, frequently exotic.

Moon in Libra people can be passive. Their desire for peace may be so strong that they avoid making any effort for fear of the disturbance it might create. This is not to say that these people are lazy. Far from it! But they may exert themselves only along channels of their own choosing. Unfortunately, such channels may lead to a dependence on others to do the dirty work.

These are friendly people with sensitive instincts. They know how to make a partnership or a relationship really work. They rely on an emotional sixth sense that makes them aware of what will please others the most.

Moon in Libra individuals are most charming, pleasing hosts and hostesses to all. They love to entertain in style and beautiful surroundings. They are particularly tolerant, accepting others as they are. But they are snobs. They would like to find their closest associates among a privileged group, people who have more money than most. Even if Libras cannot afford this kind of life, they gravitate toward it.

Moon in Libra individuals can be undependable. Their emotions blow hot and cold. They can be all over someone one day, then aloof and uninterested the next. They can be too easily influenced, unable to pursue a definite line of action for a sustained period of time.

THE MOON IN SCORPIO

Scorpio can be an emotionally hazardous placement for the Moon. The sexual appetite is likely to be stimulated. There are dangers of problems and difficulties through indiscretion. A way has to be found of directing the emotions into productive channels. There is too much tendency to use the imagination along self-indulgent lines.

With the necessary restraint and positive direction—to be found in the other planetary placements—Moon in Scorpio can produce a determined and successful person. Through the energy of the Moon, their passions can be translated into creative, artistic, and inventive work. They can have access to heights and depths of emotions unknown to others.

Moon in Scorpio people can be scientists, psychoanalysts, researchers, investigators, occultists, and deeply moving painters and writers. They are likely to excel in any occupation that requires deeper than average insight.

Such individuals are strong-willed, secretive, intense, and seldom spontaneous. Staunchly helpful and brave, nevertheless these people can be jealous and spiteful. They tend to repress their feelings so that they get tremendous buildups that can explode into anger, corruption, or near genius.

Moon in Scorpio does not produce a person with great tenderness. The urge may be there, but seldom can it be expressed. There is too much self-suppression. The sentimentality and softness of the Moon get burned up in the volcanic intensity of Mars and Pluto, planetary rulers of Scorpio. But it has to be remembered that all this will be modified by the positions of the other planets. In this way, the Moon in Scorpio placement can reflect positive and helpful values for the integral personality.

For instance, Moon in Scorpio confers great strength of will whether it is used for good or ill. The person is less dependent on others, enabling him or her to work for long hours in isolation and difficult conditions or circumstances. These people can get to the top through sheer endurance and personal discipline. They have a way of grasping difficult subjects instantly. They don't like change and are fixed in their views, often to the point of absurdity.

Moon in Scorpio individuals have a special magnetism about them. They are not the type of people who blend into a crowd. It is difficult not to be aware of their presence even though they do nothing to draw attention to themselves.

Their emotional sensitivity enables them to have deep insights into other people's characters. They are not fooled by pretense. They dislike affectation. They want people to be themselves. Yet in spite of their directness and sometimes bluntness, they are very secretive people. They never reveal their deeper feelings except in the intensity with which they approach projects they are interested in.

Sometimes Moon in Scorpio people are subject to deep depressions. They feel compelled to penetrate their souls in order to identify with their own core, the source of their feelings. At times like these, life can be difficult for their loved ones. People they live with may feel rejected or excluded. Moon in Scorpio individuals can be weird and self-tormenting.

But they do have a great capacity for getting to the bottom of things. They never give up once their emotional interest has been aroused. They like to relive their experiences. Because of this, they often make the same passionate mistakes more than once.

Moon in Scorpio people are not ones who forget or forgive quickly. Perceiving an insult, they vow to get even. It is within their nature to retaliate and get revenge no matter how long it takes.

THE MOON IN SAGITTARIUS

People with the Moon in Sagittarius often find it hard to remain in one place for long. They yearn to travel to distant and exotic places, preferably across the sea. If they can't journey physically to foreign lands, they make frequent visits through their imaginations.

These individuals are idealists. They are always looking for new horizons, new goals. They make plans in their heads, which they may have no intention of implementing at the moment. But one day they probably will.

The Moon in Sagittarius often makes a person move house a lot. Even if such people have large families, including children or elders, they are likely to pack them all up and move on to new pastures without a backward glance or any thought of inconvenience.

These people have to feel free. They will not tolerate any kind of partnership if it makes them feel tied down. They can be very good providers and family men and women, which may seem to restrict them as much as anyone. But it all depends on how *they* feel about it whether they stick at it or not.

With the Moon in Sagittarius, a person can easily become something of a wanderer. But they will never let their family down, if they have one. They will be interested in having the nicest home they can afford, a place where they can entertain friends and acquaintances. But once the family unit is established, they will be inclined to use it as a base, a place for joyous homecomings with gifts and parties—and frequent departures.

People with Moon in Sagittarius are invariably popular. They have an optimistic outlook on life that others often envy. And they seem to have more than their fair share of good luck. They can be disastrously overconfident, and lose their money gambling or backing untried business ventures. But they are not ones to worry or to blame others.

They are generous, sometimes foolishly so. But their losses have a way of being made up. Moon in Sagittarius people have spontaneous feelings. They are intuitive and quick to do others a good turn. So their generosity often is paid back, getting them out of trouble in the nick of time. Such is their good luck.

Moon in Sagittarius individuals love nature and the outdoor life. They are most active in sports and games. They are fond of animals, especially racehorses. Gambling often attracts them, and is one cause of their irresponsibility.

These people can be devils for making promises that are not kept. They can be very irresponsible. They may be a constant headache to their dependents, who have to make excuses for their easygoing casualness.

Moon in Sagittarius people are outspoken. They say exactly what they feel and very often put their foot in it. They are not the types to indulge in deception and lies. These are people with a high sense of honor and a regard for tradition. Although they sometimes want to break authoritarian rules and positions, they have a respect for established law and order.

These are freedom lovers, but they do not believe in anarchy. They can, however, be rather superficial and tend to ignore the bigger social issues for the trivial. They can be too indulgent of their need for emotional stimulation through companionship and change. They can be the tireless party types, always in search of a good time.

These people are great raconteurs. They may be successful writers about history and cultures without necessarily ever having visited other lands.

There is something of the explorer about Moon in Sagittarius people. They love to be free to roam, both mentally and physically. They do not take easily to conventional nine-to-five occupations. They need excitement in their lives, the prospect of new discoveries around every corner. They can make good professional people if their profession allows them to extend their knowledge and vision.

THE MOON IN CAPRICORN

The Moon in Capricorn is not a good position for expressing love or emotions. These feelings may be felt quite intensely, but getting them out is the problem. With this combination, people feel self-conscious about any displays of sentimentality. They can be afraid of seeming foolish.

The female side is very important to this combination. The men are likely to link up with women much older or younger. Their first attempts at marriage may not be as successful as their second, which they may studiously avoid through fears of making the same mistake. The women in their lives may lack warmth.

The women with Moon in Capricorn will not be happy unless they find a man who loves them; they should not settle for less. And it is important to have sexual rapport. It is through the act of lovemaking that all people with this combination can communicate their deeper feelings to the person they love.

But the Moon in Capricorn is a very favorable position for achieving worldly success. It may mean, though, a lot of hard work and the sacrifice of many of the normal distractions and pleasures that people enjoy. It is as if people with the Moon in Capricorn decide to put their unreleased emotions into mobilizing their ambitions. They feel more secure and confident in company when they communicate from a position of reputation or influence. So prestige becomes their aim early in life, once they discover something they are good at.

The Moon in Capricorn gives a remarkable capacity for working under pressure and in conditions that most other people would find impossible. In this way, much ground can be covered, and the favorable attention of helpful people in authority gained.

These people have an aptitude for wielding power. Instead of depending on personality and charisma, their strength lies in an extraordinary ability to know everything that is going on in the operation under their command. These are the potential captains of industry, as well as the all-seeing eyes of the bureaucratic "big brother."

Wherever the public is concerned, Moon in Capricorn individuals will eventually receive the recognition and authority so dear to their hearts.

Moon in Capricorn people have to be careful not to take too serious a view of life. They can become gloomy and brooding. They need to get out and around as often as possible, and not settle into any ruts. They can be inclined to put too much emphasis on work and achieving their ambitions. They often neglect relaxation and entertainment in which other people are involved.

These individuals are careful, sometimes too cautious. They can miss out on opportunities through a fear of taking any chances at all. They can be reluctant to venture beyond the familiar.

However, these people can be very self-demanding. They are inclined to put a great deal of pressure on themselves. They may be acutely conscious of their emotional restraint, which in turn will cause them to become even more uptight. They must find a happy way of releasing their feelings.

The sign of Capricorn energized by the Moon can make these individuals a bit self-centered in their feelings. They are inclined to relate everything to themselves. Sometimes, they appear unsympathetic. They are, however, deeply attached to their homes and families. They make a point of seeing that the people and things they love most are protected.

THE MOON IN AQUARIUS

A person with the Moon in Aquarius is usually a person with high ideals. These people are not sentimentalists, however. They believe that any good that is done should be for the benefit of all people in the community, not just for individuals. Moon in Aquarius people are the humanitarians, the reformers of the Zodiac.

A person with this combination has very strong feelings about what should and should not be done. They see things very clearly. They translate everything they feel into a mental image. In this way they are able to identify with their fellow man. They can initiate ideas that will help to solve problems rather than just relieve them.

Moon in Aquarius individuals are often scientists. The power of invention is strong. They also can make farsighted politicians, and dedicated leaders of good causes and crusades.

These people are friendly. They like to get around, to circulate, to enlarge their circle of contacts and interesting acquaintances. They are not too enthusiastic about close friendships; they prefer looser relationships.

But Moon in Aquarius folk are loyal. They love the idea of freedom and independence, for themselves and for everyone else. It is this urge that makes them so effective in their endeavors to help others. They don't want anyone to be unnecessarily dependent.

This, of course, creates its problems. Their own loved ones can feel a bit neglected. It is very hard, almost impossible, for these people to settle into a one-to-one relationship, especially if it demands a lot of their time and attention. They are not the type to cuddle up by the fire for long. They don't forget what is happening in the cold, cruel world outside.

Moon in Aquarius people live a regulated life. They seldom go to extremes, emotionally or physically. They are not self-indulgent. They may, though, be fanatical in their views of society. But they are conservative in their own affairs, which they handle with efficient detachment.

These people are interested in unusual subjects and usually have a strong intuitive flair for understanding them. They are often original thinkers, tending to use the past to demonstrate what is possible in the future.

Moon in Aquarius individuals are quietly obstinate people. For all their friendliness and understanding, they will not budge from a position or an idea once they have made up their mind. Sometimes their views are very difficult for their associates to identify with. They sometimes feel isolated. They often go out on a limb; few people really understand what they are trying to do.

These individuals have to beware of becoming eccentric. Their deeper unconventional attitudes can impel them to mix with groups that are on the fringe of established society, acquaintances who may have odd and even revolutionary inclinations.

People born with the Moon in Aquarius are good judges of character. Their instincts are well developed. They often are able to provide their associates with logical solutions to their problems that no one else may have suggested or seen.

These are individuals who can understand people undergoing stress and strain and crises of adjustment. In a helping way, they are very straightforward; they will not pull any punches in what they say if they feel it is necessary. They often use shock as a device for trying to wake people up.

Moon in Aquarius people can come on as rebels. If they want to win the support of the public, it is important for them not to display excessive independence. The public can be quick to turn against them if it is sensed that their efforts are for self and not for service.

THE MOON IN PISCES

A Moon in Pisces person is very difficult to understand. Their emotions change with the drama and frequency of a flashing light. The true person is seldom ever seen. They are a parade of different moods and personalities.

These people are dreamers. There is a great need for a strengthening influence through other planetary positions. These people find facing up to reality an excruciating experience. They can't stand pressure, disharmony, ugliness, conflict, argument, or competition. They are very happy when they are winning, but fretful and difficult when losing.

It is not so much that Moon in Pisces individuals cling to their material possessions. Just the opposite! They can be commendably philosophic about that kind of loss. But they are terribly concerned with what others think about them. They want to be liked and, even better, loved.

Moon in Pisces people usually manage to have someone strong and reliable in close contact. They need someone to depend on; they can become clinging vines. They have a happy knack of making confessions that confuse their partner but free themselves from their own feelings of guilt or doubt.

The feeling of continuous failure seems to afflict Moon in Pisces people whenever they become introspective, which is fairly often. Things that other people shrug off as the price of being human can psychologically torture these supersensitive souls.

People with the Moon in Pisces need to get out of any regular environment. Without constantly changing faces and scenes, they become highly emotional, depressed, even morbid. They need more than just the person they love—and they do love very, very deeply. They need lighter, even superficial, relationships to compensate for the depth that is in them.

These people are generous, self-sacrificing, and cooperative. They can easily be taken advantage of. They have to avoid excessive intake of alcohol or unnecessary use of drugs. They are inclined to use these aids under pressure to escape from reality.

The Moon in Pisces is an extremely creative and poetic combination. It gives people a great capacity for love and service to those less fortunate. Dedicating themselves to the hurt and needy can be an artistic and awe-inspiring mission.

Moon in Pisces individuals have a deceptive side to their nature. They have a horror of revealing their true feelings. They often adopt poses that help them release their emotions. Other people mistake the pose for the real person, only to be disappointed when this Moon child changes again. Such emotional games give the Moon in Pisces person a reputation for being unreliable and unstable.

People born with the Moon in Pisces have powerful imaginations. However, they need to channel their feelings and thoughts into constructive activities. They need to work toward definite objectives. Otherwise, they will drift off into dreamland, which is their refuge when the pressures of life become too much for them to cope with.

There is a risk of self-indulgence in food, alcohol, sex, and comfort. These people can be very sociable. They enjoy the stimulation of entertaining and visiting, at home or out. Attached to their families, they are capable of making considerable sacrifices for the ones they love—as long as they are allowed their private world.

Although gentle and kindly, Moon in Pisces individuals are often restless and seem to be inconstant in their affections. They may turn their back on an established relationship for a while, so they can enjoy the distraction of a newer or more novel one. They are usually true to lovers, mates, or friends in the long run, and certainly when a situation is serious and demands a clear show of allegiance.

Mercury in the Signs

Mercury stands for communication. Its quality is intelligence. When positive, it is discerning; when negative, cunning. This quicksilver planet can create lightning-swift intuition and heightened awareness, or mental restlessness and lack of concentration.

Mercury's influence on an individual also depends on the other planetary placements. If some planetary placements are stabilizing ones, Mercury's contribution can be positive.

Mercury gives adaptability. It intensifies the power to communicate information or knowledge. There is always a risk that without mature restraint, the influence of Mercury can make a person frivolous, superficial, and inclined to scatter mental energies. Pursuing numerous activities may interfere with an individual's ability to accomplish anything of value in one activity.

When balanced, Mercury makes a person alert, active, and quick to spot opportunities.

Mercury is strongest in association with Gemini and Virgo, the two signs it rules.

MERCURY IN ARIES

This combination makes a person mentally active and able. Their mind is seldom still. They can produce an abundance of ideas about practically any subject brought to their attention. If they do not understand something, they are inclined to head straight for the encyclopedia or the library. Ideas are as necessary to them as food.

These people often enjoy debating. They are likely to provoke arguments just for the sake of exercising their mental dexterity. They can be very clever, sometimes brilliant. But there is a tendency to become pat and stale. They may collect information for the sake of displaying knowledge instead of using it productively.

People with Mercury in Aries have a gift for summing up situations at a glance. They make good executives and administrators. They are at their best when the action is coming thick and fast, and ideas are needed for solutions. Pressure triggers their sharp wits.

But these people are not so good at making long and detailed studies. They are inclined to become bored with repetitious situations. They can bring their minds brilliantly to bear on specific problems with figures or details. But to have to concentrate on long columns of numbers day in and day out would drive them mad.

Mercury in Aries people love to read and learn subjects in which they are interested. But here, too, they are inclined to skim the surface. They will take what they think is needed off the top, then depend on their own undoubted ingenuity to fill in the rest.

This zippy approach can produce a person who may seem to know a tremendous amount. But he or she is likely to be exposed as a dabbler in any particular subject when confronted by an expert. Cornered, these individuals shift into high gear—pioneering topics, their best conversational gambit.

These people like to put forward new ideas. They are good conversationalists. But they do find it difficult to listen for long to others. Then they are compelled to put their oar in, knowledgeable or not.

Mercury in Aries can make a person blunt and outspoken. There is an impulse to say anything that is felt, even though it may offend or hurt. The excuse for this lack of diplomacy is the feeling that the truth should not hurt. But, of course, it often does, and it can hurt these people themselves.

Mercury in Aries individuals are fast movers, physically and mentally. They like to get around, making frequent short trips and visits to their friends and relatives. Friendship means a great deal to them. They are spontaneous and generous in their responses to friends. They do, however, tend to collect numerous friends, not a great many to which they are deeply attached. This tendency, of course, has to be considered against the placements of the other planets.

They have a direct and forceful manner of expression. Sometimes they are in such a hurry to communicate that their utterances become disconnected. They do not think much before they speak; what comes into the mind usually passes right out of the mouth.

These people are often impressive in engaging in repartee. Their first thoughts usually are best. Their lack of deliberation, unless their Sun is in Taurus, allows them to deliver volley after volley of clever retorts and remarks.

There may be a tendency in people with Mercury in Aries to exaggerate. They may not allow the facts to destroy a good story. It is important for them to try to cultivate greater concentration, as well as more careful regard for the truth.

These individuals are often inspired in their perceptions. But they may lack continuity. They often lack patience and restraint. When others do not agree with their ideas, they may become hostile and argumentative.

MERCURY IN TAURUS

Once Mercury in Taurus people get an idea fixed in their head, it is very difficult to change their minds. They can be as obstinate as a mule. They may take an interest in an opposite view or play the devil's advocate. If so, they appear to be won over, at least convinced of their misconception. But this is like water off a duck's back. Mercury in Taurus will only change an opinion in his or her good time.

Of course, this mental determination can be a great asset. Certainly it is helpful to a partner or a boss who relies on Mercury in Taurus individuals. When they have the right idea, they pursue it with a stubborn resolution that can produce wonderful results.

Mercury in Taurus people are methodical thinkers. They proceed cautiously from one fact to another. They are not subject to flights of fancy, unless other combinations in the chart introduce this element. They are practical. They don't jump to conclusions. They are conservative and inclined to put their faith more on what has been proven that in speculative ideas.

A person with Mercury in Taurus makes a good politician who will be known for his or her solid policies. There is a strong tendency to want to build for the future, to make provisions against possible future needs or shortages. The impulse is to resist changing the status quo. Much that has been good, and bad, in the past has been retained by the intransigence of the Mercury in Taurus individual.

These people are diplomatic and conventional in speech and writing. They may appear to be slow-thinking. But they have swift comprehension, which requires time for thought before making their responses. They are not mentally adaptable. They have to live with an idea for a long time to come around to accepting it. Even then, the attitude may be only a tentative tolerance of "newfangled" notions.

What goes into the Mercury in Taurus mind is indelibly registered. These people have a natural feeling for making money. Their ideas are usually directed toward this endeavor. They may sit on an idea for years before implementing it. When they do, the time is usually ripe. They put a lot of store in experience. They will never undertake a project unless it has been thoroughly examined. And, wherever possible, they will avoid giving snap decisions.

Mercury in Taurus folk can be a bit opinionated. They may think they have worked out the only worthwhile philosophy or approach to life. So they are inclined to ignore any other. They usually adopt a fairly dogmatic method of expression, which goes with their self-assured manner.

They are diplomatic people, however. They do not go looking for arguments even though their stubborn refusal to see the other person's point of view often puts up the backs of their associates. It is easy for Mercury in Taurus individuals to get into mental ruts.

These people lack adaptability. They tend to settle into a situation very gradually, judging it all the time on its practical advantages. They seldom embrace a new scheme or idea without a great deal of consideration. They hate to be put under pressure to make up their minds if any change is involved.

Mercury in Taurus people are intuitive. But they often lack inspiration because they will not give up their already formed hardheaded notions. They are not trustful of imagination. Everything needs to be pinned down and explainable in concrete terms.

MERCURY IN GEMINI

Now here's a person who can have a flashing wit. If the other planetary positions are favorable, Mercury in Gemini minds can be as incisive as a razor's edge. They are logical, quick-thinking, able to outdistance most of their rivals and competitors in any mental gymnastics.

But Mercury in Gemini people can be very shallow. Unless they have a solid planetary support, like the Sun in Taurus, they may be as light as feathers. They may use their mental gifts for nothing more edifying than gossip, criticism, or light reading—for example, newspaper headlines.

They want the news, near and far, but not a detailed account. They are seldom able to settle down to any serious mental activity, such as reading a good book, without having to put it down and start something else.

Without support, this combination can produce a person who is restless and lacks any powers of concentration. They may be great mimics, but cannot sustain the effort long enough to put it to any good or profitable use. They may jump from one activity to another, so nothing worthwhile is ever really accomplished.

For some Mercury in Gemini individuals, nervous problems can develop, including near breakdowns. Speech can be affected by impediments, such as stuttering or incoherence. The mind may race far ahead of the body's capability to give it voice.

Mercury in Gemini people can become con artists. The necessity to earn a living when there is no chance of sticking to one occupation turns mental dexterity into cunning. The plausibility of these people can be amazing.

But with good support from the other planets, the Mercury in Gemini person can be extremely successful. They can adapt to other people's moods in an instant without any negative reaction. As a result, other people feel they are understanding and intelligent individuals. They are often helped to get ahead by those more influential than themselves. Such allies appreciate their swift-minded versatility.

People with Mercury in Gemini are ideally suited for careers in journalism. They make first-rate linguists, interpreters, shorthand writers, typists, agents, and lecturers. They are friendly, entertaining, and fun. They have a knack for making people laugh and feel at ease.

They need travel as often as possible to change the scene and to make interesting new contacts. They have a great love of independence and freedom. Nerves get on edge when they feel hemmed in. Routine drives them up the wall. Their tolerance for repetitive tasks is almost nil.

Mercury in Gemini individuals have to guard against being slapdash. Persistence and determination to reach fixed goals are seldom among their virtues. They receive most of their life satisfaction from mental stimulation, which often is gained by going from one relationship to another.

They are not particularly easy people to live with, although the position of the other planets, especially the Sun, will have a strong bearing on this. They change their minds so often they can be very difficult to follow. They are inclined to be selfish because they take the line of least resistance. It invariably leads to new experiences, which they love so much. To resist their impulses, however, can mean a continuation of the status quo, which they hate.

There is never a dull moment when Mercury in Gemini people are around. They are inventive and curious. They sometimes act like children even in adulthood, playing tricks, joking around, and making mischief. Gemini, it has to be remembered, is the sign of the Twins. When they are stimulated by their eternal playmate Mercury, there is little time for seriousness.

These people have to guard against a tendency to become too excited. They may suffer from nerves and nervous ailments. They have a strong tendency to worry about all sorts of things, jumping from one problem to another when they are upset without any intention of pausing long enough to find practical solutions.

MERCURY IN CANCER

People with Mercury in Cancer are extremely sensitive. They want desperately to be liked and respected. This does not always show, but it is there behind their façade. They try hard to seem easygoing and nonchalant about what others think. They are tactful, discreet, and diplomatic.

The conversation of these people will usually get around to the past. They often have a repertoire of reminiscences, which can be entertaining and delightful to the ear. They have a simple way with words that communicates just the right feelings and atmosphere.

Mercury in Cancer does not confer a great amount of originality. But it does make a person a natural psychologist. Such individuals can look into people and deliver amazingly accurate descriptions of their mental states and feelings.

They love nature and can't abide cruelty to animals or people. They have strong feelings about what they like and don't like. Sometimes they can be irritable and moody. Their memory is usually first-rate. But these people can be indecisive and live in a world of fantasy if Mercury is not supported by other solid positions.

With Mercury in Cancer, a person can be an excellent scholar. They can become professors, curators, historians, lecturers, and writers of unusually perceptive autobiographies. There is a depth to these people, which shows in their manner, speech and turn of phrase.

Their mind is not busy but it is introspective. They like to go inside themselves, to explore and to interpret their own feelings. This exercise gives them a great capacity for understanding how others feel, and for describing these things.

They usually possess a strong hankering for the past. In whatever work or profession they may follow, they rely on precedent and tradition for their values and standards. They are inclined to think that things were better in the old days.

Mercury in Cancer people do not like stress and strain. They are not the competitive type. They certainly can have a surprisingly good head for business when they want to put their minds to it. But usually they are more content to stay out of the rat race. They will pursue their ambitions in areas less likely to create the feeling of competitiveness.

Although timid, Mercury in Cancer individuals are enterprising. If they can summon up the interest and the energy, they are frequently successful in influencing the public to support their schemes and business ventures. They have an appealing way of expressing themselves. Their emotional sensitivity combines with clarity of thought, as long as moodiness does not intervene.

These are people who usually have strong family ties. They also are inclined to worry and fuss about their loved ones. Their active imaginations allow them to fear the worst if loved ones are late getting home or keeping an appointment.

As parents, people with Mercury in Cancer have to learn to let go when their youngsters reach the age for venturing out into the world. They can be too protective, and may deny a teenager the freedom that is necessary for mature development.

Mercury in Cancer individuals can become very polished writers if their Sun is in Gemini. The Sun in Cancer will confer more tenacity and ambition. With the Sun in Leo, this person will be more outgoing and optimistic, alert for opportunities to organize and lead on a grand scale.

MERCURY IN LEO

Mercury in Leo instills pride of mind. And these people, proud of their ideas, do spend a lot of time putting them across to the public. They can be writers, lecturers, teachers, public-relations agents, or promoters. They favor the entertainment and amusement industries, in which they can exploit their sense of the dramatic.

Mercury in Leo people tend to be self-confident and outgoing. They have a strong regard for the worth of their own ideas, which often are quite good. But the tendency is to try to foist their opinions on others, mainly out of an impulse to give others what is good for them. This, of course, is not always appreciated. If there is not restraint indicated by other planetary positions, such a person can get a name for bossiness, boasting, and showing off.

There also is a strong tendency toward conceit. Mercury in Leo individuals think their ideas are what the world has been waiting for. They are especially haughty if the Sun also is in Leo. Although these people can be great leaders, they can make such a din about it that respect turns to laughter and derision.

Mercury in Leo people are very sensitive about how others regard them. They like plenty of praise. Anyone who doesn't react warmly and enthusiastically to their ideas is likely to be regarded as a nincompoop. There is very little leeway for intelligent criticism of their proposals. They hold their beliefs so passionately, to question them is to insult them.

Although they do not hold grudges, they are inclined to ignore anyone who disagrees with them. People can suddenly feel very much out in the cold if they have dared to question the Mercury in Leo's judgment or opinions.

The fact is that Mercury in Leo often makes a person too fixed and narrow-minded. She or he may fail to move with the times. Disdainful of detail, these individuals often make careless mistakes. They tend to take the broad and grandiose view—which has won a lot of empires, but lost a lot of friends.

The urge to be imperious has to be avoided if these people want to get their ideas accepted. Then they are more likely to reach a position of authority, in which they have the scope to express their skills and talents.

Mercury in Leo individuals are not very adaptable. Anyone who is trying to influence them has to avoid confrontations, which immediately get their backs up. Like the Lion, the symbol of Leo, they have a strong fighting spirit. At the first sign of opposition they are ready for a fight.

These people need time to think through new ideas. Even though they may oppose a viewpoint, it can be counted on that they will go away and consider it. One of their maddening habits is to come back and propose the very same action to the person who originally suggested it to them.

Mercury in Leo people have breadth of vision. But they are not the types to fill in the details, unless their Sun is in Virgo. Mercurial Leos need the backing of a good team of associates to handle the less interesting side of their plans.

There is an intolerably inflated sense of pride associated with Mercury in Leo, especially if the Sun is in Leo. These people can become very wearing on the people they live with. They are likely to be know-it-alls, and literally try to take over the other person's life. They are often badly shocked and for a while contrite when a loved one fights back, as often happens. But they soon resume their high-handed manner.

There is, throughout all, a distinct air of dignity about Mercury in Leo people. Their bearing can be impressive, and their demeanor attractive. They are magnetic personalities.

MERCURY IN VIRGO

Here Mercury is in a very strong position. It gives the person a bright and balanced intellect. There is no tendency to go to extremes, as is often the case with Mercury. And the ideas that the person holds are likely to be practical and to appeal to a wide segment of the public.

Mercury in Virgo individuals have great powers of discrimination. If they are dealing with details, they can select all that is relevant with a smooth and flowing precision. They will never allow emotional considerations to interfere with their judgment. They are capable of making decisions on the facts alone, regardless of their own personal feelings.

In their personal behavior, Mercury in Virgo people also exhibit the same discriminating faculty. They are seldom likely to be indiscreet. They are very aware of the value of a good reputation. Reliability is extremely important to them. They are not late for appointments. They enjoy doing the right thing.

People with this combination can be a bit cold and intolerant. They may be more concerned with the details of a situation than with the human element. If some compassion is called for, they will be inclined to insist on the letter of the law being followed. This can be good for business but tough for people.

A Mercury in Virgo person is strictly a no-nonsense individual. They are conscientious and serious in whatever they undertake. They respect method and order. They make very good employees. They can solve production problems at a glance, seeing all the practical alternatives and focusing on the best one.

These people have to guard against being too critical. They may strive for perfection to such a degree that they see faults everywhere, especially in people. Although they mean to be helpful, their critical observations can get others' backs up and create ill feeling against them.

People with this combination are modest and unassuming. They work extremely well under direction or without it. They can be relied upon to work, not slacking even when left alone.

Mercury in Virgo people can become unduly obsessed with their health and diet. This is the only area in which they are likely to show extreme behavior. They have a fear of ill health, mainly because it interrupts their enjoyment of their work and mental pursuits.

Mercury in Virgo individuals are often found in scientific occupations. They have a well-drilled mentality, which allows them to pursue long trails of detail toward worthwhile ends. They like to be involved in work that has humanitarian value. They make excellent laboratory workers and researchers.

However, these people can become too narrowly focused in their objectives if left to their own devices. They can put too much store on being correct in every little thing. They can become exacting and fussy. The desire for cleanliness or neatness can be accentuated to the point of getting on other people's nerves.

Mercury in Virgo confers a facility for mathematics and verbal expression. Problems are approached in a practical way, which does not allow much room for imagination. But what these people say is well worth listening to. They have a knack for putting the most complex issues into simple language.

They are quick thinkers, analytical, and systematic. Their minds work like well-arranged filing systems. They have good memories. They are best able to utilize their talents and skills when working to design or prearranged plan.

Mercury in Virgo people are easy to educate. They seldom go off into daydreams. With the Sun also in Virgo, they have to avoid suppressing their emotions and feelings. Otherwise, they become too logical.

MERCURY IN LIBRA

This is a person with a finely balanced intellect. Mercury in Libra people make extremely good judges and executives whose job is to sum up alternatives and give a balanced opinion. They are better at working with data presented to them than trying to make decisions regarding their own life.

Personally, where tne emotional element comes in, such individuals can be so torn between thought and feeling that they do nothing. Opportunities are often missed through indecision. This is especially so if these people also have the Sun in Libra.

With the Sun in Virgo, on the other hand, the mind is more practical, highly legalistic, and coldly logical. Emotional considerations are less likely to affect the judgment. But without a softening influence from other planets, there can be too much head and not enough heart.

With the Sun in Scorpio, another alternative, the logic of the mind can be used for more selfish reasons. In any judgments, points will be added up, with the weight given to personal advantage. And such individuals will definitely look for those advantages.

Mercury in Libra people usually are extremely broad-minded. They are prepared to accept people exactly as they are. They seldom try to improve or reform others, even though they may have noticed all their faults.

When confronted with a dilemma, they have a strong intuition about the right course to follow. But their nature is to weigh all the pros and cons. They do this with such precision, noting all nuances, that eventually they are back where they began. They have thus evened out the possibilities into an impeccable balance of equilibrium, or poise.

This poise is basic to Mercury in Libra people. They are often charming and serene, exceedingly friendly and diplomatic. They possess a love of refinement and artistic things. And they avoid as much as possible becoming involved in arguments.

Their intuition is sometimes brilliant. When balanced, they make very good constructive critics. They are able to provide perceptive suggestions for improving literature and works of art.

Mercury in Libra individuals are extremely social creatures. They need numerous relationships, both friendly and romantic. Their agreeable natures make them easy to talk to and get along with. They like to be liked, and so will say the kind of things that make the other person warm to them. These people have to be careful of dropping old friends for new ones.

Mercury in Libra individuals can be shallow and flighty. Libra is an air sign, mental and intellectual; it creates a need for stimulation of the mind through diverse and entertaining relationships. The presence of Mercury, the planet of swift communication, exaggerates this need. So these people may not be able to concentrate too long on one thing.

Mercury in Libra creates a personality that is enterprising and spontaneous. But unless other planetary placements give more stability, there can be a lack of direction. These people can be plagued by indecision. They are likely to compare one alternative with another so long that nothing concrete gets done. They are inclined to shove problems under the table, then hope that circumstances will eventually sort them out.

These people can be polished and persuasive speakers. They are diplomatic and able to appreciate the many sides of an argument. They are often in demand as after-dinner speakers and masters of ceremonies at weddings and celebrations. They can be extremely flattering without appearing to be insincere.

Mercury in Libra individuals are well suited for partnership ventures. They are smooth-working members of a team. They are more inclined to contribute mentally than to be much help physically; they do not generally enjoy physical exertion.

MERCURY IN SCORPIO

A person with Mercury in Scorpio can go either one of two ways—up or down. At their best they can use the extraordinary clarity and strength of their mind for the benefit of mankind. They make topnotch psychiatrists, researchers, scientists, investigators, and medical men and women. At their worst they can use their mental faculties in self-seeking and cruelly deceptive ways, so that other people are more likely to be enslaved or degraded than helped and uplifted. Such is the power of Mercury in Scorpio.

As has been mentioned frequently in these planetary descriptions, all depends on the positions of the other planets; they usually modify the undesirable propensities of any one placement. Scorpio is a sign of extremes. When considered in isolation, it can produce a totally unwarranted impression. The effects of all the planets must be synthesized into a whole, which makes up the real individual.

Mercury in Scorpio denotes a person who is active both mentally and emotionally. The emotions are usually the strongest, especially if the Sun is in Scorpio also. These people are extremely shrewd. They have a talent for spotting opportunities that will occur in the future, and for working toward them with unalterable determination. They are fixed and stubborn in their views. They often repeat the same mistakes.

Mercury in Scorpio tends to produce a person who is secretive and sly. They are able to put their finger on other people's weaknesses, which they frequently exploit. They are gifted players of the cat-and-mouse game, encouraging the foolhardy toward doom. Such a fate may be inflicted by circumstances that the Mercury in Scorpio person has perceived, even manipulated, long before.

These people often take a great interest in investigating the occult and other mysteries of life. Although they are down-to-earth and realistic, they have a fascination for trying to work out both the future and the past.

They often exhibit a steely mind, which is especially encouraging to people in emergencies. With other favorable planetary placements, they can be brilliant surgeons, fearless soldiers and commanders, and inspired mystics.

People with Mercury in Scorpio sometimes have irresistible urges to fantasize about sex. They often start their search for sexual excitement at a young age. They may get a reputation for being cool experimenters, unable to commit themselves or to achieve real intimacy.

Mercury in Scorpio people seldom give up once they have fixed their mind on an objective. They are forever probing the ground around them to make sure they have not missed anything to their advantage. They are outspoken in their relationships, not hesitating to tell another person exactly what they think. Yet their private feelings about their own life are seldom revealed.

These people do not find it easy to adapt to new ideas. They are inclined to be studious and to stick to their own opinions through thick and thin. They can be so closed to new ways of thinking that in the commercial world they may get left behind, or be forced to make costly innovations in midstream.

Mercury in Scorpio individuals can be intolerant and bitter. Intent on revenge, they can be implacable and unforgiving enemies. Without helpful contributions from other planets, they can poison their own minds brooding and plotting. They need to cultivate a positive outlook, which sees more good in the world than may be immediately apparent.

These people often have very few interests in their lives. They tend to pour themselves into a single channel of activity. Their narrow focus makes people in other areas of their lives feel secondary and neglected. They can spend too much time working and not enough on relaxing.

Mercury in Scorpio people are resourceful, especially in a crisis. But they must be confronted on a deep personal level. It often takes a whacking surprise or shock for them to see the error of their close-minded ways.

MERCURY IN SAGITTARIUS

This is a rather happy-go-lucky placement. It often marks a person who is always on the move, both mentally and physically. The urge to roam over the land or through the mind is irresistible. Mercury in Sagittarius individuals need an occupation like writing or lecturing, which can be followed without interfering with their travels and adventures.

The mind of these people is clear and sharp. They have a gift for delivering one-line observations of shattering accuracy. But their insights seem to rise from deep down in their subconscious, a place where these people seldom consciously go.

Mercury in Sagittarius can confer a great interest in gathering information, but little in expending much effort through study and mental discipline. There is a need to feel free and unfettered, which can make the person a bit of a lightweight when it comes to serious thinking.

Mercury in Sagittarius people like to do several things at once. As a result, there is a tendency to do nothing really well. Variety becomes the spice of life. And unless they can get around to putting their experiences or thoughts on paper or on the airwaves, there is not much opportunity for them to excel in anything.

If there is a stabilizing influence from other placements, Mercury in Sagittarius can be used in positive ways. It can develop in a person philosophic interests that may contribute remarkably good ideas to the store of human knowledge. Such individuals can become great defenders of the underprivileged and downtrodden.

A person with Mercury in Sagittarius believes in freedom of expression. They do not take kindly to any kind of authority, especially if there is any attempt to muzzle the truth. In spite of their freedom-loving ideas, they can be too conventional where religious beliefs are concerned. They may don the cardinal's hat or the archbishop's robe, then preach freedom of thought and not be aware of the contradiction.

This combination can make a person inclined to forget his or her promises. They can get carried away with camaraderie and so make friends of people who are not good for them. Although their business judgment can be first-rate, they may lack discretion where pleasure and amusements are concerned.

Mercury in Sagittarius people are versatile and adaptive. They can usually turn their minds to just about anything—for a while. It is not that they lack the intelligence needed for concentration, merely that they fail to find it productive in their particular case. They depend more on inspiration. Their faith in this is often vindicated by the quality of their suggestions and ideas.

These people often have the gift of gab. They are not beyond doing a bit of moralizing and preaching, which can get on the nerves of their associates. Yet they can be very casual in their approach to life, ignoring responsibilities that other people regard as essential to an ordered existence.

Mercury in Sagittarius people are always looking for pots of gold at the end of the rainbow. They may not be as interested in the spoils as in the search. They are not the types to worship money; such a love of it would tie them down to having to make it. They would rather move on and trust to luck. Luck, surprisingly, often comes their way.

These people often say the wrong thing at the wrong time. Although their insights can be inspired, their sense of timing is inappropriate, usually because they are so enthused they cannot restrain themselves. When it comes to personal observations, they can provoke embarrassment all around.

MERCURY IN CAPRICORN

Here is a person with all the mental attributes of the proverbial strong, silent type. In a man or a woman engaged heavily in worldly affairs, this combination can be impressive. But it does not allow enough free play for the expression of femininity, which is such an important part of our enjoyment of life. A woman with Mercury in Capricorn needs to work harder to bring the female lightness of touch to the surface of her personality.

But for those with serious things to do, Mercury in Capricorn is an admirable placement. These people are clear and methodical thinkers. Unless they are careful and pay tolerant attention to the views of others, they can become unimaginative and rigid.

They are cautious individuals. They will not do or say anything that might make them look foolish. But if they become too tight-lipped and guarded, they can appear to be a caricature of the strong, silent type, and so bring on themselves the derision they are endeavoring to avoid. This combination needs some lighthearted balancing, such as the Sun in Sagittarius or even the Sun in Aquarius.

Mercury in Capricorn gives the sort of mentality that enables a person to persevere to the top of any profession or trade. These people are mentally tough. They are able to withstand long hours working on detail and other tedious tasks without losing interest.

They are ambitious in a quiet and unobtrusive way. They like to get control of situations and people. They are curious about anything that might affect their future, but are not distracted by superficialities. They have a good memory, into which they pack useful information and facts, ignoring anything that is trivial or likely to sidetrack them from their objectives.

Mercury in Capricorn people have to avoid becoming bigoted. Their tendency to be diplomatic to protect themselves from being criticized can turn into bitterness and cynicism. They have a good sense of timing and are able to cultivate, through mental determination, some of the virtues that usually come through more emotional temperaments.

Mercury in Capricorn individuals have a dry and appealing sense of humor. Their tongues also can be sharp and cruel, all the more so because of their knack for encapsulating their feelings into a few words. They can be sardonic. However, because these people have a compulsive need to be respected, their method of expression usually is diplomatic.

They often have to cultivate greater faith in the human race. Sad or unhappy experiences in their younger days are never quite forgotten or outgrown. They are often the victims of neglect or other people's unhappy circumstances. It is not difficult for them to adopt a skeptical and suspicious outlook.

Mercury in Capricorn induces a high regard for tradition and law and order. These people can become staunch and brave defenders of the conventions of society. Sometimes they can be misunderstood and branded reactionaries when all they are doing is trying to preserve what is best in society.

These are not the most optimistic of people. It is easy for them to get down in the dumps. They are inclined to feel the world pressing down on them, when probably it is their own lack of flexibility and gloomy view of life.

But if Mercury in Capricorn individuals have their Sun in a more joyous sign, such as Sagittarius, they will be more optimistic. They will be less self-concerned and more enthustiastic about people. They may see the hope of the world in a religious or philosophic ideal, and devote themselves to communicating that as a means to freedom.

MERCURY IN AQUARIUS

Here is a clever and original thinker. Mercury in Aquarius individuals are the observers of the world. What they see they put together into a complete whole, so they are usually able to give very illuminating views and see solutions that other people have not even touched.

These people often are topnotch scientists and inventors. They have an unconscious urge to discover, so they are endowed with a penetrating vision. They are not so-called thinkers; they don't sit down and ponder through their perceptions and memories. They "see" things swiftly. They are able to connect seemingly isolated events and phenomena in a flash. This is true inspiration.

But, of course, there is a negative side. If Mercury is unsupported by some solid planetary influence, these people can be very superficial. They may not chatter on or make spectacles of themselves, for they are rather reserved. But they can make gossip and the trivial comings and goings of companions the center of their interests. They still observe the scene, but it lacks the penetration and depth of perception of which they are capable.

Mercury in Aquarius individuals can be vague, inquisitive, erratic, and unpredictable.

The developed Mercury in Aquarius person is an excellent judge of human nature. These individuals are able to observe a person clinically, without allowing their emotions to get in the way. So they often hit upon the truth.

They can have a special interest in trying to improve the lot of their fellow man. They are more interested in people and humanity as a whole than in individual problems. They make friends easily, liking to make contact at all levels of society, so they can absorb the total picture.

Anyone who is looking for a close personal relationship with Mercury in Aquarius people is likely to be disappointed. Even in romantic and marital situations, they seem to keep their distance. They have a detached way about them, which can appear to be cold uninterest to the more emotional types of the Zodiac.

It is this quality of detachment that allows them to be such good scientists and helpers, especially in the social field. They can focus totally, ignoring day-to-day needs, even the people around them. They can become so absorbed in a subject that they may be labeled "absent-minded."

Mercury in Aquarius folk are agreeable as a rule. If their Sun is in Capricorn, they may be more reserved and studious, with a tendency to look more on the practical side than the idealistic one. They are likely to be aware of their own position, which can make them more self-centered and self-seeking than otherwise would be the case.

With both Mercury and the Sun in Aquarius, individuals can be a little too brilliant and erratic for their own good. There is such an emphasis on intellectual pursuits and values that the person is inclined to lose touch with the more feeling and emotional side of life.

People having Mercury in Aquarius and the Sun in Pisces will be inclined to turn their attentions to artistic pursuits rather than scientific and strictly mental endeavors. These people may be entertainers or performers, who reach a wide public through television or radio. However, they tend to lack a solid opinion of themselves, and so can be inclined toward moodiness and depression. They may spend their time fighting for a sense of independence they do not really want.

Mercury in Aquarius individuals are often far ahead of their times. If they have the patience to wait, they eventually find the public embracing their ideas, which were once ignored.

MERCURY IN PISCES

Here Mercury is in danger of drowning in the emotional sea of Pisces. These people can be lacking in logical thought. But they should never be underestimated. They depend mainly on their feelings to perceive what is going on in the world. And they can be uncannily accurate and intuitive.

People with Mercury in Pisces are not easy to pin down. To argue or even debate with them can be a frustrating experience. Their mentality tends to skate over contradictions. Gaps and double-talk are normal parts of communicating. They can be infuriatingly vague, unreasonable, and indecisive.

They have wonderful memories, though. Their recollections are vivid, colored with all the emotional nuances of the moment, even if the moment was years ago. But their memory is selective.

Mercury in Pisces individuals are not anxious to remember events and things that did not appeal to them—unless there was someone or something to blame! This often is the case. Then they are unusually vindictive and unforgiving in their condemnations. They can have strong prejudices, which may last for ages, long after experiencing that they have been mistaken.

These people are subtle and ultrasensitive. They can be offended by remarks that other people accept as normal. Language has a special meaning for them. In a positive way, they can express their appreciation for things mortal and beautiful in poetry, song, and story.

They can be great talkers, spilling out their experiences and reliving them with a light that comes into their eyes. Every time they retell them, which is often, they wax more poetic. They are humorous people, easy to take to once their peculiar logic and way of seeing things are understood.

With Mercury in Pisces, a person often suffers from self-doubt. They may worry that their mind is empty and slow. In fact, their mind is crowded with keen perceptions. These people are very bright, and can demonstrate it if they will overcome their tendency to see everything through an emotional screen.

These people have a great capacity for understanding the problems of others. They are sympathetic and genuinely caring. They can pick up bad vibrations in an instant, and become distressed and disturbed. They can dwell too long and intensely on their problems, which affects their health. These people need to keep their thinking optimistic and practical.

Mercury in Pisces individuals are very good listeners. They hear people's problems with a third ear. They are capable of giving sympathy combined with good advice. They are diplomatic and subtle in tricky situations. They know how to get their way by working behind the scenes.

These people have very changeable emotions. They can be wholeheartedly in favor of one thing one moment, then opposed to it the next. They often do not know their own mind. They have to be careful making important decisions affecting their future. They need sufficient time to think through all the consequences. They can be impulsive as well as ambivalent.

Mercury in Pisces people love to fantasize and daydream. They can drift off into another world in the middle of a conversation. They often use their imagination as a means of escape when the pressures of life become too much for them, which is likely to happen fairly frequently.

With both the Sun and Mercury in Pisces, there is a tendency for a person to be lazy or listless. This combination requires practical support from the placements of other planets. Ideas, however, can be brilliant, and give rise to shrewd moneymaking schemes. But more energetic folk are likely to be required to do the physical work.

If Mercury in Pisces individuals have their Sun in Aries, their mental gymnastics keep them leaping from task to task. Action, though sometimes ineffective, replaces listlessness. If their Sun is in Aquarius, they can make rigorous intellectual productions over each and every mood. Emotion replaces reason.

Venus in the Signs

V enus stands for love and beauty. Its quality is attraction, union. Venus has a major influence on romance and love life.

At its best, Venus confers gracious, artistic, and refined sensibilities. At its worst, this planet represents sensuality. In adverse combination with other planets, such as Saturn, it can create unhappiness through lack of feeling, possessiveness, and selfishness.

Venus is considered to be the second most fortunate planet, after Jupiter. As Venus stands for beauty, love, charm, artistry, and all that is pleasing, it follows that people with a strong Venus influence are going to be popular. They will attract favorable attention and aid, giving them an easier ride in life.

But a strong Venus influence also can make individuals so desirous of comfort, ease, and freedom from the ordinary stresses and strains of life that they become dependent, lazy, demanding, indecisive, and ineffectual. In this case, too much of a good thing goes sour, for both men and women. Idealistic Venus needs to get her feet dirty in the solid, fruitful Earth. Then she has much to give in partnership, relatedness, agreeableness, serenity, charm, generosity, good humor, appreciation, and encouragement.

Venus is considered feminine, Mars masculine. All men and women have a bit of each in them, which is what gives added stimulation to love and sexual attraction. We want the opposite, we need the same. Venus takes, Mars gives. Venus represents cooperation, Mars singleness of purpose.

If a person has both Venus and Mars in the same sign, he or she will be amorous, erotic, and passionate, with a strong tendency toward impulsiveness and indiscretion. If two lovers have the same Venus or Mars placement, they are likely to achieve sexual harmony easily and naturally, spontaneously enjoying the physical side of lovemaking.

Venus is the origin of the word "veins," which according to medical lore return the "tired" blood gently to the heart, the center of the living body. The Venus principle, analogously, circulates the affections to the heart, there to be rejuvenated and to spring forth once more fresh and pure.

Venus is favorably situated in Taurus and Libra, the signs it rules.

VENUS IN ARIES

Here is a person who loves to embark on romantic ventures. Venus in Aries individuals are passionate, physical, and impulsive. They often take the initiative in love affairs. What they like they tend to go after with great gusto.

These people have the charm that comes through directness and love of action. They are too impatient to play the love game for long. They are spontaneous with their gifts, often too generous. But they want the fruits of wooing as soon as possible. Sometimes they scale up the apple tree before the fruit is ripe, and are disappointed. But they also have much enviable success.

Venus in Aries people are honest and open. Although they may seem intent on the physical side of love at times, they also need to pursue the beautiful. This is why their affections and attractions can be short-lived. They are looking for love and the exquisite. Until they find both, they do tend to have a dazzling array of lovers.

These people are often extremely good at sports and physical activity. They can become true artists of the gymnasts and ballet bar, the football and baseball fields, and the basketball court. They have a keen competitive spirit that aims just as much at excelling as at winning.

Their emotions are not so deep as to get in the way of their need for new experiences. In spite of all their activity, they do not lose sight of their objective. Many of them have a devotion to an impossible ideal. It might be finding the perfect male or female, or reaching the heights of style and artistry in creative expression.

Venus in Aries individuals are enthusiastic lovers and performers. They seek harmony through mental activity when they cannot find it in the physical. They are demonstrative people.

For a woman this combination can be a bit aggressive. Aries is the most purely masculine of all the signs. There is not much leeway here for using the feminine charms that entice by suggestion and subtlety.

In Aries, Venus is consumed before she has time to work her gentle magic.

Venus in Aries people often throw caution to the winds. They are prepared to gamble with their emotions as well as with other people's. They love the pursuit of love. The adventure often means more to them than the realization of their desires.

With the Sun in Taurus and Venus in Aries, the person is likely to become engaged at some time in his or her life in a serious secret love affair. There can be more desire for security where the emotions are concerned. The person will be more inclined to settle down and conform to domestic expectations.

With the Sun in Pisces and Venus in Aries, the person will be even more of a romantic. They are likely to put their loved ones on a pedestal and expect the impossible from them. As a result, they will frequently be disappointed, lamenting their lack of luck in love. However, there people will have quick powers of recovery from romantic disenchantment—and are likely to repeat enthusiastically the same mistakes.

Individuals with both Venus and the Sun in Aries may take many years or experiences to learn that the chase is never-ending. Eventually they discover there is no substitute for abiding love.

VENUS IN TAURUS

Taurus is the natural home of Venus. Here the planet of love and beauty can have full expression. A person with this combination can be extremely attractive, a passionate lover, charming, and gracious. But somewhere in their makeup is a touch of selfishness, of self-indulgence. They can be too attracted to the good things in life, and so make the acquisition of them their reason for living.

People with Venus in Taurus are practical. They may dream about castles in Spain, dashing princes, and alluring maidens. But they know the realities of life. If they want these things, they have to go out and get them.

They are in many ways hardheaded people. An abiding stubborn streak usually ensures that they get what they want. But it is the manner of getting that varies so much.

With Venus in Taurus, a person usually is drawn to some kind of artistic pursuit. But it will not be a flighty one. It will have a quality of earthiness about it. It will be something practical that will lead to a good living.

A woman or a man with Venus in Taurus can use their physical attractiveness to make another person work for them. They may look around to marry into money. Or they may persevere in the fields of design, handicrafts, or fashion. In such jobs they can express their artistic or creative urges, and so get to the top or a position of comfort that way.

These people have great powers of perseverance. They do not give up. Once they have fixed their target, they plod on and on. They may not be very adventurous. They do not take risks that have not been calculated. They have a great need for comfort and security. And they are prepared to work as long as it is necessary to get it.

But Venus in Taurus creates irritations if rewards are too slow in coming. Although there is loyalty in the combination, the desire for comfort can induce this person eventually to look around for an easier and more comfortable existence.

These people like to surround themselves with attractive things, which may include men or women who appeal to their senses. They have strong feelings, sensual ones. They like the feel of expensive cloth. Luxury can be more important to them than they realize.

Individuals with Venus in Taurus have a way with their lovers. They understand them and can anticipate their desires. Knowing how to please gets them the lovely things they want. There is a hint of opportunism in this placement.

Venus in Taurus people love to surround themselves with their possessions. It is impossible for them ever to imagine that they could get tired of living in the lap of luxury. Even if the placement of other planets makes their tastes less exotic, they will still exhibit a liking for what is stylish or beautiful.

These people make good nest builders. They are not inclined to move around except to better themselves. Once they have a home of their liking, they will pour all their energies and most of their money into it to make it more attractive and comfortable.

With the Sun also in Taurus, security through good investments, especially in homes and real estate, will be particularly important. With the Sun in Aries, and Venus in Taurus, there is likely to be more house moving. The love of comfort and beautiful things will be reflected in pioneering and perhaps even reckless endeavors to obtain more of them.

Venus in Taurus usually confers a love of nature. These people manage to have a lovely garden, even if it consists only of a few attractive flower boxes or potted plants in a city apartment.

These people are not known for their austere type of living. They believe in giving themselves the best even though it means living up to their income. They like to give the impression that they are doing well.

VENUS IN GEMINI

This person likes the idea of love more than the actual physical contact. Venus in Gemini individuals are flirtatious. Or they content themselves with sexual fantasies. They have extremely active imaginations, which are not dependent on actual experiences.

In Gemini, Venus is up in the air. She cannot get down to earth, where she is at her best. So the person seldom is able to make the most of her physical propensities.

There is a lack of devotion in these people. They love with their heads; they frequently experience changes of affection. They are unable to maintain a passionate relationship. Theirs is more an enthusiastic approach, which touches as it goes past on its way to the next adventure. Emotion is something these people can feel but seldom can express.

People with Venus in Gemini like to talk about art. They can be clever and popular writers of fact and fiction, seeming to have a deep insight into human emotions. But their perceptions are mostly superficial, the kind found in people who like to imagine experiences without having them. The deep reality can be missing.

But Venus in Gemini individuals are amusing and impressive conversationalists and speakers. They make fine critics. They have an appreciation of beauty that might be expressed through love of flowers, colors, music, or sketching. They can make good actors or mimics. There is a refinement about them.

These people often possess a quality of youthfulness that continues right through into old age. They are sympathetic and spontaneous. They make friends very easily and are usually found at the center of events at parties.

Venus in Gemini people need to be liked. They flee from unpleasantness or discord. They will often say what they think the other person wants to hear instead of giving a straightforward reply that might not be appreciated. They are inclined to be a bit opportunistic. It is easy for them, especially if their Sun also is in Gemini, to take life rather unseriously.

These people often marry more than once. They can have several romantic attachments going at one time. They love to travel and meet new people. They search for harmony through relationships, but can fail to give satisfaction once the initial excitement is over. They may take more out of an association than they put into it.

Venus in Gemini individuals love to travel. Their partners or close associates often have to get used to being left alone without warning—or having to pack their bags and be off on a visit or journey at a moment's notice. These fleet-footed Venus in Gemini characters find it difficult to turn down any opportunity to experience a change of scene.

It has to be remembered that Gemini is the sign of the Twins. Venus is the sign of comfort and beauty. One Twin, one side of the personality, may like to luxuriate in a well-appointed apartment. The other Twin may love to get out in the country. Often there is a fierce tug-of-war between the two, which can result in irritability, indecision, and instability.

These are people who love the fun of living but often shy away from its obligations. They do not like to be pinned down to one kind of work. Although they enjoy the trappings of wealth and success, they are not prepared to join in the often grubby rough-and-tumble climb up. They prefer to skim along the surface. Their ready wit and amusing personality often provide them with the means of making a good living and a good life.

VENUS IN CANCER

This is a person who is capable of great love and affection. And he or she expects the same in return. Family men or women will devote themselves untiringly to their loved ones. Venus in Cancer folk are the mother type.

Venus in Cancer can make a person ideally domestic. They are good homemakers and cooks. They like to bring a touch of artistry to the home. They often show admirable taste in furnishings, decor, and color schemes. Their table usually features special dishes, not just the routine home-cooked fare. They take great pleasure in being hospitable to visitors and guests.

As lovers, Venus in Cancer people can be delightful. They have a cuddly and responsive temperament. They are strongly intuitive and seem to know how to please their beloved. They work very hard at this. They like to please.

But they also can be very demanding. They need a great deal of attention and mothering themselves. They are incurably romantic. They can never be satisfied by any mortal show of love or affection. It seems they always want a little more. This can become wearying for mate or beloved.

Venus in Cancer individuals are also inclined to sink into moodiness, especially if they feel they are not being sufficiently appreciated. Whether it is a lover, their children, or their spouse, they are inclined to be clinging.

Love life does not usually run smoothly for these people. They are often too soft and romantic. They can be imposed on and exploited. They will often do anything for love. If they can't find it, they may turn mystical. Or they can wither away in fretful unhappiness.

Nevertheless, Venus in Cancer folk are kind, understanding, and comforting. They love beauty, especially nature. They can be attracted to literature, music, poetry, and art. They have a great attachment to the past. Past loves—even unhappy ones—grow gloriously in their imagination.

These people often have a mother complex. They may find it hard to break away from the home or an aging parent. They can be fortunate through real estate or land and its products. They should always try to express their emotions positively and not allow them to get bottled up.

Venus in Cancer individuals can moon around unhappily. They should try to avoid putting all their love into one person or thing.

These people can cut themselves off from the rest of society at times in order to escape pressures. They would rather ruminate in an imaginary world of their own making than try to cope with all the demands they feel are being made upon them.

Men with Venus in Cancer are often attracted to older women. These men have a definite charm and a maturity, which appeals to sophisticated women. Their manners and way of speaking have an Old World character about them. They are protective and considerate.

It is not unusual for Venus in Cancer people to be acquisitive. They may like to fill their homes with beautiful things. Sometimes money and property come to them from the maternal side of the family. They may not, however, be prepared to put a great deal of personal effort into fulfilling their materialistic appetites. They may depend on others to do the hard work, relying on their own ingratiating charm to bring them benefits.

People born with Venus in Cancer have a great need to be liked and looked up to. This often propels them into doing some kind of charity work. They are the types who will be found cheerfully working at the tables at the local church or street fair. They have many good qualities—and they want to be admired for them.

VENUS IN LEO

Here the planet of love and luxury is in the sign of romance and pleasure! The result is a person who can very easily overstep the mark in these things and make problems for himself or herself.

Venus in Leo people have a great deal of creative talent. They are dramatic, masters of the flourish and the trumpet. They love displays in which they can take a central part. They can put their ideas across to the public. They do this in love and romance.

These are people who have no problem attracting the attention of the opposite sex. They usually dress splendidly, with a touch of the flamboyant. Even though they might not have a penny to spare, they somehow manage to give the impression of being somebody or going somewhere.

They have a great talent for self-expression. They love social affairs where they can take the center of the floor, discoursing easily on this or that. Their object at all times is to be the cynosure of all eyes. They love applause and are suckers for flattery. They can become a bit tiresome with their posturing and need for compliments.

Venus in Leo people are faithful and kind. Whether it is love of a person or work, they put their whole heart into it. They may make fools of themselves sometimes in their rather childish scrambling for plaudits. But no one could ever doubt their sincerity when it comes to their affections.

They are impossibly romantic. They are inclined to believe any story about how much they are loved. Their heart rules their head. They are frequently disillusioned, heartbroken through love affairs. But they keep coming back for more, with the same ingenuous faith and trust. And probably make the same mistakes again!

As lovers, they are generous, responsive, and proud. One thing Venus in Leo lovers cannot stand is being made a fool of.

The love of pleasure and entertainment, along with the many opportunities that seem to arise to enjoy them, can make these people a bit shallow and tinselly unless there are strengthening influences in the chart.

The Sun also in Leo, for example, will impart an even greater love of pleasure but will carry with it a responsible element. The positive and creative side will be emphasized. There will then be accomplishments in which pride can be justified.

With the Sun in Virgo and Venus in Leo, there will be more emphasis on efficiency and less on imagination. The person will be more critical and inclined to look for a perfection that may never be realized. These people may dream about love affairs, but have difficulty expressing their feelings in actual romances. This combination encourages a tendency to become involved in secret emotional alliances.

The Sun in Cancer and Venus in Leo confer a softer and gentler influence, with strong sensual feelings. The emotions can get out of control more easily. Discrimination in choice of companions is necessary. These people make good lovers, but can be very possessive and jealous.

All Venus in Leo people have to beware that they do not put too much store in appearances. They can easily be distracted by glamor. In seeking romantic companions, they may fail to look for the more enduringly admirable qualities beneath the surface.

Also, Venus in Leo individuals can frequently become preoccupied with fashion and style in dress. Clothes can become so important to them that they tend to dismiss or overlook deeper values. Concern about what people are thinking can make them unpredictable, erratic, and superficial.

VENUS IN VIRGO

Venus in Virgo is a rather cool placement for love and romance. A person with this combination is exceedingly cautious about whom they give their heart to. They are nervous, almost suspicious, of anything that suggests physical contact and that may develop into intimacy. They like to put a lot of distance between themselves and the alluring suggestions of the planet of love and beauty.

These people are searching for moral beauty. In a physical and emotional world, where sex is natural, they do not feel at ease. They prefer to avoid intimate relationships. But being human, they can be tempted. Sometimes, when real love exists, they discover a reflection of the purity that means so much to them.

People with Venus in Virgo have a firm hold on their feelings and affections. They prefer to serve an idea rather than a person. They find it difficult to surrender themselves. They can change their mind at the very last moment, because they never intended to go ahead at all.

Venus in Virgo individuals are very discriminating when it comes to settling down. They are attractive people with a touch of aloofness that intrigues, increasing the suggestion of mystery. They are inclined to select their partners by rationalizing their conventional qualities. Seldom indeed do they throw themselves with abandon into the arms of love.

These people have a strong desire to be liked and accepted. But they never put themselves forward. They prefer to be a face in the crowd, to weigh the situation, before making any moves. They need to feel they are on familiar ground, among people they know before they can take the initiative.

This planetary position is very helpful for a person who wants to enter the medical profession as a doctor or nurse. The urge to be of useful service to mankind is strong in Virgo, and the presence of Venus confers an added touch of tenderness and devotion. Through self-denial these people often develop a self-fulfilling capacity for serving others.

Venus in Virgo induces a critical temperament. The person cannot help analyzing the actions and attitudes of others, especially in relation to their emotions and affections. Even though they may not say what they think, the judging still goes on in their heads.

Sometimes these people are worried by their own criticalness. Then they try to compensate by showing exaggerated concern, especially about other people's health. Venus in Virgo individuals often have a flair for improving health through natural food and diets.

Venus in Virgo men tend to be more sexually oriented than women having this placement. But the men like to think the woman they eventually marry "saved herself" for them. They have an old-fashioned respect for virginity, and a double standard for the sexes. Nevertheless, the men are controlled in their passions, atthough this may not be quite so evident if the Sun is in Leo.

With both the Sun and Venus in Virgo, the person can very easily become celibate. They either genuinely want to save themselves for the love of their life, or they have developed a strong moral conscience about sexual behavior. However, once the ice has been broken, all people with Venus in Virgo are more likely to forget their inhibitions. But if the first sexual experience is unhappy, they may never risk another.

VENUS IN LIBRA

Venus in Libra makes for harmony. Here is a person with an outstanding ability to get along with others. Such individuals are charming, sociable, and dignified. They go out of their way to please without having to try at all. Being nice, reasonable, and agreeable comes naturally to them.

Venus, the planet of love and beauty, is in its own sign. This emphasizes the artistic and refining qualities of Venus. These people have a distaste for anything that is sordid or jarring. They are always seeking to soothe and smooth their sensibilities in compatible company, for they can find this world a constantly prickling experience.

Venus in Libra people are kind and fortunately very adaptable. They have a wonderful way of accepting people exactly as they are, and of communicating this by an interested and pleasing manner. Although they prefer and usually manage to mix in the more elegant levels of their society, they are quite at home with everyone. But they cannot tolerate arguments and aggressive behavior. They make very nice excuses—and flee.

People with Venus in Libra have a love of color, proportion, and etiquette. Their good taste shows in everything they do, from the way they furnish and decorate their homes to the stylish and smart way they dress. They love the formalities of entertaining.

These people make the finest mates and partners in the Zodiac, especially if their Sun also is in Libra. Of course, this ideality is often marred by other planetary influences. But generally, Venus in Libra individuals flower in partnership. They manage to give the other person a great deal that is pleasing, even though the association may not work out or last long.

The love life of these people is not always happy. They are susceptible. In their hunger for harmony, they tend to believe every nice thing said. They are terribly romantic. They are easily misled by a show of affection. They are not fools by any means, but they are vulnerable to love and the idle flatteries of romance.

They often have beauty that is deeper than surface looks. A quality of refinement shows in their actions and manner. They are magnetic. But they can be flighty, flirtatious, selfish, self-indulgent, dependent, and sentimental. They can be too refined and delicate to cope with this hard world.

Venus in Libra individuals unconsciously impose heavy demands on their romantic partners. They are always looking for them to live up to their ideals of beauty and conduct. A constant analysis is going on behind the scenes, which often exhausts them physically and forces them to lie down, sometimes for days. This is especially so if the Sun is in Libra as well as in Venus.

The Venus in Libra combination warns against hasty and impulsive marriages. There is a great deal of variability in the temperament. The tendency is to try to compensate for this by formalizing relationships through contracts and ceremonies. It is not unlike whistling in the dark, because in the course of time the Libra changeableness may assert itself if the affections do not have a deep foundation.

Venus in Libra people are inclined to put on a show to cover up what might be lacking in a relationship or a situation. They like everything in the garden to be lovely, so much so that self-deception is a strong possibility. They live in a world of mental ideals. Of course, they can pretend that a situation lives up to their expectations. But in reality the opposite may be true, and they are dissatisfied and lonely.

VENUS IN SCORPIO

Venus in Scorpio is a highly sexual placement. Eroticism and sexual urge can be expressed in any number of ways. There can be a straightforward hunger for sexual experience, which seeks gratification in the actual act of lovemaking. Or sexual impulse can go too far to extremes. There will be a tendency not only to overindulge but also to wallow—and perhaps to sink into degrading experiences. Or the sexual urge can be associated with perversity, cruelty, and pain.

It must be understood that this is an isolated placement. Because of the modifying influence of the other planets, no one with Venus in Scorpio will be exactly as described here. But such individuals will exhibit evidence of these traits, if not to others, then to themselves.

These people have a love of sensation. They enjoy luxury, flattery, and secrecy. Their emotions are extremely strong and are almost in a constant state of arousal. They can really hate, with a venom that people without a Scorpio connection can't even imagine.

Venus in Scorpio people can be vindictive. They have tremendous powers of self-control when they have a clear objective in mind. Their aim often is to get even with someone who may have rejected them or slighted them. They can wait years for the right opportunity for revenge.

They are proud people, much more sensitive than they ever seem. They repress their seething emotions. They can appear cool, calm, and collected when just the opposite is the case.

People with Venus in Scorpio often are tactless. They say what they feel. They have an urge to discover the truth, and they don't mind dropping it on other people's toes. They often make the same mistakes twice, especially where love is concerned.

These are possessive and passionate people. Whatever is theirs they hold onto fiercely. They do not allow the person they love much freedom. They can be cruelly jealous, wildly suspicious. They are not beyond sacrificing the interests of others in order to save their own skins.

They are deeply perceptive, though not particularly artistic. They have great insights into the mysteries of life, and they accept their insights as matters of fact. Where others are amazed, Venus in Scorpio individuals can be indifferent.

Venus in Scorpio individuals are proud without being egotistical. There is a hidden side to their nature, which they do not allow others to see or suspect. They are constantly under pressure from sexual forces that might drive others to disastrous extremes. But the strength of these people in restraining their impulses is often amazing.

However, such control has its price. Venus in Scorpio people need to sublimate their desires if they do not express them. Otherwise, severe inner conflicts are possible, which can make life a misery for them as well as for the people they live with. Energies need to be redirected into productive channels.

Often these people can release themselves through activities requiring personal sacrifice. They may decide to serve a higher purpose such as the good of mankind. They are capable of great privation and dedication once the decision to serve has been made.

Venus, the planet of love and beauty, is not very comfortable in Scorpio, a sign ruled by Mars, the planet of war and destruction. The emotions and affections are too often wrenched and tortured by fate and circumstances as well as by insatiable appetites.

VENUS IN SAGITTARIUS

Venus in Sagittarius is an enthusiastic placement for romance. In love, these people hold out a great deal of promise. They are idealistic. They beckon with suggestions of heady delights just over the horizon. But if anyone can catch them, there is a strong possibility of disappointment. The moment of coming together may be splendid, or it may not. But there is little chance of a continuing and satisfying attachment.

People with Venus in Sagittarius are impulsive in their affections. One minute they want to make love, the next they have moved on to another interest or another place. Not that they are insincere. It's just that they lack the depth of persistent passion that most people expect.

Individuals with this combination want what they want when they want it. They are not too subtle in the ways of love. They don't have much time, literally, for the preambles of wooing. They are physical lovers, but only when they feel like it. They are tentative and easily rebuffed.

Venus in Sagittarius confers on a person a love of the great outdoors. They are high-spirited and fun-loving. They enjoy uncomplicated relationships that leave them free to come and go as they please. They are generous and frank and usually very popular. They make friends easily. They are better "buddies" than lovers.

These people are inclined to make promises without considering the consequences or all that is involved. This can make them unreliable when it comes to important decisions about getting married. They may think it's a great idea, but when the time comes, they split. They are hard to commit.

Venus in Sagittarius individuals love their freedom. They will not be pinned down. The urge to travel is strong. They are always seeking new horizons. They are great explorers and don't like to stay in the same place for long.

These people are often very indulgent of their loved ones in an effort to get closer to them. They can wed two or three times. If conditions become too demanding, or people emotionally binding, they are likely to solve the situation neatly and simply—by walking out.

Venus in Sagittarius suggests many passing love affairs. It is not a placement ideal for settling down, sinking roots, or nest building.

Yet people born with Venus in Sagittarius can be very sincere. Unless there are adverse planetary placements, these folk will not deliberately mislead another person. They have the best of intentions, even though their freewheeling disposition suggests otherwise at times.

Once people with Venus in Sagittarius have given their word in romantic matters, they will do their best to stick to it. They have a strong social conscience, which recognizes the need for fair play. But in a partnership they need shared interests to make a go of it. Too often people who

292 THE PLANETS IN THE SIGNS: THE MOON THROUGH PLUTO

fall in love with Venus in Sagittarius individuals mistakingly feel that once the knot is tied their spouse will alter his or her ways.

As parents, people with this combination love and indulge their children. But if they have the opportunity, they may be inclined to send the kids to boarding schools. This move can have two aims. The first is to give their youngsters the best start in life possible, with a good grounding in all the social graces and the possibility of making influential friends and acquaintances. The other is to give themselves more freedom to go their independent ways.

VENUS IN CAPRICORN

Venus in Capricorn suggests a bit of timidity in love and romance. It makes a person interestingly shy about expressing affection. They are likely to arouse the passions of the more daring types of the Zodiac. They present a challenge that is hard to resist. On the surface they may seem a bit serious. But underneath are passions waiting to be released by the right person.

Venus in Capricorn people can be very sensual. They may not be easy conquests. They generally keep their affections well locked up. No one gets a preview without some effort. They love pleasure, but don't like to admit it. They have a fear of being made to look foolish. They can be scornful of people who show too much emotion. They are easily embarrassed.

People with Venus in Capricorn are sincere. Once they fall in love, they remain true. They are usually more successful marrying later in life, when their repressed fears and emotions have had time to surface. In the early stages of life they can make mistakes by choosing partners who do not intrude on their inner world. They later discover that without deep interaction between two people, there is little chance of happiness.

These people are always aiming at self-reliance. They can feel it is a weakness to depend on someone else, even for emotional reasons. They often hold back, when they would love to reach out. The right partner can give them the means of self-expression they need so much.

Physical compatibility is very important to Venus in Capricorn individuals. Often it is only through the act of lovemaking that they are able to show their deepest feelings.

They love domestic life. They can sink into it and luxuriate. They enjoy being in familiar surroundings where there are not likely to be unexpected problems to deal with. They are creatures of habit. Too much of the family life can make them dull and uninteresting.

Venus in Capricorn people often marry someone much older or younger. They are very protective of their loved ones, especially their children. But they have to work at not becoming rigid with the younger generation. The fear of being rebuffed can prevent them from taking the initiative other people are longing for.

There is a developed and undeveloped type in this combination of Venus and Capricorn. The less developed type is more worldly and self-seeking. Such individuals want to surround themselves with possessions and material symbols of security. They like others to know how well they are doing. They are inclined to measure everything by the value of money. They frequently marry for money, prestige, or power.

The developed aspect of this combination is reflected in an ability to love through all sorts of trials. This person is not afraid to switch traditional roles in partnership. A woman will go to work to support her man. A man will do the domestic chores and raise the kids.

There is much that is appealingly old-fashioned in Venus in Capricorn people. They possess a strong sense of right and wrong. Although physically passionate, they are not as a rule the promiscuous type. They prefer to let themselves go only with a person they love. If they do have casual affairs, it is not without a sense of seriousness. They are prepared to accept their responsibilities.

These people do not look for love at first sight. They like a relationship to develop slowly, so they can be sure there will be no mistake. Often, however, they allow practical considerations to get in the way, which can unnecessarily delay their day of fulfillment and happiness.

VENUS IN AQUARIUS

People with Venus in Aquarius can be a bit erratic in their love life. Mostly they prefer a lot of distance in relationships, as far as emotion is concerned. They can't stand clinging vines, for instance. And they like their companions to be intellectual, at least able to indulge in interesting conversations. While a love mate wants to get on with the more physical side, these people may prefer a chat.

Yet they can be suddenly aroused. Without warning, they can throw their books and blueprints out the window, then plunge into splendid lovemaking. They can be interesting and exciting lovers with a fondness for experimentation.

With Venus in Aquarius, a person has a love of social life. They enjoy getting around, meeting as many interesting people as possible. They like to develop their intellect. They are friendly and good listeners. They encourage people to talk about themselves, so they can study human nature. They often make very inspired observations about living and personal relationships.

These people are idealistic. They have a very good idea of the type of person they *might* want to fall in love with, but events seldom turn out that way. They often do the unexpected, which surprises them as much as their families and associates. They can make odd and improbable marriages and alliances. The less promising, the more likely they are to succeed.

People with Venus in Aquarius usually do things in moderation. As much as they enjoy social affairs, they are unlikely to eat or drink too much. They are self-controlled. Even under stressful and unusual circumstances, they show stability.

They are tolerant people. Nothing much shocks them. They have their own fixed ideas, but don't allow these to interfere with their relationships. They accept other people's beliefs without argument. They are not prejudiced.

Venus in Aquarius people have a compulsion to be independent and free of restriction. Some of them, especially if under strong parental or family strictures, may sleep around just to make the point.

Venus in Aquarius individuals are attracted to people who are different. They do not like the run-of-the-mill type. Even if they are not particularly outstanding themselves, they will still look for extraordinariness in their closest associates, lovers, and mates.

Erratic and unpredictable behavior often turns them on. Although they may appear to be ordinary themselves, not very deep underneath lurks a most unconventional disposition. They can be attracted to far-out philosophies and to occult subjects.

These people do not have a great deal of time for personal attachments and responsibilities. They would rather be active in political groups, influencing others to work toward a life of greater independence. They cannot stand to see people bowing down to any form of authority. And for this reason they refuse to allow themselves to become the slave of their emotions.

Music, poetry, and painting can be among their interests. There is a love of beauty here, but it is the kind that does not need to possess it. These people are just as happy seeing a work of art in a museum as in having it in their own home. They have a keen sense for sharing.

Venus in Aquarius individuals often become very good parents, confounding the predictions of their friends who may be used to their preference for unfettered relationships. They can treat their kids like friends, and so enjoy sharing family life.

VENUS IN PISCES

This is a person who has an unmistakable love of beauty in some form or other. It may be music, poetry, flowers. Or it could be romantic dreams, which may reach heights of earthly unobtainability. These individuals, regardless of any modifying influences from the other planets, are tender-souled to the core.

Venus in Pisces people can be terribly vague and unworldly. They are likely to spend much of their time daydreaming, picturing themselves and their lovers in impossibly romantic situations. Venus, the planet of love and beauty, is strongest in dreamy, watery Pisces. Without a good deal of strengthening from, say, the Sun in Aries, these people can become slaves of their emotions and feelings. This is especially so if the Sun or Moon also is in Pisces.

People with Venus in Pisces are extremely sensitive, generous, and kind. Their compassion for others is easily aroused. They have a strong self-sacrificing nature, which can be used as a means of escape from pressure and reality.

In love, it is possible for these individuals to become so devoted to a lover that they are almost slavish. These people can really get a kick out of surrendering their "all." It makes them feel strangely pure, something like the sacrificial lamb. This is the way their minds work; they are either victim or villain. And as villain, they then seek punishment for their wrongs and guilt.

One guilty secret is their longing for sexual experience. Venus in Pisces individuals can be promiscuous. This is not so much out of sensuality, but out of a need to share emotional experiences with others. Unless there are strengthening factors, these people may prefer not to work. They will take any easy way out, which will give them a peaceful and comfortable life. They can be very, very lazy.

Venus in Pisces people are trusting. They are too yielding and forgiving to make enemies, except for their rivals in love and romance. Women with this placement are ultrafeminine, often possessing a remarkably soft texture of body.

These people are sociable. But they do like periods of peace and quiet. They may at times retreat into themselves. Their withdrawal is aggravating to their mates and partners, who also are frequently disconcerted by their inexplicable changes of mood.

Venus in Pisces confers a great deal of compassion. These people often get involved in some sort of caretaking or charity work. They are secretive and very sensitive to what other people may be thinking about them. They love to be loved. Without love, they sink into depression.

Venus in Pisces individuals are easily influenced. But their enthusiasms are often short-lived. They can be mad about something or someone today, and totally disinterested tomorrow. They are difficult people to follow, even harder to pin down. But they are very forgivable.

People born with Venus in Pisces have a habit of putting their loved ones on pedestals. If someone comes along who even vaguely resembles one of their idealistic images, they are inclined to regard him or her as the real thing. They can blind themselves with their own emotional projections. Needless to say, they are frequently taken for a ride and shocked into eventual disillusionment.

But they do have the long-suffering, martyr mentality. It can allow them to cling to the vine of their dreams long after autumn and winter have come and gone.

With Venus in Pisces, a person may be slow to stand up for his or her own rights. Depending on the position of the Sun and Mars, they may allow others to walk over them, feeling a greater need for peace and serenity than for justice. This can lead to involuntary frustration, which may have its release in feelings of failure and self-doubt.

Mars in the Signs

Mars is the planet of enterprise, ambition, self-assertion, combativeness, and energetic expression. Its quality is forcefulness.

At its best, it is pioneering, vigorous, courageous, strong. At its worst, it is cruel, aggressive, violent, quick-tempered. Mars is the force in us that gets things done. It is the principle of the ancient war god. It is associated with heat, blood, pain, and action.

A person with a strong Mars placement is a doer. He and she tend to be impatient and impulsive, always champing at the bit to be on the move, to get things under way.

Mars gives great organizing and executive ability. It is the dynamic business and professional man or woman.

It also is the impulse that makes heroes—not necessarily on a grand scale, when individuals think and plan, but on an everyday level. Those who just step into a gap where action or help is needed, without considering social consequences or personal safety, are demonstrating the proud Mars principle.

It is Mars that provides sexual strength in romantic desire. It drives us to go after what we want, whether we are being indiscreet or foolish. Mars sees what it wants and grabs it.

Venus loves the games, the preamble, the promise, the tantalizing fragrance of passion without contact, the exquisite contemplation of final unity. Mars can't wait. Mars thrusts through Venus's dreams, bruising the flesh, scalding the emotions, searing the sensibilities. And sometimes seems to consume the very soul, oblivious to all but the conquest of passion over restraint, ideals, and intentions.

When Saturn, the planet of depression and restriction, settles its forces on man or woman, it is Mars that can break through into the clear again, snapping bonds, shattering illusions, and pummeling obstacles into the dust with blind anger or sheer combative glee.

Mars is fierce determination once an idea or objective is targeted. But it is an energy that thrives on results. If these are slow in coming, or are not impressive enough, the dynamic attention may turn to newer and more challenging ventures.

Mars represents the body's resistance to disease, its fighting and survival capabilities. It is the iron that makes the blood red and the nerves steely.

Mars also stands for accidents and injuries through haste and impatience. It is loss of temper, burns, scalds, fevers—all that is hot, fiery, and eruptive.

Mars is especially strong in association with Aries and Scorpio, the signs it rules.

MARS IN ARIES

Mars in Aries individuals have strong desires. They are always busy doing something. Their capacity for energetic activity is enormous. They are intensely ambitious, not so much for the power and position as for the delight they get out of the rough and tumble of getting there.

They are enterprising and enthusiastic. They are always ready to fight for the things they believe in. Mars, the planet of energy and strength, is in its own sign in Aries, and so is especially powerful. These people are good organizers and executives. They can round up resources and spur others into action. Given a task to accomplish, they will seldom admit defeat. What they can't solve with their considerable mental gifts, they get around or eliminate with audacious actions.

People with Mars in Aries have to learn self-control. They continually make life difficult for themselves by being impulsive. Their often brilliant ideas never stay in their head for reflection; they are translated into action immediately, without any regard for timing. They often fall flat on their face; but they are up again instantly, hammering away at the opposition with indefatigable energy.

Mars in Aries individuals are spontaneous. They are as quick with the open hand to someone needing help as they are with a push to someone getting in their way. They love freedom and plenty of room to act in. They make superior fighting men and women, surgeons, engineers, and police officers.

Venus in Pisces gives the Mars in Aries placement a softening, artistic touch. This can make such individuals fine writers, journalists, and artists.

With Mars in Aries, a person can be accident-prone. Haste and impatience are their worst enemies. But they have an outstanding resistance to illness. If they do get sick, recovery usually is quicker than expected.

Dauntless, they often take on impossible tasks that have to be left half finished. They also are inclined to lose interest in a project once they see the end in sight. Then it is no longer a challenge.

In love, Mars in Aries people are ardent and impulsive. They need a mate who is physically compatible and understands their uncomplicated nature. They are good at sports. They need plenty of exercise to work off their great abundance of energy if their fires are not consumed in lovemaking.

In love, they also know what they want. Both the men and the women are aggressive lovers. An Aries woman is not the type to take the traditional female role of coyness and uncertainty when it comes to wooing. With more reserved men, she is the one who is likely to make the first move and set the pace.

Mars in Aries individuals are idealistic. When they decide for themselves that something has to be done to improve their community or society, there are no half measures. They have a strong sense of commitment.

A fondness for any adventure or dare is outstanding in these people. They are great vacation mates when long distances have to be traveled and numerous difficulties overcome. They will take charge right from the word go. The problem for less hardy people is not only putting up with them but also keeping up with them.

There is often a lack of sympathy and tolerance in people born with Mars in Aries. Most situations seem black and white to them. They find difficulty coping with people of finer sensibilities. They are likely to dismiss such people's feelings as weak, or just ride roughshod over them.

MARS IN TAURUS

Mars in Taurus individuals are determined to get their share of worldly goods. There is a tendency to be a bit too materialistic. Money and possessions become the main interests in life. This, of course will be offset or emphasized by the position of the other planets.

A person with Mars in Taurus is very persistent. Early in life, they form an idea of what they want. Their desires usually relate to the good things in life. And they go after them in a calm and practical manner, seldom discouraged by setbacks and hard work.

Although these people have a strong hankering for comfort and luxury, they are not dreamers. They usually know their limitations. They have made a shrewd assessment of the problems that lie ahead. Often they have to plod on for a long time before achieving worthwhile results. They can sometimes waste time by battling anticipated difficulties that may not even arise.

Mars in Taurus eventually brings financial success. These people crave security. They want money in the bank and their names on the deeds of property. They have a strong fear of being left penniless in their old age. They are often physically attractive people with good common sense. They have noted the toll that the years can take. They are not as a rule the religious or mystical type. They put their faith in tangible things. And any reward that might be coming they want in their lifetime, the sooner the better.

These people are extremely stubborn. They will never give up. Once they have an idea in their head, it's there for good, or at least until it is proved to their satisfaction that it does not work. They are doubting Thomases, not out of cynicism but out of pure hardheadedness. They don't take chances. They rely on their own judgment. They are self-contained individuals.

Sex is vital to them. They love the physical, sensual side. They are especially stimulated by touch and touching. They are possessive but good to their lovers. Jealousy can often make marriages more of a trial than should be. These people are faithful and good providers. They love children and can teach them to cope with the world.

Mars in Taurus people have great control of their emotions, but loss of temper can mean violence. Jealousy and possessiveness are their weak spots. Threatened by a mate's flirtatiousness or infidelity, they act out their rage with little restraint. They also are made anxious when their love partner seeks even innocent forms of independence.

Mars in Taurus individuals are often skilled in craftsmaking. They have a knack for designing fine and pretty things in fabric, wood, or metal. They have a good eye for practical decoration. They may do well in the building, real estate, or design industries. There is nothing flighty about their artistic and creative productions.

These people often seem to act out of character. One day they may be conservative and contented, the next impatient and discontented. They are inclined to spend extravagantly on luxuries and entertainment. Their generosity can go to extremes. They also can be wildly self-indulgent.

People with Mars in Taurus usually are prepared to work hard to get their own homes. They feel a basic need for economic security, which their impulsive actions may seem to contradict. They are often pulled between the urge to get up and go and to stay where they are. They are the types who can get in a rut and then suddenly break out.

Taurus usually confers a love of nature. But the presence of Mars there induces an urge to transform nature. These people can often be successful as developers and engineers, building highways, dams, tunnels, turnpikes, and thoroughfares.

MARS IN GEMINI

Mars in Gemini creates a forceful speaker. Such individuals have a way with words. Their ideas are often inspirational and capture the public imagination. They make good politicians, lecturers, lawyers, and teachers. As writers, they can keep the ideas coming quick and fast. They have a knack for whipping up flagging enthusiasm, which makes them admirable for addressing action groups and getting people to work together.

Mars and Gemini people can be sarcastic, satirical, and witty. They also can be blunt and bruising when it suits them. They have to be careful in company. When they mix, they tend to get hold of a pet idea and belabor everyone with it as though it were the most important invention since the wheel.

But as convincing as they are in communicating good ideas, they are not so adept at putting the ideas into action. These people have a fitful physical energy, which is not suited for prolonged activity. They tire easily. They are deft with their hands and minds. And they might have a talent for tap dancing, judo, or boxing. They are swift movers. They avoid heavy work.

People with Mars in Gemini seldom ever have one job or career. They like to do different things, either at the same time or in succession. They are sometimes ambidextrous. They love variety and change.

A person with Mars in Gemini is usually talkative. They are inclined to provoke arguments with their friends and associates for the sheer pleasure of matching wits against others. They are usually well-informed, being natural gatherers of information.

They have a way with mechanical appliances. They can repair tools and machines without special technical knowledge. Their homes usually display a host of ingenious gadgets, some of them handmade.

People with Mars in Gemini often become irritable. They build up mental energy, which is hard for them to release adequately. They become restless, discontented. Then they take out their frustrations on those around them.

Mars in Gemini, without balance from other placements, can make a person disagreeable and nasty. He or she is always having trouble with relatives or neighbors. Concentration can be difficult. Instability may develop.

Mars in Gemini people need to circulate freely. This tendency makes them poor candidates for long and committed love affairs. They see family ties as threats to their freedom. Although they love kids, they prefer to enjoy other people's.

In love, no one can take a Mars in Gemini individual for granted without being left promptly on their own and lonesome. These people do not as a rule become closely attached. They like to keep their relationships fluid, so they can move swiftly in and out as the mood takes them.

Often they do not know themselves what they are going to do the next moment. They live on a live wire, which makes them mentally and physically restless. They need to get their teeth into a project, to give it everything they have, to feel really fulfilled. But the trouble is, they are too easily distracted and dart off in new directions.

Mars in Gemini individuals work from inspirational flashes. Some of their ideas can be brilliant. These people usually gather around them an active and intelligent group of friends. They have a fondness for chat, new experiences, and late nights. There is seldom a dull moment—one way or another—when these rascals are around.

The early education of Mars in Gemini people is often erratic. They may have attended a lot of schools. Or they devoted more time to sports, hobbies, and leisure activities than to study. Concentration and continuity of thought can be more difficult to attain than their alert and observant manner suggests.

MARS IN CANCER

Mars in Cancer has produced some of the world's best writers, artists, and thinkers. The fiery energies of Mars stimulate the emotional waters of Cancer, allowing the person to dive deeper than usual into his or her own instinctive feelings. These people can discover truly original thoughts and ideas lodged in the subconscious.

Mars in Cancer gives a person strong desires. These can be sensuous, heightening the need for emotional and physical pleasure. These people can be romantic and stimulating lovers. But they can be very changeable in their moods. One minute they are all over a lover, the next peevish and resentful.

They imagine slights where none was meant. They exaggerate their hard luck and the minor problems as well. They can be very demanding and very hard to please. Irritability can create frequent arguments.

There is a strong streak of rebellion in Mars in Cancer people. They are always looking for independence, when their nature is to hold onto what they've got. They can become confused by their contradictions. They may make progress in worldly affairs by giving up one job or career after another. The stimulus of change creates even more vivid imagination, so that the natural urge for some kind of artistic expression gets released.

If Mars in Cancer individuals do not find a release, their health can be affected. There is a tendency for the emotions to disturb the digestion. If such individuals indulge food or drink to excess, or alternatively inhibit their tastes, gastritis and ulcers can develop.

With Mars in Cancer there is little chance of compatibility with maternal figures, including the real mother in this person's life. Or the women with whom they associate may cause trouble and friction.

There is, though, a powerful love of the home and a need to find peace and quiet there. But this may never be achieved to the person's satisfaction. They will be protective of their children and loved ones, but have to avoid trying to take over their lives.

There also can be a lack of direction, which increases their feelings of discontent and frustration. They may be too timid to insist on loved ones cooperating with important plans for the family or home. Or they are unsure of what they want. So progress goes by the board.

A person with Mars in Cancer is inclined to put great value on the past. They may do their utmost to bring back some of the good old days. They can muse nostalgically, but often wind up moody and brooding when the remembrances of childhood fail to materialize here and now.

Mars in Cancer folk like to fill their homes with knickknacks and bric-a-brac, especially relics in which they take considerable pride. They are often collectors of books, photographs, and souvenirs, particularly those with a martial, or warlike, flavor.

These individuals are inclined to be rigidly patriotic and prejudiced. They have a strong sense of self-preservation, which makes them suspicious of diverse groups, strangers, and unfamiliar people. Anything unknown can threaten the peace of mind and security of the Mars in Cancer individual. They fantasize striking swiftly at their imagined enemies, then brood when the moment of confrontation passes silently.

Mars in Cancer people worry too much. They are inclined to fuss around their families. They imagine the worst has happened if anyone is late arriving home. The childhood of these people is often disturbed by association with uncongenial people. Their memory constantly reflects these emotional difficulties in adult life. It is not easy for them to decide what they want to do with their lives.

Homemaking and raising families are not enough to satisfy the deeper needs of Mars in Cancer individuals. Their innate fondness for family life is too often undermined by their own forceful and aggressive attitudes. These people are likely to make a success of an occupation connected with catering—running an institution, a hotel, or a restaurant. Housing and real-estate projects also attract their interest, and provide a constructive outlet for their energies.

MARS IN LEO

Mars in Leo gives a strong sense of purpose and creative ability. The drive to outdistance and outshine any rivals is compulsive. This person is determined to get to the top of the tree, and is not too fussy about who gets pushed and shoved around in the process.

Once Mars in Leo people get an idea in their head, no one is going to change their minds for them. They tend to fix a target for their considerable ambitions, then pour enormous physical and mental energy into that objective until it is attained.

They are born showmen and showwomen. But they lack subtlety in their attempts to attract the attention and admiration of the crowd, which mean so much to them. They can be ham-fisted as well as hams. They are likely to be looking over their shoulder constantly to see what impression they are having. It is not money or social position that these people strive for. It is recognition and image.

Individuals born with Mars in Leo are extremely passionate and strongly sexed. They are born romantics. They not only imagine themselves in heroic situations, but also they like to act these out. They are often foolhardy in their desire to make an impression on members of the opposite sex. They may throw money around and show a penchant for fast and showy cars.

These people also are flamboyant dressers. Often they favor bright colors, like red and yellow, even though these shades may not suit their complexions. They are people of strong desires, who frequently go for what they like rather than for what is good for them. They are fast talkers with a great sense of the dramatic.

People with Mars in Leo seldom are happy until they reach a position of leadership. Even then, they soon become impatient to extend their authority. They love to bask in glory. And it has to be said that they are brave and courageous, depending, of course, on the influences of the other planets. These people, when they do make promises, do their utmost to deliver the goods.

They are not lazy. And they will accept responsibility. They love nothing more than to meet a challenge, especially one that exploits their vivid imagination, their undoubted initiative, and their creative turn of mind. They usually have a flair for writing and verbal expression.

Mars in Leo people are often hot-tempered and independent. They love to order other people around. They are bossy and dictatorial. They have a good idea what has to be done most times, especially in emergencies. Their conviction induces others to give them power and authority.

Their enthusiasm for projects that take their fancy is unbounded. They can inspire others into supporting their schemes through the sheer power of their personalities and their disregard for danger and discomfort.

There are seldom any back doors about people born with Mars in Leo. In fact, they are often so frank and direct as to be rude and insensitive. Tact and diplomacy are not among their virtues, unless these qualities are conferred by other planetary placements.

People with Mars in Leo tend to lack humility. They are so sure of their own infallibility that they find it difficult to listen to advice, now matter how well intended. So they are prone to make mistakes, especially of the emotional kind. They can be undisciplined in their expenditure of energy.

MARS IN VIRGO

Individuals born with Mars in Virgo have a keenness for detail. Their analytical powers fit them for a career in science. They are especially suited for working in laboratories where medical, chemical, and metallurgical problems have to be solved. These people can be dedicated researchers. In their determination to find a cure or a remedy, they put all other considerations aside.

There is usually a strong urge to serve in Mars in Virgo people. They make the most energetic employees. However, they do need a special objective to work toward. Otherwise, their considerable energies start to back up, and they can become troublemakers.

If not totally absorbed, these people can stir up teammates. They can do this by fussing about unimportant details and nonessentials. Or they may draw attention to unhygienic or unhealthy working conditions, and so create discontent among the work force.

Mars in Virgo individuals have considerable technical and executive ability. They are very good with figures. They have a special gift for analytical thought. They are able to reduce a vast amount of detail to a logical essence. They are usually exceptionally clear and fast makers of reports. They are good people to head inquiries, especially when there are attempts to conceal the facts.

One problem with Mars in Virgo is that it makes an individual extremely critical. This is an advantage if the trait is employed in constructive ways. But without direction, criticalness can degenerate into picking and nagging. Such a person also can be officious and coldly calculating.

Mars in Virgo people often have sharp tongues and are argumentative. And unless the individual is mature, he or she may lack physical courage. If their jibes or criticisms are challenged, such individuals wilt into the background, there to make intrigue and trouble.

The developed individual with Mars in Virgo is extremely capable of dealing with emergencies. They are not the types to lose their head. While others may panic or run around ineffectively, they will quietly stand their ground looking for practical solutions. They are not beyond indulging in a bit of scheming either, if it suits them.

Lack of spontaneous emotional response often makes these people seem cold and aloof. They have difficulty expressing their feelings. They will hide behind a mask of indifference rather than risk making a fool of themselves. There is often a great deal more going on deep inside than their bland appearance may suggest.

Sometimes Mars in Virgo people become health and diet faddists. They are the types to be found jogging around the park first thing in the morning. They are not exercise buffs, but their logical minds tell them it is good for them. They also can damage their health by taking diets to extreme.

These individuals are terrible worriers. They do their best not to show it and to appear cool as a cucumber. They can suffer from stomach pains and indigestion due to nerves and repressed anxieties.

People born with Mars in Virgo often like talking as a pastime more than anything else. They do not seek the public eye. They prefer to remain on the sidelines until they see a safe opportunity to put their oar in. Then they delight all and sundry with their magical ability to transform the most everyday experiences into fascinating tales of mystery and intrigue.

Mars in Virgo individuals are not great innovators or experimentalists. But they do possess a talent for solving work and production problems. They have a knack for improvising that would make them extremely handy people to have along in any environment.

MARS IN LIBRA

Mars in Libra fosters extremes in action or decision-making. This placement produces a person who is likely to swing violently to one side or another. It marks an individual who probably will be impatient and intolerant of any injustice or exploitation of others. Such people might put a great deal of energy into righting such wrongs. Or they may run around in circles, making a lot of noise but accomplishing very little.

Mars in Libra people do not like to argue or get involved in stand-up fights if they can be avoided. But in a tight spot, they will stand their ground and give as much as they receive. They prefer to solve disputes by compromise. They are adroit at maneuvering others into positions where cooperation seems to be the only sensible alternative.

These people make persuasive and firm diplomats. They are exceptionally suited for the courtroom. Here they can argue a case with telling effect. They also make excellent negotiators and go-betweens, especially if there is distinct hostility between the parties involved. In times of war, they can put on just the right show of force to make an enemy hesitate, while they increase their defenses during the pause.

As much as they love peace, truce, and moderation, individuals born with Mars in Libra usually manage to get involved in conflicts. They may seem always to strive for a state of equilibrium, especially on the domestic front. But here they often make problems for themselves by selecting a mate who is the exact opposite of themselves. So home life can be a trial or an uneasy truce.

It has to be remembered that Libra is ruled by Venus, the planet of love and beauty. When Mars, the planet of war and raw energy, is placed in this position, the result obviously involves conflict and contradiction.

These people yearn for true love, but often try too hard to obtain it. They can be attractive, passionate, skilled lovers. Mars the warrior and Venus the artist come together in an ecstasy of union.

Often these people are involved in love-at-first-sight affairs. They are impulsive and ardent. But when it comes to living with a partner, the differences start to show and the arguments begin. These individuals know instinctively what is good for them. So they often choose to move on, renouncing deeply committed relationships.

Mars in Libra people do not have a lot of physical staying power. They put tremendous energy into their projects, then burn out quickly. They can lose interest in the face of prolonged delays, aggravations, and petty conflicts.

These are rash people. It does not take much to upset their equilibrium, especially in their personal life. They can overreact. They can fall in love one day and be indifferent the next. Due to their impulsiveness, they often marry early in life—and learn to regret it. They may marry more than once. Lovers and mates seem to create the main problems in their life.

Usually, Mars in Libra confers artistic talent or a penetrating appreciation of art, as may be found in a gallery owner, dealer, or critic. Their own artistic productions may be motivated by a sense of urgency, and so come across as lacking in detail. Strong colors and broad strokes are their forte.

Mars in Libra individuals are animated talkers. They love discussions about politics and international affairs. Such topics allow them to express their particular views about the unjust treatment of others. They have to avoid a tendency to advocate extreme measures.

MARS IN SCORPIO

Mars in Scorpio is a powerful and dangerous placement. It is a bundle of dynamite that can explode at any moment. The question for the individual with this placement is whether to use the explosive energies positively or negatively.

Mars in Scorpio people give out intense vibes. They have only to be in a room to stir up reactions of dislike or attraction. They are the kind of people who cannot be ignored.

Mars, the planet of driving force and aggression, is the coruler of Scorpio, together with the mysterious, seething planet Pluto. Scorpio stands for penetration at any cost, the urge to find the secret of life even at the expense of death. There are no half measures here.

This man or woman is a hard-driving individual who knows exactly what he or she wants—and how to go about it. They are relentlessly determined. Once they start on a certain course, they never give up. They are absolutely fearless and contemptuous of any opposition. They have unlimited faith in their own self-sufficiency and their ability to overcome all obstacles.

Mars in Scorpio individuals have an unusual approach to time. Although they are impatient in their desires to keep forever moving toward the one objective they fix for themselves, they are prepared to wait years for the final result. Anything that gets in their way they are inclined to stomp on. They possess a near indestructibility. They are sustained in whatever they undertake by an unshakable sense of purpose.

These can be dangerous rivals and deadly enemies. If they are undeveloped and immature, they can be cruel, heartless, vindictive. They have a natural ability to discern the weaknesses in people. And they never fail to exploit these weaknesses in the pursuit of their own aims.

People with Mars in Scorpio can do a great deal to benefit humanity or the community in which they live. They have nerves of steel. They are just the kind of people who can dedicate themselves to eliminating criminal or corrupt practices. They make excellent spies, investigators, and undercover agents. They also make good surgeons, military leaders, and corporation heads.

These are hard-working and practical people. They have the power to command. Their physical strength and endurance are exceptional. They make fearless executives, especially the troubleshooting kind. Hardship means nothing to them. They bore unremittingly toward their goal.

It is a good idea for individuals born with Mars in Scorpio periodically to take stock of the direction their life is taking. It is not difficult for them to get on the downgrade toward an unlawful or undesirable existence. The power and resource available to them can lead them into excesses. Also, since they have very fixed ideas, they are inclined to put their head down and seldom look up to see if anything has changed since the original commitment was made.

Mars in Scorpio individuals usually like to work alone. They are not the kind to look for advice or to accept it. Their faith in their own opinions and beliefs can be so strong that they become dogmatic and even fanatical.

They often have to cultivate a more humane outlook. They can take people around them for granted, or even use them ruthlessly. They have strong sexual urges, which can be expressed or repressed. When repressed, Mars in Scorpio people must find an outlet for their energies. A constructive and self-fulfilling endeavor is an added compensation.

MARS IN SAGITTARIUS

Mars in Sagittarius people are among the most impulsive in the Zodiac. Their associates cannot predict what they will be doing next, or where they will be. Mars in Sagittarius individuals are restless, and forever on the move physically and mentally. They also can be reckless.

They are great lovers of outdoor activities. All sports and games, especially of the vigorously competitive type, appeal to them. As they grow older and their waistlines grow broader, they are likely to become good-natured coaches, the generous patrons of clubs, or jovial and active committee members.

Sagittarius normally is a sign that gives a love of the good life without much regard for tomorrow. Money is something to be used, not held onto, once the basics are provided. With Mars in Sagittarius, there is a tendency to go farther, even to extremes. These people can be extravagant to the point of foolishness. They are likely to put on weight through dietary indulgences and to drive their bodies to the limit.

Mars in Sagittarius individuals have extraordinary resources of energy, especially when it is needed to pursue a new adventure. Otherwise, their staying power is not great. They are inclined to work in fits and starts. They become easily bored with routine and cannot stand to be tied down in one place for long.

There is another side to the nature, which, if dominant, produces a more philosophically minded person. These individuals, although not particularly self-searching—unless the Sun or another planet is in Scorpio—use their experiences to look for a greater meaning to life. They are, however, inclined to stick to conventional beliefs. They may become zealous advocates of an established religion.

Mars in Sagittarius people are often distinguished by an extraordinary optimism. They have great faith in the future, especially in good luck, on which they rely. They are inclined to gamble, taking high risks with money, their careers, and positions, as well as with their own physical safety.

These are extremely independent individuals. Their love of freedom can be so pronounced that they find it difficult to work in an ordinary nine-to-five job. They are likely to switch jobs regularly. If they do not end up working for themselves, they may settle for work that gives them a minimum of responsibility and the opportunity to travel around and meet new people.

Their enthusiasm is boundless. They are usually looking for pie in the sky, one big transaction, or that surefire adventure that will solve all their financial problems forever. They do not necessarily believe this, but they live as though they do. They are people with high ambitions and a great amount of energy to use in trying to get to the top. They usually take the unconventional way up and often attain fame and fortune, confounding the dire predictions of their critics.

Mars in Sagittarius people can be pompous. They get on their associates' nerves at times with their moralizing. They may argue for the sake of hearing their own views expressed. They can be extremely tactless and blunt. They not only call a spade a spade, but also hit their audience over the head with it.

Exaggeration is often one of their main faults. They are inclined to make promises they cannot keep. They also can be boastful and slapdash. But they do have deep insights into human nature, and can often deliver jewels of wisdom in a few words.

Mars in Sagittarius individuals need to find an aim in life and keep to it.

MARS IN CAPRICORN

People with Mars in Capricorn are particularly well suited for getting ahead and eventually to the top in this world. Mars, the planet of energy, drive, and ambition, is exalted in Capricorn. That means Mars is most powerful here. Also, Capricorn is the sign of material achievement and organizing ability. Together, they represent a person to be reckoned with.

These people have great driving force. But it is controlled, contained, like the air in a tire. The pressure, although released slowly, drives inexorably forward. As hard as rocks both in determination and outlook, these individuals are prepared to plod a long, hard course that would weary any but the most dauntless competitor.

In fact, it is possible for their associates to dismiss these people for a while as being too serious and methodical ever to make it to the top. But eventually, these same people are likely to find themselves working for a Mars in Capricorn boss.

Mars in Capricorn confers a tremendous desire to obtain prestige and authority. These individuals enjoy the feeling of power, but probably more than anything they yearn to be respected. And they usually deserve whatever notch they rise to.

They are extremely conscientious. They are not the type of worker who watches the clock. While there is work to be done, they are available. Their bosses soon learn that they are most reliable employees who can be trusted to carry out instructions to the letter. No one takes their responsibilities more seriously than people born with Mars in Capricorn.

Although they are inclined to work on their own, minding their own business, they have a keen appreciation of the need for all the parts of an organization to work efficiently for the common good. When they become elevated to positions of authority, they display a rare ability to understand the workings of all departments. They know exactly what is going on in each of them and when. A company or organization can seldom become too large for a chief born with Mars in Capricorn.

These people are often strict disciplinarians. They believe in sticking to rules. Yet they would never ask another person to perform a job they would not do themselves. Usually these people on the way up have made a point of familiarizing themselves with the operations of every branch of their company. No external discipline could ever be more than what they are inclined to impose on themselves.

They are prudent, resourceful, and cautious. They are rehearsed in everything they attempt. They never risk failure by leaving anything to chance. They are not particularly imaginative or creative. But they are consummate planners, with an eye for detail and a shrewd ability to assess character.

These are not the type of people to waste time struggling against resistance. They leave that to more stubborn types who have something to prove apart from the attainment of the objective. Mars in Capricorn individuals overcome difficulties by making the best possible use of all the forces and resources at their disposal. They do not run up blind alleys or hammer on doors unless they already have planned the next move.

However, in the face of prolonged delays, these people can show evidence of frustration. They may become increasingly irritable. If their ambitions are obviously thwarted, they may be subject to violent explosions of temper.

MARS IN AQUARIUS

People born with Mars in Aquarius are usually at the hub in their community or friendship group. They seem to attract numerous acquaintances and would-be associates. Often they are members of societies and associations with humanitarian objectives. These people usually are concerned with making the world a better place to live in.

Although they are friendly and take a great interest in what others are doing and what is happening to them, they manage to keep their relationships fairly detached. They are the first to help anyone in trouble. Frequently they take home individuals who are down in their luck and give them a bed for the night. But at the first sign of any emotional demands, they lose interest.

Mars in Aquarius people are radical thinkers. They can hold strong antiauthoritarian views. They attack through writings and speeches whatever established order exists in their time or in their community. They often become involved in political agitations. They are more inclined to incite others to take action than actually to get in there themselves.

In spite of their dislike of authority, they are motivated by a strong desire for personal power. This is not obvious, because they are not interested in giving orders. Their power complex is satisfied by being in the position to change other people's views and beliefs. In this way they can be quite destructive, especially if they have a bee in their bonnet and are not objective.

Mars in Aquarius people are persuasive and plausible. They believe in freedom. They do not necessarily object to law and order, except when these are used as excuses for muzzling an individual's freedom of speech or association.

They are original thinkers and are often found in the forefront of scientific research. They are never happier than when they are experimenting either with the slide rule, the test tube, a current political idea, or an unusual hobby.

If they are not moving at great speed in their minds, they like to move around people. They take interesting journeys and make unconventional associations. They often are creditable writers. Some Mars in Aquarius individuals have well-developed musical talents.

The energy these people can put into causes is immense. But they are rather selective about the kind of work they will do. It has to offer them a good deal of freedom. They are not particularly concerned with amassing a fortune. But they do like to have a secure and comfortable home.

Because of their fiercely independent nature, Mars in Aquarius individuals are not often blessed with a great deal of domestic harmony. Much will depend on the positions of the other planets, as well as those of their mates or family members.

They can be blunt to the point of rudeness. They have strong enthusiasms. But they need a good deal of variety and intellectual stimulation to keep them interested.

They are difficult people in a close relationship, especially marriage. Disappointment awaits the partner who is looking for warmth and affection. Mars in Aquarius individuals are not particularly physical or demonstrative. They are more attracted by a marriage of minds.

These people often prefer to mix with types who have different ideas and habits from the rest of society. In this company, they can air their unusual views without risking rejection. Once they get an idea in their head, no matter how bizarre, it is usually there to stay until experience proves it to be false. They are themselves not easily swayed.

In many respects Mars in Aquarius individuals live a moderate and regular life. Yet there is something unpredictable about them. They may go along conventional lines for a time, then suddenly do something that appears completely out of character. They are sometimes the catalyst of radical change for the people they associate with.

MARS IN PISCES

Mars in Pisces is not an easy position, but it is a promising one. People born with this placement often are obliged to sort out confusing situations—both in themselves and in their environment. They have strong feelings and compulsive drives. But when it comes to expressing them or putting them into action, the result usually falls short of their expectations.

These are people who are no strangers to frustration. They have to learn to bridge the gap between feelings and mind. They must coordinate sensation with sense. What they want to do sometimes does not make sense to others, and they feel restricted and inhibited. It is not always easy for them to see basic issues.

Mars is a fiery, self-assertive planet. Pisces is a watery, self-repressive sign. And when Mars plunges into this psychological pool, there is created seething currents below, dense and steamy clouds above.

Mars in Pisces is intense, dramatic. It gives the person a determined attitude to exploit his or her artistic potential, especially talents utilized in theater and performing. These individuals also will be inclined to take more than a passing interest in the sufferings of others. They may even be attracted to working as caretakers for the sick, hurt, and needy. But there could be more sympathetic talk than action in such a role.

Mars in Pisces people have extremely fertile imaginations. They are likely to spend a good deal of their time daydreaming and living in their feelings, stimulated by thoughts of the past. They can be intuitive and kindly, prepared to involve themselves in other people's troubles.

One of the most admirable traits about these individuals is an honest secretiveness. They are likely to work assiduously for others behind the scenes. Although they may not be particularly energetic in physical ways, they can focus their heart and mind on other people's problems.

Their understanding and genuine desire to be of help can make them valuable social and charity workers. Even if other influences induce them to seek personal recognition for their efforts, it is often difficult for them to bask in glory without guilt.

It is important for Mars in Pisces people to recognize that they probably are more effective in trying to reach their goals by indirect means. They have a knack for infiltration and surreptitious maneuver. They can wheedle people, and often achieve more spectacular results than the direct methods of their associates.

Mars in Pisces does imbue a person with an interest in the occult, mysticism, or parapsychology. They often use their own sensitivity to analyze their emotions, which makes them susceptible to prophetic visions and dreams.

Mars in Pisces also heightens sensual desires. If there is a lack of control due to other planetary positions, the search for excitement and stimulation can be taken to extremes. An immature Mars in Pisces individual can become preoccupied with trying to experience every sensation the body has to offer.

They can be impressionable, easily influenced, and permissive. The strong compulsion to fantasize in the face of frustrations makes the excessive use of alcohol and drugs a danger.

Mars in Pisces people usually have a good sense of humor. They have a strong desire to please and be liked. They are diplomatic, sometimes even to the point of dishonesty. They can lack push and self-reliance. They need an aim in life or they are likely to misdirect their energies.

Jupiter in the Signs

Jupiter is the planet of good fortune. It stands for expansion through foresight. It makes a person optimistic, cheerful, generous, frank, a good friend, and a wise adviser.

Jupiter, being the planet of expansion, naturally has the reputation for bringing material gains through business, personal endeavors, and good luck. When strongly placed, it makes us the kind of people others like to be with. Like Venus, which is fortunate because it attracts, Jupiter is fortunate because it expands—friendship, good will, and joy.

Jupiter is the planet of wisdom, the kind of wisdom that comes from being able to accept trials philosophically, knowing in the end that things usually turn out for the best. For this reason, the Jupiter person often gives the impression of being too confident and easygoing.

Jupiter also gives a desire for travel and adventure. If these journeys cannot be physical or geographical, they must be mental and intellectual. The imagination must be stimulated and broadened. Jupiter likes to wander. In its wanderings, wisdom is culled.

When adverse influences are at work, the Jupiter influence can endow individuals with too much faith in the future and their own good luck. So they may take silly risks with their money or with their reputations. But being philosophical, they are able to adopt the wider view and accept things as they are. The result is they are seldom downhearted for long, and so tend to attract helpful people.

The negative side of Jupiter takes all the good influences to extremes, so like the extremes of Venus they become problems. Jupiter's expansive tendencies can make a person extravagant and too fond of the good things in life. It can mean indulgence in food or drink, with excesses causing problems of fitness and health.

Promises can be made as a matter of convenience to expand the conviviality of social occasions, with no intention ever to honor them. Gambling—again the willingness to depend on luck—can become an irresistible lure; debts are left strewn in the wake of the buoyant, good-humored, fun-loving, irresponsible Jupiter. Jupiter's travel urge, when divorced from any particular aim in life, can produce a rolling stone.

But favorably placed, Jupiter contributes dignity, justice, honesty, broad-mindedness, and fine judgment. It confers a respect for law and order and a high tone of morality expressed through a philosophic or religious ideal.

Jupiter is favorably associated with Sagittarius and Pisces, the signs it rules.

JUPITER IN ARIES

People with Jupiter in Aries have big ideas, big ambitions, and loads of energy to see them through. They are extremely independent and self-confident. Their enthusiasm for their numerous projects is boundless. They are pushers, go-getters, men and women who seldom fail to get results. But often their disdain for detail and their refusal to draw up thorough plans plunge them into disaster. Their failures are frequently as large as their successes.

These are people who love to travel and get around. They seldom spend much time in one place. They are often great car enthusiasts, speedboat fanatics, or fliers. Any activity that gives them the sensation of speed or sets the adrenalin pumping attracts them. They are the types who love sports and games. They are hikers, mountain climbers, skiers, adventurers.

These are self-made men and women. Although other planetary placements will have an effect, people with Jupiter in Aries usually end up working for themselves in their own business. Or they rise to positions of authority where they enjoy all the freedom that their individualistic natures demand.

Jupiter in Aries individuals are usually pioneers and leaders. They like to set the pace. They refuse to follow others. If they do, they manage to branch off in a spectacular way, endeavoring to improve on the original idea. They believe in whatever they do. They embrace their projects body and soul, often being captivated more by the idea of the thing than any practical considerations.

These are among the natural gamblers of the Zodiac. Their faith in themselves and the future is unlimited. They are brave and courageous. They have an almost absurd disregard for physical danger. They often succeed in their ambitions through sheer audacity. They will take chances with money, reputations, and relationships that would make their more conservative colleagues shudder.

These people are impulsive and tremendously optimistic. Wishful thinking is one of their main faults. Although they have all the zest and zeal to go with their confident expectations, they frequently fail to live up to what they have promised. Being fun-loving and seeking pleasurable social pursuits, they easily get carried away by the euphoria of an occasion.

Jupiter in Aries can produce a person with strong religious beliefs. They are inclined to preach their own unorthodox doctrines to support whom they gather around them. They are not the club-joining types, but they do like to be at the center of a group or set of which they are the acknowledged leader. These people often are seized with a personal sense of mission. They slip easily into the role of crusader.

There is a certain rebelliousness in the nature of people born with Jupiter in Aries. Although usually supporters of the need for law and order, they are inclined to be against most forms of authority without necessarily having a clear idea of why.

They are great freedom lovers. Although rash and impetuous, they have a steady side that reveals itself when they are engaged in active occupations. They are at their best having to deal with moving situations. They can adapt and change direction without disturbance, and are able to make the best of whatever is happening.

JUPITER IN TAURUS

Jupiter in Taurus produces a person who usually ends up in a fairly comfortable financial position. Jupiter is the planet symbolizing expansion through material growth. Taurus is the sign of worldly accumulation and material pleasures. Together they sound a rich note.

These people may either continuously fight against or yield to extravagant urges. They have a great love of luxury and beautiful things. They are inclined to measure a person's success by his or her material possessions. They love to relax in comfort surrounded by as many symbols of the good life as possible.

Even in the tough times, these people find it very difficult to live in economical ways. They believe firmly that the highest price usually indicates the best quality, and that nothing less than the best is a good buy. They are quite capable of going without if they have to. But their last dollar is likely to be spent on a trifle. They live in style, these Jupiter in Taurus characters, or they go without.

Jupiter in Taurus individuals have fixed opinions. They believe in supporting the establishment in all its forms. They usually become businesspeople and business owners, with some of their cash always invested in real estate or other blue-chip holdings. The establishment stands for the protection of property, so why wouldn't they be all for it?

These people are not particularly imaginative. Although solidly practical and adept at making and holding onto money, they are inclined to cling to ideas and methods that have proved to be reliable. However, what they lack in originality, they make up for in their capacity for hard work.

They are patient people with strong qualities of perseverance. They can devote themselves to a project for years, as long as they are convinced that it is going to give them a good return. They do not trust much to luck, although invariably they seem to have more than their fair share of it. This probably is because they are single-minded in their aim to make money.

They are extremely good managers and are the kind who can become millionaires. They have a flair for banking, ranching, mining, construction, and merchandising operations.

Jupiter in Taurus makes a person want value for money. Although they can be charitable, they are not the types to give handouts unless the recipient is prepared to do his or her share to help themselves.

They are very conscious of position and prestige. They like to be seen in the company of successful people. They are good mixers and love the social life. They always have an eye out for an influential person who may be helpful to them in the future. They are inclined to join prestigious professional and business clubs.

Undeveloped individuals born with Jupiter in Taurus can be so self-indulgent and lazy that they never amount to anything. They are inclined to live off others, to be greedy and possessive. They are not afraid of lying or deceiving those who befriend them.

There is a stubborn streak in all people with Jupiter in Taurus. They generally know what they want. They do not give up without a fight. They are particularly fond of having a fine residence, where they can entertain their prominent and socially acceptable friends, and show off their many lovely possessions.

In love, they are sincere, devoted, and possessive. They insist on giving their partners expensive gifts, especially clothes, as they want them to look as attractive as possible. They have expansive and sometimes ostentatious tastes. They have to watch their waistlines.

JUPITER IN GEMINI

Here the planet of expansion is in the sign of logical thought. Jupiter in Gemini people are big thinkers. Even the smallest, interesting idea they can swiftly escalate into a full-blown scheme. They have a good eye for detail and are amazingly adaptive, so any snags in their mental creations can be quickly changed without affecting the main plan.

The main trouble is that these people are often not practical, but they are bright. These are excellent individuals to bounce ideas off. But they need solid placements of the other planets to keep their feet on the ground.

A person born with Jupiter in Gemini believes in self-education. They are avid readers, conversationalists, and travelers. They are forever on the move mentally or physically. They love change and novelty.

These people often have a natural gift for writing. They should endeavor to develop any signs of this talent. It is possible for them to make their living from writing, or to add to their income through it. They can produce great volumes of thought, but the writing may suffer from lack of economy and control over their material.

The pressure of ideas keeps people born with Jupiter in Gemini continuously restless, so much so that it is sometimes difficult for them to stick to one activity for very long. Although they possess considerable power of expression, they lack perseverance. They need to see immediate results for what they do, or they get bored.

These people are extremely versatile. They have a continuous flow of new and wonderful ideas passing through their heads. As quickly as they start to develop one idea, another appears. They can make intellectual mountains out of molehills.

Jupiter in Gemini individuals often manage to get into the news. If they are not writing or lecturing to the public, the public often gets to talking or hearing about them.

These are usually clever and witty people. They make excellent company at social functions. They love to be the center of attention. They usually manage to keep a roomful of people amused and entertained with their stories and anecdotes.

They often have strong philosophic or religious beliefs. They tend to air these views to anyone who is prepared to listen. They usually have a remarkable knack for being able to talk about any subject at length without saying anything specific and yet keep it interesting and convincing.

Jupiter in Gemini individuals are especially suited for careers in politics and professions that require diplomacy and an air of knowledge. These people do have a way of being able to convey the most abstract ideas in simple-to-understand terms. They can make good teachers, but usually will require a greater sense of movement than instructing a class of children. The role of university professors, with its opportunities to make an impression on the highest circles, is more suitable to their style.

At their worst, Jupiter in Gemini people can become con artists or demagogues. They are not above using false claims to gain personal advantage.

Sometimes these people make lots of promises they cannot keep. Or they may get carried away with a situation and make commitments they mean wholeheartedly at the time but forget about.

Jupiter in Gemini individuals frequently waste their considerable energies and mental talents by scattering them over too many operations. They are inclined to get involved in numerous different activities, giving too little to each really to make a go of any. They always seem busy. But under the froth and bubble there may be very little of lasting value accomplished.

JUPITER IN CANCER

People born with Jupiter in Cancer usually dote on their families. They are intent on providing their loved ones with a secure and comfortable home. They are prepared to work very hard for those whom they regard as their own. They will accept all the responsibilities that go with being the head of a household. But they can be demanding in their need to be appreciated for what they do.

These are charitable people. They love to help anyone who stirs their sympathies. It would be very rare for anyone to ask for their assistance and not to receive it. They have a strong protective instinct. Once they take anyone or anything under their wing, they will see them through.

These Jupiter in Cancer people love to entertain at home. Their homes are often filled with their families, relatives, and friends. Jupiter in Cancer people may complain sometimes about all they have to do for others on the domestic front—but actually they love it. When someone leaves home, perhaps a teenager who is going out into the world, the Jupiter in Cancer person can be desolate.

Jupiter in Cancer individuals are often lucky. They have sharp financial judgment and business acumen. Often they have a talent for dealing in real estate or land and its products. Often they can guide a family into a business enterprise, in which every member has a particular job and responsibility.

Acquisitiveness is frequently one of their faults. They may start by accumulating household possessions, then people, then business interests. They never seem to be able to discard things that ever have meant anything to them. In the home they can become surrounded with old and worn-out possessions.

Jupiter in Cancer people are also the type to keep on faithful employees who have served them for many years. They are loyal and grateful, even though such a demonstration of gratitude may not be in their financial interests.

These are people with heart. But they are not without their faults. Sometimes they are their own worst enemies. They love food, and can be guilty of indulgence. It is very easy for them to become overweight, even at an early age. They may have strong sexual appetites and be unable to resist fantasizing, which can cause emotional problems.

The emotions of these people are more active than their minds. They are motivated by their feelings, which are strongly conditioned by the environment of their childhood. They have a binding attachment to the past, and they love to talk and reminisce about the past. Their parents mean a great deal to them, even though they may not get along with them.

People born with Jupiter in Cancer often have a deep respect for the best traditions of society. They tend to follow the religious indoctrination of their childhood. Although often interested in philosophic questions, they are inclined to be more orthodox than exploratory, even though their personal insights can be exceptionally profound and mystically revealing.

These people have a way of influencing the public if they ever enter the business scene. Even in their immediate community environment they are likely to be among the most socially active people. They tend to support worthy causes and local charities. They will generously cook and serve for social functions. They will organize an event so that everyone has a share in the work and the praise.

Cancer is the best sign for Jupiter to be placed in at a person's birth. Jupiter, the planet of expansion and benevolence, is exalted in Cancer. This means it is at its strongest and in its most compatible sign. Cancer is the sign of home and family, so Jupiter helps one to expand and the other to multiply.

JUPITER IN LEO

Jupiter in Leo produces a person of immense optimism and self-assurance. The planet of expansion in the sign of leadership makes such individuals feel they can accomplish anything. They often appear to have tremendous egos, but usually this is accompanied by an ability to carry out much of what they claim. However, depending much on the placements of the other planets, they can also be vain, boastful, and ineffectual.

These are people with high ambitions. But they are not seeking worldly wealth or possessions. They want admiration and praise. For these they will bring all their considerable talents to bear, without a great deal of thought for the material rewards.

Jupiter in Leo people love to be in the public eye. But they have a high regard for their own importance and the need of dignity to go with it. They like to dress for the occasion; they aim to attract the maximum amount of attention, without appearing to be foolish. As they are often impulsive and childish or immature in their tastes, they can select clothes and colors that are ostentatious. It is easy for these people to be show-offs.

Leo is the sign of drama. Jupiter here expands the person's sense of theater and display. These people love to mix in the higher echelons of society. Often they manage to be among the social leaders in their communities. They like to "hold court" in these situations, gathering around them their circle of admirers and handing out any favors with royal dispensation. Leo is said to be the sign of kingship. These people can be among the last to realize the age of kings is dead.

Jupiter in Leo people are fitted for running large, established businesses, and for holding top posts in government. They are not too proud to be figureheads, if necessary. Usually they manage to bring some of their own original ideas to whatever they attempt. They are not afraid of responsibility. They can be snobbish and autocratic, inclined to lord it over the people they depend on for performing the menial tasks.

However, there is much that is noble in their natures. They are generous and compassionate. They cannot help looking on the bright side, although they often risk being too confident. They are inclined to be jovial types who enjoy parties and all kinds of pleasurable activities. They can indulge drink or food to excess.

Jupiter in Leo is a propitious placement for people engaged in artistic work. Leo is the sign of imagination and self-expression. The presence of Jupiter enlarges these capacities, and adds a quality of luck that halts the disasters these fiery and impulsive characters can bring down upon themselves.

In love, these individuals are passionate, larger than life. There is nothing they will not do for the idol of their affections. They spoil, pamper, and indulge their lovers. They like their romantic companions to be attractive and desirable to other people. Then their own feelings of pride and position are enhanced.

Jupiter in Leo people are conscientious in their efforts to help others. They are quite prepared to be served; in fact, they demand homage. But they cannot stand to see a person acting in a servile way even if he or she occupies a menial position. They have a great respect for the dignity of the human race. Sometimes they consider themselves responsible for improving or saving it. They can easily become fanatical about reforms, which they feel are necessary for their fellow man.

These people often make talented writers, musicians, painters, sculptors, and entrepreneurs—always tending to be a little more dramatic and flamboyant than the next artist. Their self-confidence makes them successful actors and actresses, with a flair for obtaining publicity that is seldom rivaled.

JUPITER IN VIRGO

People born with Jupiter in Virgo accumulate knowledge as though it were a virtue. And often, in their hands and if put to worthwhile use, it can be. But frequently these people just go on and on picking over detail after detail until everyone has lost interest except themselves.

Jupiter in Virgo produces people who can be relied upon to carry out important research, especially areas that will be helpful to mankind as a whole. There is an ability to handle an amazing amount of detail, to see patterns of significance where others may discern only stunning tedium and monotony.

These individuals possess special technical skill. Problems that have gummed up the works through overload of detail and trivia can be quickly spotted and sorted out by these highly discriminating people. They make excellent laboratory workers, time-and-motion engineers, and systems analysts.

Jupiter in Virgo people can be prolific writers and talkers. Although fairly conservative and cautious, once they feel they are on secure or familiar ground, the expansive side of their nature starts to assert itself. Their imaginings can take on fantastic proportions, with every appearance of originality. But when it comes down to the world of ordinary living, they often are unable to go beyond an almost commonplace approach.

These individuals would rather talk imaginatively than live imaginatively. They can be too materialistic, inclined to hold onto their possessions as representing the highest value in life. They are practical people as a rule, and have a great respect for order and neatness.

People with Jupiter in Virgo have to cultivate a greater sense of feeling and compassion. Of course, other planetary placements may provide the warmth of emotions. But on their own, Jupiter and Virgo can be too down-to-earth and intellectual.

It is easy for Jupiter in Virgo people to be cynics. They can put too much emphasis on the importance of formalities, and overlook the human need for spontaneity, even error. In their minds, they think they have the solution to all of life's problems—if only people would listen to them.

When they do endeavor to put their thoughts into action, they are extremely good at overcoming practical difficulties. But again, the need for something more human than statistics and common sense can escape them.

These people are often drawn to the manufacturing industries. They can work with computers, machines, production lines, microcircuits—all the electronic gadgetry of modern industry. They are specialists in supplying small goods and services.

In religious outlook, people born with Jupiter in Virgo can be so skeptical that they analyze the finest teaching down to being simply words on a page. It is often beyond them even to want to see anything more than what their senses tell them.

These people often make distinguished writers. Their intellects can soar to heights that their feelings can never reach. They can lock themselves away for long stretches at a time and become lost in their own literary productions. They have a way of turning a single idea into a wonderful structure. They are the type of people who can always make the most of the materials at hand.

The minds of Jupiter in Virgo individuals are exceptionally alert and clear. They are always on the lookout to learn new things, and for opportunities to teach others. They can be painstaking in their attempts to explain the most intricate scientific theory, which, even as laypeople, they are likely to understand.

JUPITER IN LIBRA

Jupiter in Libra individuals fall over themselves to please. They are among the most socially conscious types in the Zodiac. They want to win the acceptance of others at any price. They crave for approval. They feel that they need solid external support. For this, they pin their hopes and expectations on others. They are afraid to be themselves.

But Jupiter in Libra people also are most genial and likable. They shine in the role of host or hostess. Their hospitality leaves nothing to be desired. They can be a bit lavish and certainly extravagant. But everything is always done in such good taste and with such grace that they are more often forgiven than condemned.

Libra is the sign of relationships and diplomacy. With Jupiter, the planet of expansion and excess in this sign, it is easy to understand how these people can go too far in trying to make social contacts as pleasant and harmonious as possible. They believe—and rightly so, for they are so good at it—that their effusiveness is doing a job for mankind by bringing people together.

Nevertheless, conflict does come to Jupiter in Libra individuals. Despite their best intentions, these people often find themselves in the middle of argument or strife. And they detest conflict!

But conflict is inevitable. Libra is also a sign of war as well as of peace. Alliance is Libra's strategy. It can break down, exposing the parties to battle anew. And with Jupiter in Libra, expansionist aims are freed. Trouble can come through too much of a good thing.

But again, with Jupiter's fortunate help, Jupiter in Libra individuals may slip away from relationships or situations in the nick of time. Just before conflict escalates into chaos, they escape, leaving the mess for others to clean up.

Jupiter in Libra produces a person who usually has finely balanced judgment. These people as a rule are born conciliators and judges. They are frequently found in the legal profession or in top areas of government and big business where a breadth of vision combined with an extreme delicacy of judgment are required. They can be superlatively objective. They sincerely wish to do the right thing. They are humane.

These people often carry generosity to a fault. They are inclined to give very expensive gifts. Their unconscious urge is to win approval, which means so much to them.

Jupiter in Libra individuals are humanitarians. They believe in the spirit of the law, not only the letter of it. They can be fairly orthodox in their views, but usually they strain toward the broad humanitarian outlook.

They can be great fighters for the underdog. As much as they yearn for peace and harmony, they will battle against injustice with a determination that can seem quite out of character. Nothing gets their blood up more than seeing a human being treated unfairly or exploited.

Jupiter in Libra people often have to fight against an indulgent streak in themselves. They can develop such a liking for comfort and the good life that it becomes their natural expectation. They can become lazy and effete without knowing it. They can make lovely speeches and sympathetic utterances about reforms, but fail to exert themselves in any practical way to achieve these goals.

These people usually have strong artistic impulses. Their homes reflect their expensive and refined tastes. They are fond of the best in everything. They like exotic furnishings and decor, stylish clothes and cars. They are often involved in the beautifying professions.

JUPITER IN SCORPIO

Jupiter in Scorpio is a good placement. Jupiter balances some of the less likable characteristics of Scorpio, which under worse influences can turn to bitterness and poison. Jupiter in Scorpio produces a person who usually is determined to make something worthwhile of his or her life.

These individuals have a natural feeling for business and finance. They can anticipate trends. They can predict with fair accuracy the commercial conditions that will be operating in the near future. They have a breadth of vision, but it can become stuck in one frame if they do not keep updating what they have seen.

Jupiter in Scorpio people think big and build big. Money is often their most powerful tool. These people are not intent on the pleasures that money can provide. They want the power money can give them. More power to dominate their immediate surroundings and relationships is what drives them on. They know the value of money as a means to achieve this end.

These people are often attracted to occupations connected with research and investigation. They have a way of being able to get to the bottom of things. They are relentless and untiring when they are on the trail.

They make first-rate detectives, undercover agents, and psychoanalysts. As psychologists, they dig deep to root out blocks, and so help people reconstruct their lives from within. These individuals also like to be involved in converting natural resources into useful products. They make good engineers and chemists.

Jupiter in Scorpio endows a person with considerable personal magnetism. They have tremendous willpower, which makes it necessary for them to direct their energies into worthwhile projects instead of antisocial activities. They can become devoted to whatever they pursue. They have to guard against a tendency to become fanatical about their enterprises. Their self-confidence can seem almost unlimited; this may degenerate into the pride that comes before a fall.

Jupiter in Scorpio individuals are passionate. They have strong sexual and sensual urges. There is a tendency to experiment to find new ways of heightening sensations. They can be reckless in this regard, and may be tempted to use drugs and alcohol to excess.

Yet people with Jupiter in Scorpio have an extraordinary capacity for self-control. They can hide their feelings. In fact, they can repress their emotions so much that they are in danger sometimes of exploding into rages. It is a good thing if they find an associate in whom they can confide, and let off steam before it builds up into dangerous proportions.

Jupiter in Scorpio provides artistic ability. These people find art to be an outlet for their unused energies. It is through art that they can sublimate their deeper and darker emotions, and so give the world the benefit of their extraordinary insights.

Scorpio is the sign of sex and regeneration and death. Jupiter here gives a far-seeing quality. It can enable the individual to delve beyond material and physical limitations, to envision connections of soul and sense, to "see" into psychic phenomena.

There is often an avid interest in occult matters. With their talent for getting at the essence behind the appearance, these people may make a major contribution to human knowledge of the psychic world. In this way, they calm the fears of those who dread the thought of an end to mortal existence.

People with Jupiter in Scorpio are good to be with in times of crisis. They can keep their cool and risk their necks to ensure another person's safety.

JUPITER IN SAGITTARIUS

Sagittarius is a most comfortable and fortunate place for Jupiter. Here Jupiter is in its own sign. Jupiter bestows on a person the bonuses of life, the good things that come without necessarily having to be earned. In its own sign, Sagittarius, it can make the person plain lucky!

Jupiter cannot be counted on, however. It would be silly to rush into risky and daring ventures hoping that Jupiter will provide protection and success. Strangely enough, this is just what Jupiter in Sagittarius people are inclined to do. They take chances naturally, without thought.

Jupiter in Sagittarius individuals never challenge the force of their luck. They just can't help believing in it. As a result, they often land themselves in trouble. Financial and business schemes threaten. Yet they scrape through. More often than not, they get away with it.

These people usually are genial, jovial, and generous. It could be said that they have a fair amount to smile about. But they also have their fair share of strife and trouble. They just refuse to take the setbacks and difficulties too seriously. Unlike many other people, they have great faith in the future. They are prepared to cut their losses at any time, and walk away without a backward glance.

Jupiter in Sagittarius produces an interest in religion and philosophy, and an ability to see the truth. But unfortunately these people do not like to go too deep into themselves, even though they have the faculty to do so. What they see down deep in themselves they often do not like. So they do not look too often. They prefer to remain on the surface and to express surface emotions.

Such individuals are inclined to stick to orthodox religious and philosophic beliefs. They are not nearly as daring or experimental here as they are in other areas of their life. There is a type of Jupiter in Sagittarius person who is acutely self-analyzing. But such a one is rare, and probably has other planets in Scorpio.

Jupiter in Sagittarius people usually love an active outdoor life. They have an enthusiastic interest in sports and games. If not athletes themselves, they often become promoters and coaches in spectator sports.

Travel is especially stimulating to these people. They have loads of energy. They keep on the go, mentally and physically. Visiting other countries is particularly appealing. They like to live with the people and absorb their culture. Not for them the guided tour, if they can help it. These are adventurers at heart, born trailblazers.

A person with Jupiter in Sagittarius loves freedom. They do not find it easy to settle down to a nine-to-five existence or humdrum domesticity. Even though there may be planets in the fixed and cautious signs, such a person would still feel the conflict of a settled life if his or her imagination was ever excited by a picture of distant and exotic places. The freewheeling gypsy life is for such a person.

These people often end up in positions of prestige and authority despite their nonconformity. On the way up they may have envisioned and espoused all sorts of reforms that could be made if they had the chance. But on arrival at the top, they may be too busy doing other things to get around to what they once thought so necessary. They can be guilty of hypocrisy.

With Jupiter in Sagittarius, a person has a great desire to be recognized for doing the right thing. They will placate and satisfy the demands of a group rather than risk unpopularity by going the other way. However, this man or woman has a genuine desire to do good. On a personal level, he or she can always be depended on to help anyone seeking to get out of trouble.

JUPITER IN CAPRICORN

Jupiter in Capricorn produces a fairly straitlaced, prudent, and conscientious person. He or she will have a strong sense of duty. They will conduct their affairs along conventional lines with due regard for tradition. They are quietly but determinedly ambitious, and are prepared to get to the top slowly and surely.

These are people who very often end up in charge of large business corporations. They think on an expansive scale but never overlook the immediate details. They can generate the most imaginative visions and extract the fine practical nucleus, which they then set about patiently and industriously implementing.

These are not the types of people who take chances. They work strictly to the rules, so much so that they can lose any spontaneity. They can become fixed and impersonal in their dealings with other people. There is always a danger that they will overlook the human side of a situation, and insist on the letter of the law being enforced rather than the spirit of it.

Jupiter in Capricorn individuals often become wealthy. They are the kind of people who can become married to their jobs and work, spending longer hours than are really necessary with their noses to the grindstone—and enjoying every moment of it. Their diligence and perseverance seldom escape the attention of grateful superiors. So they gradually, if not spectacularly, move up to the top of the ladder.

These people do best at managing and expanding established enterprises and businesses. They can be too cautious and lacking in self-confidence to launch a venture of their own. They have the willpower and hard-working ability, but not the flexibility. They are reluctant to take chances, an attitude that so often contributes to the success of a new operation.

Jupiter in Capricorn people want to be financially secure. They are usually thrifty and self-denying. With adverse influences from other planetary placements, they can be stingy and ever-complaining. But for the most part they are prepared to spend much of their early life scrimping and scraping as necessary to reach a position of independence through wealth or authority.

Sometimes they are subject to bouts of extravagance, but not often until they achieve their goals. When and if they do amass wealth, they are the kind of people who will spend fortunes on their homes for entertaining business associates. Yet they will argue about the milk bill! They want value for their money.

Jupiter in Capricorn individuals do have genuine unselfish urges. They can be generous patrons and sponsors. But usually they support causes that have practical value. They are not too likely to sponsor purely artistic endeavors, unless this act gains for them a high degree of prestige.

It is the desire for authority and respect that can take over the lives of these people and provide them with very little joy and simple pleasure. Everything they do is likely to be measured against what people will think of them.

They cannot stand being laughed at or ridiculed. Their sense of dignity can be so inflated that it is impossible for them eventually to act naturally. Sometimes the final reward for a life given to the pursuit of their ambitions is loneliness in a room at the top.

Jupiter in Capricorn individuals can do much good in the world, as long as they do not lose sight of themselves and their needs. Their desire for love and affection is strong, but they have to learn to give both in order to receive.

JUPITER IN AQUARIUS

Soon or later, a person born with Jupiter in Aquarius is likely to give the world, or their community, an original idea that will help to bring changes for the good. Often the ideas of these people are so far ahead of the times that the ideas are not fully appreciated until the people have gone.

Jupiter in Aquarius is a very good placement for people who are engaged in mental pursuits. It is ideal for politicians, social workers, idealists, and crusaders. Humanitarian considerations usually are very strong in these people. They are not frightened to criticize authority or to call for reforms on which the establishment may frown. They are often freedom fighters.

People with Jupiter in Aquarius have inventive minds. They are intuitive, imaginative, and fiercely dedicated when dealing with the rights of their fellow man. They like to live an active intellectual life that does not stop at airing their usually strong reformist views. They are prepared to practice what they preach. They will get in there when the going is tough with the followers they usually draw to them.

They are especially good at handling groups of people. They have a friendly, sociable way about them that makes other people feel at ease. They will accept people for what they are. But they will try to make people aware of any exploiting authority that is standing in the way of their full development.

Jupiter in Aquarius individuals are tolerant and just. They can devise important new theories that may be laughed at now but that will be hailed as great discoveries in the future. Their minds are always filled with new ideas clamoring for expression.

These people make better friends than marriage partners, as a rule. They are too inclined to circulate in groups, hanging around with their many acquaintances, exchanging views and ideas, and mounting the next offensive against ignorance or suppression.

These people make excellent scientists employed in such frontier fields as space technology, microelectronics, and atomic and nuclear research. They like to contribute to the welfare of society and humanity. They seldom will give their time to anything that is not associated with progress.

Jupiter in Aquarius produces people who are interested in philosophical questions. They have a deep desire to realize the higher potentialities of man. They are not materialists, although the placements of the other planets will have a considerable bearing on this. Even so, people with Jupiter in Aquarius will always be inclined to use their money to try to make the world in some way or other a better place in which to live.

With help from the other planets, these individuals may devote their entire lives to the welfare of other people. They are often to be found at the forefront of charitable and political movements. They are not the kind usually to preach revolution, as they believe in enlightened law and order. They would prefer to bring about improvements through more peaceful and conservative means than violence.

On the adverse side, they have to beware of a tendency to be erratic and unpredictable. Their theoretical schemes can be impractical. They have to be sure to set an example by action and not just become doctrinaire spokespeople.

People with Jupiter in Aquarius often collect odd characters among their friends. They are not the type to disown anyone just because he or she is unconventional.

JUPITER IN PISCES

Jupiter in Pisces individuals have a delicious sense of humor. Not the rollicking, life-of-the-party kind, but a quiet and subtle kind that ripples out and delights the soul. They are great observers of life, almost painfully aware of its cruel reality and yet ecstatic at times with the beauty they feel around them. These are optimistic, understanding, and charitable people.

They also have periods of gloom and deep introspection. They oscillate for much of the time between highs and lows. They are always trying to fit their individual observation and experience of life into a broad and comprehensive pattern, one that possibly would explain the mystery once and for all. They are always looking for answers that they never manage to find.

These people are often religious or have a deep interest in philosophic questions. But they are not theorists in their ideas of good. They have a strong feeling to serve others who are less fortunate, or at least to reduce their pain and misery.

They are generous to others, both in their time and with their money. They have a great amount of patience and understanding. They will listen to another person pour out their heart with a genuine sympathy that seldom fails to provide a measure of relief. These individuals born with Jupiter in Pisces can easily become devoted to a life of charitable works.

However, they enjoy the good life, too. Although there is always a touch of the saint or the martyr in them, if they are blessed with worldly wealth and possessions, they know how to enjoy them. They may at times retreat into themselves or into some sabbatical isolation, but they manage to come out smiling and eager for the next round.

Jupiter in Pisces people are fairly easygoing. They can take life as it comes. But they do not like pressure and uncongenial people or situations. These they will flee from. They use money, but they are not hungry for it. They will not work for long hours for peanuts, saving for their old age. They want to live, either delving into humanity's feelings and suffering, or getting about mixing and experiencing.

They love to get back to nature at times. They have a need to surrender themselves to simplicity. Periods spent among beautiful scenery, especially near the water, can act as a tonic to their health. These people love change. They frequently will spend as much time as possible between two homes or bases if they can afford it.

Usually, people born with Jupiter in Pisces are fairly lucky. Because of their fluctuating emotions, they often are impulsive and do things spontaneously they are likely to regret the next day. Sometimes they can even wonder how they possibly could make such a move. Naturally, some of these decisions involve money, and they often lose it. But their fortunes are frequently restored.

They can be extravagant. Their imagination knows no bounds. They are easily influenced and can be drawn into speculative ventures that would best be left alone. They have great faith in the future, so much so that they often are inclined to sit back and do nothing.

Jupiter in Pisces individuals are given to daydreaming. They live more in their emotions than in their minds. They can be very difficult to pin down. Their schemes are often unrealistic or impractical. Yet they frequently get brilliant ideas that can make them and their associates a lot of money.

Saturn in the Signs

Saturn is the planet of responsibility. Its quality is restraint. Saturn represents the power of limitation and discipline.

Saturn is the taskmaster of the Zodiac. It is cold, depressing, limiting, anxious, fearful, and conservative. At its worst it is repressive, possessive, selfish, envious, grasping, miserly, and grudging.

Saturn is the seventh and the last of the personal planets. The last three planets out from Saturn—Uranus, Neptune, and Pluto—are known as the spiritual planets. Because they take so long to traverse the Solar System, their influence mainly is expressed through eras, ages, generations. There is a tremendous gap in solar space between Saturn, which represents the outer skin of man, and the orbit of Uranus, the first spiritual planet.

Saturn, too, is very far away from the sun. So it represents all that is suppressive and least desirable to warmth-loving man. It symbolizes the bony skeleton, which keeps him upright yet is the most enduring and rigid part of the body.

Being the last personal planet from the Sun, Saturn stands at the gate to the heavens, the barrier that man has to cross to reach his final reward. Through the trials and tribulations its energy inflicts on man, Saturn provides the necessary discipline.

Saturn is the sober balance in man. It keeps in check the exuberance of the Sun, the optimism of Jupiter, the luxuriousness of Venus, the fertility of the Moon, the fire of Mars, the frivolity of Mercury. If any expectation can be spoiled, Saturn will do it. Saturn teaches us to control our passions, excitement, and enthusiasm. What the other planets give, Saturn tests.

Whereas Jupiter teaches man to be philosophical and hopeful in the bad times, Saturn teaches that there is no such thing as hope. The individual must patiently accept his lot without thought of escape. Saturn instructs the hard way, through despair and surrender. Jupiter instructs through hope and faith in the future.

Saturn is the main cause of delays and obstructions, all that drags on and complicates. Saturn turns shortcuts into long hauls, mistakes into misery. Saturn weakens the constitution, causes nervous depression, colds, arthritis, and skin diseases. It is the planetary force that blemishes beauty, reduces self-indulgent wealth to poverty or wretchedness, destroys the selfish family clique, turns self-satisfaction into self-disgust.

But when Saturn's lessons have been learned—and not one day before—the surly old planet known as Father Time and the Grim Reaper will give individuals their just rewards. These can exceed anything ever hoped for!

Saturn makes a person conscientious and industrious. There is a thoroughness, which often makes any job a little harder. But the responsibility and care shown often will attract the favorable attention of people in authority, so that position and standing are consistently advanced.

Saturn helps people to work well under pressure, but creates a dislike of change. It provides a strict public sense of right and wrong, which sometimes can be a bit puritanical. Saturn helps people to keep secrets and to give practical advice.

A weak Saturn makes a person pessimistic, fearful, slow-witted. Such individuals are inclined to miss opportunities through dithering or fear of change and progress. They can be self-pitying, backbiting, critical killjoys.

Saturn is favorably situated in Capricorn and Aquarius, the signs it rules.

SATURN IN ARIES

Saturn in Aries is not an easy placement. This person will often be at war with himself or herself. The planet of restraint in the sign of initiative and adventure gives an underlying feeling of frustration. The nature cannot be satisfactorily expressed. People may want to act, yet suppress themselves, or realize that the time is wrong for making a certain move, but find themselves doing it all the same.

Saturn in Aries does produce a person who is extremely self-reliant. They will press on indomitably in the face of all hardships and obstacles. They are likely to be too proud or afraid of being ridiculed or laughed at to ask for help. These are people who appear to have an iron will.

There is a strong sense of duty here. Saturn in Aries individuals are hard on themselves and also expect a lot of others. It is easy for these people to become disciplinarians if they have any authority. It is the sort of stressful placement that may be found in the chart of a straw boss, a drill sergeant, or a relentless servant.

These people have to avoid strain. Although they generally have great reserves of energy, they are likely to spend their lives trying too hard. Much of their exertions are likely to be due to correcting moves made at the wrong time. Their sense of timing is not strategic.

Saturn in Aries individuals are not easy to please. Often life for them consists of one obstacle after another. They surmount them, though. But doing so gets them into the habit of expecting the worst and being protectively aggressive. They can resort to authoritarian ways to compensate for their own inner frustrations.

In spite of these problems, people born with Saturn in Aries often succeed in the end. They are so persistent and persevering that they tend to wear down and exhaust the opposing forces. They are strong characters.

These people have to avoid being jealous. They may be inclined to be too guarded toward their loved ones, especially to their children when they are teenagers. Their domestic rule may need to be tempered with a bit more understanding of other people's need for freedom. Often these individuals have had to contend with a harsh or demanding parent, possibly a father, in their childhood. If so, in dealing with their children they should endeavor to remember their own unhappy experiences.

Saturn in Aries is not an influence that adds to a person's sociability. In fact, it induces a tendency to be retiring and watchfully aloof. There is a great need to be respected by others. And it can be felt that any softening of behavior or attitudes may be interpreted as a sign of weakness. These people are not the type to forgive any insult or slight, particularly if it is made in public.

Saturn in Aries can produce a certain puritanical outlook. There is a strong desire to be known for doing the accepted thing. Laws and rules may be the guiding principle. Mainly such order is used as a defense or protection against the person's own spontaneity, of which they are mistrustful. They would like to be spontaneous, but cannot bear the thought of the uncertainty it produces.

These people like to know exactly where they are going. But frequently they misjudge a situation, acting when they should not and not acting when they should. Within themselves they are likely to be a playground of emotional contradictions. These may be revealed through irritability and sudden explosions of temper.

Saturn in Aries individuals need to cultivate the habit of self-sacrifice.

SATURN IN TAURUS

Here are the makings of a very solid citizen. Saturn in Taurus people will want a good hold on the earth. Money and material possessions will mean a great deal to them. They will love saving up, putting the pennies side by side where they can watch the little mounds grow every week. This is not to say they are miserly. They are just careful, frugal, and almost fanatical about security.

Saturn, a psychologically weighty planet, is not uncomfortable in Taurus. Taurus is the sign of material wealth. And Saturn gives an even greater determination to the character to amass whatever wealth is possible, without taking any risks.

These people are not afraid of hard work. They realize that there is only one sure way of keeping the wolf from the door. They are not interested in taking shortcuts to riches. They know that there is no such thing as a free lunch. They are not interested in speculative and risky ventures. A bird in the hand is all they want. And they will gradually build their own aviary of security with patience and good, honest sweat.

Not surprisingly, Saturn in Taurus individuals often have a long haul on the way up, and frequently a difficult one. But in the end they usually win out. Their achievements do not have to be great to satisfy their desires. They possess a fondness for beautiful things, the more practical the better, but not the usual Taurus love of luxury. This, of course, will depend on whether the individual has any other planets in Taurus.

Saturn in Taurus is conducive to a purposeful personality. The tendency is to fix an overriding aim—probably to be economically independent—then butt for it. These individuals lower the head like a working bull, butt and plod resolutely toward the aim, come what may. These are not people to be deflected easily once they have made up their minds. In fact, they can become so fixed in their ideas and their way of life that they fall into a rut and seldom get out of it.

Stubbornness is one of their main faults. They can be very difficult people to live with if they do not learn the art of compromise. They also can lack spontaneity, being always inclined to follow the same old routine. These are people who can easily endure a nine-to-five existence and a fairly uneventful domestic life as long as they do not have to worry about tomorrow.

Saturn in Taurus individuals are often too cautious. Although they have a flair for handling finance and other business affairs, they often wait too long weighing the pros and cons and so miss opportunities. They would rather be slow and sure. So they will shrug off lost chances as being all for the best in the long run.

They have to avoid being possessive and avaricious. They can be inclined to live by material values, judging other people by their apparent wealth or possessions. They enjoy their homes and endeavor to make them as comfortable as possible without overdoing it.

Saturn in Taurus individuals like to entertain intimate friends, but are not too enthusiastic about public appearances. There their self-image may be challenged.

These people have due respect for law and order. They believe in tradition. They stick to tried and trusted ways. They believe in a good day's work for a good day's pay. They are conservative in their views and not particularly adventurous.

In love, they know what they want and they are prepared to wait for the right person to come along. They will have their affairs, but very seldom get carried away.

As parents, Saturn in Taurus individuals have to be careful not to become too exacting. They may confuse prudence with prudishness.

SATURN IN GEMINI

Saturn in Gemini? Unimaginably good! Saturn is the taskmaster planet of the Zodiac and usually means some hard lines for the individual in whatever sign it is placed. But Gemini is one of the best positions for this weighty

THE PLANETS IN THE SIGNS: THE MOON THROUGH PLUTO

influence to get tucked away in. Gemini normally is a flighty, scatterbrained sign, giving agility and restlessness of mind. Saturns tones all this down.

People born with Saturn in Gemini are serious, orderly thinkers. They can at time become a bit gloomy and depressed, being inclined to concentrate on minor probtems, which they can magnify into alarming proportions. They should not take their problems or themselves so seriously.

These people often make good scholars. Their disciplined way of thinking fits them for occupations in science and research. They are able to make precise comparisons and measurements. They are extremely good critics. They often find an outlet for their need to communicate at a serious level in teaching, where challenge and controversy are not frowned on.

They have a rather stern air about them that does not encourage banter or tomfoolery. Their minds are cautious and calculating, usually one jump ahead in anticipating what would be advantageous personally in any developing situation.

Saturn in Gemini individuals love to gather facts. They usually are avid readers. They enjoy serious conversations, but spend a lot of their time summing up the other person. One might, at times, get the feeling of being alone and talking alone in the presence of these studiously silent creatures.

Usually they have a talent for writing. They choose their words with great care. They are inclined to write about important and controversial current issues in politics, the law, and perhaps even religion. Specific interests will depend on the placements of the Sun and Jupiter.

Saturn in Gemini people do suffer from lack of confidence. They may at times not say what they mean for fear of being ridiculed or made to look a fool. They can be very thin-skinned about their intellectual abilities. They may take offense when none was intended.

At times, they are impulsive. Words jump out of their mouth, for which they are immediately sorry. They are inclined to be critical of their own mental efforts, and yet resent anyone else's criticism.

These people prefer to use their minds rather than move around a great deal physically. They like to get where they are going fast, though, then start concentrating on the job in hand. They travel more in the line of duty than for pleasure.

Saturn in Gemini often brings problems concerning relatives or neighbors. There can be tedious responsibilities connected with brothers or sisters. The health of other people can interfere with the daily routine of these individuals.

It often is difficult for Saturn in Gemini people to make decisions. Their minds are more peaceful when they are following a set line of inquiry. They make good secretaries, clerks, and office managers where routine is firmly established. They are very good at writing reports; they put great emphasis on reaching correct conclusions. They like to take their time, so they can be as thorough as possible.

But Saturn in Gmini individuals may lack application. Under the slightest strain or threat, they may lose their ability to concentrate. They can be quickly irritated in such situations, and so become quarrelsome or sink into sullen silence.

People born with Saturn in Gemini often grow into polished and accomplished speakers. The years seldom fail to add an attractive maturity to the speaking and writing ability. They have a remarkable power of observation, which they can convert into successful books and articles for publication.

Quite often they possess a good sense of humor, which belies their serious outlook.

SATURN IN CANCER

Saturn in Cancer can bring the moody blues. Cancer for mood, Saturn for gloom. Yet the essential dignity of both Cancer and Saturn can help the individual rise above all manner of problems and deceits, which all too often are produced when Saturn is in Cancer.

People born with Saturn in Cancer often have to contend with troublesome domestic conditions. Their childhood may have been disrupted by a broken marriage or the death or illness of one of their parents. Or a dominant parent may have instilled such a sense of self-discipline that they never really recover their buoyancy.

However, these are people who do their very best to make their homes run smoothly and orderly. They may not receive all the respect and appreciation from their families that they feel are due to them for their efforts. But they are individuals who will conscientiously work on, aware that the world is not a very thankful place.

Saturn in Cancer folk take all their responsibilities very seriously. And they worry about the slightest thing affecting the home or any member of the family. They feel it is their task to look after everyone. They are inclined to be a bit authoritarian. They will complain if others do not give a hand—and also if they do.

Sometimes these people feel inadequate in coping with home and family affairs. They can become sorry for themselves and feel like giving up. They never get enough recognition at the fact they are doing a good job and would be sadly missed.

It is not easy for Saturn in Cancer individuals to express their emotions. They care tremendously for their loved ones, but may never feel they can express this adequately. They can become depressed. It is especially important for these people in partnership to have a harmonious sexual relationship. It is through physical contact that they are best able to release their feelings and communicate the love they feel.

Despite love and tenderness from others, Saturn in Cancer people are not particularly tolerant. They have to cultivate a more sympathetic attitude if they hope to attract the kind of affection they feel they need so much. They can be too acquisitive and protective of their worldly possessions.

The homes of these people are often cluttered with old things. They find it difficult to discard anything that has an important connection with the past. They are likely to keep childhood souvenirs and toys well into their old age. They love to reminisce about the good old days, which probably were not so good at all.

These people do not like physical change. They seldom move home if they have any say about it. But frequently they are forced to move, and it takes them lots of time to settle in again.

A person born with Saturn in Cancer has to find a good reason for living to be happy. They have much to give. Often they find it difficult to discover something worthwhile and satisfying to absorb their energies. They are too self-absorbed for their own good. They have to learn to take a greater interest in the world around them.

These people have a natural ability for controlling affairs connected with the public welfare. This gift offers scope for their executive abilities. It particularly addresses their need to feel they are doing some good for others.

When occupied in a task that appeals to them, Saturn in Cancer individuals are tremendous workers. They have great powers of perseverance. They are tenacious in the pursuits of their goals. They have to be careful how they handle others, as they can be bossy and too opinionated.

These people need constant reassurance that they are needed. If they feel their efforts are unappreciated, they are likely to lose interest very quickly. They can fall back into a state of inactivity and self-pity, the moody blues being their only memory of the good life.

SATURN IN LEO

Saturn in Leo banks the fires, but keeps the coals glowing embers. Neither heat nor light nor matter is extinguished, just kept on a slow burner, a low flame. Every now and then is a sputter and burst, evidence that something is cooking.

The Saturn in Leo individual has strong qualities of leadership and an equally strong sense of moral responsibility. They tend to take themselves very seriously. They consider that they have the answer to many of the world's problems. And they are prepared to wait patiently until the public discovers how much their leadership is needed.

In other words, they have big ideas about themselves. It's justified! If given the opportunity, they frequently are capable of exercising authority on a large scale and in constructive ways. People born with Saturn in Leo can become powerful figures in government and politics. They have an inspired way of getting to the kernel of a problem, of cutting through personal considerations and inhibitions to reveal what *has* to be done.

If what *has* to be done is unpalatable to others but necessary to the welfare of an organization or a community, they are just the people to put efficiency first. They make first-rate administrators, businessmen, and businesswomen.

However, Saturn in Leo individuals do have a touch of the dictator in them. Discipline is something they understand, and they regard it as essential to any successful operation requiring people to work together. They are not individuals who believe in loose-knit, easygoing working arrangements. Although the position of the other planets will have a strong modifying influence, these people by nature tend to be aloof. Staying apart from the gang allows them to nurture the big ideas.

They have a keen sense of dignity. They feel that to let their hair down and join in beyond a certain point is to jeopardize the respect and prestige they demand and crave. Usually they are respected, but not for the reasons they may assume. Their coworkers and subordinates cannot help but admire their conscientiousness and hard-working ability.

At a party, the Saturn in Leo person is likely to be found in serious conversation on the sidelines, but always at the center of what's important. Having a good time is not likely to be the main object as far as they are concerned. Business can always be mixed with pleasure to make pleasure more pleasurable!

Close associations are not their forte, and intimate associates are few. They have trouble expressing their emotions freely. They prefer to bottle them up. This serves a dual purpose: protection and control. They will, though, adopt a compensatory façade of seemingly tolerant authority. This pose can become a dominant facet of their personality.

People born with Saturn in Leo can be badly misunderstood in love. Inside they have much affection to give. And they need love, perhaps even more than some other types. But their unbending attitude can give a potential lover the wrong impression that they are cool and calculating.

It is especially important for these individuals as parents to remember their own inner feelings and frustrations. In this way, they can be loving and tender to their children. If they are too demanding of children "for their own good," they can pass on the capacity for inhibition and frustration. Insisting on disciplined behavior can undermine a youngster's spontaneity.

Also, parents who have children with Saturn in Leo should make a point of emphasizing the togetherness and warmth of the family circle. These children should not be loaded too heavily or too early with responsibilities, which they may appear precociously willing and able to undertake. Parents must remember that these children take obligations gravely. Other children can throw them off when they feel like it, but not these children.

SATURN IN VIRGO

Saturn, the planet of restriction, makes life just a bit harder wherever it appears in a sign. But here in Virgo, its solid earthiness blends with the natural characteristics of the sign. A person with Saturn in Virgo will be practical and have a good deal of common sense.

This placement bestows mental stability. There is seldom any flightiness in these people. In fact, they can be overly concerned most of the time with the impression they are making on others, having an innate fear of appearing foolish. They can be very self-conscious, even bashful. But Saturn in Virgo individuals are not prudish, merely prudent.

Saturn in Virgo people often are very good with words. Although they may not like to become involved in public debates, once they are sure of their ground, they can express themselves with great clarity and penetration. They are often drawn to literary pursuits and are capable of working for long hours in isolation. They are the types who can produce books that are regarded as making a major contribution to solving society's problems.

Saturn in Virgo individuals are not particularly humanitarian folk, though. Personally they can lack feeling and the ability to communicate affection and love. But their minds are discriminating. They can analyze situations with tremendous precision, being especially attentive to detail. In this way, they often describe the ills of society, and come up with practical solutions or systems for dealing with them.

These people often are involved in occupations connected with diet, health, and sanitation. Virgo is the sign of work, and develops the "perfect" employee who is conscientious and receives his or her satisfaction from being able to do a good job. Saturn, the planet of perseverance, improves on the scheme. Here is an even more dogged and industrious individual.

However, there are some drawbacks. Although these people generally have a high regard for the prevailing moral code, they can carry their esteem too far and become narrow-minded and puritanical. Admirable uprightness can be turned into rigidity. They have to be careful to keep in touch with their fellow creatures. They must not lock themselves away, either in their minds through the rigidity of their opinions, or in their lifestyle, following a hermit's existence.

Saturn in Virgo individuals must beware of becoming so involved in their work that the lighter side of life and its pleasures become a bore. They can suffer down moods, depression. They have to keep active to prevent themselves from brooding on their anxieties. They are individuals who can worry over anything or nothing.

But the thing that upsets these people most is uncertainty or the unknown. Saturn in Virgo individuals need to know where they are going. They like to have the constant reassurance of material security.

However, people with Saturn in Virgo often are motivated to produce great accomplishments through their fears of insecurity. They are inclined to be more successful in later life, probably because they spend their earlier years in hard and concentrated effort, ignoring the opportunities to gamble or take a chance.

It is not unusual for Saturn in Virgo to generate hypochondria in its subjects. These people are inclined to be fastidious about their diet. If any complaint is going around, they imagine they will catch the ailment. Often they can worry so much that they suffer from digestive problems, and so bring on the chronic discomfort they dread so much.

Saturn in Virgo people can be critical. They can get on their associates' nerves by always carping about the faults they see in others. They also can be suspicious, constantly looking for the catch or the con. They need to cultivate self-confidence and a belief in other people.

A bit of faith and a lot of love for themselves and for humanity can go a long way toward making Saturn in Virgo individuals the true protectors of earthy values and rewards.

SATURN IN LIBRA

Saturn in Libra is a sobering and regularizing influence. It helps individuals strive to maintain balance in their life and their relationships. They are very much aware of the need to do the right thing. They are not going to risk upsetting the applecart in any way by their own foolish actions, if they can help it. They know how easy it is to bring trouble down on themselves. Yet they often manage to do just that.

How well Saturn works in Libra, the sign of partners and partnership, will depend on how well developed is the individual's sense of sharing. If individuals tend to be selfish and inconsiderate because of other planetary placements, they are in for some depressing circumstances in their relationships.

But if they have managed to learn the lessons of sharing and the values of harmony and togetherness, they can make this a constructive placement. They will practice a bit of self-denial.

As a rule, Saturn in Libra people are honorable. They manage their affairs with neatness and orderliness. They believe in the golden rule, honesty in marriage, integrity in business and social relationships. They can be sticklers for good form. They are inclined to frown strongly on anyone who is too demonstrative or showy.

In this lies a danger of their being intolerant. They are so intent on keeping their affairs on a solid equilibrium, they may begin to resent anything that is discordant with their own judgments and feelings. They have to learn to live and let live, especially in the little things.

Saturn in Libra people do have a tendency to become opinionated. They are particular about their style of dress; they have good taste. They have a liking for objects of art, which they may feel makes them an expert, at least a connoisseur.

They also have to guard against insincerity. Saturn in Libra individuals have an almost painful need to be accepted by others, especially at the social level. To gain this kind of treatment they may use guile and flattery. These people often encounter their own faults in their associates, especially in marriage partners. Until they have mastered these shortcomings in themselves, they have to put up with some disturbing relationships.

People born with Saturn in Libra often flourish in the legal profession. They possess extraordinarily good judgment and an ability to maintain impartiality. They make fair-minded administrators and executives. A scientific career also suits them.

Libra is the sign of art, color, and harmony. Saturn provides a realistic approach to these largely Venusian activities, which ordinarily can attract dabblers and arty types who are more interested in the show than the showing. People with Saturn in Libra have a no-nonsense approach to their creative enterprises. They take firm control of their projects, and work methodically toward worthwhile objectives.

People with less weighty planets in Libra are often flirtatious and flighty. They are inclined to have numerous affairs, not because they are so sensual but out of their sense of romance and search for the ideal of love. Saturn in Libra individuals are more realistic. They are inclined to settle for the best partner they can find without looking for the impossible.

These people like to regularize their relationships. Although they may have their share of love affairs, they like to make them lawful by marrying or avoiding involvements with people who are already attached. They are firm believers in equal rights, provided their other planetary placements are favorable.

THE PLANETS IN THE SIGNS: THE MOON THROUGH PLUTO

SATURN IN SCORPIO

Saturn in Scorpio can be a scalding combination—for the individual as well as for their close associates. But it can be a teaching influence. With Saturn in Scorpio comes the test of endurance. The individual can learn to control angry emotions and the destructive side of his or her nature. Much will depend also on the placements of the other planets; no one placement can ever be taken to represent the whole person.

Saturn in Scorpio individuals have a tremendous ability to stick to their aim. They can be relentless in the pursuit of their ambitions. Once they decide they want something, or to achieve something, they are prepared to undergo unbelievable hardships to get there.

They are exacting, cold, and calculating. They can use people to attain their own ends. They possess a talent for being able to sum people up in an instant, and especially to identify their weak points, which they then concentrate on. They can be very dangerous enemies.

These people, unless they have some strongly modifying planets elsewhere, never forget an insult. They tend to hold grudges for as long as it takes them to get even. One of the unfortunate things is that they often imagine slights and insults where none was intended. They find it very difficult to accept criticism. They can be excruciatingly thin-skinned and touchy.

It is not easy for people with Saturn in Scorpio to change their opinions. Inflexibility is one of their main faults. It often prevents them from making the success of their lives that their skills and determination would otherwise have made possible. They can be one of the most stubborn people in the Zodiac.

These individuals are intensely secretive. Their reserved exterior always conceals great emotional activity. One of their problems is that they will not allow their inner feelings any latitude or release. They are constantly in the grip of their own cool reserve. If and when they ever do release their emotions, it is usually in the form of an explosion. They have violent tempers because of this.

Saturn in Scorpio individuals can be strongly sexual. They emit a magnetism that either repels or attracts. Their pride and aloofness can act like a lure to curious members of the opposite sex. They are not the kind of people to flirt with. They mean business. And they will not play around for long.

These are highly sensitive people. In love, their passions are fixed and enduring. But they are difficult types to get away from. They tend to play for keeps. Their jealousy can amount almost to mania, and may engender cruelty.

Although intensely proud, these are not as a rule vain people. They are too hardheaded to allow themselves such an indulgence, which they regard as a weakness. They have a great talent for being able to get to the bottom of things, to see through façades and pretensions, and to solve mysteries.

People born with Saturn in Scorpio are deep and devious. They often prefer the cat-and-mouse game to the straightforward deal. They are masters at intrigue. They make good detectives, secret agents, and psychologists. They can be counted on to track down the problem or the person.

These people have considerable executive ability. They can stay cool in a crisis, and marshal the forces at their disposal. They do not lose their nerve, even when faced with imminent disaster.

SATURN IN SAGITTARIUS

Sagittarius is a bounding, forward-looking, enthusiastic sign, which can easily go to extremes. The weighty and restricting planet Saturn in this position tones all that down. Saturn in Sagittarius produces a person who is well balanced and has a lot to give to the world in the way of natural wisdom.

These people often go a long way in business. They are extremely ambitious and farsighted. They tend to work toward distant goals, which they have firmly visualized so that slipups are reduced as much as possible. Although idealistic, they keep their feet on the ground. Their plans are imaginative but practical.

Saturn in Sagittarius individuals are genial types. They enjoy getting around and meeting people, especially when it involves the possibility of making a few bucks. They prefer to mix business with pleasure and pleasure with profit.

Saturn in Sagittarius is conducive to meditation and a serious inner search for the meaning of life. They are not the kind of people who display their religious or philosophic efforts, but they often are renowned among their friends and associates as being fairly wise. If the placements of the other planets are not helpful, however, these people can spend a lot of time boring their friends by moralizing, believing they are helping others to finding a better way of life.

These are persistent people. They appreciate that their objectives may take a long time to reach. But they compensate for this by the scope of their plans, which often lead them to considerable success and possibly wealth in their later years. It is important for people with this placement to know what they want early in life and to work toward it.

Saturn in Sagittarius gives people a fear of personal restriction. They must always feel that they are going ahead. To be in a bottleneck creates tremendous inner frustrations. Such a buildup of energy can explode into a violent loss of temper.

There are times in which these people show a lack of restraint. The serious side of their nature seems to be put aside, and they can break out into seemingly uncharacteristic behavior. They can be impulsive one moment, deliberate the next. They have to avoid getting into a stop-and-go routine.

The typical Saturn in Sagittarius individual tries to be open and frank. But frequently their dread of being criticized or publicly ridiculed can prevent them from saying all that they think. They are individuals who are very much aware of other people's pain and problems. They try to be kind and compassionate.

It is usually in the later years, after these people have made a success of their lives, that they tend to take up some philanthropic activity. They may be financial patrons to struggling but practical artists and innovators. They admire people with new and workable ideas. They also may become leading members of community and charity groups, especially those sponsored by a religious organization.

These are independent people. They cannot stand relationships in which emotional demands are made on them. They are quite prepared to accept their responsibilities, but only those that they themselves select and recognize.

They have to avoid a tendency to be cynical. Unless the other planets are favorably placed, they can be destructively critical of other people's ideas. They also can cling to outdated concepts and try to force these on their work and business associates.

In love, Saturn in Sagittarius individuals are inclined to look for a reliable partner rather than be carried away by romantic dreams.

SATURN IN CAPRICORN

This is a very strong placement, for Saturn is the ruler of Capricorn. Saturn in Capricorn provides a person with great ability to persevere to the bitter, or sweet, end in whatever life objectives they set themselves.

But the trouble is that Saturn in Capricorn can make the person very materialistic, even grasping. Much depends on the placement of the Sun and the other planets. However, if the ambitions are directed and channeled along constructive and satisfying lines, this is one of the most helpful influences for an individual.

Saturn in Capricorn people may take some time in their early years to work out exactly what they want to do. It is important for them always to keep their options open while they are in this period. They should try to avoid getting settled into a dull, nine-to-five routine that offers nothing in the end or in between.

The tendency is for Saturn in Capricorn people to get into ruts. They can be inclined to take the easy way out when there is nothing special on the scene, and to sink farther and farther into a drudge routine. This may not seem so bad to them, for they are quite capable of putting up with the most difficult as well as the most boring conditions once they get used to them. But their lives can slip away from them.

Saturn in Capricorn individuals have great organizing ability. They need to be in an occupation that stretches their capabilities. Then they can discover for themselves just what they can do. They can be something like a precious stone that remains hidden in the land because no one recognizes it.

These people can be successful in business, especially in controlling large corporations, including international conglomerates. Their minds are able to retain a great amount of detail connected with various simultaneous operations. They do not waste their time or effort. They plan and aim at taking as few chances as possible. They are cautious, economical, and practical. They believe in hard work. They never fail to set an example to their associates and subordinates that is difficult to emulate.

Saturn in Capricorn individuals have great respect for the law of cause and effect. They realize that as a man sows so he reaps. There is a depth of practical wisdom in these people that often induces others to seek their advice in worldly matters.

But it must be remembered Saturn in Capricorn usually matures the individual in the latter half of life. Earlier the person may not seem to be very sure of where he or she is going. It also is inclined to bring some difficult times, which have to be patiently worked through.

One of the dangers of Saturn in Capricorn is that the person may tend to live for work. They can become so immersed in earning a living, or fulfilling their ambitions, that they have no time for other activities, especially relaxation. The loved ones of Saturn in Capricorn people have to make sure that they take their vacations and get regular exercise on the golf course or the tennis court.

These people often have a flair for writing. They can become the authors of serious and respected works, which may be regarded almost as a final authority on a subject. They can put complex ideas into simple words. This placement is also conducive to a career in science or mathematics as well as teaching.

People born with Saturn in Capricorn are often said to be success-prone, due, not in the least, to their relentless dedication to the job at hand.

SATURN IN AQUARIUS

Saturn in Aquarius individuals can do a lot of good in the world. They are not selfish types. They have high humanitarian ideals. Sooner or later they are bound to be involved in some kind of activity that makes the world, or their community, a better place to live in.

Saturn in Aquarius individuals have a knack for being objective. They can stand back from a problem and discern solutions. They do not allow personal considerations to interfere with their judgments. They look for the broader effects that their decisions will have. They can be regarded as being a bit cool and detached as far as the individual is concerned.

These people have a compulsive desire to do away with exploitive or pretentious authority. They do not like the idea of people having to kowtow to bureaucracy and officialdom, which really get their power from the masses. Although they are cautious and deliberate in their considerations, deep within the psyche of these people is a revolutionary trying to get out.

The typical Saturn in Aquarius individual has a scientific mind. Although original and inventive, they are not the types to try to rush ahead without proper preparations. They have a pronounced ability for understanding basic principles. And even in everyday life their discernment is often valuable enough for their friends and associates to seek their counsel.

These are people who generally have an admirable indifference to personal fame and success. Like the scientist who is dedicated to the task of finding the solution to a problem without worrying about who is going to get the kudos, these people can be oblivious to their own entitlement to reward. They usually gravitate to an occupation that they feel in some way or other serves the greater interests of humanity.

This indifference to success can often be infuriating for their loved ones. Saturn in Aquarius individuals are not the easiest people to live with. Although friendly and easygoing, they are inclined to put more importance on their group and altruistic activities than on family relationships. They cannot as a rule stand emotional demands being made on them.

One of their faults is they can be mentally obstinate. Once they get an idea fixed in their head, it is usually there to stay until they see it through or until experience teaches them otherwise. They also can impose their opinions on others. They have an intensity of presence, which can be a bit overpowering for people who enjoy the lighter side of life. Saturn in Aquarius folk usually have serious projects on their mind.

These are subtle people. Their intellects are finely developed. They are quick to observe the lay of the land, whether they are dealing with a person or with a situation. They also are highly intuitive.

Sometimes these people seem to lack initiative. Depending on the placements of the other planets, they may be inclined to espouse their reformative schemes loudly, but when the time comes for action, they are missing. There is a tendency to be perverse, to go in the opposite direction from everyone else, especially from established authority.

It is not unusual for Saturn in Aquarius people to court trouble. If they become involved in public agitations, they might run up against the law or get drawn into legal actions. These can be the kind that drag on interminably or are fought from court to court.

These individuals have to be careful that their zeal does not become fanaticism and ruin all their good work.

As a rule, Saturn in Aquarius people manage to keep a good balance in their lives, especially once they have found a worthwhile vocation into which to pour their talents.

SATURN IN PISCES

Saturn in Pisces is a sensitive placement and not such an easy one. It represents the coming together of the material and the immaterial. One side of the nature wants to give all, and the other side wants to hold back. Sometimes people with Saturn in Pisces despair that they will ever be able to reach their goals. Yet if they can persevere, it is almost certain that they will.

However, Saturn in Pisces is not a placement that allows for many shortcuts. Achievement has to be earned.

Saturn in Pisces individuals usually possess artistic and creative abilities, which they should strive to formulate. Too often they feel the urge to create, but do not get around to making a practical effort. They can bewail their inability to find some suitable outlet for their sensibilities when all they need to do is sit down and try.

These people are sympathetic and compassionate. They usually are drawn to an occupation that brings them in contact with people who are underprivileged or in need of help or care. They can make other people's lives happier by their sheer ability to listen and understand their problems.

People with Saturn in Pisces often lack courage and self-reliance. They are inclined to be self-pitying and evasive. They may wallow in their emotions. They can be moody and forever blaming others for their own shortcomings. Or they project their fears onto others, and so have an excuse for not trying.

Although extremely sensitive and understanding, they can be cruelly inconsiderate of their loved ones when they are under the pressure of their own emotions. They can make unbelievable demands and fly into tantrums if they are not filled to their self-indulgent satisfaction. Although perceptive of the truth most of the time, they can in their moodiness seem deliberately to avoid seeing it.

Saturn in Pisces individuals can become recluses. These are people who in their worst moments can dislike and even hate humanity. Yet in their more heightened perceptions, they can make great self-sacrifices on humanity's behalf. They are often found working in hospitals and institutions. The more psychologically evolved type is prepared to do the most menial tasks in the service of those for whom they feel compassion.

Sometimes these people can be drawn to renounce material existence. This is an extreme action, and it will be indicated also in the placements of the other planets. But Saturn in Pisces is a combination that is always in danger of running to extremes.

The need to be alone is usually very strong at times. And yet at the same time there can be a morbid fear of isolation.

These people's sufferings are also often due to others. Although they bring much upon themselves with their fluctuating moods, they are often the rather innocent bystander who gets caught up in a chaotic stream of events started by someone else.

Saturn in Pisces individuals can have a good head for business. Their ideas for making money are often brilliant. Although they find it difficult to cope with the ordinary pressures of life, in business they can play a very cool game. They can push a transaction to the limit without batting an eye or revealing the personal uncertainty they may be feeling.

Saturn in Pisces individuals may lack self-confidence. If so, they can become very dependent on the people who love them. But in their more positive moments they have much to give.

Uranus in the Signs

U ranus is the surprise packet, the anything-can-happen planet, the un-expected and eccentric force of the Zodiac. It brings drastic change and is related to science, revolution, and independence.

All this is not surprising when the events that followed the planet's discovery in 1781 are considered.

The American Revolution ended to launch what was to become the most technologically advanced nation on Earth in less than two hundred years. The first hot-air balloon flights were made (1783). The power loom was invented, heralding the Industrial Revolution. The French Revolution and the Napoleonic Wars changed the face of Europe. Britain abolished the slave trade (1807). The United States abolished slavery (1863). The first railway operated. Steamships crossed the Atlantic. Electricity, the telephone, and telegraph illuminated and shrunk the world. Antiseptic surgery eased humanity's pain. Then the airplane, radio, television, nuclear power, and space travel defied even more unimaginable limits of the natural world. And all during the nineteenth and twentieth centuries, wars of liberation spread like wildfire from one part of the globe to another.

So the discovery of Uranus marked the beginning of the scientific age and the ages of independence and liberation, fostering a brilliant succession of ideas, discoveries, and inventions, and the brilliant, often eccentric individuals who produced them.

Even the physical characteristics of Uranus are eccentric. It has peculiar markings visible through telescopes. Its axis of rotation is so tipped that it lies almost in the plane of its orbit around the Sun. So it seems to rotate on its side as it revolves around the Sun.

Also, its revolutionary path is eccentric. It was noticed by observers that Uranus didn't follow the path predicted for it. Uranus wobbles along on an irregular orbit around the Sun, slowing down and speeding up. What could cause Uranus to move in such a strange way?

Characteristic of its association with genius, invention, and discovery, the peculiar motion of Uranus itself was used to make a brilliant discovery. Two astronomers, working independently on the peculiar motion of Uranus, and using only mathematics—not observing the planet—found the answer. They suggested the presence of another planet, unknown at the time (1843–46), causing Uranus to wobble.

In 1846 astronomers sighted this new planet just where the mathematicians said it might be, and it was named Neptune. (Neptune's "hidden" presence certainly earns it the designation of planet of mystery!) But back to Uranus

Uranus takes eighty-four years to complete an orbit around the Sun, which the Earth manages in one year. This means that Uranus spends an average of seven years in each sign. But here again, Uranus refuses to conform! Due to the eccentricity of its orbit—it wobbles off path—it may spend as many as thirteen years in a sign!

The quality Uranus imparts to a person or a generation is its originality. It stands for all that is inventive, transforming, and disruptive. The planet is treated by traditional astrologers as being "malefic"—that is, it does not contribute to the peace of mind of a person. Uranus does bring unforeseeable and unalterable changes in life, but these may turn out for the better.

Just as the Uranus force in recent history has disrupted the established patterns of nations and societies, its effect is to upset the attitudes and opinions of the individual so he or she can start afresh.

Uranus is the spark of genius that often makes the brilliant person seem odd. It is unconventional, a breakaway force, which refuses to behave in established ways. Whatever sign Uranus is in at the time of birth, the lifestyle of the person will be somewhat different, a bit erratic in relation to those matters.

Uranus is more than just imaginative. It is eccentric, even nuclear, and seems to bring the blinding flash of inspiration that makes the inventor, the scientist, or the ordinary person exclaim, "Eureka!"

Uranus is an emotionally detached energy that circulates. The individual will tend to move among a wide circle of friends and acquaintants, without allowing any relationship to become too close. While the Moon and Venus tend to form cloying associations based on sentiment and erotic notions, Uranus always keeps its distance. It is concerned with the wider and broader issues that will advance the welfare of humanity as a whole, rather than personal attachments or preferences.

Uranus can provide a ripping urge for freedom, even a rip-roaring one such as opened up the American West. It is an energy that can make a person or a nation suddenly discard heartfelt traditions in favor of independence and individual expression.

Uranus is the force behind radical political movements, reforms, crusades, and worthy causes. Sometimes, though, the energy becomes too free and independent. Fanatical zeal may set the scene for dictatorships and anarchy.

Uranus can express its energy negatively in antisocial actions and in sexual perversions. Being an emotional force of nervous and mental origin, it focuses on idea and action rather than on value or consequence. Uranus is said to rule the sex glands. The sexual side of this planet's influence is more pronounced when the planet transits Scorpio (1975–81).

Uranus is especially strong in the sign of Aquarius, which it rules together with Saturn.

URANUS IN ARIES

Uranus in Aries introduces into the character an erratic and impulsive influence. These people need to learn to think twice. They should try not to act on their first impulse. The spontaneousness of Aries, the first sign of the Zodiac, can become nerve-racking unpredictability under the added stimulation of Uranus.

These are fiercely independent people. They are proud that they make a point of never bowing to anyone. They have indeflatable self-confidence. They are not the kind of person who ever asks for help if this can possibly be avoided. And then the request is likely to be made in such a way that it appears they are doing the other person the favor!

Uranus in Aries individuals are leaders. Whether asked to or not, they will usually jump into the front rank. They either will be trailblazing or haranguing a mob. They combine physical with intellectual courage.

Often these people are drawn to a political career. They are far from diplomatic, but they are experts at rough-and-tumble. They can think quickly when under attack. Instinctively they anticipate their opponent's next move. But due to their impetuous nature, they can often make the most silly blunders. It is usually only in maturity that they learn to curb this side of their nature.

Uranus in Aries people love to get involved in crusades and reforms. They are the types who may be found at the head of protest marches and demonstrations. They often champion radical changes that bring them into conflict with the ruling establishment. They are the revolutionary pioneers.

These are physically daring and adventurous people. They love meeting challenges. Once their mind is made up, they are indomitable. At least they think and act as though they are. The best of them are troubleshooters.

The less evolved type of person with Uranus in Aries tends to be intolerant and unscrupulous. They may be rabble-rousers and troublemakers. They get the thrill of power from leading gangs of inferior-minded individuals.

Uranus in Aries individuals are often responsible for new ideas and changes that mark the beginning of new epochs. Sometimes their schemes are so original that they spend their lives fighting to get them accepted. Sometimes the acceptance comes long after the individuals have gone.

Ordinarily, Uranus in Aries people do not dwell on their failures. They are not the types to cry over spilled milk. In their lives, they spill quite a few gallons with their harebrained schemes and impulsive actions. But they seldom fail to add something to the progress of the world.

These people sometimes have explosive tempers. They have little time for those who do not agree with their views and plans. They tend to gather around them groups of supporters, many of whom have ideas just as odd or unusual as their own.

Uranus in Aries individuals like to destroy sacred cows. They seem to make it a mission of their life to pull down any vulnerable authority. They believe wholeheartedly in personal freedom, especially the kind that they espouse.

Uranus in Aries confers a great deal of enthusiasm. Any project that catches the individual's fancy is embraced with great gusto. There is an impatience for results, the quicker the better. Details are often overlooked, preparations neglected. Sudden changes in direction may be made.

For their own good, Uranus in Aries people have to cultivate a sense of caution. The fires of their zeal, fanned by the currents of change, can all too easily consume their good works.

URANUS IN TAURUS

Uranus in Taurus is a solid but at times sensitive placement from the material point of view. It provides a person with a flair for discovering new ways of making money or adding to their assets. Their ideas may be far-out, perhaps ahead of their times, but they get results. So Uranus in Taurus people should not get into the habit of dismissing their ideas, which is a possibility for the more retiring types with this placement.

Taurus is a fixed and conservative sign. It does not provide any fondness for taking chances; it is unadventurous. But Uranus is the planet of flashing inspiration. All that is new and inventive it embraces. The contradictions that this placement can induce in a person are obvious. But if individuals know the ingredients in their nature, they will have a better chance of turning them into positive value.

Uranus in Taurus people have to be prepared for sudden eventualities. They are likely to undergo some radical changes in their lives. They may win a fortune or lose a fortune. Even if their life follows a fairly orderly pattern, they will have distinct periods of ups and downs in their finances.

They will often have a yearning for more comfort. They may move house more frequently than other people do, always in an effort to improve their accommodations and surroundings. They do not really like packing up and leaving familiar places and people. But it is an urge they may find hard to resist. These people may horrify themselves at times at the things they do on the spur of the moment.

Uranus in Taurus individuals often get drawn into big business. They have a way with finance, which tends to attract the attention of people who have money to invest. As long as the other planetary placements of the individual do not exaggerate the unconventionality of Uranus, they can do well as builders, farmers, bankers, industrialists, civil servants, auctioneers, economists, and architects.

Uranus in Taurus people also have a sense of art, beauty, and harmony. And they tend to bring new ideas into any projects connected with traditional forms and functions. All they have to be careful of is that their ideas are practical. Fortunately, Taurus is a down-to-earth sign, which will help to keep the fancy but sometimes erratic feet of Uranus firmly on the ground.

Individuals with Uranus in Taurus can be terribly stubborn. Once they get an idea in their head, it is usually there to stay. They can even be fanatical about their schemes. And such may range from reforming the banking system to revolutionizing the holding and protection of property. They can do a lot more talking and advocating than getting down to action.

It is not unusual for some people with Uranus in Taurus to be singers or sculptors. They endeavor to bring art into the world in practical ways. They may also have a gift for writing.

These people work well with others. Although they are independent, they enjoy being a member of a team working toward an objective that is of benefit to mankind as a whole. As well as looking after their own interests and security, they like to feel their efforts also are helping others. Scientific research may attract them.

Uranus in Taurus individuals often gather around them some odd companions. These associates are not always good for them. More often than not, their kooky pals land them in difficult situations. They are very loyal to their friends, though, and will believe nothing bad about them. They will support a mate in trouble through thick and thin.

Uranus in Taurus folk have a love of nature. They have a frequent urge to throw off their impediments and get back to the simple life. But usually this is far easier felt than done. They really like to be involved in the here and now of the world. When the time for retiring arrives, their mood has probably changed.

URANUS IN GEMINI

Uranus in Gemini can produce a person with a touch of genius about them. But like all those with a highly developed mental potential, they can be eccentric. Sometimes these people are so far ahead of the times in their thinking that they appear to be dotty. Yet an ungrateful world or community may end up employing the very ideas that were scorned—after the person has left the scene.

These people are especially well suited to a career in science, particularly those branches associated with electronics, computers, and space technology. Their minds are seldom still. They are always working out something.

These individuals like to concern themselves with the problems of humanity. They are at their happiest pitting their mental faculties against the ignorance and pretensions of fad, fashion, and controversy—especially the foolishness of authority, which they will attack with a vengeance.

Uranus in Gemini individuals love to be always on the move. They are very inquisitive people. They spend a great deal of time on the telephone. They are likely to pop in on their friends and associates at any time of the day or night. They do not believe in conventional restraints. People have to take them or leave them. They make friends very easily, and can get away with unorthodox conduct that would not be tolerated in others.

These individuals are great freedom lovers. It is not so easy for them to hold down a steady job as a result. They are impulsive and tend to say exactly what they think. Their love of independence makes it difficult for them to conform. However, if these people are employed in work that gives them ample opportunity to express their creative and inspirational talents, they can be very happy—and irreplaceable.

Anyone with Uranus in Gemini will have within them a fondness for the unusual. They may satisfy this by reading or through writing. Their imaginations are extremely inventive. They can make topnotch science-fiction authors. They are ingenious and devious and fantastic.

These people are also very persuasive. They are the types who can make inspired speeches that rally public support. But usually their ideas appeal to a minority. They are more concerned with reforms in the community than bulwarking it. They seek changes that have not been discerned by the majority. Often they have to contend with fierce opposition to their beliefs.

Uranus in Gemini is an agitated placement. Of course, the placements of the other planets and especially the Sun will have a considerable modifying effect. Nevertheless, Uranus in Gemini is a mental placement, and its agitation and restlessness may be hidden under more obvious physical and emotional influences. But those tendencies will be there.

Uranus in Gemini is inclined to make a person irritable and nervy. The flow of ideas keeps them in their head most of the time. They can be very restless. They find it difficult to relax unless they have something totally absorbing to attend to.

These people also are easily discontented unless they find occupations that are to their liking. They may change their jobs frequently. Or they may endavor to become self-employed so they can be their own boss.

They do not take easily to authority, but they do take to novel ideas. Trends are the patterns Uranus in Gemini individuals have discovered long before they are accepted as such. Frontiers of intellectual change are their battlefields.

Sudden changes in their personal lives are something that people born with Uranus in Gemini often have to contend with. Sometimes their education is interrupted in their youth. They may leave school early or be forced by domestic moves to change from one school to another. Relatives may be prominent in their early upbringing.

These people have to choose their friends with more discretion. They certainly can become involved in dubious company. The less mature Uranus in Gemini individuals may find it impossible to stick to any kind of routine. Concentration can be very difficult. Distractions take them away from the pursuit of frontier thinking that can so benefit their generation.

URANUS IN CANCER

People born with Uranus in Cancer usually make a point of equipping their home with the very latest appliances. They believe in making life as easy as possible by the use of modern gadgetry. They usually have inventive minds. Although possessing a deep respect for the achievements of the past, they are always on the lookout for something new.

Uranus in Cancer individuals have very active imaginations. They have to guard against allowing their imaginings to assume fantastic proportions. They can easily get carried away into a world of unreality. In the young or immature type, daydreaming can be a substitute for work and action.

These are people with strong instincts. They can live on their nerves and emotions. They have to guard against a tendency to get upset about every little thing. Worry and uncertainty tend to affect their digestion.

They are extrmely sensitive people. They like to be surrounded by their loved ones, whom they cherish very dearly. Yet they often yearn to be alone and to be free of their responsibilities and obligations. They can have an almost love-hate relationship with some family members, appreciating their attentive concern one moment and resisting it the next.

People with Uranus in Cancer take a great interest in their domestic affairs. They would like to work at home. Sometimes they are drawn to a literary occupation, which enables them eventually to do this. But usually they spend a good bit of their lives trying to find out what they really want to do.

They are often found in advertising and business. They are unobtrusive types as a rule. They have a way of influencing the public through their writings and unusual ideas. They work very well with groups of people. They are artistic.

One of the most impressive things about people born with Uranus in Cancer is their intuitive insights. They are very impressionable to psychic influences. Their emotions often color their thoughts.

In love, they are romantics although they do not like to be tied down. They can express themselves with a good deal of Old World charm, which makes them attractive to older people. They tend to be protective of their loved ones and to expect them to do as they say.

Uranus in Cancer folk are patriotic people. But they will not support any national policy that tends to exploit others. They believe in equality and the freedom of the individual to choose what political system he or she wants to live under. They can be inconsistent, tending to lay down the law themselves and to oppose others who do the same thing.

They are the types of people who are attracted to fighting lost causes. They are deeply affected by injustice. They have many progressive political ideas, but can be too attached to their local community scene to get out and give the wider world the benefit of their views.

Also, these people can be a bit lazy. They need to be strongly motivated to get beyond the talking and haranguing stage. They are inclined to leave the hard physical work to others. They are often restless and inclined to chase rainbows.

Uranus in Cancer individuals can be touchy and thin-skinned. The less developed type may be moody and bad-tempered. If the other planets are unfavorably placed, it is easy for these people to be untidy around the house. They may not take much care with their personal appearance. They can be domineering.

Women are often important influences in the lives of Uranus in Cancer people—for good and otherwise.

URANUS IN LEO

Uranus in Leo is conducive to a personality who loves the drama and theater of life. There is something of the showperson about them. They aim to create an effect in whatever they do. They are especially interested in putting their ideas across to large groups of people.

These people can be true revolutionaries. They may aim to bring down any kind of establishment or authority they consider to be a threat to freedom. The trouble is, however, they are likely to be guided by their own judgments alone and to ignore the opinions of others.

Uranus in Leo people can be dictatorial. If given the chance, they may be inclined to replace one tyranny with another of their own making. They are often extremists.

Uranus in Leo individuals do not do things by halves. When they become involved in a project, it is usually a total commitment. They generally reserve their enthusiasm for enterprises that they imagine will be helpful to their fellow man. The fact that they regard themselves as the natural leader of any group they affiliate with often causes resentment and ill feeling, and involves them in power struggles.

Even so, these people do have the will to command. They are not as selfish and egocentric as they may appear. As a rule, they genuinely want to improve the lot of people by making them more aware of the dangers of authority. It is one of their inconsistencies that they are prepared to overlook or ignore their own vulnerability to being similarly accused.

Uranus in Leo individuals have pride and passion. They are not afraid to give orders and to stand by them. They are prepared to mete out any punishment that may be necessary in their position as leader. They have the courage of their convictions.

But much of the time of these people is given to making speeches and airing their views. They depend a lot on their ability to sway others into supporting their schemes. They do this by the written as well as the spoken word. They are often first-rate writers and powerful speakers.

Uranus in Leo people like to get down to the grass roots. In positions of command, they are the types who will sleep with their troops. They believe strongly that all power stems from the masses. They are usually popular and magnetic.

Uranus in Leo individuals have a love of pleasure. They enjoy being at the center of a night's entertainment. They like to be admired and praised. They can easily go to excess. They are impulsive and inclined to be erratic. Much will depend on the placements of the other planets, especially the Sun.

These are people with considerable organizing ability. They have a sense of style and ceremony that can appeal to the crowd. They also make good teachers and instructors. They have a way with young people, who tend to trust and admire them. They are proud of their accomplishments.

Uranus in Leo people also are among the most stubborn in the Zodiac. They hate to admit that they are wrong. They will usually find a good excuse for any failures.

The lives of Uranus in Leo individuals often undergo radical changes. It is difficult for them to keep on a straight course for long. They tend to court disaster, or at least the unfavorable attention of those in power.

Often, their revolutionary activities are directed toward scientific achievements. These are the kind of people who inspired the conquest of space. They also were responsible for much of the new technology without which space exploration would have been impossible.

URANUS IN VIRGO

People with Uranus in Virgo usually have a deeper than normal interest in health and hygiene. Although this interest is expressed in keeping themselves fit and clean, they also desire to make the world a less toxic place in which to live. They are inclined to frown on noxious pesticides, industrial pollutants, and the addition of unnecessary artificial ingredients to processed foods.

Much depends on the favorable placements of the other planets, for if these are adverse, these same people can go the other way. They may be the very ones who create or are responsible for similar problems, which they may be endeavoring to eliminate in another area. Uranus in Virgo is not consistent.

These people can be analytical scientists, the types who introduce chemical and other devices to clean up the place, and actually make it worse. In their zeal—either in their private lives or in their professional capacities—they can upset the natural balance.

Uranus in Virgo individuals are extremely discriminating. They can mentally dissect a problem down to the finest of details. They are unconsciously motivated by a desire for purification and perfection. They have to be careful not to go to extremes. Their concern, once they get a bee in their bonnet, can be more of a nuisance than the problem they are trying to solve.

These people do have some brilliant ideas from time to time, particularly connected with solving work and production problems. This is not so surprising, as Virgo is the sign of work and service, and Uranus is the planet of invention and progress. Uranus in Virgo folk like to get their teeth into a knotty project, especially one that tests their ingenuity.

Although mentally active and discerning, these are as a rule cautious people. They like to remain on the outskirts of the crowd, observing everything that is happening but not drawing attention to themselves.

Uranus in Virgo individuals can be truly detached. They can be counted on not to take sides on an issue or in a dispute. They are inclined always to want to do the best job possible, without worrying too much about personal reward or fame.

These people are genuinely interested in helping mankind to live a fuller existence, with less dependence on external authority. They are not the revolutionary type. But they tend to feel that man has within him the potential for perfection. If he can find this, it is all the authority he really needs. As was said, Uranus in Virgo people are perfectionists.

They can also be dogmatic. With the support of other planets, they can believe that their ideas are the only correct ones. To ignore them means disaster, or at least lack of progress, for everyone. They are inclined to analyze every little thing and to erect intellectual structures that may not stand up well in the light of experience.

They also can be contrary. They may take an opposite stand to anyone they do not like, even if they secretly support their opinions. They can be very sharp-tongued and critical. It is not easy for these people to resist telling others what they should or should not be doing. And the infuriating thing about this habit is that they are very often correct.

Uranus in Virgo people mean well, but often are misunderstood. Unless the placements of the other planets give warmth and affection, they can be a bit lacking in human feeling and compassion. They may be too intellectual, and not emotional enough to enjoy truly the fruits of their works.

URANUS IN LIBRA

Uranus in Libra strives for grace under pressure. These are people with delicately balanced temperaments and minds. It does not take much to upset their equilibrium. They are easily distracted, and quick to take up new interests before older ones have been fully pursued or absorbed. They can be fickle.

This is not an unfavorable placement for Uranus, the planet of invention and inspiration. But it needs some solid practical support from the other planetary placements, particularly the Sun.

Libra is a mentally active sign. The presence here of the planet of brilliant insights, and sudden changes can upset the scales. The person can lose poise through agitation, and become eccentric in his or her ideas.

Libra gives artistic inclinations, and Uranus adds the innovative touch, which can produce progressive changes in style and form of art. These people can establish trends in art. Although they may be vogues and not long-lasting, these new forms will make a contribution to the general evolution of creative expression.

With support from the other planets, especially the Sun, Uranus in Libra individuals are the types who can easily influence groups of people, especially artists. They can be teachers or lecturers. They can begin new movements in the arts, which others may build into schools of thought that will radically change attitudes and perspectives.

However, these people often can create chaos around them. Although compulsively committed to trying to harmonize their relationships and surroundings, often they have the opposite effect. People are inclined to polarize under their influence. Libras' efforts often force people to split into camps of differing opinions.

Libra is the sign of peace—and also war. It endeavors to maintain harmony by cooperativeness. But as the whole world knows, you cannot please everyone. An unenlightened attempt will generate antagonism and friction. Uranus in Libra heightens the desire to bring peace though the written and spoken word regardless of whom the message addresses.

These are people who believe in freedom. They cannot stand any authority that exploits or oppresses mankind. They have very strong humanitarian instincts. As much as they love harmony, when their indignation at injustice is aroused they will fight to the bitter end for their principles.

Uranus in Libra individuals have to avoid stop-and-start activity. They should endeavor to follow through whatever they begin. Unless their deeper feelings are involved, which may not be very often, they are inclined to be fitful in their efforts. The need of novelty and change can lead to restlessness. Without strong support from the other planets, they can become easily discontented.

Uranus in Libra individuals can have a high turnover of friends. They can be a bit disloyal, shedding yesterday's friends for more interesting ones found today. They do not have deep attachments to people. They love to move from group to group. They are inclined to cultivate friends who are high on the social register, or who have money.

Immature individuals with Uranus in Libra do not have an easy love life. Their romantic affairs are characterized by many changes, some of which can have drastic results. They can be involved in divorces and other lawsuits. The erratic and unpredictable actions of partners can force radical changes in their lives.

There is likely to be an attraction to fashion. It is easy for these people to give the lead to a new dress style. But they also can go to extremes and experiment with way-out costumes and gear. They are the lost leaders of a current era.

Uranus in Libra is conducive to unusual unions and partnerships, both of the emotional and business kind. These people are highly tolerant of the most unconventional views and ideas. They often are stimulated by being in the company of eccentrics, and can take such far-out views a stage farther to displays or limited productions.

URANUS IN SCORPIO

Uranus in Scorpio embraces the spectrum of idea and emotion, intellectuality, and spirituality. Or this placement can seek the extreme, cutting off one way of sensing and knowing in favor of another. Uranus in Scorpio is a most decisive placement.

Scorpio is a masterful sign with great power. When Uranus, the planet of inspiration and deviation, drops into this slot at a person's birth, the results can be very good for the world at large—or very bad. This person can easily go to extremes. They can use their penetrating minds to help their fellow man, or to make his life a misery.

They are especially suited for scientific occupations. They are inventive and mechanical-minded. They have great powers of concentration. They have a sixth sense, which informs them when there is a coverup or a puzzle at the bottom of a problem. They love difficult investigations in which an important discovery might be made.

These individuals can pour over problems night and day, making infinitesimal progress but never giving up. In the laboratories of the world, such people have been responsible for some of man's most progressive and curative discoveries.

The undeveloped individual with Uranus in Scorpio can turn to crime. Much will depend on the placements of the other planets. These people can be ruthless. Once they put their minds to anything, they never give up. They are especially sensitive to criticism, and are inclined to look for insults. They do not show their feelings. And they do not forgive or forget an affront.

These people also have a heightened sensitivity and search for ways to explore sensuality. They may be drawn to experimentation, always endeavoring to reach higher intensities of feeling. They should be careful not to use drugs and alcohol to excess.

Uranus in Scorpio individuals are tenacious to a fault. They can be very obstinate. Once they make up their minds, they are not easily shifted. They can easily be unreasonable, feeling that they alone have the right answers.

People with Uranus in Scorpio are often attracted to working in groups. Although rather secretive and aloof, they appreciate that many minds are needed to make the greatest progress in any endeavor. Even so, they always tend to regard their own views as the essential ones.

These are very self-sufficient people. They have great mental stamina. They are not easily swayed. They are quite prepared to undergo any kind of trial for the sake of the principles in which they believe. They cannot be brainwashed. But they are the types who can brainwash others, and not worry about any niceties in the process. In extreme cases, they can be guilty of mental cruelty.

Uranus in Scorpio people often are very interested in metaphysics and the occult. They have an ability to discover psychic realities, or to expose pretenders. Their minds are sharply penetrative and can see through delusion.

Yet they can be self-delusive. This arises from their tendency to be compartment thinkers, refusing to see that one compartment often is the antithesis of another.

These are realists, however, when it comes to dealing with the world. They appreciate strength and are disdainful of weakness. They try to influence their associates with pressure if more subtle methods are not successful.

Although straightforward in giving their views on worldly matters, they are wily people with a great sensitivity for intrigue. It is difficult ever to be sure whether they have an ulterior motive. However, when they are straight, they are straight. And they make undeviating supporters once they have committed themselves.

Uranus in Scorpio individuals have to beware of losing their temper. They impose considerable mental pressures on themselves by not sharing their thoughts with others. Continuous suppression of this kind leads to a buildup of energy, which eventually has to break out, often quite violently.

URANUS IN SAGITTARIUS

Uranus in Sagittarius individuals as a rule have a highly developed social consciousness. They would truly like to see Utopia come to earth. They have a sense of vision that is often prophetic. But frequently their wonderful ideas and insights are too far ahead of the times to be taken seriously. Sometimes they may even have to grin and bear it while latecomers receive the credit for ideas they had earlier expressed.

These people are often excitable. They find it very difficult to remain in one place for long, either physically or mentally. They usually pursue a course that leads them from place to place, from idea to idea, or from person to person. They are not very stable types.

There is, however, a strong desire to see the world become a more moral and orderly place. Although these people may espouse what seem to be revolutionary doctrines, they are at heart conventionalists. They want to demolish in order to restore—not the old structures but the old ideas of goodness and justice. These people tend to believe wholeheartedly in the golden rule of how one person should treat another.

They have a great deal of energy. They love to get caught up in reform movements and causes in which they believe. As younger people they often can be found out front in protest marches and demonstrations. They are not afraid of a fight or a challenge.

Uranus in Sagittarius endows a person with a great love and respect for freedom. They cannot tolerate any authority that tries to brainwash its populace with foolish or bigoted propaganda. It is this that makes these basically law-supporting people often appear to be anarchists. Their high-founded motives can be easily misunderstood.

The Uranus in Sagittarius individual is often too independent-minded to accept the tenets of orthodox religion. They often tend to develop a philosophy of life for themselves that they then try to pass on to their associates. They have to be careful not to become too fanatical in their views, or they may be accused of trying to set up some kind of authority of their own.

The less developed Uranus in Sagittarius individuals can be reckless in their social experiments. They may fail to give sufficient thought to the schemes in which they involve others. They can be irresponsible and immature.

These people enjoy travel, especially to other countries. If they do not get the chance to travel, they are inclined to read about foreign places. They are inclined to write about their experiences and can become successful authors and journalists.

Uranus in Sagittarius makes a person keenly aware of the benefits of education. But they prefer an educational system that does not put too much emphasis on books. They believe people learn more quickly by doing and example. They do their best to live up to what they preach.

In love, Uranus in Sagittarius does not endow a person with a great amount of feeling or emotion. Such people are inclined to take love as it comes, but not to get too deeply involved. In fact, these individuals can be marriage-shy. They are too aware of their need for intellectual and physical freedom to roam where they please. They won't compromise without a fight.

These are generous people. They will seldom turn down a request for help from a friend. They have a wide circle of acquaintances, who usually number a good proportion of people with eccentric ideas.

URANUS IN CAPRICORN

Uranus in Capricorn is valuable for people intent on fulfilling their ambitions. It is especially helpful to business and political aspirations. It gives shrewdness and a sense of mission.

The minds of these people work very swiftly where finances are concerned. They have a way of spotting opportunities for making money in even the most commonplace situations. They are especially aware of the necessity for teamwork. They try to give everyone with whom they are involved in an enterprise a fair shake.

However, the urge to succeed in life can be very strong. Uranus in Capricorn people can be grinds. They also imagine themselves to be indispensable. They may refuse to take a break or a vacation in their desire to get a job finished. The trouble is that their lives can become completely dedicated to work. Everything else, including their closest relationships, can fail to get developed.

It is extremely important for Uranus in Capricorn individuals to keep a balance in their lives. They must try to relax and not allow their responsibilities to take them over. Without the modifying support of other planets, especially the Sun, they can become too far removed from the pleasures of life.

These people have great powers of perseverance. Anything they put their minds to they will see through to the end. Uranus, the planet of sudden change and inspiration, helps to break down the earthiness of Capricorn and introduces a greater flexibility of mind. Practicality is assisted by showers of often brilliant ideas. And a tendency to plod along in a rut is interrupted by sudden changes of direction, either self-initiated or enforced.

There is not such a fear of change and experimentation as Capricorn usually imposes. Uranus in Capricorn people are more inclined to move with the times. They can insist that organizations and subordinates do the same.

This is the kind of person who can head a very large company or corporation. They have the kind of mind that can keep up with experts in any of the many departments under their control. They encourage progressive thinking. They like to be surrounded by the latest business machines and electronic gadgetry as long as these make a contribution to efficiency.

When they do gain positions of authority, Uranus in Capricorn people treat their staff fairly. Uranus in Capricorn are not the type to encourage close personal relationships. But they do believe in a friendly and congenial atmosphere.

They can lay down the law when they want to. But usually their authority is understood without their having to make any drastic demonstrations. They have the knack of remaining aloof without being distant. Employees respect them, especially for their willingness and ability to perform the work they expect of others.

As employers, they are fair and just. They have a strong regard for the independence of others. They insist on being kept informed, but are prepared to allow a worker to use his or her initiative. They are willing to listen to advice, although they may not take it.

Uranus in Capricorn individuals often have to put up with a succession of major changes in childhood. They may move house or school many times. There can be disruptions in domestic affairs that they may never quite get over.

It is easy for them to become acquisitive if they do not marry or avoid close relationships. They have to cultivate the ability to express their feelings and emotions. They must avoid putting off making close personal contacts, as this tendency can become habitual.

URANUS IN AQUARIUS

Uranus, the planet of originality, inspiration, and independence, posited in its own sign of Aquarius at birth produces a person who is bound to be a progressive thinker. Although the placements of the other planets, especially the Sun, will have a determining influence on the overall character, this person will have a lively intelligence. How he or she uses it is the big question.

People with Uranus in Aquarius sometimes appear to be odd to more conservative types of thinkers. Uranus in Aquarius individuals do not follow accepted norms. They are for progress and reform. They believe change is best accomplished by changing people's ideas.

Their thinking can go to extremes. Once they get an idea in their head that they believe will benefit the community or the world as a whole, they will not abandon it lightly. They are often humanitarians and reformers. They tend to discern social and political problems long before others do. They advocate changes that even the people who would benefit do not fully comprehend. Their ideas can often be so far ahead of the times that they can be dismissed as eccentrics.

Uranus in Aquarius individuals have strong wills. They are likely to pit their ideas against even the strongest established conventions without worrying about the consequences to themselves if they feel that what they are doing is right. The trouble is, if other planetary placements are not favorable, they can become fanatical or their judgment may be faulty. They can propose unrealistic and even damaging reforms that would create more strife and hardship than they were trying to eradicate.

Uranus in Aquarius people can be perverse. They are the types who may oppose any proposal at all just for the sake of taking an opposite stand and hearing their own ideas being expressed. They can alienate their friends and supporters by taking too hard a line on issues. As would-be leaders of public opinion, they are often their own worst enemies.

There is a touch of the revolutionary deep down in all people born with Uranus in Aquarius. The important thing is for them to recognize this and to be selective as to which causes they champion. They can do a lot of good, as they have a powerful ability for influencing others, either through the spoken or the written word. They make topnotch politicians, writers, broadcasters, psychologists, and publishers.

These people often can appear to be a bit cool. They are detached emotionally from the people with whom they deal. They are more concerned with the welfare and goings-on of groups than of individual people. They are not the types who will put up with any emotional demands being made on them. They can be quite sharp and even rude to people who try to get too close to them.

However, when the other planetary lineups are favorable, Uranus in Aquarius individuals are friendly and easy to get along with. They have artistic tendencies, which should be developed as much as possible to compensate for their strong mental inclinations. They need to be in touch with their emotions and finer feelings.

These people are often attracted to work in the sciences. They like to feel that in whatever way they earn their living they are contributing to the overall progress of mankind. They are often in the forefront of important medical discoveries. Space research, physics, and electronics often provide suitable mediums for their inventive minds.

They are not sentimental types, as a rule. They prefer to deal in facts more than feelings. They believe in freedom for everyone, even though sometimes they have not managed to think through the ramifications of what they are proposing.

URANUS IN PISCES

People with Uranus in Pisces have to find something to do with their active minds. They need to be productive and to feel they are doing some good, for humanity as a whole or for some one in particular. They can too easily drift into an uncertain existence in which their minds may turn in on themselves, producing self-pity and vague fears.

Uranus is the planet of scientific discovery, invention, and progress. Pisces is the sign of compassion, tears, emotions, and mystical and religious impulses. They are almost opposites. The two influences can work very well together in any occupation that endeavors to serve others who are less fortunate through scientific or compassionate means.

These people have extremely vivid imaginations. Their spiritual insights are sometimes remarkable. From the scientific point of view they may receive flashes of inspiration that can solve problems that have long troubled mankind. Even in business, they have a knack for coming up with unusual ideas for making money.

The problem is they can be dilatory. They may do nothing about their good ideas. They can be too dependent on others to do the work. They may sit back and think that it is enough for them just to come up with the schemes. Also, these people can be very impractical. For every worthwhile suggestion there may be a dozen that are unworkable.

Uranus in Pisces individuals have a tendency to daydream. If they feel they are under pressure, they are inclined to slip into an imaginative world of their own making. They are so easily disillusioned with life that they can become terribly sorry for themselves.

These people have an ability for self-sacrifice. They are especially good at working in hospitals and other institutions where their understanding natures can give much solace to the sick or underprivileged.

They make very good teachers of children, especially at the infant and kindergarten stage. They can comfort as well as instruct. They are often drawn to work in orphanages. Their inventive minds can make life easier for the handicapped; they are very good at dreaming up new ways of doing things.

Uranus in Pisces people often have psychic powers. Their intuition is often remarkable. They also are likely to be interested in occult subjects. They may make first-rate astrologers. This is a placement that destroys materialism. These individuals are inclined to put humane considerations before others.

They love to be with other people. They are sociable and often are to be found taking part in group activities. They have artistic leanings, which can make them affiliate with painting, sculpting, and handicraft groups.

But they do tend to sink into reflective moods and to need to get away on their own. They are the types of people who can take up yoga and meditation seriously. They are able to combine mind and body, which makes them sometimes gifted dancers. However, their will can be uncoordinated. They may take up a pastime and quickly tire of it.

These are not as a rule ambitious people, unless the placements of the other planets give that kind of support. They would rather give than take. They are the types who genuinely would like to serve mankind if only they could find a way. Often that way is not clearly defined to their satisfaction, although the people around them who are on the receiving end of their kindly and sympathetic natures would say they have already found what they are looking for.

In love and romance, Uranus in Pisces people can be highly sensuous with a tendency to experiment for heightened sensations.

Neptune in the Signs

Neptune is the planet of mystery. It governs hidden events, peculiar forces behind the scenes. Its influences are the hardest of all to understand and get a grip on. It is regarded as the most spiritual of all the planetary forces.

Neptune brings the quality of inner vision into our lives. Its visionary quality is in direct contrast to the materialism of our own planet and our natural inclinations.

Neptune stands for idealism. It is the principle that allows a person so inclined to transcend the world. It is the mystical planet. At its worst, it represents escapism through self-delusion, drugs, alcohol, and sexual fantasy.

Neptune takes 168 years to journey around the Sun. This means it spends twelve to fifteen years in each sign. There it brings its subtle and pervasive energies to bear on the generations born in those years, causing each to follow a new course according to the sign in which it is placed.

For instance, when Neptune was first sighted in 1846, it was transiting the scientific sign Aquarius. The sighting coincided with a wave of interest around the world, scientific as well as spiritualistic, whether there was life after death. This was reflected in a great deal of research into spiritualism and psychic rappings, as well as an outbreak of the popular nineteenth-century pastime of ghost hunting.

Neptune in its own way added support to the scientific era started by Uranus half a century before. Neptune's strong deceptive and hallucinatory powers were represented by the introduction of anesthetics, and gradually the popular rise of drug taking.

Neptune gives us dreams of better things through the characteristics of the sign in which it appears. It is then up to the individual. The choice is to bring these ideas into the world through resolution and effort. Another is to go on indulgently dreaming and accomplishing little.

It has to be remembered that Neptune takes 168 years to circle the

Sun, spending an average of twelve to fifteen years in each sign. Neptune's influence in a sign applies more to the generation to which the person belongs, and to successive generations, than to the particular individual. Psychologically, the influences work at the subconscious level. In this way they affect the attitudes, beliefs, and preferences of the generation as expressed through individual character and behavior.

Neptune is strongest in association with Pisces, the sign that it rules together with Jupiter.

The following descriptions of Neptune in the signs start with Neptune in Cancer, as this era began in 1902. The Neptune eras before Cancer are not considered in this book because the Planetary Tables begin at the year 1910.

NEPTUNE IN CANCER

People with Neptune in Cancer were born between 1902 and 1916.

Neptune in Cancer individuals all like to feel they belong to something. They take pride in being members of successful movements and establishments. They were born at a time when patriotism was to be tested. They were not found to be lacking, especially in World War II, when so many of them gave so much.

This was a generation of people who had to make very difficult adjustments, passing out of the horse-and-buggy age, into the automobile age, then into the electronics age, and finally into the nuclear and space age.

Cancer is the sign of the home and the family. These people had the task of keeping both together through probably one of the most unpredictable periods in history—a period that is still challenging concepts of home and family.

There is a good deal of emotionality in the Neptune in Cancer generation. Individuals will remember the past as the good old days, forgetting the bitter times or dismissing them as a learning experience or mistake. They love to keep relics of the old days. Old photographs, books, and souvenirs are treasured possessions. Nostalgia has become an industry.

Neptune in Cancer individuals are instinctive people. They are inclined to do good turns without being asked. They like to gather their families around them as often as possible, and with as many generations as possible. They like to be at the center of warmth and affection.

Sometimes these people find it difficult to stay in one place for long. As much as they love their homes and families, they like to travel. They are especially fond of natural and rural surroundings. They would like to have a second home in the country as well if they live in the city.

Neptune in Cancer people cherish their loved ones. But they can be too demanding of attention and respect. They are not particularly materialistic, putting more value on personal attachments, belongings, and relationships than anything else.

They can be self-indulgent. They may also lack the will to engage in any heavy physical exertion. They are frequently psychic, being able to predict events as well as diagnosing illnesses from which people may be suffering.

NEPTUNE IN LEO

People with Neptune in Leo were born between 1917 and 1928.

Neptune in Leo people are great dreamers. They envision a wonderful future in which they themselves play a leading part. Many of this generation are now in the seats of power. From this position they can ensure that some of their dreams come true.

Neptune in Leo can also produce illusions of glory. These people can be distracted from practical endeavors by the enticements of glamorous people or situations. They have to guard against being drawn into speculative ventures. The urge to gamble and to take other unnecessary risks may be strong.

Neptune in Leo individuals tend to be romantics. They are usually drawn to creative work. Or they may enter politics or government and strive to make the world a better place for all to live in. They have the power to lead and inspire. They usually are able to write or speak with persuasion. They have good organizing ability and a great deal of faith in themselves.

The Neptune in Leo generation developed the motorcar and the movie industry. It also made an important contribution to psychoanalytical techniques.

Neptune in Leo individuals have a love of pleasure. They know how to play hard, and how to work for big stakes. They are often misled by people who indulge their weakness for flattery. They can put too much value on appearances.

Neptune in Leo has given rise to many revolutionaries, from the French Revolution to the American Revolution. Leo is the sign of leadership and showmanship. The addition of Neptune, the planet of illusion, can distort the vision and lead to foolhardy escapades.

These are passionate people who put their heart and soul into whatever they attempt. Sometimes they are driven by a lust for power, which can destroy the things they love most. They have to avoid being egotistical and overestimating their own worth.

Neptune in Leo people have a special gift for dealing with children. But the love life of these individuals seldom runs smoothly. They tend to put their loved ones on a pedestal and so invite disillusionment.

Neptune in Leo individuals need to find a constructive outlet for their vast energies.

NEPTUNE IN VIRGO

People with Neptune in Virgo were born between the latter part of 1928 and 1942.

These are people in whom the sense of service is usually well developed. They respond to any opportunity to implement their ideals of how social conditions can be improved. They have a way of being able to make abstract ideas more concrete and readily understandable. They usually are interested in making the community healthier, both mentally and physically. They enjoy preparing and disseminating information on nutrition and hygiene.

Neptune in Virgo individuals can be a bit scheming and cunning, but usually not out of self-interest. They are quick to discern the problems facing their immediate group. They will resort to sly behind-the-scenes maneuvering to help to right them.

There is something of the perfectionist in these individuals. They have to be sure of where they are going, or they can create more trouble and confusion than they are trying to eradicate.

There is a desire in these people to have everything in its correct place. They can be too precise and exacting. They have to avoid insisting on only the letter of the law having meaning, while ignoring the spirit of it. They can be of considerable practical help, but be a bit short on spiritual vision.

Neptune in Virgo people are usually moved to improve labor and working conditions. They believe in adult education as a means of improving the lot of everyone. They have the power to absorb and teach techniques. They are able to utilize the materials at their disposal. They are not dependent on special tools or conditions to prove their worth. It is through their talent for devising new methods that they overcome old problems.

Neptune in Virgo individuals sometimes have the healing gift. They can be in tune with inner psychic powers, which are channeled into their practical train of mind to do good work in the physical realm. The spirituality of these people, however, may not be so evident.

Neptune in Virgo people are not publicity seekers for any good work they do. Often they fail to receive the recognition of the public, even when it is due them. They are capable of making sacrifices without hullabaloo.

NEPTUNE IN LIBRA

People with Neptune in Libra were born between the latter part of 1942 and 1955.

Libra is the sign of beauty and balance. Neptune is the planet of imagination, idealism, and illusion. Neptune in Libra can inflate any desire to escape into sweetness and light.

The Neptune in Libra years produced the "flower generation," which endeavored to disarm the world with the feeling of love. Although they seem to have failed in a sense, the corrosive materialism and skepticism of the world have been challenged by that idealism.

Neptune in Libra individuals have the power to create harmony. They have high ideals about the way life should be for mankind. Sometimes their thinking is hopelessly impractical. They can get carried away with their own visions. Yet they are prepared to make the effort. They have the courage of their convictions.

Libra also is the sign of war, as well as of peace. Often these people, in spite of their altruism, create disharmony and conflict. Where they hope to spread love, they sow dissension by the sheer vagueness of their message. Neptune in Libra is not an easy placement for dealing with the determined material forces that seem to run the world.

Neptune in Libra individuals find it difficult to hide their feelings. They are compassionate. They cannot stand to see people or other creatures badly treated. They are deeply moved by the suffering of others.

In spite of their good intentions, these people do have a tendency to compromise. They may lack the will to pursue their aim to the bitter end. They feel that even a shaky peace is better than no peace at all.

Neptune in Libra people prefer to work in partnership. They are a bit lost when they are alone for long. They have refined, artistic tastes. They should not allow these to develop into extravagant appetites for the most luxurious and the most expensive.

Neptune in Libra individuals are more intellectual than physical. They may blow hot and cold in their relationships. Often they are attracted to people or situations that turn their lives upside down or inside out. Peculiar things tend to happen to them.

NEPTUNE IN SCORPIO

People with Neptune in Scorpio were born between the latter part of 1955 and early 1970.

Neptune in Scorpio stimulates a craving for any sensation. At some time in their lives, these people are likely to be drawn into a search for heightened sensations. They may learn their lessons, possibly by having their fingers burned. But they can then go beyond their limiting appetites or desires and emerge far wiser and mature human beings.

This was the generation born at a time when the world gave up a little of its hypocrisy about sex. The rigid pretensions and moral codes were challenged. Censorship was relaxed dramatically to give more reality to the movies, theater, and the daily dialogue between people.

Yet it also was a time of excess, one of the dangers of Neptune in Scorpio. Alcoholism, drug addiction, social diseases, and the crime rate soared. America fought in Vietnam, finally not quite sure itself what it had all been about. Neptune, it should be remembered, is the planet of confusion, delusion, and decay.

It is not surprising that during this period of Neptune's passage through Scorpio, the sign of sex, the Pill came into widespread use. After countless centuries of suffering, it gave women a degree of sexual freedom never before experienced. At the same time, Neptune began to confuse the appearance of and distinctions between male and female; women dressed liked men, and men began to look like women.

Neptune in Scorpio individuals have secretive tendencies. They do not take many people into their confidence. Their emotional natures are intense, but they seldom allow their exterior appearance to reveal their inner feelings. They can play a cool cat-and-mouse game.

These people like to get to the bottom of things. They have an intuition that allows them to often see through concealment. They can be confusing and seem mixed up. Yet they seldom lose control of any situation for which they are responsible.

Neptune in Scorpio people can be too indulgent of themselves. But they have a strong regenerative capability. This allows them to turn their excesses into accesses to higher knowledge.

NEPTUNE IN SAGITTARIUS

People with Neptune in Sagittarius were born or will be born between early 1970 and early 1984.

Neptune is the planet of dissolution. In Sagittarius, the sign of religion and philosophy, it tends to break down the old dogmas and creeds. Views become more liberal. The social conscience turns toward freedom, recognizing that the containments and restrictions of yesterday create explosive pressures that can destroy a society.

Yet the sense of respect for lawfulness remains, for Sagittarius, in spite of its love of liberty, believes firmly in many of the conventional values. Liberty without licence is the Sagittarius message.

This generation of young people born with Neptune in Sagittarius are responsive to any cry for frankness and openness. They are particularly concerned with greater openness in government. Gone are the days of secrecy, which bred corruption, distrust and unaccountable power—as far as they are concerned, anyway.

This generation can be sincere in its spiritual aspirations. But in its search for new dimensions of thinking, it must guard against extremes. It could become too ceremonial. It could put more emphasis on pomp and regalia when the time comes for implementing the social platforms it once believed were so urgent.

People born with Neptune in Sagittarius have the power to visualize the future as it should be. But the big question is: Do they have the strength of will and persistence to make it a reality? These individuals are restless. They tend to need constant change of surroundings and activities to keep them interested.

They are an optimistic generation, even though they will have forebodings about the future they are to control. It may be this that introduces the task of the next generation—to talk less, preach less, and do more in practical terms.

When Neptune leaves Sagittarius, the holiday is over and the new order of discipline and authority arrives. Neptune in Capricorn!

NEPTUNE IN CAPRICORN

People with Neptune in Capricorn will be born between the beginning of 1984 and 1999.

Neptune in Capricorn represents the return of the new order. It stands for more emphasis on practical down-to-earth action, and less on theorizing and abstract discussion. It may be a period in which idealism is inhibited. It will be thought that all the blueprints for a better world have already been prepared. It may be a time when traditional and conventional values are reappraised.

Some astrologers have predicted that Neptune's passage through Capricorn will see the first real moves toward world government. This will not be out of any idealistic impulse, but out of consideration for practical realities.

Capricorn is the sign of ambition and materialism. It does not need much of a negative influence from the other planets to turn this into selfishness. Capricorn also is the sign of business acumen. This may be an extremely constructive period for the economic policies of the nations.

Neptune, however, is the planet of illusion, confusion, and chaos. It also is the spiritual planet. In the face of excessive materialistic aims, Neptune is inclined to produce peculiar and unexpected situations and circumstances.

People born into this generation will have the power to persevere and to make sacrifices to reach their objectives. On the world scene, it may be a time of considerable hard work. There may be less time for leisure, probably due to the hotter pursuits of ambitions and material security.

The Neptune in Capricorn years may be rather wearying for those looking for spiritual regeneration. There can be a slackening of the drive for mystical awakening. Or there may be fewer people or groups interested.

The early years of this generation may contain some uncertainty in relation to family life. Individuals, youngsters mainly, may be neglected if parents have to give most of their time to material considerations. Parental influence, however, will be strong, with a good deal of emphasis on discipline and authority.

Pluto in the Signs

Pluto is the force of upheaval, the volcanic spewing out of emotional matter that has been pent up too long. Pluto represents the fires of hell on the surface of the Earth, the underworld coming up for air.

Pluto also represents regeneration and renewal. Its influence works at the subconscious level, and so affects the character and behavior of all people. Out of upheaval and destruction come new forces of progress, widespread throughout the consciousness of the generation.

Pluto was discovered in 1930. Its discovery coincided with gangsterism, organized crime, mobism, fascism, and Nazism, the world's worst financial crash and Great Depression, and World War II. Its discovery also coincided with racial and nationalistic struggles for nationhood and independence, and with popular or people's movements to rise from obscurity to identity, from powerlessness to autonomy.

Pluto controls mass movements, armies, and syndicates for such perverse reasons as victimizing and exterminating people in concentration camps or *pogroms*, and conquering and ruling struggling peoples in underprivileged nations.

Pluto governs large organizations and institutions for progressive purposes too, such as big business and labor, national health, welfare, and educational movements.

Pluto is responsible for mass production; the tedium of the assembly line brings yet more jobs, more goods, more time, more pay. The sweep of modern industrial life creates the need for goods and services in all areas of existence.

Pluto stands for sex and money in an abstract and universal way. Males and females wear their hair alike, dress similarly. Women demand equality and want to function in areas reserved for men. Men learn how to raise children, stay home, and keep house. Or a couple works and shares alike. The poor nations of the world and the poor individuals of a society demand equality and equity, too. Their needs create conflicts and struggles; their struggles create change. In each generation there is the sweeping away of the old and the bringing in of the new.

Pluto is the slowest-moving planet of all. Pluto's orbit is so irregular that it spends from 12 to 37 years in each sign. Its lumbering pace around the Zodiac requires 248 years to complete a full circuit.

Pluto stands for progress through irrevocable change. The change is not necessarily good or bad from the point of view of mere mortals, and most change is difficult to adjust to. But through these changes, people, communities, nations—and finally the individual—are transformed for the better in that they would never choose to return to the old ways of doing things.

So Pluto in a sign is an indicator of the basic attitudes of the generation to which the person belongs, rather than his or her individual characteristics. The influences wrought by Pluto in a sign are also passed on and affect the thinking and preferences of succeeding generations.

The sign where Pluto is at the time of birth will be the area in which the individual finds the greatest inner contradictions.

Pluto is strongest in association with Scorpio, the sign that it rules.

The following descriptions of Pluto in the signs start with Pluto in Gemini, as this era began in 1882. The Pluto eras before Gemini are not considered in this book because the Planetary Tables begin at the year 1910.

PLUTO IN GEMINI

People with Pluto in Gemini were born between 1882 and 1914, before the planet was discovered in 1930.

Pluto in Gemini individuals were a generation of people who had to make the most extraordinary adjustments in the field of communications, which Gemini represents. The telephone allowed ideas to be exchanged instantly and over long distances.

Pluto is the sign of money and wealth. The telephone was one of the most potent instruments in founding and extending the empires of the new plutocrats.

Pluto in Gemini people are inventive. They displayed in their most active days an ability to move with the times. They could adjust and adapt their thinking to the tremendous demands of a daily shrinking world.

Their times gave birth to the automobile and the airplane. And as their generation matured, they brought both to a threshold of performance that could hardly have been imagined.

This was the era that started the scramble for speedier ways to do everything. Even entertainment underwent a metamorphosis. The phonograph became popular and was mass-produced, setting the stage for a booming recording industry.

This was a generation that got used to changes. They went through two world wars, the worst depression the world had known, and entry into the nuclear and space ages.

Pluto in Gemini individuals have the power to understand what consumers need. It was they who drew up the blueprints for the miracle of mass production in many industries.

PLUTO IN CANCER

People with Pluto in Cancer were born between 1914 and 1938.

Cancer is the sign of the home and the family. With Pluto, the planet of fundamental change, in Cancer, it was to be expected that these years would see some transformations in attitudes toward domestic life, as well as physical changes in the environment and the lives of people.

World War I destroyed many homes in Europe through the actual conflict of battle. People were left rootless. Family life was unsettled. The subsequent financial crises and the Great Depression of the 1930s left people in Europe and the United States little alternative but to uproot family ties and homesteads and go in search of work. Women, among those separated from their families and mates, either went to find jobs or became the head of the household.

The Pluto in Cancer era ended just before World War II broke out. Women who never would have thought of working left their homes and family duties and poured into the factories, the military services, and other wartime work. When the war ended, woman's traditional role was over. Emancipation from the kitchen had begun.

The idea of woman's liberation, reinforced in the Pluto in Cancer era, took time to filter through to all levels of society. But the female role was never to be quite the same again. Women would continue to question, challenge, and resist being inferior to the male head of the household.

People born with Pluto traversing the sign of Cancer have this revolutionary instinct for change in them. Although they may not enjoy disruption, they tend to be catalysts for it.

They are of the era when the United States and Britain gave women the vote, when hemlines were raised, when labor-saving devices replaced servants. Improved household appliances and even prepared foods made the home modern and functional, which lightened the work of Pluto in Cancer homemakers, for whom food and comfortable furnishings are so important.

Yet people of this generation have strong attachments to the past. In spite of the changes their times effected, they are often nostalgic about the good old days. They are a deeply emotional type of people whose feelings often had to be repressed only to find release in sudden upheavals.

Pluto in Cancer individuals strive to find security. They are tenacious in their efforts to achieve it. They have strong social awareness and tend to take personal responsibility for the condition of the world. They are the types who can cherish their loved ones and what they own.

PLUTO IN LEO

People with Pluto in Leo were born between 1938 and 1957.

Leo is the sign of kings and power. In these nineteen years of Pluto's occupation, more rulers were tumbled from their thrones than probably at any other time in history. Kingship was definitely out of fashion.

But a new kind of power arose—neither vested in the people nor in the authorities who ruled: the atom bomb. Only the need for survival prevented the power-hungry nations from employing it to achieve their expansive and obsessive aims.

Leo also is the sign of young people. Pluto's compelling energy stimulated teenagers, who began to realize their own power to set up a world of their own. Soon arose the plutocratic industries and businesses catering to their fashions and fads, from music to clothes.

People born during this Pluto transit of Leo tend to have a good deal of self-confidence. They have faith in their own ideas to solve many of the problems they see around them. They like to give orders and generally possess an ability for managing and organizing.

Pluto in Leo individuals have to avoid becoming too sure of themselves, especially where their emotions are concerned. They can be self-expressive in productive ways. These are people who have contributed much to the world of art and entertainment.

Pluto in Leo people are likely to be in the forefront of movements developing in the 1980s and 1990s to establish a central world government.

PLUTO IN VIRGO

People with Pluto in Virgo were born between 1957 and 1972.

Virgo is the sign of specialization. It gives the capacity for fine analysis and the grouping of masses of detail into meaningful forms. Pluto, the planet of opportunistic wealth, applied Virgo's abilities to electronics—and the computer age was launched.

Pluto also exploited Virgo's concern for health and hygiene. The people of this era are more conscious of the industrial pollution that poisons their oceans, rivers, land forms, and atmosphere.

Pluto in Virgo individuals have an instinctive interest in order and efficiency. They appreciate the difficulties facing industry and technology, and they have a conscientious wish to help develop preventive measures.

They are the types who believe that progress does require certain sacrifices, and they are confident of their ability to devise techniques for minimizing the dangers of pollution.

The Pluto in Virgo era may prove that industry and higher standards of health are not incompatible.

Pluto is a planet of extremes and profound upheavals. It was during its transit of Virgo that many of the ills of modern terrorism—skyjacking, assassinations, holding innocents hostage—erupted. Everyone and every movement with a protest to make seemed to want to do it with accompanying violence or threat of violence.

It is not by accident that Virgo is a hypercritical sign, notorious for its fault-finding and nagging. The Pluto in Virgo age demanded some sort of move toward perfection. As a result, it often produced the extremes—for better and for worse.

PLUTO IN LIBRA

People with Pluto in Libra were or will be born between 1972 and 1984.

Libra is the sign of peace and war. With Pluto here, anything—or nothing—can happen. The old seething hatreds and divisions can suddenly rise to the surface and crack the world apart.

But Libra is a sign that endeavors always to smooth over any rents. Often peace at any price is the Libra war cry. It could easily be an age of continued stalemate.

Pluto is the planet of the underworld, not only of gangsters and terrorists, their modern counterparts, but also of mineral resources and buried treasures of oil, gold, and coal. This era saw the first oil crisis of 1973, and the subsequent ones.

Libra is the sign of balance. To redress the balance is one of its compelling aims. However, the presence of Pluto raises the danger of going too far, one way or the other.

The Pluto in Libra era is one in which huge fortunes are being made while many people of the world continue to starve. There was a great cry for social justice, and yet a reluctance to take sides to provide the necessary impetus for change by those in authority. Opportunism stepped in and filled the gap. The plutocrats grew wealthier, while economic depression tightened the belts of the people.

This generation of individuals, when they reach the seats of power, will have a compelling desire to achieve harmony in the world. They have to be careful that their well-intended efforts do not encourage greater polarization. Opposing factions and forces can lead to greater unrest and violence.

PLUTO IN SCORPIO

People with Pluto in Scorpio will be born between 1984 and 1995.

Pluto in Scorpio is in its own sign. This can be very good or very bad, with little likelihood of a happy medium.

Pluto brings sweeping changes. In the warlike, ambitious sign of Scorpio, this could be the time when man's lust for power destroys him. Pluto is the planet of nuclear power; the plutonium bomb is recognized as the ultimate of all horrors.

And yet Pluto also is the planet of gold and plenty. Gold—the age-old symbol of the powerful. The plutocrats' massive wealth could be devoted to turning this into a golden age.

Scorpio is the sign of taxation, which means that the little person may also have to pay heavily for utopian schemes. Scorpio is also the sign of insurance. So all people may want to invest in future peace and safety in order to collect real rewards on the living planet Earth.

This can be an age of awakening. Scorpio and Pluto represent the powers of spiritual regeneration. These twelve years are likely to produce great strides in psychotherapy.

The Pluto in Scorpio generation is likely to foster a shrewd business sense, as well as great determination. It will be very important that individual energies are directed along constructive channels. Individuals have the power for good or for bad.

Tables: Cusp Tables for All Signs, Ascendant Tables, and Planetary Tables

Cusp Tables
for All Signs

Y ou probably known your own Sun sign. At least you have always been under the impression that a certain Sun sign was yours. The Sun sign dates for each sign, as shown below, are generalized dates.

Generalized Sun Sign Dates

Aries	March 21 to April 20
Taurus	April 21 to May 20
Gemini	May 21 to June 20
Cancer	June 21 to July 20
Leo	July 21 to August 21
Virgo	August 22 to September 21
Libra	September 22 to October 22
Scorpio	October 23 to November 22
Sagittarius	November 23 to December 20
Capricorn	December 21 to January 19
Aquarius	January 20 to February 18
Pisces	February 19 to March 20

These generalized dates are not always the actual dates that the Sun changes sign. The actual day a sign changes differs from month to month and from year to year because the time used to measure planetary motion differs from calendar time.

In the year of your birth a sign may have changed on a day different from the generalized date. For example, if you were born on May 21 in 1942, the actual Sun sign was Taurus for that year, not Gemini.

The Cusp Tables on the next five pages give the days the signs change for the years 1910 through 1990. Check your year of birth, and see if you belong to a cusp.

The cusp period—the time it takes for a sign to give way to another sign—lasts about six days. The cusp period goes from the nineteenth to the twenty-fourth of a month. If you were born on any of these six days, you are influenced by the cusp period.

You will then certainly want to read the cusp description that applies to you in the following chapter, "Cusp Signs: Aries Through Pisces." Or you may want to consult the relevant book of the *Astroscope Profile* series for the other Sun sign. By understanding the other sign, you will learn another set of influences that make you uniquely you.

YEAR	ARIES MAR.-APR.	TAURUS APR.-MAY	GEMINI MAY-JUNE	CANCER JUNE-JULY	LEO JULY-AUG.	VIRGO AUG.-SEPT.	LIBRA SEPT.-OCT.	SCORPIO OCT.-NOV.	SAGITTARIUS NOV.-DEC.	CAPRICORN DEC.-JAN.	AQUARIUS JAN.-FEB.	PISCES FEB.-MAR.
1910	22–20	21–21	22–21	22–23	24–23	24–23	24–23	24–22	23–22	23–20	21–19	20–21
1911	22–20	21–21	22–22	23–23	24–23	24–23	24–24	25–22	23–22	23–20	21–19	20–21
1912	21–19	20–20	21–21	22–22	23–23	24–22	23–23	24–22	23–21	22–20	21–19	20–20
1913	21–20	21–21	22–21	22–23	24–23	24–23	24–23	24–22	23–21	22–20	21–18	19–20
1914	21–20	21–21	22–21	22–23	24–23	24–23	24–23	24–22	23–22	23–20	21–18	19–20
1915	22–20	21–21	22–22	23–23	24–23	24–23	24–24	25–22	23–22	23–20	21–19	20–21
1916	21–19	20–20	21–21	22–22	23–23	24–22	23–23	24–22	23–21	22–20	21–19	20–20
1917	21–20	21–21	22–21	22–22	23–23	24–23	24–23	24–22	23–21	22–20	21–19	19–20
1918	21–20	21–21	22–21	22–23	24–23	24–23	24–23	24–22	23–22	23–20	21–18	19–20
1919	22–20	21–21	22–22	22–23	24–23	24–23	23–23	24–22	23–22	23–20	21–18	20–21
1920	21–19	20–20	21–21	22–22	23–22	23–22	24–23	24–22	23–21	22–20	21–19	20–20
1921	21–20	21–21	22–21	22–22	23–23	24–23	24–23	24–22	23–21	22–20	21–18	19–20
1922	21–20	21–21	22–21	22–23	24–23	24–23	24–23	24–22	23–22	23–20	21–18	19–20

Year												
1923	20-21	21-19	23-20	23-22	24-22	24-23	24-23	24-23	22-23	22-21	21-21	22-20
1924	20-20	21-19	22-20	23-21	24-22	23-23	23-22	23-22	22-22	21-21	20-20	21-19
1925	19-20	21-18	22-20	23-21	24-22	24-23	24-23	23-23	22-22	22-21	21-21	21-20
1926	19-20	21-18	23-20	23-22	24-22	24-23	24-23	24-23	22-23	22-21	21-21	21-20
1927	20-21	21-19	23-20	23-22	24-22	24-23	24-23	24-23	22-23	22-21	21-21	22-20
1928	20-20	21-19	22-20	23-21	24-22	23-23	23-22	23-22	22-22	21-21	20-20	21-19
1929	19-20	21-18	22-20	23-21	24-22	24-23	24-23	23-23	22-22	22-21	21-21	21-20
1930	19-20	21-18	23-20	23-22	24-22	24-23	24-23	24-23	22-23	22-21	21-21	21-20
1931	20-21	21-19	23-20	23-22	24-22	24-23	24-23	24-23	22-23	22-21	21-21	22-20
1932	20-20	21-19	22-20	23-21	24-22	23-23	23-22	23-22	22-22	21-21	20-20	21-19
1933	19-20	20-18	22-19	23-21	24-22	24-23	24-23	23-23	22-22	22-21	21-21	21-20
1934	19-20	21-18	23-20	23-22	24-22	24-23	24-23	24-23	22-23	22-21	21-21	21-20
1935	20-21	21-19	23-20	23-22	24-22	24-23	24-23	24-23	22-23	22-21	21-21	22-20
1936	20-20	21-19	22-20	22-21	24-21	23-23	23-22	23-22	22-22	21-21	20-20	21-19
1937	19-20	20-18	22-19	23-21	24-22	23-23	24-22	23-23	22-22	21-21	21-21	21-20
1938	19-20	21-18	23-20	23-22	24-22	24-23	24-23	24-23	22-23	22-21	21-21	21-20
1939	20-21	21-19	23-20	23-22	24-22	24-23	24-23	24-23	22-23	22-21	21-21	22-20

Year												
1940	20–20	21–19	22–20	22–21	24–21	23–23	23–22	23–22	22–22	21–21	20–20	21–19
1941	19–20	20–18	22–19	23–21	24–22	23–23	24–22	23–23	22–22	21–21	20–20	21–19
1942	19–20	21–18	22–20	23–21	24–22	24–23	24–23	24–23	22–23	22–21	21–21	21–20
1943	20–21	21–19	23–20	23–22	24–22	24–23	24–23	24–23	22–23	22–21	21–21	22–20
1944	20–20	21–19	22–20	22–21	24–21	23–23	23–22	23–22	22–22	21–21	20–20	21–19
1945	19–20	20–18	22–19	23–21	24–22	23–23	24–22	23–23	22–22	21–21	20–20	21–19
1946	19–20	21–18	22–20	23–21	24–22	24–23	24–23	23–23	22–23	22–21	21–21	21–20
1947	19–20	21–18	23–20	23–22	24–22	24–23	24–23	24–23	22–23	22–21	21–21	21–20
1948	20–20	21–19	22–20	22–21	24–21	23–23	23–22	23–22	22–22	21–21	20–20	21–19
1949	19–20	20–18	22–19	23–21	24–22	23–23	23–22	23–22	22–22	21–21	20–20	21–19
1950	19–20	21–18	22–20	23–21	24–22	24–23	24–23	23–23	22–22	22–21	21–21	21–20
1951	20–21	21–19	23–20	24–22	25–23	24–24	24–23	24–23	23–23	22–22	21–21	22–20
1952	20–20	22–19	22–21	23–21	24–22	24–23	24–23	23–23	22–22	22–21	21–21	21–20
1953	19–20	21–18	23–20	23–22	24–22	24–23	24–23	24–23	22–23	22–21	21–21	21–20
1954	20–21	21–19	23–20	23–22	24–22	24–23	24–23	24–23	22–23	22–21	21–21	22–20
1955	20–21	21–19	23–20	24–22	25–23	24–24	24–23	24–23	23–23	22–22	21–21	22–20
1956	20–20	22–19	22–21	23–21	24–22	24–23	24–23	23–23	22–22	22–21	21–21	21–20

Year												
1957	21-20	21-21	22-21	22-23	24-23	24-23	24-23	24-22	23-22	23-20	21-18	19-20
1958	22-20	21-21	22-21	22-23	24-23	24-23	24-23	24-22	23-22	23-20	21-19	20-21
1959	22-20	21-21	22-22	23-23	24-23	24-23	24-24	25-23	24-22	23-20	21-19	20-21
1960	21-20	21-21	22-21	22-22	23-23	24-23	24-23	24-22	23-21	22-21	22-19	20-20
1961	21-20	21-21	22-21	22-23	24-23	24-23	24-23	24-22	23-22	23-20	21-18	19-20
1962	22-20	21-21	22-21	22-23	24-23	24-23	24-23	24-22	23-22	23-20	21-19	20-21
1963	22-20	21-21	22-22	23-23	24-23	24-23	24-24	25-23	24-22	23-20	21-19	20-21
1964	21-20	21-21	22-21	22-22	23-23	24-23	24-23	24-22	23-21	22-21	22-19	20-20
1965	21-20	21-21	22-21	22-23	24-23	24-23	24-23	24-22	23-22	23-20	21-18	19-20
1966	22-20	21-21	22-21	22-23	24-23	24-23	24-23	24-22	23-22	23-20	21-19	20-21
1967	22-20	21-21	22-22	23-23	24-23	24-23	24-24	25-22	23-22	23-20	21-19	20-21
1968	21-20	21-20	21-21	22-22	23-23	24-22	23-23	24-22	23-21	22-21	21-19	20-20
1969	21-20	21-21	22-21	22-23	24-23	24-23	24-23	24-22	23-22	23-20	21-18	19-20
1970	22-20	21-21	22-21	22-23	24-23	24-23	24-23	24-22	23-22	23-20	21-19	20-21
1971	22-20	21-21	22-22	23-23	24-23	24-23	24-24	25-22	23-22	23-20	21-19	20-21
1972	21-19	20-20	21-21	22-22	23-23	24-22	23-23	24-22	23-21	22-20	21-19	20-20
1973	21-20	21-21	22-21	22-22	23-23	24-23	24-23	24-22	23-22	23-20	21-18	19-20

Year												
1974	20-21	21-19	23-20	23-22	24-22	24-23	24-23	24-23	22-23	22-21	21-21	22-20
1975	20-21	21-19	23-20	23-22	25-22	24-24	24-23	24-23	23-23	22-22	21-21	22-20
1976	20-20	21-19	22-20	23-21	24-22	23-23	23-22	23-23	22-22	21-21	20-20	21-19
1977	19-20	21-18	22-20	23-21	24-22	24-23	24-23	23-23	22-22	22-21	21-21	21-20
1978	20-20	21-19	23-20	23-22	24-22	24-23	24-23	24-23	22-23	22-21	21-21	21-20
1979	20-21	21-19	23-20	23-22	25-22	24-24	24-23	24-23	22-23	22-21	21-21	22-20
1980	20-20	21-19	22-20	23-21	24-22	23-23	23-22	23-22	22-22	21-21	20-20	21-19
1981	19-20	21-18	22-20	23-21	24-22	24-23	24-23	23-23	22-22	22-21	21-21	21-20
1982	19-20	21-18	23-20	23-22	24-22	24-23	24-23	24-23	22-23	22-21	21-21	21-20
1983	20-21	21-19	23-20	23-22	24-22	24-23	24-23	24-23	22-23	22-21	21-21	22-20
1984	20-20	21-19	22-20	23-21	24-22	23-23	23-22	23-22	22-22	21-21	20-20	21-19
1985	19-20	21-18	22-20	23-21	24-22	24-23	24-23	23-23	22-22	22-21	21-21	21-20
1986	19-20	21-18	23-20	23-22	24-22	24-23	24-23	24-23	22-23	22-21	21-21	21-20
1987	20-21	21-19	23-20	23-22	24-22	24-23	24-23	24-23	22-23	22-21	21-21	22-20
1988	20-20	21-19	22-20	23-21	24-22	23-23	23-22	23-22	22-22	21-21	20-20	21-19
1989	19-20	21-18	22-20	23-21	24-22	24-23	24-23	23-23	22-22	22-21	21-21	21-20
1990	19-20	21-18	23-20	23-22	24-22	24-23	24-23	24-23	22-23	22-21	21-21	21-20

Ascendant Tables

These Ascendant Tables give the Rising sign for each hour of the day for every day that corresponds to your Sun sign.

If your Rising sign is the same as your Sun sign, you've got a double whammy going. For example, you are a "double" Aries or a "double" Capricorn or a "double" of another sign. And you probably show the tendencies of the particular sign more strongly than would be expected.

If your Sun sign and Rising sign are different, of course the approach to life is a variation. When you find your Rising sign from the tables that follow, go to the particular chapter "Your Rising Sign" that applies to you.

As you read, you will be amazed at how many facets of your own personality reveal themselves to you. You will be astounded as *Astroscope Profile* helps you on your voyage of self-discovery. And, as the mystery unfolds, you'll be startled to see just how *Astroscope Profile* is zeroing in on your character.

How can you guess your Rising sign if you do not know the time of your birth? Since each sign rises once a day, the odds are twelve to one against. Of course, you can narrow the odds if you know you were born "in the morning," or "around midnight," or "sometime in the afternoon." But the Rising sign lasts only about two hours, so you could make a big mistake. You might guess Libra, but it could be Virgo or Scorpio, depending on how far off your estimate was.

A better way to figure out your Rising sign if you do not know the hour of your birth is to read the chapters "Your Rising Sign," which start on pages 151–245. Skim through each chapter to see which Rising sign description best fits you.

DAYLIGHT SAVING TIME

The hour of birth given in the following Ascendant Tables is for Standard Time in any time zone. Between the last Sunday in April and the last Sunday in October, it has been convenient to go on Daylight Saving Time. Daylight Saving Time started in the United States during World War I, and has been used annually in most localities since 1918.

Daylight Saving Time is one hour *later* than Standard Time. If your hour of birth was recorded in Daylight Saving Time, *subtract* one hour from that recorded time. Then look up the revised hour in the Ascendant Tables.

For example, if you were born in Chicago on June 16 at 2:00 A.M., it is likely that the hour of birth recorded is in Daylight Saving Time. The Standard Time would have been one hour earlier, or 1:00 A.M. So you look up 1 A.M. as the hour for your birth in the Ascendant Tables.

CAPRICORN ASCENDANT TABLES: YOUR RISING SIGN

	December 22	December 23	December 24	December 25	December 26
Midnight	Libra	Libra	Libra	Libra	Libra
1:00 A.M.	Libra	Libra	Libra	Libra	Libra
2:00 A.M.	Libra	Libra	Libra	Libra	Libra
3:00 A.M.	Scorpio	Scorpio	Scorpio	Scorpio	Scorpio
4:00 A.M.	Scorpio	Scorpio	Scorpio	Scorpio	Scorpio
5:00 A.M.	Sagittarius	Sagittarius	Sagittarius	Sagittarius	Sagittarius
6:00 A.M.	Sagittarius	Sagittarius	Sagittarius	Sagittarius	Sagittarius
7:00 A.M.	Sagittarius	Sagittarius	Sagittarius	Sagittarius	Sagittarius
8:00 A.M.	Capricorn	Capricorn	Capricorn	Capricorn	Capricorn
9:00 A.M.	Capricorn	Capricorn	Capricorn	Capricorn	Aquarius
10:00 A.M.	Aquarius	Aquarius	Aquarius	Aquarius	Aquarius
11:00 A.M.	Pisces	Pisces	Pisces	Pisces	Pisces
Noon	Aries	Aries	Aries	Aries	Aries
1:00 P.M.	Aries	Aries	Aries	Aries	Taurus
2:00 P.M.	Taurus	Taurus	Taurus	Taurus	Taurus
3:00 P.M.	Gemini	Gemini	Gemini	Gemini	Gemini
4:00 P.M.	Gemini	Gemini	Gemini	Gemini	Gemini
5:00 P.M.	Cancer	Cancer	Cancer	Cancer	Cancer
6:00 P.M.	Cancer	Cancer	Cancer	Cancer	Cancer
7:00 P.M.	Leo	Leo	Leo	Leo	Leo
8:00 P.M.	Leo	Leo	Leo	Leo	Leo
9:00 P.M.	Leo	Leo	Leo	Leo	Leo
10:00 P.M.	Virgo	Virgo	Virgo	Virgo	Virgo
11:00 P.M.	Virgo	Virgo	Virgo	Virgo	Virgo

CAPRICORN ASCENDANT TABLES: YOUR RISING SIGN

	December 27	December 28	December 29	December 30	December 31
Midnight	Libra	Libra	Libra	Libra	Libra
1:00 A.M.	Libra	Libra	Libra	Libra	Libra
2:00 A.M.	Libra	Libra	Scorpio	Scorpio	Scorpio
3:00 A.M.	Scorpio	Scorpio	Scorpio	Scorpio	Scorpio
4:00 A.M.	Scorpio	Scorpio	Scorpio	Scorpio	Scorpio
5:00 A.M.	Sagittarius	Sagittarius	Sagittarius	Sagittarius	Sagittarius
6:00 A.M.	Sagittarius	Sagittarius	Sagittarius	Sagittarius	Sagittarius
7:00 A.M.	Capricorn	Capricorn	Capricorn	Capricorn	Capricorn
8:00 A.M.	Capricorn	Capricorn	Capricorn	Capricorn	Capricorn
9:00 A.M.	Aquarius	Aquarius	Aquarius	Aquarius	Aquarius
10:00 A.M.	Aquarius	Aquarius	Aquarius	Aquarius	Aquarius
11:00 A.M.	Pisces	Pisces	Pisces	Pisces	Pisces
Noon	Aries	Aries	Aries	Aries	Aries
1:00 P.M.	Taurus	Taurus	Taurus	Taurus	Taurus
2:00 P.M.	Taurus	Taurus	Taurus	Taurus	Taurus
3:00 P.M.	Gemini	Gemini	Gemini	Gemini	Gemini
4:00 P.M.	Gemini	Gemini	Gemini	Gemini	Gemini
5:00 P.M.	Cancer	Cancer	Cancer	Cancer	Cancer
6:00 P.M.	Cancer	Cancer	Cancer	Cancer	Cancer
7:00 P.M.	Leo	Leo	Leo	Leo	Leo
8:00 P.M.	Leo	Leo	Leo	Leo	Leo
9:00 P.M.	Leo	Leo	Leo	Virgo	Virgo
10:00 P.M.	Virgo	Virgo	Virgo	Virgo	Virgo
11:00 P.M.	Virgo	Virgo	Virgo	Virgo	Virgo

	January 1	January 2	January 3	January 4	January 5
Midnight	Libra	Libra	Libra	Libra	Libra
1:00 A.M.	Libra	Libra	Libra	Libra	Libra
2:00 A.M.	Scorpio	Scorpio	Scorpio	Scorpio	Scorpio
3:00 A.M.	Scorpio	Scorpio	Scorpio	Scorpio	Scorpio
4:00 A.M.	Scorpio	Scorpio	Scorpio	Sagittarius	Sagittarius
5:00 A.M.	Sagittarius	Sagittarius	Sagittarius	Sagittarius	Sagittarius
6:00 A.M.	Sagittarius	Sagittarius	Sagittarius	Sagittarius	Sagittarius
7:00 A.M.	Capricorn	Capricorn	Capricorn	Capricorn	Capricorn
8:00 A.M.	Capricorn	Capricorn	Capricorn	Capricorn	Capricorn
9:00 A.M.	Aquarius	Aquarius	Aquarius	Aquarius	Aquarius
10:00 A.M.	Aquarius	Pisces	Pisces	Pisces	Pisces
11:00 A.M.	Pisces	Pisces	Pisces	Pisces	Pisces
Noon	Aries	Aries	Aries	Aries	Aries
1:00 P.M.	Taurus	Taurus	Taurus	Taurus	Taurus
2:00 P.M.	Gemini	Gemini	Gemini	Gemini	Gemini
3:00 P.M.	Gemini	Gemini	Gemini	Gemini	Gemini
4:00 P.M.	Cancer	Cancer	Cancer	Cancer	Cancer
5:00 P.M.	Cancer	Cancer	Cancer	Cancer	Cancer
6:00 P.M.	Cancer	Cancer	Cancer	Cancer	Cancer
7:00 P.M.	Leo	Leo	Leo	Leo	Leo
8:00 P.M.	Leo	Leo	Leo	Leo	Leo
9:00 P.M.	Virgo	Virgo	Virgo	Virgo	Virgo
10:00 P.M.	Virgo	Virgo	Virgo	Virgo	Virgo
11:00 P.M.	Virgo	Virgo	Virgo	Virgo	Virgo

CAPRICORN ASCENDANT TABLES: YOUR RISING SIGN

	January 6	January 7	January 8	January 9	January 10
Midnight	Libra	Libra	Libra	Libra	Libra
1:00 A.M.	Libra	Libra	Libra	Libra	Libra
2:00 A.M.	Scorpio	Scorpio	Scorpio	Scorpio	Scorpio
3:00 A.M.	Scorpio	Scorpio	Scorpio	Scorpio	Scorpio
4:00 A.M.	Sagittarius	Sagittarius	Sagittarius	Sagittarius	Sagittarius
5:00 A.M.	Sagittarius	Sagittarius	Sagittarius	Sagittarius	Sagittarius
6:00 A.M.	Sagittarius	Capricorn	Capricorn	Capricorn	Capricorn
7:00 A.M.	Capricorn	Capricorn	Capricorn	Capricorn	Capricorn
8:00 A.M.	Capricorn	Aquarius	Aquarius	Aquarius	Aquarius
9:00 A.M.	Aquarius	Aquarius	Aquarius	Aquarius	Aquarius
10:00 A.M.	Pisces	Pisces	Pisces	Pisces	Pisces
11:00 A.M.	Aries	Aries	Aries	Aries	Aries
Noon	Aries	Aries	Aries	Aries	Taurus
1:00 P.M.	Taurus	Taurus	Taurus	Taurus	Taurus
2:00 P.M.	Gemini	Gemini	Gemini	Gemini	Gemini
3:00 P.M.	Gemini	Gemini	Gemini	Gemini	Gemini
4:00 P.M.	Cancer	Cancer	Cancer	Cancer	Cancer
5:00 P.M.	Cancer	Cancer	Cancer	Cancer	Cancer
6:00 P.M.	Leo	Leo	Leo	Leo	Leo
7:00 P.M.	Leo	Leo	Leo	Leo	Leo
8:00 P.M.	Leo	Leo	Leo	Leo	Leo
9:00 P.M.	Virgo	Virgo	Virgo	Virgo	Virgo
10:00 P.M.	Virgo	Virgo	Virgo	Virgo	Virgo
11:00 P.M.	Libra	Libra	Libra	Libra	Libra

	January 11	January 12	January 13	January 14	January 15
Midnight	Libra	Libra	Libra	Libra	Libra
1:00 A.M.	Libra	Libra	Scorpio	Scorpio	Scorpio
2:00 A.M.	Scorpio	Scorpio	Scorpio	Scorpio	Scorpio
3:00 A.M.	Scorpio	Scorpio	Scorpio	Scorpio	Scorpio
4:00 A.M.	Sagittarius	Sagittarius	Sagittarius	Sagittarius	Sagittarius
5:00 A.M.	Sagittarius	Sagittarius	Sagittarius	Sagittarius	Sagittarius
6:00 A.M.	Capricorn	Capricorn	Capricorn	Capricorn	Capricorn
7:00 A.M.	Capricorn	Capricorn	Capricorn	Capricorn	Capricorn
8:00 A.M.	Aquarius	Aquarius	Aquarius	Aquarius	Aquarius
9:00 A.M.	Aquarius	Aquarius	Aquarius	Aquarius	Aquarius
10:00 A.M.	Pisces	Pisces	Pisces	Pisces	Pisces
11:00 A.M.	Aries	Aries	Aries	Aries	Aries
Noon	Taurus	Taurus	Taurus	Taurus	Taurus
1:00 P.M.	Taurus	Taurus	Taurus	Taurus	Gemini
2:00 P.M.	Gemini	Gemini	Gemini	Gemini	Gemini
3:00 P.M.	Gemini	Gemini	Gemini	Gemini	Cancer
4:00 P.M.	Cancer	Cancer	Cancer	Cancer	Cancer
5:00 P.M.	Cancer	Cancer	Cancer	Cancer	Cancer
6:00 P.M.	Leo	Leo	Leo	Leo	Leo
7:00 P.M.	Leo	Leo	Leo	Leo	Leo
8:00 P.M.	Leo	Leo	Leo	Virgo	Virgo
9:00 P.M.	Virgo	Virgo	Virgo	Virgo	Virgo
10:00 P.M.	Virgo	Virgo	Virgo	Virgo	Virgo
11:00 P.M.	Libra	Libra	Libra	Libra	Libra

CAPRICORN ASCENDANT TABLES: YOUR RISING SIGN

	January 16	January 17	January 18	January 19	January 20	January 21
Midnight	Libra	Libra	Libra	Libra	Libra	Libra
1:00 A.M.	Scorpio	Scorpio	Scorpio	Scorpio	Scorpio	Scorpio
2:00 A.M.	Scorpio	Scorpio	Scorpio	Scorpio	Scorpio	Scorpio
3:00 A.M.	Scorpio	Scorpio	Scorpio	Scorpio	Scorpio	Sagittarius
4:00 A.M.	Sagittarius	Sagittarius	Sagittarius	Sagittarius	Sagittarius	Sagittarius
5:00 A.M.	Sagittarius	Sagittarius	Sagittarius	Sagittarius	Sagittarius	Sagittarius
6:00 A.M.	Capricorn	Capricorn	Capricorn	Capricorn	Capricorn	Capricorn
7:00 A.M.	Capricorn	Capricorn	Capricorn	Capricorn	Capricorn	Capricorn
8:00 A.M.	Aquarius	Aquarius	Aquarius	Aquarius	Aquarius	Aquarius
9:00 A.M.	Aquarius	Pisces	Pisces	Pisces	Pisces	Pisces
10:00 A.M.	Pisces	Pisces	Pisces	Pisces	Pisces	Aries
11:00 A.M.	Aries	Aries	Aries	Aries	Aries	Aries
Noon	Taurus	Taurus	Taurus	Taurus	Taurus	Taurus
1:00 P.M.	Gemini	Gemini	Gemini	Gemini	Gemini	Gemini
2:00 P.M.	Gemini	Gemini	Gemini	Gemini	Gemini	Gemini
3:00 P.M.	Cancer	Cancer	Cancer	Cancer	Cancer	Cancer
4:00 P.M.	Cancer	Cancer	Cancer	Cancer	Cancer	Cancer
5:00 P.M.	Cancer	Cancer	Cancer	Cancer	Cancer	Leo
6:00 P.M.	Leo	Leo	Leo	Leo	Leo	Leo
7:00 P.M.	Leo	Leo	Leo	Leo	Leo	Leo
8:00 P.M.	Virgo	Virgo	Virgo	Virgo	Virgo	Virgo
9:00 P.M.	Virgo	Virgo	Virgo	Virgo	Virgo	Virgo
10:00 P.M.	Virgo	Virgo	Virgo	Virgo	Virgo	Libra
11:00 P.M.	Libra	Libra	Libra	Libra	Libra	Libra

Planetary Tables

Our *Astroscope Profile* system of constructing a personal astroscope is really simple. Just turn to your birthday tables. These tables, on colored/banded pages, give the planetary positions for your Sun sign every day for the eighty-one years 1910–90. Once you have located your birth year and day, you can see at a glance the astrological makeup contributed by the planets of the Solar System.

HOW TO USE THE TABLES

Select the page on which your year of birth appears. Note the column headings at the top of the page. They denote each planet of the solar system: Moon (actually a satellite of Earth), Mercury, Venus, Mars, Jupiter, Saturn, Uranus, Neptune, and Pluto. Going down the column, you see the zodiacal signs in which each of the planets is located for a specific day.

Now run down the month to find your day of birth. From your birth date read across the page, stopping at each column to learn your true placement of planets in signs.

Is it a true placement? It is, except for two possible cautions. One concerns time zones around the world; the other concerns Daylight Saving Time. These cautions could apply to you, so read the sections below.

TIME ZONES AROUND THE WORLD

The times given in the tables for the Moon entering a new sign are given in New York time, which is Eastern Standard Time. If you were born in a different time zone, you may need to adjust your recorded birth time to Eastern Standard Time.

Look at the map "Time Zones Around the World" on the next page.

Time Zones Around The World

Figure 8

| +7 | +8 | +9 | +10 | +11 | +12 | +13 | +14 | +15 | +16 | +17 |

UNION OF SOVIET SOCIALIST REPUBLICS

ASIA

MONGOLIA

CHINA

NORTH KOREA
SOUTH KOREA
JAPAN

EUROPE

BLACK SEA
TURKEY
LEBANON SYRIA
ISRAEL JORDAN IRAQ
EGYPT KUWAIT
U.A.R.
SAUDI ARABIA
IRAN
AFGHANISTAN
PAKISTAN
NEPAL BHUTAN
INDIA BANGLADESH
BURMA
MUSCAT AND OMAN
YEMEN
ARABIAN SEA
SUDAN
ETHIOPIA
SOMALIA
KENYA
TANZANIA
MOZAMBIQUE
MADAGASCAR
RHODESIA
SWAZILAND
LESOTHO

LAOS
THAILAND
CAMBODIA
VIET NAM
HONG KONG TAIWAN
REPUBLIC OF THE PHILIPPINES
MALAYSIA
SINGAPORE
INDONESIA

PACIFIC OCEAN

INDIAN OCEAN

NEW GUINEA

CORAL SEA

AUSTRALIA

TASMAN SEA

NEW ZEALAND

| +7 | +8 | +9 | +10 | +11 | +12 | +13 | +14 | +15 | +16 | +17 |

For explanation of Time Zone Map, see page 396.

The time zone marked "0" is the New York, or Eastern Standard, Time Zone. If you were born in that area, you don't have to adjust your birth hour. It corresponds to Moon times given in the tables (except during Daylight Saving Time hours).

But if you were born in any other time zone, here is how you can convert your birth time.

Find on the map where you were born. Then look at the number above that place. That number tells you how many hours you must add or subtract to your birth time for the conversion.

The numbers to the left of New York (going west) are minus numbers: −1, −2, and so on. If you were born in zone −3, say, you must subtract three hours from your recorded birth time to get the correct New York time.

The numbers to the right of New York (going east) are plus numbers: +1, +2, and so on. If, for example, you were born in zone +5, you must add five hours to your recorded birth time to get the corresponding New York time.

DAYLIGHT SAVINGS TIME

As has been mentioned, the Moon times in the tables are given in New York time (Eastern Standard Time). The United States and many other nations use Daylight Savings Time during the summer, and the United States has been continuously doing so since 1918. Daylight Saving Time for any Standard Time Zone is one hour *later* than the Standard Time there. Americans go on Daylight Saving Time from the last Sunday in April through the last Sunday in October.

If your birth time is recorded in Daylight Saving Time, you may need to make an adjustment during the period April through October. If so, make sure you have first converted your birth hour for New York time (Eastern Standard) if you need to do so.

Then, *if there is one hour or less variation between the time of your birth and the time the Moon enters a new sign,* you can adjust as follows: Just subtract one hour from your birth time to correspond to the time basis used in the tables.

Here is an example for someone born in New York. Suppose you were born on September 1, 1950, and your birth time was recorded as 2:15 P.M. (Daylight Saving Time). Now imagine the tables show that the Moon entered Leo at 2:00 P.M. (Eastern Standard Time) on September 1, 1950.

You might assume you have the Moon in Leo. But your Daylight Saving Time hour of birth is really 1:15 P.M. Eastern Standard Time—an hour earlier. You actually have the Moon in Cancer—a big difference!

CAPRICORN PLANETARY TABLES

1910

January	MOON FROM	IN	MERCURY	VENUS	MARS	JUPITER	SATURN	URANUS	NEPTUNE	PLUTO
1	Virgo		Capricorn	Aquarius	Aries	Libra	Aries	Capricorn	Cancer	Gemini
2	7:37 A.M.	Libra	Capricorn	Aquarius	Aries	Libra	Aries	Capricorn	Cancer	Gemini
3			Capricorn	Aquarius	Aries	Libra	Aries	Capricorn	Cancer	Gemini
4	8:18 P.M.	Scorpio	Aquarius	Aquarius	Aries	Libra	Aries	Capricorn	Cancer	Gemini
5			Aquarius	Aquarius	Aries	Libra	Aries	Capricorn	Cancer	Gemini
6			Aquarius	Aquarius	Aries	Libra	Aries	Capricorn	Cancer	Gemini
7	8:19 A.M.	Sagittarius	Aquarius	Aquarius	Aries	Libra	Aries	Capri orn	Cancer	Gemini
8			Aquarius	Aquarius	Aries	Libra	Aries	Capricorn	Cancer	Gemini
9	5:39 P.M.	Capricorn	Aquarius	Aquarius	Aries	Libra	Aries	Capricorn	Cancer	Gemini
10			Aquarius	Aquarius	Aries	Libra	Aries	Capricorn	Cancer	Gemini
11	11:52 P.M.	Aquarius	Aquarius	Aquarius	Aries	Libra	Aries	Capricorn	Cancer	Gemini
12			Aquarius	Aquarius	Aries	Libra	Aries	Capricorn	Cancer	Gemini
13			Aquarius	Aquarius	Aries	Libra	Aries	Capricorn	Cancer	Gemini
14	3:49 A.M.	Pisces	Aquarius	Aquarius	Aries	Libra	Aries	Capricorn	Cancer	Gemini
15			Aquarius	Aquarius	Aries	Libra	Aries	Capricorn	Cancer	Gemini
16	6:45 A.M.	Aries	Aquarius	Pisces	Aries	Libra	Aries	Capricorn	Cancer	Gemini
17			Aquarius	Pisces	Aries	Libra	Aries	Capricorn	Cancer	Gemini
18	9:38 A.M.	Taurus	Aquarius	Pisces	Aries	Libra	Aries	Capricorn	Cancer	Gemini
19			Aquarius	Pisces	Aries	Libra	Aries	Capricorn	Cancer	Gemini
20	12:57 P.M.	Gemini	Aquarius	Pisces	Aries	Libra	Aries	Capricorn	Cancer	Gemini
December										
23	4:10 A.M.	Libra	Capricorn	Capricorn	Sagittarius	Scorpio	Aries	Capricorn	Cancer	Gemini
24			Capricorn	Capricorn	Sagittarius	Scorpio	Aries	Capricorn	Cancer	Gemini
25	3:35 P.M.	Scorpio	Capricorn	Capricorn	Sagittarius	Scorpio	Aries	Capricorn	Cancer	Gemini
26			Capricorn	Capricorn	Sagittarius	Scorpio	Aries	Capricorn	Cancer	Gemini
27			Capricorn	Capricorn	Sagittarius	Scorpio	Aries	Capricorn	Cancer	Gemini
28	4:40 A.M.	Sagittarius	Capricorn	Capricorn	Sagittarius	Scorpio	Aries	Capricorn	Cancer	Gemini
29			Capricorn	Capricorn	Sagittarius	Scorpio	Aries	Capricorn	Cancer	Gemini
30	5:13 P.M.	Capricorn	Capricorn	Capricorn	Sagittarius	Scorpio	Aries	Capricorn	Cancer	Gemini
31			Capricorn	Capricorn	Sagittarius	Scorpio	Aries	Capricorn	Cancer	Gemini

CAPRICORN PLANETARY TABLES

1911

	MOON FROM	IN	MERCURY	VENUS	MARS	JUPITER	SATURN	URANUS	NEPTUNE	PLUTO
January										
1		Capricorn	Capricorn	Capricorn	Sagittarius	Scorpio	Aries	Capricorn	Cancer	Gemini
2	4:01 A.M.	Aquarius	Capricorn	Capricorn	Sagittarius	Scorpio	Aries	Capricorn	Cancer	Gemini
3			Capricorn	Capricorn	Sagittarius	Scorpio	Aries	Capricorn	Cancer	Gemini
4	12:49 P.M.	Pisces	Capricorn	Capricorn	Sagittarius	Scorpio	Aries	Capricorn	Cancer	Gemini
5			Capricorn	Capricorn	Sagittarius	Scorpio	Aries	Capricorn	Cancer	Gemini
6	7:32 A.M.	Aries	Capricorn	Capricorn	Sagittarius	Scorpio	Aries	Capricorn	Cancer	Gemini
7			Capricorn	Capricorn	Sagittarius	Scorpio	Aries	Capricorn	Cancer	Gemini
8	11:59 P.M.	Taurus	Capricorn	Capricorn	Sagittarius	Scorpio	Aries	Capricorn	Cancer	Gemini
9			Capricorn	Capricorn	Sagittarius	Scorpio	Aries	Capricorn	Cancer	Gemini
10			Capricorn	Aquarius	Sagittarius	Scorpio	Aries	Capricorn	Cancer	Gemini
11	2:15 A.M.	Gemini	Capricorn	Aquarius	Sagittarius	Scorpio	Aries	Capricorn	Cancer	Gemini
12			Capricorn	Aquarius	Sagittarius	Scorpio	Aries	Capricorn	Cancer	Gemini
13	3:02 A.M.	Cancer	Capricorn	Aquarius	Sagittarius	Scorpio	Aries	Capricorn	Cancer	Gemini
14			Capricorn	Aquarius	Sagittarius	Scorpio	Aries	Capricorn	Cancer	Gemini
15	3:49 A.M.	Leo	Capricorn	Aquarius	Sagittarius	Scorpio	Aries	Capricorn	Cancer	Gemini
16			Capricorn	Aquarius	Sagittarius	Scorpio	Aries	Capricorn	Cancer	Gemini
17	6:30 A.M.	Virgo	Capricorn	Aquarius	Sagittarius	Scorpio	Aries	Capricorn	Cancer	Gemini
18			Capricorn	Aquarius	Sagittarius	Scorpio	Aries	Capricorn	Cancer	Gemini
19	12:48 P.M.	Libra	Capricorn	Aquarius	Sagittarius	Scorpio	Aries	Capricorn	Cancer	Gemini
20			Capricorn	Aquarius	Sagittarius	Scorpio	Taurus	Capricorn	Cancer	Gemini
December										
23	4:05 A.M.	Aquarius	Capricorn	Scorpio	Taurus	Sagittarius	Taurus	Capricorn	Cancer	Gemini
24			Capricorn	Scorpio	Taurus	Sagittarius	Taurus	Capricorn	Cancer	Gemini
25	4:17 P.M.	Pisces	Capricorn	Scorpio	Taurus	Sagittarius	Taurus	Capricorn	Cancer	Gemini
26			Capricorn	Scorpio	Taurus	Sagittarius	Taurus	Capricorn	Cancer	Gemini
27			Capricorn	Scorpio	Taurus	Sagittarius	Taurus	Capricorn	Cancer	Gemini
28	2:34 A.M.	Aries	Sagittarius	Scorpio	Taurus	Sagittarius	Taurus	Capricorn	Cancer	Gemini
29			Sagittarius	Scorpio	Taurus	Sagittarius	Taurus	Capricorn	Cancer	Gemini
30	9:29 P.M.	Taurus	Sagittarius	Scorpio	Taurus	Sagittarius	Taurus	Capricorn	Cancer	Gemini
31			Sagittarius	Scorpio	Taurus	Sagittarius	Taurus	Capricorn	Cancer	Gemini

1912

January	MOON FROM / IN	MERCURY	VENUS	MARS	JUPITER	SATURN	URANUS	NEPTUNE	PLUTO
1	11:59 A.M. Gemini	Sagittarius	Scorpio	Taurus	Sagittarius	Taurus	Capricorn	Cancer	Gemini
2	12:24 P.M. Cancer	Sagittarius	Scorpio	Taurus	Sagittarius	Taurus	Capricorn	Cancer	Gemini
3		Sagittarius	Scorpio	Taurus	Sagittarius	Taurus	Capricorn	Cancer	Gemini
4		Sagittarius	Scorpio	Taurus	Sagittarius	Taurus	Capricorn	Cancer	Gemini
5	11:17 A.M. Leo	Sagittarius	Sagittarius	Taurus	Sagittarius	Taurus	Capricorn	Cancer	Gemini
6		Sagittarius	Sagittarius	Taurus	Sagittarius	Taurus	Capricorn	Cancer	Gemini
7	11:24 A.M. Virgo	Sagittarius	Sagittarius	Taurus	Sagittarius	Taurus	Capricorn	Cancer	Gemini
8		Sagittarius	Sagittarius	Taurus	Sagittarius	Taurus	Capricorn	Cancer	Gemini
9	2:43 P.M. Libra	Sagittarius	Sagittarius	Taurus	Sagittarius	Taurus	Capricorn	Cancer	Gemini
10		Sagittarius	Sagittarius	Taurus	Sagittarius	Taurus	Capricorn	Cancer	Gemini
11	10:07 P.M. Scorpio	Sagittarius	Sagittarius	Taurus	Sagittarius	Taurus	Capricorn	Cancer	Gemini
12		Sagittarius	Sagittarius	Taurus	Sagittarius	Taurus	Capricorn	Cancer	Gemini
13		Sagittarius	Sagittarius	Taurus	Sagittarius	Taurus	Capricorn	Cancer	Gemini
14	8:57 A.M. Sagittarius	Sagittarius	Sagittarius	Taurus	Sagittarius	Taurus	Capricorn	Cancer	Gemini
15		Capricorn	Sagittarius	Taurus	Sagittarius	Taurus	Capricorn	Cancer	Gemini
16		Capricorn	Sagittarius	Taurus	Sagittarius	Taurus	Capricorn	Cancer	Gemini
17	2:21 A.M. Capricorn	Capricorn	Sagittarius	Taurus	Sagittarius	Taurus	Capricorn	Cancer	Gemini
18		Capricorn	Sagittarius	Taurus	Sagittarius	Taurus	Capricorn	Cancer	Gemini
19	10:06 A.M. Aquarius	Capricorn	Sagittarius	Taurus	Sagittarius	Taurus	Capricorn	Cancer	Gemini
20		Capricorn	Sagittarius	Taurus	Sagittarius	Taurus	Capricorn	Cancer	Gemini
December									
22	Gemini	Sagittarius	Aquarius	Sagittarius	Sagittarius	Taurus	Aquarius	Cancer	Gemini
23	8:10 P.M. Cancer	Sagittarius	Aquarius	Sagittarius	Sagittarius	Taurus	Aquarius	Cancer	Gemini
24		Sagittarius	Aquarius	Sagittarius	Sagittarius	Taurus	Aquarius	Cancer	Gemini
25	8:43 P.M. Leo	Sagittarius	Aquarius	Sagittarius	Sagittarius	Taurus	Aquarius	Cancer	Gemini
26		Sagittarius	Aquarius	Sagittarius	Sagittarius	Taurus	Aquarius	Cancer	Gemini
27	9:27 P.M. Virgo	Sagittarius	Aquarius	Sagittarius	Sagittarius	Taurus	Aquarius	Cancer	Gemini
28		Sagittarius	Aquarius	Sagittarius	Sagittarius	Taurus	Aquarius	Cancer	Gemini
29	11:55 P.M. Libra	Sagittarius	Aquarius	Sagittarius	Sagittarius	Taurus	Aquarius	Cancer	Gemini
30		Sagittarius	Aquarius	Sagittarius	Sagittarius	Taurus	Aquarius	Cancer	Gemini
31		Sagittarius	Aquarius	Sagittarius	Sagittarius	Taurus	Aquarius	Cancer	Gemini

1913

CAPRICORN PLANETARY TABLES

	MOON									
January	FROM	IN	MERCURY	VENUS	MARS	JUPITER	SATURN	URANUS	NEPTUNE	PLUTO
1	4:49 A.M.	Scorpio	Sagittarius	Aquarius	Sagittarius	Sagittarius	Taurus	Aquarius	Cancer	Gemini
2			Sagittarius	Aquarius	Sagittarius	Sagittarius	Taurus	Aquarius	Cancer	Gemini
3	12:01 P.M.	Sagittarius	Sagittarius	Aquarius	Sagittarius	Capricorn	Taurus	Aquarius	Cancer	Gemini
4			Sagittarius	Aquarius	Sagittarius	Capricorn	Taurus	Aquarius	Cancer	Gemini
5	9:10 P.M.	Capricorn	Sagittarius	Aquarius	Sagittarius	Capricorn	Taurus	Aquarius	Cancer	Gemini
6			Sagittarius	Aquarius	Sagittarius	Capricorn	Taurus	Aquarius	Cancer	Gemini
7			Sagittarius	Pisces	Sagittarius	Capricorn	Taurus	Aquarius	Cancer	Gemini
8	9:13 A.M.	Aquarius	Sagittarius	Pisces	Sagittarius	Capricorn	Taurus	Aquarius	Cancer	Gemini
9			Sagittarius	Pisces	Sagittarius	Capricorn	Taurus	Aquarius	Cancer	Gemini
10	8:38 P.M.	Pisces	Capricorn	Pisces	Sagittarius	Capricorn	Taurus	Aquarius	Cancer	Gemini
11			Capricorn	Pisces	Capricorn	Capricorn	Taurus	Aquarius	Cancer	Gemini
12			Capricorn	Pisces	Capricorn	Capricorn	Taurus	Aquarius	Cancer	Gemini
13	9:35 A.M.	Aries	Capricorn	Pisces	Capricorn	Capricorn	Taurus	Aquarius	Cancer	Gemini
14			Capricorn	Pisces	Capricorn	Capricorn	Taurus	Aquarius	Cancer	Gemini
15	8:45 P.M.	Taurus	Capricorn	Pisces	Capricorn	Capricorn	Taurus	Aquarius	Cancer	Gemini
16			Capricorn	Pisces	Capricorn	Capricorn	Taurus	Aquarius	Cancer	Gemini
17			Capricorn	Pisces	Capricorn	Capricorn	Taurus	Aquarius	Cancer	Gemini
18	4:05 A.M.	Gemini	Capricorn	Pisces	Capricorn	Capricorn	Taurus	Aquarius	Cancer	Gemini
19			Capricorn	Pisces	Capricorn	Capricorn	Taurus	Aquarius	Cancer	Gemini
20	7:13 A.M.	Cancer	Capricorn	Pisces	Capricorn	Capricorn	Taurus	Aquarius	Cancer	Gemini
December										
22	5:20 P.M.	Scorpio	Sagittarius	Sagittarius	Cancer	Capricorn	Gemini	Aquarius	Cancer	Cancer
23			Sagittarius	Sagittarius	Cancer	Capricorn	Gemini	Aquarius	Cancer	Cancer
24	8:27 P.M.	Sagittarius	Sagittarius	Sagittarius	Cancer	Capricorn	Gemini	Aquarius	Cancer	Cancer
25			Sagittarius	Sagittarius	Cancer	Capricorn	Gemini	Aquarius	Cancer	Gemini
26			Sagittarius	Sagittarius	Cancer	Capricorn	Gemini	Aquarius	Cancer	Gemini
27	0:36 A.M.	Capricorn	Sagittarius	Sagittarius	Cancer	Capricorn	Gemini	Aquarius	Cancer	Gemini
28			Sagittarius	Sagittarius	Cancer	Capricorn	Gemini	Aquarius	Cancer	Gemini
29	7:00 A.M.	Aquarius	Sagittarius	Sagittarius	Cancer	Capricorn	Gemini	Aquarius	Cancer	Gemini
30			Sagittarius	Sagittarius	Cancer	Capricorn	Gemini	Aquarius	Cancer	Gemini
31	4:38 P.M.	Pisces	Sagittarius	Sagittarius	Cancer	Capricorn	Gemini	Aquarius	Cancer	Gemini

1914

January	MOON FROM	IN	MERCURY	VENUS	MARS	JUPITER	SATURN	URANUS	NEPTUNE	PLUTO
1		Pisces	Sagittarius	Capricorn	Cancer	Capricorn	Gemini	Aquarius	Cancer	Gemini
2			Sagittarius	Capricorn	Cancer	Capricorn	Gemini	Aquarius	Cancer	Gemini
3	4:57 A.M.	Aries	Sagittarius	Capricorn	Cancer	Capricorn	Gemini	Aquarius	Cancer	Gemini
4			Capricorn	Capricorn	Cancer	Capricorn	Gemini	Aquarius	Cancer	Gemini
5	5:42 P.M.	Taurus	Capricorn	Capricorn	Cancer	Capricorn	Gemini	Aquarius	Cancer	Gemini
6			Capricorn	Capricorn	Cancer	Capricorn	Gemini	Aquarius	Cancer	Gemini
7			Capricorn	Capricorn	Cancer	Capricorn	Gemini	Aquarius	Cancer	Gemini
8	4:11 A.M.	Gemini	Capricorn	Capricorn	Cancer	Capricorn	Gemini	Aquarius	Cancer	Gemini
9			Capricorn	Capricorn	Cancer	Capricorn	Gemini	Aquarius	Cancer	Gemini
10	11:13 A.M.	Cancer	Capricorn	Capricorn	Cancer	Capricorn	Gemini	Aquarius	Cancer	Gemini
11			Capricorn	Capricorn	Cancer	Capricorn	Gemini	Aquarius	Cancer	Gemini
12	4:12 P.M.	Leo	Capricorn	Capricorn	Cancer	Capricorn	Gemini	Aquarius	Cancer	Gemini
13			Capricorn	Capricorn	Cancer	Capricorn	Gemini	Aquarius	Cancer	Gemini
14	5:39 P.M.	Virgo	Capricorn	Capricorn	Cancer	Capricorn	Gemini	Aquarius	Cancer	Gemini
15			Capricorn	Capricorn	Cancer	Capricorn	Gemini	Aquarius	Cancer	Gemini
16	7:52 P.M.	Libra	Capricorn	Capricorn	Cancer	Capricorn	Gemini	Aquarius	Cancer	Gemini
17			Capricorn	Capricorn	Cancer	Capricorn	Gemini	Aquarius	Cancer	Gemini
18	10:45 P.M.	Scorpio	Capricorn	Capricorn	Cancer	Capricorn	Gemini	Aquarius	Cancer	Gemini
19			Capricorn	Capricorn	Cancer	Capricorn	Gemini	Aquarius	Cancer	Gemini
20			Capricorn	Capricorn	Cancer	Capricorn	Gemini	Aquarius	Cancer	Gemini
December										
23		Pisces	Sagittarius	Scorpio	Capricorn	Aquarius	Gemini	Aquarius	Cancer	Cancer
24	0:03 A.M.	Aries	Sagittarius	Scorpio	Capricorn	Aquarius	Gemini	Aquarius	Cancer	Cancer
25			Sagittarius	Scorpio	Capricorn	Aquarius	Gemini	Aquarius	Cancer	Cancer
26	12:18 P.M.	Taurus	Sagittarius	Scorpio	Capricorn	Aquarius	Gemini	Aquarius	Cancer	Cancer
27			Sagittarius	Scorpio	Capricorn	Aquarius	Gemini	Aquarius	Cancer	Cancer
28			Capricorn	Scorpio	Capricorn	Aquarius	Gemini	Aquarius	Cancer	Cancer
29	0:52 A.M.	Gemini	Capricorn	Scorpio	Capricorn	Aquarius	Gemini	Aquarius	Cancer	Cancer
30			Capricorn	Scorpio	Capricorn	Aquarius	Gemini	Aquarius	Cancer	Cancer
31	12:01 P.M.	Cancer	Capricorn	Sagittarius	Capricorn	Aquarius	Gemini	Aquarius	Cancer	Cancer

CAPRICORN PLANETARY TABLES

1915

	MOON FROM	IN	MERCURY	VENUS	MARS	JUPITER	SATURN	URANUS	NEPTUNE	PLUTO
January 1	Cancer		Capricorn	Sagittarius	Capricorn	Aquarius	Gemini	Aquarius	Cancer	Cancer
2	9:12 P.M.	Leo	Capricorn	Sagittarius	Capricorn	Aquarius	Gemini	Aquarius	Cancer	Cancer
3			Capricorn	Sagittarius	Capricorn	Aquarius	Gemini	Aquarius	Cancer	Cancer
4			Capricorn	Sagittarius	Capricorn	Aquarius	Gemini	Aquarius	Cancer	Cancer
5	4:28 A.M.	Virgo	Capricorn	Sagittarius	Capricorn	Aquarius	Gemini	Aquarius	Cancer	Cancer
6			Capricorn	Sagittarius	Capricorn	Aquarius	Gemini	Aquarius	Cancer	Cancer
7	9:52 A.M.	Libra	Capricorn	Sagittarius	Capricorn	Aquarius	Gemini	Aquarius	Cancer	Cancer
8			Capricorn	Sagittarius	Capricorn	Aquarius	Gemini	Aquarius	Cancer	Cancer
9	1:24 P.M.	Scorpio	Capricorn	Sagittarius	Capricorn	Aquarius	Gemini	Aquarius	Cancer	Cancer
10			Capricorn	Sagittarius	Capricorn	Aquarius	Gemini	Aquarius	Cancer	Cancer
11	3:25 P.M.	Sagittarius	Capricorn	Sagittarius	Capricorn	Aquarius	Gemini	Aquarius	Cancer	Cancer
12			Capricorn	Sagittarius	Capricorn	Aquarius	Gemini	Aquarius	Cancer	Cancer
13	4:52 P.M.	Capricorn	Capricorn	Sagittarius	Capricorn	Aquarius	Gemini	Aquarius	Cancer	Cancer
14			Capricorn	Sagittarius	Capricorn	Aquarius	Gemini	Aquarius	Cancer	Cancer
15	7:17 P.M.	Aquarius	Aquarius	Sagittarius	Capricorn	Aquarius	Gemini	Aquarius	Cancer	Cancer
16			Aquarius	Sagittarius	Capricorn	Aquarius	Gemini	Aquarius	Cancer	Cancer
17			Aquarius	Sagittarius	Capricorn	Aquarius	Gemini	Aquarius	Cancer	Cancer
18	0:16 A.M.	Pisces	Aquarius	Sagittarius	Capricorn	Aquarius	Gemini	Aquarius	Cancer	Cancer
19			Aquarius	Sagittarius	Capricorn	Aquarius	Gemini	Aquarius	Cancer	Cancer
20	8:43 A.M.	Aries	Aquarius	Sagittarius	Capricorn	Aquarius	Gemini	Aquarius	Cancer	Cancer
December 23	11:23 P.M.	Leo	Capricorn	Capricorn	Leo	Pisces	Cancer	Aquarius	Leo	Cancer
24			Capricorn	Capricorn	Leo	Pisces	Cancer	Aquarius	Leo	Cancer
25			Capricorn	Capricorn	Leo	Pisces	Cancer	Aquarius	Leo	Cancer
26	10:50 A.M.	Virgo	Capricorn	Capricorn	Leo	Pisces	Cancer	Aquarius	Leo	Cancer
27			Capricorn	Aquarius	Leo	Pisces	Cancer	Aquarius	Leo	Cancer
28	7:42 P.M.	Libra	Capricorn	Aquarius	Leo	Pisces	Cancer	Aquarius	Leo	Cancer
29			Capricorn	Aquarius	Leo	Pisces	Cancer	Aquarius	Leo	Cancer
30			Capricorn	Aquarius	Leo	Pisces	Cancer	Aquarius	Leo	Cancer
31	0:54 A.M.	Scorpio	Capricorn	Aquarius	Leo	Pisces	Cancer	Aquarius	Leo	Cancer

1916

	MOON									
January	FROM	IN	MERCURY	VENUS	MARS	JUPITER	SATURN	URANUS	NEPTUNE	PLUTO
1	Scorpio		Capricorn	Aquarius	Leo	Pisces	Cancer	Aquarius	Leo	Cancer
2	2:43 A.M.	Sagittarius	Capricorn	Aquarius	Leo	Pisces	Cancer	Aquarius	Leo	Cancer
3			Capricorn	Aquarius	Leo	Pisces	Cancer	Aquarius	Leo	Cancer
4	2:26 A.M.	Capricorn	Capricorn	Aquarius	Leo	Pisces	Cancer	Aquarius	Leo	Cancer
5			Capricorn	Aquarius	Leo	Pisces	Cancer	Aquarius	Leo	Cancer
6	1:59 A.M.	Aquarius	Capricorn	Aquarius	Leo	Pisces	Cancer	Aquarius	Leo	Cancer
7			Capricorn	Aquarius	Leo	Pisces	Cancer	Aquarius	Leo	Cancer
8	3:23 A.M.	Pisces	Aquarius	Aquarius	Leo	Pisces	Cancer	Aquarius	Leo	Cancer
9			Aquarius	Aquarius	Leo	Pisces	Cancer	Aquarius	Leo	Cancer
10	8:08 A.M.	Aries	Aquarius	Aquarius	Leo	Pisces	Cancer	Aquarius	Leo	Cancer
11			Aquarius	Aquarius	Leo	Pisces	Cancer	Aquarius	Leo	Cancer
12	4:44 P.M.	Taurus	Aquarius	Aquarius	Leo	Pisces	Cancer	Aquarius	Leo	Cancer
13			Aquarius	Aquarius	Leo	Pisces	Cancer	Aquarius	Leo	Cancer
14			Aquarius	Aquarius	Leo	Pisces	Cancer	Aquarius	Leo	Cancer
15	4:19 A.M.	Gemini	Aquarius	Aquarius	Leo	Pisces	Cancer	Aquarius	Leo	Cancer
16			Aquarius	Aquarius	Leo	Pisces	Cancer	Aquarius	Leo	Cancer
17	5:07 P.M.	Cancer	Aquarius	Aquarius	Leo	Pisces	Cancer	Aquarius	Leo	Cancer
18			Aquarius	Aquarius	Leo	Pisces	Cancer	Aquarius	Leo	Cancer
19			Aquarius	Aquarius	Leo	Pisces	Cancer	Aquarius	Leo	Cancer
20	5:33 A.M.	Leo	Aquarius	Pisces	Leo	Pisces	Cancer	Aquarius	Leo	Cancer
December										
22	9:57 A.M.	Sagittarius	Capricorn	Sagittarius	Capricorn	Aries	Cancer	Aquarius	Leo	Cancer
23			Capricorn	Sagittarius	Capricorn	Aries	Cancer	Aquarius	Leo	Cancer
24	11:07 A.M.	Capricorn	Capricorn	Sagittarius	Capricorn	Aries	Cancer	Aquarius	Leo	Cancer
25			Capricorn	Sagittarius	Capricorn	Aries	Cancer	Aquarius	Leo	Cancer
26	11:05 A.M.	Aquarius	Capricorn	Sagittarius	Capricorn	Aries	Cancer	Aquarius	Leo	Cancer
27			Capricorn	Sagittarius	Capricorn	Aries	Cancer	Aquarius	Leo	Cancer
28	11:43 A.M.	Pisces	Capricorn	Sagittarius	Capricorn	Aries	Cancer	Aquarius	Leo	Cancer
29			Capricorn	Sagittarius	Capricorn	Aries	Cancer	Aquarius	Leo	Cancer
30	2:27 P.M.	Aries	Capricorn	Sagittarius	Capricorn	Aries	Cancer	Aquarius	Leo	Cancer
31			Capricorn	Sagittarius	Capricorn	Aries	Cancer	Aquarius	Leo	Cancer

CAPRICORN PLANETARY TABLES

1917

	MOON		MERCURY	VENUS	MARS	JUPITER	SATURN	URANUS	NEPTUNE	PLUTO
January	FROM	IN								
1	8:05 P.M.	Taurus	Capricorn	Sagittarius	Capricorn	Aries	Cancer	Aquarius	Leo	Cancer
2			Aquarius	Sagittarius	Capricorn	Aries	Cancer	Aquarius	Leo	Cancer
3			Aquarius	Sagittarius	Capricorn	Aries	Cancer	Aquarius	Leo	Cancer
4	4:40 A.M.	Gemini	Aquarius	Sagittarius	Capricorn	Aries	Cancer	Aquarius	Leo	Cancer
5			Aquarius	Sagittarius	Capricorn	Aries	Cancer	Aquarius	Leo	Cancer
6	3:36 P.M.	Cancer	Aquarius	Sagittarius	Capricorn	Aries	Cancer	Aquarius	Leo	Cancer
7			Aquarius	Sagittarius	Capricorn	Aries	Cancer	Aquarius	Leo	Cancer
8			Aquarius	Sagittarius	Capricorn	Aries	Cancer	Aquarius	Leo	Cancer
9	4:03 A.M.	Leo	Aquarius	Sagittarius	Aquarius	Aries	Cancer	Aquarius	Leo	Cancer
10			Aquarius	Sagittarius	Aquarius	Aries	Cancer	Aquarius	Leo	Cancer
11	5:02 P.M.	Virgo	Aquarius	Sagittarius	Aquarius	Aries	Cancer	Aquarius	Leo	Cancer
12			Aquarius	Sagittarius	Aquarius	Aries	Cancer	Aquarius	Leo	Cancer
13			Aquarius	Sagittarius	Aquarius	Aries	Cancer	Aquarius	Leo	Cancer
14	5:04 A.M.	Libra	Aquarius	Sagittarius	Aquarius	Aries	Cancer	Aquarius	Leo	Cancer
15			Aquarius	Capricorn	Aquarius	Aries	Cancer	Aquarius	Leo	Cancer
16	2:31 P.M.	Scorpio	Aquarius	Capricorn	Aquarius	Aries	Cancer	Aquarius	Leo	Cancer
17			Aquarius	Capricorn	Aquarius	Aries	Cancer	Aquarius	Leo	Cancer
18	8:17 P.M.	Sagittarius	Capricorn	Capricorn	Aquarius	Aries	Cancer	Aquarius	Leo	Cancer
19			Capricorn	Capricorn	Aquarius	Aries	Cancer	Aquarius	Leo	Cancer
20	10:28 P.M.	Capricorn	Capricorn	Capricorn	Aquarius	Aries	Cancer	Aquarius	Leo	Cancer
December										
22	Aries		Capricorn	Aquarius	Virgo	Gemini	Leo	Aquarius	Leo	Cancer
23	6:26 A.M.	Taurus	Capricorn	Aquarius	Virgo	Gemini	Leo	Aquarius	Leo	Cancer
24			Capricorn	Aquarius	Virgo	Gemini	Leo	Aquarius	Leo	Cancer
25	11:04 A.M.	Gemini	Capricorn	Aquarius	Virgo	Gemini	Leo	Aquarius	Leo	Cancer
26			Capricorn	Aquarius	Virgo	Gemini	Leo	Aquarius	Leo	Cancer
27	5:30 P.M.	Cancer	Capricorn	Aquarius	Virgo	Gemini	Leo	Aquarius	Leo	Cancer
28			Capricorn	Aquarius	Virgo	Gemini	Leo	Aquarius	Leo	Cancer
29			Capricorn	Aquarius	Virgo	Gemini	Leo	Aquarius	Leo	Cancer
30	2:16 A.M.	Leo	Capricorn	Aquarius	Virgo	Gemini	Leo	Aquarius	Leo	Cancer
31			Capricorn	Aquarius	Virgo	Gemini	Leo	Aquarius	Leo	Cancer

1918

January	MOON FROM	IN	MERCURY	VENUS	MARS	JUPITER	SATURN	URANUS	NEPTUNE	PLUTO
1	1:24 P.M.	Virgo	Capricorn	Aquarius	Virgo	Gemini	Leo	Aquarius	Leo	Cancer
2			Capricorn	Aquarius	Virgo	Gemini	Leo	Aquarius	Leo	Cancer
3			Capricorn	Aquarius	Virgo	Gemini	Leo	Aquarius	Leo	Cancer
4	1:56 A.M.	Libra	Capricorn	Aquarius	Virgo	Gemini	Leo	Aquarius	Leo	Cancer
5			Capricorn	Aquarius	Virgo	Gemini	Leo	Aquarius	Leo	Cancer
6	1:49 P.M.	Scorpio	Capricorn	Aquarius	Virgo	Gemini	Leo	Aquarius	Leo	Cancer
7			Capricorn	Aquarius	Virgo	Gemini	Leo	Aquarius	Leo	Cancer
8	10:57 P.M.	Sagittarius	Capricorn	Aquarius	Virgo	Gemini	Leo	Aquarius	Leo	Cancer
9			Capricorn	Aquarius	Virgo	Gemini	Leo	Aquarius	Leo	Cancer
10			Capricorn	Aquarius	Virgo	Gemini	Leo	Aquarius	Leo	Cancer
11	4:26 A.M.	Capricorn	Capricorn	Aquarius	Libra	Gemini	Leo	Aquarius	Leo	Cancer
12			Capricorn	Aquarius	Libra	Gemini	Leo	Aquarius	Leo	Cancer
13	6:56 A.M.	Aquarius	Capricorn	Aquarius	Libra	Gemini	Leo	Aquarius	Leo	Cancer
14			Capricorn	Aquarius	Libra	Gemini	Leo	Aquarius	Leo	Cancer
15	7:54 A.M.	Pisces	Capricorn	Aquarius	Libra	Gemini	Leo	Aquarius	Leo	Cancer
16			Capricorn	Aquarius	Libra	Gemini	Leo	Aquarius	Leo	Cancer
17	9:04 A.M.	Aries	Capricorn	Aquarius	Libra	Gemini	Leo	Aquarius	Leo	Cancer
18			Capricorn	Aquarius	Libra	Gemini	Leo	Aquarius	Leo	Cancer
19	11:50 A.M.	Taurus	Capricorn	Aquarius	Libra	Gemini	Leo	Aquarius	Leo	Cancer
20			Capricorn	Aquarius	Libra	Gemini	Leo	Aquarius	Leo	Cancer
December										
23		Virgo	Sagittarius	Capricorn	Aquarius	Cancer	Leo	Aquarius	Leo	Cancer
24	8:10 P.M.	Libra	Sagittarius	Capricorn	Aquarius	Cancer	Leo	Aquarius	Leo	Cancer
25			Sagittarius	Capricorn	Aquarius	Cancer	Leo	Aquarius	Leo	Cancer
26			Sagittarius	Capricorn	Aquarius	Cancer	Leo	Aquarius	Leo	Cancer
27	8:49 P.M.	Scorpio	Sagittarius	Capricorn	Aquarius	Cancer	Leo	Aquarius	Leo	Cancer
28			Sagittarius	Capricorn	Aquarius	Cancer	Leo	Aquarius	Leo	Cancer
29	9:03 P.M.	Sagittarius	Sagittarius	Capricorn	Aquarius	Cancer	Leo	Aquarius	Leo	Cancer
30			Sagittarius	Capricorn	Aquarius	Cancer	Leo	Aquarius	Leo	Cancer
31			Sagittarius	Capricorn	Aquarius	Cancer	Leo	Aquarius	Leo	Cancer

CAPRICORN PLANETARY TABLES

1919

January	MOON FROM	IN	MERCURY	VENUS	MARS	JUPITER	SATURN	URANUS	NEPTUNE	PLUTO
1	7:02 A.M.	Capricorn	Sagittarius	Capricorn	Aquarius	Cancer	Leo	Aquarius	Leo	Cancer
2			Sagittarius	Capricorn	Aquarius	Cancer	Leo	Aquarius	Leo	Cancer
3	2:15 P.M.	Aquarius	Sagittarius	Capricorn	Aquarius	Cancer	Leo	Aquarius	Leo	Cancer
4			Sagittarius	Capricorn	Aquarius	Cancer	Leo	Aquarius	Leo	Cancer
5	7:19 P.M.	Pisces	Sagittarius	Capricorn	Aquarius	Cancer	Leo	Aquarius	Leo	Cancer
6			Sagittarius	Capricorn	Aquarius	Cancer	Leo	Aquarius	Leo	Cancer
7	9:41 P.M.	Aries	Sagittarius	Capricorn	Aquarius	Cancer	Leo	Aquarius	Leo	Cancer
8			Sagittarius	Capricorn	Aquarius	Cancer	Leo	Aquarius	Leo	Cancer
9			Sagittarius	Capricorn	Aquarius	Cancer	Leo	Aquarius	Leo	Cancer
10	2:02 A.M.	Taurus	Sagittarius	Aquarius	Aquarius	Cancer	Leo	Aquarius	Leo	Cancer
11			Sagittarius	Aquarius	Aquarius	Cancer	Leo	Aquarius	Leo	Cancer
12	4:49 A.M.	Gemini	Sagittarius	Aquarius	Aquarius	Cancer	Leo	Aquarius	Leo	Cancer
13			Sagittarius	Aquarius	Aquarius	Cancer	Leo	Aquarius	Leo	Cancer
14	7:56 A.M.	Cancer	Capricorn	Aquarius	Aquarius	Cancer	Leo	Aquarius	Leo	Cancer
15			Capricorn	Aquarius	Aquarius	Cancer	Leo	Aquarius	Leo	Cancer
16	12:18 P.M.	Leo	Capricorn	Aquarius	Aquarius	Cancer	Leo	Aquarius	Leo	Cancer
17			Capricorn	Aquarius	Aquarius	Cancer	Leo	Aquarius	Leo	Cancer
18	6:57 P.M.	Virgo	Capricorn	Aquarius	Aquarius	Cancer	Leo	Aquarius	Leo	Cancer
19			Capricorn	Aquarius	Aquarius	Cancer	Leo	Aquarius	Leo	Cancer
20			Capricorn	Aquarius	Aquarius	Cancer	Leo	Aquarius	Leo	Cancer
December										
23	Capricorn		Sagittarius	Scorpio	Libra	Leo	Virgo	Aquarius	Leo	Cancer
24	6:20 P.M.	Aquarius	Sagittarius	Scorpio	Libra	Leo	Virgo	Aquarius	Leo	Cancer
25			Sagittarius	Scorpio	Libra	Leo	Virgo	Aquarius	Leo	Cancer
26			Sagittarius	Scorpio	Libra	Leo	Virgo	Aquarius	Leo	Cancer
27	3:55 A.M.	Pisces	Sagittarius	Scorpio	Libra	Leo	Virgo	Aquarius	Leo	Cancer
28			Sagittarius	Scorpio	Libra	Leo	Virgo	Aquarius	Leo	Cancer
29	11:05 A.M.	Aries	Sagittarius	Scorpio	Libra	Leo	Virgo	Aquarius	Leo	Cancer
30			Sagittarius	Scorpio	Libra	Leo	Virgo	Aquarius	Leo	Cancer
31	2:02 P.M.	Taurus	Sagittarius	Scorpio	Libra	Leo	Virgo	Aquarius	Leo	Cancer

1920

January	MOON FROM IN	MERCURY	VENUS	MARS	JUPITER	SATURN	URANUS	NEPTUNE	PLUTO
1	Taurus	Sagittarius	Scorpio	Libra	Leo	Virgo	Aquarius	Leo	Cancer
2	5:13 P.M. Gemini	Sagittarius	Scorpio	Libra	Leo	Virgo	Aquarius	Leo	Cancer
3		Sagittarius	Scorpio	Libra	Leo	Virgo	Aquarius	Leo	Cancer
4	5:19 P.M. Cancer	Sagittarius	Sagittarius	Libra	Leo	Virgo	Aquarius	Leo	Cancer
5		Sagittarius	Sagittarius	Libra	Leo	Virgo	Aquarius	Leo	Cancer
6	5:31 P.M. Leo	Sagittarius	Sagittarius	Libra	Leo	Virgo	Aquarius	Leo	Cancer
7		Sagittarius	Sagittarius	Libra	Leo	Virgo	Aquarius	Leo	Cancer
8	7:46 P.M. Virgo	Capricorn	Sagittarius	Libra	Leo	Virgo	Aquarius	Leo	Cancer
9		Capricorn	Sagittarius	Libra	Leo	Virgo	Aquarius	Leo	Cancer
10		Capricorn	Sagittarius	Libra	Leo	Virgo	Aquarius	Leo	Cancer
11	1:50 A.M. Libra	Capricorn	Sagittarius	Libra	Leo	Virgo	Aquarius	Leo	Cancer
12		Capricorn	Sagittarius	Libra	Leo	Virgo	Aquarius	Leo	Cancer
13	11:58 A.M. Scorpio	Capricorn	Sagittarius	Libra	Leo	Virgo	Aquarius	Leo	Cancer
14		Capricorn	Sagittarius	Libra	Leo	Virgo	Aquarius	Leo	Cancer
15		Capricorn	Sagittarius	Libra	Leo	Virgo	Aquarius	Leo	Cancer
16	0:44 A.M. Sagittarius	Capricorn	Sagittarius	Libra	Leo	Virgo	Aquarius	Leo	Cancer
17		Capricorn	Sagittarius	Libra	Leo	Virgo	Aquarius	Leo	Cancer
18	1:33 P.M. Capricorn	Capricorn	Sagittarius	Libra	Leo	Virgo	Aquarius	Leo	Cancer
19		Capricorn	Sagittarius	Libra	Leo	Virgo	Aquarius	Leo	Cancer
20		Capricorn	Sagittarius	Libra	Leo	Virgo	Aquarius	Leo	Cancer
December									
22	Taurus	Sagittarius	Aquarius	Aquarius	Virgo	Virgo	Pisces	Leo	Cancer
23	2:14 A.M. Gemini	Sagittarius	Aquarius	Aquarius	Virgo	Virgo	Pisces	Leo	Cancer
24		Sagittarius	Aquarius	Aquarius	Virgo	Virgo	Pisces	Leo	Cancer
25	2:13 A.M. Cancer	Sagittarius	Aquarius	Aquarius	Virgo	Virgo	Pisces	Leo	Cancer
26		Sagittarius	Aquarius	Aquarius	Virgo	Virgo	Pisces	Leo	Cancer
27	1:17 A.M. Leo	Sagittarius	Aquarius	Aquarius	Virgo	Virgo	Pisces	Leo	Cancer
28		Sagittarius	Aquarius	Aquarius	Virgo	Virgo	Pisces	Leo	Cancer
29	1:39 A.M. Virgo	Sagittarius	Aquarius	Aquarius	Virgo	Virgo	Pisces	Leo	Cancer
30		Sagittarius	Aquarius	Aquarius	Virgo	Virgo	Pisces	Leo	Cancer
31	5:07 A.M. Libra	Capricorn	Aquarius	Aquarius	Virgo	Virgo	Pisces	Leo	Cancer

CAPRICORN PLANETARY TABLES

1921

Day	MOON FROM	IN	MERCURY	VENUS	MARS	JUPITER	SATURN	URANUS	NEPTUNE	PLUTO
January										
1	Libra		Capricorn	Aquarius	Aquarius	Virgo	Virgo	Pisces	Leo	Cancer
2	12:28 P.M.	Scorpio	Capricorn	Aquarius	Aquarius	Virgo	Virgo	Pisces	Leo	Cancer
3			Capricorn	Aquarius	Aquarius	Virgo	Virgo	Pisces	Leo	Cancer
4	7:24 P.M.	Sagittarius	Capricorn	Aquarius	Aquarius	Virgo	Virgo	Pisces	Leo	Cancer
5			Capricorn	Aquarius	Pisces	Virgo	Virgo	Pisces	Leo	Cancer
6			Capricorn	Aquarius	Pisces	Virgo	Virgo	Pisces	Leo	Cancer
7	11:10 A.M.	Capricorn	Capricorn	Pisces	Pisces	Virgo	Virgo	Pisces	Leo	Cancer
8			Capricorn	Pisces	Pisces	Virgo	Virgo	Pisces	Leo	Cancer
9	11:50 P.M.	Aquarius	Capricorn	Pisces	Pisces	Virgo	Virgo	Pisces	Leo	Cancer
10			Capricorn	Pisces	Pisces	Virgo	Virgo	Pisces	Leo	Cancer
11			Capricorn	Pisces	Pisces	Virgo	Virgo	Pisces	Leo	Cancer
12	12:10 P.M.	Pisces	Capricorn	Pisces	Pisces	Virgo	Virgo	Pisces	Leo	Cancer
13			Capricorn	Pisces	Pisces	Virgo	Virgo	Pisces	Leo	Cancer
14	11:14 P.M.	Aries	Capricorn	Pisces	Pisces	Virgo	Virgo	Pisces	Leo	Cancer
15			Capricorn	Pisces	Pisces	Virgo	Virgo	Pisces	Leo	Cancer
16			Capricorn	Pisces	Pisces	Virgo	Virgo	Pisces	Leo	Cancer
17	7:40 A.M.	Taurus	Capricorn	Pisces	Pisces	Virgo	Virgo	Pisces	Leo	Cancer
18			Capricorn	Pisces	Pisces	Virgo	Virgo	Pisces	Leo	Cancer
19	12:22 P.M.	Gemini	Aquarius	Pisces	Pisces	Virgo	Virgo	Pisces	Leo	Cancer
20			Aquarius	Pisces	Pisces	Virgo	Virgo	Pisces	Leo	Cancer
December										
22	Libra		Sagittarius	Sagittarius	Libra	Libra	Libra	Pisces	Leo	Cancer
23	8:33 P.M.	Scorpio	Sagittarius	Sagittarius	Libra	Libra	Libra	Pisces	Leo	Cancer
24			Capricorn	Sagittarius	Libra	Libra	Libra	Pisces	Leo	Cancer
25			Capricorn	Sagittarius	Libra	Libra	Libra	Pisces	Leo	Cancer
26	3:02 A.M.	Sagittarius	Capricorn	Sagittarius	Scorpio	Libra	Libra	Pisces	Leo	Cancer
27			Capricorn	Sagittarius	Scorpio	Libra	Libra	Pisces	Leo	Cancer
28	11:17 A.M.	Capricorn	Capricorn	Sagittarius	Scorpio	Libra	Libra	Pisces	Leo	Cancer
29			Capricorn	Sagittarius	Scorpio	Libra	Libra	Pisces	Leo	Cancer
30	9:32 P.M.	Aquarius	Capricorn	Sagittarius	Scorpio	Libra	Libra	Pisces	Leo	Cancer
31			Capricorn	Sagittarius	Scorpio	Libra	Libra	Pisces	Leo	Cancer

1922

January	MOON FROM	IN	MERCURY	VENUS	MARS	JUPITER	SATURN	URANUS	NEPTUNE	PLUTO
1	Aquarius		Capricorn	Capricorn	Scorpio	Libra	Libra	Pisces	Leo	Cancer
2	9:45 A.M.	Pisces	Capricorn	Capricorn	Scorpio	Libra	Libra	Pisces	Leo	Cancer
3			Capricorn	Capricorn	Scorpio	Libra	Libra	Pisces	Leo	Cancer
4	10:42 P.M.	Aries	Capricorn	Capricorn	Scorpio	Libra	Libra	Pisces	Leo	Cancer
5			Capricorn	Capricorn	Scorpio	Libra	Libra	Pisces	Leo	Cancer
6			Capricorn	Capricorn	Scorpio	Libra	Libra	Pisces	Leo	Cancer
7	9:58 A.M.	Taurus	Capricorn	Capricorn	Scorpio	Libra	Libra	Pisces	Leo	Cancer
8			Capricorn	Capricorn	Scorpio	Libra	Libra	Pisces	Leo	Cancer
9	5:26 P.M.	Gemini	Capricorn	Capricorn	Scorpio	Libra	Libra	Pisces	Leo	Cancer
10			Capricorn	Capricorn	Scorpio	Libra	Libra	Pisces	Leo	Cancer
11	8:47 P.M.	Cancer	Capricorn	Capricorn	Scorpio	Libra	Libra	Pisces	Leo	Cancer
12			Aquarius	Capricorn	Scorpio	Libra	Libra	Pisces	Leo	Cancer
13	9:21 P.M.	Leo	Aquarius	Capricorn	Scorpio	Libra	Libra	Pisces	Leo	Cancer
14			Aquarius	Capricorn	Scorpio	Libra	Libra	Pisces	Leo	Cancer
15	9:13 P.M.	Virgo	Aquarius	Capricorn	Scorpio	Libra	Libra	Pisces	Leo	Cancer
16			Aquarius	Capricorn	Scorpio	Libra	Libra	Pisces	Leo	Cancer
17	10:23 P.M.	Libra	Aquarius	Capricorn	Scorpio	Libra	Libra	Pisces	Leo	Cancer
18			Aquarius	Capricorn	Scorpio	Libra	Libra	Pisces	Leo	Cancer
19			Aquarius	Capricorn	Scorpio	Libra	Libra	Pisces	Leo	Cancer
20	2:03 A.M.	Scorpio	Aquarius	Capricorn	Scorpio	Libra	Libra	Pisces	Leo	Cancer
December										
23	5:14 A.M.	Pisces	Capricorn	Scorpio	Pisces	Scorpio	Libra	Pisces	Leo	Cancer
24	5:23 P.M.	Aries	Capricorn	Scorpio	Pisces	Scorpio	Libra	Pisces	Leo	Cancer
25			Capricorn	Scorpio	Pisces	Scorpio	Libra	Pisces	Leo	Cancer
26			Capricorn	Scorpio	Pisces	Scorpio	Libra	Pisces	Leo	Cancer
27			Capricorn	Scorpio	Pisces	Scorpio	Libra	Pisces	Leo	Cancer
28	6:13 A.M.	Taurus	Capricorn	Scorpio	Pisces	Scorpio	Libra	Pisces	Leo	Cancer
29			Capricorn	Scorpio	Pisces	Scorpio	Libra	Pisces	Leo	Cancer
30	5:02 P.M.	Gemini	Capricorn	Scorpio	Pisces	Scorpio	Libra	Pisces	Leo	Cancer
31			Capricorn	Scorpio	Pisces	Scorpio	Libra	Pisces	Leo	Cancer

CAPRICORN PLANETARY TABLES

1923

Day	MOON (FROM / IN)	MERCURY	VENUS	MARS	JUPITER	SATURN	URANUS	NEPTUNE	PLUTO
January									
1	Gemini	Capricorn	Scorpio	Pisces	Scorpio	Libra	Pisces	Leo	Cancer
2	0:39 A.M. Cancer	Capricorn	Sagittarius	Pisces	Scorpio	Libra	Pisces	Leo	Cancer
3		Capricorn	Sagittarius	Pisces	Scorpio	Libra	Pisces	Leo	Cancer
4	5:34 A.M. Leo	Capricorn	Sagittarius	Pisces	Scorpio	Libra	Pisces	Leo	Cancer
5		Aquarius	Sagittarius	Pisces	Scorpio	Libra	Pisces	Leo	Cancer
6	8:59 A.M. Virgo	Aquarius	Sagittarius	Pisces	Scorpio	Libra	Pisces	Leo	Cancer
7		Aquarius	Sagittarius	Pisces	Scorpio	Libra	Pisces	Leo	Cancer
8	11:59 A.M. Libra	Aquarius	Sagittarius	Pisces	Scorpio	Libra	Pisces	Leo	Cancer
9		Aquarius	Sagittarius	Pisces	Scorpio	Libra	Pisces	Leo	Cancer
10	3:05 P.M. Scorpio	Aquarius	Sagittarius	Pisces	Scorpio	Libra	Pisces	Leo	Cancer
11		Aquarius	Sagittarius	Pisces	Scorpio	Libra	Pisces	Leo	Cancer
12	6:34 P.M. Sagittarius	Aquarius	Sagittarius	Pisces	Scorpio	Libra	Pisces	Leo	Cancer
13		Aquarius	Sagittarius	Pisces	Scorpio	Libra	Pisces	Leo	Cancer
14	10:57 P.M. Capricorn	Aquarius	Sagittarius	Pisces	Scorpio	Libra	Pisces	Leo	Cancer
15		Aquarius	Sagittarius	Pisces	Scorpio	Libra	Pisces	Leo	Cancer
16		Aquarius	Sagittarius	Pisces	Scorpio	Libra	Pisces	Leo	Cancer
17	5:08 A.M. Aquarius	Aquarius	Sagittarius	Pisces	Scorpio	Libra	Pisces	Leo	Cancer
18		Aquarius	Sagittarius	Pisces	Scorpio	Libra	Pisces	Leo	Cancer
19	1:58 P.M. Pisces	Aquarius	Sagittarius	Pisces	Scorpio	Libra	Pisces	Leo	Cancer
20		Aquarius	Sagittarius	Pisces	Scorpio	Libra	Pisces	Leo	Cancer
December									
23	1:39 A.M. Cancer	Capricorn	Capricorn	Scorpio	Sagittarius	Scorpio	Pisces	Leo	Cancer
24		Capricorn	Capricorn	Scorpio	Sagittarius	Scorpio	Pisces	Leo	Cancer
25	11:39 A.M. Leo	Capricorn	Capricorn	Scorpio	Sagittarius	Scorpio	Pisces	Leo	Cancer
26		Capricorn	Aquarius	Scorpio	Sagittarius	Scorpio	Pisces	Leo	Cancer
27	7:51 P.M. Virgo	Capricorn	Aquarius	Scorpio	Sagittarius	Scorpio	Pisces	Leo	Cancer
28		Capricorn	Aquarius	Scorpio	Sagittarius	Scorpio	Pisces	Leo	Cancer
29		Capricorn	Aquarius	Scorpio	Sagittarius	Scorpio	Pisces	Leo	Cancer
30	1:50 A.M. Libra	Capricorn	Aquarius	Scorpio	Sagittarius	Scorpio	Pisces	Leo	Cancer
31		Capricorn	Aquarius	Scorpio	Sagittarius	Scorpio	Pisces	Leo	Cancer

1924

January	MOON FROM	IN	MERCURY	VENUS	MARS	JUPITER	SATURN	URANUS	NEPTUNE	PLUTO
1	5:22 A.M.	Scorpio	Capricorn	Aquarius	Scorpio	Sagittarius	Scorpio	Pisces	Leo	Cancer
2	6:48 A.M.	Sagittarius	Capricorn	Aquarius	Scorpio	Sagittarius	Scorpio	Pisces	Leo	Cancer
3			Capricorn	Aquarius	Scorpio	Sagittarius	Scorpio	Pisces	Leo	Cancer
4	7:22 A.M.	Capricorn	Capricorn	Aquarius	Scorpio	Sagittarius	Scorpio	Pisces	Leo	Cancer
5			Capricorn	Aquarius	Scorpio	Sagittarius	Scorpio	Pisces	Leo	Cancer
6			Capricorn	Aquarius	Scorpio	Sagittarius	Scorpio	Pisces	Leo	Cancer
7	8:55 A.M.	Aquarius	Capricorn	Aquarius	Scorpio	Sagittarius	Scorpio	Pisces	Leo	Cancer
8			Capricorn	Aquarius	Scorpio	Sagittarius	Scorpio	Pisces	Leo	Cancer
9	1:15 P.M.	Pisces	Capricorn	Aquarius	Scorpio	Sagittarius	Scorpio	Pisces	Leo	Cancer
10			Capricorn	Aquarius	Scorpio	Sagittarius	Scorpio	Pisces	Leo	Cancer
11	9:23 P.M.	Aries	Capricorn	Aquarius	Scorpio	Sagittarius	Scorpio	Pisces	Leo	Cancer
12			Capricorn	Aquarius	Scorpio	Sagittarius	Scorpio	Pisces	Leo	Cancer
13			Capricorn	Aquarius	Scorpio	Sagittarius	Scorpio	Pisces	Leo	Cancer
14	8:49 A.M.	Taurus	Capricorn	Aquarius	Scorpio	Sagittarius	Scorpio	Pisces	Leo	Cancer
15			Capricorn	Aquarius	Scorpio	Sagittarius	Scorpio	Pisces	Leo	Cancer
16	9:28 P.M.	Gemini	Capricorn	Aquarius	Scorpio	Sagittarius	Scorpio	Pisces	Leo	Cancer
17			Capricorn	Aquarius	Scorpio	Sagittarius	Scorpio	Pisces	Leo	Cancer
18			Capricorn	Aquarius	Scorpio	Sagittarius	Scorpio	Pisces	Leo	Cancer
19	9:05 A.M.	Cancer	Capricorn	Aquarius	Scorpio	Sagittarius	Scorpio	Pisces	Leo	Cancer
20			Capricorn	Pisces	Sagittarius	Sagittarius	Scorpio	Pisces	Leo	Cancer
December										
22		Scorpio	Capricorn	Sagittarius	Aries	Capricorn	Scorpio	Pisces	Leo	Cancer
23	4:55 P.M.	Sagittarius	Capricorn	Sagittarius	Aries	Capricorn	Scorpio	Pisces	Leo	Cancer
24			Capricorn	Sagittarius	Aries	Capricorn	Scorpio	Pisces	Leo	Cancer
25	4:18 P.M.	Capricorn	Capricorn	Sagittarius	Aries	Capricorn	Scorpio	Pisces	Leo	Cancer
26			Capricorn	Sagittarius	Aries	Capricorn	Scorpio	Pisces	Leo	Cancer
27	3:42 P.M.	Aquarius	Capricorn	Sagittarius	Aries	Capricorn	Scorpio	Pisces	Leo	Cancer
28			Capricorn	Sagittarius	Aries	Capricorn	Scorpio	Pisces	Leo	Cancer
29	5:07 P.M.	Pisces	Capricorn	Sagittarius	Aries	Capricorn	Scorpio	Pisces	Leo	Cancer
30			Capricorn	Sagittarius	Aries	Capricorn	Scorpio	Pisces	Leo	Cancer
31			Capricorn	Sagittarius	Aries	Capricorn	Scorpio	Pisces	Leo	Cancer

CAPRICORN PLANETARY TABLES

1925

	MOON FROM	IN	MERCURY	VENUS	MARS	JUPITER	SATURN	URANUS	NEPTUNE	PLUTO
January										
1	3:01 A.M.	Aries	Sagittarius	Sagittarius	Aries	Capricorn	Scorpio	Pisces	Leo	Cancer
2			Sagittarius	Sagittarius	Aries	Capricorn	Scorpio	Pisces	Leo	Cancer
3	6:31 A.M.	Taurus	Sagittarius	Sagittarius	Aries	Capricorn	Scorpio	Pisces	Leo	Cancer
4			Sagittarius	Sagittarius	Aries	Capricorn	Scorpio	Pisces	Leo	Cancer
5	5:53 P.M.	Gemini	Sagittarius	Sagittarius	Aries	Capricorn	Scorpio	Pisces	Leo	Cancer
6			Sagittarius	Sagittarius	Aries	Capricorn	Scorpio	Pisces	Leo	Cancer
7			Sagittarius	Sagittarius	Aries	Capricorn	Scorpio	Pisces	Leo	Cancer
8	6:33 A.M.	Cancer	Sagittarius	Sagittarius	Aries	Capricorn	Scorpio	Pisces	Leo	Cancer
9			Sagittarius	Sagittarius	Aries	Capricorn	Scorpio	Pisces	Leo	Cancer
10	7:14 P.M.	Leo	Sagittarius	Sagittarius	Aries	Capricorn	Scorpio	Pisces	Leo	Cancer
11			Sagittarius	Sagittarius	Aries	Capricorn	Scorpio	Pisces	Leo	Cancer
12			Sagittarius	Sagittarius	Aries	Capricorn	Scorpio	Pisces	Leo	Cancer
13	6:55 A.M.	Virgo	Sagittarius	Sagittarius	Aries	Capricorn	Scorpio	Pisces	Leo	Cancer
14			Capricorn	Capricorn	Aries	Capricorn	Scorpio	Pisces	Leo	Cancer
15	4:32 P.M.	Libra	Capricorn	Capricorn	Aries	Capricorn	Scorpio	Pisces	Leo	Cancer
16			Capricorn	Capricorn	Aries	Capricorn	Scorpio	Pisces	Leo	Cancer
17	11:10 P.M.	Scorpio	Capricorn	Capricorn	Aries	Capricorn	Scorpio	Pisces	Leo	Cancer
18			Capricorn	Capricorn	Aries	Capricorn	Scorpio	Pisces	Leo	Cancer
19			Capricorn	Capricorn	Aries	Capricorn	Scorpio	Pisces	Leo	Cancer
20	2:33 A.M.	Sagittarius	Capricorn	Capricorn	Aries	Capricorn	Scorpio	Pisces	Leo	Cancer
December										
22	5:58 A.M.	Aries	Sagittarius	Aquarius	Scorpio	Capricorn	Scorpio	Pisces	Leo	Cancer
23			Sagittarius	Aquarius	Scorpio	Capricorn	Scorpio	Pisces	Leo	Cancer
24	11:26 A.M.	Taurus	Sagittarius	Aquarius	Scorpio	Capricorn	Scorpio	Pisces	Leo	Cancer
25			Sagittarius	Aquarius	Scorpio	Capricorn	Scorpio	Pisces	Leo	Cancer
26	7:19 P.M.	Gemini	Sagittarius	Aquarius	Scorpio	Capricorn	Scorpio	Pisces	Leo	Cancer
27			Sagittarius	Aquarius	Scorpio	Capricorn	Scorpio	Pisces	Leo	Cancer
28			Sagittarius	Aquarius	Sagittarius	Capricorn	Scorpio	Pisces	Leo	Cancer
29	5:27 A.M.	Cancer	Sagittarius	Aquarius	Sagittarius	Capricorn	Scorpio	Pisces	Leo	Cancer
30			Sagittarius	Aquarius	Sagittarius	Capricorn	Scorpio	Pisces	Leo	Cancer
31	5:27 P.M.	Leo	Sagittarius	Aquarius	Sagittarius	Capricorn	Scorpio	Pisces	Leo	Cancer

1926

January	MOON FROM	IN	MERCURY	VENUS	MARS	JUPITER	SATURN	URANUS	NEPTUNE	PLUTO
1	Leo		Sagittarius	Aquarius	Sagittarius	Capricorn	Scorpio	Pisces	Leo	Cancer
2			Sagittarius	Aquarius	Sagittarius	Capricorn	Scorpio	Pisces	Leo	Cancer
3	6:26 A.M.	Virgo	Sagittarius	Aquarius	Sagittarius	Capricorn	Scorpio	Pisces	Leo	Cancer
4			Sagittarius	Aquarius	Sagittarius	Capricorn	Scorpio	Pisces	Leo	Cancer
5	6:44 P.M.	Libra	Sagittarius	Aquarius	Sagittarius	Capricorn	Scorpio	Pisces	Leo	Cancer
6			Sagittarius	Aquarius	Sagittarius	Aquarius	Scorpio	Pisces	Leo	Cancer
7			Sagittarius	Aquarius	Sagittarius	Aquarius	Scorpio	Pisces	Leo	Cancer
8	4:18 A.M.	Scorpio	Sagittarius	Aquarius	Sagittarius	Aquarius	Scorpio	Pisces	Leo	Cancer
9			Sagittarius	Aquarius	Sagittarius	Aquarius	Scorpio	Pisces	Leo	Cancer
10	10:01 A.M.	Sagittarius	Sagittarius	Aquarius	Sagittarius	Aquarius	Scorpio	Pisces	Leo	Cancer
11			Capricorn	Aquarius	Sagittarius	Aquarius	Scorpio	Pisces	Leo	Cancer
12	12:08 P.M.	Capricorn	Capricorn	Aquarius	Sagittarius	Aquarius	Scorpio	Pisces	Leo	Cancer
13			Capricorn	Aquarius	Sagittarius	Aquarius	Scorpio	Pisces	Leo	Cancer
14	12:07 P.M.	Aquarius	Capricorn	Aquarius	Sagittarius	Aquarius	Scorpio	Pisces	Leo	Cancer
15			Capricorn	Aquarius	Sagittarius	Aquarius	Scorpio	Pisces	Leo	Cancer
16	11:49 A.M.	Pisces	Capricorn	Aquarius	Sagittarius	Aquarius	Scorpio	Pisces	Leo	Cancer
17			Capricorn	Aquarius	Sagittarius	Aquarius	Scorpio	Pisces	Leo	Cancer
18	1:05 P.M.	Aries	Capricorn	Aquarius	Sagittarius	Aquarius	Scorpio	Pisces	Leo	Cancer
19			Capricorn	Aquarius	Sagittarius	Aquarius	Scorpio	Pisces	Leo	Cancer
20	5:16 P.M.	Taurus	Capricorn	Aquarius	Sagittarius	Aquarius	Scorpio	Pisces	Leo	Cancer
December										
23	Leo		Sagittarius	Capricorn	Taurus	Aquarius	Sagittarius	Pisces	Leo	Cancer
24	2:03 A.M.	Virgo	Sagittarius	Capricorn	Taurus	Aquarius	Sagittarius	Pisces	Leo	Cancer
25			Sagittarius	Capricorn	Taurus	Aquarius	Sagittarius	Pisces	Leo	Cancer
26	2:31 P.M.	Libra	Sagittarius	Capricorn	Taurus	Aquarius	Sagittarius	Pisces	Leo	Cancer
27			Sagittarius	Capricorn	Taurus	Aquarius	Sagittarius	Pisces	Leo	Cancer
28			Sagittarius	Capricorn	Taurus	Aquarius	Sagittarius	Pisces	Leo	Cancer
29	2:28 A.M.	Scorpio	Sagittarius	Capricorn	Taurus	Aquarius	Sagittarius	Pisces	Leo	Cancer
30			Sagittarius	Capricorn	Taurus	Aquarius	Sagittarius	Pisces	Leo	Cancer
31	11:49 A.M.	Sagittarius	Sagittarius	Capricorn	Taurus	Aquarius	Sagittarius	Pisces	Leo	Cancer

CAPRICORN PLANETARY TABLES

1927

January	MOON FROM	IN	MERCURY	VENUS	MARS	JUPITER	SATURN	URANUS	NEPTUNE	PLUTO
1	Sagittarius		Sagittarius	Capricorn	Taurus	Aquarius	Sagittarius	Pisces	Leo	Cancer
2	5:51 P.M.	Capricorn	Sagittarius	Capricorn	Taurus	Aquarius	Sagittarius	Pisces	Leo	Cancer
3			Sagittarius	Capricorn	Taurus	Aquarius	Sagittarius	Pisces	Leo	Cancer
4	9:10 P.M.	Aquarius	Sagittarius	Capricorn	Taurus	Aquarius	Sagittarius	Pisces	Leo	Cancer
5			Capricorn	Capricorn	Taurus	Aquarius	Sagittarius	Pisces	Leo	Cancer
6	11:06 P.M.	Pisces	Capricorn	Capricorn	Taurus	Aquarius	Sagittarius	Pisces	Leo	Cancer
7			Capricorn	Capricorn	Taurus	Aquarius	Sagittarius	Pisces	Leo	Cancer
8			Capricorn	Capricorn	Taurus	Aquarius	Sagittarius	Pisces	Leo	Cancer
9	1:00 A.M.	Aries	Capricorn	Aquarius	Taurus	Aquarius	Sagittarius	Pisces	Leo	Cancer
10			Capricorn	Aquarius	Taurus	Aquarius	Sagittarius	Pisces	Leo	Cancer
11	3:56 A.M.	Taurus	Capricorn	Aquarius	Taurus	Aquarius	Sagittarius	Pisces	Leo	Cancer
12			Capricorn	Aquarius	Taurus	Aquarius	Sagittarius	Pisces	Leo	Cancer
13	8:31 A.M.	Gemini	Capricorn	Aquarius	Taurus	Aquarius	Sagittarius	Pisces	Leo	Cancer
14			Capricorn	Aquarius	Taurus	Aquarius	Sagittarius	Pisces	Leo	Cancer
15	3:00 P.M.	Cancer	Capricorn	Aquarius	Taurus	Aquarius	Sagittarius	Pisces	Leo	Cancer
16			Capricorn	Aquarius	Taurus	Aquarius	Sagittarius	Pisces	Leo	Cancer
17	11:32 P.M.	Leo	Capricorn	Aquarius	Taurus	Aquarius	Sagittarius	Pisces	Leo	Cancer
18			Capricorn	Aquarius	Taurus	Pisces	Sagittarius	Pisces	Leo	Cancer
19			Capricorn	Aquarius	Taurus	Pisces	Sagittarius	Pisces	Leo	Cancer
20	8:10 A.M.	Virgo	Capricorn	Aquarius	Taurus	Pisces	Sagittarius	Pisces	Leo	Cancer
December										
23	8:37 P.M.	Capricorn	Sagittarius	Scorpio	Sagittarius	Pisces	Sagittarius	Pisces	Leo	Cancer
24			Sagittarius	Scorpio	Sagittarius	Pisces	Sagittarius	Pisces	Leo	Cancer
25			Sagittarius	Scorpio	Sagittarius	Pisces	Sagittarius	Pisces	Leo	Cancer
26	4:54 A.M.	Aquarius	Sagittarius	Scorpio	Sagittarius	Pisces	Sagittarius	Pisces	Leo	Cancer
27			Sagittarius	Scorpio	Sagittarius	Pisces	Sagittarius	Pisces	Leo	Cancer
28	11:00 A.M.	Pisces	Sagittarius	Scorpio	Sagittarius	Pisces	Sagittarius	Pisces	Leo	Cancer
29			Capricorn	Scorpio	Sagittarius	Pisces	Sagittarius	Pisces	Leo	Cancer
30	3:18 P.M.	Aries	Capricorn	Scorpio	Sagittarius	Pisces	Sagittarius	Pisces	Leo	Cancer
31			Capricorn	Scorpio	Sagittarius	Pisces	Sagittarius	Pisces	Leo	Cancer

1928

January	MOON FROM	IN	MERCURY	VENUS	MARS	JUPITER	SATURN	URANUS	NEPTUNE	PLUTO
1	6:15 P.M.	Taurus	Capricorn	Scorpio	Sagittarius	Pisces	Sagittarius	Pisces	Leo	Cancer
2	8:20 P.M.	Gemini	Capricorn	Scorpio	Sagittarius	Pisces	Sagittarius	Pisces	Leo	Cancer
3			Capricorn	Scorpio	Sagittarius	Pisces	Sagittarius	Pisces	Leo	Cancer
4	10:28 P.M.	Cancer	Capricorn	Sagittarius	Sagittarius	Pisces	Sagittarius	Pisces	Leo	Cancer
5			Capricorn	Sagittarius	Sagittarius	Pisces	Sagittarius	Pisces	Leo	Cancer
6			Capricorn	Sagittarius	Sagittarius	Pisces	Sagittarius	Pisces	Leo	Cancer
7			Capricorn	Sagittarius	Sagittarius	Pisces	Sagittarius	Pisces	Leo	Cancer
8	1:53 A.M.	Leo	Capricorn	Sagittarius	Sagittarius	Pisces	Sagittarius	Pisces	Leo	Cancer
9			Capricorn	Sagittarius	Sagittarius	Pisces	Sagittarius	Pisces	Leo	Cancer
10	7:54 A.M.	Virgo	Capricorn	Sagittarius	Sagittarius	Pisces	Sagittarius	Pisces	Leo	Cancer
11			Capricorn	Sagittarius	Sagittarius	Pisces	Sagittarius	Pisces	Leo	Cancer
12	5:18 P.M.	Libra	Capricorn	Sagittarius	Sagittarius	Pisces	Sagittarius	Pisces	Leo	Cancer
13			Capricorn	Sagittarius	Sagittarius	Pisces	Sagittarius	Pisces	Leo	Cancer
14			Capricorn	Sagittarius	Sagittarius	Pisces	Sagittarius	Aries	Leo	Cancer
15	5:27 A.M.	Scorpio	Capricorn	Sagittarius	Sagittarius	Pisces	Sagittarius	Aries	Leo	Cancer
16			Capricorn	Sagittarius	Sagittarius	Pisces	Sagittarius	Aries	Leo	Cancer
17	6:06 P.M.	Sagittarius	Aquarius	Sagittarius	Sagittarius	Pisces	Sagittarius	Aries	Leo	Cancer
18			Aquarius	Sagittarius	Sagittarius	Pisces	Sagittarius	Aries	Leo	Cancer
19			Aquarius	Sagittarius	Capricorn	Pisces	Sagittarius	Aries	Leo	Cancer
20	4:49 A.M.	Capricorn	Aquarius	Sagittarius	Capricorn	Pisces	Sagittarius	Aries	Leo	Cancer
December										
22	6:25 A.M.	Taurus	Capricorn	Aquarius	Gemini	Taurus	Sagittarius	Aries	Virgo	Cancer
23			Capricorn	Aquarius	Gemini	Taurus	Sagittarius	Aries	Virgo	Cancer
24	7:40 A.M.	Gemini	Capricorn	Aquarius	Gemini	Taurus	Sagittarius	Aries	Virgo	Cancer
25			Capricorn	Aquarius	Gemini	Taurus	Sagittarius	Aries	Virgo	Cancer
26	7:17 A.M.	Cancer	Capricorn	Aquarius	Gemini	Taurus	Sagittarius	Aries	Virgo	Cancer
27			Capricorn	Aquarius	Gemini	Taurus	Sagittarius	Aries	Virgo	Cancer
28	7:07 A.M.	Leo	Capricorn	Aquarius	Gemini	Taurus	Sagittarius	Aries	Virgo	Cancer
29			Capricorn	Aquarius	Gemini	Taurus	Sagittarius	Aries	Virgo	Cancer
30	9:13 A.M.	Virgo	Capricorn	Aquarius	Gemini	Taurus	Sagittarius	Aries	Virgo	Cancer
31			Capricorn	Aquarius	Gemini	Taurus	Sagittarius	Aries	Virgo	Cancer

CAPRICORN PLANETARY TABLES

1929

January	MOON FROM	IN	MERCURY	VENUS	MARS	JUPITER	SATURN	URANUS	NEPTUNE	PLUTO
1	3:09 P.M.	Libra	Capricorn	Aquarius	Gemini	Taurus	Sagittarius	Aries	Virgo	Cancer
2			Capricorn	Aquarius	Gemini	Taurus	Sagittarius	Aries	Virgo	Cancer
3			Capricorn	Aquarius	Gemini	Taurus	Sagittarius	Aries	Virgo	Cancer
4	1:10 A.M.	Scorpio	Capricorn	Aquarius	Gemini	Taurus	Sagittarius	Aries	Virgo	Cancer
5			Capricorn	Aquarius	Gemini	Taurus	Sagittarius	Aries	Virgo	Cancer
6	1:50 P.M.	Sagittarius	Capricorn	Pisces	Gemini	Taurus	Sagittarius	Aries	Virgo	Cancer
7			Capricorn	Pisces	Gemini	Taurus	Sagittarius	Aries	Virgo	Cancer
8			Aquarius	Pisces	Gemini	Taurus	Sagittarius	Aries	Virgo	Cancer
9	2:51 A.M.	Capricorn	Aquarius	Pisces	Gemini	Taurus	Sagittarius	Aries	Virgo	Cancer
10			Aquarius	Pisces	Gemini	Taurus	Sagittarius	Aries	Virgo	Cancer
11	2:32 P.M.	Aquarius	Aquarius	Pisces	Gemini	Taurus	Sagittarius	Aries	Virgo	Cancer
12			Aquarius	Pisces	Gemini	Taurus	Sagittarius	Aries	Virgo	Cancer
13			Aquarius	Pisces	Gemini	Taurus	Sagittarius	Aries	Virgo	Cancer
14	0:21 A.M.	Pisces	Aquarius	Pisces	Gemini	Taurus	Sagittarius	Aries	Virgo	Cancer
15			Aquarius	Pisces	Gemini	Taurus	Sagittarius	Aries	Virgo	Cancer
16	8:07 A.M.	Aries	Aquarius	Pisces	Gemini	Taurus	Sagittarius	Aries	Virgo	Cancer
17			Aquarius	Pisces	Gemini	Taurus	Sagittarius	Aries	Virgo	Cancer
18	1:37 P.M.	Taurus	Aquarius	Pisces	Gemini	Taurus	Sagittarius	Aries	Virgo	Cancer
19			Aquarius	Pisces	Gemini	Taurus	Sagittarius	Aries	Virgo	Cancer
20	4:43 P.M.	Gemini	Aquarius	Pisces	Gemini	Taurus	Sagittarius	Aries	Virgo	Cancer
December										
22	8:03 P.M.	Libra	Capricorn	Sagittarius	Sagittarius	Gemini	Capricorn	Aries	Virgo	Cancer
23			Capricorn	Sagittarius	Sagittarius	Gemini	Capricorn	Aries	Virgo	Cancer
24	3:12 A.M.	Scorpio	Capricorn	Sagittarius	Sagittarius	Gemini	Capricorn	Aries	Virgo	Cancer
25			Capricorn	Sagittarius	Sagittarius	Gemini	Capricorn	Aries	Virgo	Cancer
26	1:12 P.M.	Sagittarius	Capricorn	Sagittarius	Sagittarius	Gemini	Capricorn	Aries	Virgo	Cancer
27			Capricorn	Sagittarius	Sagittarius	Gemini	Capricorn	Aries	Virgo	Cancer
28			Capricorn	Sagittarius	Capricorn	Gemini	Capricorn	Aries	Virgo	Cancer
29			Capricorn	Sagittarius	Capricorn	Gemini	Capricorn	Aries	Virgo	Cancer
30	0:56 A.M.	Capricorn	Capricorn	Sagittarius	Capricorn	Gemini	Capricorn	Aries	Virgo	Cancer
31			Capricorn	Capricorn	Capricorn	Gemini	Capricorn	Aries	Virgo	Cancer

1930

	MOON		MERCURY	VENUS	MARS	JUPITER	SATURN	URANUS	NEPTUNE	PLUTO
January	FROM	IN								
1	1:30 P.M.	Aquarius	Capricorn	Capricorn	Capricorn	Gemini	Capricorn	Aries	Virgo	Cancer
2			Aquarius	Capricorn	Capricorn	Gemini	Capricorn	Aries	Virgo	Cancer
3			Aquarius	Capricorn	Capricorn	Gemini	Capricorn	Aries	Virgo	Cancer
4	2:04 A.M.	Pisces	Aquarius	Capricorn	Capricorn	Gemini	Capricorn	Aries	Virgo	Cancer
5			Aquarius	Capricorn	Capricorn	Gemini	Capricorn	Aries	Virgo	Cancer
6	1:27 P.M.	Aries	Aquarius	Capricorn	Capricorn	Gemini	Capricorn	Aries	Virgo	Cancer
7			Aquarius	Capricorn	Capricorn	Gemini	Capricorn	Aries	Virgo	Cancer
8	9:58 P.M.	Taurus	Aquarius	Capricorn	Capricorn	Gemini	Capricorn	Aries	Virgo	Cancer
9			Aquarius	Capricorn	Capricorn	Gemini	Capricorn	Aries	Virgo	Cancer
10			Aquarius	Capricorn	Capricorn	Gemini	Capricorn	Aries	Virgo	Cancer
11	2:47 A.M.	Gemini	Aquarius	Capricorn	Capricorn	Gemini	Capricorn	Aries	Virgo	Cancer
12			Aquarius	Capricorn	Capricorn	Gemini	Capricorn	Aries	Virgo	Cancer
13	3:34 A.M.	Cancer	Aquarius	Capricorn	Capricorn	Gemini	Capricorn	Aries	Virgo	Cancer
14			Aquarius	Capricorn	Capricorn	Gemini	Capricorn	Aries	Virgo	Cancer
15	2:37 A.M.	Leo	Aquarius	Capricorn	Capricorn	Gemini	Capricorn	Aries	Virgo	Cancer
16			Aquarius	Capricorn	Capricorn	Gemini	Capricorn	Aries	Virgo	Cancer
17	1:58 A.M.	Virgo	Aquarius	Capricorn	Capricorn	Gemini	Capricorn	Aries	Virgo	Cancer
18			Aquarius	Capricorn	Capricorn	Gemini	Capricorn	Aries	Virgo	Cancer
19	3:46 A.M.	Libra	Aquarius	Capricorn	Capricorn	Gemini	Capricorn	Aries	Virgo	Cancer
20			Aquarius	Capricorn	Capricorn	Gemini	Capricorn	Aries	Virgo	Cancer
December										
23		Aquarius	Capricorn	Scorpio	Leo	Cancer	Capricorn	Aries	Virgo	Cancer
24	10:36 P.M.	Pisces	Capricorn	Scorpio	Leo	Cancer	Capricorn	Aries	Virgo	Cancer
25			Capricorn	Scorpio	Leo	Cancer	Capricorn	Aries	Virgo	Cancer
26			Capricorn	Scorpio	Leo	Cancer	Capricorn	Aries	Virgo	Cancer
27	11:29 A.M.	Aries	Capricorn	Scorpio	Leo	Cancer	Capricorn	Aries	Virgo	Cancer
28			Capricorn	Scorpio	Leo	Cancer	Capricorn	Aries	Virgo	Cancer
29	10:51 P.M.	Taurus	Capricorn	Scorpio	Leo	Cancer	Capricorn	Aries	Virgo	Cancer
30			Capricorn	Scorpio	Leo	Cancer	Capricorn	Aries	Virgo	Cancer
31			Capricorn	Scorpio	Leo	Cancer	Capricorn	Aries	Virgo	Cancer

CAPRICORN PLANETARY TABLES

1931

	MOON FROM IN	MERCURY	VENUS	MARS	JUPITER	SATURN	URANUS	NEPTUNE	PLUTO
January									
1	6:34 A.M. Gemini	Capricorn	Scorpio	Leo	Cancer	Capricorn	Aries	Virgo	Cancer
2		Capricorn	Scorpio	Leo	Cancer	Capricorn	Aries	Virgo	Cancer
3	10:20 A.M. Cancer	Capricorn	Scorpio	Leo	Cancer	Capricorn	Aries	Virgo	Cancer
4		Capricorn	Sagittarius	Leo	Cancer	Capricorn	Aries	Virgo	Cancer
5	11:32 A.M. Leo	Capricorn	Sagittarius	Leo	Cancer	Capricorn	Aries	Virgo	Cancer
6		Capricorn	Sagittarius	Leo	Cancer	Capricorn	Aries	Virgo	Cancer
7	12:07 P.M. Virgo	Capricorn	Sagittarius	Leo	Cancer	Capricorn	Aries	Virgo	Cancer
8		Capricorn	Sagittarius	Leo	Cancer	Capricorn	Aries	Virgo	Cancer
9	1:49 P.M. Libra	Capricorn	Sagittarius	Leo	Cancer	Capricorn	Aries	Virgo	Cancer
10		Capricorn	Sagittarius	Leo	Cancer	Capricorn	Aries	Virgo	Cancer
11	5:41 P.M. Scorpio	Capricorn	Sagittarius	Leo	Cancer	Capricorn	Aries	Virgo	Cancer
12		Capricorn	Sagittarius	Leo	Cancer	Capricorn	Aries	Virgo	Cancer
13	11:51 P.M. Sagittarius	Capricorn	Sagittarius	Leo	Cancer	Capricorn	Aries	Virgo	Cancer
14		Capricorn	Sagittarius	Leo	Cancer	Capricorn	Aries	Virgo	Cancer
15		Capricorn	Sagittarius	Leo	Cancer	Capricorn	Aries	Virgo	Cancer
16	8:02 A.M. Capricorn	Capricorn	Sagittarius	Leo	Cancer	Capricorn	Aries	Virgo	Cancer
17		Capricorn	Sagittarius	Leo	Cancer	Capricorn	Aries	Virgo	Cancer
18	6:04 P.M. Aquarius	Capricorn	Sagittarius	Leo	Cancer	Capricorn	Aries	Virgo	Cancer
19		Capricorn	Sagittarius	Leo	Cancer	Capricorn	Aries	Virgo	Cancer
20		Capricorn	Sagittarius	Leo	Cancer	Capricorn	Aries	Virgo	Cancer
December									
23	Gemini	Sagittarius	Capricorn	Capricorn	Leo	Capricorn	Aries	Virgo	Cancer
24	2:21 P.M. Cancer	Sagittarius	Capricorn	Capricorn	Leo	Capricorn	Aries	Virgo	Cancer
25		Sagittarius	Capricorn	Capricorn	Leo	Capricorn	Aries	Virgo	Cancer
26	8:16 P.M. Leo	Sagittarius	Aquarius	Capricorn	Leo	Capricorn	Aries	Virgo	Cancer
27		Sagittarius	Aquarius	Capricorn	Leo	Capricorn	Aries	Virgo	Cancer
28		Sagittarius	Aquarius	Capricorn	Leo	Capricorn	Aries	Virgo	Cancer
29	0:40 A.M. Virgo	Sagittarius	Aquarius	Capricorn	Leo	Capricorn	Aries	Virgo	Cancer
30		Sagittarius	Aquarius	Capricorn	Leo	Capricorn	Aries	Virgo	Cancer
31	4:17 A.M. Libra	Sagittarius	Aquarius	Capricorn	Leo	Capricorn	Aries	Virgo	Cancer

1932

January	MOON FROM IN	MERCURY	VENUS	MARS	JUPITER	SATURN	URANUS	NEPTUNE	PLUTO
1	Libra	Sagittarius	Aquarius	Capricorn	Leo	Capricorn	Aries	Virgo	Cancer
2	7:24 A.M. Scorpio	Sagittarius	Aquarius	Capricorn	Leo	Capricorn	Aries	Virgo	Cancer
3		Sagittarius	Aquarius	Capricorn	Leo	Capricorn	Aries	Virgo	Cancer
4	10:16 A.M. Sagittarius	Sagittarius	Aquarius	Capricorn	Leo	Capricorn	Aries	Virgo	Cancer
5		Sagittarius	Aquarius	Capricorn	Leo	Capricorn	Aries	Virgo	Cancer
6	1:37 P.M. Capricorn	Sagittarius	Aquarius	Capricorn	Leo	Capricorn	Aries	Virgo	Cancer
7		Sagittarius	Aquarius	Capricorn	Leo	Capricorn	Aries	Virgo	Cancer
8	6:44 P.M. Aquarius	Sagittarius	Aquarius	Capricorn	Leo	Capricorn	Aries	Virgo	Cancer
9		Sagittarius	Aquarius	Capricorn	Leo	Capricorn	Aries	Virgo	Cancer
10		Sagittarius	Aquarius	Capricorn	Leo	Capricorn	Aries	Virgo	Cancer
11	2:50 A.M. Pisces	Sagittarius	Aquarius	Capricorn	Leo	Capricorn	Aries	Virgo	Cancer
12		Sagittarius	Aquarius	Capricorn	Leo	Capricorn	Aries	Virgo	Cancer
13	2:07 P.M. Aries	Sagittarius	Aquarius	Capricorn	Leo	Capricorn	Aries	Virgo	Cancer
14		Sagittarius	Aquarius	Capricorn	Leo	Capricorn	Aries	Virgo	Cancer
15		Capricorn	Aquarius	Capricorn	Leo	Capricorn	Aries	Virgo	Cancer
16	3:02 A.M. Taurus	Capricorn	Aquarius	Capricorn	Leo	Capricorn	Aries	Virgo	Cancer
17		Capricorn	Aquarius	Capricorn	Leo	Capricorn	Aries	Virgo	Cancer
18	2:47 P.M. Gemini	Capricorn	Aquarius	Aquarius	Leo	Capricorn	Aries	Virgo	Cancer
19		Capricorn	Pisces	Aquarius	Leo	Capricorn	Aries	Virgo	Cancer
20	11:22 P.M. Cancer	Capricorn	Pisces	Aquarius	Leo	Capricorn	Aries	Virgo	Cancer
December									
22	8:53 P.M. Scorpio	Sagittarius	Sagittarius	Virgo	Virgo	Aquarius	Aries	Virgo	Cancer
23		Sagittarius	Sagittarius	Virgo	Virgo	Aquarius	Aries	Virgo	Cancer
24	9:42 P.M. Sagittarius	Sagittarius	Sagittarius	Virgo	Virgo	Aquarius	Aries	Virgo	Cancer
25		Sagittarius	Sagittarius	Virgo	Virgo	Aquarius	Aries	Virgo	Cancer
26	9:31 P.M. Capricorn	Sagittarius	Sagittarius	Virgo	Virgo	Aquarius	Aries	Virgo	Cancer
27		Sagittarius	Sagittarius	Virgo	Virgo	Aquarius	Aries	Virgo	Cancer
28	10:23 P.M. Aquarius	Sagittarius	Sagittarius	Virgo	Virgo	Aquarius	Aries	Virgo	Cancer
29		Sagittarius	Sagittarius	Virgo	Virgo	Aquarius	Aries	Virgo	Cancer
30		Sagittarius	Sagittarius	Virgo	Virgo	Aquarius	Aries	Virgo	Cancer
31	2:17 A.M. Pisces	Sagittarius	Sagittarius	Virgo	Virgo	Aquarius	Aries	Virgo	Cancer

CAPRICORN PLANETARY TABLES

1933

January	MOON FROM	IN	MERCURY	VENUS	MARS	JUPITER	SATURN	URANUS	NEPTUNE	PLUTO
1	Pisces		Sagittarius	Sagittarius	Virgo	Virgo	Aquarius	Aries	Virgo	Cancer
2	10:14 A.M.	Aries	Sagittarius	Sagittarius	Virgo	Virgo	Aquarius	Aries	Virgo	Cancer
3			Sagittarius	Sagittarius	Virgo	Virgo	Aquarius	Aries	Virgo	Cancer
4	9:37 P.M.	Taurus	Sagittarius	Sagittarius	Virgo	Virgo	Aquarius	Aries	Virgo	Cancer
5			Sagittarius	Sagittarius	Virgo	Virgo	Aquarius	Aries	Virgo	Cancer
6			Sagittarius	Sagittarius	Virgo	Virgo	Aquarius	Aries	Virgo	Cancer
7	10:19 A.M.	Gemini	Sagittarius	Sagittarius	Virgo	Virgo	Aquarius	Aries	Virgo	Cancer
8			Capricorn	Sagittarius	Virgo	Virgo	Aquarius	Aries	Virgo	Cancer
9	10:16 P.M.	Cancer	Capricorn	Sagittarius	Virgo	Virgo	Aquarius	Aries	Virgo	Cancer
10			Capricorn	Sagittarius	Virgo	Virgo	Aquarius	Aries	Virgo	Cancer
11			Capricorn	Sagittarius	Virgo	Virgo	Aquarius	Aries	Virgo	Cancer
12	8:26 A.M.	Leo	Capricorn	Sagittarius	Virgo	Virgo	Aquarius	Aries	Virgo	Cancer
13			Capricorn	Sagittarius	Virgo	Virgo	Aquarius	Aries	Virgo	Cancer
14	4:41 P.M.	Virgo	Capricorn	Capricorn	Virgo	Virgo	Aquarius	Aries	Virgo	Cancer
15			Capricorn	Capricorn	Virgo	Virgo	Aquarius	Aries	Virgo	Cancer
16	11:02 P.M.	Libra	Capricorn	Capricorn	Virgo	Virgo	Aquarius	Aries	Virgo	Cancer
17			Capricorn	Capricorn	Virgo	Virgo	Aquarius	Aries	Virgo	Cancer
18			Capricorn	Capricorn	Virgo	Virgo	Aquarius	Aries	Virgo	Cancer
19	3:24 A.M.	Scorpio	Capricorn	Capricorn	Virgo	Virgo	Aquarius	Aries	Virgo	Cancer
December										
22	Pisces		Sagittarius	Aquarius	Capricorn	Libra	Aquarius	Aries	Virgo	Cancer
23	12:17 P.M.	Aries	Sagittarius	Aquarius	Capricorn	Libra	Aquarius	Aries	Virgo	Cancer
24			Sagittarius	Aquarius	Capricorn	Libra	Aquarius	Aries	Virgo	Cancer
25	8:43 P.M.	Taurus	Sagittarius	Aquarius	Capricorn	Libra	Aquarius	Aries	Virgo	Cancer
26			Sagittarius	Aquarius	Capricorn	Libra	Aquarius	Aries	Virgo	Cancer
27			Sagittarius	Aquarius	Capricorn	Libra	Aquarius	Aries	Virgo	Cancer
28	7:43 A.M.	Gemini	Sagittarius	Aquarius	Aquarius	Libra	Aquarius	Aries	Virgo	Cancer
29			Sagittarius	Aquarius	Aquarius	Libra	Aquarius	Aries	Virgo	Cancer
30	8:07 P.M.	Cancer	Sagittarius	Aquarius	Aquarius	Libra	Aquarius	Aries	Virgo	Cancer
31			Sagittarius	Aquarius	Aquarius	Libra	Aquarius	Aries	Virgo	Cancer

1934

	MOON									
January	FROM	IN	MERCURY	VENUS	MARS	JUPITER	SATURN	URANUS	NEPTUNE	PLUTO
1	Cancer		Sagittarius	Aquarius	Aquarius	Libra	Aquarius	Aries	Virgo	Cancer
2	8:56 A.M.	Leo	Capricorn	Aquarius	Aquarius	Libra	Aquarius	Aries	Virgo	Cancer
3			Capricorn	Aquarius	Aquarius	Libra	Aquarius	Aries	Virgo	Cancer
4	9:08 P.M.	Virgo	Capricorn	Aquarius	Aquarius	Libra	Aquarius	Aries	Virgo	Cancer
5			Capricorn	Aquarius	Aquarius	Libra	Aquarius	Aries	Virgo	Cancer
6			Capricorn	Aquarius	Aquarius	Libra	Aquarius	Aries	Virgo	Cancer
7	7:20 A.M.	Libra	Capricorn	Aquarius	Aquarius	Libra	Aquarius	Aries	Virgo	Cancer
8			Capricorn	Aquarius	Aquarius	Libra	Aquarius	Aries	Virgo	Cancer
9	2:17 P.M.	Scorpio	Capricorn	Aquarius	Aquarius	Libra	Aquarius	Aries	Virgo	Cancer
10			Capricorn	Aquarius	Aquarius	Libra	Aquarius	Aries	Virgo	Cancer
11	5:17 P.M.	Sagittarius	Capricorn	Aquarius	Aquarius	Libra	Aquarius	Aries	Virgo	Cancer
12			Capricorn	Aquarius	Aquarius	Libra	Aquarius	Aries	Virgo	Cancer
13	5:37 P.M.	Capricorn	Capricorn	Aquarius	Aquarius	Libra	Aquarius	Aries	Virgo	Cancer
14			Capricorn	Aquarius	Aquarius	Libra	Aquarius	Aries	Virgo	Cancer
15	4:56 P.M.	Aquarius	Capricorn	Aquarius	Aquarius	Libra	Aquarius	Aries	Virgo	Cancer
16			Capricorn	Aquarius	Aquarius	Libra	Aquarius	Aries	Virgo	Cancer
17	5:17 P.M.	Pisces	Capricorn	Aquarius	Aquarius	Libra	Aquarius	Aries	Virgo	Cancer
18			Capricorn	Aquarius	Aquarius	Libra	Aquarius	Aries	Virgo	Cancer
19	8:28 P.M.	Aries	Capricorn	Aquarius	Aquarius	Libra	Aquarius	Aries	Virgo	Cancer
20			Aquarius	Aquarius	Aquarius	Libra	Aquarius	Aries	Virgo	Cancer
December										
23	6:37 A.M.	Leo	Sagittarius	Capricorn	Libra	Scorpio	Aquarius	Aries	Virgo	Cancer
24			Sagittarius	Capricorn	Libra	Scorpio	Aquarius	Aries	Virgo	Cancer
25	7:32 P.M.	Virgo	Sagittarius	Capricorn	Libra	Scorpio	Aquarius	Aries	Virgo	Cancer
26			Capricorn	Capricorn	Libra	Scorpio	Aquarius	Aries	Virgo	Cancer
27			Capricorn	Capricorn	Libra	Scorpio	Aquarius	Aries	Virgo	Cancer
28	7:59 A.M.	Libra	Capricorn	Capricorn	Libra	Scorpio	Aquarius	Aries	Virgo	Cancer
29			Capricorn	Capricorn	Libra	Scorpio	Aquarius	Aries	Virgo	Cancer
30	5:41 P.M.	Scorpio	Capricorn	Capricorn	Libra	Scorpio	Aquarius	Aries	Virgo	Cancer
31			Capricorn	Capricorn	Libra	Scorpio	Aquarius	Aries	Virgo	Cancer

CAPRICORN PLANETARY TABLES

1935

MOON January FROM	IN	MERCURY	VENUS	MARS	JUPITER	SATURN	URANUS	NEPTUNE	PLUTO
1	Scorpio	Capricorn	Capricorn	Libra	Scorpio	Aquarius	Aries	Virgo	Cancer
2	2:01 A.M. Sagittarius	Capricorn	Capricorn	Libra	Scorpio	Aquarius	Aries	Virgo	Cancer
3		Capricorn	Capricorn	Libra	Scorpio	Aquarius	Aries	Virgo	Cancer
4	1:44 A.M. Capricorn	Capricorn	Capricorn	Libra	Scorpio	Aquarius	Aries	Virgo	Cancer
5		Capricorn	Capricorn	Libra	Scorpio	Aquarius	Aries	Virgo	Cancer
6	2:04 A.M. Aquarius	Capricorn	Capricorn	Libra	Scorpio	Aquarius	Aries	Virgo	Cancer
7		Capricorn	Capricorn	Libra	Scorpio	Aquarius	Aries	Virgo	Cancer
8	2:17 A.M. Pisces	Capricorn	Capricorn	Libra	Scorpio	Aquarius	Aries	Virgo	Cancer
9		Capricorn	Aquarius	Libra	Scorpio	Aquarius	Aries	Virgo	Cancer
10	4:03 A.M. Aries	Capricorn	Aquarius	Libra	Scorpio	Aquarius	Aries	Virgo	Cancer
11		Capricorn	Aquarius	Libra	Scorpio	Aquarius	Aries	Virgo	Cancer
12	8:25 A.M. Taurus	Capricorn	Aquarius	Libra	Scorpio	Aquarius	Aries	Virgo	Cancer
13		Aquarius	Aquarius	Libra	Scorpio	Aquarius	Aries	Virgo	Cancer
14	3:43 P.M. Gemini	Aquarius	Aquarius	Libra	Scorpio	Aquarius	Aries	Virgo	Cancer
15		Aquarius	Aquarius	Libra	Scorpio	Aquarius	Aries	Virgo	Cancer
16		Aquarius	Aquarius	Libra	Scorpio	Aquarius	Aries	Virgo	Cancer
17	1:37 A.M. Cancer	Aquarius	Aquarius	Libra	Scorpio	Aquarius	Aries	Virgo	Cancer
18		Aquarius	Aquarius	Libra	Scorpio	Aquarius	Aries	Virgo	Cancer
19	1:27 P.M. Leo	Aquarius	Aquarius	Libra	Scorpio	Aquarius	Aries	Virgo	Cancer
20		Aquarius	Aquarius	Libra	Scorpio	Aquarius	Aries	Virgo	Cancer
December									
23	0:44 A.M. Sagittarius	Capricorn	Scorpio	Aquarius	Sagittarius	Pisces	Taurus	Virgo	Cancer
24		Capricorn	Scorpio	Aquarius	Sagittarius	Pisces	Taurus	Virgo	Cancer
25	7:27 A.M. Capricorn	Capricorn	Scorpio	Aquarius	Sagittarius	Pisces	Taurus	Virgo	Cancer
26		Capricorn	Scorpio	Aquarius	Sagittarius	Pisces	Taurus	Virgo	Cancer
27	11:46 A.M. Aquarius	Capricorn	Scorpio	Aquarius	Sagittarius	Pisces	Taurus	Virgo	Cancer
28		Capricorn	Scorpio	Aquarius	Sagittarius	Pisces	Taurus	Virgo	Cancer
29	2:42 P.M. Pisces	Capricorn	Scorpio	Aquarius	Sagittarius	Pisces	Taurus	Virgo	Cancer
30		Capricorn	Scorpio	Aquarius	Sagittarius	Pisces	Taurus	Virgo	Cancer
31	5:16 P.M. Aries	Capricorn	Scorpio	Aquarius	Sagittarius	Pisces	Taurus	Virgo	Cancer

1936

January	MOON FROM	IN	MERCURY	VENUS	MARS	JUPITER	SATURN	URANUS	NEPTUNE	PLUTO
1	Aries		Capricorn	Scorpio	Aquarius	Sagittarius	Pisces	Taurus	Virgo	Cancer
2	8:11 P.M.	Taurus	Capricorn	Scorpio	Aquarius	Sagittarius	Pisces	Taurus	Virgo	Cancer
3			Capricorn	Scorpio	Aquarius	Sagittarius	Pisces	Taurus	Virgo	Cancer
4			Capricorn	Sagittarius	Aquarius	Sagittarius	Pisces	Taurus	Virgo	Cancer
5	0:04 A.M.	Gemini	Capricorn	Sagittarius	Aquarius	Sagittarius	Pisces	Taurus	Virgo	Cancer
6			Aquarius	Sagittarius	Aquarius	Sagittarius	Pisces	Taurus	Virgo	Cancer
7	5:29 A.M.	Cancer	Aquarius	Sagittarius	Aquarius	Sagittarius	Pisces	Taurus	Virgo	Cancer
8			Aquarius	Sagittarius	Aquarius	Sagittarius	Pisces	Taurus	Virgo	Cancer
9	1:02 P.M.	Leo	Aquarius	Sagittarius	Aquarius	Sagittarius	Pisces	Taurus	Virgo	Cancer
10			Aquarius	Sagittarius	Aquarius	Sagittarius	Pisces	Taurus	Virgo	Cancer
11	11:05 P.M.	Virgo	Aquarius	Sagittarius	Aquarius	Sagittarius	Pisces	Taurus	Virgo	Cancer
12			Aquarius	Sagittarius	Aquarius	Sagittarius	Pisces	Taurus	Virgo	Cancer
13			Aquarius	Sagittarius	Aquarius	Sagittarius	Pisces	Taurus	Virgo	Cancer
14	11:10 A.M.	Libra	Aquarius	Sagittarius	Aquarius	Sagittarius	Pisces	Taurus	Virgo	Cancer
15			Aquarius	Sagittarius	Pisces	Sagittarius	Pisces	Taurus	Virgo	Cancer
16	11:38 P.M.	Scorpio	Aquarius	Sagittarius	Pisces	Sagittarius	Pisces	Taurus	Virgo	Cancer
17			Aquarius	Sagittarius	Pisces	Sagittarius	Pisces	Taurus	Virgo	Cancer
18			Aquarius	Sagittarius	Pisces	Sagittarius	Pisces	Taurus	Virgo	Cancer
19	10:12 A.M.	Sagittarius	Aquarius	Sagittarius	Pisces	Sagittarius	Pisces	Taurus	Virgo	Cancer
20			Aquarius	Sagittarius	Pisces	Sagittarius	Pisces	Taurus	Virgo	Cancer
December										
22	Aries		Capricorn	Aquarius	Libra	Capricorn	Pisces	Taurus	Virgo	Cancer
23	10:05 A.M.	Taurus	Capricorn	Aquarius	Libra	Capricorn	Pisces	Taurus	Virgo	Cancer
24			Capricorn	Aquarius	Libra	Capricorn	Pisces	Taurus	Virgo	Cancer
25	11:24 A.M.	Gemini	Capricorn	Aquarius	Libra	Capricorn	Pisces	Taurus	Virgo	Cancer
26			Capricorn	Aquarius	Libra	Capricorn	Pisces	Taurus	Virgo	Cancer
27	12:20 P.M.	Cancer	Capricorn	Aquarius	Libra	Capricorn	Pisces	Taurus	Virgo	Cancer
28			Capricorn	Aquarius	Libra	Capricorn	Pisces	Taurus	Virgo	Cancer
29	3:14 P.M.	Leo	Capricorn	Aquarius	Libra	Capricorn	Pisces	Taurus	Virgo	Cancer
30			Capricorn	Aquarius	Libra	Capricorn	Pisces	Taurus	Virgo	Cancer
31	8:50 P.M.	Virgo	Capricorn	Aquarius	Libra	Capricorn	Pisces	Taurus	Virgo	Cancer

CAPRICORN PLANETARY TABLES

1937

January	MOON FROM	IN	MERCURY	VENUS	MARS	JUPITER	SATURN	URANUS	NEPTUNE	PLUTO
1		Virgo	Capricorn	Aquarius	Libra	Capricorn	Pisces	Taurus	Virgo	Cancer
2			Aquarius	Aquarius	Libra	Capricorn	Pisces	Taurus	Virgo	Cancer
3	5:56 A.M.	Libra	Aquarius	Aquarius	Libra	Capricorn	Pisces	Taurus	Virgo	Cancer
4			Aquarius	Aquarius	Libra	Capricorn	Pisces	Taurus	Virgo	Cancer
5	5:59 P.M.	Scorpio	Aquarius	Aquarius	Libra	Capricorn	Pisces	Taurus	Virgo	Cancer
6			Aquarius	Pisces	Scorpio	Capricorn	Pisces	Taurus	Virgo	Cancer
7			Aquarius	Pisces	Scorpio	Capricorn	Pisces	Taurus	Virgo	Cancer
8	6:42 A.M.	Sagittarius	Aquarius	Pisces	Scorpio	Capricorn	Pisces	Taurus	Virgo	Cancer
9			Aquarius	Pisces	Scorpio	Capricorn	Pisces	Taurus	Virgo	Cancer
10	5:50 P.M.	Capricorn	Capricorn	Pisces	Scorpio	Capricorn	Pisces	Taurus	Virgo	Cancer
11			Capricorn	Pisces	Scorpio	Capricorn	Pisces	Taurus	Virgo	Cancer
12			Capricorn	Pisces	Scorpio	Capricorn	Pisces	Taurus	Virgo	Cancer
13	2:23 A.M.	Aquarius	Capricorn	Pisces	Scorpio	Capricorn	Pisces	Taurus	Virgo	Cancer
14			Capricorn	Pisces	Scorpio	Capricorn	Pisces	Taurus	Virgo	Cancer
15	8:28 A.M.	Pisces	Capricorn	Pisces	Scorpio	Capricorn	Pisces	Taurus	Virgo	Cancer
16			Capricorn	Pisces	Scorpio	Capricorn	Pisces	Taurus	Virgo	Cancer
17	12:48 P.M.	Aries	Capricorn	Pisces	Scorpio	Capricorn	Pisces	Taurus	Virgo	Cancer
18			Capricorn	Pisces	Scorpio	Capricorn	Pisces	Taurus	Virgo	Cancer
19	4:07 P.M.	Taurus	Capricorn	Pisces	Scorpio	Capricorn	Pisces	Taurus	Virgo	Cancer
December										
22		Virgo	Capricorn	Sagittarius	Pisces	Aquarius	Pisces	Taurus	Virgo	Cancer
23			Capricorn	Sagittarius	Pisces	Aquarius	Pisces	Taurus	Virgo	Cancer
24	4:55 A.M.	Libra	Capricorn	Sagittarius	Pisces	Aquarius	Pisces	Taurus	Virgo	Cancer
25			Capricorn	Sagittarius	Pisces	Aquarius	Pisces	Taurus	Virgo	Cancer
26	2:47 P.M.	Scorpio	Capricorn	Sagittarius	Pisces	Aquarius	Pisces	Taurus	Virgo	Cancer
27			Capricorn	Sagittarius	Pisces	Aquarius	Pisces	Taurus	Virgo	Cancer
28			Capricorn	Sagittarius	Pisces	Aquarius	Pisces	Taurus	Virgo	Cancer
29	3:12 A.M.	Sagittarius	Capricorn	Sagittarius	Pisces	Aquarius	Pisces	Taurus	Virgo	Cancer
30			Capricorn	Sagittarius	Pisces	Aquarius	Pisces	Taurus	Virgo	Cancer
31	4:16 P.M.	Capricorn	Capricorn	Capricorn	Pisces	Aquarius	Pisces	Taurus	Virgo	Cancer

1938

MOON		MERCURY	VENUS	MARS	JUPITER	SATURN	URANUS	NEPTUNE	PLUTO
January	FROM IN								
1	Capricorn	Capricorn	Capricorn	Pisces	Aquarius	Pisces	Taurus	Virgo	Leo
2		Capricorn	Capricorn	Pisces	Aquarius	Pisces	Taurus	Virgo	Cancer
3	4:30 A.M. Aquarius	Capricorn	Capricorn	Pisces	Aquarius	Pisces	Taurus	Virgo	Cancer
4		Capricorn	Capricorn	Pisces	Aquarius	Pisces	Taurus	Virgo	Cancer
5	3:04 P.M. Pisces	Capricorn	Capricorn	Pisces	Aquarius	Pisces	Taurus	Virgo	Cancer
6		Capricorn	Capricorn	Pisces	Aquarius	Pisces	Taurus	Virgo	Cancer
7		Sagittarius	Capricorn	Pisces	Aquarius	Pisces	Taurus	Virgo	Cancer
8	11:48 P.M. Aries	Sagittarius	Capricorn	Pisces	Aquarius	Pisces	Taurus	Virgo	Cancer
9		Sagittarius	Capricorn	Pisces	Aquarius	Pisces	Taurus	Virgo	Cancer
10	5:04 A.M. Taurus	Sagittarius	Capricorn	Pisces	Aquarius	Pisces	Taurus	Virgo	Cancer
11		Sagittarius	Capricorn	Pisces	Aquarius	Pisces	Taurus	Virgo	Cancer
12	7:49 A.M. Gemini	Sagittarius	Capricorn	Pisces	Aquarius	Pisces	Taurus	Virgo	Cancer
13		Capricorn	Capricorn	Pisces	Aquarius	Pisces	Taurus	Virgo	Cancer
14	8:21 A.M. Cancer	Capricorn	Capricorn	Pisces	Aquarius	Aries	Taurus	Virgo	Cancer
15		Capricorn	Capricorn	Pisces	Aquarius	Aries	Taurus	Virgo	Cancer
16	8:09 A.M. Leo	Capricorn	Capricorn	Pisces	Aquarius	Aries	Taurus	Virgo	Cancer
17		Capricorn	Capricorn	Pisces	Aquarius	Aries	Taurus	Virgo	Cancer
18	9:14 A.M. Virgo	Capricorn	Capricorn	Pisces	Aquarius	Aries	Taurus	Virgo	Cancer
19		Capricorn	Capricorn	Pisces	Aquarius	Aries	Taurus	Virgo	Cancer
20	1:32 P.M. Libra	Capricorn	Capricorn	Pisces	Aquarius	Aries	Taurus	Virgo	Cancer
December									
23	Capricorn	Sagittarius	Scorpio	Scorpio	Aquarius	Aries	Taurus	Virgo	Leo
24	2:59 A.M. Aquarius	Sagittarius	Scorpio	Scorpio	Aquarius	Aries	Taurus	Virgo	Leo
25		Sagittarius	Scorpio	Scorpio	Aquarius	Aries	Taurus	Virgo	Leo
26	3:40 P.M. Pisces	Sagittarius	Scorpio	Scorpio	Aquarius	Aries	Taurus	Virgo	Leo
27		Sagittarius	Scorpio	Scorpio	Aquarius	Aries	Taurus	Virgo	Leo
28		Sagittarius	Scorpio	Scorpio	Aquarius	Aries	Taurus	Virgo	Leo
29	1:15 A.M. Aries	Sagittarius	Scorpio	Scorpio	Aquarius	Aries	Taurus	Virgo	Leo
30		Sagittarius	Scorpio	Scorpio	Pisces	Aries	Taurus	Virgo	Leo
31	11:43 A.M. Taurus	Sagittarius	Scorpio	Scorpio	Pisces	Aries	Taurus	Virgo	Leo

CAPRICORN PLANETARY TABLES

1939

January	MOON FROM	IN	MERCURY	VENUS	MARS	JUPITER	SATURN	URANUS	NEPTUNE	PLUTO
1	Taurus		Sagittarius	Scorpio	Scorpio	Pisces	Aries	Taurus	Virgo	Leo
2	4:14 P.M.	Gemini	Sagittarius	Scorpio	Scorpio	Pisces	Aries	Taurus	Virgo	Leo
3			Sagittarius	Scorpio	Scorpio	Pisces	Aries	Taurus	Virgo	Leo
4	5:17 P.M.	Cancer	Sagittarius	Scorpio	Scorpio	Pisces	Aries	Taurus	Virgo	Leo
5			Sagittarius	Sagittarius	Scorpio	Pisces	Aries	Taurus	Virgo	Leo
6	4:32 P.M.	Leo	Sagittarius	Sagittarius	Scorpio	Pisces	Aries	Taurus	Virgo	Leo
7			Sagittarius	Sagittarius	Scorpio	Pisces	Aries	Taurus	Virgo	Leo
8	4:28 P.M.	Virgo	Sagittarius	Sagittarius	Scorpio	Pisces	Aries	Taurus	Virgo	Leo
9			Sagittarius	Sagittarius	Scorpio	Pisces	Aries	Taurus	Virgo	Leo
10	6:16 P.M.	Libra	Sagittarius	Sagittarius	Scorpio	Pisces	Aries	Taurus	Virgo	Leo
11			Sagittarius	Sagittarius	Scorpio	Pisces	Aries	Taurus	Virgo	Leo
12	11:58 P.M.	Scorpio	Capricorn	Sagittarius	Scorpio	Pisces	Aries	Taurus	Virgo	Leo
13			Capricorn	Sagittarius	Scorpio	Pisces	Aries	Taurus	Virgo	Leo
14			Capricorn	Sagittarius	Scorpio	Pisces	Aries	Taurus	Virgo	Leo
15	9:10 A.M.	Sagittarius	Capricorn	Sagittarius	Scorpio	Pisces	Aries	Taurus	Virgo	Leo
16			Capricorn	Sagittarius	Scorpio	Pisces	Aries	Taurus	Virgo	Leo
17	8:44 P.M.	Capricorn	Capricorn	Sagittarius	Scorpio	Pisces	Aries	Taurus	Virgo	Leo
18			Capricorn	Sagittarius	Scorpio	Pisces	Aries	Taurus	Virgo	Leo
19	9:16 P.M.	Aquarius	Capricorn	Sagittarius	Scorpio	Pisces	Aries	Taurus	Virgo	Leo
20			Capricorn	Sagittarius	Scorpio	Pisces	Aries	Taurus	Virgo	Leo
December										
23	7:32 P.M.	Gemini	Sagittarius	Capricorn	Pisces	Aries	Aries	Taurus	Virgo	Leo
24			Sagittarius	Capricorn	Pisces	Aries	Aries	Taurus	Virgo	Leo
25			Sagittarius	Aquarius	Pisces	Aries	Aries	Taurus	Virgo	Leo
26	0:01 A.M.	Cancer	Sagittarius	Aquarius	Pisces	Aries	Aries	Taurus	Virgo	Leo
27			Sagittarius	Aquarius	Pisces	Aries	Aries	Taurus	Virgo	Leo
28	2:07 A.M.	Leo	Sagittarius	Aquarius	Pisces	Aries	Aries	Taurus	Virgo	Leo
29			Sagittarius	Aquarius	Pisces	Aries	Aries	Taurus	Virgo	Leo
30	3:31 A.M.	Virgo	Sagittarius	Aquarius	Pisces	Aries	Aries	Taurus	Virgo	Leo
31			Sagittarius	Aquarius	Pisces	Aries	Aries	Taurus	Virgo	Leo

1940

	MOON		MERCURY	VENUS	MARS	JUPITER	SATURN	URANUS	NEPTUNE	PLUTO
January	**FROM**	**IN**								
1	5:44 A.M.	Libra	Sagittarius	Aquarius	Pisces	Aries	Aries	Taurus	Virgo	Leo
2			Sagittarius	Aquarius	Pisces	Aries	Aries	Taurus	Virgo	Leo
3	9:37 A.M.	Scorpio	Sagittarius	Aquarius	Pisces	Aries	Aries	Taurus	Virgo	Leo
4			Sagittarius	Aquarius	Aries	Aries	Aries	Taurus	Virgo	Leo
5	3:14 P.M.	Sagittarius	Sagittarius	Aquarius	Aries	Aries	Aries	Taurus	Virgo	Leo
6			Capricorn	Aquarius	Aries	Aries	Aries	Taurus	Virgo	Leo
7	10:32 P.M.	Capricorn	Capricorn	Aquarius	Aries	Aries	Aries	Taurus	Virgo	Leo
8			Capricorn	Aquarius	Aries	Aries	Aries	Taurus	Virgo	Leo
9			Capricorn	Aquarius	Aries	Aries	Aries	Taurus	Virgo	Leo
10	7:43 A.M.	Aquarius	Capricorn	Aquarius	Aries	Aries	Aries	Taurus	Virgo	Leo
11			Capricorn	Aquarius	Aries	Aries	Aries	Taurus	Virgo	Leo
12	7:05 P.M.	Pisces	Capricorn	Aquarius	Aries	Aries	Aries	Taurus	Virgo	Leo
13			Capricorn	Aquarius	Aries	Aries	Aries	Taurus	Virgo	Leo
14			Capricorn	Aquarius	Aries	Aries	Aries	Taurus	Virgo	Leo
15	7:55 A.M.	Aries	Capricorn	Aquarius	Aries	Aries	Aries	Taurus	Virgo	Leo
16			Capricorn	Aquarius	Aries	Aries	Aries	Taurus	Virgo	Leo
17	8:11 P.M.	Taurus	Capricorn	Aquarius	Aries	Aries	Aries	Taurus	Virgo	Leo
18			Capricorn	Aquarius	Aries	Aries	Aries	Taurus	Virgo	Leo
19			Capricorn	Pisces	Aries	Aries	Aries	Taurus	Virgo	Leo
20	5:30 A.M.	Gemini	Capricorn	Pisces	Aries	Aries	Aries	Taurus	Virgo	Leo
December										
22	Libra		Sagittarius	Sagittarius	Scorpio	Taurus	Taurus	Taurus	Virgo	Leo
23	11:29 P.M.	Scorpio	Sagittarius	Sagittarius	Scorpio	Taurus	Taurus	Taurus	Virgo	Leo
24			Sagittarius	Sagittarius	Scorpio	Taurus	Taurus	Taurus	Virgo	Leo
25			Sagittarius	Sagittarius	Scorpio	Taurus	Taurus	Taurus	Virgo	Leo
26	1:37 A.M.	Sagittarius	Sagittarius	Sagittarius	Scorpio	Taurus	Taurus	Taurus	Virgo	Leo
27			Sagittarius	Sagittarius	Scorpio	Taurus	Taurus	Taurus	Virgo	Leo
28	3:59 A.M.	Capricorn	Sagittarius	Sagittarius	Scorpio	Taurus	Taurus	Taurus	Virgo	Leo
29			Capricorn	Sagittarius	Scorpio	Taurus	Taurus	Taurus	Virgo	Leo
30	8:09 A.M.	Aquarius	Capricorn	Sagittarius	Scorpio	Taurus	Taurus	Taurus	Virgo	Leo
31			Capricorn	Sagittarius	Scorpio	Taurus	Taurus	Taurus	Virgo	Leo

CAPRICORN PLANETARY TABLES

1941

January	MOON FROM / IN	MERCURY	VENUS	MARS	JUPITER	SATURN	URANUS	NEPTUNE	PLUTO
1	Aquarius	Capricorn	Sagittarius	Scorpio	Taurus	Taurus	Taurus	Virgo	Leo
2	0:01 A.M. Pisces	Capricorn	Sagittarius	Scorpio	Taurus	Taurus	Taurus	Virgo	Leo
3		Capricorn	Sagittarius	Scorpio	Taurus	Taurus	Taurus	Virgo	Leo
4	2:36 A.M. Aries	Capricorn	Sagittarius	Sagittarius	Taurus	Taurus	Taurus	Virgo	Leo
5		Capricorn	Sagittarius	Sagittarius	Taurus	Taurus	Taurus	Virgo	Leo
6	3:27 P.M. Taurus	Capricorn	Sagittarius	Sagittarius	Taurus	Taurus	Taurus	Virgo	Leo
7		Capricorn	Sagittarius	Sagittarius	Taurus	Taurus	Taurus	Virgo	Leo
8		Capricorn	Sagittarius	Sagittarius	Taurus	Taurus	Taurus	Virgo	Leo
9	3:25 A.M. Gemini	Capricorn	Sagittarius	Sagittarius	Taurus	Taurus	Taurus	Virgo	Leo
10		Capricorn	Sagittarius	Sagittarius	Taurus	Taurus	Taurus	Virgo	Leo
11	12:31 P.M. Cancer	Capricorn	Sagittarius	Sagittarius	Taurus	Taurus	Taurus	Virgo	Leo
12		Capricorn	Sagittarius	Sagittarius	Taurus	Taurus	Taurus	Virgo	Leo
13	6:36 P.M. Leo	Capricorn	Sagittarius	Sagittarius	Taurus	Taurus	Taurus	Virgo	Leo
14		Capricorn	Capricorn	Sagittarius	Taurus	Taurus	Taurus	Virgo	Leo
15	10:45 P.M. Virgo	Capricorn	Capricorn	Sagittarius	Taurus	Taurus	Taurus	Virgo	Leo
16		Capricorn	Capricorn	Sagittarius	Taurus	Taurus	Taurus	Virgo	Leo
17		Aquarius	Capricorn	Sagittarius	Taurus	Taurus	Taurus	Virgo	Leo
18	2:00 A.M. Libra	Aquarius	Capricorn	Sagittarius	Taurus	Taurus	Taurus	Virgo	Leo
19		Aquarius	Capricorn	Sagittarius	Taurus	Taurus	Taurus	Virgo	Leo
December									
22	3:38 P.M. Pisces	Capricorn	Aquarius	Aries	Gemini	Taurus	Taurus	Virgo	Leo
23		Capricorn	Aquarius	Aries	Gemini	Taurus	Taurus	Virgo	Leo
24	11:27 P.M. Aries	Capricorn	Aquarius	Aries	Gemini	Taurus	Taurus	Virgo	Leo
25		Capricorn	Aquarius	Aries	Gemini	Taurus	Taurus	Virgo	Leo
26		Capricorn	Aquarius	Aries	Gemini	Taurus	Taurus	Virgo	Leo
27	10:44 A.M. Taurus	Capricorn	Aquarius	Aries	Gemini	Taurus	Taurus	Virgo	Leo
28		Capricorn	Aquarius	Aries	Gemini	Taurus	Taurus	Virgo	Leo
29	11:26 P.M. Gemini	Capricorn	Aquarius	Aries	Gemini	Taurus	Taurus	Virgo	Leo
30		Capricorn	Aquarius	Aries	Gemini	Taurus	Taurus	Virgo	Leo
31		Capricorn	Aquarius	Aries	Gemini	Taurus	Taurus	Virgo	Leo

1942

	MOON									
January	FROM / IN	MERCURY	VENUS	MARS	JUPITER	SATURN	URANUS	NEPTUNE	PLUTO
1	8:01 A.M. Cancer	Capricorn	Aquarius	Aries	Gemini	Taurus	Taurus	Virgo	Leo
2		Capricorn	Aquarius	Aries	Gemini	Taurus	Taurus	Virgo	Leo
3	10:30 P.M. Leo	Capricorn	Aquarius	Aries	Gemini	Taurus	Taurus	Virgo	Leo
4		Capricorn	Aquarius	Aries	Gemini	Taurus	Taurus	Virgo	Leo
5		Capricorn	Aquarius	Aries	Gemini	Taurus	Taurus	Virgo	Leo
6	7:41 A.M. Virgo	Capricorn	Aquarius	Aries	Gemini	Taurus	Taurus	Virgo	Leo
7		Capricorn	Aquarius	Aries	Gemini	Taurus	Taurus	Virgo	Leo
8	2:45 P.M. Libra	Capricorn	Aquarius	Aries	Gemini	Taurus	Taurus	Virgo	Leo
9		Capricorn	Aquarius	Aries	Gemini	Taurus	Taurus	Virgo	Leo
10	7:20 P.M. Scorpio	Aquarius	Aquarius	Taurus	Gemini	Taurus	Taurus	Virgo	Leo
11		Aquarius	Aquarius	Taurus	Gemini	Taurus	Taurus	Virgo	Leo
12	9:29 P.M. Sagittarius	Aquarius	Aquarius	Taurus	Gemini	Taurus	Taurus	Virgo	Leo
13		Aquarius	Aquarius	Taurus	Gemini	Taurus	Taurus	Virgo	Leo
14	10:07 P.M. Capricorn	Aquarius	Aquarius	Taurus	Gemini	Taurus	Taurus	Virgo	Leo
15		Aquarius	Aquarius	Taurus	Gemini	Taurus	Taurus	Virgo	Leo
16	10:55 P.M. Aquarius	Aquarius	Aquarius	Taurus	Gemini	Taurus	Taurus	Virgo	Leo
17		Aquarius	Aquarius	Taurus	Gemini	Taurus	Taurus	Virgo	Leo
18		Aquarius	Aquarius	Taurus	Gemini	Taurus	Taurus	Virgo	Leo
19	1:46 A.M. Pisces	Aquarius	Aquarius	Taurus	Gemini	Taurus	Taurus	Virgo	Leo
20		Aquarius	Aquarius	Taurus	Gemini	Taurus	Taurus	Virgo	Leo
December									
22	9:46 A.M. Cancer	Capricorn	Capricorn	Sagittarius	Cancer	Gemini	Gemini	Libra	Leo
23	10:35 P.M. Leo	Capricorn	Capricorn	Sagittarius	Cancer	Gemini	Gemini	Libra	Leo
24		Capricorn	Capricorn	Sagittarius	Cancer	Gemini	Gemini	Libra	Leo
25		Capricorn	Capricorn	Sagittarius	Cancer	Gemini	Gemini	Libra	Leo
26		Capricorn	Capricorn	Sagittarius	Cancer	Gemini	Gemini	Libra	Leo
27	11:08 A.M. Virgo	Capricorn	Capricorn	Sagittarius	Cancer	Gemini	Gemini	Libra	Leo
28		Capricorn	Capricorn	Sagittarius	Cancer	Gemini	Gemini	Libra	Leo
29	9:40 P.M. Libra	Capricorn	Capricorn	Sagittarius	Cancer	Gemini	Gemini	Libra	Leo
30		Capricorn	Capricorn	Sagittarius	Cancer	Gemini	Gemini	Libra	Leo
31		Capricorn	Capricorn	Sagittarius	Cancer	Gemini	Gemini	Libra	Leo

CAPRICORN PLANETARY TABLES

1943

	MOON FROM	IN	MERCURY	VENUS	MARS	JUPITER	SATURN	URANUS	NEPTUNE	PLUTO
January										
1	4:37 A.M.	Scorpio	Capricorn	Capricorn	Sagittarius	Cancer	Gemini	Gemini	Libra	Leo
2			Capricorn	Capricorn	Sagittarius	Cancer	Gemini	Gemini	Libra	Leo
3	7:34 A.M.	Sagittarius	Aquarius	Capricorn	Sagittarius	Cancer	Gemini	Gemini	Libra	Leo
4			Aquarius	Capricorn	Sagittarius	Cancer	Gemini	Gemini	Libra	Leo
5	7:35 A.M.	Capricorn	Aquarius	Capricorn	Sagittarius	Cancer	Gemini	Gemini	Libra	Leo
6			Aquarius	Capricorn	Sagittarius	Cancer	Gemini	Gemini	Libra	Leo
7	6:41 A.M.	Aquarius	Aquarius	Capricorn	Sagittarius	Cancer	Gemini	Gemini	Libra	Leo
8			Aquarius	Aquarius	Sagittarius	Cancer	Gemini	Gemini	Libra	Leo
9	7:03 A.M.	Pisces	Aquarius	Aquarius	Sagittarius	Cancer	Gemini	Gemini	Libra	Leo
10			Aquarius	Aquarius	Sagittarius	Cancer	Gemini	Gemini	Libra	Leo
11	10:23 A.M.	Aries	Aquarius	Aquarius	Sagittarius	Cancer	Gemini	Gemini	Libra	Leo
12			Aquarius	Aquarius	Sagittarius	Cancer	Gemini	Gemini	Libra	Leo
13	5:26 P.M.	Taurus	Aquarius	Aquarius	Sagittarius	Cancer	Gemini	Gemini	Libra	Leo
14			Aquarius	Aquarius	Sagittarius	Cancer	Gemini	Gemini	Libra	Leo
15			Aquarius	Aquarius	Sagittarius	Cancer	Gemini	Gemini	Libra	Leo
16	3:40 A.M.	Gemini	Aquarius	Aquarius	Sagittarius	Cancer	Gemini	Gemini	Libra	Leo
17			Aquarius	Aquarius	Sagittarius	Cancer	Gemini	Gemini	Libra	Leo
18	3:55 P.M.	Cancer	Aquarius	Aquarius	Sagittarius	Cancer	Gemini	Gemini	Libra	Leo
19			Aquarius	Aquarius	Sagittarius	Cancer	Gemini	Gemini	Libra	Leo
20			Aquarius	Aquarius	Sagittarius	Cancer	Gemini	Gemini	Libra	Leo
December										
23		Scorpio	Capricorn	Scorpio	Gemini	Leo	Gemini	Gemini	Libra	Leo
24	12:40 P.M.	Sagittarius	Capricorn	Scorpio	Gemini	Leo	Gemini	Gemini	Libra	Leo
25			Capricorn	Scorpio	Gemini	Leo	Gemini	Gemini	Libra	Leo
26	3:21 P.M.	Capricorn	Capricorn	Scorpio	Gemini	Leo	Gemini	Gemini	Libra	Leo
27			Capricorn	Scorpio	Gemini	Leo	Gemini	Gemini	Libra	Leo
28	4:21 P.M.	Aquarius	Capricorn	Scorpio	Gemini	Leo	Gemini	Gemini	Libra	Leo
29			Capricorn	Scorpio	Gemini	Leo	Gemini	Gemini	Libra	Leo
30	5:19 P.M.	Pisces	Capricorn	Scorpio	Gemini	Leo	Gemini	Gemini	Libra	Leo
31			Capricorn	Scorpio	Gemini	Leo	Gemini	Gemini	Libra	Leo

1944

January	MOON FROM / IN	MERCURY	VENUS	MARS	JUPITER	SATURN	URANUS	NEPTUNE	PLUTO
1	Pisces	Capricorn	Scorpio	Gemini	Leo	Gemini	Gemini	Libra	Leo
2	0:01 A.M. Aries	Capricorn	Scorpio	Gemini	Leo	Gemini	Gemini	Libra	Leo
3		Capricorn	Sagittarius	Gemini	Leo	Gemini	Gemini	Libra	Leo
4	2:37 A.M. Taurus	Capricorn	Sagittarius	Gemini	Leo	Gemini	Gemini	Libra	Leo
5		Capricorn	Sagittarius	Gemini	Leo	Gemini	Gemini	Libra	Leo
6	6:45 A.M. Gemini	Capricorn	Sagittarius	Gemini	Leo	Gemini	Gemini	Libra	Leo
7		Capricorn	Sagittarius	Gemini	Leo	Gemini	Gemini	Libra	Leo
8	3:50 P.M. Cancer	Capricorn	Sagittarius	Gemini	Leo	Gemini	Gemini	Libra	Leo
9		Capricorn	Sagittarius	Gemini	Leo	Gemini	Gemini	Libra	Leo
10		Capricorn	Sagittarius	Gemini	Leo	Gemini	Gemini	Libra	Leo
11	2:59 A.M. Leo	Capricorn	Sagittarius	Gemini	Leo	Gemini	Gemini	Libra	Leo
12		Capricorn	Sagittarius	Gemini	Leo	Gemini	Gemini	Libra	Leo
13	3:39 P.M. Virgo	Capricorn	Sagittarius	Gemini	Leo	Gemini	Gemini	Libra	Leo
14		Capricorn	Sagittarius	Gemini	Leo	Gemini	Gemini	Libra	Leo
15		Capricorn	Sagittarius	Gemini	Leo	Gemini	Gemini	Libra	Leo
16	4:29 A.M. Libra	Capricorn	Sagittarius	Gemini	Leo	Gemini	Gemini	Libra	Leo
17		Capricorn	Sagittarius	Gemini	Leo	Gemini	Gemini	Libra	Leo
18	3:23 P.M. Scorpio	Capricorn	Sagittarius	Gemini	Leo	Gemini	Gemini	Libra	Leo
19		Capricorn	Sagittarius	Gemini	Leo	Gemini	Gemini	Libra	Leo
20	10:47 P.M. Sagittarius	Capricorn	Sagittarius	Gemini	Leo	Gemini	Gemini	Libra	Leo
December									
22	9:42 A.M. Aries	Capricorn	Aquarius	Sagittarius	Virgo	Cancer	Gemini	Libra	Leo
23		Capricorn	Aquarius	Sagittarius	Virgo	Cancer	Gemini	Libra	Leo
24	12:25 P.M. Taurus	Sagittarius	Aquarius	Sagittarius	Virgo	Cancer	Gemini	Libra	Leo
25		Sagittarius	Aquarius	Sagittarius	Virgo	Cancer	Gemini	Libra	Leo
26	3:28 P.M. Gemini	Sagittarius	Aquarius	Sagittarius	Virgo	Cancer	Gemini	Libra	Leo
27		Sagittarius	Aquarius	Sagittarius	Virgo	Cancer	Gemini	Libra	Leo
28	7:47 P.M. Cancer	Sagittarius	Aquarius	Sagittarius	Virgo	Cancer	Gemini	Libra	Leo
29		Sagittarius	Aquarius	Sagittarius	Virgo	Cancer	Gemini	Libra	Leo
30		Sagittarius	Aquarius	Sagittarius	Virgo	Cancer	Gemini	Libra	Leo
31	2:22 A.M. Leo	Sagittarius	Aquarius	Sagittarius	Virgo	Cancer	Gemini	Libra	Leo

CAPRICORN PLANETARY TABLES

1945

	MOON FROM	MOON IN	MERCURY	VENUS	MARS	JUPITER	SATURN	URANUS	NEPTUNE	PLUTO
January										
1	Leo		Sagittarius	Aquarius	Sagittarius	Virgo	Cancer	Gemini	Libra	Leo
2	11:52 A.M.	Virgo	Sagittarius	Aquarius	Sagittarius	Virgo	Cancer	Gemini	Libra	Leo
3			Sagittarius	Aquarius	Sagittarius	Virgo	Cancer	Gemini	Libra	Leo
4	11:45 P.M.	Libra	Sagittarius	Aquarius	Sagittarius	Virgo	Cancer	Gemini	Libra	Leo
5			Sagittarius	Aquarius	Sagittarius	Virgo	Cancer	Gemini	Libra	Leo
6			Sagittarius	Pisces	Capricorn	Virgo	Cancer	Gemini	Libra	Leo
7	12:11 P.M.	Scorpio	Sagittarius	Pisces	Capricorn	Virgo	Cancer	Gemini	Libra	Leo
8			Sagittarius	Pisces	Capricorn	Virgo	Cancer	Gemini	Libra	Leo
9	10:52 P.M.	Sagittarius	Sagittarius	Pisces	Capricorn	Virgo	Cancer	Gemini	Libra	Leo
10			Sagittarius	Pisces	Capricorn	Virgo	Cancer	Gemini	Libra	Leo
11			Sagittarius	Pisces	Capricorn	Virgo	Cancer	Gemini	Libra	Leo
12	6:27 A.M.	Capricorn	Sagittarius	Pisces	Capricorn	Virgo	Cancer	Gemini	Libra	Leo
13			Sagittarius	Pisces	Capricorn	Virgo	Cancer	Gemini	Libra	Leo
14	10:55 A.M.	Aquarius	Capricorn	Pisces	Capricorn	Virgo	Cancer	Gemini	Libra	Leo
15			Capricorn	Pisces	Capricorn	Virgo	Cancer	Gemini	Libra	Leo
16	1:26 P.M.	Pisces	Capricorn	Pisces	Capricorn	Virgo	Cancer	Gemini	Libra	Leo
17			Capricorn	Pisces	Capricorn	Virgo	Cancer	Gemini	Libra	Leo
18	3:22 P.M.	Aries	Capricorn	Pisces	Capricorn	Virgo	Cancer	Gemini	Libra	Leo
19			Capricorn	Pisces	Capricorn	Virgo	Cancer	Gemini	Libra	Leo
December										
22	Leo		Sagittarius	Sagittarius	Leo	Libra	Cancer	Gemini	Libra	Leo
23	9:46 A.M.	Virgo	Sagittarius	Sagittarius	Leo	Libra	Cancer	Gemini	Libra	Leo
24			Sagittarius	Sagittarius	Leo	Libra	Cancer	Gemini	Libra	Leo
25	6:49 P.M.	Libra	Sagittarius	Sagittarius	Leo	Libra	Cancer	Gemini	Libra	Leo
26			Sagittarius	Sagittarius	Leo	Libra	Cancer	Gemini	Libra	Leo
27			Sagittarius	Sagittarius	Cancer	Libra	Cancer	Gemini	Libra	Leo
28	6:42 A.M.	Scorpio	Sagittarius	Sagittarius	Cancer	Libra	Cancer	Gemini	Libra	Leo
29			Sagittarius	Sagittarius	Cancer	Libra	Cancer	Gemini	Libra	Leo
30	7:30 P.M.	Sagittarius	Sagittarius	Capricorn	Cancer	Libra	Cancer	Gemini	Libra	Leo
31			Sagittarius	Capricorn	Cancer	Libra	Cancer	Gemini	Libra	Leo

1946

MOON										
January	FROM	IN	MERCURY	VENUS	MARS	JUPITER	SATURN	URANUS	NEPTUNE	PLUTO
1	Sagittarius		Sagittarius	Capricorn	Cancer	Libra	Cancer	Gemini	Libra	Leo
2	7:10 A.M.	Capricorn	Sagittarius	Capricorn	Cancer	Libra	Cancer	Gemini	Libra	Leo
3			Sagittarius	Capricorn	Cancer	Libra	Cancer	Gemini	Libra	Leo
4	4:32 P.M.	Aquarius	Sagittarius	Capricorn	Cancer	Libra	Cancer	Gemini	Libra	Leo
5			Sagittarius	Capricorn	Cancer	Libra	Cancer	Gemini	Libra	Leo
6	11:42 P.M.	Pisces	Sagittarius	Capricorn	Cancer	Libra	Cancer	Gemini	Libra	Leo
7			Sagittarius	Capricorn	Cancer	Libra	Cancer	Gemini	Libra	Leo
8			Sagittarius	Capricorn	Cancer	Libra	Cancer	Gemini	Libra	Leo
9	4:52 A.M.	Aries	Sagittarius	Capricorn	Cancer	Libra	Cancer	Gemini	Libra	Leo
10			Capricorn	Capricorn	Cancer	Libra	Cancer	Gemini	Libra	Leo
11	8:23 A.M.	Taurus	Capricorn	Capricorn	Cancer	Libra	Cancer	Gemini	Libra	Leo
12			Capricorn	Capricorn	Cancer	Libra	Cancer	Gemini	Libra	Leo
13	10:43 A.M.	Gemini	Capricorn	Capricorn	Cancer	Libra	Cancer	Gemini	Libra	Leo
14			Capricorn	Capricorn	Cancer	Libra	Cancer	Gemini	Libra	Leo
15	12:34 P.M.	Cancer	Capricorn	Capricorn	Cancer	Libra	Cancer	Gemini	Libra	Leo
16			Capricorn	Capricorn	Cancer	Libra	Cancer	Gemini	Libra	Leo
17	3:11 P.M.	Leo	Capricorn	Capricorn	Cancer	Libra	Cancer	Gemini	Libra	Leo
18			Capricorn	Capricorn	Cancer	Libra	Cancer	Gemini	Libra	Leo
19	7:50 P.M.	Virgo	Capricorn	Capricorn	Cancer	Libra	Cancer	Gemini	Libra	Leo
20			Capricorn	Capricorn	Cancer	Libra	Cancer	Gemini	Libra	Leo
December										
22	Sagittarius		Sagittarius	Scorpio	Capricorn	Scorpio	Leo	Gemini	Libra	Leo
23	5:51 A.M.	Capricorn	Sagittarius	Scorpio	Capricorn	Scorpio	Leo	Gemini	Libra	Leo
24			Sagittarius	Scorpio	Capricorn	Scorpio	Leo	Gemini	Libra	Leo
25	6:27 P.M.	Aquarius	Sagittarius	Scorpio	Capricorn	Scorpio	Leo	Gemini	Libra	Leo
26			Sagittarius	Scorpio	Capricorn	Scorpio	Leo	Gemini	Libra	Leo
27			Sagittarius	Scorpio	Capricorn	Scorpio	Leo	Gemini	Libra	Leo
28	5:40 A.M.	Pisces	Sagittarius	Scorpio	Capricorn	Scorpio	Leo	Gemini	Libra	Leo
29			Sagittarius	Scorpio	Capricorn	Scorpio	Leo	Gemini	Libra	Leo
30	2:23 P.M.	Aries	Sagittarius	Scorpio	Capricorn	Scorpio	Leo	Gemini	Libra	Leo
31			Sagittarius	Scorpio	Capricorn	Scorpio	Leo	Gemini	Libra	Leo

CAPRICORN PLANETARY TABLES

1947

January	MOON FROM IN	MERCURY	VENUS	MARS	JUPITER	SATURN	URANUS	NEPTUNE	PLUTO
1	Aries	Sagittarius	Scorpio	Capricorn	Scorpio	Leo	Gemini	Libra	Leo
2	0:01 A.M. Taurus	Sagittarius	Scorpio	Capricorn	Scorpio	Leo	Gemini	Libra	Leo
3	10:22 P.M. Gemini	Capricorn	Scorpio	Capricorn	Scorpio	Leo	Gemini	Libra	Leo
4		Capricorn	Scorpio	Capricorn	Scorpio	Leo	Gemini	Libra	Leo
5	10:27 P.M. Cancer	Capricorn	Scorpio	Capricorn	Scorpio	Leo	Gemini	Libra	Leo
6		Capricorn	Sagittarius	Capricorn	Scorpio	Leo	Gemini	Libra	Leo
7	9:56 P.M. Leo	Capricorn	Sagittarius	Capricorn	Scorpio	Leo	Gemini	Libra	Leo
8		Capricorn	Sagittarius	Capricorn	Scorpio	Leo	Gemini	Libra	Leo
9	10:50 P.M. Virgo	Capricorn	Sagittarius	Capricorn	Scorpio	Leo	Gemini	Libra	Leo
10		Capricorn	Sagittarius	Capricorn	Scorpio	Leo	Gemini	Libra	Leo
11		Capricorn	Sagittarius	Capricorn	Scorpio	Leo	Gemini	Libra	Leo
12	2:59 A.M. Libra	Capricorn	Sagittarius	Capricorn	Scorpio	Leo	Gemini	Libra	Leo
13		Capricorn	Sagittarius	Capricorn	Scorpio	Leo	Gemini	Libra	Leo
14	11:19 A.M. Scorpio	Capricorn	Sagittarius	Capricorn	Scorpio	Leo	Gemini	Libra	Leo
15		Capricorn	Sagittarius	Capricorn	Scorpio	Leo	Gemini	Libra	Leo
16	11:06 P.M. Sagittarius	Capricorn	Sagittarius	Capricorn	Scorpio	Leo	Gemini	Libra	Leo
17		Capricorn	Sagittarius	Capricorn	Scorpio	Leo	Gemini	Libra	Leo
18		Capricorn	Sagittarius	Capricorn	Scorpio	Leo	Gemini	Libra	Leo
19	12:11 P.M. Capricorn	Capricorn	Sagittarius	Capricorn	Scorpio	Leo	Gemini	Libra	Leo
20		Capricorn	Sagittarius	Capricorn	Scorpio	Leo	Gemini	Libra	Leo
December									
23	1:08 A.M. Taurus	Sagittarius	Capricorn	Virgo	Sagittarius	Leo	Gemini	Libra	Leo
24		Sagittarius	Capricorn	Virgo	Sagittarius	Leo	Gemini	Libra	Leo
25	5:46 A.M. Gemini	Sagittarius	Aquarius	Virgo	Sagittarius	Leo	Gemini	Libra	Leo
26		Sagittarius	Aquarius	Virgo	Sagittarius	Leo	Gemini	Libra	Leo
27	7:03 A.M. Cancer	Capricorn	Aquarius	Virgo	Sagittarius	Leo	Gemini	Libra	Leo
28		Capricorn	Aquarius	Virgo	Sagittarius	Leo	Gemini	Libra	Leo
29	6:43 A.M. Leo	Capricorn	Aquarius	Virgo	Sagittarius	Leo	Gemini	Libra	Leo
30		Capricorn	Aquarius	Virgo	Sagittarius	Leo	Gemini	Libra	Leo
31	6:47 A.M. Virgo	Capricorn	Aquarius	Virgo	Sagittarius	Leo	Gemini	Libra	Leo

1948

January	MOON FROM	IN	MERCURY	VENUS	MARS	JUPITER	SATURN	URANUS	NEPTUNE	PLUTO
1		Virgo	Capricorn	Aquarius	Virgo	Sagittarius	Leo	Gemini	Libra	Leo
2	10:12 A.M.	Libra	Capricorn	Aquarius	Virgo	Sagittarius	Leo	Gemini	Libra	Leo
3			Capricorn	Aquarius	Virgo	Sagittarius	Leo	Gemini	Libra	Leo
4	2:54 P.M.	Scorpio	Capricorn	Aquarius	Virgo	Sagittarius	Leo	Gemini	Libra	Leo
5			Capricorn	Aquarius	Virgo	Sagittarius	Leo	Gemini	Libra	Leo
6	11:44 P.M.	Sagittarius	Capricorn	Aquarius	Virgo	Sagittarius	Leo	Gemini	Libra	Leo
7			Capricorn	Aquarius	Virgo	Sagittarius	Leo	Gemini	Libra	Leo
8			Capricorn	Aquarius	Virgo	Sagittarius	Leo	Gemini	Libra	Leo
9	10:42 A.M.	Capricorn	Capricorn	Aquarius	Virgo	Sagittarius	Leo	Gemini	Libra	Leo
10			Capricorn	Aquarius	Virgo	Sagittarius	Leo	Gemini	Libra	Leo
11	10:54 P.M.	Aquarius	Capricorn	Aquarius	Virgo	Sagittarius	Leo	Gemini	Libra	Leo
12			Capricorn	Aquarius	Virgo	Sagittarius	Leo	Gemini	Libra	Leo
13			Capricorn	Aquarius	Virgo	Sagittarius	Leo	Gemini	Libra	Leo
14	11:39 A.M.	Pisces	Aquarius	Aquarius	Virgo	Sagittarius	Leo	Gemini	Libra	Leo
15			Aquarius	Aquarius	Virgo	Sagittarius	Leo	Gemini	Libra	Leo
16	11:41 P.M.	Aries	Aquarius	Aquarius	Virgo	Sagittarius	Leo	Gemini	Libra	Leo
17			Aquarius	Aquarius	Virgo	Sagittarius	Leo	Gemini	Libra	Leo
18			Aquarius	Pisces	Virgo	Sagittarius	Leo	Gemini	Libra	Leo
19	9:53 A.M.	Taurus	Aquarius	Pisces	Virgo	Sagittarius	Leo	Gemini	Libra	Leo
20			Aquarius	Pisces	Virgo	Sagittarius	Leo	Gemini	Libra	Leo
December										
22	10:00 P.M.	Libra	Capricorn	Sagittarius	Capricorn	Capricorn	Virgo	Gemini	Libra	Leo
23			Capricorn	Sagittarius	Capricorn	Capricorn	Virgo	Gemini	Libra	Leo
24			Capricorn	Sagittarius	Capricorn	Capricorn	Virgo	Gemini	Libra	Leo
25	1:40 A.M.	Scorpio	Capricorn	Sagittarius	Capricorn	Capricorn	Virgo	Gemini	Libra	Leo
26			Capricorn	Sagittarius	Capricorn	Capricorn	Virgo	Gemini	Libra	Leo
27	6:28 A.M.	Sagittarius	Capricorn	Sagittarius	Capricorn	Capricorn	Virgo	Gemini	Libra	Leo
28			Capricorn	Sagittarius	Capricorn	Capricorn	Virgo	Gemini	Libra	Leo
29	12:49 P.M.	Capricorn	Capricorn	Sagittarius	Capricorn	Capricorn	Virgo	Gemini	Libra	Leo
30			Capricorn	Sagittarius	Capricorn	Capricorn	Virgo	Gemini	Libra	Leo
31			Capricorn	Sagittarius	Capricorn	Capricorn	Virgo	Gemini	Libra	Leo

1949

CAPRICORN PLANETARY TABLES

	MOON FROM	IN	MERCURY	VENUS	MARS	JUPITER	SATURN	URANUS	NEPTUNE	PLUTO
January										
1	3:01 A.M.	Aquarius	Capricorn	Sagittarius	Capricorn	Capricorn	Virgo	Gemini	Libra	Leo
2	7:58 A.M.	Pisces	Capricorn	Sagittarius	Capricorn	Capricorn	Virgo	Gemini	Libra	Leo
3			Capricorn	Sagittarius	Capricorn	Capricorn	Virgo	Gemini	Libra	Leo
4	8:39 P.M.	Aries	Capricorn	Sagittarius	Capricorn	Capricorn	Virgo	Gemini	Libra	Leo
5			Capricorn	Sagittarius	Aquarius	Capricorn	Virgo	Gemini	Libra	Leo
6			Aquarius	Sagittarius	Aquarius	Capricorn	Virgo	Gemini	Libra	Leo
7			Aquarius	Sagittarius	Aquarius	Capricorn	Virgo	Gemini	Libra	Leo
8	9:01 A.M.	Taurus	Aquarius	Sagittarius	Aquarius	Capricorn	Virgo	Gemini	Libra	Leo
9			Aquarius	Sagittarius	Aquarius	Capricorn	Virgo	Gemini	Libra	Leo
10	6:25 P.M.	Gemini	Aquarius	Sagittarius	Aquarius	Capricorn	Virgo	Gemini	Libra	Leo
11			Aquarius	Sagittarius	Aquarius	Capricorn	Virgo	Gemini	Libra	Leo
12	11:52 P.M.	Cancer	Aquarius	Capricorn	Aquarius	Capricorn	Virgo	Gemini	Libra	Leo
13			Aquarius	Capricorn	Aquarius	Capricorn	Virgo	Gemini	Libra	Leo
14			Aquarius	Capricorn	Aquarius	Capricorn	Virgo	Gemini	Libra	Leo
15	2:06 A.M.	Leo	Aquarius	Capricorn	Aquarius	Capricorn	Virgo	Gemini	Libra	Leo
16			Aquarius	Capricorn	Aquarius	Capricorn	Virgo	Gemini	Libra	Leo
17	2:52 A.M.	Virgo	Aquarius	Capricorn	Aquarius	Capricorn	Virgo	Gemini	Libra	Leo
18			Aquarius	Capricorn	Aquarius	Capricorn	Virgo	Gemini	Libra	Leo
19	4:04 A.M.	Libra	Aquarius	Capricorn	Aquarius	Capricorn	Virgo	Gemini	Libra	Leo
December										
22	Aquarius		Capricorn	Aquarius	Virgo	Aquarius	Virgo	Cancer	Libra	Leo
23			Capricorn	Aquarius	Virgo	Aquarius	Virgo	Cancer	Libra	Leo
24	4:22 A.M.	Pisces	Capricorn	Aquarius	Virgo	Aquarius	Virgo	Cancer	Libra	Leo
25			Capricorn	Aquarius	Virgo	Aquarius	Virgo	Cancer	Libra	Leo
26	3:07 P.M.	Aries	Capricorn	Aquarius	Libra	Aquarius	Virgo	Cancer	Libra	Leo
27			Capricorn	Aquarius	Libra	Aquarius	Virgo	Cancer	Libra	Leo
28			Capricorn	Aquarius	Libra	Aquarius	Virgo	Cancer	Libra	Leo
29	3:59 A.M.	Taurus	Capricorn	Aquarius	Libra	Aquarius	Virgo	Cancer	Libra	Leo
30			Capricorn	Aquarius	Libra	Aquarius	Virgo	Cancer	Libra	Leo
31	4:13 P.M.	Gemini	Capricorn	Aquarius	Libra	Aquarius	Virgo	Cancer	Libra	Leo

1950

MOON		MERCURY	VENUS	MARS	JUPITER	SATURN	URANUS	NEPTUNE	PLUTO
January	**FROM IN**								
1	Gemini	Capricorn	Aquarius	Libra	Aquarius	Virgo	Cancer	Libra	Leo
2		Aquarius	Aquarius	Libra	Aquarius	Virgo	Cancer	Libra	Leo
3	1:54 A.M. Cancer	Aquarius	Aquarius	Libra	Aquarius	Virgo	Cancer	Libra	Leo
4		Aquarius	Aquarius	Libra	Aquarius	Virgo	Cancer	Libra	Leo
5	8:56 A.M. Leo	Aquarius	Aquarius	Libra	Aquarius	Virgo	Cancer	Libra	Leo
6		Aquarius	Aquarius	Libra	Aquarius	Virgo	Cancer	Libra	Leo
7	2:05 P.M. Virgo	Aquarius	Aquarius	Libra	Aquarius	Virgo	Cancer	Libra	Leo
8		Aquarius	Aquarius	Libra	Aquarius	Virgo	Cancer	Libra	Leo
9	6:07 P.M. Libra	Aquarius	Aquarius	Libra	Aquarius	Virgo	Cancer	Libra	Leo
10		Aquarius	Aquarius	Libra	Aquarius	Virgo	Cancer	Libra	Leo
11	9:26 P.M. Scorpio	Aquarius	Aquarius	Libra	Aquarius	Virgo	Cancer	Libra	Leo
12		Aquarius	Aquarius	Libra	Aquarius	Virgo	Cancer	Libra	Leo
13		Aquarius	Aquarius	Libra	Aquarius	Virgo	Cancer	Libra	Leo
14	0:16 A.M. Sagittarius	Aquarius	Aquarius	Libra	Aquarius	Virgo	Cancer	Libra	Leo
15		Capricorn	Aquarius	Libra	Aquarius	Virgo	Cancer	Libra	Leo
16	3:07 A.M. Capricorn	Capricorn	Aquarius	Libra	Aquarius	Virgo	Cancer	Libra	Leo
17		Capricorn	Aquarius	Libra	Aquarius	Virgo	Cancer	Libra	Leo
18	7:07 A.M. Aquarius	Capricorn	Aquarius	Libra	Aquarius	Virgo	Cancer	Libra	Leo
19		Capricorn	Aquarius	Libra	Aquarius	Virgo	Cancer	Libra	Leo
20	1:45 P.M. Pisces	Capricorn	Aquarius	Libra	Aquarius	Virgo	Cancer	Libra	Leo
December									
22	Gemini	Capricorn	Capricorn	Aquarius	Pisces	Libra	Cancer	Libra	Leo
23		Capricorn	Capricorn	Aquarius	Pisces	Libra	Cancer	Libra	Leo
24	1:17 A.M. Cancer	Capricorn	Capricorn	Aquarius	Pisces	Libra	Cancer	Libra	Leo
25		Capricorn	Capricorn	Aquarius	Pisces	Libra	Cancer	Libra	Leo
26	12:44 P.M. Leo	Capricorn	Capricorn	Aquarius	Pisces	Libra	Cancer	Libra	Leo
27		Capricorn	Capricorn	Aquarius	Pisces	Libra	Cancer	Libra	Leo
28	10:38 P.M. Virgo	Capricorn	Capricorn	Aquarius	Pisces	Libra	Cancer	Libra	Leo
29		Capricorn	Capricorn	Aquarius	Pisces	Libra	Cancer	Libra	Leo
30		Capricorn	Capricorn	Aquarius	Pisces	Libra	Cancer	Libra	Leo
31	6:20 A.M. Libra	Capricorn	Capricorn	Aquarius	Pisces	Libra	Cancer	Libra	Leo

1951

CAPRICORN PLANETARY TABLES

	MOON		MERCURY	VENUS	MARS	JUPITER	SATURN	URANUS	NEPTUNE	PLUTO
January	FROM	IN								
1		Libra	Capricorn	Capricorn	Aquarius	Pisces	Libra	Cancer	Libra	Leo
2	11:00 A.M.	Scorpio	Capricorn	Capricorn	Aquarius	Pisces	Libra	Cancer	Libra	Leo
3			Capricorn	Capricorn	Aquarius	Pisces	Libra	Cancer	Libra	Leo
4	12:36 P.M.	Sagittarius	Capricorn	Capricorn	Aquarius	Pisces	Libra	Cancer	Libra	Leo
5			Capricorn	Capricorn	Aquarius	Pisces	Libra	Cancer	Libra	Leo
6	12:32 P.M.	Capricorn	Capricorn	Capricorn	Aquarius	Pisces	Libra	Cancer	Libra	Leo
7			Capricorn	Capricorn	Aquarius	Pisces	Libra	Cancer	Libra	Leo
8	12:38 P.M.	Aquarius	Capricorn	Aquarius	Aquarius	Pisces	Libra	Cancer	Libra	Leo
9			Capricorn	Aquarius	Aquarius	Pisces	Libra	Cancer	Libra	Leo
10	3:02 P.M.	Pisces	Capricorn	Aquarius	Aquarius	Pisces	Libra	Cancer	Libra	Leo
11			Capricorn	Aquarius	Aquarius	Pisces	Libra	Cancer	Libra	Leo
12	8:24 P.M.	Aries	Capricorn	Aquarius	Aquarius	Pisces	Libra	Cancer	Libra	Leo
13			Capricorn	Aquarius	Aquarius	Pisces	Libra	Cancer	Libra	Leo
14			Capricorn	Aquarius	Aquarius	Pisces	Libra	Cancer	Libra	Leo
15	7:10 A.M.	Taurus	Capricorn	Aquarius	Aquarius	Pisces	Libra	Cancer	Libra	Leo
16			Capricorn	Aquarius	Aquarius	Pisces	Libra	Cancer	Libra	Leo
17	7:36 P.M.	Gemini	Capricorn	Aquarius	Aquarius	Pisces	Libra	Cancer	Libra	Leo
18			Capricorn	Aquarius	Aquarius	Pisces	Libra	Cancer	Libra	Leo
19			Capricorn	Aquarius	Aquarius	Pisces	Libra	Cancer	Libra	Leo
20	8:06 A.M.	Cancer	Capricorn	Aquarius	Aquarius	Pisces	Libra	Cancer	Libra	Leo
December										
23	6:31 P.M.	Scorpio	Sagittarius	Scorpio	Libra	Aries	Libra	Cancer	Libra	Leo
24			Sagittarius	Scorpio	Libra	Aries	Libra	Cancer	Libra	Leo
25	9:22 P.M.	Sagittarius	Sagittarius	Scorpio	Libra	Aries	Libra	Cancer	Libra	Leo
26			Sagittarius	Scorpio	Libra	Aries	Libra	Cancer	Libra	Leo
27	9:22 P.M.	Capricorn	Sagittarius	Scorpio	Libra	Aries	Libra	Cancer	Libra	Leo
28			Sagittarius	Scorpio	Libra	Aries	Libra	Cancer	Libra	Leo
29	8:38 P.M.	Aquarius	Sagittarius	Scorpio	Libra	Aries	Libra	Cancer	Libra	Leo
30			Sagittarius	Scorpio	Libra	Aries	Libra	Cancer	Libra	Leo
31			Sagittarius	Scorpio	Libra	Aries	Libra	Cancer	Libra	Leo

1952

January	MOON FROM	IN	MERCURY	VENUS	MARS	JUPITER	SATURN	URANUS	NEPTUNE	PLUTO
1	3:01 A.M.	Pisces	Sagittarius	Scorpio	Libra	Aries	Libra	Cancer	Libra	Leo
2	0:47 A.M.	Aries	Sagittarius	Scorpio	Libra	Aries	Libra	Cancer	Libra	Leo
3			Sagittarius	Sagittarius	Libra	Aries	Libra	Cancer	Libra	Leo
4	7:57 A.M.	Taurus	Sagittarius	Sagittarius	Libra	Aries	Libra	Cancer	Libra	Leo
5			Sagittarius	Sagittarius	Libra	Aries	Libra	Cancer	Libra	Leo
6	6:13 P.M.	Gemini	Sagittarius	Sagittarius	Libra	Aries	Libra	Cancer	Libra	Leo
7			Sagittarius	Sagittarius	Libra	Aries	Libra	Cancer	Libra	Leo
8			Sagittarius	Sagittarius	Libra	Aries	Libra	Cancer	Libra	Leo
9	6:00 A.M.	Cancer	Sagittarius	Sagittarius	Libra	Aries	Libra	Cancer	Libra	Leo
10			Sagittarius	Sagittarius	Libra	Aries	Libra	Cancer	Libra	Leo
11			Sagittarius	Sagittarius	Libra	Aries	Libra	Cancer	Libra	Leo
12	6:42 P.M.	Leo	Sagittarius	Sagittarius	Libra	Aries	Libra	Cancer	Libra	Leo
13			Sagittarius	Sagittarius	Libra	Aries	Libra	Cancer	Libra	Leo
14			Capricorn	Sagittarius	Libra	Aries	Libra	Cancer	Libra	Leo
15	7:12 A.M.	Virgo	Capricorn	Sagittarius	Libra	Aries	Libra	Cancer	Libra	Leo
16			Capricorn	Sagittarius	Libra	Aries	Libra	Cancer	Libra	Leo
17	6:14 P.M.	Libra	Capricorn	Sagittarius	Libra	Aries	Libra	Cancer	Libra	Leo
18			Capricorn	Sagittarius	Libra	Aries	Libra	Cancer	Libra	Leo
19			Capricorn	Sagittarius	Libra	Aries	Libra	Cancer	Libra	Leo
20	2:28 A.M.	Scorpio	Capricorn	Sagittarius	Libra	Aries	Libra	Cancer	Libra	Leo
21			Capricorn	Sagittarius	Scorpio	Aries	Libra	Cancer	Libra	Leo
December										
22	Pisces		Sagittarius	Aquarius	Aquarius	Taurus	Libra	Cancer	Libra	Leo
23	11:21 A.M.	Aries	Sagittarius	Aquarius	Aquarius	Taurus	Libra	Cancer	Libra	Leo
24			Sagittarius	Aquarius	Aquarius	Taurus	Libra	Cancer	Libra	Leo
25	3:53 P.M.	Taurus	Sagittarius	Aquarius	Aquarius	Taurus	Libra	Cancer	Libra	Leo
26			Sagittarius	Aquarius	Aquarius	Taurus	Libra	Cancer	Libra	Leo
27	9:58 P.M.	Gemini	Sagittarius	Aquarius	Aquarius	Taurus	Libra	Cancer	Libra	Leo
28			Sagittarius	Aquarius	Aquarius	Taurus	Libra	Cancer	Libra	Leo
29			Sagittarius	Aquarius	Aquarius	Taurus	Libra	Cancer	Libra	Leo
30	6:15 A.M.	Cancer	Sagittarius	Aquarius	Aquarius	Taurus	Libra	Cancer	Libra	Leo
31			Sagittarius	Aquarius	Pisces	Taurus	Libra	Cancer	Libra	Leo

CAPRICORN PLANETARY TABLES

1953

MOON FROM	IN	MERCURY	VENUS	MARS	JUPITER	SATURN	URANUS	NEPTUNE	PLUTO
January									
1	Cancer	Sagittarius	Aquarius	Pisces	Taurus	Libra	Cancer	Libra	Leo
2	0:01 A.M. Leo	Sagittarius	Aquarius	Pisces	Taurus	Libra	Cancer	Libra	Leo
3		Sagittarius	Aquarius	Pisces	Taurus	Libra	Cancer	Libra	Leo
4	5:36 A.M. Virgo	Sagittarius	Aquarius	Pisces	Taurus	Libra	Cancer	Libra	Leo
5		Sagittarius	Aquarius	Pisces	Taurus	Libra	Cancer	Libra	Leo
6	5:30 P.M. Libra	Sagittarius	Pisces	Pisces	Taurus	Libra	Cancer	Libra	Leo
7		Capricorn	Pisces	Pisces	Taurus	Libra	Cancer	Libra	Leo
8		Capricorn	Pisces	Pisces	Taurus	Libra	Cancer	Libra	Leo
9	4:53 A.M. Scorpio	Capricorn	Pisces	Pisces	Taurus	Libra	Cancer	Libra	Leo
10		Capricorn	Pisces	Pisces	Taurus	Libra	Cancer	Libra	Leo
11	12:29 P.M. Sagittarius	Capricorn	Pisces	Pisces	Taurus	Libra	Cancer	Libra	Leo
12		Capricorn	Pisces	Pisces	Taurus	Libra	Cancer	Libra	Leo
13	4:11 P.M. Capricorn	Capricorn	Pisces	Pisces	Taurus	Libra	Cancer	Libra	Leo
14		Capricorn	Pisces	Pisces	Taurus	Libra	Cancer	Libra	Leo
15	5:10 P.M. Aquarius	Capricorn	Pisces	Pisces	Taurus	Libra	Cancer	Libra	Leo
16		Capricorn	Pisces	Pisces	Taurus	Libra	Cancer	Libra	Leo
17	5:19 P.M. Pisces	Capricorn	Pisces	Pisces	Taurus	Libra	Cancer	Libra	Leo
18		Capricorn	Pisces	Pisces	Taurus	Libra	Cancer	Libra	Leo
19	6:17 P.M. Aries	Capricorn	Pisces	Pisces	Taurus	Libra	Cancer	Libra	Leo
20		Capricorn	Pisces	Pisces	Taurus	Libra	Cancer	Libra	Leo
December									
23	Leo	Sagittarius	Sagittarius	Scorpio	Gemini	Scorpio	Cancer	Libra	Leo
24		Sagittarius	Sagittarius	Scorpio	Gemini	Scorpio	Cancer	Libra	Leo
25	0:15 A.M. Virgo	Sagittarius	Sagittarius	Scorpio	Gemini	Scorpio	Cancer	Libra	Leo
26		Sagittarius	Sagittarius	Scorpio	Gemini	Scorpio	Cancer	Libra	Leo
27	12:18 P.M. Libra	Sagittarius	Sagittarius	Scorpio	Gemini	Scorpio	Cancer	Libra	Leo
28		Sagittarius	Sagittarius	Scorpio	Gemini	Scorpio	Cancer	Libra	Leo
29		Sagittarius	Sagittarius	Scorpio	Gemini	Scorpio	Cancer	Libra	Leo
30	1:07 A.M. Scorpio	Sagittarius	Capricorn	Scorpio	Gemini	Scorpio	Cancer	Libra	Leo
31		Capricorn	Capricorn	Scorpio	Gemini	Scorpio	Cancer	Libra	Leo

1954

January	MOON FROM IN	MERCURY	VENUS	MARS	JUPITER	SATURN	URANUS	NEPTUNE	PLUTO
1	9:00 A.M. Sagittarius	Capricorn	Capricorn	Scorpio	Gemini	Scorpio	Cancer	Libra	Leo
2		Capricorn	Capricorn	Scorpio	Gemini	Scorpio	Cancer	Libra	Leo
3	8:06 P.M. Capricorn	Capricorn	Capricorn	Scorpio	Gemini	Scorpio	Cancer	Libra	Leo
4		Capricorn	Capricorn	Scorpio	Gemini	Scorpio	Cancer	Libra	Leo
5		Capricorn	Capricorn	Scorpio	Gemini	Scorpio	Cancer	Libra	Leo
6	1:01 A.M. Aquarius	Capricorn	Capricorn	Scorpio	Gemini	Scorpio	Cancer	Libra	Leo
7		Capricorn	Capricorn	Scorpio	Gemini	Scorpio	Cancer	Libra	Leo
8	4:59 A.M. Pisces	Capricorn	Capricorn	Scorpio	Gemini	Scorpio	Cancer	Libra	Leo
9		Capricorn	Capricorn	Scorpio	Gemini	Scorpio	Cancer	Libra	Leo
10	7:31 A.M. Aries	Capricorn	Capricorn	Scorpio	Gemini	Scorpio	Cancer	Libra	Leo
11		Capricorn	Capricorn	Scorpio	Gemini	Scorpio	Cancer	Libra	Leo
12	10:15 A.M. Taurus	Capricorn	Capricorn	Scorpio	Gemini	Scorpio	Cancer	Libra	Leo
13		Capricorn	Capricorn	Scorpio	Gemini	Scorpio	Cancer	Libra	Leo
14	1:40 P.M. Gemini	Capricorn	Capricorn	Scorpio	Gemini	Scorpio	Cancer	Libra	Leo
15		Capricorn	Capricorn	Scorpio	Gemini	Scorpio	Cancer	Libra	Leo
16	6:22 P.M. Cancer	Capricorn	Capricorn	Scorpio	Gemini	Scorpio	Cancer	Libra	Leo
17		Capricorn	Capricorn	Scorpio	Gemini	Scorpio	Cancer	Libra	Leo
18		Capricorn	Capricorn	Scorpio	Gemini	Scorpio	Cancer	Libra	Leo
19	0:20 A.M. Leo	Aquarius	Capricorn	Scorpio	Gemini	Scorpio	Cancer	Libra	Leo
20		Aquarius	Capricorn	Scorpio	Gemini	Scorpio	Cancer	Libra	Leo
December									
23	Sagittarius	Sagittarius	Scorpio	Pisces	Cancer	Scorpio	Cancer	Libra	Leo
24	8:46 P.M. Capricorn	Capricorn	Scorpio	Pisces	Cancer	Scorpio	Cancer	Libra	Leo
25		Capricorn	Scorpio	Pisces	Cancer	Scorpio	Cancer	Libra	Leo
26		Capricorn	Scorpio	Pisces	Cancer	Scorpio	Cancer	Libra	Leo
27	6:49 A.M. Aquarius	Capricorn	Scorpio	Pisces	Cancer	Scorpio	Cancer	Libra	Leo
28		Capricorn	Scorpio	Pisces	Cancer	Scorpio	Cancer	Libra	Leo
29	2:56 P.M. Pisces	Capricorn	Scorpio	Pisces	Cancer	Scorpio	Cancer	Libra	Leo
30		Capricorn	Scorpio	Pisces	Cancer	Scorpio	Cancer	Libra	Leo
31	8:46 P.M. Aries	Capricorn	Scorpio	Pisces	Cancer	Scorpio	Cancer	Libra	Leo

CAPRICORN PLANETARY TABLES

1955

January	MOON FROM / IN	MERCURY	VENUS	MARS	JUPITER	SATURN	URANUS	NEPTUNE	PLUTO
1	Aries	Capricorn	Scorpio	Pisces	Cancer	Scorpio	Cancer	Libra	Leo
2		Capricorn	Scorpio	Pisces	Cancer	Scorpio	Cancer	Libra	Leo
3	0:29 A.M. Taurus	Capricorn	Scorpio	Pisces	Cancer	Scorpio	Cancer	Libra	Leo
4		Capricorn	Scorpio	Pisces	Cancer	Scorpio	Cancer	Libra	Leo
5	1:59 A.M. Gemini	Capricorn	Scorpio	Pisces	Cancer	Scorpio	Cancer	Libra	Leo
6		Capricorn	Scorpio	Pisces	Cancer	Scorpio	Cancer	Libra	Leo
7	3:06 A.M. Cancer	Capricorn	Sagittarius	Pisces	Cancer	Scorpio	Cancer	Libra	Leo
8		Capricorn	Sagittarius	Pisces	Cancer	Scorpio	Cancer	Libra	Leo
9	4:43 A.M. Leo	Capricorn	Sagittarius	Pisces	Cancer	Scorpio	Cancer	Libra	Leo
10		Capricorn	Sagittarius	Pisces	Cancer	Scorpio	Cancer	Libra	Leo
11	8:49 A.M. Virgo	Aquarius	Sagittarius	Pisces	Cancer	Scorpio	Cancer	Libra	Leo
12		Aquarius	Sagittarius	Pisces	Cancer	Scorpio	Cancer	Libra	Leo
13	4:12 P.M. Libra	Aquarius	Sagittarius	Pisces	Cancer	Scorpio	Cancer	Libra	Leo
14		Aquarius	Sagittarius	Pisces	Cancer	Scorpio	Cancer	Libra	Leo
15		Aquarius	Sagittarius	Pisces	Cancer	Scorpio	Cancer	Libra	Leo
16	3:48 A.M. Scorpio	Aquarius	Sagittarius	Aries	Cancer	Scorpio	Cancer	Libra	Leo
17		Aquarius	Sagittarius	Aries	Cancer	Scorpio	Cancer	Libra	Leo
18	4:24 P.M. Sagittarius	Aquarius	Sagittarius	Aries	Cancer	Scorpio	Cancer	Libra	Leo
19		Aquarius	Sagittarius	Aries	Cancer	Scorpio	Cancer	Libra	Leo
20		Aquarius	Sagittarius	Aries	Cancer	Scorpio	Cancer	Libra	Leo
December									
23	Aries	Capricorn	Capricorn	Scorpio	Virgo	Scorpio	Leo	Libra	Leo
24	10:26 A.M. Taurus	Capricorn	Capricorn	Scorpio	Virgo	Scorpio	Leo	Libra	Leo
25	12:27 P.M. Gemini	Capricorn	Aquarius	Scorpio	Virgo	Scorpio	Leo	Scorpio	Leo
26		Capricorn	Aquarius	Scorpio	Virgo	Scorpio	Leo	Scorpio	Leo
27	12:11 P.M. Cancer	Capricorn	Aquarius	Scorpio	Virgo	Scorpio	Leo	Scorpio	Leo
28		Capricorn	Aquarius	Scorpio	Virgo	Scorpio	Leo	Scorpio	Leo
29	11:41 A.M. Leo	Capricorn	Aquarius	Scorpio	Virgo	Scorpio	Leo	Scorpio	Leo
30		Capricorn	Aquarius	Scorpio	Virgo	Scorpio	Leo	Scorpio	Leo
31		Capricorn	Aquarius	Scorpio	Virgo	Scorpio	Leo	Scorpio	Leo

1956

Day	MOON FROM	IN	MERCURY	VENUS	MARS	JUPITER	SATURN	URANUS	NEPTUNE	PLUTO
January										
1	1:01 P.M.	Virgo	Capricorn	Aquarius	Scorpio	Virgo	Scorpio	Leo	Scorpio	Leo
2			Capricorn	Aquarius	Scorpio	Virgo	Scorpio	Leo	Scorpio	Leo
3	5:11 P.M.	Libra	Capricorn	Aquarius	Scorpio	Virgo	Scorpio	Leo	Scorpio	Leo
4			Capricorn	Aquarius	Scorpio	Virgo	Scorpio	Leo	Scorpio	Leo
5			Aquarius	Aquarius	Scorpio	Virgo	Scorpio	Leo	Scorpio	Leo
6	1:38 A.M.	Scorpio	Aquarius	Aquarius	Scorpio	Virgo	Scorpio	Leo	Scorpio	Leo
7			Aquarius	Aquarius	Scorpio	Virgo	Scorpio	Leo	Scorpio	Leo
8	1:16 P.M.	Sagittarius	Aquarius	Aquarius	Scorpio	Virgo	Scorpio	Leo	Scorpio	Leo
9			Aquarius	Aquarius	Scorpio	Virgo	Scorpio	Leo	Scorpio	Leo
10			Aquarius	Aquarius	Scorpio	Virgo	Scorpio	Leo	Scorpio	Leo
11	1:55 A.M.	Capricorn	Aquarius	Aquarius	Scorpio	Virgo	Scorpio	Leo	Scorpio	Leo
12			Aquarius	Aquarius	Scorpio	Virgo	Scorpio	Leo	Scorpio	Leo
13	2:33 P.M.	Aquarius	Aquarius	Aquarius	Scorpio	Virgo	Sagittarius	Leo	Scorpio	Leo
14			Aquarius	Aquarius	Sagittarius	Virgo	Sagittarius	Leo	Scorpio	Leo
15			Aquarius	Aquarius	Sagittarius	Virgo	Sagittarius	Leo	Scorpio	Leo
16	1:53 A.M.	Pisces	Aquarius	Aquarius	Sagittarius	Virgo	Sagittarius	Leo	Scorpio	Leo
17			Aquarius	Aquarius	Sagittarius	Virgo	Sagittarius	Leo	Scorpio	Leo
18	11:19 A.M.	Aries	Aquarius	Pisces	Sagittarius	Virgo	Sagittarius	Leo	Scorpio	Leo
19			Aquarius	Pisces	Sagittarius	Leo	Sagittarius	Leo	Scorpio	Leo
20	6:17 P.M.	Taurus	Aquarius	Pisces	Sagittarius	Leo	Sagittarius	Leo	Scorpio	Leo
21			Aquarius	Pisces	Sagittarius	Leo	Sagittarius	Leo	Scorpio	Leo
December										
22	Virgo		Capricorn	Sagittarius	Aries	Libra	Sagittarius	Leo	Scorpio	Virgo
23			Capricorn	Sagittarius	Aries	Libra	Sagittarius	Leo	Scorpio	Virgo
24	1:16 A.M.	Libra	Capricorn	Sagittarius	Aries	Libra	Sagittarius	Leo	Scorpio	Virgo
25			Capricorn	Sagittarius	Aries	Libra	Sagittarius	Leo	Scorpio	Virgo
26	6:29 A.M.	Scorpio	Capricorn	Sagittarius	Aries	Libra	Sagittarius	Leo	Scorpio	Virgo
27			Capricorn	Sagittarius	Aries	Libra	Sagittarius	Leo	Scorpio	Virgo
28	2:38 P.M.	Sagittarius	Capricorn	Sagittarius	Aries	Libra	Sagittarius	Leo	Scorpio	Virgo
29			Capricorn	Sagittarius	Aries	Libra	Sagittarius	Leo	Scorpio	Virgo
30			Capricorn	Sagittarius	Aries	Libra	Sagittarius	Leo	Scorpio	Virgo
31	0:43 A.M.	Capricorn	Capricorn	Sagittarius	Aries	Libra	Sagittarius	Leo	Scorpio	Virgo

CAPRICORN PLANETARY TABLES

1957

January	MOON FROM	IN	MERCURY	VENUS	MARS	JUPITER	SATURN	URANUS	NEPTUNE	PLUTO
1		Capricorn	Capricorn	Sagittarius	Aries	Libra	Sagittarius	Leo	Scorpio	Virgo
2	12:18 P.M.	Aquarius	Capricorn	Sagittarius	Aries	Libra	Sagittarius	Leo	Scorpio	Virgo
3			Capricorn	Sagittarius	Aries	Libra	Sagittarius	Leo	Scorpio	Virgo
4			Capricorn	Sagittarius	Aries	Libra	Sagittarius	Leo	Scorpio	Virgo
5	0:57 A.M.	Pisces	Capricorn	Sagittarius	Aries	Libra	Sagittarius	Leo	Scorpio	Virgo
6			Capricorn	Sagittarius	Aries	Libra	Sagittarius	Leo	Scorpio	Virgo
7	1:01 P.M.	Aries	Capricorn	Sagittarius	Aries	Libra	Sagittarius	Leo	Scorpio	Virgo
8			Capricorn	Sagittarius	Aries	Libra	Sagittarius	Leo	Scorpio	Virgo
9	11:23 P.M.	Taurus	Capricorn	Sagittarius	Aries	Libra	Sagittarius	Leo	Scorpio	Virgo
10			Capricorn	Sagittarius	Aries	Libra	Sagittarius	Leo	Scorpio	Virgo
11			Capricorn	Sagittarius	Aries	Libra	Sagittarius	Leo	Scorpio	Virgo
12	5:27 A.M.	Gemini	Capricorn	Sagittarius	Aries	Libra	Sagittarius	Leo	Scorpio	Virgo
13			Capricorn	Capricorn	Aries	Libra	Sagittarius	Leo	Scorpio	Virgo
14	7:58 A.M.	Cancer	Capricorn	Capricorn	Aries	Libra	Sagittarius	Leo	Scorpio	Virgo
15			Capricorn	Capricorn	Aries	Libra	Sagittarius	Leo	Scorpio	Virgo
16	7:48 A.M.	Leo	Capricorn	Capricorn	Aries	Libra	Sagittarius	Leo	Scorpio	Leo
17			Capricorn	Capricorn	Aries	Libra	Sagittarius	Leo	Scorpio	Leo
18	7:29 A.M.	Virgo	Capricorn	Capricorn	Aries	Libra	Sagittarius	Leo	Scorpio	Leo
19			Capricorn	Capricorn	Aries	Libra	Sagittarius	Leo	Scorpio	Leo
20	8:22 A.M.	Libra	Capricorn	Capricorn	Aries	Libra	Sagittarius	Leo	Scorpio	Leo
December										
23	10:07 A.M.	Aquarius	Capricorn	Aquarius	Scorpio	Libra	Sagittarius	Leo	Scorpio	Virgo
24			Capricorn	Aquarius	Sagittarius	Libra	Sagittarius	Leo	Scorpio	Virgo
25	8:53 P.M.	Pisces	Capricorn	Aquarius	Sagittarius	Libra	Sagittarius	Leo	Scorpio	Virgo
26			Capricorn	Aquarius	Sagittarius	Libra	Sagittarius	Leo	Scorpio	Virgo
27			Capricorn	Aquarius	Sagittarius	Libra	Sagittarius	Leo	Scorpio	Virgo
28	9:27 A.M.	Aries	Capricorn	Aquarius	Sagittarius	Libra	Sagittarius	Leo	Scorpio	Virgo
29			Sagittarius	Aquarius	Sagittarius	Libra	Sagittarius	Leo	Scorpio	Virgo
30	9:38 P.M.	Taurus	Sagittarius	Aquarius	Sagittarius	Libra	Sagittarius	Leo	Scorpio	Virgo
31			Sagittarius	Aquarius	Sagittarius	Libra	Sagittarius	Leo	Scorpio	Virgo

1958

January	MOON FROM	IN	MERCURY	VENUS	MARS	JUPITER	SATURN	URANUS	NEPTUNE	PLUTO
1		Taurus	Sagittarius	Aquarius	Sagittarius	Libra	Sagittarius	Leo	Scorpio	Virgo
2	7:33 A.M.	Gemini	Sagittarius	Aquarius	Sagittarius	Libra	Sagittarius	Leo	Scorpio	Virgo
3			Sagittarius	Aquarius	Sagittarius	Libra	Sagittarius	Leo	Scorpio	Virgo
4	1:16 P.M.	Cancer	Sagittarius	Aquarius	Sagittarius	Libra	Sagittarius	Leo	Scorpio	Virgo
5			Sagittarius	Aquarius	Sagittarius	Libra	Sagittarius	Leo	Scorpio	Virgo
6	3:37 P.M.	Leo	Sagittarius	Aquarius	Sagittarius	Libra	Sagittarius	Leo	Scorpio	Virgo
7			Sagittarius	Aquarius	Sagittarius	Libra	Sagittarius	Leo	Scorpio	Virgo
8	6:35 P.M.	Virgo	Sagittarius	Aquarius	Sagittarius	Libra	Sagittarius	Leo	Scorpio	Virgo
9			Sagittarius	Aquarius	Sagittarius	Libra	Sagittarius	Leo	Scorpio	Virgo
10	8:36 P.M.	Libra	Sagittarius	Aquarius	Sagittarius	Libra	Sagittarius	Leo	Scorpio	Virgo
11			Sagittarius	Aquarius	Sagittarius	Libra	Sagittarius	Leo	Scorpio	Virgo
12	11:28 P.M.	Scorpio	Sagittarius	Aquarius	Sagittarius	Libra	Sagittarius	Leo	Scorpio	Virgo
13			Sagittarius	Aquarius	Sagittarius	Libra	Sagittarius	Leo	Scorpio	Virgo
14			Sagittarius	Aquarius	Sagittarius	Scorpio	Sagittarius	Leo	Scorpio	Virgo
15	3:56 A.M.	Sagittarius	Capricorn	Aquarius	Sagittarius	Scorpio	Sagittarius	Leo	Scorpio	Virgo
16			Capricorn	Aquarius	Sagittarius	Scorpio	Sagittarius	Leo	Scorpio	Virgo
17	10:10 A.M.	Capricorn	Capricorn	Aquarius	Sagittarius	Scorpio	Sagittarius	Leo	Scorpio	Virgo
18			Capricorn	Aquarius	Sagittarius	Scorpio	Sagittarius	Leo	Scorpio	Virgo
19	6:18 P.M.	Aquarius	Capricorn	Aquarius	Sagittarius	Scorpio	Sagittarius	Leo	Scorpio	Virgo
20			Capricorn	Aquarius	Sagittarius	Scorpio	Sagittarius	Leo	Scorpio	Virgo
December										
23	5:12 A.M.	Gemini	Sagittarius	Capricorn	Taurus	Scorpio	Sagittarius	Leo	Scorpio	Virgo
24			Sagittarius	Capricorn	Taurus	Scorpio	Sagittarius	Leo	Scorpio	Virgo
25	3:35 P.M.	Cancer	Sagittarius	Capricorn	Taurus	Scorpio	Sagittarius	Leo	Scorpio	Virgo
26			Sagittarius	Capricorn	Taurus	Scorpio	Sagittarius	Leo	Scorpio	Virgo
27	11:47 P.M.	Leo	Sagittarius	Capricorn	Taurus	Scorpio	Sagittarius	Leo	Scorpio	Virgo
28			Sagittarius	Capricorn	Taurus	Scorpio	Sagittarius	Leo	Scorpio	Virgo
29			Sagittarius	Capricorn	Taurus	Scorpio	Sagittarius	Leo	Scorpio	Virgo
30	5:57 A.M.	Virgo	Sagittarius	Capricorn	Taurus	Scorpio	Sagittarius	Leo	Scorpio	Virgo
31			Sagittarius	Capricorn	Taurus	Scorpio	Sagittarius	Leo	Scorpio	Virgo

CAPRICORN PLANETARY TABLES

1959

MOON FROM	IN	MERCURY	VENUS	MARS	JUPITER	SATURN	URANUS	NEPTUNE	PLUTO
January									
1	6:39 A.M. Libra	Sagittarius	Capricorn	Taurus	Scorpio	Sagittarius	Leo	Scorpio	Virgo
2		Sagittarius	Capricorn	Taurus	Scorpio	Sagittarius	Leo	Scorpio	Virgo
3	1:47 P.M. Scorpio	Sagittarius	Capricorn	Taurus	Scorpio	Sagittarius	Leo	Scorpio	Virgo
4		Sagittarius	Capricorn	Taurus	Scorpio	Sagittarius	Leo	Scorpio	Virgo
5	3:41 P.M. Sagittarius	Sagittarius	Capricorn	Taurus	Scorpio	Sagittarius	Leo	Scorpio	Virgo
6		Sagittarius	Capricorn	Taurus	Scorpio	Capricorn	Leo	Scorpio	Virgo
7	5:48 P.M. Capricorn	Sagittarius	Capricorn	Taurus	Scorpio	Capricorn	Leo	Scorpio	Virgo
8		Sagittarius	Aquarius	Taurus	Scorpio	Capricorn	Leo	Scorpio	Virgo
9	9:07 P.M. Aquarius	Sagittarius	Aquarius	Taurus	Scorpio	Capricorn	Leo	Scorpio	Virgo
10		Sagittarius	Aquarius	Taurus	Scorpio	Capricorn	Leo	Scorpio	Virgo
11		Capricorn	Aquarius	Taurus	Scorpio	Capricorn	Leo	Scorpio	Virgo
12	2:56 A.M. Pisces	Capricorn	Aquarius	Taurus	Scorpio	Capricorn	Leo	Scorpio	Virgo
13		Capricorn	Aquarius	Taurus	Scorpio	Capricorn	Leo	Scorpio	Virgo
14	12:21 P.M. Aries	Capricorn	Aquarius	Taurus	Scorpio	Capricorn	Leo	Scorpio	Virgo
15		Capricorn	Aquarius	Taurus	Scorpio	Capricorn	Leo	Scorpio	Virgo
16		Capricorn	Aquarius	Taurus	Scorpio	Capricorn	Leo	Scorpio	Virgo
17	0:45 A.M. Taurus	Capricorn	Aquarius	Taurus	Scorpio	Capricorn	Leo	Scorpio	Virgo
18		Capricorn	Aquarius	Taurus	Scorpio	Capricorn	Leo	Scorpio	Virgo
19	1:16 P.M. Gemini	Capricorn	Aquarius	Taurus	Scorpio	Capricorn	Leo	Scorpio	Virgo
20		Capricorn	Aquarius	Taurus	Scorpio	Capricorn	Leo	Scorpio	Virgo
December									
23	Libra	Sagittarius	Scorpio	Sagittarius	Sagittarius	Capricorn	Leo	Scorpio	Virgo
24	1:44 A.M. Scorpio	Sagittarius	Scorpio	Sagittarius	Sagittarius	Capricorn	Leo	Scorpio	Virgo
25		Sagittarius	Scorpio	Sagittarius	Sagittarius	Capricorn	Leo	Scorpio	Virgo
26		Sagittarius	Scorpio	Sagittarius	Sagittarius	Capricorn	Leo	Scorpio	Virgo
27	2:48 A.M. Sagittarius	Sagittarius	Scorpio	Sagittarius	Sagittarius	Capricorn	Leo	Scorpio	Virgo
28		Sagittarius	Scorpio	Sagittarius	Sagittarius	Capricorn	Leo	Scorpio	Virgo
29	2:30 A.M. Capricorn	Sagittarius	Scorpio	Sagittarius	Sagittarius	Capricorn	Leo	Scorpio	Virgo
30		Sagittarius	Scorpio	Sagittarius	Sagittarius	Capricorn	Leo	Scorpio	Virgo
31	2:40 A.M. Aquarius	Sagittarius	Scorpio	Sagittarius	Sagittarius	Capricorn	Leo	Scorpio	Virgo

1960

January	MOON FROM	IN	MERCURY	VENUS	MARS	JUPITER	SATURN	URANUS	NEPTUNE	PLUTO
1		Aquarius	Sagittarius	Scorpio	Sagittarius	Sagittarius	Capricorn	Leo	Scorpio	Virgo
2	5:00 A.M.	Pisces	Sagittarius	Scorpio	Sagittarius	Sagittarius	Capricorn	Leo	Scorpio	Virgo
3			Sagittarius	Sagittarius	Sagittarius	Sagittarius	Capricorn	Leo	Scorpio	Virgo
4	10:57 A.M.	Aries	Sagittarius	Sagittarius	Sagittarius	Sagittarius	Capricorn	Leo	Scorpio	Virgo
5			Capricorn	Sagittarius	Sagittarius	Sagittarius	Capricorn	Leo	Scorpio	Virgo
6	8:42 P.M.	Taurus	Capricorn	Sagittarius	Sagittarius	Sagittarius	Capricorn	Leo	Scorpio	Virgo
7			Capricorn	Sagittarius	Sagittarius	Sagittarius	Capricorn	Leo	Scorpio	Virgo
8			Capricorn	Sagittarius	Sagittarius	Sagittarius	Capricorn	Leo	Scorpio	Virgo
9	9:14 A.M.	Gemini	Capricorn	Sagittarius	Sagittarius	Sagittarius	Capricorn	Leo	Scorpio	Virgo
10			Capricorn	Sagittarius	Sagittarius	Sagittarius	Capricorn	Leo	Scorpio	Virgo
11	9:52 P.M.	Cancer	Capricorn	Sagittarius	Sagittarius	Sagittarius	Capricorn	Leo	Scorpio	Virgo
12			Capricorn	Sagittarius	Sagittarius	Sagittarius	Capricorn	Leo	Scorpio	Virgo
13			Capricorn	Sagittarius	Sagittarius	Sagittarius	Capricorn	Leo	Scorpio	Virgo
14	9:33 A.M.	Leo	Capricorn	Sagittarius	Sagittarius	Sagittarius	Capricorn	Leo	Scorpio	Virgo
15			Capricorn	Sagittarius	Capricorn	Sagittarius	Capricorn	Leo	Scorpio	Virgo
16	7:34 P.M.	Virgo	Capricorn	Sagittarius	Capricorn	Sagittarius	Capricorn	Leo	Scorpio	Virgo
17			Capricorn	Sagittarius	Capricorn	Sagittarius	Capricorn	Leo	Scorpio	Virgo
18			Capricorn	Sagittarius	Capricorn	Sagittarius	Capricorn	Leo	Scorpio	Virgo
19	3:32 A.M.	Libra	Capricorn	Sagittarius	Capricorn	Sagittarius	Capricorn	Leo	Scorpio	Virgo
20			Capricorn	Sagittarius	Capricorn	Sagittarius	Capricorn	Leo	Scorpio	Virgo
21	9:05 A.M.	Scorpio	Capricorn	Sagittarius	Capricorn	Sagittarius	Capricorn	Leo	Scorpio	Virgo
December										
22	12:21 P.M.	Pisces	Sagittarius	Aquarius	Cancer	Capricorn	Capricorn	Leo	Scorpio	Virgo
23			Sagittarius	Aquarius	Cancer	Capricorn	Capricorn	Leo	Scorpio	Virgo
24	4:00 P.M.	Aries	Sagittarius	Aquarius	Cancer	Capricorn	Capricorn	Leo	Scorpio	Virgo
25			Sagittarius	Aquarius	Cancer	Capricorn	Capricorn	Leo	Scorpio	Virgo
26	10:38 P.M.	Taurus	Sagittarius	Aquarius	Cancer	Capricorn	Capricorn	Leo	Scorpio	Virgo
27			Sagittarius	Aquarius	Cancer	Capricorn	Capricorn	Leo	Scorpio	Virgo
28			Capricorn	Aquarius	Cancer	Capricorn	Capricorn	Leo	Scorpio	Virgo
29	8:11 A.M.	Gemini	Capricorn	Aquarius	Cancer	Capricorn	Capricorn	Leo	Scorpio	Virgo
30			Capricorn	Aquarius	Cancer	Capricorn	Capricorn	Leo	Scorpio	Virgo
31	5:00 P.M.	Cancer	Capricorn	Aquarius	Cancer	Capricorn	Capricorn	Leo	Scorpio	Virgo

CAPRICORN PLANETARY TABLES

1961

MOON FROM	IN	MERCURY	VENUS	MARS	JUPITER	SATURN	URANUS	NEPTUNE	PLUTO
January									
1	Cancer	Capricorn	Aquarius	Cancer	Capricorn	Capricorn	Leo	Scorpio	Virgo
2		Capricorn	Aquarius	Cancer	Capricorn	Capricorn	Leo	Scorpio	Virgo
3	8:24 A.M. Leo	Capricorn	Aquarius	Cancer	Capricorn	Capricorn	Leo	Scorpio	Virgo
4		Capricorn	Aquarius	Cancer	Capricorn	Capricorn	Leo	Scorpio	Virgo
5	8:49 P.M. Virgo	Capricorn	Aquarius	Cancer	Capricorn	Capricorn	Leo	Scorpio	Virgo
6		Capricorn	Pisces	Cancer	Capricorn	Capricorn	Leo	Scorpio	Virgo
7		Capricorn	Pisces	Cancer	Capricorn	Capricorn	Leo	Scorpio	Virgo
8	8:22 A.M. Libra	Capricorn	Pisces	Cancer	Capricorn	Capricorn	Leo	Scorpio	Virgo
9		Capricorn	Pisces	Cancer	Capricorn	Capricorn	Leo	Scorpio	Virgo
10	5:05 P.M. Scorpio	Capricorn	Pisces	Cancer	Capricorn	Capricorn	Leo	Scorpio	Virgo
11		Capricorn	Pisces	Cancer	Capricorn	Capricorn	Leo	Scorpio	Virgo
12	9:32 P.M. Sagittarius	Capricorn	Pisces	Cancer	Capricorn	Capricorn	Leo	Scorpio	Virgo
13		Capricorn	Pisces	Cancer	Capricorn	Capricorn	Leo	Scorpio	Virgo
14	10:57 P.M. Capricorn	Capricorn	Pisces	Cancer	Capricorn	Capricorn	Leo	Scorpio	Virgo
15		Aquarius	Pisces	Cancer	Capricorn	Capricorn	Leo	Scorpio	Virgo
16	10:20 P.M. Aquarius	Aquarius	Pisces	Cancer	Capricorn	Capricorn	Leo	Scorpio	Virgo
17		Aquarius	Pisces	Cancer	Capricorn	Capricorn	Leo	Scorpio	Virgo
18	9:59 P.M. Pisces	Aquarius	Pisces	Cancer	Capricorn	Capricorn	Leo	Scorpio	Virgo
19		Aquarius	Pisces	Cancer	Capricorn	Capricorn	Leo	Scorpio	Virgo
20	11:53 P.M. Aries	Aquarius	Pisces	Cancer	Capricorn	Capricorn	Leo	Scorpio	Virgo
December									
23	Cancer	Capricorn	Sagittarius	Sagittarius	Aquarius	Capricorn	Virgo	Scorpio	Virgo
24	5:39 A.M. Leo	Capricorn	Sagittarius	Sagittarius	Aquarius	Capricorn	Virgo	Scorpio	Virgo
25		Capricorn	Sagittarius	Capricorn	Aquarius	Capricorn	Virgo	Scorpio	Virgo
26	5:30 P.M. Virgo	Capricorn	Sagittarius	Capricorn	Aquarius	Capricorn	Virgo	Scorpio	Virgo
27		Capricorn	Sagittarius	Capricorn	Aquarius	Capricorn	Virgo	Scorpio	Virgo
28		Capricorn	Sagittarius	Capricorn	Aquarius	Capricorn	Virgo	Scorpio	Virgo
29	6:24 A.M. Libra	Capricorn	Capricorn	Capricorn	Aquarius	Capricorn	Virgo	Scorpio	Virgo
30		Capricorn	Capricorn	Capricorn	Aquarius	Capricorn	Virgo	Scorpio	Virgo
31	5:39 P.M. Scorpio	Capricorn	Capricorn	Capricorn	Aquarius	Capricorn	Virgo	Scorpio	Virgo

1962

January	MOON FROM	IN	MERCURY	VENUS	MARS	JUPITER	SATURN	URANUS	NEPTUNE	PLUTO
1	Scorpio		Capricorn	Capricorn	Capricorn	Aquarius	Capricorn	Virgo	Scorpio	Virgo
2			Capricorn	Capricorn	Capricorn	Aquarius	Capricorn	Virgo	Scorpio	Virgo
3	1:53 A.M.	Sagittarius	Capricorn	Capricorn	Capricorn	Aquarius	Capricorn	Virgo	Scorpio	Virgo
4			Capricorn	Capricorn	Capricorn	Aquarius	Aquarius	Virgo	Scorpio	Virgo
5	5:38 A.M.	Capricorn	Capricorn	Capricorn	Capricorn	Aquarius	Aquarius	Virgo	Scorpio	Virgo
6			Capricorn	Capricorn	Capricorn	Aquarius	Aquarius	Virgo	Scorpio	Virgo
7	7:20 A.M.	Aquarius	Capricorn	Capricorn	Capricorn	Aquarius	Aquarius	Virgo	Scorpio	Virgo
8			Aquarius	Capricorn	Capricorn	Aquarius	Aquarius	Virgo	Scorpio	Virgo
9	8:09 A.M.	Pisces	Aquarius	Capricorn	Capricorn	Aquarius	Aquarius	Virgo	Scorpio	Virgo
10			Aquarius	Capricorn	Capricorn	Aquarius	Aquarius	Virgo	Scorpio	Virgo
11	9:23 A.M.	Aries	Aquarius	Capricorn	Capricorn	Aquarius	Aquarius	Leo	Scorpio	Virgo
12			Aquarius	Capricorn	Capricorn	Aquarius	Aquarius	Leo	Scorpio	Virgo
13	12:50 P.M.	Taurus	Aquarius	Capricorn	Capricorn	Aquarius	Aquarius	Leo	Scorpio	Virgo
14			Aquarius	Capricorn	Capricorn	Aquarius	Aquarius	Leo	Scorpio	Virgo
15	7:04 P.M.	Gemini	Aquarius	Capricorn	Capricorn	Aquarius	Aquarius	Leo	Scorpio	Virgo
16			Aquarius	Capricorn	Capricorn	Aquarius	Aquarius	Leo	Scorpio	Virgo
17			Aquarius	Capricorn	Capricorn	Aquarius	Aquarius	Leo	Scorpio	Virgo
18	2:53 A.M.	Cancer	Aquarius	Capricorn	Capricorn	Aquarius	Aquarius	Leo	Scorpio	Virgo
19			Aquarius	Capricorn	Capricorn	Aquarius	Aquarius	Leo	Scorpio	Virgo
20	1:10 P.M.	Leo	Aquarius	Capricorn	Capricorn	Aquarius	Aquarius	Leo	Scorpio	Virgo
December										
23	Scorpio		Capricorn	Scorpio	Leo	Pisces	Aquarius	Virgo	Scorpio	Virgo
24	1:03 A.M.	Sagittarius	Capricorn	Scorpio	Leo	Pisces	Aquarius	Virgo	Scorpio	Virgo
25			Capricorn	Scorpio	Leo	Pisces	Aquarius	Virgo	Scorpio	Virgo
26	9:34 A.M.	Capricorn	Capricorn	Scorpio	Leo	Pisces	Aquarius	Virgo	Scorpio	Virgo
27			Capricorn	Scorpio	Leo	Pisces	Aquarius	Virgo	Scorpio	Virgo
28	3:53 P.M.	Aquarius	Capricorn	Scorpio	Leo	Pisces	Aquarius	Virgo	Scorpio	Virgo
29			Capricorn	Scorpio	Leo	Pisces	Aquarius	Virgo	Scorpio	Virgo
30			Capricorn	Scorpio	Leo	Pisces	Aquarius	Virgo	Scorpio	Virgo
31	8:29 P.M.	Pisces	Capricorn	Scorpio	Leo	Pisces	Aquarius	Virgo	Scorpio	Virgo

1963

CAPRICORN PLANETARY TABLES

	MOON FROM	IN	MERCURY	VENUS	MARS	JUPITER	SATURN	URANUS	NEPTUNE	PLUTO
January										
1		Pisces	Capricorn	Scorpio	Leo	Pisces	Aquarius	Virgo	Scorpio	Virgo
2	2:01 A.M.	Aries	Capricorn	Scorpio	Leo	Pisces	Aquarius	Virgo	Scorpio	Virgo
3			Aquarius	Scorpio	Leo	Pisces	Aquarius	Virgo	Scorpio	Virgo
4	2:43 A.M.	Taurus	Aquarius	Scorpio	Leo	Pisces	Aquarius	Virgo	Scorpio	Virgo
5			Aquarius	Scorpio	Leo	Pisces	Aquarius	Virgo	Scorpio	Virgo
6	5:19 A.M.	Gemini	Aquarius	Pisces	Leo	Pisces	Aquarius	Virgo	Scorpio	Virgo
7			Aquarius	Sagittarius	Leo	Pisces	Aquarius	Virgo	Scorpio	Virgo
8	9:15 A.M.	Cancer	Aquarius	Sagittarius	Leo	Pisces	Aquarius	Virgo	Scorpio	Virgo
9			Aquarius	Sagittarius	Leo	Pisces	Aquarius	Virgo	Scorpio	Virgo
10	2:07 P.M.	Leo	Aquarius	Sagittarius	Leo	Pisces	Aquarius	Virgo	Scorpio	Virgo
11			Aquarius	Sagittarius	Leo	Pisces	Aquarius	Virgo	Scorpio	Virgo
12	10:03 P.M.	Virgo	Aquarius	Sagittarius	Leo	Pisces	Aquarius	Virgo	Scorpio	Virgo
13			Aquarius	Sagittarius	Leo	Pisces	Aquarius	Virgo	Scorpio	Virgo
14			Aquarius	Sagittarius	Leo	Pisces	Aquarius	Virgo	Scorpio	Virgo
15	8:37 A.M.	Libra	Aquarius	Sagittarius	Leo	Pisces	Aquarius	Virgo	Scorpio	Virgo
16			Aquarius	Sagittarius	Leo	Pisces	Aquarius	Virgo	Scorpio	Virgo
17	9:27 P.M.	Scorpio	Aquarius	Sagittarius	Leo	Pisces	Aquarius	Virgo	Scorpio	Virgo
18			Aquarius	Sagittarius	Leo	Pisces	Aquarius	Virgo	Scorpio	Virgo
19			Aquarius	Sagittarius	Leo	Pisces	Aquarius	Virgo	Scorpio	Virgo
20	9:21 A.M.	Sagittarius	Aquarius	Sagittarius	Leo	Pisces	Aquarius	Virgo	Scorpio	Virgo
December										
23	12:29 P.M.	Aries	Capricorn	Capricorn	Capricorn	Aries	Aquarius	Virgo	Scorpio	Virgo
24			Capricorn	Aquarius	Capricorn	Aries	Aquarius	Virgo	Scorpio	Virgo
25	3:50 P.M.	Taurus	Capricorn	Aquarius	Capricorn	Aries	Aquarius	Virgo	Scorpio	Virgo
26			Capricorn	Aquarius	Capricorn	Aries	Aquarius	Virgo	Scorpio	Virgo
27	4:58 P.M.	Gemini	Capricorn	Aquarius	Capricorn	Aries	Aquarius	Virgo	Scorpio	Virgo
28			Capricorn	Aquarius	Capricorn	Aries	Aquarius	Virgo	Scorpio	Virgo
29	5:16 P.M.	Cancer	Capricorn	Aquarius	Capricorn	Aries	Aquarius	Virgo	Scorpio	Virgo
30			Capricorn	Aquarius	Capricorn	Aries	Aquarius	Virgo	Scorpio	Virgo
31	6:20 P.M.	Leo	Capricorn	Aquarius	Capricorn	Aries	Aquarius	Virgo	Scorpio	Virgo

1964

January	MOON FROM	IN	MERCURY	VENUS	MARS	JUPITER	SATURN	URANUS	NEPTUNE	PLUTO
1	Leo		Capricorn	Aquarius	Capricorn	Aries	Aquarius	Virgo	Scorpio	Virgo
2	9:50 P.M.	Virgo	Capricorn	Aquarius	Capricorn	Aries	Aquarius	Virgo	Scorpio	Virgo
3			Capricorn	Aquarius	Capricorn	Aries	Aquarius	Virgo	Scorpio	Virgo
4			Capricorn	Aquarius	Capricorn	Aries	Aquarius	Virgo	Scorpio	Virgo
5	5:19 A.M.	Libra	Capricorn	Aquarius	Capricorn	Aries	Aquarius	Virgo	Scorpio	Virgo
6			Capricorn	Aquarius	Capricorn	Aries	Aquarius	Virgo	Scorpio	Virgo
7	4:29 P.M.	Scorpio	Capricorn	Aquarius	Capricorn	Aries	Aquarius	Virgo	Scorpio	Virgo
8			Capricorn	Aquarius	Capricorn	Aries	Aquarius	Virgo	Scorpio	Virgo
9			Capricorn	Aquarius	Capricorn	Aries	Aquarius	Virgo	Scorpio	Virgo
10	5:24 A.M.	Sagittarius	Capricorn	Aquarius	Capricorn	Aries	Aquarius	Virgo	Scorpio	Virgo
11			Capricorn	Aquarius	Capricorn	Aries	Aquarius	Virgo	Scorpio	Virgo
12	5:34 P.M.	Capricorn	Capricorn	Aquarius	Capricorn	Aries	Aquarius	Virgo	Scorpio	Virgo
13			Capricorn	Aquarius	Capricorn	Aries	Aquarius	Virgo	Scorpio	Virgo
14			Capricorn	Aquarius	Aquarius	Aries	Aquarius	Virgo	Scorpio	Virgo
15	3:35 A.M.	Aquarius	Capricorn	Aquarius	Aquarius	Aries	Aquarius	Virgo	Scorpio	Virgo
16			Capricorn	Aquarius	Aquarius	Aries	Aquarius	Virgo	Scorpio	Virgo
17	11:54 A.M.	Pisces	Capricorn	Aquarius	Aquarius	Aries	Aquarius	Virgo	Scorpio	Virgo
18	6:08 P.M.	Aries	Capricorn	Pisces	Aquarius	Aries	Aquarius	Virgo	Scorpio	Virgo
19			Capricorn	Pisces	Aquarius	Aries	Aquarius	Virgo	Scorpio	Virgo
20	10:26 P.M.	Taurus	Capricorn	Pisces	Aquarius	Aries	Aquarius	Virgo	Scorpio	Virgo
21			Capricorn	Pisces	Aquarius	Aries	Aquarius	Virgo	Scorpio	Virgo
December										
22	Leo		Sagittarius	Sagittarius	Virgo	Taurus	Pisces	Virgo	Scorpio	Virgo
23	2:54 A.M.	Virgo	Sagittarius	Sagittarius	Virgo	Taurus	Pisces	Virgo	Scorpio	Virgo
24	7:22 A.M.	Libra	Sagittarius	Sagittarius	Virgo	Taurus	Pisces	Virgo	Scorpio	Virgo
25			Sagittarius	Sagittarius	Virgo	Taurus	Pisces	Virgo	Scorpio	Virgo
26			Sagittarius	Sagittarius	Virgo	Taurus	Pisces	Virgo	Scorpio	Virgo
27	3:37 P.M.	Scorpio	Sagittarius	Sagittarius	Virgo	Taurus	Pisces	Virgo	Scorpio	Virgo
28			Sagittarius	Sagittarius	Virgo	Taurus	Pisces	Virgo	Scorpio	Virgo
29			Sagittarius	Sagittarius	Virgo	Taurus	Pisces	Virgo	Scorpio	Virgo
30	2:51 A.M.	Sagittarius	Sagittarius	Sagittarius	Virgo	Taurus	Pisces	Virgo	Scorpio	Virgo
31			Sagittarius	Sagittarius	Virgo	Taurus	Pisces	Virgo	Scorpio	Virgo

CAPRICORN PLANETARY TABLES

1965

January	MOON FROM	IN	MERCURY	VENUS	MARS	JUPITER	SATURN	URANUS	NEPTUNE	PLUTO
1	3:21 P.M.	Capricorn	Sagittarius	Sagittarius	Virgo	Taurus	Pisces	Virgo	Scorpio	Virgo
2			Sagittarius	Sagittarius	Virgo	Taurus	Pisces	Virgo	Scorpio	Virgo
3			Sagittarius	Sagittarius	Virgo	Taurus	Pisces	Virgo	Scorpio	Virgo
4	3:59 A.M.	Aquarius	Sagittarius	Sagittarius	Virgo	Taurus	Pisces	Virgo	Scorpio	Virgo
5			Sagittarius	Sagittarius	Virgo	Taurus	Pisces	Virgo	Scorpio	Virgo
6	4:02 P.M.	Pisces	Sagittarius	Sagittarius	Virgo	Taurus	Pisces	Virgo	Scorpio	Virgo
7			Sagittarius	Sagittarius	Virgo	Taurus	Pisces	Virgo	Scorpio	Virgo
8			Sagittarius	Sagittarius	Virgo	Taurus	Pisces	Virgo	Scorpio	Virgo
9	2:23 A.M.	Aries	Sagittarius	Sagittarius	Virgo	Taurus	Pisces	Virgo	Scorpio	Virgo
10			Sagittarius	Sagittarius	Virgo	Taurus	Pisces	Virgo	Scorpio	Virgo
11	9:18 A.M.	Taurus	Sagittarius	Sagittarius	Virgo	Taurus	Pisces	Virgo	Scorpio	Virgo
12			Sagittarius	Sagittarius	Virgo	Taurus	Pisces	Virgo	Scorpio	Virgo
13	12:43 P.M.	Gemini	Sagittarius	Capricorn	Virgo	Taurus	Pisces	Virgo	Scorpio	Virgo
14			Capricorn	Capricorn	Virgo	Taurus	Pisces	Virgo	Scorpio	Virgo
15	1:32 P.M.	Cancer	Capricorn	Capricorn	Virgo	Taurus	Pisces	Virgo	Scorpio	Virgo
16			Capricorn	Capricorn	Virgo	Taurus	Pisces	Virgo	Scorpio	Virgo
17	12:25 P.M.	Leo	Capricorn	Capricorn	Virgo	Taurus	Pisces	Virgo	Scorpio	Virgo
18			Capricorn	Capricorn	Virgo	Taurus	Pisces	Virgo	Scorpio	Virgo
19	1:03 P.M.	Virgo	Capricorn	Capricorn	Virgo	Taurus	Pisces	Virgo	Scorpio	Virgo
20			Capricorn	Capricorn	Virgo	Taurus	Pisces	Virgo	Scorpio	Virgo
December										
23		Capricorn	Sagittarius	Aquarius	Capricorn	Gemini	Pisces	Virgo	Scorpio	Virgo
24			Sagittarius	Aquarius	Aquarius	Gemini	Pisces	Virgo	Scorpio	Virgo
25	1:37 A.M.	Aquarius	Sagittarius	Aquarius	Aquarius	Gemini	Pisces	Virgo	Scorpio	Virgo
26			Sagittarius	Aquarius	Aquarius	Gemini	Pisces	Virgo	Scorpio	Virgo
27	1:59 P.M.	Pisces	Sagittarius	Aquarius	Aquarius	Gemini	Pisces	Virgo	Scorpio	Virgo
28			Sagittarius	Aquarius	Aquarius	Gemini	Pisces	Virgo	Scorpio	Virgo
29			Sagittarius	Aquarius	Aquarius	Gemini	Pisces	Virgo	Scorpio	Virgo
30	2:46 A.M.	Aries	Sagittarius	Aquarius	Aquarius	Gemini	Pisces	Virgo	Scorpio	Virgo
31			Sagittarius	Aquarius	Aquarius	Gemini	Pisces	Virgo	Scorpio	Virgo

1966

MOON		MERCURY	VENUS	MARS	JUPITER	SATURN	URANUS	NEPTUNE	PLUTO
January	FROM / IN								
1	1:15 P.M. Taurus	Sagittarius	Aquarius	Aquarius	Gemini	Pisces	Virgo	Scorpio	Virgo
2		Sagittarius	Aquarius	Aquarius	Gemini	Pisces	Virgo	Scorpio	Virgo
3	7:05 P.M. Gemini	Sagittarius	Aquarius	Aquarius	Gemini	Pisces	Virgo	Scorpio	Virgo
4		Sagittarius	Aquarius	Aquarius	Gemini	Pisces	Virgo	Scorpio	Virgo
5	9:28 P.M. Cancer	Sagittarius	Aquarius	Aquarius	Gemini	Pisces	Virgo	Scorpio	Virgo
6		Sagittarius	Aquarius	Aquarius	Gemini	Pisces	Virgo	Scorpio	Virgo
7	10:03 P.M. Leo	Sagittarius	Aquarius	Aquarius	Gemini	Pisces	Virgo	Scorpio	Virgo
8		Capricorn	Aquarius	Aquarius	Gemini	Pisces	Virgo	Scorpio	Virgo
9	10:03 P.M. Virgo	Capricorn	Aquarius	Aquarius	Gemini	Pisces	Virgo	Scorpio	Virgo
10		Capricorn	Aquarius	Aquarius	Gemini	Pisces	Virgo	Scorpio	Virgo
11	11:37 P.M. Libra	Capricorn	Aquarius	Aquarius	Gemini	Pisces	Virgo	Scorpio	Virgo
12		Capricorn	Aquarius	Aquarius	Gemini	Pisces	Virgo	Scorpio	Virgo
13		Capricorn	Aquarius	Aquarius	Gemini	Pisces	Virgo	Scorpio	Virgo
14	3:38 A.M. Scorpio	Capricorn	Aquarius	Aquarius	Gemini	Pisces	Virgo	Scorpio	Virgo
15		Capricorn	Aquarius	Aquarius	Gemini	Pisces	Virgo	Scorpio	Virgo
16	11:03 A.M. Sagittarius	Capricorn	Aquarius	Aquarius	Gemini	Pisces	Virgo	Scorpio	Virgo
17		Capricorn	Aquarius	Aquarius	Gemini	Pisces	Virgo	Scorpio	Virgo
18	8:50 P.M. Capricorn	Capricorn	Aquarius	Aquarius	Gemini	Pisces	Virgo	Scorpio	Virgo
19		Capricorn	Aquarius	Aquarius	Gemini	Pisces	Virgo	Scorpio	Virgo
20		Capricorn	Aquarius	Aquarius	Gemini	Pisces	Virgo	Scorpio	Virgo
December									
23	Taurus	Sagittarius	Capricorn	Libra	Leo	Pisces	Virgo	Scorpio	Virgo
24	8:19 P.M. Gemini	Sagittarius	Capricorn	Libra	Leo	Pisces	Virgo	Scorpio	Virgo
25		Sagittarius	Capricorn	Libra	Leo	Pisces	Virgo	Scorpio	Virgo
26		Sagittarius	Capricorn	Libra	Leo	Pisces	Virgo	Scorpio	Virgo
27	2:52 A.M. Cancer	Sagittarius	Capricorn	Libra	Leo	Pisces	Virgo	Scorpio	Virgo
28		Sagittarius	Capricorn	Libra	Leo	Pisces	Virgo	Scorpio	Virgo
29	7:00 A.M. Leo	Sagittarius	Capricorn	Libra	Leo	Pisces	Virgo	Scorpio	Virgo
30		Sagittarius	Capricorn	Libra	Leo	Pisces	Virgo	Scorpio	Virgo
31	10:03 A.M. Virgo	Sagittarius	Capricorn	Libra	Leo	Pisces	Virgo	Scorpio	Virgo

CAPRICORN PLANETARY TABLES

1967

MOON FROM	IN	MERCURY	VENUS	MARS	JUPITER	SATURN	URANUS	NEPTUNE	PLUTO
January 1	Virgo	Sagittarius	Capricorn	Libra	Leo	Pisces	Virgo	Scorpio	Virgo
2	12:42 P.M. Libra	Capricorn	Capricorn	Libra	Leo	Pisces	Virgo	Scorpio	Virgo
3		Capricorn	Capricorn	Libra	Leo	Pisces	Virgo	Scorpio	Virgo
4	3:35 P.M. Scorpio	Capricorn	Capricorn	Libra	Leo	Pisces	Virgo	Scorpio	Virgo
5		Capricorn	Capricorn	Libra	Leo	Pisces	Virgo	Scorpio	Virgo
6	7:37 P.M. Sagittarius	Capricorn	Capricorn	Libra	Leo	Pisces	Virgo	Scorpio	Virgo
7		Capricorn	Aquarius	Libra	Leo	Pisces	Virgo	Scorpio	Virgo
8		Capricorn	Aquarius	Libra	Leo	Pisces	Virgo	Scorpio	Virgo
9	0:51 A.M. Capricorn	Capricorn	Aquarius	Libra	Leo	Pisces	Virgo	Scorpio	Virgo
10		Capricorn	Aquarius	Libra	Leo	Pisces	Virgo	Scorpio	Virgo
11	8:08 A.M. Aquarius	Capricorn	Aquarius	Libra	Leo	Pisces	Virgo	Scorpio	Virgo
12		Capricorn	Aquarius	Libra	Leo	Pisces	Virgo	Scorpio	Virgo
13	5:49 P.M. Pisces	Capricorn	Aquarius	Libra	Leo	Pisces	Virgo	Scorpio	Virgo
14		Capricorn	Aquarius	Libra	Leo	Pisces	Virgo	Scorpio	Virgo
15		Capricorn	Aquarius	Libra	Leo	Pisces	Virgo	Scorpio	Virgo
16	6:00 A.M. Aries	Capricorn	Aquarius	Libra	Leo	Pisces	Virgo	Scorpio	Virgo
17		Capricorn	Aquarius	Libra	Cancer	Pisces	Virgo	Scorpio	Virgo
18	6:36 P.M. Taurus	Capricorn	Aquarius	Libra	Cancer	Pisces	Virgo	Scorpio	Virgo
19		Capricorn	Aquarius	Libra	Cancer	Pisces	Virgo	Scorpio	Virgo
20		Aquarius	Aquarius	Libra	Cancer	Pisces	Virgo	Scorpio	Virgo
December 23	Virgo	Sagittarius	Scorpio	Aquarius	Virgo	Aries	Virgo	Scorpio	Virgo
24	2:39 A.M. Libra	Sagittarius	Scorpio	Aquarius	Virgo	Aries	Virgo	Scorpio	Virgo
25	5:41 A.M. Scorpio	Capricorn	Scorpio	Aquarius	Virgo	Aries	Virgo	Scorpio	Virgo
26		Capricorn	Scorpio	Aquarius	Virgo	Aries	Virgo	Scorpio	Virgo
27		Capricorn	Scorpio	Aquarius	Virgo	Aries	Virgo	Scorpio	Virgo
28	6:50 A.M. Sagittarius	Capricorn	Scorpio	Aquarius	Virgo	Aries	Virgo	Scorpio	Virgo
29		Capricorn	Scorpio	Aquarius	Virgo	Aries	Virgo	Scorpio	Virgo
30	8:00 A.M. Capricorn	Capricorn	Scorpio	Aquarius	Virgo	Aries	Virgo	Scorpio	Virgo
31		Capricorn	Scorpio	Aquarius	Virgo	Aries	Virgo	Scorpio	Virgo

1968

January	MOON FROM	IN	MERCURY	VENUS	MARS	JUPITER	SATURN	URANUS	NEPTUNE	PLUTO
1	10:47 A.M.	Aquarius	Capricorn	Scorpio	Aquarius	Virgo	Aries	Virgo	Scorpio	Virgo
2			Capricorn	Sagittarius	Aquarius	Virgo	Aries	Virgo	Scorpio	Virgo
3	3:55 P.M.	Pisces	Capricorn	Sagittarius	Aquarius	Virgo	Aries	Virgo	Scorpio	Virgo
4			Capricorn	Sagittarius	Aquarius	Virgo	Aries	Virgo	Scorpio	Virgo
5			Capricorn	Sagittarius	Aquarius	Virgo	Aries	Virgo	Scorpio	Virgo
6	1:15 A.M.	Aries	Capricorn	Sagittarius	Aquarius	Virgo	Aries	Virgo	Scorpio	Virgo
7			Capricorn	Sagittarius	Aquarius	Virgo	Aries	Virgo	Scorpio	Virgo
8	1:22 P.M.	Taurus	Capricorn	Sagittarius	Aquarius	Virgo	Aries	Virgo	Scorpio	Virgo
9			Capricorn	Sagittarius	Aquarius	Virgo	Aries	Virgo	Scorpio	Virgo
10			Capricorn	Sagittarius	Pisces	Virgo	Aries	Virgo	Scorpio	Virgo
11	1:51 A.M.	Gemini	Capricorn	Sagittarius	Pisces	Virgo	Aries	Virgo	Scorpio	Virgo
12			Capricorn	Sagittarius	Pisces	Virgo	Aries	Virgo	Scorpio	Virgo
13	12:58 P.M.	Cancer	Capricorn	Sagittarius	Pisces	Virgo	Aries	Virgo	Scorpio	Virgo
14			Aquarius	Sagittarius	Pisces	Virgo	Aries	Virgo	Scorpio	Virgo
15	9:21 P.M.	Leo	Aquarius	Sagittarius	Pisces	Virgo	Aries	Virgo	Scorpio	Virgo
16			Aquarius	Sagittarius	Pisces	Virgo	Aries	Virgo	Scorpio	Virgo
17			Aquarius	Sagittarius	Pisces	Virgo	Aries	Virgo	Scorpio	Virgo
18	3:29 A.M.	Virgo	Aquarius	Sagittarius	Pisces	Virgo	Aries	Virgo	Scorpio	Virgo
19			Aquarius	Sagittarius	Pisces	Virgo	Aries	Virgo	Scorpio	Virgo
20	8:13 A.M.	Libra	Aquarius	Sagittarius	Pisces	Virgo	Aries	Virgo	Scorpio	Virgo
December										
22		Aquarius	Capricorn	Aquarius	Libra	Libra	Aries	Libra	Scorpio	Virgo
23	6:34 P.M.	Pisces	Capricorn	Aquarius	Libra	Libra	Aries	Libra	Scorpio	Virgo
24			Capricorn	Aquarius	Libra	Libra	Aries	Libra	Scorpio	Virgo
25			Capricorn	Aquarius	Libra	Libra	Aries	Libra	Scorpio	Virgo
26	0:14 A.M.	Aries	Capricorn	Aquarius	Libra	Libra	Aries	Libra	Scorpio	Virgo
27			Capricorn	Aquarius	Libra	Libra	Aries	Libra	Scorpio	Virgo
28	8:01 A.M.	Taurus	Capricorn	Aquarius	Libra	Libra	Aries	Libra	Scorpio	Virgo
29			Capricorn	Aquarius	Libra	Libra	Aries	Libra	Scorpio	Virgo
30	8:11 P.M.	Gemini	Capricorn	Aquarius	Scorpio	Libra	Aries	Libra	Scorpio	Virgo
31			Capricorn	Aquarius	Scorpio	Libra	Aries	Libra	Scorpio	Virgo

1969

CAPRICORN PLANETARY TABLES

January	MOON FROM / IN	MERCURY	VENUS	MARS	JUPITER	SATURN	URANUS	NEPTUNE	PLUTO
1	Gemini	Capricorn	Aquarius	Scorpio	Libra	Aries	Libra	Scorpio	Virgo
2	11:04 A.M. Cancer	Capricorn	Aquarius	Scorpio	Libra	Aries	Libra	Scorpio	Virgo
3		Capricorn	Aquarius	Scorpio	Libra	Aries	Libra	Scorpio	Virgo
4	11:01 P.M. Leo	Capricorn	Aquarius	Scorpio	Libra	Aries	Libra	Scorpio	Virgo
5		Aquarius	Pisces	Scorpio	Libra	Aries	Libra	Scorpio	Virgo
6		Aquarius	Pisces	Scorpio	Libra	Aries	Libra	Scorpio	Virgo
7	10:05 A.M. Virgo	Aquarius	Pisces	Scorpio	Libra	Aries	Libra	Scorpio	Virgo
8		Aquarius	Pisces	Scorpio	Libra	Aries	Libra	Scorpio	Virgo
9	6:32 P.M. Libra	Aquarius	Pisces	Scorpio	Libra	Aries	Libra	Scorpio	Virgo
10		Aquarius	Pisces	Scorpio	Libra	Aries	Libra	Scorpio	Virgo
11		Aquarius	Pisces	Scorpio	Libra	Aries	Libra	Scorpio	Virgo
12	0:23 A.M. Scorpio	Aquarius	Pisces	Scorpio	Libra	Aries	Libra	Scorpio	Virgo
13		Aquarius	Pisces	Scorpio	Libra	Aries	Libra	Scorpio	Virgo
14	2:52 A.M. Sagittarius	Aquarius	Pisces	Scorpio	Libra	Aries	Libra	Scorpio	Virgo
15		Aquarius	Pisces	Scorpio	Libra	Aries	Libra	Scorpio	Virgo
16	3:32 A.M. Capricorn	Aquarius	Pisces	Scorpio	Libra	Aries	Libra	Scorpio	Virgo
17		Aquarius	Pisces	Scorpio	Libra	Aries	Libra	Scorpio	Virgo
18	3:16 A.M. Aquarius	Aquarius	Pisces	Scorpio	Libra	Aries	Libra	Scorpio	Virgo
19		Aquarius	Pisces	Scorpio	Libra	Aries	Libra	Scorpio	Virgo
20	4:50 A.M. Pisces	Aquarius	Pisces	Scorpio	Libra	Aries	Libra	Scorpio	Virgo
December									
23	5:37 A.M. Cancer	Capricorn	Sagittarius	Pisces	Scorpio	Taurus	Libra	Scorpio	Virgo
24		Capricorn	Sagittarius	Pisces	Scorpio	Taurus	Libra	Scorpio	Virgo
25	9:32 P.M. Leo	Capricorn	Sagittarius	Pisces	Scorpio	Taurus	Libra	Scorpio	Virgo
26		Capricorn	Sagittarius	Pisces	Scorpio	Taurus	Libra	Scorpio	Virgo
27		Capricorn	Sagittarius	Pisces	Scorpio	Taurus	Libra	Scorpio	Virgo
28	10:13 A.M. Virgo	Capricorn	Sagittarius	Pisces	Scorpio	Taurus	Libra	Scorpio	Virgo
29		Capricorn	Capricorn	Pisces	Scorpio	Taurus	Libra	Scorpio	Virgo
30	10:01 P.M. Libra	Capricorn	Capricorn	Pisces	Scorpio	Taurus	Libra	Scorpio	Virgo
31		Capricorn	Capricorn	Pisces	Scorpio	Taurus	Libra	Scorpio	Virgo

1970

January	MOON FROM	IN	MERCURY	VENUS	MARS	JUPITER	SATURN	URANUS	NEPTUNE	PLUTO
1	Libra		Capricorn	Capricorn	Pisces	Scorpio	Taurus	Libra	Scorpio	Virgo
2	7:00 A.M.	Scorpio	Capricorn	Capricorn	Pisces	Scorpio	Taurus	Libra	Scorpio	Virgo
3			Capricorn	Capricorn	Pisces	Scorpio	Taurus	Libra	Scorpio	Virgo
4	11:30 A.M.	Sagittarius	Capricorn	Capricorn	Pisces	Scorpio	Taurus	Libra	Scorpio	Virgo
5			Capricorn	Capricorn	Pisces	Scorpio	Taurus	Libra	Sagittarius	Virgo
6	12:41 P.M.	Capricorn	Capricorn	Capricorn	Pisces	Scorpio	Taurus	Libra	Sagittarius	Virgo
7			Capricorn	Capricorn	Pisces	Scorpio	Taurus	Libra	Sagittarius	Virgo
8	12:25 P.M.	Aquarius	Capricorn	Capricorn	Pisces	Scorpio	Taurus	Libra	Sagittarius	Virgo
9			Capricorn	Capricorn	Pisces	Scorpio	Taurus	Libra	Sagittarius	Virgo
10	12:17 P.M.	Pisces	Capricorn	Capricorn	Pisces	Scorpio	Taurus	Libra	Sagittarius	Virgo
11			Capricorn	Capricorn	Pisces	Scorpio	Taurus	Libra	Sagittarius	Virgo
12	2:15 P.M.	Aries	Capricorn	Capricorn	Pisces	Scorpio	Taurus	Libra	Sagittarius	Virgo
13			Capricorn	Capricorn	Pisces	Scorpio	Taurus	Libra	Sagittarius	Virgo
14	7:38 P.M.	Taurus	Capricorn	Capricorn	Pisces	Scorpio	Taurus	Libra	Sagittarius	Virgo
15			Capricorn	Capricorn	Pisces	Scorpio	Taurus	Libra	Sagittarius	Virgo
16			Capricorn	Capricorn	Pisces	Scorpio	Taurus	Libra	Sagittarius	Virgo
17	4:19 A.M.	Gemini	Capricorn	Capricorn	Pisces	Scorpio	Taurus	Libra	Sagittarius	Virgo
18			Capricorn	Capricorn	Pisces	Scorpio	Taurus	Libra	Sagittarius	Virgo
19	3:48 P.M.	Cancer	Capricorn	Capricorn	Pisces	Scorpio	Taurus	Libra	Sagittarius	Virgo
20			Capricorn	Capricorn	Pisces	Scorpio	Taurus	Libra	Sagittarius	Virgo
December										
23	6:37 A.M.	Scorpio	Capricorn	Scorpio	Scorpio	Scorpio	Taurus	Libra	Sagittarius	Virgo
24			Capricorn	Scorpio	Scorpio	Scorpio	Taurus	Libra	Sagittarius	Virgo
25	2:38 P.M.	Sagittarius	Capricorn	Scorpio	Scorpio	Scorpio	Taurus	Libra	Sagittarius	Virgo
26			Capricorn	Scorpio	Scorpio	Scorpio	Taurus	Libra	Sagittarius	Virgo
27	7:16 P.M.	Capricorn	Capricorn	Scorpio	Scorpio	Scorpio	Taurus	Libra	Sagittarius	Virgo
28			Capricorn	Scorpio	Scorpio	Scorpio	Taurus	Libra	Sagittarius	Virgo
29	9:54 P.M.	Aquarius	Capricorn	Scorpio	Scorpio	Scorpio	Taurus	Libra	Sagittarius	Virgo
30			Capricorn	Scorpio	Scorpio	Scorpio	Taurus	Libra	Sagittarius	Virgo
31			Capricorn	Scorpio	Scorpio	Scorpio	Taurus	Libra	Sagittarius	Virgo

CAPRICORN PLANETARY TABLES

1971

	MOON FROM	MOON IN	MERCURY	VENUS	MARS	JUPITER	SATURN	URANUS	NEPTUNE	PLUTO
January										
1	3:21 A.M.	Pisces	Capricorn	Scorpio	Scorpio	Scorpio	Taurus	Libra	Sagittarius	Virgo
2	1:46 A.M.	Aries	Capricorn	Scorpio	Scorpio	Scorpio	Taurus	Libra	Sagittarius	Virgo
3			Sagittarius	Scorpio	Scorpio	Scorpio	Taurus	Libra	Sagittarius	Virgo
4			Sagittarius	Scorpio	Scorpio	Scorpio	Taurus	Libra	Sagittarius	Virgo
5	4:59 A.M.	Taurus	Sagittarius	Scorpio	Scorpio	Scorpio	Taurus	Libra	Sagittarius	Virgo
6			Sagittarius	Scorpio	Scorpio	Scorpio	Taurus	Libra	Sagittarius	Virgo
7	10:26 A.M.	Gemini	Sagittarius	Scorpio	Scorpio	Scorpio	Taurus	Libra	Sagittarius	Virgo
8			Sagittarius	Sagittarius	Scorpio	Scorpio	Taurus	Libra	Sagittarius	Virgo
9	5:30 P.M.	Cancer	Sagittarius	Sagittarius	Scorpio	Scorpio	Taurus	Libra	Sagittarius	Virgo
10			Sagittarius	Sagittarius	Scorpio	Scorpio	Taurus	Libra	Sagittarius	Virgo
11			Sagittarius	Sagittarius	Scorpio	Scorpio	Taurus	Libra	Sagittarius	Virgo
12	2:55 A.M.	Leo	Sagittarius	Sagittarius	Scorpio	Scorpio	Taurus	Libra	Sagittarius	Virgo
13			Sagittarius	Sagittarius	Scorpio	Scorpio	Taurus	Libra	Sagittarius	Virgo
14	2:04 P.M.	Virgo	Sagittarius	Sagittarius	Scorpio	Scorpio	Taurus	Libra	Sagittarius	Virgo
15			Capricorn	Sagittarius	Scorpio	Sagittarius	Taurus	Libra	Sagittarius	Virgo
16			Capricorn	Sagittarius	Scorpio	Sagittarius	Taurus	Libra	Sagittarius	Virgo
17	2:35 A.M.	Libra	Capricorn	Sagittarius	Scorpio	Sagittarius	Taurus	Libra	Sagittarius	Virgo
18			Capricorn	Sagittarius	Scorpio	Sagittarius	Taurus	Libra	Sagittarius	Virgo
19	2:59 P.M.	Scorpio	Capricorn	Sagittarius	Scorpio	Sagittarius	Taurus	Libra	Sagittarius	Virgo
20			Capricorn	Sagittarius	Scorpio	Sagittarius	Taurus	Libra	Sagittarius	Virgo
December										
23		Pisces	Sagittarius	Capricorn	Pisces	Sagittarius	Gemini	Libra	Sagittarius	Libra
24	4:03 P.M.	Aries	Sagittarius	Aquarius	Pisces	Sagittarius	Gemini	Libra	Sagittarius	Libra
25			Sagittarius	Aquarius	Pisces	Sagittarius	Gemini	Libra	Sagittarius	Libra
26	6:36 P.M.	Taurus	Sagittarius	Aquarius	Pisces	Sagittarius	Gemini	Libra	Sagittarius	Libra
27			Sagittarius	Aquarius	Aries	Sagittarius	Gemini	Libra	Sagittarius	Libra
28	8:50 P.M.	Gemini	Sagittarius	Aquarius	Aries	Sagittarius	Gemini	Libra	Sagittarius	Libra
29			Sagittarius	Aquarius	Aries	Sagittarius	Gemini	Libra	Sagittarius	Libra
30	11:21 P.M.	Cancer	Sagittarius	Aquarius	Aries	Sagittarius	Gemini	Libra	Sagittarius	Libra
31			Sagittarius	Aquarius	Aries	Sagittarius	Gemini	Libra	Sagittarius	Libra

1972

	MOON									
January	**FROM**	**IN**	**MERCURY**	**VENUS**	**MARS**	**JUPITER**	**SATURN**	**URANUS**	**NEPTUNE**	**PLUTO**
1		Cancer	Sagittarius	Aquarius	Aries	Sagittarius	Gemini	Libra	Sagittarius	Libra
2	3:38 A.M.	Leo	Sagittarius	Aquarius	Aries	Sagittarius	Gemini	Libra	Sagittarius	Libra
3	11:01 A.M.	Virgo	Sagittarius	Aquarius	Aries	Sagittarius	Gemini	Libra	Sagittarius	Libra
4			Sagittarius	Aquarius	Aries	Sagittarius	Gemini	Libra	Sagittarius	Libra
5	9:32 P.M.	Libra	Sagittarius	Aquarius	Aries	Sagittarius	Gemini	Libra	Sagittarius	Libra
6			Sagittarius	Aquarius	Aries	Sagittarius	Gemini	Libra	Sagittarius	Libra
7			Sagittarius	Aquarius	Aries	Sagittarius	Gemini	Libra	Sagittarius	Libra
8			Sagittarius	Aquarius	Aries	Sagittarius	Gemini	Libra	Sagittarius	Libra
9	10:16 A.M.	Scorpio	Sagittarius	Aquarius	Aries	Sagittarius	Gemini	Libra	Sagittarius	Libra
10			Sagittarius	Aquarius	Aries	Sagittarius	Gemini	Libra	Sagittarius	Libra
11	10:33 P.M.	Sagittarius	Sagittarius	Aquarius	Aries	Sagittarius	Taurus	Libra	Sagittarius	Libra
12			Capricorn	Aquarius	Aries	Sagittarius	Taurus	Libra	Sagittarius	Libra
13			Capricorn	Aquarius	Aries	Sagittarius	Taurus	Libra	Sagittarius	Libra
14	7:56 A.M.	Capricorn	Capricorn	Aquarius	Aries	Sagittarius	Taurus	Libra	Sagittarius	Libra
15			Capricorn	Aquarius	Aries	Sagittarius	Taurus	Libra	Sagittarius	Libra
16	2:18 P.M.	Aquarius	Capricorn	Aquarius	Aries	Sagittarius	Taurus	Libra	Sagittarius	Libra
17			Capricorn	Pisces	Aries	Sagittarius	Taurus	Libra	Sagittarius	Libra
18	6:30 P.M.	Pisces	Capricorn	Pisces	Aries	Sagittarius	Taurus	Libra	Sagittarius	Libra
19			Capricorn	Pisces	Aries	Sagittarius	Taurus	Libra	Sagittarius	Libra
20	9:35 P.M.	Aries	Capricorn	Pisces	Aries	Sagittarius	Taurus	Libra	Sagittarius	Libra
December										
22	7:51 A.M.	Leo	Sagittarius	Sagittarius	Scorpio	Capricorn	Gemini	Libra	Sagittarius	Libra
23			Sagittarius	Sagittarius	Scorpio	Capricorn	Gemini	Libra	Sagittarius	Libra
24	11:18 A.M.	Virgo	Sagittarius	Sagittarius	Scorpio	Capricorn	Gemini	Libra	Sagittarius	Libra
25			Sagittarius	Sagittarius	Scorpio	Capricorn	Gemini	Libra	Sagittarius	Libra
26	6:24 P.M.	Libra	Sagittarius	Sagittarius	Scorpio	Capricorn	Gemini	Libra	Sagittarius	Libra
27			Sagittarius	Sagittarius	Scorpio	Capricorn	Gemini	Libra	Sagittarius	Libra
28			Sagittarius	Sagittarius	Scorpio	Capricorn	Gemini	Libra	Sagittarius	Libra
29	5:37 A.M.	Scorpio	Sagittarius	Sagittarius	Scorpio	Capricorn	Gemini	Libra	Sagittarius	Libra
30			Sagittarius	Sagittarius	Scorpio	Capricorn	Gemini	Libra	Sagittarius	Libra
31	6:24 P.M.	Sagittarius	Sagittarius	Sagittarius	Sagittarius	Capricorn	Gemini	Libra	Sagittarius	Libra

CAPRICORN PLANETARY TABLES

1973

| | MOON | | | | | | | | | |
January	FROM	IN	MERCURY	VENUS	MARS	JUPITER	SATURN	URANUS	NEPTUNE	PLUTO
1	Sagittarius		Sagittarius	Sagittarius	Sagittarius	Capricorn	Gemini	Libra	Sagittarius	Libra
2			Sagittarius	Sagittarius	Sagittarius	Capricorn	Gemini	Libra	Sagittarius	Libra
3	7:00 A.M.	Capricorn	Sagittarius	Sagittarius	Sagittarius	Capricorn	Gemini	Libra	Sagittarius	Libra
4			Sagittarius	Sagittarius	Sagittarius	Capricorn	Gemini	Libra	Sagittarius	Libra
5	5:46 P.M.	Aquarius	Capricorn	Sagittarius	Sagittarius	Capricorn	Gemini	Libra	Sagittarius	Libra
6			Capricorn	Sagittarius	Sagittarius	Capricorn	Gemini	Libra	Sagittarius	Libra
7			Capricorn	Sagittarius	Sagittarius	Capricorn	Gemini	Libra	Sagittarius	Libra
8	3:02 A.M.	Pisces	Capricorn	Sagittarius	Sagittarius	Capricorn	Gemini	Libra	Sagittarius	Libra
9			Capricorn	Sagittarius	Sagittarius	Capricorn	Gemini	Libra	Sagittarius	Libra
10	6:29 P.M.	Aries	Capricorn	Sagittarius	Sagittarius	Capricorn	Gemini	Libra	Sagittarius	Libra
11			Capricorn	Sagittarius	Sagittarius	Capricorn	Gemini	Libra	Sagittarius	Libra
12	2:25 P.M.	Taurus	Capricorn	Capricorn	Sagittarius	Capricorn	Gemini	Libra	Sagittarius	Libra
13			Capricorn	Capricorn	Sagittarius	Capricorn	Gemini	Libra	Sagittarius	Libra
14	4:32 P.M.	Gemini	Capricorn	Capricorn	Sagittarius	Capricorn	Gemini	Libra	Sagittarius	Libra
15			Capricorn	Capricorn	Sagittarius	Capricorn	Gemini	Libra	Sagittarius	Libra
16	5:38 P.M.	Cancer	Capricorn	Capricorn	Sagittarius	Capricorn	Gemini	Libra	Sagittarius	Libra
17			Capricorn	Capricorn	Sagittarius	Capricorn	Gemini	Libra	Sagittarius	Libra
18	6:29 P.M.	Leo	Capricorn	Capricorn	Sagittarius	Capricorn	Gemini	Libra	Sagittarius	Libra
19			Capricorn	Capricorn	Sagittarius	Capricorn	Gemini	Libra	Sagittarius	Libra
20	9:24 P.M.	Virgo	Capricorn	Capricorn	Sagittarius	Capricorn	Gemini	Libra	Sagittarius	Libra
December										
23	Sagittarius		Sagittarius	Aquarius	Aries	Aquarius	Cancer	Libra	Sagittarius	Libra
24	4:57 A.M.	Capricorn	Sagittarius	Aquarius	Aries	Aquarius	Cancer	Libra	Sagittarius	Libra
25			Sagittarius	Aquarius	Taurus	Aquarius	Cancer	Libra	Sagittarius	Libra
26	5:18 P.M.	Aquarius	Sagittarius	Aquarius	Taurus	Aquarius	Cancer	Libra	Sagittarius	Libra
27			Sagittarius	Aquarius	Taurus	Aquarius	Cancer	Libra	Sagittarius	Libra
28			Sagittarius	Aquarius	Taurus	Aquarius	Cancer	Libra	Sagittarius	Libra
29	5:37 A.M.	Pisces	Capricorn	Aquarius	Taurus	Aquarius	Cancer	Libra	Sagittarius	Libra
30			Capricorn	Aquarius	Taurus	Aquarius	Cancer	Libra	Sagittarius	Libra
31	4:25 P.M.	Aries	Capricorn	Aquarius	Taurus	Aquarius	Cancer	Libra	Sagittarius	Libra

1974

MOON		MERCURY	VENUS	MARS	JUPITER	SATURN	URANUS	NEPTUNE	PLUTO
January	**FROM** **IN**								
1	Aries	Capricorn	Aquarius	Taurus	Aquarius	Cancer	Libra	Sagittarius	Libra
2	11:39 P.M. Taurus	Capricorn	Aquarius	Taurus	Aquarius	Cancer	Libra	Sagittarius	Libra
3		Capricorn	Aquarius	Taurus	Aquarius	Cancer	Libra	Sagittarius	Libra
4		Capricorn	Aquarius	Taurus	Aquarius	Cancer	Libra	Sagittarius	Libra
5	2:59 A.M. Gemini	Capricorn	Aquarius	Taurus	Aquarius	Cancer	Libra	Sagittarius	Libra
6		Capricorn	Aquarius	Taurus	Aquarius	Cancer	Libra	Sagittarius	Libra
7	3:16 A.M. Cancer	Capricorn	Aquarius	Taurus	Aquarius	Cancer	Libra	Sagittarius	Libra
8		Capricorn	Aquarius	Taurus	Aquarius	Cancer	Libra	Sagittarius	Libra
9	2:54 A.M. Leo	Capricorn	Aquarius	Taurus	Aquarius	Gemini	Libra	Sagittarius	Libra
10		Capricorn	Aquarius	Taurus	Aquarius	Gemini	Libra	Sagittarius	Libra
11	2:55 A.M. Virgo	Capricorn	Aquarius	Taurus	Aquarius	Gemini	Libra	Sagittarius	Libra
12		Capricorn	Aquarius	Taurus	Aquarius	Gemini	Libra	Sagittarius	Libra
13	5:48 A.M. Libra	Capricorn	Aquarius	Taurus	Aquarius	Gemini	Libra	Sagittarius	Libra
14		Capricorn	Aquarius	Taurus	Aquarius	Gemini	Libra	Sagittarius	Libra
15	12:32 P.M. Scorpio	Capricorn	Aquarius	Taurus	Aquarius	Gemini	Libra	Sagittarius	Libra
16		Capricorn	Aquarius	Taurus	Aquarius	Gemini	Libra	Sagittarius	Libra
17	10:33 P.M. Sagittarius	Aquarius	Aquarius	Taurus	Aquarius	Gemini	Libra	Sagittarius	Libra
18		Aquarius	Aquarius	Taurus	Aquarius	Gemini	Libra	Sagittarius	Libra
19		Aquarius	Aquarius	Taurus	Aquarius	Gemini	Libra	Sagittarius	Libra
20	11:15 A.M. Capricorn	Aquarius	Aquarius	Taurus	Aquarius	Gemini	Libra	Sagittarius	Libra
December									
23	Aries	Capricorn	Capricorn	Sagittarius	Pisces	Cancer	Scorpio	Sagittarius	Libra
24	1:51 A.M. Taurus	Capricorn	Capricorn	Sagittarius	Pisces	Cancer	Scorpio	Sagittarius	Libra
25	8:21 A.M. Gemini	Capricorn	Capricorn	Sagittarius	Pisces	Cancer	Scorpio	Sagittarius	Libra
26		Capricorn	Capricorn	Sagittarius	Pisces	Cancer	Scorpio	Sagittarius	Libra
27	11:09 A.M. Cancer	Capricorn	Capricorn	Sagittarius	Pisces	Cancer	Scorpio	Sagittarius	Libra
28		Capricorn	Capricorn	Sagittarius	Pisces	Cancer	Scorpio	Sagittarius	Libra
29	11:52 A.M. Leo	Capricorn	Capricorn	Sagittarius	Pisces	Cancer	Scorpio	Sagittarius	Libra
30		Capricorn	Capricorn	Sagittarius	Pisces	Cancer	Scorpio	Sagittarius	Libra
31		Capricorn	Capricorn	Sagittarius	Pisces	Cancer	Scorpio	Sagittarius	Libra

CAPRICORN PLANETARY TABLES

1975

| MOON | | | | | | | | | |
FROM / IN	MERCURY	VENUS	MARS	JUPITER	SATURN	URANUS	NEPTUNE	PLUTO
January								
1 — 1:03 P.M. Virgo	Capricorn	Capricorn	Sagittarius	Pisces	Cancer	Scorpio	Sagittarius	Libra
2	Capricorn	Capricorn	Sagittarius	Pisces	Cancer	Scorpio	Sagittarius	Libra
3 — 3:01 P.M. Libra	Capricorn	Capricorn	Sagittarius	Pisces	Cancer	Scorpio	Sagittarius	Libra
4	Capricorn	Capricorn	Sagittarius	Pisces	Cancer	Scorpio	Sagittarius	Libra
5 — 7:21 P.M. Scorpio	Capricorn	Capricorn	Sagittarius	Pisces	Cancer	Scorpio	Sagittarius	Libra
6	Capricorn	Capricorn	Sagittarius	Pisces	Cancer	Scorpio	Sagittarius	Libra
7	Capricorn	Aquarius	Sagittarius	Pisces	Cancer	Scorpio	Sagittarius	Libra
8 — 2:12 A.M. Sagittarius	Capricorn	Aquarius	Sagittarius	Pisces	Cancer	Scorpio	Sagittarius	Libra
9	Aquarius	Aquarius	Sagittarius	Pisces	Cancer	Scorpio	Sagittarius	Libra
10 — 11:09 A.M. Capricorn	Aquarius	Aquarius	Sagittarius	Pisces	Cancer	Scorpio	Sagittarius	Libra
11	Aquarius	Aquarius	Sagittarius	Pisces	Cancer	Scorpio	Sagittarius	Libra
12 — 10:05 P.M. Aquarius	Aquarius	Aquarius	Sagittarius	Pisces	Cancer	Scorpio	Sagittarius	Libra
13	Aquarius	Aquarius	Sagittarius	Pisces	Cancer	Scorpio	Sagittarius	Libra
14	Aquarius	Aquarius	Sagittarius	Pisces	Cancer	Scorpio	Sagittarius	Libra
15 — 10:26 A.M. Pisces	Aquarius	Aquarius	Sagittarius	Pisces	Cancer	Scorpio	Sagittarius	Libra
16	Aquarius	Aquarius	Sagittarius	Pisces	Cancer	Scorpio	Sagittarius	Libra
17 — 11:00 P.M. Aries	Aquarius	Aquarius	Sagittarius	Pisces	Cancer	Scorpio	Sagittarius	Libra
18	Aquarius	Aquarius	Sagittarius	Pisces	Cancer	Scorpio	Sagittarius	Libra
19	Aquarius	Aquarius	Sagittarius	Pisces	Cancer	Scorpio	Sagittarius	Libra
20 — 10:37 A.M. Taurus	Aquarius	Aquarius	Sagittarius	Pisces	Cancer	Scorpio	Sagittarius	Libra
December								
23 — 1:54 A.M. Virgo	Capricorn	Scorpio	Gemini	Aries	Leo	Scorpio	Sagittarius	Libra
24	Capricorn	Scorpio	Gemini	Aries	Leo	Scorpio	Sagittarius	Libra
25 — 5:00 A.M. Libra	Capricorn	Scorpio	Gemini	Aries	Leo	Scorpio	Sagittarius	Libra
26	Capricorn	Scorpio	Gemini	Aries	Leo	Scorpio	Sagittarius	Libra
27 — 7:51 A.M. Scorpio	Capricorn	Scorpio	Gemini	Aries	Leo	Scorpio	Sagittarius	Libra
28	Capricorn	Scorpio	Gemini	Aries	Leo	Scorpio	Sagittarius	Libra
29 — 10:59 A.M. Sagittarius	Capricorn	Scorpio	Gemini	Aries	Leo	Scorpio	Sagittarius	Libra
30	Capricorn	Scorpio	Gemini	Aries	Leo	Scorpio	Sagittarius	Libra
31 — 3:19 P.M. Capricorn	Capricorn	Scorpio	Gemini	Aries	Leo	Scorpio	Sagittarius	Libra

1976

January	MOON FROM IN	MERCURY	VENUS	MARS	JUPITER	SATURN	URANUS	NEPTUNE	PLUTO
1	Capricorn	Capricorn	Scorpio	Gemini	Aries	Leo	Scorpio	Sagittarius	Libra
2	9:28 P.M. Aquarius	Capricorn	Sagittarius	Gemini	Aries	Leo	Scorpio	Sagittarius	Libra
3		Aquarius	Sagittarius	Gemini	Aries	Leo	Scorpio	Sagittarius	Libra
4		Aquarius	Sagittarius	Gemini	Aries	Leo	Scorpio	Sagittarius	Libra
5	6:37 A.M. Pisces	Aquarius	Sagittarius	Gemini	Aries	Leo	Scorpio	Sagittarius	Libra
6		Aquarius	Sagittarius	Gemini	Aries	Leo	Scorpio	Sagittarius	Libra
7	6:29 P.M. Aries	Aquarius	Sagittarius	Gemini	Aries	Leo	Scorpio	Sagittarius	Libra
8		Aquarius	Sagittarius	Gemini	Aries	Leo	Scorpio	Sagittarius	Libra
9		Aquarius	Sagittarius	Gemini	Aries	Leo	Scorpio	Sagittarius	Libra
10	7:36 A.M. Taurus	Aquarius	Sagittarius	Gemini	Aries	Leo	Scorpio	Sagittarius	Libra
11		Aquarius	Sagittarius	Gemini	Aries	Leo	Scorpio	Sagittarius	Libra
12	6:24 P.M. Gemini	Aquarius	Sagittarius	Gemini	Aries	Leo	Scorpio	Sagittarius	Libra
13		Aquarius	Sagittarius	Gemini	Aries	Leo	Scorpio	Sagittarius	Libra
14		Aquarius	Sagittarius	Gemini	Aries	Leo	Scorpio	Sagittarius	Libra
15	1:47 A.M. Cancer	Aquarius	Sagittarius	Gemini	Aries	Cancer	Scorpio	Sagittarius	Libra
16		Aquarius	Sagittarius	Gemini	Aries	Cancer	Scorpio	Sagittarius	Libra
17	6:20 A.M. Leo	Aquarius	Sagittarius	Gemini	Aries	Cancer	Scorpio	Sagittarius	Libra
18		Aquarius	Sagittarius	Gemini	Aries	Cancer	Scorpio	Sagittarius	Libra
19	8:49 A.M. Virgo	Aquarius	Sagittarius	Gemini	Aries	Cancer	Scorpio	Sagittarius	Libra
20		Aquarius	Sagittarius	Gemini	Aries	Cancer	Scorpio	Sagittarius	Libra
December									
22	Capricorn	Capricorn	Aquarius	Sagittarius	Taurus	Leo	Scorpio	Sagittarius	Libra
23	0:02 A.M. Aquarius	Capricorn	Aquarius	Sagittarius	Taurus	Leo	Scorpio	Sagittarius	Libra
24		Capricorn	Aquarius	Sagittarius	Taurus	Leo	Scorpio	Sagittarius	Libra
25	5:00 A.M. Pisces	Capricorn	Aquarius	Sagittarius	Taurus	Leo	Scorpio	Sagittarius	Libra
26		Capricorn	Aquarius	Sagittarius	Taurus	Leo	Scorpio	Sagittarius	Libra
27	1:57 P.M. Aries	Capricorn	Aquarius	Sagittarius	Taurus	Leo	Scorpio	Sagittarius	Libra
28		Capricorn	Aquarius	Sagittarius	Taurus	Leo	Scorpio	Sagittarius	Libra
29		Capricorn	Aquarius	Sagittarius	Taurus	Leo	Scorpio	Sagittarius	Libra
30	2:02 A.M. Taurus	Capricorn	Aquarius	Sagittarius	Taurus	Leo	Scorpio	Sagittarius	Libra
31		Capricorn	Aquarius	Sagittarius	Taurus	Leo	Scorpio	Sagittarius	Libra

CAPRICORN PLANETARY TABLES

1977

Date	MOON FROM	IN	MERCURY	VENUS	MARS	JUPITER	SATURN	URANUS	NEPTUNE	PLUTO
January 1	2:47 P.M.	Gemini	Capricorn	Aquarius	Sagittarius	Taurus	Leo	Scorpio	Sagittarius	Libra
2			Capricorn	Aquarius	Capricorn	Taurus	Leo	Scorpio	Sagittarius	Libra
3			Capricorn	Aquarius	Capricorn	Taurus	Leo	Scorpio	Sagittarius	Libra
4	2:10 A.M.	Cancer	Capricorn	Aquarius	Capricorn	Taurus	Leo	Scorpio	Sagittarius	Libra
5			Capricorn	Pisces	Capricorn	Taurus	Leo	Scorpio	Sagittarius	Libra
6	11:33 A.M.	Leo	Capricorn	Pisces	Capricorn	Taurus	Leo	Scorpio	Sagittarius	Libra
7			Capricorn	Pisces	Capricorn	Taurus	Leo	Scorpio	Sagittarius	Libra
8	6:54 P.M.	Virgo	Capricorn	Pisces	Capricorn	Taurus	Leo	Scorpio	Sagittarius	Libra
9			Capricorn	Pisces	Capricorn	Taurus	Leo	Scorpio	Sagittarius	Libra
10			Capricorn	Pisces	Capricorn	Taurus	Leo	Scorpio	Sagittarius	Libra
11	0:15 A.M.	Libra	Capricorn	Pisces	Capricorn	Taurus	Leo	Scorpio	Sagittarius	Libra
12			Capricorn	Pisces	Capricorn	Taurus	Leo	Scorpio	Sagittarius	Libra
13	3:47 A.M.	Scorpio	Capricorn	Pisces	Capricorn	Taurus	Leo	Scorpio	Sagittarius	Libra
14			Capricorn	Pisces	Capricorn	Taurus	Leo	Scorpio	Sagittarius	Libra
15	4:39 A.M.	Sagittarius	Capricorn	Pisces	Capricorn	Taurus	Leo	Scorpio	Sagittarius	Libra
16			Capricorn	Pisces	Capricorn	Taurus	Leo	Scorpio	Sagittarius	Libra
17	7:40 A.M.	Capricorn	Capricorn	Pisces	Capricorn	Taurus	Leo	Scorpio	Sagittarius	Libra
18			Capricorn	Pisces	Capricorn	Taurus	Leo	Scorpio	Sagittarius	Libra
19	10:18 A.M.	Aquarius	Capricorn	Pisces	Capricorn	Taurus	Leo	Scorpio	Sagittarius	Libra
20			Capricorn	Pisces	Capricorn	Taurus	Leo	Scorpio	Sagittarius	Libra
December 22	11:53 A.M.	Gemini	Sagittarius	Sagittarius	Leo	Cancer	Virgo	Scorpio	Sagittarius	Libra
23			Sagittarius	Sagittarius	Leo	Cancer	Virgo	Scorpio	Sagittarius	Libra
24			Sagittarius	Sagittarius	Leo	Cancer	Virgo	Scorpio	Sagittarius	Libra
25	0:33 A.M.	Cancer	Sagittarius	Sagittarius	Leo	Cancer	Virgo	Scorpio	Sagittarius	Libra
26			Sagittarius	Sagittarius	Leo	Cancer	Virgo	Scorpio	Sagittarius	Libra
27	12:51 P.M.	Leo	Sagittarius	Sagittarius	Leo	Cancer	Virgo	Scorpio	Sagittarius	Libra
28			Sagittarius	Capricorn	Leo	Cancer	Virgo	Scorpio	Sagittarius	Libra
29			Sagittarius	Capricorn	Leo	Cancer	Virgo	Scorpio	Sagittarius	Libra
30	0:25 A.M.	Virgo	Sagittarius	Capricorn	Leo	Cancer	Virgo	Scorpio	Sagittarius	Libra
31			Sagittarius	Capricorn	Leo	Gemini	Virgo	Scorpio	Sagittarius	Libra

1978

January	MOON FROM	IN	MERCURY	VENUS	MARS	JUPITER	SATURN	URANUS	NEPTUNE	PLUTO
1	9:43 A.M.	Libra	Sagittarius	Capricorn	Leo	Gemini	Virgo	Scorpio	Sagittarius	Libra
2			Sagittarius	Capricorn	Leo	Gemini	Virgo	Scorpio	Sagittarius	Libra
3	3:18 P.M.	Scorpio	Sagittarius	Capricorn	Leo	Gemini	Virgo	Scorpio	Sagittarius	Libra
4			Sagittarius	Capricorn	Leo	Gemini	Virgo	Scorpio	Sagittarius	Libra
5	5:38 P.M.	Sagittarius	Sagittarius	Capricorn	Leo	Gemini	Leo	Scorpio	Sagittarius	Libra
6			Sagittarius	Capricorn	Leo	Gemini	Leo	Scorpio	Sagittarius	Libra
7	5:51 P.M.	Capricorn	Sagittarius	Capricorn	Leo	Gemini	Leo	Scorpio	Sagittarius	Libra
8			Sagittarius	Capricorn	Leo	Gemini	Leo	Scorpio	Sagittarius	Libra
9	5:16 P.M.	Aquarius	Sagittarius	Capricorn	Leo	Gemini	Leo	Scorpio	Sagittarius	Libra
10			Sagittarius	Capricorn	Leo	Gemini	Leo	Scorpio	Sagittarius	Libra
11	6:35 P.M.	Pisces	Sagittarius	Capricorn	Leo	Gemini	Leo	Scorpio	Sagittarius	Libra
12			Sagittarius	Capricorn	Leo	Gemini	Leo	Scorpio	Sagittarius	Libra
13	10:24 P.M.	Aries	Sagittarius	Capricorn	Leo	Gemini	Leo	Scorpio	Sagittarius	Libra
14			Capricorn	Capricorn	Leo	Gemini	Leo	Scorpio	Sagittarius	Libra
15			Capricorn	Capricorn	Leo	Gemini	Leo	Scorpio	Sagittarius	Libra
16	6:38 A.M.	Taurus	Capricorn	Capricorn	Leo	Gemini	Leo	Scorpio	Sagittarius	Libra
17			Capricorn	Capricorn	Leo	Gemini	Leo	Scorpio	Sagittarius	Libra
18	6:24 P.M.	Gemini	Capricorn	Capricorn	Leo	Gemini	Leo	Scorpio	Sagittarius	Libra
19			Capricorn	Capricorn	Leo	Gemini	Leo	Scorpio	Sagittarius	Libra
20			Capricorn	Capricorn	Leo	Gemini	Leo	Scorpio	Sagittarius	Libra
December										
23		Libra	Sagittarius	Scorpio	Capricorn	Leo	Virgo	Scorpio	Sagittarius	Libra
24	8:12 P.M.	Scorpio	Sagittarius	Scorpio	Capricorn	Leo	Virgo	Scorpio	Sagittarius	Libra
25			Sagittarius	Scorpio	Capricorn	Leo	Virgo	Scorpio	Sagittarius	Libra
26			Sagittarius	Scorpio	Capricorn	Leo	Virgo	Scorpio	Sagittarius	Libra
27	0:53 A.M.	Sagittarius	Sagittarius	Scorpio	Capricorn	Leo	Virgo	Scorpio	Sagittarius	Libra
28			Sagittarius	Scorpio	Capricorn	Leo	Virgo	Scorpio	Sagittarius	Libra
29	2:18 A.M.	Capricorn	Sagittarius	Scorpio	Capricorn	Leo	Virgo	Scorpio	Sagittarius	Libra
30			Sagittarius	Scorpio	Capricorn	Leo	Virgo	Scorpio	Sagittarius	Libra
31	2:25 A.M.	Aquarius	Sagittarius	Scorpio	Capricorn	Leo	Virgo	Scorpio	Sagittarius	Libra

CAPRICORN PLANETARY TABLES

1979

	MOON FROM	IN	MERCURY	VENUS	MARS	JUPITER	SATURN	URANUS	NEPTUNE	PLUTO
January										
1	Aquarius		Sagittarius	Scorpio	Capricorn	Leo	Virgo	Scorpio	Sagittarius	Libra
2	2:40 A.M.	Pisces	Sagittarius	Scorpio	Capricorn	Leo	Virgo	Scorpio	Sagittarius	Libra
3			Sagittarius	Scorpio	Capricorn	Leo	Virgo	Scorpio	Sagittarius	Libra
4	5:00 A.M.	Aries	Sagittarius	Scorpio	Capricorn	Leo	Virgo	Scorpio	Sagittarius	Libra
5			Sagittarius	Scorpio	Capricorn	Leo	Virgo	Scorpio	Sagittarius	Libra
6	10:12 A.M.	Taurus	Sagittarius	Scorpio	Capricorn	Leo	Virgo	Scorpio	Sagittarius	Libra
7			Sagittarius	Sagittarius	Capricorn	Leo	Virgo	Scorpio	Sagittarius	Libra
8	7:13 P.M.	Gemini	Sagittarius	Sagittarius	Capricorn	Leo	Virgo	Scorpio	Sagittarius	Libra
9			Capricorn	Sagittarius	Capricorn	Leo	Virgo	Scorpio	Sagittarius	Libra
10			Capricorn	Sagittarius	Capricorn	Leo	Virgo	Scorpio	Sagittarius	Libra
11	6:37 A.M.	Cancer	Capricorn	Sagittarius	Capricorn	Leo	Virgo	Scorpio	Sagittarius	Libra
12			Capricorn	Sagittarius	Capricorn	Leo	Virgo	Scorpio	Sagittarius	Libra
13	6:24 P.M.	Leo	Capricorn	Sagittarius	Capricorn	Leo	Virgo	Scorpio	Sagittarius	Libra
14			Capricorn	Sagittarius	Capricorn	Leo	Virgo	Scorpio	Sagittarius	Libra
15			Capricorn	Sagittarius	Capricorn	Leo	Virgo	Scorpio	Sagittarius	Libra
16	6:14 A.M.	Virgo	Capricorn	Sagittarius	Capricorn	Leo	Virgo	Scorpio	Sagittarius	Libra
17			Capricorn	Sagittarius	Capricorn	Leo	Virgo	Scorpio	Sagittarius	Libra
18	6:31 P.M.	Libra	Capricorn	Sagittarius	Capricorn	Leo	Virgo	Scorpio	Sagittarius	Libra
19			Capricorn	Sagittarius	Capricorn	Leo	Virgo	Scorpio	Sagittarius	Libra
20			Capricorn	Sagittarius	Capricorn	Leo	Virgo	Scorpio	Sagittarius	Libra
December										
23	3:01 P.M.	Pisces	Sagittarius	Aquarius	Virgo	Virgo	Virgo	Scorpio	Sagittarius	Libra
24			Sagittarius	Aquarius	Virgo	Virgo	Virgo	Scorpio	Sagittarius	Libra
25	5:31 P.M.	Aries	Sagittarius	Aquarius	Virgo	Virgo	Virgo	Scorpio	Sagittarius	Libra
26			Sagittarius	Aquarius	Virgo	Virgo	Virgo	Scorpio	Sagittarius	Libra
27	8:59 P.M.	Taurus	Sagittarius	Aquarius	Virgo	Virgo	Virgo	Scorpio	Sagittarius	Libra
28			Sagittarius	Aquarius	Virgo	Virgo	Virgo	Scorpio	Sagittarius	Libra
29			Sagittarius	Aquarius	Virgo	Virgo	Virgo	Scorpio	Sagittarius	Libra
30	1:30 A.M.	Gemini	Sagittarius	Aquarius	Virgo	Virgo	Virgo	Scorpio	Sagittarius	Libra
31			Sagittarius	Aquarius	Virgo	Virgo	Virgo	Scorpio	Sagittarius	Libra

1980

	MOON		MERCURY	VENUS	MARS	JUPITER	SATURN	URANUS	NEPTUNE	PLUTO
January	FROM	IN								
1	7:56 A.M.	Cancer	Sagittarius	Aquarius	Virgo	Virgo	Virgo	Scorpio	Sagittarius	Libra
2			Sagittarius	Aquarius	Virgo	Virgo	Virgo	Scorpio	Sagittarius	Libra
3	4:07 P.M.	Leo	Capricorn	Aquarius	Virgo	Virgo	Virgo	Scorpio	Sagittarius	Libra
4			Capricorn	Aquarius	Virgo	Virgo	Virgo	Scorpio	Sagittarius	Libra
5			Capricorn	Aquarius	Virgo	Virgo	Virgo	Scorpio	Sagittarius	Libra
6	3:00 A.M.	Virgo	Capricorn	Aquarius	Virgo	Virgo	Virgo	Scorpio	Sagittarius	Libra
7			Capricorn	Aquarius	Virgo	Virgo	Virgo	Scorpio	Sagittarius	Libra
8	3:39 P.M.	Libra	Capricorn	Aquarius	Virgo	Virgo	Virgo	Scorpio	Sagittarius	Libra
9			Capricorn	Aquarius	Virgo	Virgo	Virgo	Scorpio	Sagittarius	Libra
10			Capricorn	Aquarius	Virgo	Virgo	Virgo	Scorpio	Sagittarius	Libra
11	3:52 A.M.	Scorpio	Capricorn	Aquarius	Virgo	Virgo	Virgo	Scorpio	Sagittarius	Libra
12			Capricorn	Aquarius	Virgo	Virgo	Virgo	Scorpio	Sagittarius	Libra
13	1:37 P.M.	Sagittarius	Capricorn	Aquarius	Virgo	Virgo	Virgo	Scorpio	Sagittarius	Libra
14			Capricorn	Aquarius	Virgo	Virgo	Virgo	Scorpio	Sagittarius	Libra
15	7:06 P.M.	Capricorn	Capricorn	Aquarius	Virgo	Virgo	Virgo	Scorpio	Sagittarius	Libra
16			Capricorn	Aquarius	Virgo	Virgo	Virgo	Scorpio	Sagittarius	Libra
17	9:12 P.M.	Aquarius	Capricorn	Pisces	Virgo	Virgo	Virgo	Scorpio	Sagittarius	Libra
18			Capricorn	Pisces	Virgo	Virgo	Virgo	Scorpio	Sagittarius	Libra
19	10:11 P.M.	Pisces	Capricorn	Pisces	Virgo	Virgo	Virgo	Scorpio	Sagittarius	Libra
20			Capricorn	Pisces	Virgo	Virgo	Virgo	Scorpio	Sagittarius	Libra
December										
22		Cancer	Sagittarius	Sagittarius	Capricorn	Libra	Libra	Scorpio	Sagittarius	Libra
23	5:03 P.M.	Leo	Sagittarius	Sagittarius	Capricorn	Libra	Libra	Scorpio	Sagittarius	Libra
24			Sagittarius	Sagittarius	Capricorn	Libra	Libra	Scorpio	Sagittarius	Libra
25	11:35 P.M.	Virgo	Sagittarius	Sagittarius	Capricorn	Libra	Libra	Scorpio	Sagittarius	Libra
26			Capricorn	Sagittarius	Capricorn	Libra	Libra	Scorpio	Sagittarius	Libra
27			Capricorn	Sagittarius	Capricorn	Libra	Libra	Scorpio	Sagittarius	Libra
28	10:25 A.M.	Libra	Capricorn	Sagittarius	Capricorn	Libra	Libra	Scorpio	Sagittarius	Libra
29			Capricorn	Sagittarius	Capricorn	Libra	Libra	Scorpio	Sagittarius	Libra
30	10:48 P.M.	Scorpio	Capricorn	Sagittarius	Capricorn	Libra	Libra	Scorpio	Sagittarius	Libra
31			Capricorn	Sagittarius	Aquarius	Libra	Libra	Scorpio	Sagittarius	Libra

CAPRICORN PLANETARY TABLES

1981

January	MOON FROM	IN	MERCURY	VENUS	MARS	JUPITER	SATURN	URANUS	NEPTUNE	PLUTO
1		Scorpio	Capricorn	Sagittarius	Aquarius	Libra	Libra	Scorpio	Sagittarius	Libra
2	11:09 A.M.	Sagittarius	Capricorn	Sagittarius	Aquarius	Libra	Libra	Scorpio	Sagittarius	Libra
3			Capricorn	Sagittarius	Aquarius	Libra	Libra	Scorpio	Sagittarius	Libra
4	9:11 P.M.	Capricorn	Capricorn	Sagittarius	Aquarius	Libra	Libra	Scorpio	Sagittarius	Libra
5			Capricorn	Sagittarius	Aquarius	Libra	Libra	Scorpio	Sagittarius	Libra
6			Capricorn	Sagittarius	Aquarius	Libra	Libra	Scorpio	Sagittarius	Libra
7	4:38 A.M.	Aquarius	Capricorn	Sagittarius	Aquarius	Libra	Libra	Scorpio	Sagittarius	Libra
8			Capricorn	Sagittarius	Aquarius	Libra	Libra	Scorpio	Sagittarius	Libra
9	9:47 A.M.	Pisces	Capricorn	Sagittarius	Aquarius	Libra	Libra	Scorpio	Sagittarius	Libra
10			Capricorn	Sagittarius	Aquarius	Libra	Libra	Scorpio	Sagittarius	Libra
11	1:48 P.M.	Aries	Capricorn	Sagittarius	Aquarius	Libra	Libra	Scorpio	Sagittarius	Libra
12			Capricorn	Capricorn	Aquarius	Libra	Libra	Scorpio	Sagittarius	Libra
13	4:37 P.M.	Taurus	Capricorn	Capricorn	Aquarius	Libra	Libra	Scorpio	Sagittarius	Libra
14			Aquarius	Capricorn	Aquarius	Libra	Libra	Scorpio	Sagittarius	Libra
15	7:26 P.M.	Gemini	Aquarius	Capricorn	Aquarius	Libra	Libra	Scorpio	Sagittarius	Libra
16			Aquarius	Capricorn	Aquarius	Libra	Libra	Scorpio	Sagittarius	Libra
17	10:23 P.M.	Cancer	Aquarius	Capricorn	Aquarius	Libra	Libra	Scorpio	Sagittarius	Libra
18			Aquarius	Capricorn	Aquarius	Libra	Libra	Scorpio	Sagittarius	Libra
19			Aquarius	Capricorn	Aquarius	Libra	Libra	Scorpio	Sagittarius	Libra
20	2:36 A.M.	Leo	Aquarius	Capricorn	Aquarius	Libra	Libra	Scorpio	Sagittarius	Libra
December										
22		Scorpio	Capricorn	Aquarius	Libra	Scorpio	Libra	Sagittarius	Sagittarius	Libra
23	7:49 A.M.	Sagittarius	Capricorn	Aquarius	Libra	Scorpio	Libra	Sagittarius	Sagittarius	Libra
24			Capricorn	Aquarius	Libra	Scorpio	Libra	Sagittarius	Sagittarius	Libra
25	8:19 P.M.	Capricorn	Capricorn	Aquarius	Libra	Scorpio	Libra	Sagittarius	Sagittarius	Libra
26			Capricorn	Aquarius	Libra	Scorpio	Libra	Sagittarius	Sagittarius	Libra
27			Capricorn	Aquarius	Libra	Scorpio	Libra	Sagittarius	Sagittarius	Libra
28	7:47 A.M.	Aquarius	Capricorn	Aquarius	Libra	Scorpio	Libra	Sagittarius	Sagittarius	Libra
29			Capricorn	Aquarius	Libra	Scorpio	Libra	Sagittarius	Sagittarius	Libra
30	5:47 P.M.	Pisces	Capricorn	Aquarius	Libra	Scorpio	Libra	Sagittarius	Sagittarius	Libra
31			Capricorn	Aquarius	Libra	Scorpio	Libra	Sagittarius	Sagittarius	Libra

1982

January	FROM (MOON)	IN	MERCURY	VENUS	MARS	JUPITER	SATURN	URANUS	NEPTUNE	PLUTO
1		Pisces	Capricorn	Aquarius	Libra	Scorpio	Libra	Sagittarius	Sagittarius	Libra
2	1:31 A.M.	Aries	Capricorn	Aquarius	Libra	Scorpio	Libra	Sagittarius	Sagittarius	Libra
3			Capricorn	Aquarius	Libra	Scorpio	Libra	Sagittarius	Sagittarius	Libra
4	6:00 A.M.	Taurus	Capricorn	Aquarius	Libra	Scorpio	Libra	Sagittarius	Sagittarius	Libra
5			Capricorn	Aquarius	Libra	Scorpio	Libra	Sagittarius	Sagittarius	Libra
6	7:49 A.M.	Gemini	Aquarius	Aquarius	Libra	Scorpio	Libra	Sagittarius	Sagittarius	Libra
7			Aquarius	Aquarius	Libra	Scorpio	Libra	Sagittarius	Sagittarius	Libra
8	8:08 A.M.	Cancer	Aquarius	Aquarius	Libra	Scorpio	Libra	Sagittarius	Sagittarius	Libra
9			Aquarius	Aquarius	Libra	Scorpio	Libra	Sagittarius	Sagittarius	Libra
10	8:19 A.M.	Leo	Aquarius	Aquarius	Libra	Scorpio	Libra	Sagittarius	Sagittarius	Libra
11			Aquarius	Aquarius	Libra	Scorpio	Libra	Sagittarius	Sagittarius	Libra
12	10:50 A.M.	Virgo	Aquarius	Aquarius	Libra	Scorpio	Libra	Sagittarius	Sagittarius	Libra
13			Aquarius	Aquarius	Libra	Scorpio	Libra	Sagittarius	Sagittarius	Libra
14	4:22 P.M.	Libra	Aquarius	Aquarius	Libra	Scorpio	Libra	Sagittarius	Sagittarius	Libra
15			Aquarius	Aquarius	Libra	Scorpio	Libra	Sagittarius	Sagittarius	Libra
16			Aquarius	Aquarius	Libra	Scorpio	Libra	Sagittarius	Sagittarius	Libra
17	2:15 A.M.	Scorpio	Aquarius	Aquarius	Libra	Scorpio	Libra	Sagittarius	Sagittarius	Libra
18			Aquarius	Aquarius	Libra	Scorpio	Libra	Sagittarius	Sagittarius	Libra
19	2:36 P.M.	Sagittarius	Aquarius	Aquarius	Libra	Scorpio	Libra	Sagittarius	Sagittarius	Libra
20			Aquarius	Aquarius	Libra	Scorpio	Libra	Sagittarius	Sagittarius	Libra
December										
23	6:27 A.M.	Aries	Capricorn	Capricorn	Aquarius	Scorpio	Scorpio	Sagittarius	Sagittarius	Libra
24			Capricorn	Capricorn	Aquarius	Scorpio	Scorpio	Sagittarius	Sagittarius	Libra
25	1:29 P.M.	Taurus	Capricorn	Capricorn	Aquarius	Scorpio	Scorpio	Sagittarius	Sagittarius	Libra
26			Capricorn	Capricorn	Aquarius	Scorpio	Scorpio	Sagittarius	Sagittarius	Libra
27	4:51 P.M.	Gemini	Capricorn	Capricorn	Aquarius	Sagittarius	Scorpio	Sagittarius	Sagittarius	Libra
28			Capricorn	Capricorn	Aquarius	Sagittarius	Scorpio	Sagittarius	Sagittarius	Libra
29	5:09 P.M.	Cancer	Capricorn	Capricorn	Aquarius	Sagittarius	Scorpio	Sagittarius	Sagittarius	Libra
30			Capricorn	Capricorn	Aquarius	Sagittarius	Scorpio	Sagittarius	Sagittarius	Libra
31	4:41 P.M.	Leo	Capricorn	Capricorn	Aquarius	Sagittarius	Scorpio	Sagittarius	Sagittarius	Libra

1983

CAPRICORN PLANETARY TABLES

January	MOON FROM / IN	MERCURY	VENUS	MARS	JUPITER	SATURN	URANUS	NEPTUNE	PLUTO
1	Leo	Capricorn	Capricorn	Aquarius	Sagittarius	Scorpio	Sagittarius	Sagittarius	Libra
2	5:13 P.M. Virgo	Aquarius	Capricorn	Aquarius	Sagittarius	Scorpio	Sagittarius	Sagittarius	Libra
3		Aquarius	Capricorn	Aquarius	Sagittarius	Scorpio	Sagittarius	Sagittarius	Libra
4	8:14 P.M. Libra	Aquarius	Capricorn	Aquarius	Sagittarius	Scorpio	Sagittarius	Sagittarius	Libra
5		Aquarius	Capricorn	Aquarius	Sagittarius	Scorpio	Sagittarius	Sagittarius	Libra
6		Aquarius	Aquarius	Aquarius	Sagittarius	Scorpio	Sagittarius	Sagittarius	Libra
7	2:37 A.M. Scorpio	Aquarius	Aquarius	Aquarius	Sagittarius	Scorpio	Sagittarius	Sagittarius	Libra
8		Aquarius	Aquarius	Aquarius	Sagittarius	Scorpio	Sagittarius	Sagittarius	Libra
9	11:32 A.M. Sagittarius	Aquarius	Aquarius	Aquarius	Sagittarius	Scorpio	Sagittarius	Sagittarius	Libra
10		Aquarius	Aquarius	Aquarius	Sagittarius	Scorpio	Sagittarius	Sagittarius	Libra
11	11:08 P.M. Capricorn	Aquarius	Aquarius	Aquarius	Sagittarius	Scorpio	Sagittarius	Sagittarius	Libra
12		Aquarius	Aquarius	Aquarius	Sagittarius	Scorpio	Sagittarius	Sagittarius	Libra
13		Capricorn	Aquarius	Aquarius	Sagittarius	Scorpio	Sagittarius	Sagittarius	Libra
14	11:29 A.M. Aquarius	Capricorn	Aquarius	Aquarius	Sagittarius	Scorpio	Sagittarius	Sagittarius	Libra
15		Capricorn	Aquarius	Aquarius	Sagittarius	Scorpio	Sagittarius	Sagittarius	Libra
16		Capricorn	Aquarius	Aquarius	Sagittarius	Scorpio	Sagittarius	Sagittarius	Libra
17	1:39 P.M. Pisces	Capricorn	Aquarius	Aquarius	Sagittarius	Scorpio	Sagittarius	Sagittarius	Libra
18		Capricorn	Aquarius	Pisces	Sagittarius	Scorpio	Sagittarius	Sagittarius	Libra
19	1:00 P.M. Aries	Capricorn	Aquarius	Pisces	Sagittarius	Scorpio	Sagittarius	Sagittarius	Libra
20		Capricorn	Aquarius	Pisces	Sagittarius	Scorpio	Sagittarius	Sagittarius	Libra
December									
23	Leo	Capricorn	Scorpio	Libra	Sagittarius	Scorpio	Sagittarius	Sagittarius	Scorpio
24	4:24 A.M. Virgo	Capricorn	Scorpio	Libra	Sagittarius	Scorpio	Sagittarius	Sagittarius	Scorpio
25		Capricorn	Scorpio	Libra	Sagittarius	Scorpio	Sagittarius	Sagittarius	Scorpio
26	6:31 A.M. Libra	Capricorn	Scorpio	Libra	Sagittarius	Scorpio	Sagittarius	Sagittarius	Scorpio
27		Capricorn	Scorpio	Libra	Sagittarius	Scorpio	Sagittarius	Sagittarius	Scorpio
28	10:47 A.M. Scorpio	Capricorn	Scorpio	Libra	Sagittarius	Scorpio	Sagittarius	Sagittarius	Scorpio
29		Capricorn	Scorpio	Libra	Sagittarius	Scorpio	Sagittarius	Sagittarius	Scorpio
30	4:55 P.M. Sagittarius	Capricorn	Scorpio	Libra	Sagittarius	Scorpio	Sagittarius	Sagittarius	Scorpio
31		Capricorn	Scorpio	Libra	Sagittarius	Scorpio	Sagittarius	Sagittarius	Scorpio

1984

January

	MOON FROM / IN	MERCURY	VENUS	MARS	JUPITER	SATURN	URANUS	NEPTUNE	PLUTO
1	Sagittarius	Capricorn	Scorpio	Libra	Sagittarius	Scorpio	Sagittarius	Sagittarius	Scorpio
2	1:20 A.M. Capricorn	Capricorn	Sagittarius	Libra	Sagittarius	Scorpio	Sagittarius	Sagittarius	Scorpio
3		Capricorn	Sagittarius	Libra	Sagittarius	Scorpio	Sagittarius	Sagittarius	Scorpio
4	11:42 A.M. Aquarius	Capricorn	Sagittarius	Libra	Sagittarius	Scorpio	Sagittarius	Sagittarius	Scorpio
5		Capricorn	Sagittarius	Libra	Sagittarius	Scorpio	Sagittarius	Sagittarius	Scorpio
6	11:20 P.M. Pisces	Capricorn	Sagittarius	Libra	Sagittarius	Scorpio	Sagittarius	Sagittarius	Scorpio
7		Capricorn	Sagittarius	Libra	Sagittarius	Scorpio	Sagittarius	Sagittarius	Scorpio
8		Capricorn	Sagittarius	Libra	Sagittarius	Scorpio	Sagittarius	Sagittarius	Scorpio
9	12:15 P.M. Aries	Capricorn	Sagittarius	Libra	Sagittarius	Scorpio	Sagittarius	Sagittarius	Scorpio
10		Capricorn	Sagittarius	Libra	Sagittarius	Scorpio	Sagittarius	Sagittarius	Scorpio
11	11:56 P.M. Taurus	Capricorn	Sagittarius	Scorpio	Sagittarius	Scorpio	Sagittarius	Sagittarius	Scorpio
12		Capricorn	Sagittarius	Scorpio	Sagittarius	Scorpio	Sagittarius	Sagittarius	Scorpio
13		Capricorn	Sagittarius	Scorpio	Sagittarius	Scorpio	Sagittarius	Sagittarius	Scorpio
14	7:43 A.M. Gemini	Capricorn	Sagittarius	Scorpio	Sagittarius	Scorpio	Sagittarius	Sagittarius	Scorpio
15		Capricorn	Sagittarius	Scorpio	Sagittarius	Scorpio	Sagittarius	Sagittarius	Scorpio
16	11:38 A.M. Cancer	Capricorn	Sagittarius	Scorpio	Sagittarius	Scorpio	Sagittarius	Sagittarius	Scorpio
17		Capricorn	Sagittarius	Scorpio	Sagittarius	Scorpio	Sagittarius	Sagittarius	Scorpio
18	12:41 P.M. Leo	Capricorn	Sagittarius	Scorpio	Sagittarius	Scorpio	Sagittarius	Sagittarius	Scorpio
19		Capricorn	Sagittarius	Scorpio	Sagittarius	Scorpio	Sagittarius	Sagittarius	Scorpio
20	12:58 P.M. Virgo	Capricorn	Sagittarius	Scorpio	Sagittarius	Scorpio	Sagittarius	Capricorn	Scorpio
December									
22	5:17 A.M. Capricorn	Sagittarius	Aquarius	Aquarius	Capricorn	Scorpio	Sagittarius	Capricorn	Scorpio
23		Sagittarius	Aquarius	Aquarius	Capricorn	Scorpio	Sagittarius	Capricorn	Scorpio
24	10:52 A.M. Aquarius	Sagittarius	Aquarius	Aquarius	Capricorn	Scorpio	Sagittarius	Capricorn	Scorpio
25		Sagittarius	Aquarius	Aquarius	Capricorn	Scorpio	Sagittarius	Capricorn	Scorpio
26	7:17 P.M. Pisces	Sagittarius	Aquarius	Pisces	Capricorn	Scorpio	Sagittarius	Capricorn	Scorpio
27		Sagittarius	Aquarius	Pisces	Capricorn	Scorpio	Sagittarius	Capricorn	Scorpio
28		Sagittarius	Aquarius	Pisces	Capricorn	Scorpio	Sagittarius	Capricorn	Scorpio
29	7:12 A.M. Aries	Sagittarius	Aquarius	Pisces	Capricorn	Scorpio	Sagittarius	Capricorn	Scorpio
30		Sagittarius	Aquarius	Pisces	Capricorn	Scorpio	Sagittarius	Capricorn	Scorpio
31	7:49 P.M. Taurus	Sagittarius	Aquarius	Pisces	Capricorn	Scorpio	Sagittarius	Capricorn	Scorpio

CAPRICORN PLANETARY TABLES

1985

MOON		MERCURY	VENUS	MARS	JUPITER	SATURN	URANUS	NEPTUNE	PLUTO
January	FROM	IN								
1	Taurus	Sagittarius	Aquarius	Pisces	Capricorn	Scorpio	Sagittarius	Capricorn	Scorpio
2		Sagittarius	Aquarius	Pisces	Capricorn	Scorpio	Sagittarius	Capricorn	Scorpio
3	7:23 A.M. Gemini	Sagittarius	Aquarius	Pisces	Capricorn	Scorpio	Sagittarius	Capricorn	Scorpio
4		Sagittarius	Aquarius	Pisces	Capricorn	Scorpio	Sagittarius	Capricorn	Scorpio
5	3:13 P.M. Cancer	Sagittarius	Pisces	Pisces	Capricorn	Scorpio	Sagittarius	Capricorn	Scorpio
6		Sagittarius	Pisces	Pisces	Capricorn	Scorpio	Sagittarius	Capricorn	Scorpio
7	8:33 P.M. Leo	Sagittarius	Pisces	Pisces	Capricorn	Scorpio	Sagittarius	Capricorn	Scorpio
8		Sagittarius	Pisces	Pisces	Capricorn	Scorpio	Sagittarius	Capricorn	Scorpio
9		Sagittarius	Pisces	Pisces	Capricorn	Scorpio	Sagittarius	Capricorn	Scorpio
10	0:10 A.M. Virgo	Sagittarius	Pisces	Pisces	Capricorn	Scorpio	Sagittarius	Capricorn	Scorpio
11		Sagittarius	Pisces	Pisces	Capricorn	Scorpio	Sagittarius	Capricorn	Scorpio
12	2:57 A.M. Libra	Capricorn	Pisces	Pisces	Capricorn	Scorpio	Sagittarius	Capricorn	Scorpio
13		Capricorn	Pisces	Pisces	Capricorn	Scorpio	Sagittarius	Capricorn	Scorpio
14	5:19 A.M. Scorpio	Capricorn	Pisces	Pisces	Capricorn	Scorpio	Sagittarius	Capricorn	Scorpio
15		Capricorn	Pisces	Pisces	Capricorn	Scorpio	Sagittarius	Capricorn	Scorpio
16	8:55 A.M. Sagittarius	Capricorn	Pisces	Pisces	Capricorn	Scorpio	Sagittarius	Capricorn	Scorpio
17		Capricorn	Pisces	Pisces	Capricorn	Scorpio	Sagittarius	Capricorn	Scorpio
18	1:32 P.M. Capricorn	Capricorn	Pisces	Pisces	Capricorn	Scorpio	Sagittarius	Capricorn	Scorpio
19		Capricorn	Pisces	Pisces	Capricorn	Scorpio	Sagittarius	Capricorn	Scorpio
20	7:34 P.M. Aquarius	Capricorn	Pisces	Pisces	Capricorn	Scorpio	Sagittarius	Capricorn	Scorpio
December									
22	Taurus	Sagittarius	Sagittarius	Scorpio	Aquarius	Sagittarius	Sagittarius	Capricorn	Scorpio
23		Sagittarius	Sagittarius	Scorpio	Aquarius	Sagittarius	Sagittarius	Capricorn	Scorpio
24	3:46 A.M. Gemini	Sagittarius	Sagittarius	Scorpio	Aquarius	Sagittarius	Sagittarius	Capricorn	Scorpio
25		Sagittarius	Sagittarius	Scorpio	Aquarius	Sagittarius	Sagittarius	Capricorn	Scorpio
26	3:41 P.M. Cancer	Sagittarius	Sagittarius	Scorpio	Aquarius	Sagittarius	Sagittarius	Capricorn	Scorpio
27		Sagittarius	Sagittarius	Scorpio	Aquarius	Sagittarius	Sagittarius	Capricorn	Scorpio
28		Sagittarius	Capricorn	Scorpio	Aquarius	Sagittarius	Sagittarius	Capricorn	Scorpio
29	1:51 A.M. Leo	Sagittarius	Capricorn	Scorpio	Aquarius	Sagittarius	Sagittarius	Capricorn	Scorpio
30		Sagittarius	Capricorn	Scorpio	Aquarius	Sagittarius	Sagittarius	Capricorn	Scorpio
31	10:06 A.M. Virgo	Sagittarius	Capricorn	Scorpio	Aquarius	Sagittarius	Sagittarius	Capricorn	Scorpio

1986

	MOON FROM	MOON IN	MERCURY	VENUS	MARS	JUPITER	SATURN	URANUS	NEPTUNE	PLUTO
January										
1		Virgo	Sagittarius	Capricorn	Scorpio	Aquarius	Sagittarius	Sagittarius	Capricorn	Scorpio
2	3:08 P.M.	Libra	Sagittarius	Capricorn	Scorpio	Aquarius	Sagittarius	Sagittarius	Capricorn	Scorpio
3			Sagittarius	Capricorn	Scorpio	Aquarius	Sagittarius	Sagittarius	Capricorn	Scorpio
4	7:42 P.M.	Scorpio	Sagittarius	Capricorn	Scorpio	Aquarius	Sagittarius	Sagittarius	Capricorn	Scorpio
5			Sagittarius	Capricorn	Scorpio	Aquarius	Sagittarius	Sagittarius	Capricorn	Scorpio
6	9:28 P.M.	Sagittarius	Capricorn	Capricorn	Scorpio	Aquarius	Sagittarius	Sagittarius	Capricorn	Scorpio
7			Capricorn	Capricorn	Scorpio	Aquarius	Sagittarius	Sagittarius	Capricorn	Scorpio
8	10:31 P.M.	Capricorn	Capricorn	Capricorn	Scorpio	Aquarius	Sagittarius	Sagittarius	Capricorn	Scorpio
9			Capricorn	Capricorn	Scorpio	Aquarius	Sagittarius	Sagittarius	Capricorn	Scorpio
10			Capricorn	Capricorn	Scorpio	Aquarius	Sagittarius	Sagittarius	Capricorn	Scorpio
11	0:18 A.M.	Aquarius	Capricorn	Capricorn	Scorpio	Aquarius	Sagittarius	Sagittarius	Capricorn	Scorpio
12			Capricorn	Capricorn	Scorpio	Aquarius	Sagittarius	Sagittarius	Capricorn	Scorpio
13	3:36 A.M.	Pisces	Capricorn	Capricorn	Scorpio	Aquarius	Sagittarius	Sagittarius	Capricorn	Scorpio
14			Capricorn	Capricorn	Scorpio	Aquarius	Sagittarius	Sagittarius	Capricorn	Scorpio
15	11:19 A.M.	Aries	Capricorn	Capricorn	Scorpio	Aquarius	Sagittarius	Sagittarius	Capricorn	Scorpio
16			Capricorn	Capricorn	Scorpio	Aquarius	Sagittarius	Sagittarius	Capricorn	Scorpio
17	10:32 P.M.	Taurus	Capricorn	Capricorn	Scorpio	Aquarius	Sagittarius	Sagittarius	Capricorn	Scorpio
18			Capricorn	Capricorn	Scorpio	Aquarius	Sagittarius	Sagittarius	Capricorn	Scorpio
19			Capricorn	Capricorn	Scorpio	Aquarius	Sagittarius	Sagittarius	Capricorn	Scorpio
20	11:25 A.M.	Gemini	Capricorn	Capricorn	Scorpio	Aquarius	Sagittarius	Sagittarius	Capricorn	Scorpio
December										
23		Virgo	Sagittarius	Scorpio	Pisces	Pisces	Sagittarius	Sagittarius	Capricorn	Scorpio
24	0:11 A.M.	Libra	Sagittarius	Scorpio	Pisces	Pisces	Sagittarius	Sagittarius	Capricorn	Scorpio
25	5:51 A.M.	Scorpio	Sagittarius	Scorpio	Pisces	Pisces	Sagittarius	Sagittarius	Capricorn	Scorpio
26			Sagittarius	Scorpio	Pisces	Pisces	Sagittarius	Sagittarius	Capricorn	Scorpio
27			Sagittarius	Scorpio	Pisces	Pisces	Sagittarius	Sagittarius	Capricorn	Scorpio
28	8:08 A.M.	Sagittarius	Sagittarius	Scorpio	Pisces	Pisces	Sagittarius	Sagittarius	Capricorn	Scorpio
29			Sagittarius	Scorpio	Pisces	Pisces	Sagittarius	Sagittarius	Capricorn	Scorpio
30	7:47 A.M.	Capricorn	Capricorn	Scorpio	Pisces	Pisces	Sagittarius	Sagittarius	Capricorn	Scorpio
31			Capricorn	Scorpio	Pisces	Pisces	Sagittarius	Sagittarius	Capricorn	Scorpio

CAPRICORN PLANETARY TABLES

1987

MOON FROM	IN	MERCURY	VENUS	MARS	JUPITER	SATURN	URANUS	NEPTUNE	PLUTO
January									
1	5:29 A.M. Aquarius	Capricorn	Scorpio	Pisces	Pisces	Sagittarius	Sagittarius	Capricorn	Scorpio
2		Capricorn	Scorpio	Pisces	Pisces	Sagittarius	Sagittarius	Capricorn	Scorpio
3	8:22 A.M. Pisces	Capricorn	Scorpio	Pisces	Pisces	Sagittarius	Sagittarius	Capricorn	Scorpio
4		Capricorn	Scorpio	Pisces	Pisces	Sagittarius	Sagittarius	Capricorn	Scorpio
5	12:17 P.M. Aries	Capricorn	Scorpio	Pisces	Pisces	Sagittarius	Sagittarius	Capricorn	Scorpio
6		Capricorn	Scorpio	Pisces	Pisces	Sagittarius	Sagittarius	Capricorn	Scorpio
7	8:31 P.M. Taurus	Capricorn	Scorpio	Pisces	Pisces	Sagittarius	Sagittarius	Capricorn	Scorpio
8		Capricorn	Sagittarius	Pisces	Pisces	Sagittarius	Sagittarius	Capricorn	Scorpio
9		Capricorn	Sagittarius	Aries	Pisces	Sagittarius	Sagittarius	Capricorn	Scorpio
10	7:49 A.M. Gemini	Capricorn	Sagittarius	Aries	Pisces	Sagittarius	Sagittarius	Capricorn	Scorpio
11		Capricorn	Sagittarius	Aries	Pisces	Sagittarius	Sagittarius	Capricorn	Scorpio
12	8:30 P.M. Cancer	Capricorn	Sagittarius	Aries	Pisces	Sagittarius	Sagittarius	Capricorn	Scorpio
13		Capricorn	Sagittarius	Aries	Pisces	Sagittarius	Sagittarius	Capricorn	Scorpio
14		Capricorn	Sagittarius	Aries	Pisces	Sagittarius	Sagittarius	Capricorn	Scorpio
15	9:10 A.M. Leo	Capricorn	Sagittarius	Aries	Pisces	Sagittarius	Sagittarius	Capricorn	Scorpio
16		Capricorn	Sagittarius	Aries	Pisces	Sagittarius	Sagittarius	Capricorn	Scorpio
17	8:35 P.M. Virgo	Capricorn	Sagittarius	Aries	Pisces	Sagittarius	Sagittarius	Capricorn	Scorpio
18		Aquarius	Sagittarius	Aries	Pisces	Sagittarius	Sagittarius	Capricorn	Scorpio
19		Aquarius	Sagittarius	Aries	Pisces	Sagittarius	Sagittarius	Capricorn	Scorpio
20	6:15 A.M. Libra	Aquarius	Sagittarius	Aries	Pisces	Sagittarius	Sagittarius	Capricorn	Scorpio
December									
23	Aquarius	Capricorn	Aquarius	Scorpio	Aries	Sagittarius	Sagittarius	Capricorn	Scorpio
24	5:48 P.M. Pisces	Capricorn	Aquarius	Scorpio	Aries	Sagittarius	Sagittarius	Capricorn	Scorpio
25		Capricorn	Aquarius	Scorpio	Aries	Sagittarius	Sagittarius	Capricorn	Scorpio
26	8:17 P.M. Aries	Capricorn	Aquarius	Scorpio	Aries	Sagittarius	Sagittarius	Capricorn	Scorpio
27		Capricorn	Aquarius	Scorpio	Aries	Sagittarius	Sagittarius	Capricorn	Scorpio
28		Capricorn	Aquarius	Scorpio	Aries	Sagittarius	Sagittarius	Capricorn	Scorpio
29	1:38 A.M. Taurus	Capricorn	Aquarius	Scorpio	Aries	Sagittarius	Sagittarius	Capricorn	Scorpio
30		Capricorn	Aquarius	Scorpio	Aries	Sagittarius	Sagittarius	Capricorn	Scorpio
31	9:29 A.M. Gemini	Capricorn	Aquarius	Scorpio	Aries	Sagittarius	Sagittarius	Capricorn	Scorpio

1988

January	MOON FROM / IN	MERCURY	VENUS	MARS	JUPITER	SATURN	URANUS	NEPTUNE	PLUTO
1	Gemini	Capricorn	Aquarius	Scorpio	Aries	Sagittarius	Sagittarius	Capricorn	Scorpio
2	7:30 P.M. Cancer	Capricorn	Aquarius	Scorpio	Aries	Sagittarius	Sagittarius	Capricorn	Scorpio
3		Capricorn	Aquarius	Scorpio	Aries	Sagittarius	Sagittarius	Capricorn	Scorpio
4		Capricorn	Aquarius	Scorpio	Aries	Sagittarius	Sagittarius	Capricorn	Scorpio
5	7:00 A.M. Leo	Capricorn	Aquarius	Scorpio	Aries	Sagittarius	Sagittarius	Capricorn	Scorpio
6		Capricorn	Aquarius	Scorpio	Aries	Sagittarius	Sagittarius	Capricorn	Scorpio
7	7:37 P.M. Virgo	Capricorn	Aquarius	Scorpio	Aries	Sagittarius	Sagittarius	Capricorn	Scorpio
8		Capricorn	Aquarius	Scorpio	Aries	Sagittarius	Sagittarius	Capricorn	Scorpio
9		Capricorn	Aquarius	Sagittarius	Aries	Sagittarius	Sagittarius	Capricorn	Scorpio
10	8:12 A.M. Libra	Capricorn	Aquarius	Sagittarius	Aries	Sagittarius	Sagittarius	Capricorn	Scorpio
11		Aquarius	Aquarius	Sagittarius	Aries	Sagittarius	Sagittarius	Capricorn	Scorpio
12	6:21 P.M. Scorpio	Aquarius	Aquarius	Sagittarius	Aries	Sagittarius	Sagittarius	Capricorn	Scorpio
13		Aquarius	Aquarius	Sagittarius	Aries	Sagittarius	Sagittarius	Capricorn	Scorpio
14		Aquarius	Aquarius	Sagittarius	Aries	Sagittarius	Sagittarius	Capricorn	Scorpio
15	0:28 A.M. Sagittarius	Aquarius	Aquarius	Sagittarius	Aries	Sagittarius	Sagittarius	Capricorn	Scorpio
16		Aquarius	Pisces	Sagittarius	Aries	Sagittarius	Sagittarius	Capricorn	Scorpio
17	3:20 A.M. Capricorn	Aquarius	Pisces	Sagittarius	Aries	Sagittarius	Sagittarius	Capricorn	Scorpio
18		Aquarius	Pisces	Sagittarius	Aries	Sagittarius	Sagittarius	Capricorn	Scorpio
19	3:08 A.M. Aquarius	Aquarius	Pisces	Sagittarius	Aries	Sagittarius	Sagittarius	Capricorn	Scorpio
20		Aquarius	Pisces	Sagittarius	Aries	Sagittarius	Sagittarius	Capricorn	Scorpio
December									
22	9:42 P.M. Cancer	Capricorn	Sagittarius	Aries	Taurus	Capricorn	Capricorn	Capricorn	Scorpio
23		Capricorn	Sagittarius	Aries	Taurus	Capricorn	Capricorn	Capricorn	Scorpio
24		Capricorn	Sagittarius	Aries	Taurus	Capricorn	Capricorn	Capricorn	Scorpio
25	5:08 A.M. Leo	Capricorn	Sagittarius	Aries	Taurus	Capricorn	Capricorn	Capricorn	Scorpio
26		Capricorn	Sagittarius	Aries	Taurus	Capricorn	Capricorn	Capricorn	Scorpio
27	3:36 P.M. Virgo	Capricorn	Sagittarius	Aries	Taurus	Capricorn	Capricorn	Capricorn	Scorpio
28		Capricorn	Sagittarius	Aries	Taurus	Capricorn	Capricorn	Capricorn	Scorpio
29		Capricorn	Sagittarius	Aries	Taurus	Capricorn	Capricorn	Capricorn	Scorpio
30	3:58 A.M. Libra	Capricorn	Sagittarius	Aries	Taurus	Capricorn	Capricorn	Capricorn	Scorpio
31		Capricorn	Sagittarius	Aries	Taurus	Capricorn	Capricorn	Capricorn	Scorpio

CAPRICORN PLANETARY TABLES

1989

January	MOON FROM IN	MERCURY	VENUS	MARS	JUPITER	SATURN	URANUS	NEPTUNE	PLUTO
1	4:27 P.M. Scorpio	Capricorn	Sagittarius	Aries	Taurus	Capricorn	Capricorn	Capricorn	Scorpio
2		Capricorn	Sagittarius	Aries	Taurus	Capricorn	Capricorn	Capricorn	Scorpio
3		Aquarius	Sagittarius	Aries	Taurus	Capricorn	Capricorn	Capricorn	Scorpio
4	2:26 A.M. Sagittarius	Aquarius	Sagittarius	Aries	Taurus	Capricorn	Capricorn	Capricorn	Scorpio
5		Aquarius	Sagittarius	Aries	Taurus	Capricorn	Capricorn	Capricorn	Scorpio
6	8:24 A.M. Capricorn	Aquarius	Sagittarius	Aries	Taurus	Capricorn	Capricorn	Capricorn	Scorpio
7		Aquarius	Sagittarius	Aries	Taurus	Capricorn	Capricorn	Capricorn	Scorpio
8	11:44 A.M. Aquarius	Aquarius	Sagittarius	Aries	Taurus	Capricorn	Capricorn	Capricorn	Scorpio
9		Aquarius	Sagittarius	Aries	Taurus	Capricorn	Capricorn	Capricorn	Scorpio
10	1:40 P.M. Pisces	Aquarius	Capricorn	Aries	Taurus	Capricorn	Capricorn	Capricorn	Scorpio
11		Aquarius	Capricorn	Aries	Taurus	Capricorn	Capricorn	Capricorn	Scorpio
12	3:58 P.M. Aries	Aquarius	Capricorn	Aries	Taurus	Capricorn	Capricorn	Capricorn	Scorpio
13		Aquarius	Capricorn	Aries	Taurus	Capricorn	Capricorn	Capricorn	Scorpio
14	6:34 P.M. Taurus	Aquarius	Capricorn	Aries	Taurus	Capricorn	Capricorn	Capricorn	Scorpio
15		Aquarius	Capricorn	Aries	Taurus	Capricorn	Capricorn	Capricorn	Scorpio
16	11:03 P.M. Gemini	Aquarius	Capricorn	Aries	Taurus	Capricorn	Capricorn	Capricorn	Scorpio
17		Aquarius	Capricorn	Aries	Taurus	Capricorn	Capricorn	Capricorn	Scorpio
18		Aquarius	Capricorn	Aries	Taurus	Capricorn	Capricorn	Capricorn	Scorpio
19	4:50 A.M. Cancer	Aquarius	Capricorn	Aries	Taurus	Capricorn	Capricorn	Capricorn	Scorpio
20		Aquarius	Capricorn	Taurus	Taurus	Capricorn	Capricorn	Capricorn	Scorpio
December									
22	11:27 A.M. Scorpio	Capricorn	Aquarius	Sagittarius	Cancer	Capricorn	Capricorn	Capricorn	Scorpio
23		Capricorn	Aquarius	Sagittarius	Cancer	Capricorn	Capricorn	Capricorn	Scorpio
24		Capricorn	Aquarius	Sagittarius	Cancer	Capricorn	Capricorn	Capricorn	Scorpio
25	0:01 A.M. Sagittarius	Capricorn	Aquarius	Sagittarius	Cancer	Capricorn	Capricorn	Capricorn	Scorpio
26		Capricorn	Aquarius	Sagittarius	Cancer	Capricorn	Capricorn	Capricorn	Scorpio
27	10:18 A.M. Capricorn	Capricorn	Aquarius	Sagittarius	Cancer	Capricorn	Capricorn	Capricorn	Scorpio
28		Capricorn	Aquarius	Sagittarius	Cancer	Capricorn	Capricorn	Capricorn	Scorpio
29	6:42 P.M. Aquarius	Capricorn	Aquarius	Sagittarius	Cancer	Capricorn	Capricorn	Capricorn	Scorpio
30		Capricorn	Aquarius	Sagittarius	Cancer	Capricorn	Capricorn	Capricorn	Scorpio
31		Capricorn	Aquarius	Sagittarius	Cancer	Capricorn	Capricorn	Capricorn	Scorpio

1990

January	MOON FROM IN	MERCURY	VENUS	MARS	JUPITER	SATURN	URANUS	NEPTUNE	PLUTO
1	3:01 A.M. Pisces	Capricorn	Aquarius	Sagittarius	Cancer	Capricorn	Capricorn	Capricorn	Scorpio
2		Capricorn	Aquarius	Sagittarius	Cancer	Capricorn	Capricorn	Capricorn	Scorpio
3	5:48 A.M. Aries	Capricorn	Aquarius	Sagittarius	Cancer	Capricorn	Capricorn	Capricorn	Scorpio
4		Capricorn	Aquarius	Sagittarius	Cancer	Capricorn	Capricorn	Capricorn	Scorpio
5	6:51 A.M. Taurus	Capricorn	Aquarius	Sagittarius	Cancer	Capricorn	Capricorn	Capricorn	Scorpio
6		Capricorn	Aquarius	Sagittarius	Cancer	Capricorn	Capricorn	Capricorn	Scorpio
7	11:00 A.M. Gemini	Capricorn	Aquarius	Sagittarius	Cancer	Capricorn	Capricorn	Capricorn	Scorpio
8		Capricorn	Aquarius	Sagittarius	Cancer	Capricorn	Capricorn	Capricorn	Scorpio
9	12:54 P.M. Cancer	Capricorn	Aquarius	Sagittarius	Cancer	Capricorn	Capricorn	Capricorn	Scorpio
10		Capricorn	Aquarius	Sagittarius	Cancer	Capricorn	Capricorn	Capricorn	Scorpio
11	4:26 P.M. Leo	Capricorn	Aquarius	Sagittarius	Cancer	Capricorn	Capricorn	Capricorn	Scorpio
12		Capricorn	Aquarius	Sagittarius	Cancer	Capricorn	Capricorn	Capricorn	Scorpio
13	9:47 P.M. Virgo	Capricorn	Aquarius	Sagittarius	Cancer	Capricorn	Capricorn	Capricorn	Scorpio
14		Capricorn	Aquarius	Sagittarius	Cancer	Capricorn	Capricorn	Capricorn	Scorpio
15		Capricorn	Aquarius	Sagittarius	Cancer	Capricorn	Capricorn	Capricorn	Scorpio
16	7:12 A.M. Libra	Capricorn	Aquarius	Sagittarius	Cancer	Capricorn	Capricorn	Capricorn	Scorpio
17		Capricorn	Capricorn	Sagittarius	Cancer	Capricorn	Capricorn	Capricorn	Scorpio
18	7:19 P.M. Scorpio	Capricorn	Capricorn	Sagittarius	Cancer	Capricorn	Capricorn	Capricorn	Scorpio
19		Capricorn	Capricorn	Sagittarius	Cancer	Capricorn	Capricorn	Capricorn	Scorpio
20		Capricorn	Capricorn	Sagittarius	Cancer	Capricorn	Capricorn	Capricorn	Scorpio
December									
23	Pisces	Capricorn	Capricorn	Taurus	Leo	Capricorn	Capricorn	Capricorn	Scorpio
24	4:19 P.M. Aries	Capricorn	Capricorn	Taurus	Leo	Capricorn	Capricorn	Capricorn	Scorpio
25		Capricorn	Capricorn	Taurus	Leo	Capricorn	Capricorn	Capricorn	Scorpio
26	8:47 P.M. Taurus	Sagittarius	Capricorn	Taurus	Leo	Capricorn	Capricorn	Capricorn	Scorpio
27		Sagittarius	Capricorn	Taurus	Leo	Capricorn	Capricorn	Capricorn	Scorpio
28	10:19 P.M. Gemini	Sagittarius	Capricorn	Taurus	Leo	Capricorn	Capricorn	Capricorn	Scorpio
29		Sagittarius	Capricorn	Taurus	Leo	Capricorn	Capricorn	Capricorn	Scorpio
30	9:54 P.M. Cancer	Sagittarius	Capricorn	Taurus	Leo	Capricorn	Capricorn	Capricorn	Scorpio
31		Sagittarius	Capricorn	Taurus	Leo	Capricorn	Capricorn	Capricorn	Scorpio